DRUGS, SOCIETY, AND BEHAVIOR
94/95

Ninth Edition

Editor

Erich Goode
State University of New York at Stony Brook

Erich Goode received his undergraduate degree from
Oberlin College and his Ph.D. in sociology from Columbia
University. He is currently professor of sociology at the State
University of New York at Stony Brook; he has also taught
courses at Columbia, New York University, Florida Atlantic
University, and the University of North Carolina, Chapel
Hill, and, during the spring semester of 1993, Hebrew
University in Jerusalem. He is the author of a number of
books, articles, and chapters on drug use and abuse,
including *The Marijuana Smokers* (Basic Books, 1970), *The
Drug Phenomenon* (Bobbs-Merrill, 1973), and *Drugs in
American Society* (4th edition, McGraw-Hill, 1993).
Professor Goode has taught several courses on alcoholism
and drug abuse.

Annual Editions
A Library of Information from the Public Press

The Dushkin Publishing Group, Inc.
Sluice Dock, Guilford, Connecticut 06437

Cover illustration by Mike Eagle

The Annual Editions Series

Annual Editions is a series of over 60 volumes designed to provide the reader with convenient, low-cost access to a wide range of current, carefully selected articles from some of the most important magazines, newspapers, and journals published today. Annual Editions are updated on an annual basis through a continuous monitoring of over 300 periodical sources. All Annual Editions have a number of features designed to make them particularly useful, including topic guides, annotated tables of contents, unit overviews, and indexes. For the teacher using Annual Editions in the classroom, an Instructor's Resource Guide with test questions is available for each volume.

VOLUMES AVAILABLE

Africa
Aging
American Foreign Policy
American Government
American History, Pre-Civil War
American History, Post-Civil War
Anthropology
Biology
Business Ethics
Canadian Politics
Child Growth and Development
China
Comparative Politics
Computers in Education
Computers in Business
Computers in Society
Criminal Justice
Drugs, Society, and Behavior
Dying, Death, and Bereavement
Early Childhood Education
Economics
Educating Exceptional Children
Education
Educational Psychology
Environment
Geography
Global Issues
Health
Human Development
Human Resources
Human Sexuality
India and South Asia
International Business
Japan and the Pacific Rim

Latin America
Life Management
Macroeconomics
Management
Marketing
Marriage and Family
Mass Media
Microeconomics
Middle East and the Islamic World
Money and Banking
Multicultural Education
Nutrition
Personal Growth and Behavior
Physical Anthropology
Psychology
Public Administration
Race and Ethnic Relations
Russia, Eurasia, and Central/Eastern Europe
Social Problems
Sociology
State and Local Government
Third World
Urban Society
Violence and Terrorism
Western Civilization, Pre-Reformation
Western Civilization, Post-Reformation
Western Europe
World History, Pre-Modern
World History, Modern
World Politics

Library of Congress Cataloging in Publication Data
Main entry under title: Annual Editions: Drugs, Society, and Behavior. 1994/95.
  1. Drugs—Periodicals. 2. Drug abuse—United States—Periodicals. 3. Alcohol—Periodicals. 4. Drunk driving—Periodicals. I. Goode, Erich, *comp.* II. Title: Drugs, Society, and Behavior.
ISBN 1–56134–253–X   362.2′92′0973′05

© 1994 by The Dushkin Publishing Group, Inc., Guilford, CT 06437

Ninth Edition

Printed in the United States of America

Printed on Recycled Paper

Editors/ Advisory Board

EDITOR

Erich Goode
SUNY, Stony Brook

ADVISORY BOARD

Members of the Advisory Board are instrumental in the final selection of articles for each edition of Annual Editions. Their review of articles for content, level, currentness, and appropriateness provides critical direction to the editor and staff. We think you'll find their careful consideration well reflected in this volume.

STAFF

To the Reader

In publishing ANNUAL EDITIONS we recognize the enormous role played by the magazines, newspapers, and journals of the *public press* in providing current, first-rate educational information in a broad spectrum of interest areas. Within the articles, the best scientists, practitioners, researchers, and commentators draw issues into new perspective as accepted theories and viewpoints are called into account by new events, recent discoveries change old facts, and fresh debate breaks out over important controversies.

Many of the articles resulting from this enormous editorial effort are appropriate for students, researchers, and professionals seeking accurate, current material to help bridge the gap between principles and theories and the real world. These articles, however, become more useful for study when those of lasting value are carefully *collected, organized, indexed,* and *reproduced* in a *low-cost format,* which provides easy and permanent access when the material is needed. That is the role played by *Annual Editions.* Under the direction of each volume's *Editor,* who is an expert in the subject area, and with the guidance of an *Advisory Board,* we seek each year to provide in each *ANNUAL EDITION* a current, well-balanced, carefully selected collection of the best of the public press for your study and enjoyment. We think you'll find this volume useful, and we hope you'll take a moment to let us know what you think.

Interest in and concern about drug use comes in cycles. In certain decades, little concern is evidenced about the issue; people rarely talk about drugs, they are rarely news—few articles are written in newspapers and magazines about their use, and little drug activity is reported in the broadcast media—and hardly anyone considers drug abuse the most important social problem facing the country. In other decades, drug use emerges as a central social issue; it provides a major topic of conversation, the newspapers, magazines, and broadcast media are filled with news and commentary on the subject, and a substantial proportion of the population regards drug abuse as the number one problem the country faces.

In the mid- to late 1980s, public concern over drug abuse fairly exploded. While this concern declined as a result of the Persian Gulf crisis and war, and later the economic recession, it remains, relative to many pressing issues, fairly high. In many quarters, our society is intensely concerned about the problem of drug use and abuse. Among some of the public, this concern borders on panic. Is this panic justified? Are drugs as central a problem as much of the public believes? What are drugs in the first place? What short-term effects do they have? How do they affect the individual and the society over the long run? How should we deal with drugs and drug abuse? The articles included in *Annual Editions: Drugs, Society, and Behavior 94/95* represent a sampling of current thinking on the subject of drug use. The selections are intended to be thought-provoking and informative. I hope that reading them will help the student meet the challenge that drug use poses and permit him or her to reach reasonable, well-informed conclusions on this troubling issue.

Unit 1 provides the student with a general framework for what follows; it makes four basic points. First, our society tolerates certain (legal) drugs, but is concerned about, and arrests, users of other (illegal) drugs. Second, drug use has a long history, both around the world generally and in this society specifically. Third, illegal drug use generates a worldwide network of sellers that makes use extremely difficult to eradicate, but it is the consumer, ultimately, on which this enterprise is based. And fourth, all drug use is a sociological or anthropological phenomenon that has to be understood before the problem can be attacked. Unit 2 emphasizes the fact that drug use and abuse—or physical dependence—form a continuum or spectrum. Too often, we assume that if someone is a user of a given (usually illegal) drug, he or she is chemically dependent, indeed, high nearly all the time. Unit 2 shows that users come in all degrees of involvement, from experimenters to heavy, chronic, dependent abusers. Unit 3 explores a variety of explanations for drug use: Why do people use and abuse drugs? Why do *some* people use certain drugs—while the rest of us do not? In short, *why drugs*? Unit 4 demonstrates that drug use is highly patterned and variable over time and according to social characteristics. Who uses? Who does not? What are some basic recent *trends* in drug use?

Unit 5 emphasizes the fact that drugs are not unitary phenomena, but can be classified according to type. Too often we refer to drugs—illegal drugs, that is—in a generic fashion, as if they all had identical or extremely similar effects. This is false; in fact, certain drugs do certain things to us, others do very different things. Unit 6 looks at the long-run impact of drugs on society and individuals. Unit 7 focuses on a crucial aspect of drug use: buying and selling. Drug consumption is an economic enterprise, and that fact influences many features of the drug scene. Why? How? In what specific ways? Unit 8 looks at how our society is attacking the problem of drug abuse, what is wrong with what we are doing, and what should be done about it. Is legalization a viable option? Several observers support this option, while others do not. Last, Unit 9 deals with the treatment of drug abusers and the people they hurt and with educational programs that convince young people to avoid becoming involved in the first place.

We would like to have your comments and suggestions about the articles in this edition. Please complete and return the article rating form at the end of the book.

Erich Goode
Editor

Contents

Unit 1

Thinking About Drugs

Four articles in this section examine how drugs are defined today. The history of drugs in our culture is also discussed.

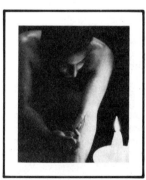

Unit 2

Use, Addiction, and Dependence

Five selections in this section discuss what is meant by drug addiction. Topics examined include physical dependency and drugs such as crack, alcohol, and nicotine.

The concepts in bold italics are developed in the article. For further expansion please refer to the Topic Guide, the Index, and the Glossary.

Unit 3

Why Drugs?

Six articles in this section discuss how and why individuals get "hooked" on drugs.

Unit 4

Patterns and Trends in Drug Use

Six articles in this section discuss the divergent patterns in the use of drugs as they lose and gain popularity.

Unit 5

The Major Drugs of Use and Abuse

Nine articles in this section examine some of the major drugs in use today. The drugs discussed include cocaine, marijuana, crack, methamphetamine (speed, crank, or "ice"), prescription drugs, and steroids.

The concepts in bold italics are developed in the article. For further expansion please refer to the Topic Guide, the Index, and the Glossary.

Unit 6

The Impact of Drug Use on Society

Five selections in this section discuss how drugs have devastated some portions of our society.

The concepts in bold italics are developed in the article. For further expansion please refer to the Topic Guide, the Index, and the Glossary.

Unit 7

The Economy of Drug Use

Five selections in this section discuss the enormous driving economic force behind the marketing of both legal and illegal drugs.

The concepts in bold italics are developed in the article. For further expansion please refer to the Topic Guide, the Index, and the Glossary.

Unit 8

Fighting the Drug War

Six articles in this section examine the current state of the war on drug usage. Topics include today's drug scene, new programs to combat drugs, and drug legalization.

The concepts in bold italics are developed in the article. For further expansion please refer to the Topic Guide, the Index, and the Glossary.

Unit 9

Drug Prevention and Treatment

Six selections in this section discuss drug dependence and treatment. Topics covered include educational programs, live-in therapeutic communities, and new methods for breaking addiction.

Topic Guide

This topic guide suggests how the selections in this book relate to topics of traditional concern to students and professionals involved with the study of drugs, society, and behavior. It is useful for locating articles that relate to each other for reading and research. The guide is arranged alphabetically according to topic. Articles may, of course, treat topics that do not appear in the topic guide. In turn, entries in the topic guide do not necessarily constitute a comprehensive listing of all the contents of each selection.

TOPIC AREA	TREATED IN:	TOPIC AREA	TREATED IN:
Addiction	2. Opium, Cocaine, and Marijuana 5. Addiction and Dependence 6. Battlefield of Addiction 7. High and Hooked 8. Smoking—Why Is It So Hard to Quit? 9. Drugs and Free Will 10. Intoxicating Habits 12. Lure of Drugs 13. Probing the Complex Genetics of Alcoholism 14. Pleasurable Chemistry 15. Executive's Secret Struggle 18. Increase in Drug-Caused Emergencies 20. Supply and Purity Up 22. How and Why of a Cocaine High 33. Alcohol and the Family 42. Pregnant, Addicted—and Guilty? 47. Getting Junkies to Clean Up 50. Maintenance Isn't Cure 51. Trying to Break Addictions	Attitudes and Drugs (cont'd)	19. Up in Smoke 21. Smoking, Drinking, and Illicit Drug Use 23. New View from on High 24. Choose Your Poison 26. Selling Pot 27. High Anxiety 31. Dealing with Demons 32. Alcohol and Kids 37. Tobacco Lobby 39. Pushing Drugs to Doctors 42. Pregnant, Addicted—and Guilty? 43. Should We Legalize Drugs? 44. Testing Workers for Drugs 45. Toward a Policy on Drugs 48. Alonzo's Battle 52. Hard Sell in the Drug War
Advertising	19. Up in Smoke 32. Alcohol and Kids 37. Tobacco Lobby 39. Pushing Drugs to Doctors 52. Hard Sell in the Drug War	Biological Factors	5. Addiction and Dependence 7. High and Hooked 8. Smoking—Why Is It So Hard to Quit? 9. Drugs and Free Will 10. Intoxicating Habits 11. High Times in the Wild Kingdom 13. Probing the Complex Genetics of Alcoholism 14. Pleasurable Chemistry 22. How and Why of a Cocaine High 25. Prozac Backlash 30. Pumped Up 34. Cocaine Effect on Babies Questioned
Alcohol	1. Drugs 'R' Us 3. Alcohol in America 10. Intoxicating Habits 13. Probing the Complex Genetics of Alcoholism 17. With Teens and Alcohol, It's Just Say When 21. Smoking, Drinking, and Illicit Drug Use 28. Alcohol in Perspective 31. Dealing with Demons 32. Alcohol and Kids 33. Alcohol and the Family	Children/Teenagers	17. With Teens and Alcohol, It's Just Say When 19. Up in Smoke 21. Smoking, Drinking, and Illicit Drug Use 30. Pumped Up 32. Alcohol and Kids 33. Alcohol and the Family 34. Cocaine Effect on Babies Questioned 35. Families vs. the Lure of the Streets 42. Pregnant, Addicted—and Guilty? 48. Alonzo's Battle 52. Hard Sell in the Drug War
Alcoholics Anonymous (AA)	10. Intoxicating Habits 12. Lure of Drugs	Cigarettes	*See* Nicotine
Alcoholism	3. Alcohol in America 10. Intoxicating Habits 13. Probing the Complex Genetics of Alcoholism 17. With Teens and Alcohol, It's Just Say When 31. Dealing with Demons 32. Alcohol and Kids 33. Alcohol and the Family	Cocaine	2. Opium, Cocaine, and Marijuana 4. Coke Inc. 5. Addiction and Dependence 18. Increase in Drug-Caused Emergencies 21. Smoking, Drinking, and Illicit Drug Use 22. How and Why of a Cocaine High 34. Cocaine Effect on Babies Questioned 40. Cocaine Money Market 46. U.S. Aid Hasn't Stopped Drug Flow
Amphetamines	21. Smoking, Drinking, and Illicit Drug Use 29. Drug Scene's New "Ice" Age	Crack	4. Coke Inc. 5. Addiction and Dependence 34. Cocaine Effect on Babies Questioned
Attitudes and Drugs	1. Drugs 'R' Us 2. Opium, Cocaine, and Marijuana 9. Drugs and Free Will 12. Lure of Drugs 16. Just Say Maybe 17. With Teens and Alcohol, It's Just Say When	Decriminalization	*See* Legalization

TOPIC AREA	TREATED IN:	TOPIC AREA	TREATED IN:
Epidemiology	2. Opium, Cocaine, and Marijuana 3. Alcohol in America 16. Just Say Maybe 17. With Teens and Alcohol, It's Just Say When 18. Increase in Drug-Caused Emergencies 19. Up in Smoke 20. Supply and Purity Up 21. Smoking, Drinking, and Illicit Drug Use	Nicotine	1. Drugs 'R' Us 8. Smoking—Why Is It So Hard to Quit? 19. Up in Smoke 21. Smoking, Drinking, and Illicit Drug Use
		Race, Drug Use and	2. Opium, Cocaine, and Marijuana 21. Smoking, Drinking, and Illicit Drug Use 35. Families vs. the Lure of the Streets 42. Pregnant, Addicted—and Guilty?
Etiology	5. Addiction and Dependence 8. Smoking—Why Is It So Hard to Quit? 9. Drugs and Free Will 10. Intoxicating Habits 11. High Times in the Wild Kingdom 12. Lure of Drugs 13. Probing the Complex Genetics of Alcoholism 14. Pleasurable Chemistry 22. How and Why of a Cocaine High	Research, Drug	5. Addiction and Dependence 9. Drugs and Free Will 10. Intoxicating Habits 11. High Times in the Wild Kingdom 13. Probing the Complex Genetics of Alcoholism 14. Pleasurable Chemistry 16. Just Say Maybe 18. Increase in Drug-Caused Emergencies 20. Supply and Purity Up 21. Smoking, Drinking, and Illicit Drug Use 22. How and Why of a Cocaine High 26. Selling Pot 33. Alcohol and the Family 34. Cocaine Effect on Babies Questioned 39. Pushing Drugs to Doctors
Family	31. Dealing with Demons 32. Alcohol and Kids 33. Alcohol and the Family 34. Cocaine Effect on Babies Questioned 35. Families vs. the Lure of the Streets 42. Pregnant, Addicted—and Guilty?		
Heroin	2. Opium, Cocaine, and Marijuana 4. Coke Inc. 5. Addiction and Dependence 7. High and Hooked 9. Drugs and Free Will 14. Pleasurable Chemistry 20. Supply and Purity Up 21. Smoking, Drinking, and Illicit Drug Use 36. Worldwide Drug Scourge 47. Getting Junkies to Clean Up 50. Maintenance Isn't Cure	Socioeconomic Issues	1. Drugs 'R' Us 2. Opium, Cocaine, and Marijuana 21. Smoking, Drinking, and Illicit Drug Use 34. Cocaine Effect on Babies Questioned 35. Families vs. the Lure of the Streets 42. Pregnant, Addicted—and Guilty?
		Treatment, Drug	9. Drugs and Free Will 10. Intoxicating Habits 12. Lure of Drugs 25. Prozac Backlash 31. Dealing with Demons 33. Alcohol and the Family 34. Cocaine Effect on Babies Questioned 39. Pushing Drugs to Doctors 44. Testing Workers for Drugs 47. Getting Junkies to Clean Up 49. Prisoners and Prisons 50. Maintenance Isn't Cure 51. Trying to Break Addictions
History of Drug Use	1. Drugs 'R' Us 2. Opium, Cocaine, and Marijuana 3. Alcohol in America 20. Supply and Purity Up 21. Smoking, Drinking, and Illicit Drug Use 41. U.S. Drug Laws: Two Views 43. Should We Legalize Drugs?		
Law Enforcement	1. Drugs 'R' Us 2. Opium, Cocaine, and Marijuana 4. Coke Inc. 38. High in the Hollows 42. Pregnant, Addicted—and Guilty? 43. Should We Legalize Drugs? 45. Toward a Policy on Drugs 46. U.S. Aid Hasn't Stopped Drug Flow 49. Prisoners and Prisons	War on Drugs	1. Drugs 'R' Us 2. Opium, Cocaine, and Marijuana 3. Alcohol in America 4. Coke Inc. 19. Up in Smoke 27. High Anxiety 32. Alcohol and Kids 38. High in the Hollows 41. U.S. Drug Laws: Two Views 42. Pregnant, Addicted—and Guilty? 43. Should We Legalize Drugs? 44. Testing Workers for Drugs 45. Toward a Policy on Drugs 46. U.S. Aid Hasn't Stopped Drug Flow 47. Getting Junkies to Clean Up 48. Alonzo's Battle 49. Prisoners and Prisons 50. Maintenance Isn't Cure 52. Hard Sell in Drug War
Legalization	16. Just Say Maybe 41. U.S. Drug Laws: Two Views 43. Should We Legalize Drugs? 45. Toward a Policy on Drugs		
Marijuana	1. Drugs 'R' Us 2. Opium, Cocaine, and Marijuana 5. Addiction and Dependence 21. Smoking, Drinking, and Illicit Drug Use 26. Selling Pot 38. High in the Hollows		

Thinking About Drugs

Everything that exists can be looked at or thought about in a variety of ways, through the lens of different perspectives. Although each perspective tells us something different about what we are looking at, some are more relevant, insightful, and powerful than others. The phenomena of drug use and abuse follow this rule. Some ways of looking at drugs and drug use tell us a great deal about their reality; others focus on marginal, less central issues, while still others tell us little beyond the biases of the observers.

How should we think about drug use? What perspectives tell us about the reality of drugs? The first thing we should know is that drugs encompass an extremely wide range of substances. Ask the man and woman in the street what "drugs" are and, in all likelihood, most of the answers you get will include illegal substances—crack, cocaine, heroin, perhaps LSD, marijuana, and PCP or "angel dust." Answers you will be less likely to receive will be the legal drugs—alcohol, tobacco, our morning cup of coffee, prescription drugs, and routinely available over-the-counter (OTC) medications. But in at least two respects, legal substances such as alcohol, tobacco, and tranquilizers are drugs in the same way as illegal substances such as LSD, heroin, and crack are. First, drugs that are used to achieve a certain psychic state are *psychoactive*, that is, mind-active. They influence the workings of the human mind—how we think, feel, and even act; the way drugs work on the mind cuts across the legal-illegal boundary. Second, both legal and illegal drugs are often overused, misused, and abused, thereby causing a great deal of damage to human life and to society generally. In fact, legal drugs—cigarettes and alcohol specifically—kill 20 to 30 times as many people as illegal drugs. Clearly, the distinction between legal and illegal drugs is an artificial, humanly created one, not crucial in most respects to the student of drug use. "Drugs 'R' Us" emphasizes the fuzziness of the line between legal and illegal drugs and the damage the use and abuse of legal drugs cause to our society.

The second lesson is that there is a great deal of widely disseminated misinformation about drug use; much of what most of the public believes about the subject is wrong. We tend to exaggerate the dangers of illegal drug use and minimize the dangers of legal drug use.

Another important conclusion we have to draw is that drug use and abuse are not confined to the twentieth century. Drug abuse is an ancient problem; humans have been ingesting psychoactive substances since the Stone Age—and possibly longer—over 10,000 or 12,000 years ago, when alcohol was first discovered. In the United States, alcohol was consumed in vastly greater quantities in the late 1700s and early 1800s than it is today, and, in the second half of the nineteenth century, addiction to narcotics, such as morphine and opium, was far more common, on a per-population basis, than heroin addiction is today. Problems associated with drug use and abuse have always been with us and, in all likelihood, always will be. "Opium, Cocaine, and Marijuana in American History" and "Alcohol in America" provide a detailed picture of drug use in this country's past, quite different from what most of us thought.

The next lesson we learn is that illegal drug use generates an immense network of social relations that exert a powerful influence worldwide. The base on which this network rests is the purchase and use of illegal substances by the consumer. The drug problem will not go away until people stop using drugs; it is futile to denounce drug dealers when the demand—and the profits—are so huge. "Coke Inc.: Inside the Big Business of Drugs" discusses the size, appeal, and impact of the drug trade for powdered cocaine, crack, and heroin.

The fifth lesson is that drug use is a sociological, psychological, and even anthropological phenomenon, generated and sustained by the people interacting in a specific setting and their customs and social networks. While drug use may be universal, or nearly so, the specific qualities it possesses in a particular community or society are dependent on the characteristics of the users themselves, that community, and that society. Too often, drug use and abuse are looked upon as a simple pathology—a sickness—in need of removal. Given this limited perspective, we will never be able to understand what sustains them, what they grow out of. When we begin asking who uses drugs and in what social situations and contexts, we begin to understand why drugs are so difficult to eradicate and what part they play for users and abusers.

Looking Ahead: Challenge Questions

What is a drug? How are psychoactive drugs different from drugs that only influence the workings of the human body? From the viewpoint of a drug's effects, is it meaningful to distinguish between legal and illegal drugs? Why are certain legal psychoactive substances not widely regarded as drugs?

Why is a study of drug use and law enforcement in the past important? Does it tell us something important about the current drug scene? Why have the lessons of history been lost on the present generation?

How would you go about studying drug use? What issues and questions are important to you?

Why do drugs, drug use, and drug sales make such a powerful impact on our society?

DRUGS 'R' US

Daniel Lazare

Judging from what one hears in Washington these days, there are two theories as to why people use drugs. One is the Republican theory, advanced most vehemently by drug czar William Bennett, that people indulge in heroin, cocaine and the like because law and order has broken down, and families, churches and schools are disintegrating. The other is the Democratic theory, which holds that people do drugs because they're poor, downtrodden and longing for escape. "Up with hope, down with dope," says Jesse Jackson, appearing to imply that once social conditions are ameliorated, the drug problem will vanish like a puff of smoke.

But rarely are things so simple. While racism and poverty help explain why some Americans resort to ultra-potent substances like crack, they're hardly the whole story. Throughout history people have resorted to various mind-altering substances, from beer to peyote, for reasons that are as varied as human experience itself. They've taken drugs to get closer to God or to heighten their experiences here on Earth; to sharpen their senses or anesthetize their brains; to blend in with the crowd or to distinguish themselves from the pack.

During the '20s, middle-class kids drank bathtub gin to show their contempt for the repressive, puritanical America of Calvin Coolidge. Forty years later, they demonstrated revulsion for American consumerism by turning their nose up at booze and puffing away happily on pot. In the '70s, yuppies snorted coke because it seemed to go with the quickening pace on Wall Street, while, more recently, aspiring arbitrageurs have downed gallons of black coffee in imitation of caffeine-junkie Ivan Boesky.

Thus, the question of intoxication turns out to be as complex as sex, death, money or other fundamental aspects of the human condition. One generation's meat quite frequently turns out to be another's poison. The only constant is that most people do something to alter their conscious state. While Mormons eschew all mind-altering substances right down to coffee, tea and chocolate, they and people like them are a distinct minority.

What's your drug? In fact, all of us may be hooked in one way or another, teetotalers included, whether we know it or not. Since the '70s, medical researchers have zeroed in on a group of internally generated mood-control agents known as endogenous morphines, or endorphins, that are believed to play a key role in determining whether we're anxious or relaxed, unable to concentrate or immersed in thought.

Ironically, endorphins are chemically related to forbidden exogenous opiates such as opium, morphine and heroin, and produce a similar psychological state—a sense of bliss, floating and transcendence of ego.

For centuries, people who have spoken of "losing" themselves in their work, of shutting out the world while they concentrate on an intellectual problem, may actually have describing a heightened mental state brought on by an internally generated drug. They may not be so much devoted to their profession as devoted to a chemical high that scientists now believe may be brought on by hard work or vigorous physical exercise.

Committed joggers, of course, are so devoted to their daily "runner's high" that many injure themselves through over-training. When ordered by a doctor to stop, they may often display such classic symptoms of withdrawal as irritability, nervousness and loss of concentration.

When doctors speak of being addicted to their work, according to *Messengers of Paradise: Opiates and the Brain,* an interesting new book by Charles F. Levinthal, they may mean it quite literally. One surgeon interviewed as part of a 1975 study said operating was "like taking narcotics." Another compared it to heroin. A third confessed that he never felt under more stress than when he was vacationing with his family in the Bahamas. A fourth said he was so nervous after two days of sight-seeing in Mexico—the first vacation for him and his wife in years—that he volunteered his services to a local hospital and spent the rest of his vacation in surgery.

Surgeons are not the only ones who describe work in such terms. A world-class chess master quoted by Levinthal said that whenever he sits down to a game, "Time passes a hundred times faster . . . it resembles a dream state. A whole story can unfold in seconds, it seems." In his 1934 novel, *The Search,* C. P. Snow described the ecstasy of scientific discovery in terms bordering on the hallucinatory: "It was as though I had looked for a truth outside myself, and finding it had become for a moment a part of the truth I sought; as though all the world, the atoms and the stars, were wonderfully clear and close to me, and I to them. . . ." This may have been literary hyperbole—or an accurate description of a scientist who has made the breakthrough of a lifetime and is soaring on opiates as a result.

Whatever their political or moral value, hard work and self-discipline may also be routes to self-medication. Similarly, those dependent on outside sources to satisfy their

 From *In These Times,* October 18-24, 1989, pp. 12-13. Reprinted by permission of *In These Times,* a weekly newspaper based in Chicago.

opiate craving may never have learned to generate their own. Conventional solutions to the "problem" of addiction frequently make it worse. By throwing exogenous-opiate junkies in jail or depriving them of employment—one goal of militant organizations like Partnership for a Drug-Free America—they likely will remain locked in their exogenous addiction and will never be able to produce their own drugs in ways that society deems legitimate.

Alcohol—the legal high: If opiates, internal or external, are the most common mind-altering substances, then alcohol is a close second. We celebrate anniversaries with champagne, the end of the work day with beer and a good meal with wine. In 1954, the French government estimated that a third of the electorate derived all or part of its income from the production or sale of alcoholic beverages, while in Italy a few years later an estimated 10 percent of arable land was said to be given over to viticulture.

According to archaeologists, beer-making is as old as agriculture; in neolithic times, it was probably the only method of preserving the nutritive value of grain. Since then, alcohol has been brewed from just about every conceivable fruit or vegetable—mead from honey, sake from rice, wine from palm, mezcal and Central American pulque from agave and cactus. North American Indians even made a liquor from maple syrup, while South American Indians made one from various jungle fruits.

According to the Book of Genesis, grape wine was discovered by Noah, who promptly got drunk and threw off all his clothes, presumably in celebration. Approximately 1,000 years later, the Book of Proverbs advised: "Give strong drink to him who is perishing, and wine to those in bitter distress; let them drink and forget their poverty, and remember their misery no more"—a reminder that seeking escape from oppressive social conditions through intoxication is not necessarily a cardinal sin.

Why is alcohol so popular? For one thing, users have learned to savor the taste of beer, wine, cognac, eau de vie and so on that goes with inebriation. For another, it is a source of nutrients, goes well with food and, as a common agricultural byproduct, is all but unavoidable in a wide range of cultures. It is also a highly sociable drug that a vast range of societies have used to bring people together to laugh, talk, sing, dance and worship (e.g. the Passover seder, in which inebriation is a *mitzvah* or commandment).

Finally, alcohol has the advantage of being highly modulatory. Whether at a party or dinner, experienced users know how much to drink in order to attain an appropriate level of intoxication. They may happily gulp down one and another, but then wait until their mind has settled a bit before venturing on to a third. At a business gathering, they may decide not to drink at all.

Of course, alcohol has its dark side—18 million problem drinkers in the U.S. alone, 23,000 alcohol-related traffic deaths per year, tens of thousands of work-related injuries—but it also has benefits that are frequently overlooked. While everyone knows of marriages destroyed by alcohol, how about the marriages it helps save? Who speaks up for the worker who, after a hard day, fortifies him or herself with a drink or two before facing up to the rigors at home?

Whereas feudal peasants worked to exhaustion and then, on feast days, drank to collapse, industrial man uses alcohol in smaller amounts to fine-tune the means of production—himself. After working eight hours, he uses it as a reward and relaxant. Would the same worker be more productive if he didn't settle himself down with a beer, but instead fidgeted nervously in front of the TV or yelled at the kids? Perhaps. But considering that periods of peak economic growth have sometimes coincided with periods of peak alcohol consumption (e.g. the U.S. in the '50s), the answer, very possibly, is that productivity would not be enhanced.

By the same token, despite a pronounced shift since the '70s from hard liquor to white wine, low-alcohol beer and the ubiquitous Perrier-with-a-twist, industrial productivity has been stagnant. Americans are drinking less, but not working better as a result.

Dying for a smoke: Then there is nicotine, a mood-control agent whose popularity worldwide is only slightly less than that of alcohol. Beginning in 1493, when Columbus returned from the New World with an interesting new plant called tobacco, nicotine's progress has, until recent years, been unchecked. Users were executed in 17th-Century Russia, while Bavaria, Saxony and Zurich decreed bans. Whenever Sultan Murad IV traveled around the Ottoman Empire during this period, he delighted in executing his subjects for the heinous offense of lighting up. "Even on the battlefield . . . he would punish them by beheading, hanging, quartering or crushing their hands or feet," according to one account.

Nevertheless, the popular will has prevailed. When the director general of New Amsterdam tried to impose a smoking ban in 1639, virtually the entire male population camped outside his office in protest. While fond of wine, Thomas Jefferson inveighed against tobacco (which he called "productive of infinite wretchedness"), yet after the revolution it emerged as a major cash crop.

Besides being useful as a fumigant, nicotine has a mild calming effect that can be used to promote sociability, which is why it quickly became a fixture in coffee houses and taverns. Rip Van Winkle, everybody's favorite peaceful layabout, was, according to his creator, Washington Irving, never to be seen without his hunting rifle, his dog and his pipe. Gen. Douglas MacArthur smoked a corncob pipe, a homely touch that was immediately picked up by the press, while college men in the '50s favored briars because it gave them the firm-jawed look appropriate to the American Century.

Since then, however, nicotine in general, and cigarettes in particular, have been under sustained assault. Smokers nowadays are segregated in restaurants, barred from lighting up on airplanes, shunned by co-workers and harassed by friends. Yuppies pollute the air with their BMWs, but nonetheless are aghast at the thought of soiling their lungs with so much as a whiff of someone else's "sidestream" smoke. Yet, in a certain roundabout sense, we owe a debt of

For centuries, people who have spoken of losing themselves in their work or shutting out the world may have been describing an elevated state brought on by an internally generated drug.

gratitude to nicotine for helping to show how to run a proper anti-drug campaign. Smokers are encouraged by an array of government subsidies, but millions of nicotine addicts have been persuaded to quit through means that stop somewhat short of driving them into the arms of Uzi-toting drug dealers.

Rather than driving users underground, the anti-smoking forces have mounted a nonstop propaganda campaign that has proved devastatingly effective simply because it is true. Outside the tobacco lobby, few people doubt that cigarettes cause lung cancer and are a prime contributor to heart and respiratory diseases causing hundreds of thousands of deaths in the U.S. each year. The credible campaign appeals to people's self-interest, rather than bludgeoning them into obedience.

Meanwhile, amid all the hysteria over crack, no one seems to notice the growing amount of tobacco advertising pitched directly at the inner-urban market. Faced with declining sales, cigarette manufacturers have tried to recoup by appealing to blacks and Hispanics, a strategy as devastating in terms of health and mortality as the efforts of the Medellin and Cali cartels. Yet, if affluence and education rise, it seems reasonable to presume that nicotine addiction will decline in these areas as well.

Reefer madness: On the other hand, probably no drug has been the subject of more lies than marijuana. The 1936 propaganda film *Reefer Madness* is valuable both as a camp classic and a window onto the obsessions of a middle-class society then terrified of sex, jazz and "letting go." Although American society seemed to be coming to its senses in the '70s, when marijuana came within a hair's breadth of decriminalization, it has since beaten a hasty retreat behind a curtain of disinformation and lies.

Due to the war on drugs, marijuana is back as an official "gateway" drug leading inexorably, according to official dogma, to cocaine, heroin and a lifetime of addiction. Yet millions of students have used marijuana since the '60s with no noticeable ill-effect. Millions of adults with kids, jobs and mortgages relax occasionally with a joint without winding up in the gutter. But simple facts like these mean little to a Republican-Democratic establishment hopelessly hooked on rhetoric and revenge.

The curious thing about marijuana, though, is that just as its evils have been vastly inflated by the government, its virtues have probably been exaggerated by supporters as well. In Holland, where marijuana is decriminalized, surveys indicate that a smaller percentage of people smoke than in the U.S. In India and the Caribbean, where marijuana is

ubiquitous, those with the economic means prefer booze. Steve Hagar, editor of *High Times* magazine, the pot-smoker's bible, tells of an American traveler who, when offered palm wine in an African village, asked for some potent local herb instead. The villagers were puzzled: why would anyone prefer something as lowly as marijuana to a delicacy like palm wine?

Why indeed? If drug prohibition were lifted, marijuana would undoubtedly find a niche in American society, but probably not much more. Laborers, taxi drivers and construction workers might find it useful in relieving boredom, but others might find that its hypnotic quality makes them feel groggy. Some might prefer it on weekends, while others might find that its effects are not very sociable. It makes many people quiet and withdrawn, which is why the noise level at a party usually drops whenever joints begin circulating. People opposed to noisy parties on principle might appreciate marijuana for precisely that reason. But judging from the experience in Holland, where marijuana is neither stigmatized by the government nor glamorized by the underground, a majority, arguably, would not.

Just say yes: Given the multiplicity of drugs and uses, what is one to make of a slogan like "Just Say No," endorsed by nearly the entire political spectrum, from Jesse Jackson to Jesse Helms? What's most apparent about the slogan is its arbitrariness. It does not ask Americans to forgo all mind-altering substances, obviously, since drugs like caffeine, nicotine or highly addictive Valium are still freely available.

It does not ask them to steer clear of only the most dangerous since, in terms of sheer bodies, alcohol and nicotine kill approximately 150 Americans for every one who succumbs to the effects of heroin, coke or other prohibited substances. (According to the National Council on Alcoholism, alcohol and tobacco were implicated in more than half a million deaths in 1985, while illicit substances were found to be factors in only 3,562.) Banning one without the other is like banning deer rifles while permitting sales of automatic weapons to go forward unimpeded.

Rather, the purpose of the "Just Say No" campaign is to shore up political authority. Using the circular logic favored by authoritarian governments, the campaign asks Americans to forgo those substances that have been prohibited not for reasons of health but for reasons of custom and politics. It urges them to just say no for no other reason than that their leaders have just said no.

The results may be unreasonable, but that's exactly the point. Right-wing authoritarianism is, in the final analysis, irrationality by decree. Those on top seek to limit debate not because it's disruptive but because it may lead to something more intelligent and democratic, and thereby upset their rule. Similarly, if drug czar William Bennett succeeds in enforcing unthinking drug obedience, he and other conservative hardliners no doubt will try to achieve it in other areas as well, such as abortion rights, collective bargaining, race relations and foreign policy.

The goal is mass cerebral anesthetization, more complete than that achieved by any drug.

Opium, Cocaine and Marijuana in American History

Over the past 200 years, Americans have twice accepted and then vehemently rejected drugs. Understanding these dramatic historical swings provides perspective on our current reaction to drug use

David F. Musto

DAVID F. MUSTO is professor of psychiatry at the Child Study Center and professor of the history of medicine at Yale University. He earned his medical degree at the University of Washington and received his master's in the history of science and medicine from Yale. Musto began studying the history of drug and alcohol use in the U.S. when he worked at the National Institute of Mental Health in the 1960s. He has served as a consultant for several national organizations, including the Presidential Commission on the HIV epidemic. From 1981 until 1990, Musto was a member of the Smithsonian Institution's National Council.

Dramatic shifts in attitude have characterized America's relation to drugs. During the 19th century, certain mood-altering substances, such as opiates and cocaine, were often regarded as compounds helpful in everyday life. Gradually this perception of drugs changed. By the early 1900s, and until the 1940s, the country viewed these and some other psychoactive drugs as dangerous, addictive compounds that needed to be severely controlled. Today, after a resurgence of a tolerant attitude toward drugs during the 1960s and 1970s, we find ourselves, again, in a period of drug intolerance.

America's recurrent enthusiasm for recreational drugs and subsequent campaigns for abstinence present a problem to policymakers and to the public. Since the peaks of these episodes are about a lifetime apart, citizens rarely have an accurate or even a vivid recollection of the last wave of cocaine or opiate use.

Phases of intolerance have been fueled by such fear and anger that the record of times favorable toward drug taking has been either erased from public memory or so distorted that it becomes useless as a point of reference for policy formation. During each attack on drug taking, total denigration of the preceding, contrary mood has seemed necessary for public welfare. Although such vigorous rejection may have value in further reducing demand, the long-term effect is to destroy a realistic perception of the past and of the conflicting attitudes toward mood-altering substances that have characterized our national history.

The absence of knowledge concerning our earlier and formative encounters with drugs unnecessarily impedes the already difficult task of establishing a workable and sustainable drug policy. An examination of the period of drug use that peaked around 1900 and the decline that followed it may enable us to approach the current drug problem with more confidence and reduce the likelihood that we will repeat past errors.

Until the 19th century, drugs had been used for millennia in their natural form. Cocaine and morphine, for example, were available only in coca leaves or poppy plants that were chewed, dissolved in alcoholic beverages or taken in some way that diluted the impact of the active agent. The ad-vent of organic chemistry in the 1800s changed the available forms of these drugs. Morphine was isolated in the first decade and cocaine by 1860; in 1874 diacetylmorphine was synthesized from morphine (although it became better known as heroin when the Bayer Company introduced it in 1898).

By mid-century the hypodermic syringe was perfected, and by 1870 it had become a familiar instrument to American physicians and patients [see "The Origins of Hypodermic Medication," by Norman Howard-Jones; SCIENTIFIC AMERICAN, January 1971]. At the same time, the astounding growth of the pharmaceutical industry intensified the ramifications of these accomplishments. As the century wore on, manufacturers grew increasingly adept at exploiting a marketable innovation and moving it into mass production, as well as advertising and distributing it throughout the world.

During this time, because of a peculiarity of the U.S. Constitution, the powerful new forms of opium and cocaine were more readily available in America than in most nations. Under the Constitution, individual states assumed responsibility for health issues, such as regulation of medical practice and the availability of pharmacological products. In fact, America had as many laws regarding health professions as it had states. For much of the 19th century, many states chose to have no controls at all; their legislatures reacted to the claims of contradictory health care

1. THINKING ABOUT DRUGS

philosophies by allowing free enterprise for all practitioners. The federal government limited its concern to communicable diseases and the provision of health care to the merchant marine and to government dependents.

Nations with a less restricted central government, such as Britain and Prussia, had a single, preeminent pharmacy law that controlled availability of dangerous drugs. In those countries, physicians had their right to practice similarly granted by a central authority. Therefore, when we consider consumption of opium, opiates, coca and cocaine in 19th-century America, we are looking at an era of wide availability and unrestrained advertising. The initial enthusiasm for the purified substances was only slightly affected by any substantial doubts or fear about safety, long-term health injuries or psychological dependence.

History encouraged such attitudes. Crude opium, alone or dissolved in some liquid such as alcohol, was brought by European explorers and settlers to North America. Colonists regarded opium as a familiar resource for pain relief. Benjamin Franklin regularly took laudanum—opium in alcohol extract—to alleviate the pain of kidney stones during the last few years of his life. The poet Samuel Taylor Coleridge, while a student at Cambridge in 1791, began using laudanum for pain and developed a lifelong addiction to the drug. Opium use in those early decades constituted an "experiment in nature" that has been largely forgotten, even repressed, as a result of the extremely negative reaction that followed.

Americans had recognized, however, the potential danger of continually using opium long before the availability of morphine and the hypodermic's popularity. The American Dispensatory of 1818 noted that the habitual use of opium could lead to "tremors, paralysis, stupidity and general emaciation." Balancing this danger, the text proclaimed the extraordinary value of opium in a multitude of ailments ranging from cholera to asthma. (Considering the treatments then in vogue—blistering, vomiting and bleeding—we can understand why opium was as cherished by patients as by their physicians.)

Opium's rise and fall can be tracked through U.S. import-consumption statistics compiled while importation of the drug and its derivative, morphine, was unrestricted and carried moderate tariffs. The per capita consumption of crude opium rose gradually during the

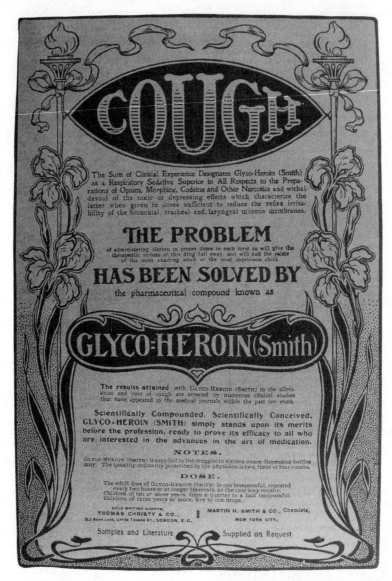

1800s, reaching a peak in the last decade of the century. It then declined, but after 1915 the data no longer reflect trends in drug use, because that year new federal laws severely restricted legal imports. In contrast, per capita consumption of smoking opium rose until a 1909 act outlawed its importation.

Americans had quickly associated smoking opium with Chinese immigrants who arrived after the Civil War to work on railroad construction. This association was one of the earliest examples of a powerful theme in the American perception of drugs: linkage between a drug and a feared or rejected group within society. Cocaine would be similarly linked with blacks and marijuana with Mexicans in the first third of the 20th century. The association of a drug with a racial group or a political cause, however, is not unique to America. In the 19th century, for instance, the Chinese came to regard opium as

HEROIN COUGH SYRUP was one of many pharmaceuticals at the turn of the century that contained mood-altering substances. The name "heroin" was coined by Bayer in 1898, a year before the company introduced aspirin.

a tool and symbol of Western domination. That perception helped to fuel a vigorous antiopium campaign in China early in the 20th century.

During the 1800s, increasing numbers of people fell under the influence of opiates—substances that demanded regular consumption or the penalty of withdrawal, a painful but rarely life-threatening experience. Whatever the cause—overprescribing by physicians, over-the-counter medicines, self-indulgence or "weak will"—opium addiction brought shame. As consumption increased, so did the frequency of addiction.

At first, neither physicians nor their patients thought that the introduction of the hypodermic syringe or pure

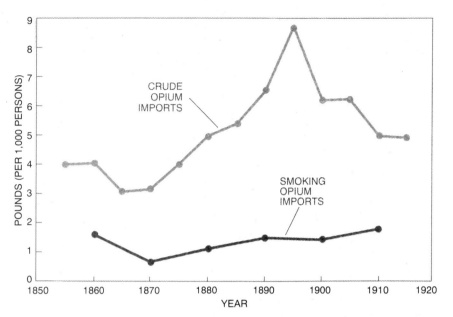

OPIATE CONSUMPTION was documented by the Treasury and the Commerce Departments, starting in the mid-19th century. The importation of smoking opium became illegal in 1909, and crude opium and its derivatives were severely restricted in 1915. After 1915, the data reflected medicinal use.

morphine contributed to the danger of addiction. On the contrary, because pain could be controlled with less morphine when injected, the presumption was made that the procedure was less likely to foster addiction.

Late in the century some states and localities enacted laws limiting morphine to a physician's prescription, and some laws even forbade refilling these prescriptions. But the absence of any federal control over interstate commerce in habit-forming drugs, of uniformity among the state laws and of effective enforcement meant that the rising tide of legislation directed at opiates—and later cocaine—was more a reflection of changing public attitude toward these drugs than an effective reduction of supplies to users. Indeed, the decline noted after the mid-1890s was probably related mostly to the public's growing fear of addiction and of the casual social use of habit-forming substances rather than to any successful campaign to reduce supplies.

At the same time, health professionals were developing more specific treatments for painful diseases, finding less dangerous analgesics (such as aspirin) and beginning to appreciate the addictive power of the hypodermic syringe. By now the public had learned to fear the careless, and possibly addicted, physician. In *A Long Day's Journey into Night*, Eugene O'Neill dramatized the

painful and shameful impact of his mother's physician-induced addiction.

In a spirit not unlike that of our times, Americans in the last decade of the 19th century grew increasingly concerned about the environment, adulterated foods, destruction of the forests and the widespread use of mood-altering drugs. The concern embraced alcohol as well. The Anti-Saloon League, founded in 1893, led a temperance movement toward prohibition, which later was achieved in 1919 and became law in January 1920.

After overcoming years of resistance by over-the-counter, or patent, medicine manufacturers, the federal government enacted the Pure Food and Drug Act in 1906. This act did not prevent sales of addictive drugs like opiates and cocaine, but it did require accurate labeling of contents for all patent remedies sold in interstate commerce. Still, no national restriction existed on the availability of opiates or cocaine. The solution to this problem would emerge from growing concern, legal ingenuity and the unexpected involvement of the federal government with the international trade in narcotics.

Responsibility for the Philippines in 1898 added an international dimension to the

2. Opium, Cocaine, and Marijuana

growing domestic alarm about drug abuse. It also revealed that Congress, if given the opportunity, would prohibit nonmedicinal uses of opium among its new dependents. Civil Governor William Howard Taft proposed reinstituting an opium monopoly—through which the previous Spanish colonial government had obtained revenue from sales to opium merchants—and using those profits to help pay for a massive public education campaign. President Theodore Roosevelt vetoed this plan, and in 1905 Congress mandated an absolute prohibition of opium for any purpose other than medicinal use.

To deal efficiently with the antidrug policy established for the Philippines, a committee from the Islands visited various territories in the area to see how others dealt with the opium problem. The benefit of controlling narcotics internationally became apparent.

In early 1906 China had instituted a campaign against opium, especially smoking opium, in an attempt to modernize and to make the Empire better able to cope with continued Western encroachments on its sovereignty. At about the same time, Chinese anger at maltreatment of their nationals in the U.S. seethed into a voluntary boycott of American goods. Partly to appease the Chinese by aiding their antiopium efforts and partly to deal with uncontrollable smuggling within the Philippine Archipelago, the U.S. convened a meeting of regional powers. In this way, the U.S. launched a campaign for worldwide narcotics traffic control that would extend through the years in an unbroken diplomatic sequence from the League of Nations to the present efforts of the United Nations.

The International Opium Commission, a gathering of 13 nations, met in Shanghai in February 1909. The Protestant Episcopal bishop of the Philippines, Charles Henry Brent, who had been instrumental in organizing the meeting, was chosen to preside. Resolutions noting problems with opium and opiates were adopted, but they did not constitute a treaty, and no decisions bound the nations attending the commission. In diplomatic parlance, what was needed now was a conference not a commission. The U.S. began to pursue this goal with determination.

The antinarcotics campaign in America had several motivations. Appeasement of China was certainly one factor for officials of the State Department. The department's opium commissioner, Hamilton Wright, thought the whole matter could be "used as oil to smooth the troubled water of our aggressive commercial policy there." Another reason was the belief, strongly held by the federal government today, that controlling crops and traffic in producing countries could most efficiently stop U.S. nonmedical consumption of drugs.

To restrict opium and coca production required worldwide agreement and, thus, an international conference. After intense diplomatic activity, one was convened in the Hague in December 1911. Brent again presided, and on January 23, 1912, the 12 nations represented signed a convention. Provision was made for the other countries to comply before the treaty was brought into force. After all, no producing or manufacturing nation wanted to leave the market open to nonratifying nations.

The convention required each country to enact domestic legislation controlling narcotics trade. The goal was a world in which narcotics were restricted to medicinal use. Both the producing and consuming nations would have control over their boundaries.

After his return from Shanghai, Wright labored to craft a comprehensive federal antinarcotics law. In his path loomed the problem of states' rights. The health professions were considered a major cause of patient addiction. Yet how could federal law interfere with the prescribing practices of physicians or require that pharmacists keep records? Wright settled on the federal government's power to tax; the result, after prolonged bargaining with pharmaceutical, import, export and medical interests, was the Harrison Act of December 1914.

Representative Francis Burton Harrison's association with the act was an accidental one, the consequence of his introduction of the administration's bill. If the chief proponent and negotiator were to be given eponymic credit, it should have been called the Wright Act. It could even have been called a second Mann Act, after Representative James Mann, who saw the bill through to passage in the House of Representatives, for by that time Harrison had become governor-general of the Philippines.

The act required a strict accounting of opium and coca and their derivatives from entry into the U.S. to dispensing to a patient. To accom-

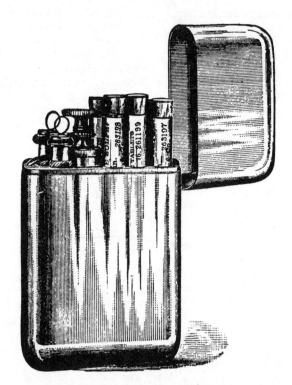

1894 EMERGENCY KIT by the Parke-Davis Company carried cocaine, morphine, atropine and strychnine as well as a hypodermic syringe.

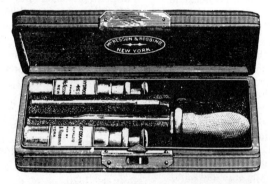

POCKET COCAINE CASE manufactured by pharmacists McKesson & Robbins was one of many drug kits on the market in the late 1800s.

plish this control, a small tax had to be paid at each transfer, and permits had to be obtained by applying to the Treasury Department. Only the patient paid no tax, needed no permit and, in fact, was not allowed to obtain one.

Initially Wright and the Department of Justice argued that the Harrison Act forbade indefinite maintenance of addiction unless there was a specific medical reason such as cancer or tuberculosis. This interpretation was rejected in 1916 by the Supreme Court—even though the Justice Department argued that the Harrison Act was the domestic implementation of the Hague Opium Convention and therefore took precedence over states' rights. Maintenance was to be allowed.

That decision was short-lived. In 1919 the Supreme Court, led by Oliver Wendell Holmes and Louis Brandeis, changed its mind by a 5-4 vote. The court declared that indefinite maintenance for "mere addiction" was outside legitimate medical practice and that, consequently, prohibiting it did not constitute interference with a state's right to regulate physicians. Second, because the person receiving the drugs for maintenance was not a bona fide patient but just a recipient of drugs, the transfer of narcotics defrauded the government of taxes required under the Harrison Act.

During the 1920s and 1930s, the opiate problem, chiefly morphine and heroin, declined in the U.S., until much of the problem was confined to the periphery of society and the outcasts of urban areas. There were exceptions: some health professionals and a few others of middle class or higher status continued to take opiates.

America's international efforts continued. After World War I, the British and U.S. governments proposed adding the Hague Convention to the Versailles Treaty. As a result, ratifying the peace treaty meant ratifying the Hague Convention and enacting a domestic law controlling narcotics. This incorporation led to the British Dangerous Drugs Act of 1920, an act often misattributed to a raging heroin epidemic in Britain. In the 1940s some Americans argued that the British system provided heroin to addicts and, by not relying on law enforcement, had almost eradicated the opiate problem. In fact, Britain had no problem to begin with. This argument serves as an interesting example of how the desperate need to solve the drug problem in the U.S. tends to create misperceptions of a foreign drug situation.

The story of cocaine use in America is somewhat shorter than that of opium, but it follows a similar plot. In 1884 purified cocaine became commercially available in the U.S. At first the wholesale cost was very high—$5 to $10 a gram—but it soon fell to 25 cents a gram and remained there until the price inflation of World War I. Problems with cocaine were evident almost from the beginning, but popular opinion and the voices of leading medical experts depicted cocaine as a remarkable, harmless stimulant.

William A. Hammond, one of America's most prominent neurologists, extolled cocaine in print and lectures. By 1887 Hammond was assuring audiences that cocaine was no more habit-forming than coffee or tea. He also told them of the "cocaine wine" he had perfected with the help of a New York druggist: two grains of cocaine to a pint of wine. Hammond claimed that this tonic was far more effective than the popular French coca wine, probably a reference to Vin Mariani, which he complained had only half a grain of cocaine to the pint.

Coca-Cola was also introduced in 1886 as a drink offering the advantages of coca but lacking the danger of alcohol. It amounted to a temperance coca beverage. The cocaine was removed in 1900, a year before the city of Atlanta, Ga., passed an ordinance (and a state statute the following year) prohibiting provision of any cocaine to a consumer without a prescription.

Cocaine is one of the most powerful of the central nervous system euphoriants. This fact underlay cocaine's quickly growing consumption and the ineffectiveness of the early warnings. How could anything that made users so confident and happy be bad? Within a year of cocaine's introduction, the Parke-Davis Company provided coca and cocaine in 15 forms, including coca cigarettes, cocaine for injection and cocaine for sniffing. Parke-Davis and at least one other company also offered consumers a handy cocaine kit. (The Parke-Davis kit contained a hypodermic syringe.) The firm proudly supplied a drug that, it announced, "can supply the place of food, make the coward brave, the silent eloquent and . . . render the sufferer insensitive to pain."

Cocaine spread rapidly throughout the nation. In September 1886 a physician in Puyallup, Washington Territory, reported an adverse reaction to cocaine during an operation. Eventually reports of overdoses and idiosyncratic reactions shifted to accounts of the social and behavioral effects of long-term cocaine use. The ease with which experimenters became regular users and the increasing instances of cocaine being linked with violence and paranoia gradually took hold in popular and medical thought.

In 1907 an attempt was made in New York State to shift the responsibility for cocaine's availability from the open market to medical control. Assemblyman Alfred E. Smith, later the governor of New York and in 1928 the Democratic party's presidential candidate, sponsored such a bill. The cost of cocaine on New York City streets, as revealed by newspaper and police accounts after the law's enactment, was typically 25 cents a packet, or "deck."

Although 25 cents may seem cheap, it was actually slightly higher than the average industrial wage at that time, which was about 20 cents an hour. Packets, commonly glycine envelopes, usually contained one to two grains (65 to 130 milligrams), or about a tenth of a gram. The going rate was roughly 10 times that of the wholesale price, a ratio not unlike recent cocaine street prices, although in the past few years the street price has actually been lower in real value than what it was in 1910.

Several similar reports from the years before the Harrison Act of 1914 suggest that both the profit margin and the street price of cocaine were unaffected by the legal availability of cocaine from a physician. Perhaps the formality of medical consultation and the growing antagonism among physicians and the public toward cocaine helped to sustain the illicit market.

In 1910 William Howard Taft, then president of the U.S., sent to Congress a report that cocaine posed the most serious drug problem America had ever faced. Four years later President Woodrow Wilson signed into law the Harrison Act, which, in addition to its opiate provisions, permitted the sale of cocaine only through prescriptions. It also forbade any trace of cocaine in patent remedies, the most severe restriction on any habit-forming drug to that date. (Opiates, including heroin, could still be present in small amounts in nonprescription remedies, such as cough medicines.)

Although the press continued to reveal Hollywood scandals and underworld cocaine practices during the 1920s, cocaine use gradually declined as a societal problem. The laws probably hastened the trend, and certainly the tremendous public fear reduced demand. By 1930 the New York City Mayor's Committee on Drug Addiction was reporting that "during the last 20 years cocaine as an addiction has ceased to be a problem."

Unlike opiates and cocaine, marijuana was introduced during a period of drug intolerance. Consequently, it was not until the 1960s, 40 years after marijuana cigarettes had arrived in America, that it was widely used. The practice of smoking cannabis leaves came to the U.S. with Mexican immigrants, who had come North during the 1920s to work in agriculture, and it soon extended to white and black jazz musicians.

As the Great Depression of the 1930s settled over America, the immigrants became an unwelcome minority linked with violence and with growing and smoking marijuana. Western states pressured the federal government to control marijuana use. The first official response was to urge adoption of a uniform state antinarcotics law. Then a new approach became feasible in 1937, when the Supreme Court upheld the National Firearms Act. This act prohibited the transfer of machine guns between private citizens without purchase of a transfer tax stamp—and the government would not issue the necessary stamp. Prohibition was implemented through the taxing power of the federal government.

Within a month of the Supreme Court's decision, the Treasury Department testified before Congress for a bill to establish a marijuana transfer tax. The bill became law, and until the Comprehensive Drug Abuse Act of 1970, marijuana was legally controlled through a transfer tax for which no stamps or licenses were available to private citizens. Certainly some people were smoking marijuana in the 1930s, but not until the 1960s was its use widespread.

Around the time of the Marihuana Tax Act of 1937, the federal government released dramatic and exaggerated portrayals of marijuana's effects. Scientific publications during the 1930s also fearfully described marijuana's dangers. Even Walter Bromberg, who thought that marijuana made only a small contribution to major crimes, nevertheless reported the drug was "a primary stimulus to the impulsive life with direct expression in the motor field."

Marijuana's image shifted during the 1960s, when it was said that its use at the gigantic Woodstock gathering kept peace—as opposed to what might have happened if alcohol had been the drug of choice. In the shift to drug toleration in the late 1960s and early 1970s, investigators found it difficult to associate health problems with marijuana use. The 1930s and 1940s had marked the nadir of drug toleration in the U.S., and possibly the mood of both times affected professional perception of this controversial plant.

After the Harrison Act, the severity of federal laws concerning the sale and possession of opiates and cocaine gradually rose. As drug use declined, penalties increased until 1956, when the death penalty was introduced as an option by the federal government for anyone older than 18 providing heroin to anyone younger than 18 (apparently no one was ever executed under this statute). At the same time, mandatory minimum prison sentences were extended to 10 years.

After the youthful counterculture discovered marijuana in the 1960s, demand for the substance grew until about 1978, when the favorable attitude toward it reached a peak. In 1972 the Presidential Commission on Marihuana and Drug Abuse recommended "decriminalization" of marijuana, that is, legal possession of a small amount

for personal use. In 1977 the Carter administration formally advocated legalizing marijuana in amounts up to an ounce.

The Gallup Poll on relaxation of laws against marijuana is instructive. In 1980, 53 percent of Americans favored legalization of small amounts of marijuana; by 1986 only 27 percent supported that view. At the same time, those favoring penalties for marijuana use rose from 43 to 67 percent. This reversal parallels the changes in attitude among high school students revealed by the Institute of Social Research at the University of Michigan.

The decline in favorable attitudes toward marijuana that began in the late 1970s continues. In the past few years we have seen penalties rise again against users and dealers. The recriminalization of marijuana possession by popular vote in Alaska in 1990 is one example of such a striking reversal.

In addition to stricter penalties, two

MARIHUANA TAX STAMP of 1937 established governmental control over the transfer and sale of the plant. The stamp was never available for private use.

other strategies, silence and exaggeration, were implemented in the 1930s to keep drug use low and prevent a recurrence of the decades-long, frustrating and fearful antidrug battle of the late 19th and early 20th centuries. Primary and secondary schools instituted educational programs against drugs. Then policies shifted amid fears that talking about cocaine or heroin to young people, who now had less exposure to drugs, would arouse their curiosity. This concern led to a decline in drug-related information given during school instruc-

tion as well as to the censorship of motion pictures.

The Motion Picture Association of America, under strong public and religious pressure, decided in 1934 to refuse a seal of approval for any film that showed narcotics. This prohibition was enforced with one exception—*To the Ends of the Earth,* a 1948 film that lauded the Federal Bureau of Narcotics—until *Man with a Golden Arm* was successfully exhibited in 1956 without a seal.

Associated with a decline in drug information was a second, apparently paradoxical strategy: exaggerating the effects of drugs. The middle ground was abandoned. In 1924 Richmond P. Hobson, a nationally prominent campaigner against drugs, declared that one ounce of heroin could addict 2,000 persons. In 1936 an article in the *American Journal of Nursing* warned that a marijuana user "will suddenly turn with murderous violence upon whomever is nearest to him. He will run amuck with knife, axe, gun, or anything else that is close at hand, and will kill or maim without any reason."

A goal of this well-meaning exaggeration was to describe drugs so repulsively that anyone reading or hearing of them would not be tempted to experiment with the substances. One contributing factor to such a publicity campaign, especially regarding marijuana, was that the Depression permitted little money for any other course of action.

Severe penalties, silence and, if silence was not possible, exaggeration became the basic strategies against drugs after the decline of their first wave of use. But the effect of these tactics was to create ignorance and false images that would present no real obstacle to a renewed enthusiasm for drugs in the 1960s. At the time, enforcing draconian and mandatory penalties would have filled to overflowing all jails and prisons with the users of marijuana alone.

Exaggeration fell in the face of the realities of drug use and led to a loss of credibility regarding any government pronouncement on drugs. The lack of information erased any awareness of the first epidemic, including the gradually obtained and hard-won public insight into the hazards of cocaine and opiates. Public memory, which would have provided some context for the antidrug laws, was a casualty of the antidrug strategies.

The earlier and present waves of drug use have much in common, but there is at least one major difference. During the first wave of drug use, anti-drug laws were not enacted until the public demanded them. In contrast, today's most severe antidrug laws were on the books from the outset; this gap between law and public opinion made the controls appear ridiculous and bizarre. Our current frustration over the laws' ineffectiveness has been greater and more lengthy than before because we have lived through many years in which antidrug laws lacked substantial public support. Those laws appeared powerless to curb the rise in drug use during the 1960s and 1970s.

The first wave of drug use involved primarily opiates and cocaine. The nation's full experience with marijuana is now under way (marijuana's tax regulation in 1937 was not the result of any lengthy or broad experience with the plant). The popularity and growth in demand for opiates and cocaine in mainstream society derived from a simple factor: the effect on most people's physiology and emotions was enjoyable. Moreover, Americans have recurrently hoped that the technology of drugs would maximize their personal potential. That opiates could relax and cocaine energize seemed wonderful opportunities for fine-tuning such efforts.

Two other factors allowed a long and substantial rise in consumption during the 1800s. First, casualties accumulate gradually; not everyone taking cocaine or opiates becomes hooked on the drug. In the case of opiates, some users have become addicted for a lifetime and have still been productive.

Yet casualties have mounted as those who could not handle occasional use have succumbed to domination by drugs and by drug-seeking behavior. These addicts become not only miserable themselves but also frightening to their families and friends. Such cases are legion today in our larger cities, but the percentage of those who try a substance and acquire a dependence or get into serious legal trouble is not 100 percent. For cocaine, the estimate varies from 3 to 20 percent, or even higher, and so it is a matter of time before cocaine is recognized as a likely danger.

Early in the cycle, when social tolerance prevails, the explanation for casualties is that those who succumb to addiction are seen as having a physiological idiosyncrasy or "foolish trait." Personal disaster is thus viewed as an

 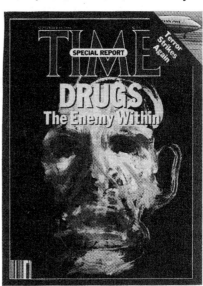

TIME MAGAZINE COVERS from 1981 and from 1986 reflect a clear change in American views toward mood-altering drugs, specifically cocaine.

exception to the rule. Another factor minimizing the sense of risk is our belief in our own invulnerability—that general warnings do not include us. Such faith reigns in the years of greatest exposure to drug use, ages 15 to 25. Resistance to a drug that makes a user feel confident and exuberant takes many years to permeate a society as large and complex as the U.S.

The interesting question is not why people take drugs, but rather why they stop taking them. We perceive risk differently as we begin to reject drugs. One can perceive a hypothetical 3 percent risk from taking cocaine as an assurance of 97 percent safety, or one can react as if told that 3 percent of New York/Washington shuttle flights crash. Our exposure to drug problems at work, in our neighborhood and within our families shifts our perception, gradually shaking our sense of invulnerability.

Cocaine has caused the most dramatic change in estimating risk. From a grand image as the ideal tonic, cocaine's reputation degenerated into that of the most dangerous of drugs, linked in our minds with stereotypes of mad, violent behavior. Opiates have never fallen so far in esteem, nor were they repressed to the extent cocaine had been between 1930 and 1970.

Today we are experiencing the reverse of recent decades, when the technology of drug use promised an extension of our natural potential. Increasingly we see drug consumption as reducing what we could achieve on our own with healthy food and exercise. Our change of attitude about drugs is connected to our concern over air pollution, food adulteration and fears for the stability of the environment.

Ours is an era not unlike that early in this century, when Americans made similar efforts at self-improvement accompanied by an assault on habit-forming drugs. Americans seem to be the least likely of any people to accept the inevitability of historical cycles. Yet if we do not appreciate our history, we may again become captive to the powerful emotions that led to draconian penalties, exaggeration or silence.

FURTHER READING

AMERICAN DIPLOMACY AND THE NARCOTICS TRAFFIC, 1900–1939. Arnold H. Taylor. Duke University Press, 1969.

DRUGS IN AMERICA: A SOCIAL HISTORY, 1800–1980. H. Wayne Morgan. Syracuse University Press, 1981.

DARK PARADISE: OPIATE ADDICTION IN AMERICA BEFORE 1940. David T. Courtwright. Harvard University Press, 1982.

THE AMERICAN DISEASE: ORIGINS OF NARCOTIC CONTROL. Expanded Edition. David F. Musto. Oxford University Press, 1987.

AMERICA'S FIRST COCAINE EPIDEMIC. David F. Musto in *Wilson Quarterly*, pages 59–65; Summer 1989.

ILLICIT PRICE OF COCAINE IN TWO ERAS: 1908–14 AND 1982–89. David F. Musto in *Connecticut Medicine*, Vol. 54, No. 6, pages 321–326; June 1990.

Alcohol in America

W. J. Rorabaugh

W. J. Rorabaugh is professor of history at the University of Washington in Seattle, and author of The Alcoholic Republic.

F or centuries Europeans have downed large quantities of beer, wine, and hard liquor. When Europeans began to migrate to North America in the early 1600s they brought along their hearty drinking habits. Thus Americans have been heavy users of alcohol for more than three hundred years.

English colonists in Massachusetts and Virginia imported beer, but this was expensive, and for a time they brewed their own. After 1700 the colonists drank fermented peach juice, hard apple cider, and rum, which they imported from the West Indies or distilled from West Indian molasses.

Virginians had a carefree attitude about alcohol. Drinking was an important part of the culture, and people passed around jugs or bowls of liquor at barbecues, on market days, and at elections. Candidates gave away free drinks. A stingy candidate had no chance of winning. Practically everyone drank.

Even restrained New Englanders consumed great quantities of liquor. The Puritans called alcohol the "Good Creature of God," a holy substance to be taken proudly yet cautiously. Though unopposed to the use of alcohol, New England ministers did declare public drunkenness a sin that led to poverty, crime, and violence, especially wife beating.

By 1770 Americans consumed alcohol, mostly in the form of rum and cider, routinely with every meal. Many people began the day with an "eye opener" and closed it with a nightcap. People of all ages drank, including toddlers who finished off

> *By 1770 Americans consumed alcohol routinely with every meal. Many people began the day with an "eye opener" and closed it with a nightcap.*

the heavily sugared portion at the bottom of a parent's mug of rum toddy. Each person consumed about three and a half gallons of alcohol per year. This is about double the present rate of consumption.

The American Revolution drastically changed drinking habits. When the British blockaded the seacoast and thereby cut off molasses and rum imports, Americans looked for a substitute. Scot-Irish immigrants who had settled on the western frontier provided whiskey.

After the revolution whiskey replaced rum, since the British refused to supply it and the new federal government began to tax it in the 1790s. Whiskey also thrived because it was cheap. The settlement of the corn belt in Kentucky and Ohio created a corn glut. Western farmers could make no profit shipping corn overland to eastern markets, so they distilled corn into "liquid assets." By the 1820s whiskey sold for twenty-five cents a gallon, making it cheaper than beer, wine, coffee, tea, or milk. In many places whiskey was also less

dangerous than water, which was frequently contaminated.

By 1830 consumption of alcohol, mostly in the form of whiskey, had reached more than seven gallons a year for every person over age fifteen or three times the current rate.

Liquor tended to be taken in small quantities throughout the day, often with meals. Instead of a morning coffee break, Americans stopped work at 11:00 a.m. to drink. A lot of work went undone but in this slow paced, preindustrial age this was not always a problem. A drunken stage coach driver posed little threat, since the horses knew the route and made their own way home. However, there was growing opposition to alcohol.

The earliest attacks on alcohol came during the late 1700s from Methodists and Quakers. Dr. Benjamin Rush, a prominent Philadelphia physician, led this first temperance movement. Rush believed that overuse of hard liquor was unhealthy, but that small quantities of weak mixed drinks

From *OAH Magazine of History*, Fall 1991, pp. 17-19. Reprinted by permission.

were harmless. Most Americans ignored the doctor's warnings.

Protestant ministers shifted the attack against alcohol from the issue of health to the question of sin. Arguing that any drinking easily led to drunkenness, they demanded teetotalism, or total abstinence from alcohol. Soon churches required members to take a pledge not to drink.

By 1850 the consumption of alcohol had dropped by more than half. This decline did not mean that the average American drank only half as much. Rather, half the population had stopped drinking. Other people continued to drink as they had before the temperance movement.

As early as the 1830s temperance leaders resorted to government power to coerce the remaining drinkers to give up liquor. Temperance became prohibition, and in 1838 Massachusetts passed the first prohibition law. Ignoring beer, cider, and wine, the state legislature banned the sale of hard liquor in any quantity under fifteen gallons. Retailers dodged the law. One enterprising seller sold the right to see his blind pig for six cents. The purchaser also got a free drink. This is the origin of the term "blind pig" to describe an illegal drinking establishment. Two years later the prohibition statute was repealed.

In 1851 Neal Dow, a crusading dry Quaker who had served as mayor of Portland, Maine, persuaded his state to enact a prohibition law. Although several states copied the Maine Law, as it was called, they all found that effective enforcement was impossible and consequently rescinded the legislation.

During the Civil War northern soldiers turned from traditional hard liquor to a preferred new German light lager beer, which enjoyed great popularity after the war. This period saw the emergence of today's largest breweries, including Anheuser-Busch, Schlitz, Pabst, and Miller (originally Mueller).

In 1873-1874 women living in several small towns in Ohio started the Women's Crusade. Lacking the vote and feeling powerless, they turned to direct action. Locally prominent women invaded all-male saloons, dropped to their knees, and said loud prayers. Customers fled, but the crusading women stayed to demand that each saloon be closed. Any retailer who had the women arrested faced public out-

rage. Many saloons closed. These tactics failed, however, in large cities. Cincinnati saloon-keepers' wives attacked the prohibitionists.

Frances Willard then organized the Woman's Christian Temperance Union, which gained more than a million members and became the world's largest women's organization. The WCTU decided to "do everything." Willard advocated making children take the pledge, banning drinkers from jobs as school teachers, legislating prohibition, and giving women the vote.

After Willard's death in 1898, anti-liquor leadership passed to the Anti-Saloon League. This organization, which included both men and women, operated as a political pressure group. Elected officials who favored prohibition were rewarded with campaign funds and workers while those against prohibition risked defeat. After 1900 the ASL, in cooperation with the WCTU, succeeded in drying up most of the country. National prohibition, however, still looked unlikely.

There was little support in the country's large cities for national prohibition. The cities were run by corrupt political machines that used saloons owned by the brewers as the basis of their power. Prohibitionists attacked the connection between saloons and corrupt politics with only limited success.

Prohibition was finally adopted not because of women's groups, but because of World War I. German-American brewers lost their political effectiveness amid anti-German hysteria, and in 1917 prohibitionists persuaded Congress to pass a temporary war time dry law. Food was in short supply, and anti-liquor forces warned that brewing or distilling grain threatened the war effort. In this milieu the Eighteenth Amendment was proposed and took effect after three-fourths of the states ratified it in January 1920.

The amendment did have its oddities, however. It outlawed the manufacture, sale, or transportation of intoxicating liquors for beverage purposes but did **not** prohibit consumption. Congress also had to define the percentage of alcohol that was intoxicating. Many people hoped that beer and light wine might be kept legal, but the Volstead Act of 1919 banned any beverage that contained over one half of one percent alcohol.

In the 1920s enforcement proceeded in earnest, at least in some areas. In cities such as New York or San Francisco, however, prohibition was not successful. The law did reduce consumption, perhaps by half, and it did change the ways in which people drank. For example, the all-male saloon disappeared and was replaced by the speakeasy, where men and women drank together out of teacups. People also drank in hotel rooms and in private homes where arrest was unlikely.

Liquor was imported illegally, largely from Canada. Soon rum runners' boats outraced the Coast Guard's, and Canadian distillers Hiram Walker and Seagrams—still major forces in the American liquor business—profited mightily.

By the late 1920s, because of corrupt and incompetent Prohibition agents, and because of public opposition, the Eighteenth Amendment was impossible to enforce. In Chicago, where Al Capone was making an estimated $200 million a year, at least 400 policemen were "on the take." Although the "dry" Herbert Hoover called prohibition a noble experiment and defeated the "wet" Al Smith for the presidency in 1928, a sense of exasperation about prohibition was growing.

Public opinion had turned against prohibition, and in 1933 Congress passed and the states ratified the Twenty-first Amendment which ended America's dry years. Newly elected President Franklin D. Roosevelt celebrated in the White House by mixing the first of many nightly martinis.

The end of prohibition did not mean a resurgence of the saloon. Many states, especially in the South and Midwest, prohibited sales of alcohol by the drink, while other states discouraged consumption by creating state liquor stores that restricted advertising, locations, and business hours. Both the federal government and the states imposed high taxes on alcoholic products.

From the 1950s through the 1970s alcohol consumption rose steadily. The post-World War II economic boom stimulated the market, which has always correlated with wealth. The poor drank the least, the rich drank the most. Doctors and lawyers, as befitted their status, were the heartiest topers. Whites drank more than blacks. The young drank more than the old. Alcohol use peaked between ages twenty-five and thirty-five, especially for single males. The large number of baby boomers in the prime drinking age bracket in the 1960s and 1970s accounted for much of the consumption.

Drinking styles changed as well. Not only did more women drink, they drank more. Women preferred sweet drinks like ready-mixed canned cocktails, wine coolers, or white wine. Wine sales, especially of upscale, expensive wines, soared, and white wines marched past red. Hard liquor tastes shifted from American whiskey to Canadian whiskey and Scotch, and by the 1970s to vodka, gin, and white rum.

Imported beers, often darker and more flavorful than American-style lager, gained a market, and regional brewers collapsed under pressure from a half dozen nationally advertised giants. Anheuser-Busch became the industry leader by its early decision to sponsor sporting events on television. Shrewd advertising techniques created a huge market for light beers that appealed to the calorie-conscious.

During the past two decades teenage drinking has become a major issue. In the 1970s, many states reduced the legal drinking age to eighteen, and in some states liquor-related teen auto accidents then grew rapidly. The age of taking a first drink dropped into the early teens. More alarming was evidence of severe alcohol-related problems, including physical addiction among older teens who had been drinking only a few years. Patterns of alcohol abuse that took a decade or more to develop in an adult emerged among teens in far shorter periods. These trends produced a backlash against teen drinking amid charges that the liquor industry's advertising enticed young people to drink.

In the 1980s changing demographics spurred a decline in alcohol consumption. In addition, there were rising health concerns, especially about the effects of alcohol on the health of the unborn children of pregnant mothers. Any woman at a particular early stage of pregnancy who consumed a small number of drinks was at risk for fetal alcohol syndrome.

A major social cost associated with alcohol abuse continued to be drunken driving. Each year intoxicated drivers caused about half of nearly 50,000 automobile accident fatalities. Mothers Against Drunk Driving (MADD) lobbied to raise the drinking age to twenty-one. Eventually, Congress coerced the states to adopt such a policy. State legislatures also imposed stricter definitions of legal drunkenness. Those convicted of driving under the influence found it harder to keep their licenses and were more likely to serve time in jail.

Attitudes toward alcohol in the 1990s are more intolerant than at any time since the early 1930s. Although legal, liquor has not become entirely respectable. The acceptance of alcohol has always depended upon the social context surrounding its use. American attitudes have varied considerably and may be said to express widespread ambivalence. Simultaneously, Americans have accepted alcohol as part of a European heritage, but have rejected it as a destructive substance. When Americans react to the mention of alcohol, they typically respond with an uneasy laugh that is symbolic of both the joy and sorrow of alcohol in American culture.

COKE INC.

INSIDE THE BIG BUSINESS OF DRUGS

MICHAEL STONE

CTING ON A TIP FROM THE BROOKLYN DISTRICT ATTORney, federal Customs agents raided a warehouse on 44th Drive in Long Island City early last November. They were looking for cocaine, and they found it— 400 pounds stuffed in cardboard boxes lying in plain view. But that was only the start. Against a wall, the agents found hundreds of twenty-gallon cans filled with bricks of cocaine packed in lye so corrosive it had begun to eat through the metal containers. It took a police unit seven days to move out the drugs. By then, the agents had uncovered nearly 5,000 bricks: 4,840 kilograms—5.3 tons—of cocaine.

Richard Mercier, the agent in charge of the operation, says that in 1973, he put a dealer away for 34 years for possession of three ounces of cocaine. In those days, the seizure of a kilogram of drugs—2.2 pounds—was a major bust. After the Long Island City raid, Mercier recalls, he surveyed a 24-foot truck piled four feet high with cocaine. "How much more is out there?" he wondered.

Three months after that bust, in the early-morning hours of February 3, a police anti-crime unit rounded the corner at Lenox Avenue and 128th Street in Harlem and saw a young man we'll call Willie waving a .357 Magnum at a group of youths across the street. Someone yelled, "Yo, burgundy!"—the code name for the officers' red Chevy—and Willie darted into a nearby tenement. The cops cornered him in a second-floor apartment, and Willie dropped a brown bag containing almost 300 vials of crack. On a bench next to him, police found a plastic bag containing 2,900 more vials of crack. In a wastebasket they discovered more than $12,000 in small bills. It was Willie's second arrest. He was fifteen.

These events evoke the images New Yorkers most commonly associate with the city's drug trade: mountains of white powder smuggled by a faceless international cartel, and the dead-end kid hawking crack in the ghetto. But the smuggler and the street dealer are only the most obvious players in the city's bustling drug business. Between them, an army of unseen workers— middlemen, money counters, couriers, chemists, money launderers, labelers, and arm-breakers—tend the vast machinery of New York's dope trade. Seven days a week, 24 hours a day, they process, package, and distribute the hundreds of kilos of heroin and cocaine required to feed the city's habit.

A legion of entrepreneurs also supply New Yorkers with tons of marijuana, as well as a dazzling assortment of pharmaceuticals: barbiturates, amphetamines, LSD, ecstasy. You can still buy PCP on West 127th Street, and officials have run across "ice," a potent new methamphetamine derivative, in East New York. But today, the huge heroin and cocaine/crack markets are the focus of law-enforcement efforts, for these are the drugs that are corroding city life.

During the past decade, New York's drug business has undergone a revolution. Ten years ago, cocaine was still exotic, a drug popular with celebrities and people trying to be hip. Crack wasn't even an idea. Though heroin was plentiful, users tended to be older and more discreet about their habits. A *Times* survey in December 1981 asked New Yorkers to rate the most important problems facing the city, and drugs didn't make the top ten. The appetite for drugs that's since sprung up has developed together with a business that aggressively marketed its products and worked feverishly to keep pace with the demand it was creating. At times, dealer and user seemed locked in a fatal embrace, each egging the other on to new and dangerous highs.

The breakneck expansion in sales and revenues destabilized New York's entrenched distribution networks, ushered in an era of intense competition, and sparked episodes of unprecedented violence. Thousands of organizations—from mom-and-pop candy-store operations to vast criminal conspiracies—sprouted to meet the demand. The drug trade also became an equal-opportunity employer: As the Mafia pulled back from—or was muscled out of—the business, blacks and other minority-group members who'd previously been relegated to the lower levels of distribution were drafted into key roles. And with cocaine and heroin selling at several times the price of gold, street-smart young men suddenly found themselves awash in cash.

At the same time, these dealers influenced the type, price, availability, and quality of drugs in the city. Crack was an immediate success here, though in Boston and Chicago the drug is relatively rare. The taboo on selling dangerous drugs to minors, observed a generation ago, was breached, and now teenagers and even younger children play important roles in the trade.

Despite the efforts of the authorities and the opposition of community groups, the city's drug lords—many of them unedu-

The city's drug lords—many of them uneducated and seemingly unemployable—have built and managed amazingly efficient markets.

cated and seemingly unemployable—have developed and managed remarkably efficient markets. Gone are the periodic shortages that hit the city when organized crime ran the drug supply. The new traffickers not only increased profits but lowered prices and raised product quality. One wonders what might have been accomplished if all that energy, innovation, and daring had been harnessed to a worthy enterprise.

EVERYONE AGREES THAT THE DRUG BUSINESS IS BIG BUSIness, but there's wide disagreement over its exact size. The most quoted estimate—which comes from the House Narcotics Committee—is that retail drug sales nationally for 1987 amounted to $150 billion, a figure that one committee aide claims has grown substantially since then. There are no official figures for New York, but Sterling Johnson Jr., the city's special narcotics prosecutor, thinks the city's share may be as much as $80 billion.

Other experts argue that these numbers are grossly inflated. "If New Yorkers were spending $80 billion a year on drugs," says Peter Reuter, a researcher at the Rand Corporation, "then every man, woman, and child in the city would have a habit." Reuter calls the government's estimates "mythical numbers," created by agencies whose budgets and influence grow with the perceived size of the problem.

In fact, there simply isn't enough information to get an accurate reading of the size of the drug trade, although there are ways to make rough guesses. The most common method estimates the amount of drugs smuggled into the area and then multiplies that figure by the street value of the drugs to get a total price. For example, on the basis of figures from several law-enforcement agencies, it's estimated that officials intercepted around 14,000 kilograms of cocaine in the metropolitan area in the past twelve months, an amount experts assume to be around 10 percent of all the cocaine shipped here. Since the street value of a kilogram of cocaine runs from $80,000 to $190,000, cocaine sales in the city, according to the formula, ranged between $11.2 billion and $26.6 billion.

There are several problems with this method, however. For one thing, different government agencies often take credit for the same bust, thus inflating the overall figure for the amount seized. What's more, recent studies indicate that a substantial portion—perhaps 40 percent—of the cocaine and heroin brought into the country never reaches the street. Instead, it's consumed by dealers and their cronies or used as payments for services like prostitution. Finally, there's no good reason to believe that there's a fixed ratio between seizures and imports.

A second method for computing the size of the drug business focuses on heroin and is based on the number of users and the average cost of their daily habit. The state Division of Substance Abuse Services estimates that there are 200,000 heroin addicts (as opposed to recreational users) living in the city. If they spend an average of $50 a day to satisfy their habits, then addicts alone account for $3.6 billion in heroin sales each year.

Once again, however, the experts disagree on the data. Working from studies of the criminal activities of narcotics addicts, Reuter calculates that the common estimate of the number of heroin addicts and the cost of their addiction is far too high. "If there were 200,000 addicts in New York, each spending $50 a day, the city would have ceased to exist," he says. "The junkies would have stolen it long ago."

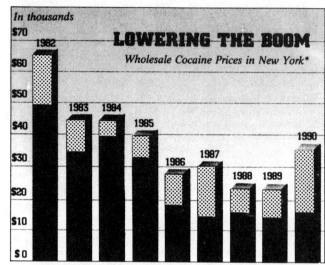

Per kilogram. Prices vary depending on the location of the deal and the status of the buyer. The annual range is indicated in dots. By way of comparison, the consumer price index has risen 58 percent in the past decade.

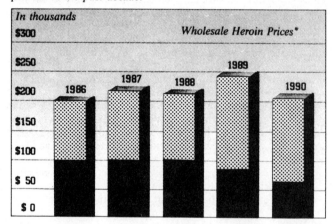

The average cost of a heroin habit is anybody's guess. "It might be $150 to $200 per day," says Paul Dinella, a former addict who until recently worked for the Division of Substance Abuse. "All I know is that a junkie will spend whatever he can get." Dinella also points out that most addicts vary their drug use over time. Some "dry out" periodically; around 40,000 heroin users entered treatment facilities around the state last year. Thousands more were jailed. When surveyed, though, addicts tend to exaggerate their habits, citing what they spend when they're binging. One study found that a group of addicts overstated the amount they spent on drugs by a factor of four.

A third approach attempts to place drug sales within the context of the economy as a whole. New York's gross economic product is about $180 billion. Given Sterling Johnson's drug-trade figure—$80 billion—that would mean that New Yorkers spend nearly half of what they produce on drugs. Many experts think that's impossible. Rather, they estimate that the city's underground economy is around $18 billion and that drug revenues are some fraction of that.

The wild card here is out-of-town sales. New York is a shipping point for many drugs, one of three or four main distribution centers in the United States. Revenues from these wholesale deals add billions to the total drug trade here and go some ways toward reconciling the difference between estimates based on interception and consumption.

Inevitably, the experts view the size of the drug problem through their personal lenses. The cop and the prosecutor see the crack crews on every corner and think the world has gone crazy. The economists and academicians look for the paper trail that tens of billions of dollars should leave and can't find it. Still, even moderate estimates place drug sales in New York at around $12 billion; by contrast, restaurant and bar revenues in the metropolitan area total around $7 billion.

In any case, the business has grown explosively in the past decade. Even heroin use is on the rise after declining for years. There are a few small positive signs: a recent reduction in casual cocaine use among high-school seniors, a decline in cocaine-related emergency-room visits after a dramatic rise, and a flattening out of the growth rate of crack consumption. But these developments may simply show that the market is saturated. "So we've stabilized crack use at record levels of consumption," says a House Narcotics Committee aide. "Is that something to be proud of?"

ALMOST EVERY COCAINE DEAL THAT takes place in New York begins in Colombia. Although the coca plant grows mainly in Peru and Bolivia, Colombians process about 80 percent of the region's crop and export it around the world. Of the estimated 450 tons of cocaine produced last year, as much as 75 tons may have passed through New York, says Arthur Stiffel, top Customs agent at Kennedy airport.

The Colombians smuggle cocaine in ways limited only by the imagination. Government agents have found the drug concealed in the cages of poisonous snakes and in blocks of chocolate. Every year, they intercept hundreds of human "mules" who swallow cocaine-filled condoms to sneak the stuff past Customs. Typically, Colombia's cartels smuggle boat- or planeloads of cocaine into a southern border state, then truck the drug up to New York. Recently, according to Stiffel, the smugglers have also been flying shipments directly into local airports. In June 1988, a Customs unit in Miami seized 1,200 kilos of cocaine that were en route to Suffolk County Airport in Westhampton, the first installment of a 15-ton load targeted for Long Island's East End summer population. The huge cargo ships that visit New York-area ports are another favorite vehicle for traffickers. "Not even counting what's hidden in the merchandise, a one-inch dropped ceiling in a standard container could hold thousands of pounds of cocaine," says Customs agent Richard Mercier. "But we only have the resources to inspect 3 percent of the containers that come in."

Mercier's arithmetic explains the government's dilemma. Because the markup on cocaine is so high—a kilo that costs $4,000 to produce in Colombia sells in New York at wholesale for $14,000 to $23,000 and recently even as high as $35,000—the cartels would make a hefty profit even if Mercier's colleagues beat the odds and intercepted half the illegal drugs entering the city. The Colombians, of course, aren't indifferent to government seizures, but it costs them more to lose customers and sales to competitors than to lose an occasional shipment.

Some officials attribute a recent rise in the wholesale price of cocaine to the effectiveness of the war on drugs here and in Latin America. Others say it's too soon to tell if the war is helping, and in any case, drug prices vary widely depending on the location of the deal and the status of the buyer.

OST OF THE COCAINE BROUGHT INTO NEW YORK—80 to 90 percent, says the DEA—is imported by the Cali cartel, an association of traffickers from Colombia's third-largest city. Headed by the two Rodriguez-Orjuela brothers and José Santa Cruz–Londoño, the group was formed in the early eighties to set drug policy and coordinate smuggling.

Before the cartel took over, most traffickers shipped their drugs to Miami, then sold them to middlemen with connections around the country. This arrangement worked fine as long as the market remained small and import prices stayed high. But as more and more traffickers got into the act and production levels jumped, import prices in Miami plummeted. As a result, the demand for cocaine rocketed, and local distributors racked up huge profits.

Today, the DEA maintains that the Cali cartel controls the first line of distribution in New York. Operating through teams, or "cells," of salaried employees, the cartel sells to the legions of mid-level dealers who ultimately supply the city's street dealers and retail organizations. Kenneth Robinson, one of the DEA's Cali experts, says that each cell typically includes a supervisor, or underboss, six to eight managers, and assorted workers. The supervisor takes possession of the drug shipments and stores them in safe houses—generally, private homes or warehouses. The managers place their orders through coded phone calls directly to the cartel in Colombia, which relays them to the supervisor. The supervisor then contacts the managers and arranges delivery at a safe house or at some public place, such as a mall, where the proliferation of shopping bags can help hide the transfer of drugs and money.

The cartel managers are the bureaucrats of the drug business. Contrary to the popular image of cocaine cowboys with flashy life-styles and flamboyant personalities, typical managers live modestly, blending into the suburbs where they often live. Overall, the cartel's operations are disciplined and difficult to trace. Money and drugs are kept separately, beepers are leased from legitimate businesses, written records are limited, and workers are trained in countersurveillance. When FBI undercover agents posing as money launderers recently met with cartel members, the Colombians brought along their lawyers.

But beneath the corporate veneer, the Colombians operate according to a code of violence and intimidation. Stiffel speculates that many of the cartel leaders came of age during Colombia's civil wars, when killing was a way of life. "They're not like the Mafia," says Robinson. "The Mafia isn't going to touch your family. But the Colombians will kill you, your wife, your children, and your dog. They're not going to leave anyone to take revenge later on."

Their methods are effective. Robinson points out that of the 400 or so cartel members arrested in the United States, only a handful have cooperated with the police. And in a business often disrupted by ripoffs and blunders, the Colombian operation seems to run smoothly. "I've busted dozens of Colombians over

ON THE TRAIL			
Kilograms of Cocaine Seized by the DEA in New York State.			
Fiscal Year		Fiscal Year	
1990	8,715*	1985	332
1989	4,468	1984	1,119
1988	8,817	1983	229
1987	1,430	1982	335
1986	1,960	1981	149
	* To date	1980	160

the years—peasants guarding rooms with tens, twenties, fifties piled floor to ceiling," Stiffel says. "But I've never yet found one of them with more than a few dollars in his pocket."

Government officials don't know how much money the cartel actually makes from its New York operations. DEA agents busted a Cali money-laundering outfit in Great Neck and found records that indicated revenues of $44 million in less than two months. The 5.3-ton load in Long Island City—also identified as part of a Cali operation, though no one has been arrested in connection with the raid—would have brought around $200-million at wholesale prices. Robinson thinks that the Cali cartel has three or four cells operating independently of one another in the New York area and that, on average, it takes two or three months to distribute a major delivery.

One drug ring busted in Manorville, Long Island, is thought to have generated revenues of $200 million to $250 million a year.

New York's huge market has attracted other importers as well. In fact, Stiffel disputes the view that the Cali cartel controls New York's cocaine hierarchy. Rather, he argues that New York's traffickers are caught up in a kind of feeding frenzy, with all of Colombia's major cartels, as well as other groups and individual importers, competing for coca dollars. Two years ago, an apparent turf dispute between Cali and the Medellín cartel, the world's largest cocaine producer, sparked a rash of murders in Queens.

Last May, FBI agents busted a Medellín-operated ring based in Manorville, Long Island, that supplied cocaine to Jackson Heights, Flushing, and Jamaica, Queens. Agents say the group handled 6,400 kilos of cocaine during one five-month period in 1988. Jules Bonavolonta, the agent in charge of the investigation, estimates conservatively that the ring was generating revenues of $200 million to $250 million a year.

The Mafia has also continued to bring cocaine into the city. Law-enforcement officials speculate that at the time former Bonanno-family soldier Costabile "Gus" Farace murdered DEA undercover agent Everett Hatcher in February 1989 ("Death of a Hood," *New York*, January 29, 1990), he was building a cocaine-distribution ring in South Brooklyn and Staten Island. Farace was allegedly supplied from Miami by Gerard Chilli, his former prison mate and a reputed capo in the Bonanno family. Farace was gunned down last November because his actions had brought too much heat on the mob, investigators say.

After cocaine leaves the cartel's cell, it generally passes through a series of middlemen before reaching the street. Along the way, a dealer—who generally works on consignment—has three ways to make money. He can broker his supply intact and tack on a commission. He can divide it into smaller units and mark up the price. Or he can "cut" (dilute) the cocaine with harmless adulterants like milk sugar—in effect, increasing the amount of cocaine he has to sell.

In one typical sequence, using low-end prices, a high-level broker buys 100 kilos of pure cocaine at $17,000 per kilo and sells them in ten-kilo lots at an average price of $19,000 per kilo, earning $200,000. The second dealer sells the ten kilos for $23,000 a kilo, earning $40,000. His customers cut the cocaine by a third, producing, in all, 133 kilos, which they break into around 4,700 one-ounce units and sell to dealers for $800 each, for a total profit of about $1,460,000. Finally, these dealers add another one-half cut, creating in all 200 kilos, or about 7,050 ounces, of adulterated cocaine. That cocaine is converted into crack at a rate of about 350 vials per ounce of cocaine. The crack vials are sold on the street for, say, $5 each, earning the dealers $8,577,500, of which around 20 percent goes to the street sellers.

This pyramid form of distribution has two main virtues: It maximizes the dealer's access to his market while minimizing his involvement in potentially dangerous transactions. No one at an intermediate level deals with more than a handful of contacts. Yet, after just five transfers, the system has supplied hundreds of street sellers who are reaching tens of thousands of customers. And the original 100 kilos of cocaine valued at $1.7-million have produced more than $12 million in revenues—a markup of around 700 percent.

SHARING IN THESE PROFITS ARE LITERALLY THOUSANDS of new, ethnically diverse mid-level dealers. Until the cartels arrived, cocaine distribution had been a closed shop, largely controlled by Cubans. But when the Colombians opened up the market in the early eighties, they created what one dealer at the time called the "ethnicization" of cocaine. Saddled with an oversupply of drugs, the cartels fronted "trusted friends" and associates, who sold to anyone—Latinos, blacks, Italians, even cops—who could deliver the cash. "Our undercover guys were always being told by dealers, 'I think you're "the man," ' " says Joseph Lisi, a New York police captain. "They'd say, 'Right, I'm the man. But I've got $80,000 in this briefcase, and if you don't want to deal with me, I'm out of here right now.' They'd never make it to the door."

Meanwhile, as prices began to fall, demand surged, and small-time street sellers suddenly found business soaring. If the Colombians were looking for dealers who could move "weight"—large quantities—those dealers were looking for high-level suppliers who could help them expand. All over the city, small cocaine retail outfits began cropping up—Dominicans in Washington Heights, blacks in Harlem and South Jamaica, Jamaicans in Brownsville, Bedford-Stuyvesant, and East New York.

The appearance of crack in late 1984 accelerated the process. No one group could control its spread. An ounce of cocaine that could be bought on the street for $1,000 yielded 320 to 360 vials of crack—more if cut—that sold for $10 each in hot locations. (The price is lower in poor neighborhoods that don't get suburban traffic.) Anyone with a few hundred dollars and a hot plate could go into business and triple his money overnight. Thousands of people did, and the old order—already shaken—crumbled completely. Crack turned the lower level of the cocaine trade into a freewheeling, decentralized business, with new outfits springing up and established groups growing into multi-million-dollar, citywide organizations.

DEA agents discovered just how sophisticated some of these groups had become when they started investigating the Basedballs organization in 1985. The brainchild of Santiago Polanco, now 29, Basedballs started out in 1982 as an outfit selling grams and half-grams of cocaine along Audubon Avenue, east of the George Washington Bridge—a prime drug location because of its suburban traffic from New Jersey. The operation was small, but profitable enough to enable Polanco to walk into an Englewood Cliffs car dealership in 1984 and plunk down $43,000 in cash for a Mercedes-Benz.

When crack appeared on the scene, Polanco was one of the first dealers to recognize its potential and aggressively market the drug. He packaged his product in red-topped vials, calling the stuff Basedballs—a play on the term "free-basing"—and took pains to ensure brand quality. He hired "cooks" to process the cocaine, and when one dealer was caught tampering with the product, Polanco had him beaten with a baseball bat. Among the customers driving over from New Jersey, Basedballs quickly became one of the most sought-after brands.

Though they often handle substantial sums, most street

dealers make only modest profits for the roughest work in the business.

Basedballs employees were the only dealers on Audubon Avenue around 173rd, 174th, and 175th Streets. Organization members later told DEA agents that they had bought the territory from its former owners, but, just in case, Polanco imported a team of hit men from his family's village in the Dominican Republic to protect Basedballs's turf and ease its expansion. By 1986, the organization had wrested control of the intersection of Edgecombe Avenue and 145th Street—a prime spot, easily accessible to the Bronx across the 145th Street Bridge—from a group of black dealers and opened a string of new spots in Harlem and the South Bronx.

As Basedballs's business expanded, so did its organization. Polanco secured a major supplier, a Dominican who dealt directly with the cartels in Colombia. Polanco also centralized Basedballs's operations in a headquarters at 2400 Webb Avenue in the Bronx. There, his workers cooked, packaged, and stockpiled crack in separate apartments. And he arranged with one of the dozens of money-changing companies along upper Broadway to launder Basedballs's revenues through an investment company he set up in the Dominican Republic.

Meanwhile, Polanco began distancing himself from Basedballs's day-to-day operations, adding layers of bureaucracy and spending more and more time in the Dominican Republic. By the summer of 1986, Basedballs employed as many as nine mid-level managers to deal with street-level managers at a score of locations around the city. Each location manager, in turn, supervised teams of dealers, none of whom were supposed to know the people more than one level above them.

It took law-enforcement agents and their informants nearly two years to penetrate the highest levels of Basedballs's organization. They can only guess how much money the operation made, but by one estimate, Polanco may have been clearing $20-million a year. One DEA agent saw the fruits of Polanco's activities in the Dominican Republic: two nightclubs, a jeans company, a 30-unit condominium complex, an office building, a palatial home, and a gold-plated gull-wing Mercedes. Today, Polanco is believed to be serving a 30-year sentence in a Dominican prison for homicide, and U.S. law-enforcement officials have dismantled his organization and locked up more than 30 of his associates. But agents estimate that there may be dozens of organizations as large as, or larger than, Basedballs operating in New York.

A T THE BOTTOM OF THE distribution pyramid stands the street seller, subject to arrest, to ripoffs, to calculated violence by competitors. This is especially true for crack dealers. Over the past five years, law enforcement has focused on the cocaine trade, with street dealers the most visible target. They are also the first to get shot when a fight breaks out over turf, which is far more common in the cocaine trade than in the older, more established heroin business. Even the crack dealer's clients present special risks. "I wouldn't deal that crack s—-," says Reuben, a former heroin dealer in the South Bronx. "Once a [heroin addict] gets his fix, he's cool. But when those crackheads start bugging out, you don't know what they're going to do."

In contrast to the myth, most street dealers make only modest profits. The stories about their vast incomes probably arise in part because they generally don't point out the distinction between the large sums of cash they handle and the relatively small commissions they earn. "After factoring in the long hours, they

may come out a couple of dollars an hour ahead of the minimum wage," says Philippe Bourgois, an anthropologist studying East Harlem's drug culture.

Willie, the fifteen-year-old caught on gun- and drug-possession charges in Harlem last February, was probably earning about $300 to $350 per week, according to his arresting officer, Terry McGhee. "We see these kids out there in the cold, not moving from one spot, selling for ten hours at a stretch with nothing but a space heater. Maybe at the end of the night, they'll get paid $50," McGhee says. "I'll tell you one thing: You couldn't get a cop to do that."

But to compare dealing to a mainstream job may miss the point. Many youngsters drift in and out of the drug trade as a way of making pocket money or supporting their own drug habits. Part-time work is hard to find in the slum neighborhoods where most dealers live, and a full-time job often means a long commute and menial work. What's more, though a dealer's hours are long, they are often spent with friends on the streets. Willie, for example, belonged to a group called Boogie-Down Productions—the BDP—a gang of up to twenty teenagers that still pushes drugs on 128th Street and Lenox Avenue. "A lot of these young kids who become dealers are joining a crew," says McGhee. "It gives them access to power. Access to guns. It means no one can push them around anymore."

Crews like these are not simple throwbacks to the gangs of the fifties. They're richer and far better armed, and they're manipulated by adult criminals for profit. But their gang structure ensures discipline and loyalty. The graffiti on the walls of an abandoned BDP hangout—THIS BLOCK BELONGS TO THE BDP—indicate that Willie and his pals were protecting their turf, not just a business enterprise.

In even the poorest markets, however, some dealers make out well. "Everyone who goes into the crack business perceives that he's going to get rich," Bourgois says. "And some of them will. Kids who are responsible or street-smart or especially tough can still get promoted very quickly to manager and get a cut of the profits." Also, street dealing is the entry point into the trade, a way to make contacts or amass enough capital to go into business for oneself. Some street dealers get regular salaries or per diems, but many work on commission—usually between 10 and 20 percent. One of Basedballs's dealers boasted to DEA agents that he cleared $1,400 in commissions during one eight-hour shift on Audubon Avenue.

B EFORE CRACK, HEROIN WAS THE DRUG OF CHOICE IN THE slums, and its popularity is said to be rebounding. According to Division of Substance Abuse data, roughly one in every sixteen working-age men in New York is a heroin addict. The ratio has remained constant over the past five years, but the high mortality rate associated with heroin—especially since the outbreak of AIDS among IV-drug users—may conceal an increase in new addicts. Meanwhile, heroin use among twenty-year-olds—a better indicator of trends in demand—has been rising.

Some experts think the change comes as a reaction to crack, as former crack users switch to a relatively milder drug. Others attribute the comeback to an improvement in the quality of heroin. Greater purity not only gives users a better high but enables them to snort the drug instead of shooting it. At least two factors account for heroin's better quality. For one, Southeast Asia—noted for its pure heroin—now supplies about 70 percent of the New York market. For another, the recent decentralization of heroin distribution in the city has increased the supply and fostered competition among dealers.

THROUGHOUT THE SIXTIES AND SEVENTIES, THE MAFIA dominated the heroin market as the major importer and distributor. In the early eighties, however, the so-called Pizza Connection prosecutions weakened the mob's hold and cut the flow of heroin from Sicily into the United States. Law-enforcement officials say that the ethnic Chinese took over as the industry's new leaders.

In fact, New York's Chinese have been smuggling heroin into the city for years, but until recently, they distrusted the distributors—most of them black—who supplied the street networks; as a result, Chinese smugglers delegated a few of their elders to broker the drug through the Mafia. But around the time that the Mafia began pulling out of the trade, Chinatown began to change.

"Thirty to 40 years ago, Chinatown was very provincial," says Michael Shum, an agent in the DEA's New York Southeast Asian Heroin Task Force. "People from different regions spoke different dialects. In my grandmother's day, if you were Fukienese and you went into a store owned by Toy Shanese, they wouldn't sell you groceries. Forget about drugs—if you didn't speak their language, you couldn't buy a tomato."

Today, Shum says, the old rivalries have broken down and cash has become a universal language. In one recent case, DEA agents turned up a connection between Puerto Rican heroin dealers and members of a Chinese youth gang; the young men had met in school and later "married up" in jail.

The big Chinese move into heroin has had two profound effects on the market. By stepping up their smuggling activities, the Chinese have flooded the city with Southeast Asian heroin. And by dealing directly with minority distributors, they have bypassed the Mafia middlemen who were notorious for heavily cutting their product. As a result, the average drug sold on the street has gone from being as low as 2 percent pure heroin in the early eighties to around 40 percent today.

Still, the heroin trade remains highly profitable. A kilo of pure heroin that costs around $11,000 in Bangkok can be sold for between $85,000 and $125,000 to an Asian broker in the United States or for $150,000 to $240,000 to a mid-level dealer acting as an intermediary between the importer and the street. Markups like these have attracted a grab bag of international trafficking organizations in addition to the Chinese, and even diplomats and businessmen have joined the trade. "We map out ten to twenty major trafficking routes and find out there are ten to twenty more," says DEA agent Dwight Rabb. "We're being inundated with dope."

Because of the huge markup, the drug cartels can afford to lose an occasional shipment to a bust.

Government agents have seized heroin hidden in imported cars, wheelbarrow tires, and the caskets of servicemen killed overseas. The "condom eaters" have also been busy. "Last year, we arrested 123 Nigerians alone at JFK, most of them carrying internally," says Arthur Stiffel, whose Customs agents use X-ray machines to search suspects. "This year, they're running at double the rate."

Though the Chinese dominate the heroin trade in the city, no single group controls the supply. Various foreign nationals—including Nigerians, Ghanaians, Pakistanis, Indians, Thais, and Vietnamese—and assorted American organized-crime groups all smuggle heroin independently of one another. What's more, the Chinese in the trade often operate separately. Unlike the Mafia, Chinatown's criminal organizations—descended from Hong Kong's ruthless triads—do not require their members to pay tribute or even, in many cases, to get permission to deal. Indeed, the new generation of Chinese traffickers may have broken into the violent American market at the expense of their ties to traditional criminal hierarchies. "When the young American Chinese go to Hong Kong now, the guys over there don't want to have anything to do with them," says Dwight Rabb. "The Hong Kong Chinese call them 'bananas'—yellow on the outside, white on the inside."

From the mid-level to the street, heroin distribution has mainly been controlled by black organizations. However, law-enforcement officials report that lately Chinese gangs have been selling in northern Queens and that Hispanic groups—often backed by cocaine money—have broken into the business. But the big heroin markets are found in the predominantly black slums, and dealers from outside are unwelcome.

Older and more established than their crack counterparts, these networks give the heroin business a stability unique in the drug trade. Many of them were Mafia franchises and developed along the same organizational lines as the mob. Until their recent bust, a handful of powerful dealers in southeastern Queens divided the lucrative market there into territories. In Harlem where several groups often run outlets on the same street or even in the same building, agreements over turf are strictly regulated.

WHAT'S MORE, HEROIN'S HIGH PRICE AND NARROW DIStribution make the business easier to control than the crack trade. For one thing, there's simply less heroin around. For another, top distributors are especially guarded about the people with whom they deal. Even if an enterprising young street dealer could find a connection, a kilo of heroin might cost him $200,000 or more wholesale—about six times as much as a similar amount of cocaine.

Heroin's high prices are reflected in the dealer's huge profit margins. While cocaine is rarely cut more than once, heroin can be "stepped on" two or three times. Mid-level transactions are based entirely on relationships; a trusted broker need never touch the product and only rarely the cash. From 1985 until recently, Lorenzo "Fat Cat" Nichols, the legendary Queens drug trafficker, ran a multi-million-dollar operation from prison. In 1988, according to the FBI, he was moving an average of 25 kilos of cocaine and 3 kilos of heroin a month. He bought the heroin from Chinese broker "John" Man Sing Eng—whom he'd met in prison—and, using two lieutenants as go-betweens, sold them to more than a dozen customers.

The big heroin money, however, is made by the dealers who process the drug and market it through networks of street sellers. Take the case of Earl Gibson, a veteran black dealer whose operation included a heroin mill in Queens and selling locations in Brooklyn, in the Bronx, and on the Lower East Side. Before his conviction on drug charges two years ago, Gibson cut, packaged, and sold about a kilo of heroin every four days, earning $150,000 to $200,000 a week. Gibson's occasional partner, Raymond Sanchez "Shorty" Rivera, a Puerto Rican dealer based on the Lower East Side, generated that kind of revenue every day. Based on the testimony of workers for Rivera—who has also been convicted—the FBI estimates that he was grossing more than $60 million a year.

WITH MONEY LIKE THAT TO BE MADE, THE DRUG BUSINESS is a powerful lure. In 1987, when he was seventeen, a young Dominican we'll call Pedro had already tried several times to get into the drug business, passing his requests through an acquaintance who worked as a courier for one of the leading distributors in the Bushwick–East New York section of Brooklyn. The distributor, a fellow Dominican in his mid-twenties who knew Pedro and his family, eventually agreed to front him a small supply of heroin.

Pedro took in a partner who knew a location for selling—a spot on his East New York block that had opened up when the previous dealer was nabbed by police. Since neither youth had any extensive experience, they hired a seller recently out of jail. In those days, two distributors in the area were selling different brands, one called Goodyear and the other Airborne; Pedro handled Airborne.

The distributor supplied Pedro with heroin already cut and packaged in units called packs, each of which contained 100 $10 bags. Pedro took the packs on consignment and eventually returned 80 percent of the proceeds to the wholesaler. He paid a further 10 percent to his seller and split the remaining 10 percent with his partner—leaving him just $50 profit per pack sold.

Nevertheless, business was solid—on a good day, he could sell fifteen packs. Most clients were local addicts who could afford only a bag or two at a time, but, Pedro recalls, some were middle-class men in business suits. Others were out-of-town dealers who bought in bulk and who got discounts from Pedro.

Over the next two years, Pedro was able to open five locations, including spots on Knickerbocker Avenue and in Bushwick Park—prime areas that are restricted to well-connected dealers. At the height of his operation, he was personally clearing $600 a day.

Over time, though, competition picked up and cut into Pedro's revenues. By the time he got out last year, he was making $200 a day; now, he says, most dealers are just trying to survive.

"They're making $1,000 a week, if they're lucky," he says. "That may seem like a lot, but to a dealer, that's nothing." In Pedro's world, a successful dealer must project a certain image: He's got to be tough and free-spending. Fancy cars, gold jewelry, and designer warm-up gear are only the most obvious marks of his position. He's also got to pay for trips to Florida (stressed-out street dealers like to relax at theme parks) and pick up the tab at restaurants and clubs.

Beyond all that, a high-flying life-style can be especially expensive in the slums. Pedro's Cutlass Supreme was stolen right after he'd sunk $3,000 into customizing the tires and sound system. At a party, his $1,500 gold chain and medallion were lifted at gunpoint. And several times, he says, he was ripped off for the drugs he was carrying.

Meanwhile, Pedro's risks were high. Once, early on, some competing dealers tried to move in on one of his locations. Under the terms of their agreement, Pedro's wholesaler was supposed to provide him with protection. Instead, he supplied him with guns—expecting Pedro and his cronies to take care of themselves.

"Like most young guys from the neighborhood, carrying a gun made me feel power," he recalls. "At the time, I only thought about shooting other people. I never thought about getting shot myself."

Over time, twelve of the young men he worked with were arrested and jailed. He says that since their release, two have been killed trying to re-enter the drug trade and another was killed because he owed money to Pedro's former supplier. In fact, the police have determined that more than quarter of New York City's record 1,905 homicides last year were drug related.

The demise of his associates and the decline of his business finally led Pedro to give up dealing. But he still recalls the many times he rebuffed his mother's tearful pleas to stop. "That really made me sad, to see my mother cry," he says. "But not my mother or any job was ever going to give me the money that drugs was bringing to me."

Use, Addiction, and Dependence

Of all approaches to drug use and abuse, perhaps the least fruitful and most fallacious is the *either-or* perspective, that is, the view that one is either a complete abstainer *or* an addict, with no in-between territory; that as soon as one "fools around" with drugs, one becomes "hooked for life." The reality is quite otherwise. In fact, drug use is a continuum, not an either-or proposition. Experimentation does not necessarily lead to regular use, and regular use does not necessarily lead to compulsive use or addiction. For every drug, it is possible to find users at every point along the spectrum—from experimentation to occasional use to regular use to outright addiction. There is no inevitable "slide" from less to more involved levels of use.

At the same time, there is a biological and biochemical *basis* for physical dependence or addiction. Certain drugs possess unique properties that influence how—and how often—they are used. Most researchers today believe that addiction, or physical dependence, is strongly linked to how *reinforcing* drugs are. Some drugs are highly reinforcing, which means that it is extremely pleasurable to take them; these drugs are likely to generate a physical dependence in the user. With other drugs, the pleasure is less immediate, more diluted, less sensuous, and more of an acquired taste; these drugs are less likely to generate a physical dependence.

Physical dependence can be demonstrated even in laboratory animals in experiments. If certain drugs are available, these animals will take them again and again and will undergo a great deal of pain and deprivation to do so; on the other hand, certain other drugs are difficult for researchers to get animals to self-administer, and animals will discontinue them readily when they can. Drugs that animals will self-administer extremely readily and which, it can be inferred, are highly reinforcing are heroin, amphetamines, and cocaine (including, presumably, crack). Drugs that animals have relatively little interest in taking in the laboratory and which, it may be inferred, are far less reinforcing, are alcohol, marijuana, and the hallucinogens. In biological terms, then, looking at the factor of reinforcement alone, it can be said that heroin, amphetamines, and cocaine possess a high addiction potential, while that of alcohol, marijuana, and the hallucinogens is fairly low.

Another factor has to be emphasized: *route of administration*, or, *how* a drug is taken. Certain methods of use are highly reinforcing, that is, the drug's effects are immediate and highly sensuous; other methods are less so, that

is, the drug's effects are slower, more muted, less immediately sensuous. Intravenous injection and smoking are more immediate, more highly reinforcing methods of use; oral (swallowing a pill, for instance, or drinking alcohol) and nasal (sniffing or "snorting" cocaine or heroin) ingestion are slower, less reinforcing techniques. When a highly reinforcing drug is taken in a highly reinforcing fashion, its addiction potential is large; when a less immediately pleasurable drug is taken in a less reinforcing fashion, its addiction potential is far smaller.

These two factors—the characteristics of the drug and the mechanism of use—help explain why heroin, crack, and injected cocaine are likely to generate a high proportion of drug-dependent users. However, many features of the drug scene are not fully explained by the biological model. Why, for instance, are there so many alcoholics, since the drug is not especially reinforcing and is nearly always taken in a not-especially reinforcing fashion? Why does nicotine, a psychoactive chemical found in tobacco, generate so many addicts when laboratory animals avoid taking it altogether? Why is marijuana, taken via a highly reinforcing technique, unlikely to generate users dependent on the drug? Clearly, sociological, cultural, and individual factors come into play here, and they determine how, and how often, certain drugs are taken. Each of our readings emphasizes the complexity of use, addiction, and dependence. On the one hand, drugs are chemical substances with pharmacological properties; they have the *potential* to do things to the human body, as the articles "Addiction and Dependence," "Smoking—Why Is It So Hard to Quit?" and "High and Hooked" emphasize. On the other hand, "Drugs and Free Will" emphasizes that biological explanations can take the observer only so far in understanding drug use; after all, immense variation can be seen among different drug users—and even from one laboratory animal to another. Clearly, to understand use and dependence, we need a broad, eclectic approach.

Looking Ahead: Challenge Questions

What is the difference between dependence on a legal drug and dependence on an illegal drug?

What is the most addicting drug known?

Is alcohol addicting? Are cigarettes?

Why is the degree of immediate pleasure generated by different drugs so strongly related to a drug's potential for chemical dependence?

ADDICTION AND DEPENDENCE

Erich Goode

Although it has been well known for at least 2,000 years that certain drugs "have the power to enslave men's minds," it was not until the nineteenth century that the nature of physical addiction began to be clearly understood. At that time, a "classic" conception of addiction was formed, based on the opiates—at first, opium and morphine; then, after the turn of the century, heroin as well. Much later, it was recognized that alcohol, sedatives (such as barbiturates), and tranquilizers also produced most of the symptoms of "classic" addiction.

What is "classic" addition? If a person takes a certain drug in sufficient quantity over a sufficiently long period of time and then stops taking it abruptly, the user will experience a set of physical symptoms known as *withdrawal*. These symptoms—depending on the dose and the duration—include chills, fever, diarrhea, muscular twitching, nausea, vomiting, cramps, and general bodily aches and pains, especially in the bones and the joints. It does not much matter what one thinks of how one feels about the drug, or even whether one knows one has been taking an addicting drug. (One may not attribute one's discomfort to the drug, but these physical symptoms will occur nonetheless.) These symptoms are not psychological—that is, "all in the mind." They are physiological, and most of them can be replicated in laboratory animals. The withdrawal syndrome is the nervous system's way of "compensating" for the removal of the drug after the body has become acclimated to its presence and effects.

Although the label "addicting" has been pinned at some time or another on practically every drug ever ingested, it began to be recognized that certain drugs simply do not have physically addicting properties. Regardless of the dose administered or the length of time the drug is ingested, the same sort of withdrawal symptoms exhibited with heroin, alcohol, or the barbiturates cannot be induced in humans or animals taking LSD, marijuana or cocaine. Users will not become physically sick in this way upon the discontinuation of the use or administration of these drugs. In a word, these substances are not addicting in the "classic" sense of the word. If we mean by "addicting" the appearance of "classic" withdrawal symptoms after prolonged use and abrupt discontinuation, then certain drugs are addicting and others are not. (*Other* symptoms may appear, of course.)

This bothered a number of officials and experts a great deal. Saying that a drug is not addicting seemed to border perilously close on stating that it is not very dangerous. Something had to be done. Some new concept or terminology had to be devised to make nonaddicting drugs sound as if they were in fact addicting. In the early 1950s, the World Health Organization, in an effort to devise a new terminology that would apply to the "abuse" of all drugs, and not simply those that are physically addicting, adopted the term "drug dependence." As it appeared in its final form in a later statement, drug dependence was defined as

> . . . a state of psychic dependence or physical dependence, or both, on a drug, arising in a person following administration of that drug on a periodic or continued basis. The characteristics of such a state will vary with the agent involved, and these characteristics must always be made clear by designating the particular type of drug dependence in each specific case. . . . All of these drugs have one effect in common: they are capable of creating, in certain individuals, a particular state of mind that is termed "psychic dependence." In this situation, there is a feeling of satisfaction and psychic drive that requires periodic or continuous administration of the drug to produce pleasure or to avoid discomfort (Eddy et al., 1965, p. 723).

Under the new terminology, each drug has its own characteristic type of dependence: There is a "drug dependence of the morphine type," a "drug dependence of the cannabis [marijuana] type," a "drug dependence of the alcohol type," and so on. In other words, the new terminology is a definition, or a series of definitions, by enumeration, for it was felt that no single term could possibly cover the diverse actions of the many drugs in use (or "abuse").

The new terminology was extremely imprecise and clearly biased. The intent of the drug experts who devised this terminology seemed to be ideological: to make sure that a discrediting label was attached to as many widely used drugs as possible. Under the old terminology of "classic" addiction, it was not possible to label a wide range of drugs as "addicting." It thus became necessary to stigmatize substances such as marijuana and LSD with a new term that resembled "addicting." In other words, the scientists and physicians who devised the new terminology of "dependence" were, in effect, disseminating propaganda to convince people that nonaddicting substances were just as "bad" for them, that they could be just as dependent on them as on the truly addicting drugs. Medical authorities labeled the continued (or even the sporadic) use of nonaddicting drugs as "dependence" in large part because they were unable to understand why anyone would want to take them in the first place.

Physical dependence is a powerful concept. With a great deal of accuracy, it predicts what will happen physiologically to an organism that takes enough of a certain drug for a long enough period of time. Can psychological dependence be an equally useful concept? Does the fact that it was devised for propagandistic purposes mean that it is automatically meaningless?

During the 1970s and 1980s, researchers began to see some strong parallels between physical and psychological dependence. To put it another way, the fact that one drug is physically addicting and another is not does not seem to predict the patterns of their use very well. Some crucial facts and findings have emerged in the past generation—since the World Health Organization's notion of psychological dependence was formulated—to suggest that perhaps the concept of psychological dependence may not be meaningless.

First, . . . most regular users of heroin are not physically addicted in the classic sense. They take wildly varying amounts of heroin on a day-by-day basis, often go a day or two without the drug and do not suffer powerful withdrawal symptoms, take several doses a day for the next several days, and so on (Johnson et al., 1985; Johnson, 1984; Zinberg, 1984). If physical addiction were so crucial in determining use, this pattern would be unlikely, perhaps even impossible.

Second, even the heroin users who are physically addicted and withdrawn—whether because of imprisonment, the intervention of a treatment program, or self-imposed withdrawal—usually go back to using heroin; roughly nine addicts in 10 who withdraw become readdicted within two years. If physical dependence were the major factor in continued use, we would predict a much lower relapse rate than this. If the physical compulsion or craving is absent, why return to a life of addiction?

Third, many of the drugs that are not physically addicting are often used in much the same way as the addicting drugs are—that is, frequently, compulsively, in large doses, at an enormous personal and physical toll on the user. How could an addicting drug like heroin and a nonaddicting drug like amphetamine or cocaine produce similar use patterns? If addiction—the product of a biochemically induced craving—is the principal explanation for compulsive use, then how is this possible?

Fourth, and perhaps most crucial, is the hold that cocaine, a supposedly nonaddicting drug, was found to have on laboratory animals. The researchers who conducted the experiments wanted to answer several basic questions: How reinforcing is cocaine? How dependent do animals become on the drug? How much will they go through or put up with to continue receiving it? The researchers discovered that animals will go through practically anything to continue receiving their "coke."

Three key sets of experiments establishing cocaine's dependence potential were conducted. In all three, a catheter was inserted into the vein of a laboratory animal (rats, monkeys, and dogs were used). A mechanism, usually a lever, was rigged up so that animals could self-regulate intravenous (IV) administration of the drug. In one set of experiments, animals were given a choice between cocaine and food; they could have one or the other but not both. Consistently, laboratory animals chose to continue receiving cocaine instead of food, to the point where they literally died of starvation.

In a second set of experiments, the cocaine was abruptly withdrawn; pressing a bar no longer produced any cocaine. The researchers reasoned that the longer the unreinforced bar-pressing behavior continued, the more dependency-producing a drug is: The more frequently animals press the bar before they give up—before bar-pressing is "extinguished"—the greater the dependence potential of the drug. Not only did animals that had taken cocaine over a period of time continue to press the bar many times after the drug was withdrawn, but, even more remarkable, they did so far longer than did those animals that had taken heroin—a clearly addicting drug! (A summary of the experiments conducted on the dependence potential of cocaine in animals may be found in Johanson, 1984; see also Clouet et al., 1988; Brady and Lucas, 1984.)

In a third experiment, one set of laboratory rats was allowed to self-administer cocaine; and a second set, heroin. Both groups could do this continuously and ad libitum—that is, at will, as much or as little as they chose. Those rats that self-administered heroin developed a stable pattern of use, maintained their pretest weight, continued good grooming behavior, and tended to be in good health. Their mortality rate was 36 percent after 30 days. Those self-administering cocaine ad libitum exhibited an extremely erratic pattern of use, with binges of heavy use alternating with brief periods of abstinence. They lost 47 percent of their body weight, ceased grooming behavior, and maintained extremely poor physical health. After 3 days, 90 percent were dead (Bozarth and Wise, 1985).

It is absolutely crucial to emphasize that humans are not rats and that experimental conditions are not the same as everyday life. What animals do in the laboratory may not tell us even in a rough way what humans do in real life. At the same time, laboratory experiments give us the framework within which drug effects can be understood. They establish the inherent pharmacological properties of drugs. Just *how* people take them is another matter; for that we have to examine drug use in naturalistic settings. Laboratory experiments give us an important clue as to how drugs might be taken in real life; they do not provide the whole story.

The facts and findings that these experiments brought to light point to the inescapable conclusion that the concept of psychological, or psychic, dependence is a meaningful, powerful mechanism. In fact the results of the many studies conducted on the subject "indicate that psychological dependence might be more important than physical dependence" in much drug use, including narcotic addiction (Ray and Ksir, 1990, p. 29). "Psychological dependence, based on reinforcement, is apparently the real driving force behind even narcotic addiction, and tolerance and physical dependence are less important contributors to the problem" (p. 29). Taking a highly reinforcing or intensely pleasurable drug over a period of time does not necessarily lead to physical addiction, but it does lead to a powerful desire to repeat the experience and to make enormous sacrifices in order to do so. The more intensely pleasurable or reinforcing the experience is, the more psychologically dependency-producing it is.

But aren't many activities or substances pleasurable? In a letter to the editor of *Trans-action* magazine, one observer commented on the assertion that marijuana produces a "psychic dependence" by saying: "What does this phrase mean? It means that the drug is pleasurable, as is wine, smoked sturgeon, poetry, comfortable chairs, and *Trans-action*. Once people use it, and like it, they will tend to continue to do so if they can. But they can get along without it if they must, which is why it cannot be called physically addicting" (Freidson, 1968, p. 75).

Clearly, we run into a conceptual dilemma here. On the one hand, many activities or substances are pleasurable; does it make any sense to dub all of them psychologically dependency-producing? To do so is to be guilty of using a concept that is so broad as to be all but meaningless. On the other hand, certain drugs do produce a syndrome that is clearly distinct from, but as powerful as—indeed, in some ways, even more powerful than—physical dependence. Unlike the case with several of the activities or substances mentioned above, such as comfortable chairs, poetry, and smoked sturgeon, an alarmingly high proportion of users cannot get along without certain drugs—cocaine being the outstanding example. We are led to the following inescapable conclusions with respect to drugs and dependence.

First, psychic dependence and physical dependence are two separate and to some degree independent phenomena. That is, someone, or an organism of any species, can be psychologically dependent on a given drug without being physically dependent. Likewise, the reverse is also true: It is possible to be physically dependent on a drug without being psychologically dependent—for instance, as a result of having been administered that drug without realizing it (in an experiment, for instance, or in the form of a medicine or painkiller in a hospital).

Second, substances vary in their potential for causing psychological dependence—with cocaine ranking highest, heroin next, possibly the amphetamines after that, and the other drugs trailing considerably behind these three. It is highly likely that this potential is closely related to how reinforcing each drug is—that is, the intensity of the pleasure that each delivers to the user. The more reinforcing the drug, the higher its potential for psychic dependency.

Third, psychological dependence is a continuum, with gradations between substances, whereas physical dependence is probably more of an all-or-nothing affair. The potential for psychological dependence is a matter of degree. Heroin, barbiturates, and alcohol are clearly dependency-producing drugs; this property can be demonstrated in laboratory animals. Drugs either are or are not physically addicting. In contrast, drugs can be arranged along a continuum of psychic dependency—with cocaine ranking high on this dimension and marijuana ranking considerably lower on it.

Fourth, substances vary in their "immediate sensuous appeal" (Lasagna, von Felsigner, and Beecher, 1955; Grinspoon and Bakalar, 1976, pp. 191–194). This is not quite the same thing as the capacity to generate pleasure. It is, more precisely, *the capacity to generate intense pleasure without the intervention of learning or other cognitive processes.* For the most part, one has to learn to enjoy marijuana (Becker, 1953; Goode, 1970, pp. 234ff.). The same is true of alcohol. It has been asserted for heroin, but it may be less true than has been previously assumed (McAuliffe and Gordon, 1974). Certainly it is true of many pleasurable activities and substances—including eating smoked sturgeon, reading certain books and magazines, and appreciating fine art. Here, the pleasure is great but cultivated. In any case, it is not true of cocaine and, to a lesser degree, amphetamines. Subjects who take these substances without knowing what they are taking tend to enjoy them the very first time and want to take them again. In short, they have an immediate sensuous appeal (Lasagna, von Felsinger, and Beecher, 1955).

Fifth, different routes of administration are differentially capable of generating intense and immediate pleasure in individuals who take drugs by these means. As we've seen, intravenous injection is one of the fastest ways to deliver a drug to the brain; smoking—especially of cocaine—is also an extremely rapid and efficient means of drug-taking and is therefore highly reinforcing and likely to cause psychological dependence. Injecting and smoking cocaine have been described as being like "a jolt of electricity to the brain." On the other hand, chewing coca leaves, which contain less than 1 percent cocaine, is far less instantly reinforcing and is far less likely to lead to dependency (Weil and Rosen, 1983, p. 46).

And sixth, individuals vary with regard to their degree of susceptibility or vulnerability to becoming psychologically dependent on varying substances or activities. Clearly, the variation from one person to another in this respect is vastly greater than from one animal to another of the same species, or even from representatives of some animal species as compared with those of others.

The term "behavioral dependence" is sometimes used as a synonym for psychological dependence (Ray and Ksir, 1990, p. 28). This is not entirely accurate. Psychological dependence can refer to both a potentiality and an actuality: We can say that cocaine has a high potential for psychological dependence, and we can infer that a specific individual, John Doe, is psychologically dependent on cocaine. On the other hand, the concept of behavioral dependence always refers to an actuality. It makes no sense to refer to a drug as having a high potential for behavioral dependence; we can only say that John Doe is behaviorally dependent on a particular drug.

Behavioral dependence refers to actual, concrete behavior enacted by an actual, concrete person taking an actual, concrete drug. What has John Doe gone through or given up in order to take or continue taking a specific drug? What is John Doe now going through to do so? What will John Doe go through? To continue taking their drug of choice, some individuals have lost their jobs, destroyed their marriages, given up all their material possessions, gone into enormous debt, ruined their health, threatened their very lives. They exhibit behavioral dependence. While psychological dependence can be inferred from someone's behavior, behavioral dependence is what we see concretely—an actual person sabotaging or giving up concrete values and possessions previously held in esteem to take a specific drug. We recognize behavioral dependence by the sacrifices a particular user makes to get high. Behavioral dependence has been known for some time to be common among alcoholics and heroin addicts. It is now know that cocaine causes similar manifestations in users as well.

Clearly, there are parallels with other forms of behavior that lack the direct physical reinforcement of drugs such as cocaine and heroin. One can, for example, be said to be behaviorally dependent on compulsive gambling (Lesieur, 1977) or bulemia/anorexia (Polivy and Herman, 1983, pp. 168ff.; Orbach, 1986) if one continues engaging in the activity in spite of the fact that it threatens or destroys that which one values dearly—such as one's health, a marriage, one's job, a bank account, financial solvency, friendships, and so on. Consequently, even though the mechanism of direct physiological reinforcement is absent, *addictlike* behavior may be exhibited in a wide range of areas—behavior that may not be qualitatively different from that exhibited by the drug-dependent. On the other hand, this concept of behavioral dependence can be stretched so far that it becomes useless and unrecognizable (Goleman, 1992). For instance, can one be behaviorally dependent on watching television, as is so often asserted? On having sex (Carnes, 1983; Goleman, 1984; Levine and Troiden, 1988)? On being in love (Bireda, 1985)? Eating Pepperidge Farm cookies? On the other hand, when confined to internally rewarding, repetitive, self-destructive behaviors, it remains useful.

In short, although physical dependence (or classic addiction) is a very real and very concrete phenomenon, behavioral dependence does not depend on physical addiction alone. In many ways, the distinction between physical dependence and true psychological dependence—for the drugs that are powerfully reinforcing—is largely irrelevant. Chronic users of drugs that produce "only" psychological dependence behave in much the same way that addicts of physically dependency-producing drugs do. On the other hand, to throw drugs that produce a weak psychological dependence (such as marijuana) into the same category as drugs that produce a powerful one (such as cocaine) is misleading. Many experts "now regret" the distinction they one drew between cocaine as a "psychologically addictive" drug and narcotics like heroin that are "physiologically addictive." Heroin is addictive in a different way—it is both physically and psychologically dependency-producing. But both drugs activate pleasure centers in the brain in such a way that users feel impelled to take them again and again. Some users can overcome this message, but it is a factor that all users have to contend with. "We should define addiction in terms of the compulsion to take the drug rather than whether it causes withdrawal," says Michael A. Bozarth, an addiction specialist (Eckholm, 1986).

REFERENCES

Becker, Howard S. 1953. "Becoming a Marijuana User." *American Journal of Sociology,* 59 (November): 235–242.

Bireda, Martha R. 1985. *Love Addiction.* Oakland, Calif.: New Harbinger.

Bozarth, Michael A., and Roy A. Wise, 1985. "Toxicity Associated with Long-Term Intravenous Heroin and Cocaine Self-Administration in the Rat." *Journal of the American Medical Association.* 254 (July 5): 81–83.

Brady, Joseph V., and Scott E. Lucas (eds.). 1984. *Testing Drugs for Physical Dependence Potential and Abuse Liability.* Rockville, Md.: National Institute on Drug Abuse.

Carnes, Patrick. 1983. *Out of the Shadows: Understanding Sexual Addiction.* Minneapolis, Minn.: CompCare.

Clouet, Doris, Khursheed Asghar, and Robert Brown (eds.). 1988. *Mechanisms of Cocaine Abuse and Toxicity.* Rockville, Md.: National Institute on Drug Abuse.

Eckholm, Erik. 1986. "Cocaine's Vicious Spirals: Highs, Lows, Desperation." *The New York Times,* August 17, p. 2E.

Eddy, Nathan B., H. Halbach, Harris Isbell, and Maurice H. Seevers. 1965. "Drug Dependence: Its Significance and Characteristics." *Bulletin of the World Health Organization,* 32: 721–733.

Freidson, Eliot. 1968. "Ending Campus Drug Incidents." *Transaction,* 5 (July–August): 75, 81.

Goleman, Daniel. 1984. "Some Sexual Behavior Viewed as an Addiction." *The New York Times,* March 31, p. C3.

Goleman, Daniel. 1992. "As Addiction Medicine Gains, Experts Debate What It Should Cover." *The New York Times,* March 31, p. C3.

Goode, Erich, 1970. *The Marijuana Smokers.* New York: Basic Books.

Grinspoon, Lester, and James B. Bakalar. 1976. *Cocaine: A Drug and Social Evolution.* New York: Basic Books.

2. USE, ADDICTION, AND DEPENDENCE

Johnson, Bruce D. 1984. "Empirical Patterns of Heroin Consumption Among Selected Street Heroin Users." In G. Serban (ed.), *The Social and Medical Aspects of Drug Abuse.* New York: Spectrum Publications, pp. 101–122.

Johnson, Bruce D., et al. 1985. *Taking Care of Business: The Economics of Crime by Heroin Abusers.* Lexington, Mass.: Lexington Books.

Johanson, Chris E. 1984. "Assessment of the Abuse Potential of Cocaine in Animals." In John Grabowski (ed.), *Cocaine: Pharmacology, Effects, and Treatment of Abuse.* Rockville, Md.: National Institute on Drug Abuse, pp. 110–119.

Lasagna, Louis, J. M. von Felsinger, and H. K. Beecher. 1955. "Drug-Induced Changes in Man." *Journal of the American Medical Association,* 157 (March 19): 1006–1020.

Lesieur, Henry R. 1977. *The Chase: Career of the Compulsive Gambler.* Garden City, N.Y.: Anchor Press/Doubleday.

Levine, Martin P., and Richard R. Troiden. 1988. "The Myth of Sexual Compulsivity." *The Journal of Sex Research,* 25 (August): 347–363.

McAuliffe, William E., and Robert A. Gordon. 1974. "A Test of Lindesmith's Theory of Addiction: The Frequency of Euphoria Among Long-Term Addicts." *American Journal of Sociology,* 79 (January): 795–840.

Orbach, Susie. 1986. *Hunger Strike: The Anorectic's Struggle as a Metaphor for Our Age.* New York. W. W. Norton.

Polivy, Janet, and C. Peter Herman. 1983. *Breaking the Diet Habit: The Natural Weight Alternative.* New York: Basic Books.

Ray, Oakley, and Charles Ksir. 1990. *Drugs, Society and Human Behavior* (5th ed.). St. Louis: Times-Mirror/Mosby.

Weil, Andres, and Winifred Rosen, 1983. *Chocolate to Morphine: Understanding Mind-Active Drugs.* Boston: Houghton Mifflin.

Zinberg, Norman E. 1984. *Drug, Set, and Setting: The Basis for Controlled Intoxicant Use.* New Haven, Conn.: Yale University Press.

THE BATTLEFIELD
OF ADDICTION

Science and treatment offer some hope for people trapped by alcohol and drugs

He is polite, articulate and well-dressed. He has a job at city hall in Toronto and money in the bank. He and his girlfriend share an apartment and a close relationship. For 41-year-old Eric, the job, the savings and the relationship are major accomplishments, if not minor miracles. Three years ago, after half a lifetime of smoking, drinking and injecting drugs daily—and using morphine and alcohol to endure withdrawal—Eric had become severely addicted. For years, he had distributed drugs, hung around with prostitutes and pushers, and carried a gun to protect himself. "Of all the drugs I did over 23 or 24 years, cocaine took me to my bottom," he said. "I could never get enough of it. I was totally morally bankrupt."

'I was totally out of control. It was only a matter of time before I was dead.'

On his harrowing downhill slide, Eric had plenty of company. Year after year, thousands of Canadians cross the line between social drinking and alcoholism, between taking an occasional sleeping pill and handfuls of them, between normal living and the endless nightmare of addiction to mood-altering chemicals of one kind or another. But at the same time, medical researchers in Canada and the United States are beginning to understand how chemical addiction affects the brain—findings that one day may have clinical application. Rehabilitation centres are employing new and promising methods of treatment for substance abuse. But perhaps even more significant in the battle against alcohol abuse are recent surveys showing declines in the number of Canadians who drink, how many are categorized as alcoholics and the nation's overall consumption.

Although most Canadians do not become hooked on alcohol or drugs, those who do, like Eric, inflict incalculable damage on themselves, their families, their employers and the nation's health and social services. Addicts out of control usually wind up sooner or later in hospital emergency departments, detox or treatment centres, jails or mental institutions. Every year,

thousands die—by suicide, on highways, from exposure, of alcohol-induced cirrhosis of the liver or drug-induced brain seizures. Yet hundreds more, prepared to seek help, do recover. For many, the road back has led them to Alcoholics Anonymous, which this year is celebrating its 50th anniversary in Canada, to Narcotics Anonymous or elsewhere in the panorama of self-help groups. Some respond to psychotherapy, some to religion.

Still others, also like Eric, combine professional treatment and self-discipline. But like every addict who overcomes dependence, Eric first had to hit a personal bottom—physically, emotionally, psychologically and spiritually. He reached that bottom, he recalls, in the fall of 1990 during a tearful conversation with his younger sister, who convinced him that either cocaine or his companions in the drug trade were going to kill him. "I was totally out of control," says Eric. "It was only a matter of time before I was dead."

Despite the well-publicized notoriety surrounding such drugs as cocaine, and its lethal derivative known as crack, alcohol abuse remains a far larger problem than addiction to street drugs or to such prescription medications as barbiturates and sedatives. A national drug and alcohol survey, done for Health and Welfare Canada by Statistics Canada and published in 1990, showed that Canadians spend about $10 billion a year on alcohol. The survey also estimated that almost 80 per cent of Canadians aged 15 and over drink alcohol. In 1989, Ontario's Addiction Research Foundation (ARF) estimated on the basis of trends in deaths from cirrhosis that there were close to 477,000 alcoholics in Canada, down from nearly 623,000 a decade earlier. Other estimates range as high as two million.

Nobody knows even roughly how many Canadians may be addicted to illicit and prescription drugs. The Health and Welfare survey found that cannabis (marijuana and hashish) remains the most popular street drug among Canadians. Almost one-quarter of 11,634 people aged 15 and over who took part in the national survey had used the drug at some time during their lives, and 6.5 per cent were current users. The survey reported that only 1.4 per cent of the respondents currently used cocaine or crack. Less than one per cent were using the hallucinogenic chemical LSD, amphetamines or heroin. But at the same time, almost 21 per cent of those surveyed had recently used mood-altering prescription drugs.

By almost any measure, the social costs of excessive alcohol and drug consumption are enormous. Every year, substance abuse directly or indirectly leads to thousands of deaths. The ARF reported that in 1989, the latest year for which national figures were available, 3,062 people died from diseases directly related to alcohol consumption, such as cirrhosis. Alcohol was also involved in almost 16,000 other deaths in fires, motor vehicle accidents, acts of violence and other incidents. There were 428 deaths directly attributable to drug use. In Alberta, the Alcohol and Drug Abuse Commission (AADAC) reports that alcohol is a factor in about 80 per cent of the province's domestic disputes. Moreover, substance abuse imposes a huge financial burden on the Canadian economy—according to the ARF, almost $34 billion annually (or five cents out of every dollar of wealth generated by the entire country) in extra health care, policing and lost productivity.

In an attempt to address the consequences of active addiction, companies across the country are introducing what have come to be known as employee assistance programs. Shell Canada Ltd. established a full-scale program at its Calgary headquarters in 1983 and four years ago, in defining its alcohol and drug policy, rejected employee testing and assured workers with dependency problems that they could expect assistance "without fear of discrimination." Shell's consultants have found that alcohol abuse ranks second behind work-related stress as the most common problem among 5,500 employees. David Chisholm, manager of Shell's occupational and environmental health department, said that "we believe alcohol is a bigger problem than all other drugs." Although mandatory drug screening is uncommon in Canada, Transport Canada has prepared draft legislation to require compulsory drug testing in four federally regulated transportation sectors: marine, aviation, rail and trucking.

'There's a lot more female alcoholism out there than we think there is.'

Drugs and alcohol also play a major role in the commission of crime. Since 1990, the Correctional Service of Canada, the federal agency that runs the country's penitentiaries, has studied the pre-prison living habits of every inmate entering the system. John Weekes, a research manager for the Correctional Service, said that the studies show that more than half of the 5,500 individuals given penitentiary sentences since 1990 used drugs or alcohol on the day they committed their crime. More than two-thirds entered prison with drug and alcohol problems that required professional treatment.

Addiction can develop from prolonged use of alcohol or experimentation with street drugs. It can also begin with a visit to a doctor's office. Norma, a forty-something mother of two and the wife of a small-town Ontario doctor, began suffering severe migraine headaches after an operation in 1970. Her doctor prescribed Fiorinal, a painkiller containing codeine. Fiorinal relieved her headaches but it made her feel overly energetic and euphoric. Norma said that she began taking the drug even before she experienced any migraine symptoms. Her consumption grew from the prescribed three pills a day to 14. She developed a dependence on the drug that lasted for 20 years.

According to many experts in the field of addiction research and counselling, female dependence on drugs or alcohol is a huge but largely hidden problem. Treatment centres have only begun in the past decade to design programs for women. Women are more likely to keep their alcoholism or drug addiction hidden for a number of reasons. For one thing, the experts say, they tend to experience more fear, shame and guilt than men. Many are also afraid that social service agencies or the courts will take their children away. "There's a lot more female alcoholism out there than we think there is," said Lucille Toth, director of development and public relations for the Renascent Centres, an organization that operates three treatment facilities in the Toronto area. "We just don't know about it."

A woman called Amy is perhaps typical. For almost 20 years, she was a closet alcoholic who concealed her drinking from everyone but her immediate family. A former teacher and the mother of two grown children, Amy lives in a suburban community west of Toronto. She took her first drink in her early 20s, then gradually progressed from social drinking to occasional binges to daily consumption—as much as a 26-ounce bottle of vodka and a dozen bottles of beer—most of it at home. "I had to have the drink," she recalls, "no matter about the fights with my husband and children."

One of Amy's few public displays of drunkenness convinced her she had hit bottom and had to quit drinking. At mid-morning on a chilly fall day in 1990, while supervising six children in the school kindergarten, she became desperate for a drink. She got the youngsters dressed and took them to a nearby shopping centre where there was a liquor store. She bought them snacks at a fast-food restaurant and left them at a food-court table while she slipped into the liquor store for a bottle of vodka. By noon, she was visibly drunk and had to be removed from the school by her daughter. She subsequently spent a month in a treatment centre and has been a sober member of AA ever since.

But the emergence of more female addicts is only one of the shifts that have occurred in the ranks of those entering treatment programs. Addiction counsellors say that over the past decade they have been seeing more young people and more patients generally who are addicted to both drugs and alcohol. Dennis James, director of the health recovery program at the Donwood Institute in Toronto—the first publicly funded hospital in Canada devoted solely to treating substance abuse—said that, in that time, the average age of patients has dropped to 35 from 42. Ten years ago, 75 per cent of Donwood's patients were exclusively alcoholics; now, only 45 per cent are. The rest are addicted to other substances as well.

Characteristic of that trend is a construction company supervisor named Geoff, who lives in a medium-sized Ontario manufacturing city east of Toronto, who was addicted to both alcohol and cocaine. In his early 30s and the father of two preschool children, he had become what addiction experts define as a "poly user." Geoff, who spent 28 days in a Toronto-area treatment centre in the spring, started drinking at age 15 and four years ago began using cocaine. Geoff's final binge occurred shortly before he entered treatment. He got up on a Thursday morning, phoned his employer to complain of illness and by noon was in a local bar. He and a couple of friends woke up in jail on Saturday morning in a small town in New York state across the St. Lawrence River from Gananoque, Ont. They were escorted to the border and were back in a bar on the Canadian side by early afternoon. "I didn't know how I'd got there or what had happened," he said.

For every alcoholic and drug addict who overcomes his or her problem, several others fail and many never even try. And those who seek treatment represent only a small minority of the addicted population. Brian Rush, the ARF's head of treatment systems research and development, said that U.S. surveys have consistently shown that only 10 to 15 per cent of those with alcohol or drug problems come forward asking for help. Applied to Ontario, where about 75,000 people seek some form of treatment each year, those percentages would suggest that the province has as many as 750,000 people with addictions—more than seven per cent of the total population. Those determined to overcome their dependence generally apply for admission to a structured program, which can involve weekly counselling sessions, or a 28- to 40-day stay in a treatment centre.

An alternative is the 12-step recovery program offered by Alcoholics Anonymous. Indeed, most residential treatment centres now encourage clients to regularly attend meetings of AA or similar organizations. Patients are strongly urged to continue those affiliations after they are released. AA, the oldest of the self-help groups, was founded in Akron, Ohio, in 1935, following an encounter between a hard-drinking physician and a recently sober New York stockbroker—who, although deceased, remain anonymous in keeping with the philosophy of the program. The broker had discovered that his compulsion to drink was overcome so long as he tried to help other alcoholics by sharing his experiences with them. AA now estimates that it has about 2.2 million members worldwide. The first AA group in Canada was formed in Toronto in 1943. There are now 5,275 groups across the nation, with a total membership of about 95,000.

A loosely structured fellowship, AA has only one requirement for membership: a desire to stop drinking. Members are encouraged to attend AA meetings and follow a program of 12 steps, the first of which is to admit that "we admitted we were powerless over alcohol, that our lives had become unmanageable." The steps also suggest that members make "a searching and fearless moral inventory of ourselves," and make amends directly to all those harmed by their drinking. Joe C., a 73-year-old retired Toronto businessman, said that he joined AA 48 years ago and still attends meetings, for "peace of mind and serenity."

Associated with AA, but functioning independently of it, are two organizations devoted to helping family members cope with the emotional turmoil of having lived with an alcoholic. The Al-Anon Family Groups for spouses were first organized by the wife of one of AA's co-founders. Alateen, formed more recently, offers help to the children of alcoholics. Members of both groups apply AA's 12 steps as a way to deal with what the science of addiction calls "co-dependency"—the pervasive and victimizing compulsion among family members to shield an alcoholic in their midst, often for years, from the consequences of his or her actions.

AA makes no claims about its success, and professional addiction counsellors are equally reserved about how well their techniques work. They contend that it is difficult to assess the effectiveness of treatment because many patients fail to complete prescribed courses, others only achieve temporary sobriety and some lapse back into their addictions several months or even years afterward. Garth Martin, assistant director of the ARF's Clinical Research and Treatment Institute, claimed that, as a rule, one-third of those who enter a program will achieve complete abstinence or sharply reduce their use of drugs or alcohol. Another third will cut back but continue to have problems. And one-third, said Martin, show no improvement at all.

'Isolation is the core of addiction. The key to beating the addiction is to smash that isolation.'

Most counsellors agree that treatment works best when an individual recognizes his problem early in his addiction. They also claim that a middle-aged alcoholic with a stable family, job and community life is more likely to overcome a dependence than someone younger from a disrupted social background. Dr. David Korn, president of Toronto's Donwood Institute, said that many youthful addicts must be taught basic life skills because they are poorly educated, unemployed and have never formed lasting relationships. However, Dr. Graeme Cunningham, director of alcohol and drug services at the Homewood Health Centre in Guelph, Ont., said that the results of short-term treatment among people addicted mainly to street drugs "are abysmal."

People addicted to street drugs, particularly those who began using them in their early teens, have social and emotional problems that must be addressed along with their substance abuse. Donwood's James said that they usually have difficulty resolving conflicts, tolerating criticism or expressing feelings. "If someone starts using chemicals early, it influences their learning capacity and ability to form relationships," said James. "Many have limited social skills and a limited ability to tolerate differences in other people. They become angry and frustrated easily."

In the scores of treatment programs across the country, the central element in most is to have the alcoholic or drug addict talk candidly about his dependence, either with a counsellor, or with fellow addicts. AA also emphasizes the healing power of open, honest disclosure. In addition to closed meetings for members only, the organization holds some meetings that are open to the public, at which a recovered alcoholic talks about his or her experiences.

Group therapy sessions, led by a treatment centre addiction counsellor who guides the conversation, can be a powerful experience for an individual addict, said Cunningham. Many addicts spend years feeling lonely and isolated, he said. They usually abandon social and recreational pursuits because alcohol or drugs have come to dominate their lives. They alienate spouses and children and become consumed by fear and shame. "Isolation is the core of addiction," Cunningham said. "The key to beating the addiction is to smash that isolation. It takes incredible courage for many of these people to speak publicly for the first time about themselves in front of a room full of strangers."

If there is one reason for optimism in the shadow of addiction, it is that Canadians are drinking less than they were a decade ago. Some of the havoc caused by excessive drinking is also declining. Figures published by Statistics Canada reveal that although 111,300 people were charged with impaired driving in 1991, that total was a 31-per-cent decrease from 1981. During the same period, drug use among young Canadians also showed a sharp decline.

Still, thousands of Canadians remain tormented by their addictions. For many, life is a vicious cycle of consumption, sickness and depression and renewed craving for alcohol or drugs, or both. Experts concede that, despite all the research on the subject and the prevalence of treatment programs, addiction remains a baffling phenomenon. There is no reliable way of determining who is likely to become an alcoholic or drug addict. And most addiction counsellors readily admit that they can never predict who will beat the problem and who will succumb to it. For those who don't make it, addiction to chemicals—in bottles, pills or needles—promises an inevitable downward slide to an institution. Or oblivion.

D'ARCY JENISH

BARS OF ANOTHER KIND

His home is a cramped cubicle in a grim sandstone building on a forlorn New Brunswick hillside. His neighbors are murderers and other violent criminals—many of them serving life sentences. But Randy (not his real name), 27, a lifer convicted of murder, asked to be transferred to Dorchester Penitentiary, a multilevel security federal prison in Dorchester, N.B. "This is known as a good place to do your time," explained the tall curly-haired Nova Scotia native, who spoke to *Maclean's* on the understanding that he would not be identified. His main reason for preferring Dorchester: the institution's hardline efforts to stamp out drug and alcohol abuse within its walls. Explained Randy: "The institutions which have the most problems are the ones which do not come down on drugs and booze."

And he should know: in other prisons he has been in, he said, drug use—and drug-inspired violence—have been commonplace. They are problems that the prisoners bring into the system with them. Almost seventy per cent of inmates in any federal prison have problems with drugs and alcohol, notes Claudette Shea, who runs a substance abuse program at Dorchester. Inmates routinely smuggle marijuana, Valium, LSD and cocaine past sometimes complacent guards. Equally popular are stills hidden in toilet bowls and air ducts that transform a mixture of vegetables, sugar, yeast and water into a mixture of 90-proof homebrew. "It makes street alcohol look like crap," says Randy, who claims to have tried it only once. "You get 10 or 15 guys that are doing six or seven glasses apiece, the next thing you know there's anger coming out and it's turned into a full-scale riot."

In a way, the need for an outlet is understandable. Alcohol and drugs help relieve, if only briefly, the boredom and hopelessness of prison life. As well, for most of the inmates substance abuse has long been a way of life. "I turned to alcohol and drugs to forget my problems," explained one 27-year-old inmate who is serving a life sentence for murder and has been using drugs and alcohol since he was 13. "But that only fuelled the fire that was inside and after a while the fire got so big that it let go." He said that Dorchester's guards occasionally find "some home-made stuff [alcohol], but as far as drugs go the place is clean."

Dorchester's strict policy of keeping its 236 inmates as clean as possible is a far cry from a few years back, when drugs and alcohol were as big a problem there as in any other institution, at times leading to violence among inmates. Its substance abuse programs treat at least 40 inmates a year. It also houses a chapter of Alcoholics Anonymous, although Shea acknowledges that most inmates attend because they think that it will lead to quicker parole—not because they sincerely want to control their addiction. The authorities have also stemmed the supply of illicit drugs. Brenda Hastie, Dorchester's chief administrator, says that information supplied by the RCMP from outside sources has virtually halted the flow of narcotics into the prison. Randy, meanwhile, has another explanation for the disappearance of the problem in Dorchester: "Everyone knows that if they are caught with the stuff they're out of here"—possibly to a prison where violence related to drinking and drugs is commonplace. That is a prospect that even some of the most hardened criminals don't want to contemplate.

JOHN DeMONT *in Dorchester*

High and hooked

A better understanding of how addictions work could provide benefits for science, for medicine and for recreation

IN 1964 Aryeh Routtenberg stuck electrodes into the brains of his experimental rats. The electrodes were so positioned that current flowing through them caused a particular pleasure. For one hour a day, each rat could control this current by means of a lever in its cage. Another lever, which also worked for just that one hour, controlled the food supply. There was no contest between the levers. The rats, too busy mainlining current to stop for food, wasted away to ecstatic death.

The link between pleasure and addiction is not always so extreme, but more mundane addictions have brought about millions of less dramatic deaths outside the laboratory, and caused untold misery and pain. The substances to which people get addicted, though, also bring great pleasure to billions—some addicted, some not. They are the basis of several multi-billion dollar industries around the world. Some 60m Americans smoke tobacco; three-quarters of West European adults drink alcohol; no one knows how many people around the world consume caffeine in tea, coffee or cola. Figures for illegal drugs are harder to come by, but around 2m Americans are thought to take cocaine, and many more than that have smoked marijuana.

Not all the people who indulge in these tastes are addicts—that is, they do not depend on their habit in a way that seems clearly abnormal to the bulk of people who do not share their tastes. Though almost everyone who smokes tobacco is hooked, drinkers are not necessarily alcoholics and not all heroin users are hopeless junkies. Pleasure and the addiction need not come together—either can be present without the other. Yet the two are obviously connected. Neuroscientists are now using the tools of molecular biology to find the links between them, deep in the recesses of the brain.

The kick from cocaine

The cerebral nooks and crannies of interest are those between nerve cells—synapses. To jump over the gap between two cells, a nerve impulse has to be translated from electricity to chemicals and back. The first cell releases a chemical called a neurotransmitter into the synaptic gap. These molecules are then picked up by receptor proteins on the surface of the second cell. The neurotransmitter fits the receptor as a key fits a lock. The unlocking of the receptor leads to the creation or suppression of a nerve impulse in the second cell.

There are many different types of neurotransmitter, and thus of synapse; different pathways in the brain need their different properties. It is by subverting some of these synapses, and thus some of the brain's pathways, that drugs produce pleasure. It is through changing them in a more fundamental way that the drugs cause addiction.

The first evidence for this is almost 20 years old. Recently it has started to pile up quite quickly. In 1975 Solomon Snyder, at Johns Hopkins University in Baltimore, Hans Kosterlitz of the University of Aberdeen in Scotland and John Hughes of Parke-Davis, an English pharmaceuticals company, found out how heroin, then drug-*du-jour* for worried policy-makers, works. Dr Snyder discovered there was a receptor protein in mammalian brains which heroin would stick to. Dr Kosterlitz and Dr Hughes reasoned that nature was unlikely to have produced such a lock without also evolving a key.

Working independently, they found a chemical in the body that fitted into the same receptor as heroin; Dr Kosterlitz named it "endorphin". This type of neurotransmitter (there are, it turns out, at least three different endorphins) damps down pain by suppressing the signals which transmit it; it also provides feelings of well-being. Heroin acts as an ill-fitting key which can open the lock but cannot then be withdrawn. The synapse is over-stimulated. Unusually pleasurable sensations result.

If you replace heroin and endorphins with nicotine and the neurotransmitter acetylcholine, or with caffeine and adenosine, or Valium and gamma-amino butyric acid, or marijuana and anadamide, the same story can be told. Other drugs work in slightly more subtle ways. Alcohol does not mimic a neurotransmitter, but at least some of its effects come from messing up the same synapses that heroin works on.

Cocaine, which has replaced heroin as the drug of concern in America, and has thus been extensively researched, works on nerves that use the neurotransmitter dopamine. These nerves are found in, among other places, the mesolimbic system—the part of the brain which seems to generate emotion. Cocaine subverts the pathway not by binding to dopamine receptors, but by sticking to a molecule called, inelegantly, the dopamine re-uptake transporter.

Nerve cells, canny little things, recycle their neurotransmitters. Receptor molecules spit out their neurotransmitters once they have served their purpose, and the cell whence they came mops them up for reuse. Block this re-uptake, and the transmitters will just sit in the synaptic gap, stimulating the receptors again and again and again. Another strategy is to jam the re-uptake system open, so that dopamine flows through it the wrong way all the time, keeping the gap suffused with the neurotransmitter. That is what amphetamines do.

The fact that amphetamines and cocaine work in similar ways will come as no surprise to anyone who has tried both. The nature of the high a drug provides depends on the type of neurotransmitter it interferes with. But the brain is a complex place; the separate systems within it that use different neurotransmitters all interact. A drug acting on one set of synapses can have secondary and tertiary effects all over the place. That is why drug experiences are so varied.

The range of things that can be addictive, though, is wider even than the range of available drugs. Foreign bodies in the synapses are not an absolute prerequisite for an addiction. Something as straightforward as

From *The Economist*, May 15, 1993, pp. 105-107. © 1993 by The Economist, Ltd. Distributed by The New York Times Special Features.

2. USE, ADDICTION, AND DEPENDENCE

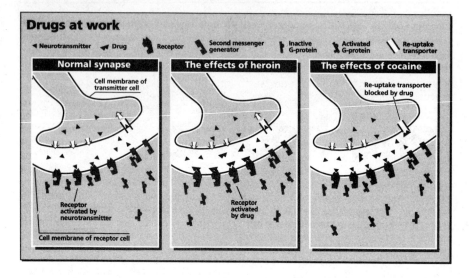

Drugs at work

◄ Neurotransmitter   ◄ Drug   Receptor   Second messenger generator   Inactive G-protein   Activated G-protein   Re-uptake transporter

Normal synapse

Cell membrane of transmitter cell

Receptor activated by neurotransmitter

Cell membrane of receptor cell

The effects of heroin

Receptor activated by drug

The effects of cocaine

Re-uptake transporter blocked by drug

healthy exercise can, in the extreme, hook. In the case of exercise it appears that the body becomes addicted to the endorphins it produces to ameliorate the pain and stress.

Other behaviours that carry an intensity with them—and thus presumably over-stimulate some parts of the brain's wiring—can produce similar effects, though the synapses involved have yet to be charted. Gambling has many of the characteristics of drug taking—a euphoric high, and a craving in the addict. Some people believe themselves addicted to sex; lawyers in England recently convinced a jury that a teenage hacker was addicted to computing.

It is easy to see some such "addictions" as excuses, especially as the term resists strict definition. But addiction to chemicals is clearly real, and there seems no reason to believe that compulsive chemical-taking is necessarily in a different class from other acquired compulsive habits. Anyway, chemical dependency is easier to study than other sorts. That is why it has been possible to locate the roots of pleasure in the synapses—and why it has been possible to find the roots of withdrawal there, too.

Cold turkey

Clinically, addiction can be characterised by two things: craving and withdrawal. Craving is still the subject of a certain amount of scientific handwaving. The best the psychologists can do is describe the process as one of positive re-inforcement—which means that if you like something, you will tend to do it again. Having their receptors overstimulated is something people tend to like a lot. How this "liking" translates into neural circuitry is not yet clear.

Withdrawal, the physical and mental turmoil that follows when an addiction is interrupted, is proving more tractable to experimental analysis. A suggestive picture of how it works can be pieced together, as long as you do not mind taking the pieces from different studies of different drugs: work on cocaine by Nora Volcow at Brookhaven Na-

tional Laboratory, among others; on cocaine and amphetamines by Bruce Cohen of McLean Hospital in Boston; on heroin by Zvi Vogel at the Weizmann Institute in Rehovot in Israel and Anton Shofelmeer at the Free University in Amsterdam; and on benzodiazepines (such as Valium) by Erick Sigel at the University of Berne.

Again, the synapse is the scene of the action. Most biological systems have feedback mechanisms that help smooth out the little fluctuations that life throws at them. Synapses are no exception. The receiving cell can adjust itself to changes in the behaviour of the transmitting cell in two ways. It can fine-tune the signal the receptors pass on, and it can change the number of receptors.

The receptor molecules are conduits for information, with one end outside the cell and the other inside. When a neurotransmitter attaches itself outside, the part on the inside changes its shape. In this new shape, it can accommodate molecules called G-proteins, which hang around inside the cell. These G-proteins are, themselves, also shape-changers. Interacting with the receptor activates the G-proteins; these then head off to spread the word via yet more molecules, called second messengers.

The second messengers tell the cell about the signal from the neurotransmitters. One part of the cell that listens is the system which sends out and suppresses nerve impulses. Another avid audience is made up of the enzymes which add phosphate groups to proteins, some of which help in the production of impulses. More messages make them more active, and more likely to add phosphate to receptor molecules. A phosphorylated receptor is an unhappy receptor. It is reluctant to accommodate G-proteins and thus to bring information in from the outside.

The nucleus, which controls the production of proteins, also listens to the second messengers. Lots of chatter from them suggests to the nucleus that there are too many receptors at the synapse, so it brings their

manufacture to a halt. Insert an addictive drug into the system and the din from the second messengers becomes deafening. The result is fewer receptor molecules.

Both the phosphorylation of receptors and their absence means that it takes more of the drug to obtain the same effect. Those higher doses, in turn, lead to even less sensitive synapses. And they also lead to synapses that can no longer function without the drug. The cell gets used to damming the flood of drug-induced noise in order to be able to deal with the faint whispers of reality that float on top of it. Remove the drug, and the normal signals can no longer get over the barrier that has been erected. The system goes from getting too much of the neurotransmitter's effects to not enough; heaven turns to hell.

Put this way, the molecular picture seems obvious. It fits with a common experience of addiction, that of needing to do more and more of the drug just to keep from feeling bad. Of course, it cannot be that simple—after all drugs that work on the same neurotransmitter may vary in their addictiveness. And people vary, too, in their susceptibility to addiction. Then again, addictions to substances that affect different types of synapse can be quite similar—and some people seem to be prone to addiction *per se*, rather than just to have a weakness for a particular substance. And the fact that addiction remains after withdrawal has ended—a fact attested to at Alcoholics Anonymous every day—suggests there is a more general problem to look at.

Dopamine heads

For more evidence that addictions have something in common in the way they act on the brain as a whole, no matter which pathways they stimulate . . . Edythe London, who works at America's National Institute on Drug Abuse, studies glucose metabolism in the brains of people with addictions. Glucose is the body's principal fuel, so its use is a good index of how active an area is. Dr London's [studies] show that, in certain parts of the brain, addicts use less glucose than non-addicts do. The difference applies regardless of what drug is being used, and it is still visible when they are not under the influence.

Other clues to a general theory of addiction have led researchers to focus on the dopamine system—even when looking at drugs which do not affect dopamine receptors. There is evidence that many, and possibly all, addictions affect the dopamine cells in the brain's mesolimbic system. In the case of cocaine this effect is direct, which may account for the drug's peculiar potency. For other drugs it seems to be indirect, brought about by connections between the dopamine system and the other neurotransmitter systems.

Inside the dopamine system, the researchers' attention has lighted on D2. It should come as no surprise by now to hear that D2 is a protein found in synapses, one of the three different receptor proteins for dopamine. The detailed make-up of these proteins can vary from person to person—variation that comes from differences in the gene which describes the protein. So the different variants of D2 are inherited.

It was inheritance that led the researchers to D2. In the 1970s a series of Danish studies compared the children and stepchildren of alcoholic fathers. The former proved more likely to succumb to the same addiction. This, and the evidence that identical twins are more likely to share an alcoholic fate than are non-identical twins, suggested that genes were playing a role. In 1990, to great excitement, Kenneth Blum of the University of Texas at San Antonio, and Ernest Noble of the University of California, Los Angeles, announced that they had found a gene peculiarly common among alcoholics. It described a form of the D2 receptor known as A1.

This was challenged by several researchers, most notably Kenneth Kidd, of Yale. Dr Kidd points out that different ethnic groups have different frequencies of A1, which could confuse the statistics. Others, convinced by Dr Blum, Dr Noble and subsequent work, have suggested that A1 frequencies may actually explain differences in alcoholism between ethnic groups, though this is far from certain.

In 1992 George Uhl, of Johns Hopkins, found that a second variant of D2, known as B1, seemed peculiarly common in people addicted to tobacco, cocaine, heroin, tranquillisers, marijuana and amphetamines as well as alcohol—almost the whole list of commonly addictive substances. This is at least as controversial as the original finding; its meaning is not clear, nor is the nature of the difference between the different D2s.

To link small variations in a single protein with the existence of an all-purpose "addictive personality" is to go a long way too far. But there is evidence in one case for a link between personality and withdrawal symptoms—and to link withdrawal symptoms to specific molecules is not too farfetched. About 40% of people prescribed courses of benzodiazepines to treat anxiety or insomnia can suffer some withdrawal symptoms—souped-up versions of the symptoms the drugs are used to treat—after the course of medication is finished. Peter Tyrer, who works at St Charles' Hospital in London, has found that the people who suffer withdrawal share not a specific protein, but rather specific personality traits: insecurity, inability to make decisions, an over-reliance on the opinions of others. Spot them, and you can save people from withdrawal.

Better living through chemistry

The links between proteins, the lowly building blocks of the brain, and personalities, the high abstractions of the mind, are undoubtedly going to be convoluted—but evidence from both ends suggests they are there to be found. What are the pharmaceutical companies, to which this should be of interest, doing about it?

Some work is going into drugs to treat drug addiction. Naltrexone keeps heroin from activating endorphin receptors, without activating them itself. Methadone works in the same way as heroin, but less effectively; it thus provides a way off heroin that minimises withdrawal symptoms. Similar approaches to cocaine are being tried. Drugs which act on dopamine pathways in general may have wide-spread effects on addiction. But drugs to defeat dependence are not the only possibilities.

Some of the damage that comes from drug addiction, especially the physical damage, comes from secondary aspects of the drug. Lung cancer, for example, is caused by the substances that accompany nicotine in tobacco smoke, not by nicotine itself. It might be possible to get rid of some of these problems without getting rid of the pleasure, even if it is not possible to get rid of the addictions. Another option is to develop tests which could tell people if they were at risk of falling under a particular spell so that they could choose their pleasures wisely.

Eventually, an understanding of neurotransmitters, receptors, G-proteins and second messengers might allow pleasure and addiction to be decoupled—or at least allow withdrawal to be suppressed. Though, on the face of it, the effects that cause pleasure in the short term are those that cause addiction in the long term, there is a lot of variability in the system that might be exploited. Techniques like those used to target specific dopamine receptors in the treatment of Parkinson's disease, might, at least in principle, be used to fine tune a drug's effects at the synapse and produce low-addiction highs. And pure substances tailored to neurotransmitter sites would have a good chance of being free of unpleasant side effects elsewhere in the body. That would not create a brave new world; it might, perhaps, create a slightly happier one.

SMOKING –
Why is it so hard to QUIT?

David Krogh

DAVID KROGH, AUTHOR OF THE NEW BOOK *SMOKING: THE ARTIFICIAL PASSION* PUBLISHED BY W.H. FREEMAN AND COMPANY, IS AN SCIENCE WRITER AND EDITOR AT THE UNIVERSITY OF CALIFORNIA.

Almost everyone has watched someone try to quit smoking. They charge into the effort with optimism because of some new-found belief that hypnotism, nicotine gum or acupuncture will do the trick this time. They quit for a week or two, maybe even a few months, but then suddenly they're… *smoking again*. And, it's not just one cigarette here and there, their all-consuming habit has returned. It's as if the whole effort to stop never took place.

Why does this happen? How can someone not choose whether to continue this strange ritual of inhalation and exhalation? The mystery behind the inability to quit relates to the nature of the drug. Nicotine has almost no effect on a smoker that an onlooker can perceive. We believe we *know* why heroin is attractive: it makes people euphoric. In a slightly different way, the

ticeable effect and yet, to judge by its number of users, is easily the world's most addictive substance?

Why Do People Smoke?

To understand these contradictions we must drop our preconceived notions about what constitutes an attractive mental or physical state for most people.

Most of us believe, that drugs will be attractive in direct proportion to how euphoric they make us feel; but this is not the case. Jack Henningfield of the National Institute on Drug Abuse points out that if we gave heroin to 50 randomly selected people, most would get sick and would never want any again. We actually have a massive test-case that proves this every day: Thousands of hospital patients receive painkilling dependence-producing drugs in large quantities, yet almost none become serious drug abusers as a result.

It's clear that what makes a drug attractive is not only that people get high with it; but rather that people find it *useful* — perhaps for getting high, but also for other, less exotic reasons.

The important reason with nicotine is

Wald asked some 3,600 workers to detail when they actually smoked cigarettes from the time they awoke until they went to bed. The results showed that these people smoked most of their cigarettes and had their two highest hourly rates of smoking while on the job.

So, what do people want from a drug? To judge by this evidence, they want to be able to *function*. It is work, after all, that calls upon us to perform in a way that will keep a paycheck coming in. The work environment is likely to present us with situations that make us feel uncomfortable, *abnormal*. We may feel hammering tension from having too much to do or drowsiness and boredom from having too little to do.

The findings scientists have uncovered in the past 30 years regarding the effects of nicotine depict a drug that is almost perfectly suited to returning people to a state which might be called psychological neutrality, no matter whether they have been removed from this state by stress or boredom.

Electroencephalograph studies show that nicotine generally arouses human beings. Give a subject a dose of nicotine and his brainwave activity will increase in fre-

THE ADDICTIVE QUALITIES OF NICOTINE OFTEN OVERPOWER A SMOKER'S FEAR OF PREMATURE DEATH.

same thing is true of alcohol or cocaine. It would make sense that the more a drug does for us, the more alluring it would be. But if this is true, how can we explain nicotine, which hardly seems to have any noticeable effect on a smoker that an onlooker can perceive. We believe we know

that the drug helps the user maintain his or her daily routine, especially at work. We have some telling information about smoking in the workplace. In the early 1970s, British researchers T.W. Meade and N.J.

quency, a sign of increased arousal. However, we also have some evidence that nicotine sedates or depresses smokers, depending on the dosage and environment. (In general, larger doses of nicotine tend to

From *Priorities,* Spring 1992, pp. 29-31. Reprinted with permission from *Priorities,* a publication of the American Council on Science and Health, Inc., New York, NY.

ONE MUST REGARD AN UNSUCCESSFUL ATTEMPT TO QUIT AS AN EXERCISE IN GETTING TO KNOW ONE'S HABIT.

sedate while smaller doses tend to arouse.)

Consider that smokers may be able to move themselves up or down at will on a stimulation/sedation continuum by simply taking in a given amount of nicotine in a given situation. The ability to do this — and do it almost instantaneously — would obviously be a very attractive proposition for almost anyone. Is there little wonder that nicotine has found such favor in the workplace?

Any drug that can function in such different ways might be expected to have varied effects when people actually perform tasks under its influence. This is just what we find with nicotine. There is evidence that people's physical reactions can actually speed up with nicotine. For example, non-smokers given nicotine can tap on a keyboard about five percent faster under its influence. Concentration during a long, boring task may also improve with nicotine. In one study, smokers and nonsmokers were asked to note pauses in the sweep hand of a clock. The smokers could maintain their vigilance remarkably well over an 80-minute test, while the nonsmokers' concentration steadily waned. We also have reason to believe that nicotine may moderate aggressive or anxious mood states. It may, in fact, have effects much like those of the milder tranquilizers.

These various research results cannot be regarded as conclusive. The idea that smoking provides absolute benefits in mental and emotional functioning has a number of critics. But, smoking research continues. Nevertheless, these findings do present a consistent picture of why nicotine is seemingly so attractive. Nicotine is the all-time addictive drug of choice because so many people use it in so many different ways.

Nicotine Has Deadly Addictive Power

Regardless of the smoker's perceived benefits from tobacco, one would assume that an overwhelming consideration must be the likelihood of an early grave after a life of gnawing addiction. However, the addictive qualities of nicotine often overpower a smoker's fear of premature death.

Thanks in large part to work done at the National Institute on Drug Abuse in the 1980s, it is now clear that all the elements of addiction found with "serious" drugs like heroin and cocaine are also found with nicotine. Smokers trying to quit are likely to become as psychologically distressed as the average psychiatric outpatient. In animal experiments, squirrel monkeys will press levers as many as 250 times to get a single intravenous dose of nicotine. Human smokers under the same conditions will dose themselves at orderly, predictable rates depending on how much nicotine they are getting — the very hallmark of an activity controlled by a substance.

People tend to think of nicotine addiction as a kind of lap-dog version of addiction — the real thing existing only with *truly* addictive substances, such as heroin or cocaine. The smokers everyone knows don't live in squalid crash-pads, rob people, or worse. How similar can heroin addiction and nicotine addiction be?

Such reasoning ignores the fact that nicotine is legal and thus easily available at a low cost. Were this not the case, nicotine addicts might demonstrate all the depraved trappings of drug culture that we now see with harder drugs. Consider, for example, the account of a Mr. N.A. Photiades, who wrote to the *Times* of London in 1957, looking back on his experience in World War II:

> I had the misfortune to be a prisoner for nearly four years during the war and found that the one thing that men were unable to give up was cigarette smoking. There was, in fact, a very active market in bartering the handful of rice we received daily for the two cigarettes our hosts so kindly gave us. I have actually seen men die of starvation because they had sold their food for cigarettes.

CONSIDER THAT SMOKERS MAY BE ABLE TO MOVE THEMSELVES UP OR DOWN AT WILL ON A STIMULATION/SEDATION CONTINUUM BY SIMPLY TAKING IN A GIVEN AMOUNT OF NICOTINE IN A GIVEN SITUATION.

Such stories have been repeated at various intervals in history when tobacco has been unavailable or available only at the most prohibitive cost. The message from these accounts is: Whatever the cost of nicotine, people will pay it.

Given the probable benefits of nicotine and its addictive power, it's understandable why quitting is so difficult. Smoking works itself into every facet of waking life, essentially as an unhealthy means of relating to one's environment. It is a drug of physical dependence, as surely as cocaine or heroin.

Nicotine Addiction Can Be Beat

On the face of it, this would seem to present a forbidding set of circumstances for anyone who wants to quit. But while it is true that most individual attempts to quit smoking will end in failure, it is also true that 42 million Americans have quit smoking. Clearly it is possible, though quitting may take several attempts and some clever strategy.

This is important to keep in mind when trying to quit. It is a rare smoker who can stop for good on his or her first attempt. Smokers should not feel that there is something wrong with them — that they are more hooked or less resolute than others — if they don't succeed on the first go around. One must regard an unsuccessful attempt to quit as an exercise in getting to know one's habit. (*i.e.,* When did temptations to smoke arise and when were they absent?)

Nicotine gum or the new nicotine skin patch (both available by prescription) are useful tools in the quitting arsenal. Initial clinical trials on the nicotine patch look very promising. Nicotine gum, which has been around for years, lessens the early withdrawal symptoms smokers are likely to feel. Nicotine substitutes allow the quitter to conquer the habitual behavioral aspects of smoking before dealing with the physical symptoms of withdrawal.

Another piece of advice: People trying to quit should stay away from people who smoke. Nearly three quarters of all quitters who relapse do so in the presence of people who are smoking — usually after having *asked* one of these people for a cigarette.

Finally, smokers who want to quit should attempt to develop a repertoire of *coping strategies* as the research literature phrases it. Saul Shiffman, perhaps the nation's leading expert on smoking relapse, has found that people who develop such strategies are far less likely to relapse in a given "crisis" than those who don't. Such strategies can be divided into the "cognitive" and "behavioral". They involve "thinking" or "doing" something specific to overcome those moments when the ex-smoker really craves a cigarette. Thinking: about the effort you've invested so far; about how much your kids will benefit; about your uncle who died from emphysema. Doing: Getting up and leaving a bar; going out for a walk; sitting down to play with a video game.

Even the person who mixes and matches these and other strategies is not likely to find quitting easy. Smoking is a tenacious habit precisely because it is so intimately tied to the everyday acts in our lives. Nevertheless, with determination and a smart strategy, it is possible to quit smoking.

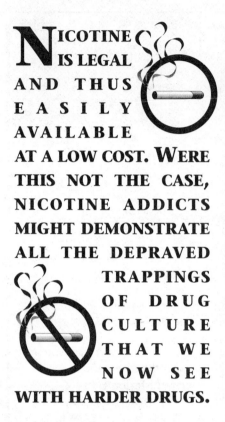

NICOTINE IS LEGAL AND THUS EASILY AVAILABLE AT A LOW COST. WERE THIS NOT THE CASE, NICOTINE ADDICTS MIGHT DEMONSTRATE ALL THE DEPRAVED TRAPPINGS OF DRUG CULTURE THAT WE NOW SEE WITH HARDER DRUGS.

WHILE IT IS TRUE THAT MOST INDIVIDUAL ATTEMPTS TO QUIT SMOKING WILL END IN FAILURE, IT IS ALSO TRUE THAT 42 MILLION AMERICANS HAVE QUIT SMOKING.

Drugs and Free Will

Jeffrey A. Schaler

Jeffrey A. Schaler is a psychotherapist in Silver Spring, Maryland. He is a doctoral candidate in human development at the University of Maryland. He lectures on drugs, alcoholism, and society in the department of justice, law, and society at American University, Washington, D. C.

That was the disease talking. . .I was a victim." So declared Marion Barry, 54, mayor of the District of Columbia. Drug addiction is the disease. Fourteen charges were lodged against him by the U.S. attorney's office, including three counts of perjury, a felony offense for lying about drug use before a grand jury; ten counts of cocaine possession, a misdemeanor; and one count of conspiracy to possess cocaine.

Barry considered legal but settled for moral sanctuary in what has come to be known as the disease-model defense. He maintained that he "was addicted to alcohol and had a chemical dependency on Valium and Xanax." These are diseases, he asserted, "similar to cancer, heart disease and diabetes." The implication: It is as unfair to hold him responsible for drug-related criminal behavior as it is to hold a diabetic responsible for diabetes.

The suggestion was that his disease of addiction forced him to use drugs, which in turn eroded his volition and judgment. He did not voluntarily break the law. According to Barry, "the best defense to a lie is truth," and the truth, he contended, is that he was powerless in relation to drugs, his life unmanageable and "out of control." His behaviors or acts were purportedly the result, that is, symptomatic, of his disease. And jail, say those who agree with him, is not the answer to the "product of an illness."

This disease alibi has become a popular defense. Baseball's Pete Rose broke through his "denial" to admit he has a "gambling disease." Football's Dexter Manley claimed his drug use was caused by addiction disease. Addiction treatment professionals diagnosed televangelist Jimmy Swaggart as having "lost control"

of his behavior and as being "addicted to the chemical released in his brain from orgasm." They assert that Barry, Rose, Manley and Swaggart all need "twelve-step treatment" for addiction, the putative disease that, claims the multimillion-dollar addiction treatment industry, is reaching epidemic proportions and requires medical treatment. To view addiction-related behaviors as a function of free will, they often say, is cruel, stigmatizing and moralistic, an indication that one does not really understand the disease.

Others are more reluctant to swallow the disease model. After testing positive for cocaine in 1987, Mets pitcher Dwight Gooden said he could moderate his use of the drug and was not addicted. This is heresy according to disease-model proponents, a sign of denial, the salient symptom of the disease of addiction and considered by some to be a disease itself. There is no such thing as responsible drug taking or controlled drinking for an addict or an alcoholic, they assert.

The tendency to view unusual or questionable behavior as part of a disease process is now being extended, along with the characteristic theory of "loss of control," to include all sorts of "addictive" behaviors. We are currently experiencing the "diseasing of America," as social-clinical psychologist Stanton Peele describes it in his recent book of the same name (1989). The disease model is being applied to any socially unacceptable behavior as a means of absolving people of responsibility for their actions, criminal or otherwise. The practice is justified on this basis: Drug use constitutes an addiction. Addiction is a disease. Acts stemming from the disease are called symptoms. Since the symptoms of a disease are involuntary, the symptoms of drug addiction disease are likewise involuntary. Addicts are thus not responsible for their actions.

Is this analogizing of drug addiction to real diseases like diabetes, heart disease and cancer scientifically valid? Or is the word "disease" simply a misused metaphor? Does drug use truly equal addiction? Are the symptoms of drug addiction really involuntary?

Loss of Control

At the heart of the idea that drug use equals addiction is a theory known as "loss of control." This theory may have originated among members of Alcoholics Anonymous "to denote," as described by researcher E.M. Jellinek in his book The Disease Concept of Alcoholism (1960), "that stage in the development of [alcoholics'] drinking history when the ingestion of one alcoholic drink sets up a chain reaction so that they are unable to adhere to their intention to 'have one or two drinks only' but continue to ingest more and more—often with quite some difficulty and disgust—contrary to their volition."

Loss of control also suggests that addictive drugs can start a biochemical chain reaction experienced by an addict as an uncontrollable physical demand for more drugs. Drug addicts are people who have allegedly lost their ability to control their ingestion of drugs.

In a speech in San Diego two years ago, National Drug Policy Director William Bennett explained that a drug "addict is a man or woman whose power to exercise. . .rational volition has. . .been seriously eroded by drugs, and whose life is instead organized largel—even exclusively—around the pursuit and satisfaction of his addiction."

Yet, there is a contradiction in Bennett's point of view. If an addict's power to exercise rational volition is seriously eroded, on what basis does the addict organize life "largely even exclusively around the pursuit and satisfaction of his addiction"? An act of organizing is clearly a volitional act, an act of will.

Three Models of Drug Use

Etiological paradigms for understanding drug use can be distilled into three models. Aside from the disease model, there are two other ways of looking at drug addiction: the free-will model and the moralistic model.In the free-will model drug use is envisioned as a means of coping with environmental experience, a behavioral choice and a function of psychological and environmental factors combined. The nervous system of the body is conceived of as a lens, modulating experience as self and environment interact. The self is like the film in a camera, where experience is organized and meaning is created. The self is not the brain.

Individual physiological differences affect the experience of self. They do not create it. The quality of a camera lens affects the image of the environment transposed to the film. When the image is unpleasant, drugs are used to modify the lens.

The self is the executor of experience in this model, not the nervous system. Drug use may or may not be an effective means of lens modification. The assessment of drug effectiveness and the price of drug use are viewed as moral, not medical, judgments.

The recommended therapy for the drug user is: 1) a matter of choice; 2) concerned with awareness and responsibility; 3) a process of values clarification; 4) a means of support to achieve specific behavior goals; and 5) an educational process that involves the learning of coping strategies.

The moralistic model harkens back to the days of the temperance movement and is often erroneously equated with the free-will model. Here, addiction is considered to be the result of low moral standards, bad character and weak will. Treatment consists of punishment for drug-using behavior. The punitive nature of America's current war on drugs with its call for "user accountability" is typical of the moralistic perspective.

Addicts are viewed as bad people who need to be rehabilitated in "boot camps." They are said to be lacking in values. President Bush gave a clear example of this during the televised debates of the 1988 presidential campaign. When asked how to solve the drug problem, he answered, "by instilling values."

The drug user's loss of values is often attributed to the presence of a disease. A "plague" and "epidemic" of drug use are said to be spreading across the land. Since users are sick and supposedly unaware of their disease, many people feel justified in coercing them into treatment, treatment that is primarily religious in nature. Thus, the moralistic model is paternalistic.

In the disease or medical model, addicts are considered to have physiological differences from normal people, differences based in a genetic source or created through the chemical effects of drugs. Instead of focusing on the interaction between the self and the environment, advocates of the disease model view the interaction between physiology and the chemicals in drugs as both the disease and the executor of behavior and experience. In this sense the model is mechanistic. The person is viewed as a machine, a highly complex machine, but a machine nevertheless. The disease of addiction is considered to be incurable. People in treatment can only reach a state of perpetual recovery. Treatment of symptoms involves admitting that one is ill by breaking through denial of the disease and turning over one's life to a "higher power" in a spiritual sense and psychological support to achieve sobriety. Addicts are not bad but sick people. Intervention is required because the machine has broken. Thus, the disease model is both paternalistic and mechanistic.

Addiction Redefined

Proponents of the will and the disease models disagree with the moralistic perspective, but for different reasons. The former believe addicts should not be punished for having unconventional values. They believe treatment should focus on changing the psychological and environmental conditions conducive to drug use. Coping skills should be taught along with the building of self-esteem and self-efficacy. The latter believe that addicts should not be punished for being sick and that treatment should focus on the biological factors that cause and reinforce drug use.

James R. Milam and Katherine Ketcham, authors of *Under the Influence* (1981), are popular spokespersons for the disease-model camp. They argue that alcoholics should not be held accountable for their actions because these are the "outpourings of a sick brain...They are sick, unable to think rationally, and incapable of giving up alcohol by themselves."

Similarly, physician Mark S. Gold, an expert on cocaine use and treatment, says in his book *800-CO-CAINE* (1984) that cocaine should not be regarded as a benign recreational drug because it can cause addiction. As with alcoholism, says Gold, there is no cure for cocaine addiction except permanent and total abstention from its use. Cocaine produces "an irresistible compulsion to use the drug at increasing doses and frequency in the face of serious physical and/or psychological side effects and the extreme disruption of the user's personal relationships and system of values." According to Gold "if you feel addicted, you are addicted." Addiction, be it to alcohol or cocaine, is, as far as Milam, Ketcham and Gold are concerned, identical to loss of control. The drug itself and physiological changes in the addict's body are said to control further ingestion of drugs in what is viewed as an involuntary process.

It may be helpful to look at how the term "addiction" has developed. Its use in conjunction with drugs, disease, loss of control, withdrawal and tolerance developed out of the moralistic rhetoric of the temperance and anti-opium movements of the nineteenth century, not through scientific inquiry. Such a restrictive use of the word served multiple purposes according to psychologist Bruce Alexander of Simon Fraser University in British Columbia, lead author of an article on the subject. Linking addiction to drugs and illness suggested it was a medical problem. It also helped to scare people away from drug use, a tactic that became increasingly important with anti-opium reformers. Etymologically, the word "addiction" comes from the Latin "dicere" (infinitive form) and, combined with the preposition "ad," means "to say yes to," "consent." Consent implies voluntary acceptance.

The idea of choice, volition or voluntariness inherent in the meaning of the word "addiction" is significant to will-model proponents because the concept of addiction as a disease depends so much on the loss-of-control theory. Most people think of addiction with the element of volition decidedly absent. Studies of alcoholics and cocaine and heroin addicts conducted over the past twenty-six years appear to refute this claim, however.

The Myth of Loss of Control

In 1962 British physician and alcohol researcher D.L. Davies rocked the alcoholism field by publishing the results of a long-term follow-up study of patients treated for alcoholism at the Maudsley Hospital in London. Abstinence, long considered the only cure for alcoholism, was seriously questioned as the only form of treatment when seven out of ninety-three male alcoholics studied exhibited a pattern of normal drinking. Physiological differences purportedly present in alcoholics did not seem to affect their ability to control drinking.

Four years later, *The Lancet* published an important study by British psychiatrist Julius Merry that supported Davies's findings. Alcoholics who were unaware they were drinking alcohol did not develop an uncontrollable desire to drink more, undermining the assertion by supporters of the disease model that a small amount of alcohol triggers uncontrollable craving. If alcoholics truly experience loss of control, then the subjects of the study should have reported higher craving whether they believed their beverages contained alcohol or not.

According to the loss-of-control theory, those with the disease of alcoholism cannot plan their drinking especially when going through a period of excessive craving. Yet, psychologist Nancy Mello and physician Jack Mendelson, leading alcoholism researchers and editors of the *Journal of Studies on Alcohol*, reported in 1972 that he found alcoholics bought and stockpiled alcohol to be able to get as drunk as they wanted even while undergoing withdrawal from previous binges. In other words, they could control their drinking for psychological reasons; their drinking behavior was not determined by a physiologically uncontrollable force, sparked by use of alcohol.

As Mello and Mendelson wrote in summary of their study of twenty-three alcoholics published in *Psychosomatic Medicine:* "It is important to emphasize that even in the unrestricted alcohol-access situation, no subject drank all the alcohol available or tried to 'drink to oblivion.' These data are inconsistent with predictions from the craving hypothesis so often invoked to account for an alcoholic's perpetuation of drinking. No empirical support has been provided for the notion of craving by directly observing alcoholic subjects in a situation where they can choose to drink alcohol in any volume at any time by working at a simple task. There has been no confirmation of the notion that once drinking starts, it proceeds autonomously."

A significant experiment conducted by Alan Marlatt of the University of Washington in Seattle and his colleagues in 1973 supported these findings by showing that alcoholics' drinking is correlated with their beliefs about alcohol and drinking. Marlatt successfully disguised beverages containing and not containing alcohol among a randomly assigned group of sixty-four alcoholic and social drinkers (the control group) asked to participate in a "taste-rating task." One group of subjects was given a beverage with alcohol but was told that although it tasted like alcohol it actually contained none. Subjects in another group were given a beverage with no alcohol (tonic) but were told that it did contain alcohol.

As Marlatt and co-authors reported in the *Journal of Abnormal Psychology*, they found "the consumption rates were higher in those conditions in which subjects were led to believe that they would consume alcohol, regardless of the actual beverage administered." The finding was obtained among both alcoholic and social drinker subjects. Marlatt's experiment suggests that according to their findings the ability of alcoholics to stop drinking alcohol is not determined by a physiological reaction to alcohol. A psychological fact—the belief that they were drinking alcohol—was operationally significant, not alcohol itself.

Similar findings have been reported in studies of cocaine addiction. Patricia G. Erickson and her colleagues at the Addiction Research Foundation in Ontario concluded, in their book *The Steel Drug* (1987), after reviewing many studies on cocaine that most social-recreational users are able to maintain a low-to-moderate use pattern without escalating to dependency and that users can essentially "treat themselves." They state, "Many users particularly appreciated that they could benefit from the various appealing effects of cocaine without a feeling of loss of control."

Erickson and co-authors cite in support a study by Spotts and Shontz (1980) that provides "the most in-depth profile of intravenous cocaine users to date." They state: "Most users felt a powerful attachment to cocaine, but not to the extent of absolute necessity. [A]ll agreed that cocaine is not physically addicting. . . [and] many reported temporary tolerance."

In a study by Siegel (1984) of 118 users, 99 of whom were social-recreational users, described by Erickson et al. as the only longitudinal study of cocaine users in North America, "all users reported episodes of cocaine abstinence."

These results thus further support the hypothesis that drug use is a function of psychological, not physiological, variables. Even the use of heroin, long considered "the hardest drug," can be controlled for psychological and environmental reasons that are important to heroin addicts. A notable study of 943 randomly selected Vietnam veterans, 495 of whom "represented a 'drug-positive' sample whose urine samples had been positive for opiates at the time of departure" from Vietnam, was commissioned by the U.S. Department of Defense and led by epidemiologist Lee N. Robins. The study shows that only 14 percent of those who used heroin in Vietnam became re-addicted after returning to the United States. Her findings, reported in 1975, support the theory that drug use is a function of environmental stress, which in this example ceased when the veterans left Vietnam. Veterans said they used heroin to cope with the harrowing experience of war. As Robins and co-authors wrote in *Archives of General Psychiatry*:

> . . .[I]t does seem clear that the opiates are not so addictive that use is necessarily followed by addiction nor that once addicted, an individual is necessarily addicted permanently. At least in certain circumstances, individuals can use narcotics regularly and even become addicted to them but yet be able to avoid use in other social circumstances. . .How generalizable these results are is currently unknown. No previous study has had so large and so unbiased a sample of heroin users.

The cocaine and heroin studies are important for several reasons. They challenge the contention that drug addiction is primarily characterized by loss of control. Moreover, these and similar studies support the idea that what goes on outside of a person's body is more significant in understanding drug use, including alcoholism, than what goes on inside the body.

Consider for a moment how a person enters and exits drug use. While disease-model proponents such as Milam, Ketcham and Gold, claim that abstinence is the only cure for this "special disease," implying that strength of will is irrelevant, we must recognize drug use, and abstinence from it, for what they really are —volitional acts.

Addiction and the Law

This is a markedly different process from that in real diseases. A person cannot will the onset of cancer, diabetes or epilepsy. Nor can these diseases be willed away. While people may exercise responsibility in relation to their diseases, they cannot be held responsible for actually creating them. Research supports the idea that drug use does not automatically lead to loss of control—a drug-ingestion frenzy devoid of any volitional component. Unfortunately, viewing addiction as a disease has often led to attempts to absolve drug users of their responsibility for criminal actions.

The extent of an addict's responsibility for criminal behavior has been debated in the courts for more than twenty-five years. Recently, in *Traynor v. Turnage* (1988), the Supreme Court upheld the right of the Veterans Administration (VA) to define alcoholism to be the result of willful misconduct. The petitioner in this case asserted he was unable to claim VA education benefits because he was an alcoholic; he further claimed that he suffered from a disease called alcoholism and that the law prohibits discrimination on the basis of a disease. The VA called his alcoholism "willful misconduct." Soon thereafter, however, Congress passed a law for veterans that expressly forbids considering the disabling effects of chronic alcoholism to be the result of willful misconduct. However, this law does not define alcoholism as a disease, nor does it prohibit drug addiction from being regarded as "willful misconduct."

According to Herbert Fingarette, a professor of philosophy at the University of California in Santa Barbara and an expert on addiction and criminal responsibility, much of the controversy arising from *Traynor* and similar cases—such as *Powell v. Texas* (1968), a case involving the disease-model defense of a man convicted for public intoxication—stemmed from a Supreme Court ruling in *Robinson v. California* (1962).

In this case the Court decided that narcotics addiction is a disease and held that criminal punishment of a person thus afflicted violates the Eighth Amendment's prohibition against cruel and unusual punishment. As Justice William O. Douglas concurred, "The addict is a sick person." But the Court ruled only insofar as Robinson's status as a drug addict was concerned. Its decision had nothing to do with any acts stemming from that status.

In *Powell* the Court held against the use of status as an alcoholic as exculpatory. Powell, an alcoholic, was held to be responsible for his criminal actions. In *Traynor,* the Court upheld the decision made in *Powell.* Traynor and Powell were not absolved of responsibility for their actions because of their alcoholism disease. Robinson, however, was absolved of criminal responsibility because of his status as a drug addict. In *Robinson,* the Court equated punishment for the status of narcotics addiction with punishment for disease afflic-

tion. From this viewpoint, an addict's acts are considered to be inseparable from his status as an addict because they are a symptom of the disease and thus an involuntary result of status.

The critical point here is the inseparability of status and act. Certain acts are considered to be part of disease status. Disease is involuntary. Therefore, acts stemming from the disease are exculpable. Are the acts that stem from status really involuntary? This belief is the legal corollary to Jellinek's notion of loss of control.

Disease vs. Behavior

According to professor of psychiatry Thomas Szasz at the State University of New York in Syracuse, a disease, as textbooks on pathology state, is a phenomenon limited to the body. It has no relationship to a behavior such as drug addiction, except as a metaphor. Szasz argues against the disease model of addiction on the basis of the following distinction between disease and behavior. In *Insanity: The Idea and Its Consequences* (1987) he writes:

> [B]y behavior we mean the person's 'mode of conducting himself' or his 'deportment'. . .the name we attach to a living being's conduct in the daily pursuit of life. . . [B]odily movements that are the products of neurophysiological discharges or reflexes are not behavior. . . The point is that behavior implies action, and action implies conduct pursued by an agent seeking to attain a goal.

The products of neurophysiological discharges or reflexes become behavior when they are organized through intent, a willful act. Drug-taking behavior is not like epilepsy. The former involves intentional, goal-seeking behavior. An epileptic convulsion is an unconscious, unorganized neurophysiological discharge or reflex, not a behavior.

In another example, smoking cigarettes and drinking alcohol are behaviors that can lead to the diseases we call cancer of the lungs and cirrhosis of the liver. Smoking and drinking are behaviors. Cancer and cirrhosis are diseases. Smoking and drinking are not cancer and cirrhosis.

The alleged absence of voluntariness or willfulness forms the basis of legal rulings that extend beyond the minimalist interpretation of *Robinson,* exculpating criminal behavior on the basis of a person's supposed disease status. Yet because behavior such as drug use involves voluntariness it seems an individual who uses drugs should not be absolved of responsibility for criminal behavior on the grounds that his actions are involuntary symptoms of drug addiction disease.

Many advocates of the disease model cite as further evidence for their view the results of genetic studies involving the heritability of alcoholism. Recently, the dopamine D2 receptor gene was found to be associated with alcoholism. A study by Kenneth Blum and co-authors, published in the Journal of the American Medical Association, suggests that this gene confers susceptibility to at least one form of alcoholism. The goal of this and similar studies is to identify the at-risk population in order to prevent people from becoming alcoholics and drug addicts.

What such studies do not tell us is why people who are not predisposed become alcoholics and why those who are predisposed do not. It seems more than reasonable to attribute this variance to psychological factors such as will, volition and choice, as well as to environmental variables such as economic opportunity, racism and family settings, to name just a few. Experimental controls accounting for genetic versus environmental influences on alcoholic behavior are sorely lacking in these studies.

The basis upon which people with alleged alcoholism disease are distinguished from mere heavy drinkers is arbitrary. No reliable explanation has yet been put forth of how the biological mechanisms theoretically associated with alcoholism and other forms of drug addiction translate into drug-taking behavior. Moreover, Annabel M. Bolos and co-authors, in a rigorous attempt to replicate the Blum findings, reported higher frequencies of the D2 receptor gene found in their control population than in the alcoholic population in the same journal seven months later.

Treatment

Finally, the contribution of treatment to exposing the myth of addiction disease warrants mention. Since his arrest at the Vista Hotel in Washington, D.C., Marion Barry has undergone treatment for alcohol addiction and chemical dependency at the Hanley-Hazelden clinic in West Palm Beach, Florida, and at the Fenwick Hall facility near Charleston, South Carolina. Barry said he needs treatment because he has "not been spiritual enough." His plan is to turn his "entire will and life over to the care of God . . . using the twelve-step method and consulting with treatment specialists." He said he will then "become more balanced and a better person."

The twelve-step program Barry is attempting to follow is the one developed by Alcoholics Anonymous (AA), a spiritual self-help fellowship. AA is the major method dealing with alcoholism today. All good addiction treatment facilities and treatment programs aim at getting the patient into AA and similar programs such as Narcotics Anonymous. Yet several courts throughout the United States have determined that AA is a religion and not a form of medicine, in cases involving First Amendment violations, most recently in *Maryland v. Norfolk* (1989). Anthropologist Paul Antze at York University in Ontario has written extensively on AA and describes the "point-by-point homology between AA's dramatic model of the alcoholic's predicament and the venerable Protestant drama of sin and salvation."

Successful treatment from this perspective is dependent upon a religious conversion experience. In addition, patients are required to adopt a disease identity. If they do not, they are said to be in denial. But such an approach is a psychologically coercive remedy for a moral problem, not a medical one. And here—in their concepts of treatment —is where the disease model and moralistic model of addiction seem to merge.

With so much evidence to refute it, why is the view of drug addiction as a disease so prevalent? Incredible as it may seem, because doctors say so. One leading alcoholism researcher asserts that alcoholism is a disease simply because people go to doctors for it. Undoubtedly, addicts seek help from doctors for two reasons. Addicts have a significant psychological investment in maintaining this view, having learned that their sobriety depends on believing they have a disease. And treatment professionals have a significant economic investment at stake. The more behaviors are diagnosed as diseases, the more they will be paid by health insurance companies for treating these diseases.

Most people say we need more treatment for drug addiction. But few people realize how ineffective treatment programs really are. Treatment professionals know this all too well. In fact, the best predictor of treatment success, says Charles Schuster, director of the National Institute on Drug Abuse, is whether the addict has a job or not.

George Vaillant, professor of psychiatry at Dartmouth Medical School, describes his first experience , using the disease model and its effectiveness in diagnosing alcoholism, in *The Natural History of Alcoholism* (1983):

". . . I learned for the first time how to diagnose alcoholism as an illness. . . Instead of pondering the sociological and psychodynamic complexities of alcoholism. . . [A]lcoholism became a fascinating disease. . . [B]y inexorably moving patients into the treatment system of AA, I was working for the most exciting alcohol program in the world . . . After initial discharge, only five patients in the Clinic sample never relapsed to alcoholic drinking, and there is compelling evidence that the results of our treatment were no better than the natural history of the disease."

This is important information because the definition of who an alcoholic or drug addict is and what constitutes treatment as well as treatment success can affect the lives of people who choose not to use drugs as well as those who choose to. For example, Stanton Peele has written extensively on how studies show that most people arrested for drinking and driving are directed into treatment for alcoholism disease, yet the majority are not alcoholics. Those receiving treatment demonstrate higher recidivism rates, including accidents, driving violations, and arrests, than those who are prosecuted and receive ordinary legal sanctions.

Furthermore, in a careful review of studies on treatment success and follow-up studies of heroin addicts at the United States Public Health Service hospital for narcotics addicts at Lexington, Kentucky, where "tens of thousands of addicts have been treated," the late Edward M. Brecher concluded in Licit & Illicit Drugs (1972) that "[a]lmost all [addicts] became readdicted and reimprisoned . . . for most the process is repeated over and over again . . . [and] no cure for narcotics addiction, and no effective deterrent, was found there— or anywhere else."

Brecher explained the failure of treatment in terms of the addictive property of heroin. Vaillant suggested that tuberculosis be considered as an analogy. Treatment, he said, rests entirely on recognition of the factors contributing to the "resistance" of the patient. And here is the "catch-22" of the disease model. Addiction is a disease beyond volitional control except when it comes to treatment failure, wherein "resistance" comes into play.

Neither Brecher nor Vaillant recognized that treatment does not work because there is nothing to treat. There is no medicine and there is no disease. The notions that heroin as an addictive drug causes addicts not to be treated successfully, or that "resistance" causes alcoholics to be incurable, are mythical notions that only serve to reinforce an avoidance of the facts: Addicts and alcoholics do not "get better" because they do not want to. Their self-destructive behaviors are not disturbed. They are disturbing.

All of this is not to suggest that the people we call addicts are bad, suffering from moral weakness and lack of willpower, character or values. Drug addicts simply have different values from the norm and often refuse to take responsibility for their actions. Public policy based on the disease model of addiction enables this avoidance to continue by sanctioning it in the name of helping people. As a result, criminals are absolved of responsibility for their actions, drug prevention and treatment programs end up decreasing feelings of personal self-worth and power instead of increasing them, and people who choose not to use drugs pay higher taxes and health insurance premiums to deal with the consequences of those who do.

Drug use is a choice, not a disease. Still, our current drug policies give the drug user only two options: treatment or jail. But if the drug user is sick, that is, is not responsible for his behavior, why should he go to jail for his illness? And if the drug user is someone who chooses to use drugs because he finds meaning in doing so, why should he be forced into treatment for having unconventional values? "Unconventional values" is not a disease.

"Treatment" for drug addiction is a misnomer. Education is a more appropriate term. In this modality a drug addict is given psychological and environmental support to achieve goals based on an identification of values and behavior-value dissonance. Behavioral accountability is stressed insofar as people learn about the consequences of their actions.

The legal arguments set forth to exculpate criminals because of addiction disease do not seem to be supported by scientific findings. Quite to the contrary, research suggests that drug addiction is far from a real disease. And as long as drug addiction can be blamed on a mythical disease, the real reasons why people use drugs—those related to socioeconomic, existential and psychological conditions including low self-esteem, self-worth and self-efficacy—can be ignored.

Readings Suggested by the Author:

Alexander, B.K. *Peaceful Measures: Canada's Way Out of the "War on Drugs."* Toronto: University of Toronto Press, 1990.

Douglas, M. (ed.). *Constructive Drinking: Perspectives on Drink from Anthropology.* New York: Cambridge University Press, 1987.

Fingarette, H. *Heavy Drinking: The Myth of Alcoholism as a Disease.* Berkeley, Calif.: University of California Press, 1988.

Institute of Medicine. *Broadening the Base of Treatment for Alcohol Problems.* Washington, D. C.: National Academy Press, 1990.

Peele, S., Brodsky, A. and Arnold, M. *The Truth about Addiction and Recovery.* New York: Simon and Schuster, 1991.

Szasz, T. S. *Ceremonial Chemistry: The Ritual Persecution of Drugs, Addicts, and Pushers.* Holmes Beach, Fla.: Learning Publications, 1985.

Why Drugs?

Why do people use and abuse drugs? And why do some people use, abuse, and become dependent on certain psychoactive substances while others do not? What explanations account for drug use? The medical profession calls explanations that attempt to answer the "why" question, *etiology*; what is the etiology or cause of drug use and abuse? In short, *why drugs*?

A variety of perspectives attempt to answer the "why" question. In the early 1980s, a federal agency, the National Institute on Drug Abuse, published a nearly 500-page monograph entitled *Theories of Drug Abuse*, which described some 40 different explanations of why people abuse drugs. Clearly, a definitive explanation of drug use and abuse—one on which nearly all informed observers will agree—has not yet been devised. This issue is still fraught with controversy.

Some experts believe that drug use is a universal human need—indeed, an instinct that is characteristic of all, or most, members of the animal kingdom. "High Times in the Wild Kingdom" summarizes this perspective, originally put forth by Andrew Weil in his book, *The Natural Mind* (1972), and later expanded by Ronald Siegel in *Intoxication: Life in Pursuit of Artificial Paradise* (1989). Siegel concludes that since humans have a universal need to get high, and since all currently known intoxicating substances have dangerous side effects, scientists ought to search for one that is completely safe. While most experts do not agree, this theory is worthy of attention.

The "animal instinct" theory, however, does not address the question of the *variability* of drug use among humans. After all, instinct or not, some of us are lifetime abstainers, others use drugs (alcohol and coffee, for instance) safely, moderately, and without untoward effect, and still others are compulsive, drug-dependent abusers. How do we account for the difference? For answers, we have to look at differences among individuals.

Some experts believe that there is a genetic basis to dependence and addiction—that some people are born with a genetic propensity to abuse and become dependent on addictive drugs such as alcohol. What exactly does this "genetic propensity" consist of? With respect to alcohol, some observers believe that an unusual insensitivity to the effects of alcohol causes some people to drink to excess; their insensitivity causes them to feel only slightly drunk when they are very drunk, which influences them to drink more than others do. The same could be true of drugs generally, some argue. "Probing the Complex Genetics of Alcoholism" explores the difficulties in drawing conclusions in this controversial area.

The controversial genetic theory is not accepted by most drug abuse experts. Some observers argue that there is a syndrome known as the "addictive personality." Those individuals who become chemically dependent do so because, to quote Benjamin Stein, author of "The Lure of Drugs: They 'Organize' an Addict's Life," they are "lonely, sad, frightened people" who have a basic personality flaw for which drugs offer a crutch that "organizes" their lives. Still other experts argue that alcohol and other chemical dependencies are "intoxicating habits," that the chemically dependent have simply learned to do the wrong things with the substances they use and abuse. Just as Pavlov's dogs learned to salivate at the sound of a bell, the stimuli in the addict's environment serve as cues that generate a drug craving. Addicts associate these cues with pleasure because they have been associated with reinforcement in the past; such associations can be unlearned as readily as they were learned. Still other experts point to more natural causes. The brain produces a set of morphine-like chemicals called endorphins (or "endogenous morphines") which, under certain circum-

stances, give us a "natural high." When endorphins are released, the body feels pleasure and wants to repeat what caused it; could these endorphins be a clue to the etiology of drug use and abuse?

Sociological perspectives stress the influence of the society, the culture, social contexts or settings, and subcultures within a given society on drug dependence. Certain categories in the population are more likely than others to use and abuse drugs; certain drugs penetrate poorer neighborhoods more readily than more affluent ones; men learn that it is acceptable and normative to drink at higher levels than women do; drinking in some societies takes place in family settings and tends to be moderate, whereas in other societies, drinking typically takes place among single men in a bar setting, and tends to be more excessive; and so on. In any explanation of drug and alcohol abuse, it is incomplete and misleading to leave sociological factors out of the picture.

Recently, many observers have concluded that several explanations are necessary for a complete understanding of the "why" question. Perhaps, one day, an integrated theory may emerge.

Looking Ahead: Challenge Questions

Why do people use drugs? Why do some people use certain drugs? Why do some people who use drugs abuse and become dependent on them—while others do not? Why do so many drug users not become drug abusers? Where does use end and abuse begin?

Is abuse a chemical, a genetic, a psychological, or a sociological phenomenon? Is it a combination of all of these factors? In what way? Is it a different combination for different individuals?

Is drug abuse rational or irrational behavior? Why?

If drug abuse can be explained by factors beyond the individual's control, are we therefore not responsible for our abuse of drugs?

If the supply of a certain drug suddenly dried up, would the users and abusers of that drug simply stop taking drugs altogether—or turn to another chemical substance?

Do we need a different explanation for use than we do for abuse? Abuse than for addiction and dependence? Do we need a different explanation for the abuse of each drug separately?

If alcoholism is genetically caused, how can one member of the same family become an alcoholic, one an abstainer, and the third a moderate drinker? If drug abuse is hereditary, what about other factors?

Why can some people handle alcohol while others cannot?

Intoxicating Habits

Some alcoholism researchers say they are studying a learned behavior, not a disease

BRUCE BOWER

Most alcoholism treatment programs in the United States operate on the assumption that people seeking their help have a disease characterized by physical dependency and a strong genetic predisposition. The goal of treatment, therefore, is total abstinence.

Herbert Fingarette, a philosophy professor at the University of California, Santa Barbara, pored over alcoholism and addiction research and came up with a suggestion for the many proponents of this approach: Forget it.

In a controversial new book (*Heavy Drinking: The Myth of Alcoholism as a Disease*, University of California Press, 1988), Fingarette says alcoholism has no single cause and no medical cure, and is the result of a range of physical, personal and social characteristics that predispose a person to drink excessively.

"Let's view the persistent heavy drinking of the alcoholic not as a sin or disease but as a central activity of the individual's way of life," he contends. Seen in this context, alcoholism treatment must focus not just on the drinking problem, but on developing a satisfying way of life that does not revolve around heavy drinking. Total abstinence — the goal of medical treatment centers as well as Alcoholics Anonymous — is unrealistic for many heavy drinkers, holds Fingarette.

Disputes over the nature of alcoholism have a long and vitriolic history. But Fingarette's arguments reflect a growing field of research, populated mainly by psychologists, in which alcoholism and other addictions — including those that do not involve drugs, such as compulsive gambling — are viewed more as habits than as diseases. Addictive behavior, in this scheme, typically revolves around an immediate gratification followed by delayed, harmful effects. The habitual behavior nevertheless continues and is often experienced by the addict as uncontrollable.

"Addiction occurs in the environment, not in the liver, genes or synapses," says psychologist Timothy B. Baker of the University of Wisconsin in Madison. Biology may, in some cases, increase a person's risk of developing a dependency, but "an individual chooses to take drugs in the world. The likelihood of a person trying a drug or eventually becoming addicted is influenced by his or her friends, marital happiness, the variety and richness of alternatives to drug use and so on," Baker contends.

Expectations and beliefs about alcohol's power to make one feel better shape the choices leading to alcohol addiction, according to one line of investigation. The most notable of these beliefs, says psychologist G. Alan Marlatt of the University of Washington in Seattle, is that alcohol acts as a magical elixir that enhances social and physical pleasure, increases sexual responsiveness and assertiveness, and reduces tension (SN: 10/3/87, p.218).

The initial physical arousal stimulated by low doses of alcohol pumps up positive expectations, explains Marlatt. But higher alcohol doses dampen arousal, sap energy and result in hangovers that, in turn, lead to a craving for alcohol's stimulating effects. As tolerance to the drug develops, a person requires more and more alcohol to get a short-term "lift" and a vicious cycle of abuse picks up speed.

Despite falling into this addictive trap, Marlatt says, some people drastically cut back their drinking or stop imbibing altogether without the help of formal treatment. In these cases, he maintains, external events often conspire to change an individual's attitude toward alcohol. Examples include an alcohol-related injury, the departure of a spouse, financial and legal problems stemming from drinking or the alcohol-related death of another person.

When treatment is sought out, Marlatt advises, the focus should be on teaching ways to handle stress without drinking and developing realistic expectations about alcohol's effects. Marlatt and his co-workers are now developing an "alcohol skills-training program" for college students, described more fully in *Issues in Alcohol Use and Misuse by Young Adults* (G. Howard, editor, Notre Dame University Press, 1988). Preliminary results indicate many students who consume large amounts of alcohol every week cut down considerably after completing the eight-session course. In fact, says Marlatt, children of alcoholics show some of the best responses to the program and are highly motivated to learn how to drink in moderation.

Psychologists teach the students how to set drinking limits and cope with peer pressure at parties and social events. Realistic expectations about alcohol's mood-enhancing powers are developed, and participants learn alternative methods of stress reduction, such as meditation and aerobic exercise.

The program does not promote drinking, says Marlatt, and students showing signs of hard-core alcohol dependency are referred for treatment that stresses abstinence. "But it's inappropriate to insist that all students abusing alcohol are in the early stages of a progressive disease," he contends. "Our approach acknowledges that drinking occurs regularly and gives students more options and choices for safer drinking."

A similar approach to helping adult alcoholics has been developed by psychologists W. Miles Cox of the Veterans Administration Medical Center in Indianapolis and Eric Klinger of the University of Minnesota in Morris. Their model, described in the May JOURNAL OF ABNORMAL PSYCHOLOGY, holds that although a number of biological and social factors influence alcohol abuse, the final decision to drink is motivated by conscious or unconscious expectations that alcohol will brighten one's emotional state and wipe away stress. An alcoholic's expected pleasure or relief from a drinking binge, for example, may outweigh fears that it eventually will lead to getting fired or divorced.

Cox and Klinger's technique aims at providing alternative sources of emotional satisfaction. They have developed a questionnaire to assess an alcoholic's major life goals and concerns. A counselor then helps the alcoholic formulate weekly goals based on his or her responses. Counseling also attempts to reduce the tendency to use alcohol as a crutch when faced with frustration. "Alcoholics often have unrealistically high standards and lack the capacity to forgive themselves for not meeting these standards," Cox says.

The focus on an alcoholic's concerns and motivation is intended to complement other treatments, say the researchers. It is consistent, they note, with the efforts of Alcoholics Anonymous to drive home the negative side of drinking and the benefits of not drinking.

The context in which people consume alcohol is another part of the addictive process under study. Any combination of drinking and mildly pleasant activity, such as television viewing, conversation or card games, appears to provide the best protection against anxiety and stress, report psychologists Claude M. Steele and Robert A. Josephs of the University of Michigan's Institute of Social Research in Ann Arbor. Alcohol's ability to draw attention away from stressful thoughts and onto immediate activity may play a key role in its addictive power, they suggest.

Steele and Joseph tested this theory in their laboratory. They gave enough vodka and tonic to adult subjects to induce mild intoxication. Another group expected to receive vodka and tonic, but was given tonic in glasses rubbed with alcohol to create the odor of a real drink. Everyone was told that in 15 minutes they would have to give a speech on "What I dislike about my body and physical appearance." Researchers asked some from each group to sit quietly before making the speech, while others were asked to rate a series of art slides before speaking.

Those subjects who drank alcohol and rated slides reported significantly less anxiety over the speech than the other participants. Viewing the slides when sober had no anxiety-reducing effects.

According to the researchers, this supports the notion that alcohol's reduction of psychological stress has less to do with its direct pharmacological effects than with its knack for shifting attention with the aid of distractions.

On the other hand, being intoxicated and doing nothing before the speech significantly increased subjects' anxiety, note the investigators in the May JOURNAL OF ABNORMAL PSYCHOLOGY. Without any distraction, alcohol appears to narrow attention to the upcoming situation.

Recent investigations also suggest alcohol users are motivated by alcohol's ability to reduce psychological stress among people who are highly self-conscious and constantly evaluating themselves. Steele and Josephs did not, however, evaluate the "self-awareness" of their subjects.

A different approach to unraveling drinking behavior involves the search for cues that set off an alcoholic's craving or irresistible urge to drink. Just as Pavlov's dogs were conditioned to salivate after hearing a bell that previously had preceded the appearance of food, there are internal and external "bells" that provoke craving in many alcoholics, explains psychiatrist Arnold M. Ludwig of the University of Kentucky Medical Center in Lexington.

These cues are often quite specific, he says. For instance, recovered alcoholic and major league baseball pitcher Bob Welch has reported experiencing a craving to drink during airplane flights, after a game of golf and after pitching.

In a survey of 150 abstinent alcoholics reported in the fall 1986 ALCOHOL HEALTH & RESEARCH WORLD, Ludwig finds nearly all of them can identify one or more "bells" that trigger craving. With the exception of "internal tension," mentioned as a cue by more than half the subjects, there was considerable individual difference in reported drinking "bells." These included going to a dance, feeling lonely, having a barbecue, seeing a drink in an advertisement and driving past former drinking hangouts.

Alcoholics Anonymous, notes Ludwig, teaches that four general conditions — hunger, anger, loneliness and tiredness — make recovered alcoholics more vulnerable to drinking urges, an observation supported by research on craving.

Other evidence, Ludwig says, suggests that the more times uncomfortable withdrawal symptoms — shakiness, agitation, hallucinations or confusion — have been relieved by drinking in the past, the greater the likelihood that familiar drinking cues will elicit craving in alcoholics.

Many alcoholics feel helpless and bewildered when craving strikes, seemingly out of the blue. "But craving is not the elusive, mysterious force many believe it to be," says Ludwig. To successfully recover, he contends, alcoholics must become aware of the emotional and situational cues that trigger drinking urges.

The first drink in the right setting, he adds, often whets the appetite for more. Alcoholics should seek out "safe havens" where drinking is discouraged, he suggests, such as workplaces, Alcoholics Anonymous and outdoor activities.

Whereas Ludwig sees drinking cues as stoking the internal embers of craving, other researchers focus solely on external "reinforcers" that affect an alcoholic's drinking behavior. When important reinforcers outside the realm of drinking, such as a job or marriage, are lost, say psychologists Rudy E. Vuchinich and Jalie A. Tucker of Wayne State University in Detroit, a recovered alcoholic becomes more likely to resume drinking.

"The growing consensus from clinical studies [points to] the important role of environmental variables and changes in life circumstances in influencing the drinking behavior of alcoholics," they write in the May JOURNAL OF ABNORMAL PSYCHOLOGY. But the development of appropriate environmental measures to study drinking is still in the early stages, the investigators add.

While research into the psychology of alcohol addiction is beginning to mature, it remains largely ignored by the biologically oriented advocates of alcoholism-as-disease, says Marlatt. The research and clinical communities are especially polarized over suggestions from addiction studies that some alcoholics — about 15 to 20 percent, according to Marlatt — can safely engage in moderate or social drinking.

The characteristics of alcohol abusers who can handle controlled drinking are not clear, but Marlatt and other researchers see milder alcoholics as prime candidates for this treatment approach.

Given that most current alcoholism treatment is based on the disease model of total abstinence, which has been endorsed by the American Medical Association and the American Psychiatric Association for many years, reconciliation between opposing theoretical camps is not imminent.

"But biological and genetic approaches to alcoholism need to be integrated with psychological and social approaches," Marlatt says. "This really hasn't been done yet."

High Times in the Wild Kingdom

Is drug abuse natural?

One of the surest ways to kill a rat is to let it shoot cocaine. Teach a rat, or a dog or a monkey, to dose itself at will, and it typically becomes just as helpless as any urban junkie. Addicted animals will give up food or companionship, even endure electrical shocks, to get another fix. And they'll continue to dose themselves as their lungs and nervous systems start to fail.

This is in the lab, of course. Such depravity would never occur in nature, right? Wrong, says Ronald Siegel, a psychopharmacologist at UCLA. In a recent book titled "Intoxication: Life in Pursuit of Artificial Paradise,"* Siegel argues that the urge to get high is as basic and universal as the desire for food or sex—and that it has some of the same consequences in the wild as it has in urban America. "The entire animal kingdom is driven by the same pursuit," he says. "It is part of our nature."

Siegel traces the roots of today's drug problem back 135 million years to the Cretaceous Period, when angiosperm plants started manufacturing toxic chemicals as a defense against herbivores. By the time humans discovered the pleasing effects of certain plant toxics, some 5,000 years ago, other animals were already forging "the new chemical bond we call addiction." Humans have recently carried the relationship to new extremes, of course, by extracting and refining the poisons of choice. But modern drug taking remains part of a "long natural tradition." Siegel doesn't always back his assertions with data, and his prose style is a bizarre amalgam of Scientific American and the New York Post. Yet despite its flaws, his treatise offers a refreshing perspective on the drug problem, and it's full of amusing yarns.

Addiction, as Siegel makes clear, is not always a bad thing. Australian koalas spend their lives feeding exclusively on eucalyptus leaves, not just for nutrition but to alter their body temperatures and make themselves unpalatable to parasites and predators. The leaves are bitter medicine: infants have to start out on a predigested pulp excreted by their mothers. But once they learn the habit, there's no giving it up. They die when deprived of eucalyptus, because their addicted bodies have no other way to get nutrients.

Other animals use drugs for sheer pleasure. In the Canadian Rockies, bighorn sheep grind their teeth to the gums nibbling at a narcotic lichen that grows on bare rocks. And various creatures eat the hallucinogenic mescal beans that grow in the Texas desert, even though the beans lack usable nutrients. When Siegel led a group of goats to a patch of shrubs to gauge the veracity of this rumor, several munched themselves into a daylong delirium. So did one of his pack horses (he had to restrain the others). Small wonder that the Wichita Indians, who developed an entire pharmacology by observing animals, became mescal eaters themselves.

Drunk elephants: Psychedelics don't have a broad animal following, but drunkenness seems ubiquitous. It often results from a chance encounter with fermented fruit or grain, yet many creatures actively lust after alcohol. Farm animals are notorious for breaking into vats of moonshine mash. So are elephants. Siegel recounts how a herd of 150 once raided an illegal still in West Bengal, drank liberally, then "rampaged across the land, killing five people, injuring a dozen, demolishing seven concrete buildings and trampling twenty village huts." Baboons can get carried away, too. In "The Descent of Man," Darwin recounts how a troupe in North Africa "held their aching heads with both hands and wore a pitiable expression" a day after gulping down bowls of strong beer. "When beer or wine was offered them, they turned away with disgust."

Luckily, natural forces usually converge to keep animals from wasting their lives, even when they lack a sense of restraint. When flocks of migrating robins arrive in southern California each February, they gorge themselves on ripening firethorn and toyon berries. For a few weeks the birds go utterly berserk, and many die in high-speed flying accidents. But because the berries are seasonal, sobriety prevails the rest of the year. In the Andes, llamas, birds, snails, insects and people all consume cocaine by eating leaves or seeds from the coca plant. But the drug's natural packaging effectively prohibits harmful doses.

Insect anarchy: There are exceptions to this pattern, however—instances in which drug use tears at the fabric of animal society. Ranchers have known since the 19th century that locoweed, a flowering plant native to the American Southwest, can turn cattle and horses into crazed, hopeless junkies. Many addicts die of starvation or thirst, as they give up food and water in favor of the drug. And their offspring tend to perpetuate the cycle of dependency. *Lasius flavus,* or yellow ant, suffers similarly from its appetite for beetle juice. Colonies of yellow ants typically feed and care for *Lomechusa* beetles in exchange for the chance to lick an intoxicating goo from their abdomens. If the worker ants drink too much, they get careless and damage the ant larvae in their care. The workers' addiction also compromises their loyalties: in a crisis, they tend to safeguard the beetles' larvae instead of their own kin's. Entire societies can collapse as a result.

The fact that drug use is natural doesn't mean it's good, then, just that chanting "no" isn't likely to rid us of it anytime soon. The most controversial alternative—to haul off and legalize currently controlled substances—could prove disastrous, given the deadly pharmacopia we've amassed. The obvious solution, in Siegel's view, is to restructure our chemical environment—to fabricate drugs that "balance optimal positive effects, such as stimulation or pleasure, with minimal . . . toxic consequences." If medical science could perform that feat, he reasons, everyone could have a good time and no one would get hurt. It's a fanciful notion, a bit like that of erecting a high-tech global missile shield. The difference is that, in this case, a partial success would represent progress.

Geoffrey Cowley

The Lure of Drugs:

They 'Organize' An Addict's Life

Benjamin Stein

Benjamin Stein, an aide in the Nixon-Ford White Houses, is a lawyer and freelance writer in Los Angeles. His latest book is "Hollywood Days, Hollywood Nights" (Bantam).

AND NOW for a few words about drugs . . .

Everyone in America talks on television and at political gatherings about drugs — politicians, preachers, teachers, lawyers, law enforcement officials, even parents. Everyone talks about drugs, that is, except for the one group most directly affected by drugs: drug addicts and users. It might make sense for the nation to listen to what they think.

Now, I am not exactly a drug addict. But I do take a variety of tranquilizing and sleeping pills, and in my past life, when I was a '60s kind of guy, I used my share

of what was hip. That was a while ago, but for whatever reasons since the days of law school, through the days in Washington, in the bureaucracy, in the White House, at a university, and the days in New York, at a great newspaper, and in Los Angeles, around the studios, and the cars and the bars and the flash and the cash and the trash, I have spent much time with drug users. Even now, I am involved in a number of self-help programs for major, heavy-duty drug abusers. These are not people I am studying. These are my friends, and this is a big part of my life.

In a word, I know something about drugs and drug users from the inside out.

I'd like to share a little bit of what I know, and correct a few wrong impressions. Some of these have public

policy implications, and some of them are just interesting in the way learning about any new kind of people is interesting.

First, drug addicts do not become drug addicts by mistake, by accident or because someone lurks on a corner offering reefers. Drug addicts do not get high just because they have nothing else to do and getting high would be a cool way of spitting on the bourgeoisie.

Drug addicts (and by that is meant, without any doubt, alcohol addicts) get that way because drugs have a way of, temporarily, organizing an otherwise disordered life. I have heard hundreds, maybe thousands of drug addicts talk about how they got into drugs so heavily that drugs ruled their lives.

Every single one of them wanted

some outside power to take over his life. Each man or woman felt that his or her life was grossly defective, that he or she was severely lacking the basic equipment needed to cope with existence. "I feel like I was dropped here from another planet without any travel brochure," one particularly articulate young man once said. "I have felt like a lonely, heartbroken child my whole life," said another man, who spoke for every addict I have ever known. "I never felt like I even belonged in my own skin, let alone in my family or in my high school," said another young woman. I defy anyone to find a drug addict who had a happy childhood or who emerged from childhood with a well-integrated personality.

Drugs — and again, this includes alcohol in a big way — made the psychically split feel whole again. "When I first started to use coke, I felt six-feet tall and bulletproof," said one diminutive man. "I used blow (cocaine) in eighth grade, and I wondered where it had been all my life," said another man. "For the first time, I felt like I belonged, like I could talk to people, like I was going somewhere," is a sort of synthesis of hundreds of comments by addicts about how the felt when they got onto drugs. In other words, drugs that are illegal do exactly what prescription psychoactive drugs do.

Drugs are not like going to a dance or having a vacation or getting a great stereo or even like having sex. They are not interludes in otherwise different lives. For the drug addict, the effect of the drug, the knowledge that a drink or a shot or a snort or a pill can change their relation to the universe is the overwhelming fact of their lives for the time they are allowing drugs to organize their lives. They genuinely believe that their lives would be unbearable without drugs.

In other words, you will not stop drug addiction by nuclear bombing Peru. The drug addict will find something legal, something by prescription, something that will organize his life again and take his shattered self and make it real.

That is, drug addiction is not a problem made by smugglers. It is a problem of lonely, sad, frightened people — some of them truly wonderful people — who want something to help, and if they can't get it from Colombia, they will get it from the corner liquor store or from a doctor, and they will be addicts all the same.

The problem in America is not the importation of illegal drugs. The problem is the minds and hearts and

bodies of broken people who need to be made whole by something, and drugs come easily to hand.

Second, and this is crucial, drug addiction in each case is usually self-limiting in either tragic or miraculous ways. The tragic way in which drugs are self-limiting is obvious: People die from them sooner or later.

The miraculous way comes from the fact that drugs simply do not keep on succesfully organizing addicts' lives. Addicts come to know that. At some point, early or late, the drug addict sees that the negative effects of the habit are far more dangerous than whatever life he had before he took up drugs. He finds that sleepless nights, car crashes, nights in jail, loss of family, loss of job, loss of self-respect, loss of home are worse than what he had before. In other words, the drug has lost its ability to put the addict back into one piece again. The drug addiction has made him far more shattered than he ever was before he began to get high.

Drug addicts get saved by having something to organize themselves without drugs. This can be religion, self-help groups, new friends, a new environment, new creative challenges or some combination. Those who felt themselves psychically crippled before they used drugs or alcohol will still feel incomplete when they stop using or drinking. They need something to fill up the empty spaces inside.

To an astonishingly impressive extent, Alcoholics Anonymous (by far the largest active multi-faith non-profit organization in Southern California) gives men and women a reason to live, and organizing principles (their famous and inspiring 12-step program) to glue splintered egos together. (Every drug addict and alcoholic knows of at least one person whose life has been saved by AA, and knows that the opportunity is out there.) I have no doubt that there are religious organizations outside AA that do excellent work as well.

The point is that drug addiction is something that comes from inside

'The point is that drug addiction is something that comes from inside individuals. It will never be stopped by speedboats, helicopters or search dogs.'

millions of individuals. It will never be stopped by speedboats and helicopters and search dogs, nor by defoliating marijuana acreage in Humboldt County, California. It will be slowed down (not stopped, because realistically it is never going to be stopped altogether) when millions of individuals realize that there are alternatives to drugs for binding up wounds, alternatives that do not cut still deeper lacerations, alternatives that build lives.

It's a happy sign that the Congress has realized this, in an election year, and has increased funding for drug treatment centers. But the continuing illusion that pouring money into high-tech search gear for border patrols — the path Washington took in earlier legislation — will stop drug abuse when drugs are available freely inside the stores of America is a joke.

The idea that drug addicts will stop booting up because of appeals by movie stars or politicians' wives simply bears no relation to the reality of the problem. Drug addicts need to be brought back to sanity one by one, from the inside out. To the extent that the government can help addicts by helping hospitals, drug treatment centers and self-help groups make their services more widely available, then it can help the addicts I know. (It is deeply instructive to know, however, that AA, which has probably saved more addicts than every other public or private program put together, proudly will not accept any outside contributions, and is entirely self-supporting from the dollars and quarters placed onto plates at the meetings.)

There are more truths that can be learned by listening to the people most directly affected by addiction — the addicts. I have only touched on a few. But it is clear that the huge volume of knowledge of what drug addiction is and how it can be stopped lies mainly in the experience of drug addicts, present and recovering, grateful or still suffering. It might make sense to listen to them.

Probing the Complex Genetics of Alcoholism

Recent findings of an "alcoholism gene" haven't held up—but a huge new study funded by NIH may help to nail down the basis of this costly condition

LAST APRIL, RESEARCHERS CAUSED A FLURRY in the media when they announced in the *Journal of the American Medical Association* that they had for the first time identified a gene—an allele of the D2 dopamine receptor—that they believed to be implicated in severe cases of alcoholism. But the first test of the finding, reported last month by researchers at the National Institute on Alcohol Abuse and Alcoholism (NIAAA), has failed to confirm it.*

Frustrating findings are common in the world of alcoholism research, where for the past two decades researchers have been trying, so far without success, to identify biological markers—and more recently, actual genes—signaling a predisposition to alcoholism. Indeed, some scientists are beginning to suspect that there may be no genes for alcoholism per se, but rather for a general susceptibility to compulsive behaviors whose specific expression is shaped by environmental and temperamental factors.

Definitive answers may be on the horizon: The NIAAA, in an attempt to crack the biological riddles of the disease, has launched a massive study—massive for the behavioral sciences anyway—a kind of Manhattan Project on the genetics of alcoholism. Budgeted at $25 million for the first 5 years, it's a multisite, multilevel study including everything from psychological tests to DNA probes that will involve 600 alcoholics and potentially thousands of their family members.

The study will take off from the fragments of knowledge scientists now have about society's most costly disease. For example, it

is now widely accepted that a vulnerability to the disorder can be partly inherited. (This certainty is based on results of adoption, twin, and family studies that have been rolling in since the mid-1970s, as well as by success in breeding strains of rats that prefer alcohol over water in their drinks.) Scientists are also now certain that many genes are involved, and that they are different for different groups of individuals.

But the tremendous variability shown in alcoholism has prevented researchers from pinning those genes down more specifically.

20's to under 20, and although some alcoholics stick to alcohol, more and more are taking advantage of the availability of illicit drugs.

What kinds of genes can account for even a part of this variability? Are the functions they mediate metabolic or behavioral? The principal investigator of the NIAAA study,† neuroscientist Henri Begleiter of the State University of New York's Health Science Center at Brooklyn, says he has come to the conclusion that no genes specific to alcoholism exist. Noting that it is getting harder and harder to find a "pure" alcoholic, he suspects that the disorder results from an underlying "behavioral disregulation that is not specific to alcoholism...a set of biological factors which are heavily influenced by environmental events and can lead to very different adverse outcomes." These outcomes include problems that look like addictions, such as gambling and eating disorders, as well as other compulsions and disorders of impulse control.

There is no evidence to contradict this

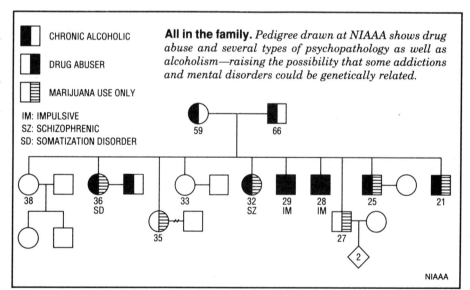

All in the family. *Pedigree drawn at NIAAA shows drug abuse and several types of psychopathology as well as alcoholism—raising the possibility that some addictions and mental disorders could be genetically related.*

CHRONIC ALCOHOLIC

DRUG ABUSER

MARIJUANA USE ONLY

IM: IMPULSIVE
SZ: SCHIZOPHRENIC
SD: SOMATIZATION DISORDER

NIAAA

For many alcoholics, the disease is associated with psychiatric problems: childhood conduct disorder, for example, which is marked by aggression and other antisocial activities, has emerged as one behavioral predictor for alcoholism. But there are also many alcoholics who apparently function normally until they end up in the hospital with cirrhosis. Other mysteries: why alcoholism can set in either early and fast, or gradually develop over decades; and why some alcoholics are binge drinkers, and others "maintenance" drinkers. And the epidemiology is actually changing: the average age of onset has moved from the mid-

idea, says Begleiter: For example, low levels of platelet monoamine oxidase (MAO) have long been suspected to be related to alcoholism, but now it seems they may correspond better to compulsive disorders in general. Furthermore, although he has

*The study, "Allelic Association of Human Dopamine D2 Receptor Gene in Alcoholism," was reported in the 18 April 1990 *JAMA* by a team headed by Kenneth Blum of the University of Texas Health Science Center and Ernest Noble of the University of California at Los Angeles. The NIAAA study, "Population and Pedigree Studies Reveal a Lack of Association Between the Dopamine D2 Receptor Gene and Alcoholism," by Annabel M. Bolos et al., appeared in the 26 December 1990 *JAMA*. Two other research teams, at Washington University and McGill University, are also testing the Blum-Noble finding with family studies of alcoholics.

†Principal investigators at the six sites in the National Collaborative Studies on the Genetics of Alcoholism are neuroscientist Bernice Porjesz at SUNY; psychiatric geneticist Theodore Reich at Washington University in St. Louis; psychologist Victor Hesselbrock at the University of Connecticut; psychiatrist Marc Schuckit of the University of California at San Diego; neuroscientist Floyd Bloom of Scripps Clinic and Research Foundation; geneticist Michael Conneally and psychiatrist John Nurnberger at Indiana University, and psychiatrist Raymond Crowe, University of Iowa.

identified anomalies in the brain waves of young sons of alcoholics, Begleiter doesn't think the phenomenon is specific to alcoholics, pointing to the fact that similar results have been found with cocaine abusers.

Psychologist Victor Hesselbrock of the University of Connecticut, one study investigator who agrees with Begleiter, says he thinks a number of scientists are "privately" leaning to the same view. But other researchers, while open to the idea of a generalized susceptibility, continue to place emphasis on the possibility that there are genes specific to alcoholism. Kenneth Blum of the University of Texas Health Science Center, for example, believes there may be genes for "compulsive disease" (he and his colleagues suspect their dopamine gene is one), but also "subgenes"—what biologists call modifier genes—that dictate susceptibilities to particular substances. The NIAAA study's co-principal investigator Theodore Reich, psychiatric geneticist at Washington University, is even more emphatic: He contradicts study leader Begleiter by saying, "I am convinced there is a pharmacogenetics of alcoholism." He predicts, "We'll begin to see the [reemergence] of primary alcoholics" as the crack epidemic wanes.

Psychiatrist Marc Schuckit of the University of California at San Diego is also in this camp, based on his research with high-risk sons of alcoholics. Many subjects, he says, experience a "decreased intensity" of response to alcohol, suggesting that people drink too much because they are getting "less feedback." Since a recent study using Valium with the same subjects failed to show these decreased responses, Schuckit believes they are specific to alcohol.

The genetic picture is enormously complicated by the fact that mental disorders, particularly anxiety, depression, manic depression, and personality disorders are seen in close to half of alcoholics, according to the National Institute of Mental Health's epidemiologic Catchment Area Study. But which conditions precede alcoholic drinking, and the circumstances under which they lead to alcoholism, are not understood. Possible genetic linkages with alcoholism cannot be ruled out in some cases—most notably with antisocial personality disorder, which by definition begins in adolescence and which often includes criminal activity and substance abuse.

Schuckit, for one, says most alcoholics do not have mental disorders and that the search for a genetic predisposition should focus on this group. But other researchers disagree, in large part because so many alcoholics have antisocial personality characteristics—about one-quarter, according to the NIAAA (only 1.5% of the general population qualifies for the diagnosis). Many scientists, therefore, view the disorder as part and parcel of the puzzle of alcoholism.

Enter the NIAAA collaborative study which was started a year ago in hopes of fitting together all the disparate pieces. Principal investigator Begleiter characterizes it as part of a "new era of research on the genetics of predisposition" that is "much more complex, challenging, and interesting" than the search for "typical Mendelian disorders."

Indeed, the study involves an elaborate design in which state-of-the-art behavioral and biological assessments will be applied to an unprecedentedly large population. All six sites will follow the same research protocols, and technical people have been trained to carry out all tests in an identical manner. The first phase has involved the development of several new assessment instruments, including a 71-page diagnostic questionnaire covering drinking and drug habits, medical history, and psychiatric problems. These, along with tests of cognitive and motor skills, electrophysiological measurements, and biochemical assays, will be administered to the 600 alcoholics and their immediate families as well as to members of 200 control families where no addictions (as far as can be ascertained) exist. One-third of the subjects will be women, who have hitherto received short shrift in genetics studies. Says Reich: "We'll be trying to put together the whole phenotype" of alcoholism.

The next phase will involve segregation analysis to model potential mechanisms of inheritance and to characterize the effect of genes suspected to be involved in alcoholism and other familial disorders. Finally, there will be formal linkage studies, involving dozens of members each from between 100 and 200 families of alcoholics, for an in-depth look at candidate genes and their association with diagnoses and with possible biological markers. These include blood platelet enzymes such as adenylate cyclase and monoamine oxidase, neurotransmitters, and brain waves. Perhaps the most promising candidate as marker at the moment, according to several investigators, is a decrement in a certain brain wave, called the P3 wave, that Begleiter has identified in studies of young sons of alcoholics. The anomaly, which is linked to the processing of significant sensory stimuli, is also evident in alcoholics.

Ultimately, the study will result in the creation of a tissue bank of blood cells from alcoholics and family members that will "capture the full range of variation" in alcoholism, says Reich. That will enable the products of the study to be used for many years, to be available for the rapid testing of new hypotheses as they come along. Psychiatrist Robert Cloninger of Washington University says the study design "has a lot of information." For example, "If we find a linkage in St. Louis, we can tell Indiana and New York to check it." So, although baseline data will be collected for prospective research, "We'll be able to replicate within the study without doing follow-up."

The field of behavioral genetics, says NIAAA director Enoch Gordis, "is ripe for this attack" because of advances in computerized pedigree analysis and biotechnology. Cloninger points out that such a study wouldn't have flown 10 years ago because not enough of the human genome had been explored; but now, he says, "There are markers spanning 95% of the human genome. If there are major susceptibility genes, the probability of finding them approaches one." Whether that will happen in 5 years depends on luck, but "it really is a matter of time."

In any case, investigators say the study will help researchers agree on a typology for alcoholics that will sort out which cases are strongly genetically influenced. It may lead to new pharmacological treatments, and to the development of tests combining biological and psychological indicators to predict individuals at risk for alcoholism and other addictions. Another likely outcome, says Cloninger, will be closer coordination between what have been the separate domains of alcoholism and drug abuse research.

Begleiter says he will be "overjoyed" if, as he suspects, it turns out that all addictions stem from "the same biological core of anomalies." In that case, he says, the study "will tell us a hell of a lot more than just about alcoholism." It would imply the same research model could be extended to "many other disorders," and would justify a much broader application of the basic model of alcoholism treatment. Indeed, it could mean nothing less than a major reconceptualization of the disease.

CONSTANCE HOLDEN

A Pleasurable Chemistry

Endorphins, the body's natural narcotics, aren't something we have to run after.
They're everywhere.

Janet L. Hopson

Janet L. Hopson, who lives in Oakland, California, gets endorphin highs by contributing to Psychology Today.

Welcome aboard the biochemical bandwagon of the 1980s. The magical, morphine-like brain chemicals called endorphins are getting a lot of play. First we heard they were responsible for runner's high and several other cheap thrills. Now we're hearing that they play a role in almost every human experience from birth to death, including much that is pleasurable, painful and lusty along the way.

Consider the following: crying, laughing, thrills from music, acupuncture, placebos, stress, depression, chili peppers, compulsive gambling, aerobics, trauma, masochism, massage, labor and delivery, appetite, immunity, near-death experiences, playing with pets. Each, it is claimed, is somehow involved with endorphins. Serious endorphin researchers pooh-pooh many or most of these claims but, skeptics notwithstanding, the field has clearly sprinted a long way past runner's high.

Endorphin research had its start in the early 1970s with the unexpected discovery of opiate receptors in the brain. If we have these receptors, researchers reasoned, then it is likely that the body produces some sort of opiate- or morphine-like chemicals. And that's exactly what was found, a set of relatively small biochemicals dubbed "opioid peptides" or "endorphins" (short for "endogenous morphines") that plug into the receptors. In other words, these palliative peptides are sloshing around in our brains, spines and bloodstreams, apparently acting just like morphine. In fact, morphine's long list of narcotic effects was used as a treasure map for where scientists might hunt out natural opiates in the body. Morphine slows the pulse and depresses breathing, so they searched in the heart and lungs. Morphine deadens pain, so they looked in the central and peripheral nervous systems. It disturbs digestion and elimination, so they explored the gut. It savages the sex drive, so they probed the reproductive and endocrine systems. It triggers euphoria, so they scrutinized mood.

Nearly everywhere researchers looked, endorphins or their receptors were present. But what were they doing: transmitting nerve impulses, alleviating pain, triggering hormone release, doing several of these things simultaneously or disintegrating at high speed and doing nothing at all? In the past decade, a trickle of scientific papers has become a tidal wave, but still no one seems entirely certain of what, collectively, the endorphins are doing to us or for us at any given time.

Researchers do have modern-day sextants for their search, including drugs such as naloxone and naltrexone. These drugs, known as opiate blockers, pop into the endorphin receptors and block the peptides' normal activity, giving researchers some idea of what their natural roles might be. Whatever endorphins are doing, however, it must be fairly subtle. As one researcher points out, people injected with opiate blockers may feel a little more pain or a little less "high," but no one gasps for breath, suffers a seizure or collapses in a coma.

Subtle or not, endorphins are there, and researchers are beginning to get answers to questions about how they touch our daily lives—pain, exercise, appetite, reproduction and emotions.

•ANSWERS ON ANALGESIA: A man falls off a ladder, takes one look at his right hand—now cantilevered at a sickening angle—and knows he has a broken bone. Surprisingly, he feels little pain or anxiety until hours later, when he's home from the emergency room. This physiological grace period, which closely resembles a sojourn on morphine, is a common survival mechanism in the animal world, and researchers are confident that brain opiates are responsible for such cases of natural pain relief. The question is how do they work and, more to the point, how can we make them work for us?

The answers aren't in, but researchers have located a pain control system in the periaquaductal gray (PAG), a tiny region in the center of the brain, and interestingly, it produces opioid peptides. While no one fully understands how this center operates, physicians can now jolt it with electric current to lessen chronic pain.

One day in 1976, as Navy veteran Dennis Hough was working at a hospital's psychiatric unit, a disturbed patient snapped Hough's back and ruptured three of his vertebral discs. Five years later, after two failed back operations, Hough was bedridden with constant shooting pains in his legs, back and shoulders and was depressed to the point of suicide. Doctors were just then pioneering a technique of implanting platinum electrodes in the PAG, and Hough soon underwent the skull drilling and emplacement. He remembers it as "the most barbaric thing I've ever experienced, including my tour of duty in Vietnam," but the results were worth the ordeal; For the past seven years, Hough has been able to stimulate his brain's own endorphins four times a day by producing a radio signal from a transmitter on his belt. The procedure is delicate—too much current and his eyes flutter, too little and the pain returns in less than six hours. But it works dependably, and Hough not only holds down an office job now but is engaged to be married.

Researchers would obviously like to find an easier way to stimulate the brain's own painkillers, and while they have yet to find it, workers in many labs are actively developing new drugs and treatments. Some physicians have tried direct spinal injections of endorphins to alleviate postoperative pain. And even the most cynical now seem to agree that acupuncture works its magic by somehow triggering the release of endorphins. There may, however, be an even easier path to pain relief: the power of the mind.

Several years ago, neurobiologist Jon Levine, at the University of California, San Francisco, discovered that the placebo effect (relief) based on no known action other than the patient's belief in a treatment) can itself be blocked by naloxone and must therefore be based on endorphins. Just last year Levine was able to quantify the effects: One shot of placebo can equal the relief of 6 to 8 milligrams of morphine, a low but fairly typical dose.

Another line of research suggests that endorphins may be involved in self-inflicted injury—a surprisingly common veterinary and medical complaint and one that, in many cases, can also be prevented with naloxone. Paul Millard Hardy, a behavioral neurologist at Boston's New England Medical Center, believes that animals may boost endorphin levels through self-inflicted pain and then "get caught in a self-reinforcing positive feedback loop." He thinks something similar may occur in compulsive daredevils and in some cases of deliberate self-injury. One young woman he studied had injected pesticide into her own veins by spraying Raid into an intravenous needle. This appalling act, she told Hardy, "made her feel better, calmer and almost high."

Hardy also thinks endorphin release might explain why some autistic children constantly injure themselves by banging their heads. Because exercise is believed to be an alternate route to endorphin release, Hardy and physician Kiyo Kitahara set up a twice-a-day exercise program for a group of autistic children. He qualifies the evidence as "very anecdotal at this point" but calls the results "phenomenal."

•RUNNER'S HIGH, RUNNER'S CALM: For most people, "endorphins" are synonymous with "runner's high," a feeling of well-being that comes after an aerobic workout. Many people claim to have experienced this "high," and remarkable incidents are legion. Take, for example, San Francisco runner Don Paul, who placed 10th in the 1979 San Francisco Marathon and wound up with his ankle in a cast the next day. Paul had run the 26 miles only vaguely aware of what turned out to be a serious stress fracture. Observers on the sidelines had to tell him he was "listing badly to one side for the last six miles." He now runs 90 miles per week in preparation for the U.S. men's Olympic marathon trial and says that when he trains at the level, he feels "constantly great. Wonderful."

Is runner's high a real phenomenon based on endorphins? And can those brain opiates result in "exercise addiction"? Or, as many skeptics hold, are the effects on mood largely psychological? Most studies with humans have found rising levels of endorphins in the blood during exercise.

However, says exercise physiologist Peter Farrell of Pennsylvania State University, "when we look at animal studies, we don't see a concurrent increase in the brain." Most circulating peptides fail to cross into the brain, he explains, so explaining moods like runner's high based on endorphin levels in the blood is questionable. Adds placebo expert Jon Levine, "Looking for mood changes based on the circulating blood is like putting a voltmeter to the outside of a computer and saying 'Now I know how it works.'" Nevertheless, Farrell exercises religiously: "I'm not going to waste my lifetime sitting around getting sclerotic just because something's not proven yet."

Murray Allen, a physician and kinesiologist at Canada's Simon Fraser University, is far more convinced about the endorphin connection. He recently conducted his own study correlating positive moods and exercise—moods that could be blocked by infusing the runner with naloxone. Allen thinks these moods are "Mother Nature's way of rewarding us for staying fit" but insists that aerobic exercisers don't get "high." Opioid peptides "slow down and inhibit excess activity in the brain," he says. "Many researchers have been chasing after psychedelic, excitable responses." The actual effect, he says, is "runner's calm" and extremes leading to exhaustion usually negate it.

In a very similar experiment last year, a research team at Georgia State University found the mood-endorphin link more elusive. Team member and psychologist Wade Silverman of Atlanta explains that only those people who experience "runner's high" on the track also noticed it in the lab. Older people and those who ran fewer, not more, miles per week were also more likely to show a "high" on the test. "People who run a lot—50 miles per week or more—are often drudges, masochists, running junkies," says Silverman. "They don't really enjoy it. It hurts." For optimum benefits. Silverman recommends running no more than three miles per day four times a week.

Silverman and Lewis Maharam, a sports medicine internist at Manhattan's New York Infirmary/Beekman Downtown Hospital, both agree that powerful psychological factors—including heightened sense of self-esteem and self-discipline—contribute to the "high" in those who exercise moderately. Maharam would still like to isolate and quantify the role of endorphins, however, so he could help patients "harness the high." He would like to give people "proper exercise prescriptions," he says, "to stimulate the greatest enjoyment and benefit from exercise. If we could encourage the 'high' early on, maybe we could get people to want to keep exercising from the start."

The questions surrounding exercise, mood and circulating endorphins remain. But even if opioids released into the bloodstream from, say, the adrenal glands don't enter the brain and give a "high" or a "calm," several studies show that endorphins in the blood do bolster the immune system's activity. One way or the other, regular moderate exercise seems destined to make us happy.

•APPETITE CLOCKS AND BLOCKS: Few things in life are more basic to survival and yet more pleasurable than eating good food—and where survival and pleasure intersect, can the endorphins be far behind? To keep from starving, an animal needs to know when, what and how much to eat, and researchers immediately suspected that opioid peptides might help control appetite and satiety. People, after all, have long claimed that specific foods such as chili peppers or sweets give them a "high." And those unmistakably "high" on morphine or heroin experience constipation, cravings and other gastrointestinal glitches.

Indeed, investigators quickly located opiate receptors in the alimentary tract and found a region of the rat's hypothalamus that—when injected with tiny amounts of beta endorphin—will trigger noshing of particular nutrients. Even a satiated rat will dig heartily into fats, proteins or sweets when injected with the peptide. Neurobiologist Sarah Leibowitz and her colleagues at Rockefeller University produced this result and also found that opiate blockers would prevent the snack attack—strong evidence that endorphins help regulate appetite. The opiates "probably enhance the hedonic, pleasurable, rewarding properties" of fats, proteins and sweets—foods that can help satiate an animal far longer than carbohydrates so it can survive extended periods without eating.

Intriguingly, rats crave carbohydrates at the beginning of their 12-hour activity cycles, but they like fats, proteins or sweets before retiring—a hint that endorphins control not just the nature but the timing of appetites. Leibowitz suspects that endorphins also help control cravings in response to stress and starva-

tion, and that disturbed endorphin systems may, in part, underlie obesity and eating disorders. Obese people given opiate blockers, for example, tend to eat less; bulimics often gorge on fat-rich foods; both bulimics and anorexics often have abnormal levels of endorphins; and in anorexics, food deprivation enhances the release of opiates in the brain. This brain opiate reward, some speculate, may reinforce the anorexic's self-starvation much as self-injury seems to be rewarding to an autistic child.

Researchers such as Leibowitz are hoping to learn enough about the chemistry of appetite to fashion a binge-blocking drug as well as more effective behavioral approaches to over- or undereating. In the meantime, people who try boosting their own endorphins through exercise, mirth or music may notice a vexing increase in their taste for fattening treats.

•PUBERTY, PREGNANCY AND PEPTIDES: Evolution has equipped animals with two great appetites—the hunger for food to prevent short-term disintegration and the hunger for sex and reproduction to prevent longer-term genetic oblivion. While some endorphin researchers were studying opioids and food hunger, others began searching for a sex role—and they found it.

Once again, drug addiction pointed the way: Users of morphine and heroin often complain of impotence and frigidity that fade when they kick their habits. Could natural opioids have some biochemical dampening effect on reproduction? Yes, says Theodore Cicero of Washington University Medical School. Endorphins, he says, "play an integral role—probably the dominant role—in regulating reproductive hormone cycles."

This formerly small corner of endorphin research has "exploded into a huge area of neurobiology," Cicero says, and researchers now think the opioid peptides help fine-tune many—perhaps all—of the nervous and hormonal pathways that together keep the body operating normally.

Cicero and his colleagues have tracked the byzantine biochemical loops through which endorphins, the brain, the body's master gland (the pituitary), the master's master (the hypothalamus) and the gonads exchange signals to ensure that an adult animal can reproduce when times are good but not when the environment is hostile. Cicero's work helped show that beta endorphin rules the hypothalamus and thus, indirectly, the pituitary and gonads.

The Washington University group also sees "a perfect parallel" between the brain's ability to produce endorphins and the onset of puberty: As the opioid system matures, so does the body sexually. A juvenile rat with endorphins blocked by naloxone undergoes puberty earlier; a young rat given opiates matures far later than normal and its offspring can have disturbed hormonal systems. Cicero calls the results "frightening" and adds, "there couldn't possibly be a worse time for a person to take drugs than during late childhood or adolescence."

Endorphins play a critical role in a later reproductive phase, as well: pregnancy and labor. Women in their third trimester sometimes notice that the pain and pressure of, say, a blood pressure cuff, is far less pronounced than before or after pregnancy. Alan Gintzler and his colleagues at the State University of New York Health Science Center in Brooklyn found that opioid peptides produced inside the spinal cord probably muffle pain and perhaps elevate mood to help a woman deal with the increasing physical stress of pregnancy. Endorphin activity builds throughout pregnancy and reaches a peak just before and during labor. Some have speculated that the tenfold drop from peak endorphin levels within 24 hours of delivery may greatly contribute to postpartum depression.

•CHILLS, THRILLS, LAUGHTER AND TEARS: Just as the effects of morphine go beyond the physical, claims for the opioid peptides extend to purely esthetic and emotional, with speculation falling on everything from the pleasure of playing with pets and the transcendence of near-death experiences to shivers over sonatas and the feeling of well-being that comes with a rousing laugh or a good cry.

Avram Goldstein of Stanford University, a pioneer in peptide research, recently collected a group of volunteers who get a spine-tingling thrill from their favorite music and gave them either a placebo or an opiate blocker during a listening session. Their shivers declined with the blocker—tantalizing evidence that endorphins mediate rapture, even though the mechanics are anyone's guess.

Former *Saturday Review* editor Norman Cousins may have spawned a different supposition about endorphins and emotion when he literally laughed himself out of the sometimes fatal disease ankylosing spondylitis. He found that 10 minutes of belly laughing before bed gave him two hours of painfree sleep. Before long, someone credited endorphins with the effect, and by now the claim is commonplace. For example, Matt Weinstein, a humor consultant from Berkeley, California, frequently mentions a possible link between endorphins, laughter and health in his lectures on humor in the workplace. His company's motto: If you take yourself too seriously, there's an excellent chance you may end up seriously ill.

Weinstein agrees with laughter researcher William Fry, a psychiatrist at Stanford's medical school, that evidence is currently circumstantial. Fry tried to confirm the laughter-endorphin link experimentally, but the most accurate way to assess it would be to tap the cerebrospinal fluid. That, Fry says, "is not only a difficult procedure but it's not conducive to laughter" and could result in a fountain of spinal fluid gushing out with the first good guffaw. Confirmation clearly awaits a less ghoulish methodology. But in the meantime, Fry is convinced that mirth and playfulness can diminish fear, anger and depression. At the very least, he says, laughter is a good aerobic exercise that ventilates the lungs and leaves the muscles relaxed. Fry advises patients to take their own humor inventory, then amass a library of books, tapes and gags that dependably trigger hilarity.

Another William Frey, this one at the University of Minnesota, studies the role of tears in emotion, stress and health. "The physiology of the brain when we experience a change in emotional state from sad to angry to happy or vice versa is an absolutely unexplored frontier," Frey says. And emotional tears are a fascinating guidepost because "they are unique to human beings and are our natural excretory response to strong emotion." Since all other bodily fluids are involved in removing something, he reasons, logic dictates that tears wash something away, too. Frey correctly predicted that tears would contain the three biochemicals that build up during stress: leucine-enkephalin, an endorphin, and the hormones prolactin and ACTH. These biochemicals are found in both emotional tears and tears from chopping onions, a different sort of stress.

Frey is uncertain whether tears simply carry off excess endorphins that collect in the stressed brain or whether those peptides have some activity in the tear ducts, eyes, nose or throat. Regardless, he cites evidence that people with ulcers and colitis tend to cry less than the average, and he concludes that a person who feels like crying "should go ahead and do it! I can't think of any other physical excretory process that humans alone can do, so why suppress it and its possibly healthful effects?"

All in all, the accumulated evidence suggests that if you want to use your endorphins, you should live the unfettered natural life. Laugh! Cry! Thrill to music! Reach puberty. Get pregnant. Get aerobic. Get hungry. Eat! Lest this sound like a song from *Fiddler on the Roof*, however, remember that stress or injury may be even quicker ways to pump out home-brew opioids. The bottom line is this: Endorphins are so fundamental to normal physiological functioning that we don't have to seek them out at all. We probably surf life's pleasures and pains on a wave of endorphins already.

Test yourself by imagining the following: the sound of chalk squeaking across a blackboard; a pink rose sparkling with dew; embracing your favorite movie star; chocolate-mocha mousse cake; smashing your thumb with a hammer. If any of these thoughts sent the tiniest tingle down your spine, then you have have just proved the point.

Executive's Secret Struggle With Heroin's Powerful Grip

Joseph B. Treaster

He is an executive in a company in New York, lives in a condo on the Upper East Side of Manhattan, drives an expensive car, plays tennis in the Hamptons and vacations with his wife in Europe and the Caribbean.

But unknown to office colleagues, friends and most of his family, the man is also a longtime heroin user. He says he finds heroin relaxing and pleasurable and has seen no reason to stop using it until the woman he recently married insisted that he do so.

"The drug is an enhancement to my life," he said. "I see it as similar to a guy coming home and having a drink of alcohol. Only alcohol has never done it for me."

Nearly everything about the 44-year-old executive, who spoke on the condition that he not be identified, seems to fly in the face of widely held perceptions about heroin users. But drug experts say perhaps as many as a third of the estimated 750,000 heroin addicts in America are juggling habitual use of what has long been thought of as the most debilitating and enslaving of drugs, managing jobs and even families with few if any outward signs of addiction.

But they are flirting with disaster. The businessman, for example, col-lapsed on the bathroom floor of his condo after an overdose of heroin 11 years ago. He lost a job at least partly because of his involvement with drugs, and his marriage is in trouble.

Doctors say that while heroin does not damage the organs as, for instance, heavy alcohol use does, there are many other dangers. Heroin users are always at risk of overdose and arrest, and those who inject the drug are especially susceptible to infections, as well as such diseases as hepatitis and AIDS.

Still, experts say, some heroin users are able to avoid the pitfalls for long periods of time. "There are enormous numbers of people in all walks of life who have integrated heroin use with their lives," said Dr. Robert B. Millman, the director of drug and alcohol abuse programs at New York Hospital–Payne Whitney Psychiatric Clinic.

The executive, who used marijuana and LSD in college and once sold cocaine to friends and business associates, said he has been using heroin for 20 years. Three years ago, when he began to worry that the drug was threatening to control his life, he developed an alternating cycle in which he would use heroin for a week or two, then break off for three weeks and resume again.

For the last two months, the businessman says, he has managed to stay away from his favorite drug. But he's not sure he will be able to resist its allure for long or that he even wants to. Four weeks ago he dropped out of a drug-treatment program, but each day he has been taking a drug called naltrexone, intended to discourage heroin use.

"In my heart," he said, "I really don't feel there's anything wrong with using heroin. But there doesn't seem to be any way in the world I can persuade my wife to grant me this space in our relationship. I don't want to lose her, so I'm making this effort. I wish I believed in the effort more."

The businessman agreed to talk with a reporter in response to a request made through Carl Castagna, the director of a Cornell University drug treatment program that the man attended for three months. He told his story over the course of a half-dozen telephone interviews. Mr. Castagna confirmed the basic facts of the man's life and said he had no reason to doubt the man's account of his drug use.

Heroin Is Returning, With Lighter Image

Until recently, the issue of illegal drugs in America has been dominated by cocaine. But as cocaine use has declined, heroin, the country's most feared drug in the 1960's and 70's, has been making a comeback. Production has increased in Asia and Latin America, and the drug is becoming increasingly available on the streets of America.

Dr. Millman said many people find they can experiment with heroin or even use it regularly on weekends or on special occasions without developing a compulsion to take it more frequently and in greater amounts.

Dr. Arnold M. Washton, the author of several books, who operates a private outpatient drug clinic on Park Avenue in midtown, said sampling heroin or crack, which is even more addicting, is like playing Russian roulette. "Not everyone will become addicted," he said, "but you can't predict who will and who won't."

Dr. Millman said people like the businessman who are "reasonably affluent and enjoy their work and their lives" are less likely to fall under the spell of heroin.

"These people are somewhat adventurous or, you might say, reckless," he said. "But instead of getting in deeper with the drug, they've got lots of reasons for pulling back. Even then, though, not everyone can pull back."

The Drug's Revenge: Painful Withdrawal

Heroin users develop a tolerance for the drug, which means they have to take more and more to achieve the calm, relaxed and sometimes euphoric state for which it is renowned. At the same time, the drug changes the body's chemistry so that as a dose wears off, painful withdrawal symptoms begin.

Those who become addicted find that as their tolerance for heroin increases, it becomes difficult to achieve a pleasurable feeling from the drug. Yet they are driven to take it, or feed their habit, to stave off the sickness that begins to set in four to six hours after a dose.

The businessman developed his on-again, off-again cycle at a time when he was using heroin every day and had been periodically dropping into drug-treatment programs to force down his tolerance and loosen the drug's control.

"It's like hide and seek," he said of his system. "You touch home base and you're free: Once you're clean and straight, you're in control again. Once you're in control, it's O.K. to indulge again."

Invariably, he said, he goes through a few days of withdrawal. But for him the symptoms have never been severe. "I don't ball up on the floor and throw up like you see in the movies," he said. Instead, his legs ache the way they might after jogging, he said, and he feels chilly and enervated, sometimes restless at night.

"For the first two weeks after I've stopped, it does not occupy my thoughts in an overwhelming sense," he said. "But by the third week it is creeping in there and it just gets to the point where I want it. I say: 'It's time. I've been good enough. I want my reward.' "

He may be at home, he may be at work. But at that point he dials the telephone number of a friend, a maintenance crew supervisor who is also a heroin user and who, for years, has been his supplier.

"I can't afford to go up to the South Bronx or wherever and put myself in that kind of jeopardy," he said. "For me, the ultimate jeopardy is discovery."

With the corner of a credit card or the clip of a ballpoint pen, he scoops a few grains up to his nose and inhales. During a cycle of use, he typically spends $300 a week on the drug.

For 10 years, the businessman injected heroin. But in 1981 he suffered the overdose. He recovered in an emergency room, but the incident scared him into treatment. Within a few months, though, he was back on heroin.

The businessman, who dresses in stylish suits and ties and is still almost as trim as when he earned varsity letters in high school sports, said he heads a department with several employees and receives a salary plus production bonuses. Last year, he said, he earned $200,000, up from $130,000 the preceding year and $70,000 the year before that.

Back in the 1980's, he was using a lot of cocaine along with the heroin and selling cocaine to friends and colleagues. His superiors learned about the cocaine and told him he was through. But the businessman said he did not believe drugs were the main issue. "They were just looking for an excuse," he said. "I actually believe it was more of a personality conflict."

Thinking that it would be wise to cut down on his drug use, mainly because it was becoming so expensive, but with no intention of quitting, the executive went into a treatment program. While under treatment he found a new job. No one asked about drugs and he didn't mention them. Within a short time he was back on heroin.

Choosing Between Life and Habit

When the businessman decided he wanted to end his long bachelorhood, he chose a woman who had been a friend for a decade and who was among a handful of people to whom he had disclosed his heroin habit. When they began seriously dating, she told him she could not abide his affair with heroin. "I told her I didn't honestly know if I could stop, but I would try," he said. "Ultimately, I went underground. She would catch me every now and then and there would be trouble."

Shortly after he proposed, he and his fiancée, at her suggestion, went into therapy together. She has been worried, he said, that he will be arrested and will lose his job. And, he said, "She says she likes me better without the drugs."

Under the influence of heroin, the businessman said, he tends to turn inward. "When I'm not using," he said, "I'm the first to say, 'Let's go out for dinner; let's call someone.'

When I'm using, I'm quite content to order in and watch television."

Sometimes heroin causes drowsiness, and, occasionally, when the businessman and his wife have been out at a restaurant together, he has nodded off.

"She would say, 'Are you high?' and I would either deny it or acknowledge it," he said. "When the meal was over we would probably go home and go into separate rooms. We do not have a screaming, yelling relationship."

But he knew this could not go on indefinitely. "The question," he said, "is what's more important, her or the drug? I wouldn't be honest if I didn't tell you that I have lain awake nights wondering what I'd have to do to get out of this marriage."

The businessman, who has a degree in psychology, first smoked marijuana as a college sophomore in the late 1960's, when he went home to an affluent suburb of New York City for the summer. Back on campus at a large state university in the Northeast, he smoked marijuana regularly and took about 100 trips on LSD.

After college, he and some friends decided they needed a break before beginning careers, and they rented a house on the California coast. He calls it "my hippie period." He was the only one in the house not injecting heroin.

"It was driving me crazy," he said.

"In my opinion heroin was an evil drug, and I believed these friends were doing something that would injure them."

But one day he suddenly said to the others: "Give me some of that stuff. I want to find out what you're doing."

The first time, he said: "I didn't feel that much. I tried it again, alone, and I actually thought I was overdosing. I thought I was dying. I had to actually work at liking it."

Twenty years later, he is working at stopping. But the ambivalence endures. "Part of me wants everything to be all right," he said. "But another part of me says, 'You're not a bad person. Why do you have to change?' "

Patterns and Trends in Drug Use

Drug use is socially patterned; different drugs are used in different frequencies by different social categories in the population. In addition, drug use displays trends: It varies over time. Consequently, in order to understand the phenomenon of drug use, we must examine its pattern and trends. Who uses drugs? How frequently? And how does this change from year to year?

More basically, how do we study drug use? Will people simply lie about their use, which, with respect to illegal drugs, is a criminal act? With the legal drugs, our job is relatively easy. All officially tabulated sales are taxable, which means that there are detailed and precise records on how many purchases of what quantities of which legal drugs available for inspection. Legal drug sales are a matter of public record, so, in order to know how much alcohol, tobacco, prescription drugs, and over-the-counter drugs are used, we look at their official sales.

The matter is not *quite* this easy, of course. There are unofficial sales of legal drugs—moonshine whiskey, cigarettes, and cigars smuggled into the United States from abroad, legal drug use by American tourists on vacation in other countries, and so on—that do not get recorded anywhere. And someone may purchase a bottle of liquor, put it on the shelf, and never drink it at all; this represents a sale, but no use. Because of these and other complexities, scientists refer to sales as "apparent" consumption; sales are not *exactly* consumption, but they are very close to it.

With alcohol, there is another complexity: Different alcoholic beverages contain different percentages of alcohol, which scientists call *ethanol* or ethyl alcohol. In the United States, the "proof" of an alcoholic beverage designates the percentage of ethanol it contains; to get that percentage, simply divided the proof by a factor of two. So, 100–proof vodka is 50 percent ethanol; 80–proof whiskey is 40 percent alcohol. Each type of drink contains its own specific percentage of ethanol. Beer is 4–5 percent ethanol; wine is 12–13 percent; "fortified" wines, such as sherry and port, are nearly 20 percent; distilled beverages, such as vodka, gin, rum, scotch, and tequila, are 40–50 percent ethanol. Thus, for the many types of alcoholic drinks it is necessary to apply a "conversion factor": For beer, to determine the consumption of alcohol or ethanol itself, one must divide the total quantity of beer sold by 20 or 25; for wine, one must divide by 8; for whiskey, divide by 2 or 2.5, depending on the proof; and so on.

With illegal drugs, the matter is more difficult. Here, we have no official record of sales. How do we know who

uses and who does not, and whether use changes over time? Many social scientists believe that, to answer these questions, we can conduct surveys. Simply ask a sample consisting of an accurate cross section of Americans about their own use, these experts advise. Would people lie about their own drug use? The evidence suggests that most people tell the truth about matters like that. It is important to sample a fairly large number of respondents, and that they reflect the composition of the population at large. But study after study has shown that the answers people give in a survey tell us a great deal about their drug-use patterns.

What patterns do we see in drug use, judging from the many currently available surveys on the subject? Many of the findings are fairly commonsensical. Men tend to use illegal drugs—and alcohol as well—more than women. The young use more than the old, urban residents more than rural dwellers, residents of the East and the West coasts more than those living in the South and the Midwest, high school and college drop-outs more than those who graduate, and—especially very recently—the poor more than the affluent.

One dramatic change took place in the 1980s that is still ongoing: Drug use, both legal and illegal, is declining significantly and dramatically. The peak for illegal drug use was the late 1970s; not only are Americans using less, they also disapprove of drug use, were more likely to believe that it is harmful, and less likely to favor legalization, even of marijuana. Alcohol and, somewhat less so, tobacco use also declined during the 1980s and into the 1990s, although far less sharply than was true for the illegal drugs.

But in addition to this downhill overall trend, we also notice a less heartening one. That is the growing *divergence* in drug use patterns between the poor and the affluent, between middle- and lower-class Americans. While drug use declined among members of the middle classes, among the lower and working classes it increased, remained stable, or declined much more slowly. Thus, the people with the most resources to deal with the problem of drug use are giving it up, while those with the fewest resources are most likely to continue.

The early 1990s witnessed a slight reversal in this trend: a small but significant upturn in the illegal use of recreational drugs. Among eighth-graders, college students, and young adults not in college (but not among high school seniors), slightly more were likely to use illegal drugs in 1992 than in 1991, as the selection, "Smoking, Drinking, and Illicit Drug Use among American Secondary

Toxic Waste Dump.

School Students, College Students, and Young Adults, 1975–1992" shows. Will this trend continue? At this point, all we have is speculation.

Looking Ahead: Challenge Questions

What changes have taken place in the drug use and abuse patterns in the United States during the past generation or so? Why do certain drugs experience ups and downs in popularity over time? Do you think that these variations are a matter of availability, cultural preference, stresses and strains—or what?

Why are certain categories in the population more likely to use and abuse certain drugs? Why are others less likely to do so?

How accurate are surveys on drug use?

Why do you think that members of the middle and the lower classes are diverging in their drug use patterns over time?

What do you foresee as the "drug of the future"? What will the drug use patterns be in the near future? Will drug use and abuse remain high in the United States a decade from now? Or do you foresee a decline? Why?

Just Say Maybe

Drugs: For a decade, the drug culture was demonized. But it's staging a strong return.

JOHN LELAND

B-REAL HAD A QUESTION FOR HIS audience. As the stage lights went down at Memorial Hall in Kansas City, Kans., he stepped in front of a curtain bearing a giant marijuana leaf and asked, "What do you want?" It was a rhetorical question; B-Real and his musical group, the multimillion-selling Cypress Hill, have but a small handful of tricks in their bag, and the audience was already declaring its intentions. "I wanna get hiiiiigh," they chanted, united beneath a cloud of grayish-brown smoke, "So hiiiigh." Rita Marley first sang these words 11 years ago after her husband, the Jamaican reggae star Bob Marley, died of brain cancer—words of defiance in the face of death. But here in Kansas City, where better than 3,000 mostly white, mostly suburban teenagers had gathered last Wednesday night, the words were a benign generational rallying cry. In response, B-Real wheeled out a giant brown hand holding a joint the size of a baseball bat. The crowd roared. On the floor of the hall, Kevin Divine, 14, from suburban Olathe, Kans., sized things up. "It's a good beat," he said, in the approving language teens have used since the days of "American Bandstand." "And it promotes the use of marijuana."

Here's a flashback: after a decade of being demonized and driven underground, the drug culture is suddenly back on display, buoyed by entertainers like Cypress Hill. A University of Michigan survey of college students and young adults found that in 1992, the most recent year studied, a 12-year decline in drug use came abruptly to a halt. Marijuana use increased very slightly, and LSD use rose for the third consecutive year. Marijuana seizures are up nationwide, and hospital emergency-room episodes have risen sharply for many drugs. Groups that advocate legalizing pot have seen their memberships skyrocket. "We have a hard time keeping up with demand," says Richard Cowan, 53, the national director of NORML, the National Organization for the Reform of Marijuana Laws. Heroin also appears to be making a comeback (next page).

Sea change: It is too soon to say what all these numbers mean; many of the upticks are small, and may be just statistical accidents. Casual drug use is still way down from the late '70s, when more than half the high-school seniors tested said they'd smoked pot in the last year. "Whether this is a pause or the beginning of a turnaround, we cannot say," says Lloyd Johnston, coauthor of the Michigan studies. Adrienne Jordan, 17, a high-school senior in Ferndale, Wash., is not so reserved about what she sees. A former heavy pot smoker, she has noticed a sharp rise in drug use among her friends and classmates. "Especially this year, there is a lot more pot," she says. "It's very noticeable."

What is clear, and arresting, is the rise of a popular culture that actively glorifies drug use. There is a sea change in attitudes, if not in actual use: an emerging population that openly espouses that drugs—at least some drugs—are no big deal. In Boston's Mission Hill district, a teen in a White Sox windbreaker and Duke baseball hat, smoking a cigar filled with marijuana, sums up a growing attitude: "I don't consider it a drug. It's a plant. Coke, I don't do that sh-t. That's a drug." Studies of junior-high and high-school students show that the percentage who believe that use of marijuana is very harmful has dropped, in some cases as much as 10 percent over a two-year period. When Jon Bonne, 21, arrived at Columbia University in New York three years ago, marijuana use on campus was nearly invisible, and uncool. "The image of the pot smoker was very much a hippie thing," he says. "Now it's completely different. There's a whole mode of dress, music and style that didn't exist three years ago."

Devil's horns: Music, television, movies and fashion are all embracing this change. For most of the 1980s, drugs either vanished from popular entertainments or appeared in the role of the villain: the murderous cocaine warriors of "Miami Vice" or "Scarface," the craven psychopaths of "RoboCop." Even archetypal stoner characters—Bill and Ted, Wayne and Garth—never touched the stuff; it was taboo. No more. In the last year, drug use has gone prime time, and without the cautionary alarm bells or Devil's horns. On a recent episode of "Roseanne," one of the top-rated sitcoms in the country, the principal characters found a stash of marijuana and lit up, spending half the show laughing themselves silly. Recent skits on "Saturday Night Live" and the Comedy Central program "The Kids in the Hall" present innocuous pot humor. MTV's top-rated Beavis and Butt-head sniff paint thinner.

Pot has made a benign re-entry in the movies as well. In the film "True Romance," Brad Pitt plays a stoner who knows his navel more intimately with each passing scene. And Richard Linklater's "Dazed and Confused," about a bunch of high-school students on the last day of class in 1976, celebrates pot smoking from beginning to end. Asked why the studio agreed to finance such a supportive depiction of drug use, Linklater says, "I think they've been spurred on by the supposed media resurgence of marijuana." Gramercy Pictures certainly used the pot connection as a selling point. The press kits for the movie included custom rolling papers and marijuana-leaf earrings, and the ad campaign ran, "See it with a bud." A second slogan, "Finally! A movie for everyone who *did* inhale," was nixed by the Motion Picture Association of America.

But it is rock musicians who have most heartily taken up the pot banner. Musicians have long played an intimate role in our national attitudes toward illicit drugs. In the 1960s and '70s, rockers were the voice of the burgeoning drug culture. During the '80s, strung out or in 12-step programs, musicians like Aerosmith, Keith Richards, Ozzy Osbourne and Mötley Crüe helped fuel the backlash against their past vices. Now a new generation of musicians is turning that around. Foremost is Cypress Hill, the multiracial rap group from South Gate, a Los Angeles suburb. Peppered with anthems bearing titles like "Hits From the Bong" and "Legalize It," the group's most recent album, "Black Sunday," entered the Billboard charts at No. 1 this summer, and has remained in the top 15 ever since. The group is relentless in its support of cannabis, or hemp. "We wanted to do something bold and take a stance on pot and the liberations of smokers," says rapper Sen Dog (Senen Reyes), 27. Cypress Hill even has its own line of clothes and drug paraphernalia; sales this year have reached $6 million. "They just let it all hang out and they tell it like it is," says Scott Altman, 17, a Cypress Hill fan from suburban St. Louis. A varsity ice-hockey player, Altman likes the music but skips the drugs. "It may promote marijuana but it brings everyone closer together to have a good time." A suburban 15-year-old at the group's Kansas City show had a different perspective. "When you're pulling hits from the bong," he said, "it's good to listen to 'Hits From the Bong'."

Other pop groups have jumped on the bandwagon. The platinum-selling Atlanta rock band the Black Crowes performed on their last tour before a giant marijuana leaf, and sold their own rolling papers in the lobby. The rapper Dr. Dre has sold more than 2 million copies of his album "The Chronic," named after a particularly potent strain of marijuana. Members of the Seattle bands Nirvana and Soundgarden, the multi-million-selling Spin Doctors and Faith No More have all come out publicly for legalization; Guns N' Roses and Metallica had NORML tables at their last tour. Other acts are using pot iconography in their marketing. The hard-rock band Sacred Reich, signed to a music subsidiary of Disney, sent out bongs with promotional copies of its last album. Rick Krim, vice president of music and talent at MTV, says he gets a video a

Heroin Makes an Ominous Comeback

THE 31-YEAR-OLD SCREEN-writer looks like she's en route to a dinner party in her $300 dress. Then she opens the gold compact inside her purse and pulls out a tiny wax-paper bag labeled NASTY BOY. It's her preferred brand of heroin. Inside a bathroom at a bar on New York's Lower East Side, she draws out two half-inch lines of heroin with a razor blade on the mirrored top of the compact and offers the cut-off end of a straw to a less-experienced friend. "Be careful," she jokes. "It'll lead to other things."

Diesel. Dynamite. White Death. They're new names for an old enemy making a dangerous comeback. While there are no reliable national statistics, local authorities report increases in heroin-related arrests and hospital admissions. In New York City, emergency-room visits involving heroin were up 34 percent in 1992 and arrests were 16 percent higher. In Seattle, methadone centers are filled for the first time in years. Customs officials say smugglers are thriving because demand is now flourishing.

These statistics may just be a storm warning. Certainly, the conditions are right for a heroin epidemic reminiscent of the 1970s. A worldwide opium glut has pushed heroin prices to a 30-year low; the drug now costs about as much as crack. Today's heroin is purer—and more insidious. Twenty years ago the typical sample was only 3 to 4 percent pure. Now agents are turning up samples with purity levels as high as 80 percent. The drug is so potent that users can get high by snorting or smoking—eliminating messy, HIV-carrying needles. Now, everyone from street kids to Yuppies "[feels] they're safe from AIDS, so they generalize to thinking that heroin's safe," says Dr. David R. Gastfriend of Massachusetts General Hospital in Boston.

The mellowness of a heroin high is appealing, especially after a decade of crack-induced anxiety. "People are getting tired of the roller-coaster high," says Ed Fresquez of Cenikor Foundation, a Houston drug-treatment facility. Many of today's users are too young to remember the strung-out junkies of the '70s, so they don't see the ugly downside of heroin until it's too late. The 31-year-old New York screen-writer still has fond memories of her first night. "I was dancing alone in the middle of a cluttered living room with the lights on bright and I couldn't have been happier," she recalls. Two years later, her habit is costing her hundreds of dollars a month.

On campus: Counselors say drug-education programs concentrate too much on crack, neglecting heroin's dangers. As a result, the drug has acquired an almost romantic mystique, especially on campus. "If you take someone who likes the movies of Quentin Tarantino, listens to Kurt Cobain and reads William Burroughs, it's almost automatic he's tried heroin," claims a former Bennington College student.

He could take a lesson from Angel, a 20-year-old Chicago street hustler, who must feed his habit several times a day to ward off the "sickness"— waves of pain and nausea as the high wears off. He usually buys at a house on the city's West Side, where armed gang members watch over desperate junkies waiting for a hit. Angel says the heroin-hungry lines grow longer every day. "I see pregnant ladies snorting," he says. "There's people who look like they're dying of AIDS. I see it eating the younger minds like me." Heroin may be cheaper and purer in 1993, but it's just as devastating.

BARBARA KANTROWITZ *with* DEBRA ROSENBERG *in Boston,* PATRICK ROGERS *and* LUCILLE BEACHY *in New York and* STANLEY HOLMES *in Chicago* week that refers to marijuana. The network asks acts to edit the references before the videos can air. "If there were ever anything with an anti-drug message, that might be a different story, " says Krim. "But this stuff pretty much glorifies it."

Fashion statement: Along with the music has come a boom in pot fashion. At the high end, about two dozen manufacturers are offering clothing made from hemp, the same plant that produces marijuana. Because it is illegal to grow hemp in the United States, all of the fabric is imported. But it is at the low, popular end that pot fashion makes its strongest statement. After a decadelong absence from American iconography, the marijuana leaf is popping up on clothing, jewelry, even tattoos. Pot fashion, not long ago the province of losers or outcasts, has suddenly become hip, blossoming into an estimated $10 million to $15 million business. "I see guys wearing white baseball hats with a bright-green pot leaf, girls in tie-dyed T shirts with pot-leaf motifs, and necklaces and earrings with pot leaves," says Dave, 23, a supermarket clerk in Evanston, Ill. "You never saw that two years ago. And if you did, you looked away, as if it was a secret. Now it's not a secret. It's out in the open."

Lee Brown, the new drug czar, is outraged by this fashion statement. Brown, former top cop of New York, last week unveiled the Clinton administration's drug policy, a sketchy program that points toward greater emphasis on treatment; he has yet to say where the money will come from. "It angers me when I see" the drug wear, he says. "It's a mistake for parents to allow their children to get caught in that culture."

Ironically, though, part of the easing of attitudes toward drugs has come from government circles. Bill Clinton's claim that he didn't inhale became the best joke of the campaign; suddenly, a presidential candidate's history of illegal drug use was something to snicker about, not grounds to disqualify him from the Oval Office. One popular T shirt reads INHALE TO THE CHIEF. Surgeon General Joycelyn Elders has advocated making marijuana available for medicinal purposes. And the federal government has softened its anti-drug propaganda campaigns. As silly as they sometimes

seemed, they worked. "When Clinton got elected, I knew weed was going to come back," says Eric Bonerz, 28, the manager of a trendy downtown New York clothing boutique that sells pot-leaf hats by the dozen—many of them, he avers, to people who don't smoke. "Now you can smoke it, wear it, whatever . . . It's less illegal now."

At the same time, the drug itself is undergoing an image makeover, in step with the health and environmental consciousness of the '90s. Smokers argue, echoing an old line, that it is natural, nonaddictive and not associated with violence or domestic abuse. For generations who have seen firsthand the ravages of both crack and alcohol, this combination can be very appealing. One slang term for desirable marijuana is "kind bud." "Frank," 33, who runs a Los Angeles landscaping company, is a typical thirty-something user. After smoking in school, he gave it up for most of his 20s, as he and his friends got into drinking, cocaine and other drugs. Now he's back. "Drinking gets me blotto. With pot my mind still functions." He finds marijuana a healthier alternative to his past habits. "On coke, I would take all kinds of risks: go places that were dangerous and do things I shouldn't." Pot, he says, is "probably less dangerous."

Pot activists go this claim one better. The bible of the legalization movement, "The Emperor Wears No Clothes," by Jack Herer, argues that until it was declared illegal in 1937, the hemp plant provided fuel oil, fabric and paper in a more efficient and ecologically sound way than our currently available resources. Since being published in 1985, according to Herer, 54, his book has sold 193,000 copies. Its acolytes—smokers and nonsmokers alike—are gushing in their idealism. "This means more than going to a party, smoking a joint and having a good time," says John Birrenbach, president of the Institute for Hemp, a St. Paul-based advocacy group that sells cannabis products via a mail-order catalog. "It means saving the planet."

But it is wrong to think of pot as risk-free. Although much is still unknown about the drug's effects, and even more muddied by decades of "Reefer Madness" hysteria, there are a few undisputed health risks as-

sociated with the drug. Carcinogenic tars and benzopyrenes are at much higher levels in marijuana than in tobacco, and chronic use impairs short-term memory. Smoking also suppresses the immune system. (Many other fears, such as physical addiction, genetic damage or reduced fertility, are either unsupported or rarely borne out, says Christine Hartel of the National Institute on Drug Abuse.) Some of the risks, however, may be higher today than at the height of the drug culture. Back in the '70s and '80s, average marijuana was about 1.5 to 2 percent THC, the main psychoactive ingredient; now it's twice as high and can even reach 30 percent THC, according to NIDA. The Center on Addiction and Substance Abuse at Columbia University estimates that substance abuse and addiction claim nearly 500,000 lives a year, and drain $250 billion from the health-care system. Though most of this is from alcohol and cigarettes, a new boom in the drug culture means more than just a nostalgic smell in the air.

Hemp culture: Lofty Bullock, a 22-year-old British deejay and entrepreneur, already thinks the trend may be turning. Bullock runs Headflows, a natty enclave of hemp culture on Washington, D.C.'s, bohemian "New" U Street. Earlier this year, he says, he was selling hundreds of T shirts a week. Now, in a slower market, he has sold most of his stock to British retailers. "I reached a peak about six months ago," he says. There is still some interest, he finds. "But being a hip, underground thing—that's over."

Whether this means the drug culture is expanding to mall dimensions or beginning its last inhale remains to be seen. At the Cypress Hill show in Kansas City, Blake Overt, 15, offered one hint. Blake does not smoke marijuana, but likes the music anyway. "It's words everybody can relate to," he says. "Except my mom." Drug trends may or may not be cyclical. But kids embracing music and fashions to bug their parents—well, that's eternal.

With DEBRA ROSENBERG *in Boston,* ROXIE HAMMILL *in Kansas City,* PATRICK ROGERS *in New York,* STANLEY HOLMES *in Chicago,* FARAI CHIDEYA, MELINDA LIU *and* MARY HAGER *in Washington,* ANDREW MURR *in Los Angeles,* PHYLLIS LIBRACH *in St. Louis,* GINNY CARROLL *and* PETER ANNIN *in Houston and bureau reports*

Youthful Drinking Persists

With Teens and Alcohol, It's Just Say When

Felicity Barringer

The 13-year-old, the daughter of two lawyers, had been drinking for about four years when she showed up for gymnastics practice at her private school in Massachusetts, too drunk to perform. A 15-year-old boy told a juvenile court judge: "I'm not a problem drinker. I only have a six-pack of beer an evening." A 16-year-old regularly consumed enough vodka and beer to have hallucinations in her kitchen, seeing skeletons, knives and images she took for visions of Satan's realm.

These are the children of alcohol, whose numbers have waxed and waned over the centuries, from the days when ancient Greeks worshiped Dionysus, the god of wine, to London's Gin Lane in the late 18th century, to America's suburban malls and fraternity houses today. They are the inheritors—some would say the victims—of the country's ambivalence about the intoxicant of the ages.

While experts say that the use of other recreational drugs has diminished since the end of the 1970's, alcohol use has diminished far more slowly. Its staying power as the intoxicant of choice among the young has made it the nation's most persistent problem drug.

In recent days and months, public officials, like the nation's drug control policy director, Bob Martinez, have had more and more to say about the dangers of alcohol use by young people, and researchers have brought out some new figures, some heartening, others disturbing.

Even as alcohol use has diminished over the last decade, a Federal survey of students in eight states shows that 10.6 million of 20.7 million 7th through 12th graders drink, though all states now prohibit drinking before the age of 21. Eight million of them drink at least once a week, and 450,000 drink at least five or more drinks at a sitting.

"Cocaine has become unacceptable for a lot of teens," said Peter Rogers, a Youngstown, Ohio, pediatrician who heads the Child-Adolescent Committee of the American Society of Addictive Medicine. "Marijuana's becoming unacceptable. Teenage drinking has never been unacceptable."

The peak years for all drug use, he said, were 1978 and 1979. "About 10 percent of high school seniors used marijuana daily back then," he said. Now the figure is 2.3 percent. In 1978 and 1979 about 6 percent of high school seniors drank daily. "It was 4.8 percent in 1990. And the percentage of seniors who drank five or more drinks in a row at least once a week is the same as it was back then."

For Lloyd Johnston, a University of Michigan social science researcher whose annual survey of high school seniors was the source of Dr. Rogers's figures, alcohol, once a "safe," familiar drug in the view of many parents who saw cocaine and other hard drugs as the alternatives, no longer hides in the shadow. "The illicit drug problem has subsided," he said. "We've been standing by this mountain all the time, but now we have a chance to look at the mountain. It's a constant, and we're more conscious of it now."

Helping to focus people's attention, he said, are widely publicized criminal trials involving incidents in which alcohol played a role, such as the one currently under way in Queens, where a group of St. John's University schoolmates are charged with sexually abusing a young woman. With the publicizing of the acquaintance-rape issue, it has become clear that most such assaults involve heavy drinking by the man or the woman or both.

Generally, the young drinkers who need the most help to change their behavior are those who started drinking earliest, experts in public health and adolescent psychology say. But other than that, they say, it is difficult to predict the course of adolescent drinking.

Children who experiment with liquor in early teens could be off it by high school, but most are not. Young men and women who wait until college to do their heavy drinking may be more destructive in their drinking habits than those who drank earlier but more moderately.

Most drinking begins at the liquor cabinet at home, experts say.

"By 12, most kids know someone who drinks, and they probably know a significant number who drink," said Dr. Johnston of the University of Michigan. His extensive annual survey, which has involved high school students since 1979, is being extended to eighth graders, but no data is yet available.

"The commonest reason for kids using alcohol," said Margaret Bean-Bayog, a psychiatrist in private practice in Newton, Mass., "is that it's in the subculture around them. Kids in a grade school where everyone is drinking are more likely to drink. For kids whose parents use it, they don't have a reference point that doesn't include alcohol.

"The age of first alcohol use in the 1930's was 17 for boys and 19 for women," she said. "It has drifted steadily down. Now it's much more common for a 13-year-old to have had a drink." What parents need to be alert for, Dr. Bean-Bayog and other experts say, are changes in behavior, secretiveness, declining grades and desertion of old friends for a heavy-drinking crowd.

What is most alarming, she said, is not the simple fact of drinking, but the tendency of some adolescents to drink simply to get drunk. Although binge drinking has declined somewhat among high school students, it is still common behavior among college-age drinkers. Dr. Johnston's survey shows that 93 percent of college students have tried alcohol, 75 percent drink regularly and 4 percent drink daily. The percentage of those who drank five or more drinks at a sitting in the last two weeks now stands at 41, down from 45 percent in the late 1970's.

Some adolescents drink simply to get drunk.

Henry Wechsler, a lecturer in social psychology at Harvard University's School of Public Health, said that studies he has done in 1977 and 1990 show that among college freshmen, "the one group that has disappeared are the frequent light drinkers, those likely to have one or two drinks regularly. What's happened is a polarization between the

binge drinkers and the abstainers."

Dr. Johnston's surveys indicate that the students bound for college tend to drink less than those who are not. But by the age of 19 or 20, the college group is drinking just as much as their non-college peers, and bingeing more often.

"There's a massive amount of advertising that tells youngsters that if you want to have a good time with your friends, have camaraderie, go to good beach parties, you better drink," Dr. Johnston said. Dr. Rogers said a teenager watching an average amount of television sees 2,500 alcohol advertisements a year.

What then, to tell teens about the dangers of alcohol abuse? Dr. Wechsler feels that a prohibitionist approach would be a mistake. "When you start campaigns among the young focused on 'Just say no,' you lose credibility because so many people are saying yes," he said.

His remedy is peer pressure. Cigarettes, once a badge of maturity, has lost much of this status among adolescents. Eventually, he said, drunkenness could become so stigmatized that the bingers melt away. "Given enough time and enough attention to the problems of heavy drinking, you're going to have a change," he said.

U.S. Reports Sharp Increase in Drug-Caused Emergencies

Joseph B. Treaster

Federal health officials in Washington yesterday reported sharp increases in the number of medical emergencies resulting from drug use. They said the numbers underscored the need for more rehabilitation programs and more effective prevention efforts.

While casual drug use has continued to decline, heavy users of cocaine, heroin and marijuana have been streaming into hospital emergency rooms in unprecedented numbers, the officials said.

The number of those seeking help for adverse reactions to cocaine in 1992 increased 18 percent over the previous year, to 119,800. At the same time, heroin overdoses and other reactions to the drug rose 34 percent, to 48,000, and casualties of marijuana jumped 48 percent, to 24,000.

"These are the highest levels ever," said Daniel Melnick, a senior official in the Substance Abuse and Mental Health Services Administration, which released the data yesterday.

'Desperation of Use'

Dr. Mitchell S. Rosenthal, the president of Phoenix House, the largest residential treatment organization in the country, said: "These kinds of big rises suggest a desperation of use and a kind of hopelessness among users. They think they are trapped and can see no alternative but to keep using."

Data show a need for more drug prevention, experts say.

The emergency-room cases resulting from heroin and marijuana use included people of all ages, from adolescence up. But cases among cocaine users 12 to 17 years old declined, the data showed.

While the emergency-room visits were attributed mainly to chronic drug users, Mark A. R. Kleiman, a drug expert who teaches public policy at Harvard University, said the data appeared to reinforce the notion "that heroin is coming back in a serious way and that marijuana may also be coming back."

The unrelenting rise in drug cases in hospital emergency rooms from the mid-1980's goes to the heart of the national health crisis, many drug experts said.

Emergency-room treatment is among the most expensive kind of care, the experts pointed out, and it has little affect in reversing chronic drug use.

Cry for More Treatment

Both Donna E. Shalala, the Secretary of Health and Human Services, the parent organization of the substance abuse agency, and Lee P. Brown, President Clinton's chief anti-drug aide, said the soaring drug casualties cried out for more spending on treatment and anti-drug education.

But President Clinton's proposed $13 billion anti-drug budget for the coming year sticks with the pattern established by Presidents Ronald Reagan and George Bush, in which the biggest share of the money goes to trying to stop the flow of drugs rather than to programs aimed at rehabilitation and discouraging drug use. With the President's consent, Congress trimmed from his proposal $100 million that had been earmarked for treatment and $143 million designated for anti-drug education.

White House officials had promised that the Administration's national health system overhaul would include substantial increases in money for drug treatment. But the proposals include no provisions for the kind of long-term residential treatment that most experts say is needed to deal with the kind of chronic drug users now flooding emergency rooms. Instead, Mr. Clinton's health insurance proposal would cover two periods of 30 days of hospital or clinic treatment in any year, along with 30 days of outpatient care.

"We're not talking about people who can use 30 days of inpatient treatment," Dr. Rosenthal said. "We're talking about people here who, if they are not in the emergency room, they are likely to be getting into all kinds of anti-social behavior that can lead to prisons, courts and everything else."

Many experts say that curtailing heavy drug use would sharply cut national health costs. The Center on Addiction and Substance Abuse at Columbia University, for example, recently found that 20 percent of all Medicaid costs were related to drug abuse. Medicaid is the Federal-state program for the poor.

"Trying to cut health care costs without solving the drug crisis is like trying to sail a sinking ship without fixing the hole on the bottom," said Paul Samuels, the president of the Legal Action Center, a national drug policy organization based in New York.

Many experts said Mr. Clinton appeared to be avoiding the drug issue. The President has seldom addressed the issue in public and has not presented a comprehensive national strategy.

'Feeling of Being Left Out'

Herbert D. Kleber, the executive vice president of the Center on Addiction and Substance Abuse, said, "the President is so concerned about health care reform that he is not paying enough attention to drug abuse."

Dr. Kleber added: "And it is going to be hard to reform health care in a cost-effective way if he doesn't pay adequate attention to this group of heavy users that we're hearing about today. It's also going to be hard to stop violence."

A number of studies have shown that heavy drug users consume most of the illegal drugs sold in this country, and that they are often involved in property crimes and violence.

Representative Charles B. Rangel, the Manhattan Democrat who heads the House Caucus on Narcotics Abuse, said there was clearly a relationship between the steep increases in emergency-room cases due to drugs and "the feeling of being left out economically."

"If you plot the hospitals where the highest amounts of casualties are coming from," Mr. Rangel said, "you will also find the highest concentrations of AIDS, of unemployment, of people going off to jail, of teen-age pregnancies and of violent crime."

Drugs and Emergency Room Visits

THE NUMBER OF PATIENTS HAS RISEN . . .

■ '91
'92

	Marijuana Hashish	Heroin Morphine	Cocaine
Atlanta	610 / 957	157 / 232	3,266 / 5,118
Baltimore	355 / 672	3,892 / 5,106	6,687 / 8,078
Boston	616 / 1,006	1,165 / 2,061	2,992 / 4,266
Chicago	808 / 1,488	2,262 / 2,958	5,575 / 8,214
Detroit	807 / 1,487	1,828 / 1,843	5,919 / 6,939
Los Angeles	1,055 / 1,331	1,674 / 2,944	4,901 / 5,337
New York	1,195 / 2,004	6,019 / 8,382	16,099 / 20,414
Philadelphia	692 / 1,648	2,424 / 2,364	8,769 / 10,986
Washington	959 / 1,259	1,480 / 1,152	4,572 / 4,236

. . . AND HAS BECOME A LARGER PERCENTAGE OF ALL EMERGENCY ROOM PATIENTS

All emergency room patients

Patients admitted for cocaine

Patients admitted for heroin

'78 '79 '80 '81 '82 '83 '84 '85 '86 '87 '88 '89 '92

Sources: Drug Abuse Warning Network

The New York Times

Up In Smoke

Why do so many kids ignore all the evidence condemning cigarettes?

Sandy Rovner

Washington Post Staff Writer

On the seventh floor of Leonard Hall at American University in Washington, D.C., is the room of Chuck Salloum, a 19-year-old sophomore from Brooklyn, N.Y. Aside from the requisite clutter of dirty laundry, notebooks and textbooks, the room is virtually overflowing with cigarette memorabilia featuring Marlboro motifs and Joe Camel, the hip cartoon mascot for the popular cigarettes. Salloum has posters from the New York subway, mugs, playing cards, and a T-shirt that he sent for with Camel "cash," the coupons R. J. Reynolds proffers with each pack.

Salloum, the anointed jester of the dormitory floor, smokes two packs of Camels a day and has no intention of quitting. He talks about sending 500 empty packs to R. J. Reynolds to get a cordless phone.

"Maybe I'm addicted," he says, "but so what? I don't want to be caught 90 years old playing bingo in a church."

"He doesn't have to worry," a classmate suggests.

"I do my best thinking when I'm smoking," says Salloum.

Dion Algeri, 19, from Scotchplains, N.J., agrees. "It's like I think all the best conversations I've ever had in my life have been with a drink in one hand and a cigarette in the other."

Federal officials report that more than 3,000 youngsters a day start smoking, a figure that angers the health specialists. Despite far-reaching public health campaigns showing the links between smoking and lung and heart disease, about a third of all U.S. teenagers do some smoking by the time they are 18, according to recent surveys from the federal Centers for Disease Control. Youngsters buy 947 million packs of cigarettes a year, says the CDC.

And for many of these youngsters, it is a habit that will be hard to break. Up to 90 percent of adult smokers began puffing before they were 20, half of them before they were 14, says Democratic Rep. Mike Synar of Oklahoma, who has made tobacco one of his primary legislative concerns.

The overall number of smokers is declining in the United States, but anti-smoking forces are concerned by the fact that those who do opt to smoke are doing so earlier.

The only encouraging trend in the anti-smoking campaign geared toward teenagers is an apparent decline in smoking among black high school students. A survey released this fall showed that white high school seniors were twice as likely to smoke as blacks, but health specialists caution that those results might be misleading. Although health officials are pleased by the decline among black students, they are hard pressed to explain the numbers.

Gary Giovino, the chief epidemiologist at the Office on Smoking and Health in Atlanta, speculates that it might reflect the high cost of cigarettes, which run about $1.50 a pack.

"But this is a phenomenon we really have to look into," he says. "It's something that has been happening for a few years, but we've only just become aware of it."

CDC has found, however, that more blacks tend to start smoking after adolescence and have a higher relapse rate when they try to quit.

Smoking had been declining among white teens until about six years ago. Since then it has remained flat, a great disappointment to anti-smoking forces, including federal agencies, national health and anti-tobacco groups. They blame the advertising efforts of the tobacco industry, bitterly charging that cigarette ads are aimed at young people.

The tobacco industry, through its trade association, the Tobacco Institute, denies that its ads target youth.

Walker Merriman, the spokesman from the Tobacco Institute, says the cartoons that are so popular in the tobacco ads are no more aimed at children than "the Peanuts characters in the Metropolitan Life insurance ads are aimed at kids or the Garfield the cat cartoon for Embassy Suite hotel rooms or the Pink Panther for insulation. I don't know how many kids are buying insulation today."

The industry also argues that models in its advertisements are over the age of 24 and the ads appear only in adult magazines.

Such arguments inflame the anti-smoking coalition. "Teens aren't reading Ranger Rick and Highlights for Children," says Robert Jaffe, a Seattle family practitioner and head of the Washington state chapter of "Doctors Ought to Care" or DOC. "They're reading Cosmopolitan, Mademoiselle, Glamour, Sports Illustrated. The tobacco people say they're shooting for an 18-to-24-year-old audience. I think it's more like 11 to 18."

Giovino agrees that advertising has much to do with teenagers smoking. "The ads portray tobacco, something that is subversive and deleterious, paired with glamourous and with slim and with sexy and with cool and with macho and successful," he says. "You do that often enough, and the cigarettes take on the attributes of the rest of the ad."

Nonetheless, he cautions that no one reason can explain the phenomenon. "It's a multi-multi-factorial thing," he says. "Some females smoke to try to keep their weight down; some males may smoke to try to appear cool; some of everybody may smoke to try to feel part of the social group."

"Listen," says Tina Burnell to a group of her peers at Walter Johnson High School in Bethesda, Md., "I'll stop smoking when I'm pregnant."

She says it with unswerving confidence, although a bit defensively. Tina, who is 14, has been smoking for two years, at least partly, she says, because it is something to do with her hands.

"You mean," asks Todd Cohen, 16, "you have to kill yourself in order to kill time?"

"That is a really stupid reason," pronounces classmate Amy Georgatsos, 16.

Tina's friend, Karin Dynner, 16, shows some tolerance for Tina's habit. Although a nonsmoker, Karin says all her friends smoke but she has not joined their ranks because she lost an uncle "who was very close to the family" to lung cancer.

"I know it will make me sick, I know all that stuff," says Tina. "After all I'm not stupid. I know I'll stop when I'm pregnant."

"What makes you think you'll be any different?" demands Tina's classmate Stephanie Evans, 17.

"I know it's not going to be easy," responds Tina. "I mean that right now it's part of my life—after I eat, I have a cigarette. When I'm stressed out, I have a cigarette. I'm used to it. I'm addicted. It calms me down. But I know I'll stop. It's like I wouldn't hurt my children."

Tina's predictions are mirrored by American University student Kartik Singh, 18, from India and Kansas City, Kan. He started smoking heavily while in college in the Netherlands. He smokes Marlboro Reds, the strongest in tar and nicotine, and the brand that youths consider the most macho. "Now I wish I could quit. I probably will this summer," he says.

Giovino says Kartik's and Tina's attitude is not unusual—just unrealistic.

"A lot of kids think they can experiment around with this stuff and quit any time they want," he says. "The reality is they get addicted pretty quick, and eventually they find out how hard it is to quit."

Polls have asked youngsters if they think they'll still be smoking in two years, and overwhelmingly they predict that they will not. But, says Giovino, "when you go back in two years and check, of course most of them still are."

And there is mounting evidence that for reasons still not completely understood, girls become addicted faster and find it more difficult to stop than boys, says Richard Evans, director of the social psychology behavioral medicine program at the University of Houston.

When she was a sophomore in high school, Sarah Dupree, 19, spent a year in France. That's where she started smoking. "I didn't smoke much when I got home [to Newtown, Conn.] but it built up, little by little," says Dupree, another resident of Leonard Hall's seventh floor. "I know that I want to quit, and sometimes I'll light a cigarette and it won't even taste good. And other times, I'll light up and it will be the best I ever had."

Statistically, the number of boys and girls using tobacco products appears in federal surveys to be about equal, but officials point out that the number of boys includes those using smokeless tobacco. Teenage girls are actually the heaviest smokers since few of them use smokeless tobacco.

Experts say they do not know why teenagers, especially teenage girls, keep smoking. But getting or staying thin is clearly a major factor, they say. The CDC has found that 34 percent of female high school students think they're overweight and 44 percent are trying to lose weight. Perhaps 20 percent are actually overweight, CDC officials estimate.

Jaffe says the link between smoking and thinness is unquestionably "a reflection of very successful advertising campaigns. The tobacco industry should be congratulated on it. The fear of fat is a huge issue among teenagers," so you find cigarettes like "Superslims, Lights, Extra Lights, Ultra Lights, what I call ultra-bulemic-anorexic lights."

The models in the ads for these various incarnations, he notes, are "ungodly skinny," and in some cases the models in the ads are photographically altered to appear stretched as long and slim as the cigarette itself.

Right up there with keeping thin, the experts say, is "appearing cool."

"Let's face it," says Mike Michaelson, the student ombudsman in the Montgomery County, Md., school system, "smoking is still made to look like it is a swishy habit."

A lot of the advertising is by indirection, says Jaffe. "If you were from the planet Mars, you wouldn't even know

Smoking is portrayed by advertisers as a fashionable habit, the "in" thing to do, or as something that revolves around an image that does not identify with the actual product. Researchers have found that the Camel cartoon character is as recognizable to 6-year-olds as the Mickey Mouse silhouette that denotes television's Disney Channel; it is so familiar to many 3-year-olds that it is more identifiable to children than to adults.

what the product is. All you know is that whatever it is, the person is having a good time and they look really sexy and attractive and this is what kids are attracted to."

Nicole Lee is 18, a freshman at American University from Pittsburgh. She has been smoking since junior high school.

"It was a cool thing back then, like sneaking a butt in the girls' bathroom without getting caught and everything," she recalls. "And I really wasn't inhaling. It was just, like, to see if you could get away with it, rebelling against the system kind of thing.

"People say, 'Oh, do you think you're cool when you smoke?' And maybe to begin with, I thought so, but now it's kind of like, no, I don't think it's cool, but if I don't have a cigarette I'm going to be having, like, a massive nic-fit in a few minutes."

Most of the two dozen teenagers who smoke and were interviewed for this story say that either a parent, both parents or older brothers and sisters are smokers as well. And their friends smoke. This, the experts believe, is

probably the best predictor of a new smoker, but "there is no definitive answer to why any given kid begins to smoke," says Giovino.

Walter Johnson High School's Tina has an older sister who smokes and a best friend. She has, as the experts put it, "smoking in her environment."

But Stephanie Evans notes that it is pretty hard to escape it. "You always see people on TV, when they're stressed out, they light up." Stephanie tried it once, but it was such an unpleasant experience that she never did it again. Now, she says, "it's just a turn-off."

Nyck.E Sims is a senior at the Maret School in Washington, D.C. She is 17, has never smoked and has neither sympathy nor patience for her classmates who do.

Nyck.E says with some passion, "I just can't see it. I just can't see anyone getting addicted to cigarettes. I know it happens, but I don't know why. Smokers stink. They really stink. They have it in their hair, in their clothes."

One of Nyck.E's classmates, an ex-smoker, admits she

started in the fourth grade. "But don't say who I am. My parents think it was the 9th grade." She's not smoking anymore, but she's having a hard time stopping.

Another Maret student, Andrea Clemente, 15, continues to smoke, although she has tried a time or two to quit. It's getting harder at school because Maret recently changed its policy. Once, there was a lounge for 11th and 12th graders where smoking was permitted. "It de facto became a smoking lounge," says Sally Collier, student counselor and part-time smoking cessation leader at Maret, "because the nonsmokers couldn't stand to be there."

The students voted to turn the lounge back to the nonsmokers, and this year Maret, like many other schools, banned smoking everywhere on the grounds—for teachers as well as students.

Andrea doesn't like the smell of her own cigarettes either. She carries a lemon-scented body spray that she uses to cover up the stale smoke odor. "My mother knew I was smoking again," she says, "not because of the smell of smoke on my clothes but because of the smell of lemon."

American University's health counselor, Jody Gan, says she is appalled by the amount of smoking on campus.

Smokers are grouped together on certain floors in dormitories, such as Leonard Hall's seventh floor. The lounge gives new meaning to a smoke-filled room: dozens of cigarettes with their smoke curling up to the ceiling and whooshing outside every 15 minutes or so when someone is driven to open a window.

The smoke alarm goes off every couple of hours. "Turn that thing off," yells somebody down the corridor.

"I am struck by the numbers of people who smoke here," Gan says. "These students are so concerned with their appearance and working out. Aerobics classes are packed; gyms are packed, and yet I see students walking around in workout clothes and smoking. Even as they come out of the aerobics classes, they're lighting up, not even seeing the connection or not even caring."

The federal government recently announced a $135 million, seven-year program to encourage states to set up anti-smoking programs in 17 states. This will be augmented by another $30 million or so from the American Cancer Society. Its goal is to help 5 million smokers to stop and to prevent another 2 million young people from starting.

The Robert Wood Johnson Foundation has just given a $1.2 million grant to the group called Stop Teenage Addiction to Tobacco (STAT) to work in four U.S. cities—San Jose; Springfield, Mass.; Perth Amboy, N.J.; and Seattle.

But, says STAT official Susan Godfrey, that can't compare to the tobacco industry's $3 billion a year for advertising.

Godfrey got involved with STAT one day two years ago when her 6-year-old daughter Megan spotted a Camel ad on the side of a bus.

"She got all excited," Godfrey recalls. "She squealed something like, 'ooh look at those cute little camels. I want

one.' I looked at those camels playing pool, and I suddenly realized what the ad was for and I went right back to the hospital and told Joe Tye, [founder of STAT] that I'd do whatever I could."

Smooth Joe Camel has become a ubiquitous symbol, plastered all over billboards and magazine ads in both English and Spanish. Most recently, he was featured in a four-page color pop-up ad in probably one of the year's most popular People magazine issues, the one with Liz Taylor's wedding on the cover.

Last week, the Journal of the American Medical Association (JAMA) reported that the Camel cartoon character is as recognizable to 6-year-olds as the Mickey Mouse silhouette that denotes the Disney Channel. The character is familiar to many 3-year-olds and in general is more identifiable to children than to adults, according to the research.

"I think what we can conclude is that kids are aware of cigarette advertising, and that this should be viewed as a risk," says Paul M. Fischer, a researcher at the Medical College of Georgia, who directed one of three studies on smoking and brand recognition in the JAMA.

Next to Joe Camel in the cigarette cartoon world comes the hip "younger cousin" of Kool cigarette's Willie the Penguin, a kind of penguin Bart Simpson, head feathers in a buzz cut and a Kool hanging out of his mouth. He was quickly attacked by Health and Human Services Secretary Louis W. Sullivan and Surgeon General Antonia C. Novello.

A press release written as though by the new "spokes-symbol" says Kool was looking for a younger advocate. "My older cousin, Willie the Penguin, represented Kool for three decades. Let's face it, he's gotten on in years," the press release says. "Yes, I'm a star . . . *the* star of a test to give Kool cigarettes a new look for the '90s."

How do the anti-smoking forces fight back?

In Canada, cigarettes sell now for up to $6 a pack, mostly because of excise taxes. That has had a perceptible effect in lowering the number of smokers, says Godfrey.

California has imposed a special 25-cent-per-pack tax which it is devoting, in part, to anti-smoking efforts. By last June, the fund contained $1.4 billion of which $264 million was set aside for anti-tobacco health programs, according to Larry C. White, who wrote about the program in "Priorities," a publication of the American Council on Science and Health.

In one TV spot paid for by the California fund, White says, a group of executives is sitting in a smoky room. One says: "Gentlemen, gentlemen, the tobacco industry has a very serious, multi-billion dollar problem. We need more cigarette smokers. Pure and simple. Every day 2,000 Americans stop smoking and another 1,100 quit. Actually, technically, they die. That means that this business needs 3,000 fresh new volunteers every day. So forget about all that cancer, heart disease, emphysema, stroke stuff."

Laughter. Then, "Gentlemen, we're not in this for our health."

White, who lives in Berkeley, says his 14-year-old daughter, Becky, is participating in a program underwritten by the fund in which she spends a semester learning about tobacco and public speaking and then is sent to talk to 4th and 7th grade classes.

"You have to get them before they're teens," says White.

In the District of Columbia, a program in grade schools and junior high schools is looking toward a smoke-free year 2000. A videotape, based on a rap song written and performed by students at Alice Deal High School, is being distributed by the D.C. Lung Association.

The rap tells kids: "There's something bad in that cigarette/It's nicotine, and boy you can bet/That if you start now/And do not quit/You're going to be/A nicotine/Addict Addict Addict."

The message of the video is powerful, but a lung association official acknowledges that by the end of the 18 months it took to make the tape, some participants were smoking themselves.

With Supply and Purity Up, Heroin Use Expands

Joseph B. Treaster

Even with her striking beauty, hardly anyone seemed to notice the young model as she glided through the swarm of heroin dealers and glassy-eyed addicts on a patch of steamy pavement in East Harlem.

This was not her crowd, but they had what she needed and she would endure what she had to to get her drug. She was one of the new ones, drawn to a high grade of heroin that does not need to be pumped into the body with a hypodermic needle but can be inhaled like cocaine without the slightest damage to a finely turned nose, at least in the beginning.

For several years, drug experts and law-enforcement officials have been saying that bumper crops of opium poppies, the raw material for heroin, foreshadowed a resurgence of heroin use. Now, evidence is accumulating that the scary potential is becoming a scary reality.

Although unable to quantify the problem, police officials, drug researchers and social workers in cities like New York, Chicago, Newark, Detroit, Los Angeles and San Diego say they are seeing numerous signs of growing availability, heightened use and increased medical problems associated with heroin.

In many cities, they say, heroin is being sold in places where only crack and powdered cocaine had been available, while dealers who previously handled cocaine exclusively have added heroin to their inventories.

"People buying crack would say, 'Do you know where I can get some heroin?' and it took off like that," said Anthony Davis, a counselor at the McAlister Institute drug treatment center in San Diego. As a result, many users have become addicted to both drugs, experts say.

Moreover, researchers say that some dealers have borrowed a tactic from the highly successful crack trade: selling heroin in smaller packages at lower prices. And because of the drug's growing availability, officials said, the purity, or concentration, of heroin is at an all-time high.

Purer Heroin in Boston

Thomas F. O'Grady, chief of the heroin investigations section of the Federal Drug Enforcement Administration, said that as recently as 10 years ago, a $10 bag of heroin was only 3 or 4 percent pure; it consisted mainly of dilutants. Now, he said, the average purity of heroin nationwide is almost 35 percent.

The mix sold in New York is nearly 64 percent heroin, he said, and in Boston, where the nation's purest heroin is being sold, the heroin content is 81 percent.

Such pure blends make the drug both more desirable and more dangerous. Although researchers have not reported a surge in overdose deaths across the country, increases in such deaths have been reported recently in Connecticut and Florida.

"There has unquestionably been a significant increase in the use of heroin in the United States, and it appears to be continuing to expand," said Robert C. Bonner, the head of the Federal drug agency in Washington.

A Shift in Emphasis

In response to the increase, Mr. Bonner said, the agency was nearly doubling its efforts against heroin.

An aide to Mr. Bonner said the agency would increase heroin investigations to approximately 25 percent of its work, while cutting back on measures to counter marijuana and methamphetamines. Cocaine trafficking still commands most of the agency's attention.

Unlike the crack explosion in the 1980's, the new wave of heroin has spread across the country gradually, like the rising waters of a flooding river.

"Two years ago, if young people were using drugs, it was cocaine," said Dr. Lawrence J. Ouellet, a sociologist at the University of Illinois, who has been studying drug use in the streets of Chicago. "Now many of them are using heroin. It's happening little by little."

Federal officials say heroin has also found its way into smaller cities

 From *The New York Times*, August 1, 1993, pp. 1, 41. © 1993 by The New York Times Company. Reprinted by permission.

like Springfield, Mass., and Milwaukee, where it had previously been a rarity, and has been showing up on college campuses on the East Coast.

The growing use is also being reflected in the nation's hospitals. In April, in its latest report on people seeking help in hospital emergency rooms for drug-related problems, the Substance Abuse and Mental Health Services Administration reported that an all-time high of 13,387 men and women sought help because of heroin in the summer of 1992, up 30 percent from the previous summer. While most of those were longtime heroin users, many were young people, relatively new to the drug, the agency said.

The rising prevalence of heroin can also be seen in police statistics. In 1988, 28 percent of the New York City Police Department's drug arrests involved heroin, while 55 percent involved cocaine.

By last year, heroin arrests represented 36 percent of the total, against 51.9 for cocaine. In the first two months of this year, 40 percent of the drug arrests were for heroin, 47 percent for cocaine.

Bumper crops of poppies set off changes now hitting the drug trade.

Drug experts estimate that there may have been as many as a million heroin users in the United States, 200,000 of them in New York, before the start of the latest rise. But they emphasize that that is only an estimate, saying that national drug surveys do not reach many of the people who have traditionally used heroin.

Memories Are Short

After crippling millions of Americans, cocaine has, for many, become a dreaded substance. Heroin, though, seems to be another matter.

ON THE STREET

Cleaner Heroin

Ten years ago, officials say, a bag of heroin consisted mainly of dilutants and contained only 3 or 4 percent of the drug. In samples taken in the third quarter of 1992, the Drug Enforcement Administration found that the average purity of heroin in selected United States locations was 38.7 percent.

Location	Purity
Boston	81.7
New York	64.7
Puerto Rico	61.9
Newark	59.6
Philadelphia	55.7
San Diego	50.4
Phoenix	44.2
San Francisco	30.9
Atlanta	29.5
New Orleans	22.1
Los Angeles	21.3
Denver	18.7
Seattle	16.8
Washington	15.4
Detroit	11.2
Dallas	9.0
St. Louis	7.8
Houston	6.3

Source: Drug Enforcement Administration

It has been 20 years since President Richard Nixon called it Public Enemy No. 1, and memories are short.

"Heroin is not the bad boy it used to be," said John Galea, the director of a team of state researchers that work the streets of New York City. In many circles, he said, "snorting heroin is almost the same as drinking a Coke."

Nevertheless, cocaine is not on the brink of vanishing. After marijuana, it remains the second most widely used illegal drug, and it remains

stubbornly entrenched among poor people in the inner cities. Dr. Herbert D. Kleber, the medical director of the Center on Addiction and Substance Abuse at Columbia University, said cocaine abuse was likely to remain a problem as heroin use rose.

While some of the new heroin users are young people with relatively little drug experience, the experts say, others are crack and cocaine addicts who have discovered that by taking heroin they can ease the anxiety created by these stimulants as well as the steep depression that often sets in as the effects of cocaine wear off.

Some people develop dual addictions, the experts say, routinely injecting, sniffing or smoking a mixture of cocaine and heroin often referred to as a speed ball. Others, however, are swept away by the heroin.

'It Mellows You Out'

"I see a lot of my old acquaintances who were so hooked on crack," said Lena Rivera, a recovering addict who works for the Center for AIDS Outreach and Prevention in New York. "Now they're shooting heroin. They got hooked on heroin and left the crack alone."

Denise Diaz, 32, who said she had been a receptionist in a New York law firm until drugs got the better of her, talked about the sensations of crack and heroin.

"When you take crack you're real hyper," she said as she rested on a park bench in the courtyard of a high-rise public housing project in Manhattan. "Then you do some heroin and it mellows you out. It gives you a real even high. You don't get paranoid. You just get nice. You can conversate. It gives you energy."

But, she said, it does not take long before the body becomes dependent upon heroin. "You wake up one morning with aches and pains," she said. "By the time you realize you've got a habit, it's too late."

New York is the nation's biggest

clearing house for heroin. It pours in from the Golden Triangle in Southeast Asia, a vast sweep of Myanmar, Laos and Thailand, as well as from Pakistan, Afghanistan, Lebanon, Mexico and, lately, Colombia, which has added heroin to its enormous exports of cocaine.

Avoiding the Needle

Besides gaining an edge on the market of old-time addicts by offering high-grade heroin, dealers, at the same time, have been developing a new clientele by making the drug easier to use.

"At high levels of purity, you can snort heroin and get a pretty good high," said Dr. Robert B. Millman, the director of drug and alcohol abuse programs at the New York Hospital-Payne Whitney Clinic. "But when the purity was 3 or 4 percent, you had to inject the drug to get the desired effect. The needle always scared away some people. Now that barrier is gone."

But, Dr. Millman said, heroin users immediately begin developing a tolerance for the drug and require larger and larger doses to approximate the original impact. The larger the dose, the greater the cost. As a result, Dr. Millman said, most users reach a point where they begin the more efficient practice of injecting the drug.

The thought of a tidal wave of new heroin injectors terrifies health care workers, since intravenous drug users have the highest rate of infection of the virus that causes AIDS. More than half of the intravenous users in New York are infected.

But a surge in the use of hypodermic needles as a way of taking heroin is by no means a certainty. Indeed, it has been a fear of contracting AIDS that has contributed to a sharp increase in snorting the drug.

In New York, for example, 46 percent of the heroin users who entered treatment centers last year said they inhaled the drug compared with 25 percent four years earlier.

Some of those were newcomers,

state officials said. Some were longtime heroin users who had stopped injecting out of fear of AIDS, the officials said, and others were veterans who had never progressed from snorting to the needle.

Proof of the needle's lure is abundant. Dee Dee Torres, 25, a prostitute working the streets of the Bushwick neighborhood in Brooklyn, said she started sniffing heroin two years ago. Seven months ago, she said, she began injecting the drug. Doris Perez, another Brooklyn prostitute, said she had been sniffing heroin for six years. But 20 months ago, she said, she succumbed to the needle.

The hypodermic needle crept up, too, on the young model who bought her heroin at the teeming drug bazaar in East Harlem. She had been introduced to heroin by her boyfriend, a musician, two and a half years ago. "We sniffed," she said.

But three weeks ago, she said, she started injecting. "It's cheaper," she said, "I was sniffing three or four bags a day. Now I shoot one bag."

Smoking, Drinking, and Illicit Drug Use Among American Secondary School Students, College Students, and Young Adults, 1975–1992

Lloyd D. Johnston, Patrick M. O'Malley and Jerald G. Bachman

The nation may have been taking progress in the war against drugs too much for granted over the past two years, according to University of Michigan scientists who conduct the annual national surveys of secondary school students. They point to some troublesome warning signals in the results from their 1992 survey of nearly 50,000 eighth-, 10th-, and 12th-grade students across the country.

The study, which is funded under research grants from the National Institute on Drug Abuse, found modest but statistically significant increases in the use of a number of drugs by eighth-graders, most of whom are only 13 or 14 years old. Increases are reported in their use of marijuana, cocaine, crack, LSD, other hallucinogens, stimulants, and inhalants.

Reporting on their 18th national survey of 12th-graders and second national survey of eighth- and 10th-graders, social psychologists Lloyd D. Johnston, Patrick M. O'Malley, and Jerald G. Bachman conclude that these survey results provide an important early warning signal to the nation.

"We and others have warned that, as the peak years of the drug epidemic pass, there will be replacement cohorts of young Americans who did not have the chance to learn vicariously by observing the experiences of their drug-using contemporaries, including those they see in the mass media," says Johnston. "As this opportunity for informal learning subsides, formal or intentional mechanisms become all the more important. That means that what children learn in school, from their families, through the media (including advertising campaigns), and from the nation's leaders determines whether they see drugs as being as dangerous and as unacceptable as their predecessors did."

The U-M investigators previously demonstrated that changes in the perceived dangers of drugs have played a major role in reducing the use of a number of them—in particular, marijuana and cocaine and probably LSD, PCP, and crack. Peer norms have also shifted in the direction of greater restraint as these drugs came to be seen as more dangerous. The three investigators argue that perceived risk and peer norms, taken together, have been critical to reducing drug use. They have found no evidence that reduced availability accounted for the declines.

In 1992 eighth-graders were significantly less likely to see cocaine or crack as dangerous and (nonsignificantly) less likely to see marijuana use as dangerous than eighth-graders in 1991. (The question was not asked for LSD.) Their personal disapproval of marijuana, cocaine, and crack also fell significantly in 1992. These shifts may well explain the increase in the use of these drugs among eighth-graders.

"While the long-term decline in the use of a number of drugs among the 12th-graders continued in 1992, some of their key beliefs and attitudes began to move in the wrong direction, perhaps presaging a reversal of the previous declines in drug use among seniors, as well," Johnston states. For the first time in recent years, there was a statistically significant decline among 12th-graders in the perceived risk of LSD, heroin, and amphetamines;

From *The University of Michigan News and Information Services*, April 13, 1993, and July 13, 1993. This paper is originally from the National Institute on Drug Abuse, U.S. Department of Health and Human Services. Reprinted by permission.

4. PATTERNS AND TRENDS IN DRUG USE

and there were statistically nonsignificant declines for marijuana, cocaine, and barbiturates.

"The drug abuse issue has pretty much 'fallen off the screen' in this country, both figuratively and literally," Johnson states. "Ever since the buildup to the Gulf War, political leaders and the press talk about it less, television networks have backed off on their prime time placement of anti-drug ads, and in general, national attention has moved away from the issue.

"In the past these sources of influence have been instrumental in bringing about the kind of attitudinal and normative changes necessary to reduce drug use, so their letting up on the issue may well lead to some reversals. We may be seeing the first of those here."

While none of the changes in drug use among eighth-graders is as yet very large in absolute terms, they represent large proportional changes in the numbers of users at that grade level, which means that this newest wave of adolescents entering the teen years may be at the vanguard of a reversal of previously improving conditions, the investigators note.

The U-M researchers draw particular attention to LSD.

Use of Selected Illicit Drugs by Eighth, Tenth, and Twelfth Graders, 1992

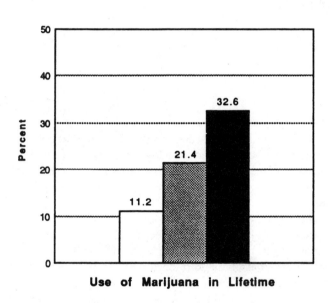

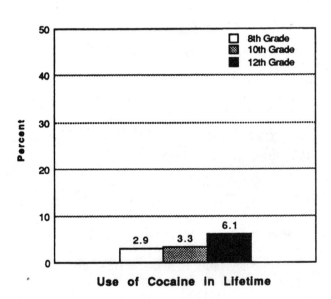

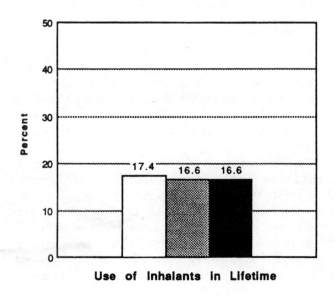

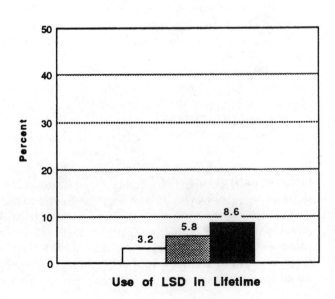

Trends in Annual Prevalence for Five Populations: Marijuana

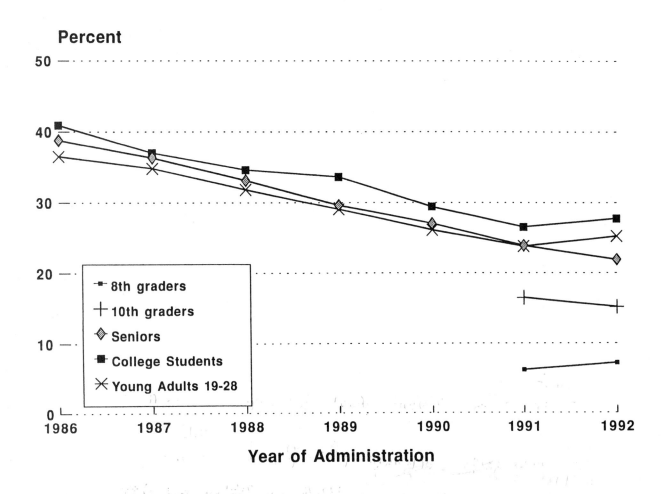

Percent

Year of Administration

They reported last year that LSD use had risen significantly among American college students over a two-year period (1989-1991). Among the 1992 high school seniors the use of LSD rose to its highest level since 1985 (with annual prevalence at 5.6 percent in 1992 compared with a low of 4.4 percent in 1985). The one-year increase of 0.4 percent in 1992 did not reach statistical significance, but use rose in all three grade levels and the eighth-grade increase (from 1.7 percent to 2.1 percent) was significant.

"LSD may be a prime example of generational forgetting," states Johnston, "since it was perhaps the first drug in the epidemic of the past 25 years to decline as a result of concerns about its consequences. Today's youngsters don't hear what an earlier generation heard—that LDS causes bad trips, flashbacks, schizophrenia, brain damage, chromosomal damage, and so on. While some of those early assertions never were substantiated, some were, and young people today are not as likely to know about the dangers of the drug. As mentioned earlier, the perceived risk of LSD is down among seniors in 1992 and is not yet measured among eighth- and 10th-graders.

"We also see inhalant use increasing in recent years, and youngsters don't fully understand the lethal potential of using such substances as butane, solvents, glues, nitrous oxide, and so on." This class of drugs is most commonly used in the early teens, the investigators note, and is the most widely used of the illicitly used drugs among eighth-graders. Tragically, as a result, overdose deaths resulting from inhalant use are often children in their early teens.

One in every six eighth-graders (17.4 percent) used some inhalant in their lifetime; and one in every 20 (4.7 percent) used one in the past 30 days. In 1992, annual inhalant use was up slightly (not significantly) among eighth- and 10th-graders. Among 12th-graders there was no increase in 1992, but use had been rising through the 1980s.

4. PATTERNS AND TRENDS IN DRUG USE

One drug class showed an abrupt increase in the proportion of students associating risk with its use—anabolic steroids. At all three grade levels the proportion of students who associated great risk with steroid use jumped sharply, by five to six percentage points. The investigators credit this change both to increased media coverage of the issue between 1991 and 1992 and to Lyle Alzado's effort to have youngsters learn from his experience. (Alzado was a professional football player who attributed his development of an incurable brain tumor to his use of steroids.) In general, the use of steroids is quite low, and use among 12th-graders has been declining gradually since 1989, very likely because of continuing attention to its dangers.

Turning to the licit drugs, cigarette smoking did not show any significant changes across any of the three grade levels in 1992. Thirty-day prevalence rates for smoking thus remain quite high: 16 percent for eighth-graders, 22 percent for 10th-graders, and 28 percent for 12th-graders. "The lack of change is itself noteworthy, considering the substantial declines in use in recent years for most other drugs by young people, the increased rates of quitting among adults, and the proliferation of smoking prevention efforts in the nation's schools," the investigators say.

The 30-day rate of smoking among 12th-graders, for whom longer term data are available, has fallen by only 1.6 percentage points since 1981, to 28 percent in 1992. "The implications of this lack of change in smoking initiation rates for disease, mortality, and the nation's health care costs will be enormous," the investigators note. Johnston adds that he thinks that the massive advertising and promotion of cigarettes, much of it aimed at young people, is a major reason that cigarette smoking has not been falling among adolescents.

With regard to alcohol use, among seniors the longer term declines in drinking and binge drinking continued in 1992, though the one-year changes did not always reach statistical significance. The proportion of 12th-graders reporting any drinking during the past 30-days fell significantly by 2.7 percentage points to 51 percent—down substantially from the high point of 72 percent in 1980. The proportion of 12th-graders reporting having five or more drinks in a row on at least one occasion during the prior two weeks fell by 1.9 percentage points, to 28 percent—again, down substantially from a high of 41 percent in 1980. The investigators attribute some, though not all, of this decline to changes in the minimum drinking age laws in a number of states. (All states now have a minimum drinking age of 21.)

There were declines in drinking and drunkenness in 1992 among 10th-graders as well; but among eighth-graders there were no such declines in alcohol use. In fact, they showed some modest (not statistically significant) increases.

"No one can deny that over the last 13 years we have made a lot of progress in reducing the numbers of young Americans using illicit drugs—in particular, marijuana, cocaine, and crack," Johnston says, "but we may now be in danger of losing some of that hard-won ground as a new, more naive, generation of youngsters enter adolescence, and as society eases up on its many communications to young people of all ages about drugs. Further, there are several classes of drugs—LSD, inhalants, and cigarettes—on which we have either been losing ground or not making much progress in recent years."

The policy implications of these findings are, Johnston says: "Just as we think of drug dependence for the individual as a chronic, sometimes relapsing disease, we need to think of drug problems in society as chronic, relapsing problems. That means that we can never eliminate them once and for all, but rather must work to reduce and contain them on an ongoing basis. For the foreseeable future American youngsters are going to be aware of a smorgasbord of abusable drugs, and those drugs are going to remain available to some degree. In the face of that, each new cohort of youngsters must be given the knowledge, skills, and motivation to resist using these drugs, which means that adult society needs to become more effective, and more committed for the long term, as it continues to persuade and educate youngsters with regard to drugs. Like it or not, we are in this for the long term."

The long-term decline in illicit drug use by American college students halted in 1992 and may have begun to reverse. Based on the 1992 survey of a nationally representative sample of some 1,500 college students, University of Michigan social scientists Lloyd Johnston, Jerald Bachman, and Patrick O'Malley report that nearly one-third of all college students used some illicit drug at least once in the prior 12 months.

This represents a slight rise—from 29.2 percent in 1991 to 30.6 percent in 1992—in the proportion using any illicit drug. The change, which is not statistically significant, was due largely to an increase in the proportion of college students using marijuana, for which annual use rose from 26 percent to 27 percent.

One in every eight college students (13 percent) reported using an illicit drug other than marijuana, representing virtually no change from 1991.

The use of one class of illicit drugs did rise, however.

Hallucinogen use rose among college students for the third year in a row—a cumulative change that is statistically significant. In 1989, 5.1 percent used an hallucinogen in the prior year; by 1992, 6.8 percent reported such use. One of the major hallucinogens, LSD, accounted for most or all of this increase, rising from 3.4 percent to 5.7 percent over the same interval.

Cocaine use continued to decline, dropping from 3.6 percent of 1991 college students reporting use in the prior 12 months to 3 percent of the 1992 students. This one-year change was not statistically significant.

Crack, stimulants, barbiturates, tranquilizers, inhalants, heroin, opiates other than heroin, and other illicitly used

Use of Selected Licit Drugs by Eighth, Tenth and Twelfth Graders, 1992

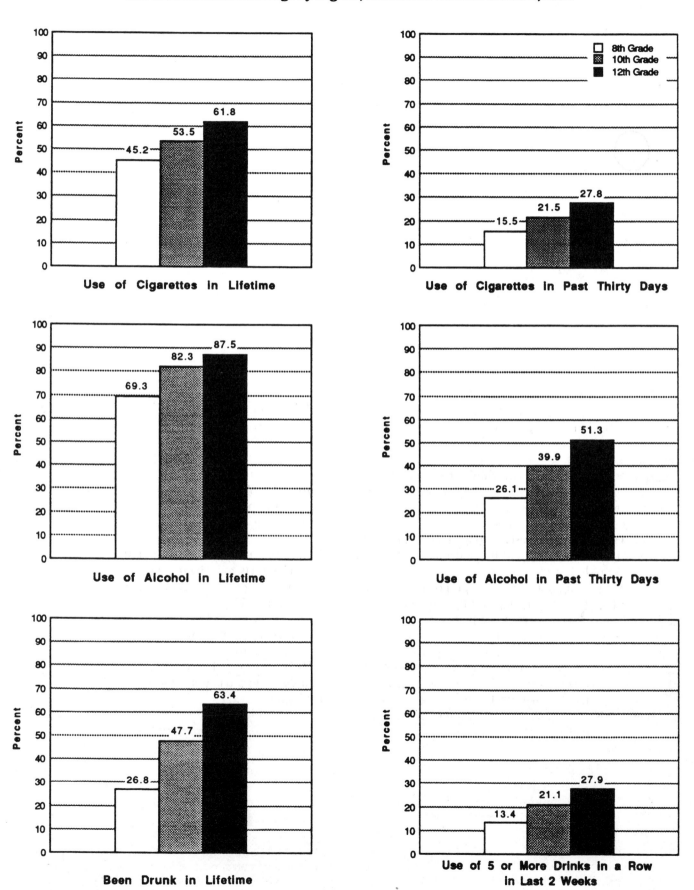

drugs showed little or no further decline in active use in 1992 among college students, even though a number of them had been declining previously.

The U-M Monitoring the Future study, which is funded through research grants from the National Institute on Drug Abuse, also reports on trends in drug use among all young adult high school graduates between the ages of 19 and 28. The young adults, a nationally representative sample of about 6,800 respondents per year, showed results similar to the college students. (The college student sample comprised about one-fifth of this larger young adult population.) The decline among young adults in the use of any illicit drug in the prior year halted in 1992—in fact, their use actually increased slightly, by 1.3 percent, due to an increase of the same magnitude in marijuana use. Marijuana use climbed by 1.4 percentage points to 25 percent. (Again, neither of these increases were large enough to reach statistical significance.)

One in every seven of the young adults (14.1 percent) reported using some illicit drug other than marijuana during the prior year. This proportion is virtually unchanged from 1991.

Cocaine use continued to decline slightly: the proportion saying they used any cocaine in the prior 12 months fell from 6.2 percent in 1991 to 5.7 percent in 1992 (not a statistically significant one-year change, but a continuation of a long-term trend).

Perhaps most important, the use of LSD rose among 19- to 28-year-olds for the third year in a row, going from 2.7 percent of the 1989 sample saying they used in the prior 12 months to 4.3 percent in 1992. The use of any hallucinogen rose similarly from 3.6 percent to 5 percent.

There was little change in the active use of the other illicit drugs among the 19- to 28-year-olds.

"Whether this is a pause, or the beginning of a turnaround we cannot say," cautions Johnston, "but it clearly contrasts with the steady declines in drug use we have been seeing since 1985. Taken along with the upturn in drug use among eighth-grade students, which we reported earlier this year, it certainly presents the basis for some concern.

"There is no question that the use of LSD is up among secondary school and college students. All five populations we study have shown increases in use in recent years," adds Johnston. The five national populations are eighth-, 10th-, and 12th-grade students, as well as college students and young adults. "Three of these five populations also showed some increase in marijuana use in 1992."

"As we have said earlier, drug use has fallen on the national agenda since the Gulf War, and it has not been a very visible issue in the media either. We may now be seeing the effects of this lack of public attention.

"I think it's fair to say from our previous research findings that the country has been working its way out of the most serious drug epidemic in its history because the dangers of drug use were becoming known to our young people and because society had been speaking loudly and consistently about its disapproval of drug use. But this must be an ongoing process if new replacement cohorts of young people are to get the message.

"The message need not be shrill, and it need not be exaggerated, but it must be repeated."

Johnston adds, "It is useful to be reminded that it was among American college students that the massive drug epidemic of the last 25 years began. They are often the harbingers of change in behavior and norms for young people more generally, and a reversal in drug use in this population would not bode well for the country."

The study also looks at use of the licit drugs alcohol and tobacco. It found that heavy party drinking remains widespread among American college students. In 1992, 41 percent of them (51 percent of the males and 33 percent of the females) indicated that in the prior two weeks they had consumed five or more drinks in a row on at least one occasion. There has been little change in this statistic since 1984, when it peaked at 45 percent.

"College students appear to be buffered somehow from the forces in society which have lowered heavy drinking among high school students, those of college age who are not in college, and older age groups," notes Johnston. "Many colleges and universities are actively trying to deal with the problem, but in the aggregate they have not been all that successful."

While cigarette smoking is much lower among college students than among their age peers who are not in college, they have shown no decline in their smoking rate since 1985. If anything, their smoking rates may have risen a little in the past couple of years. One in seven college students (14 percent) is a daily smoker, with college women a little more likely to smoke than college men (15 percent vs. 12 percent, respectively, report smoking daily).

SUMMARY

The study, titled "Monitoring the Future," is also widely known as the National High School Senior Survey. It has been conducted under a series of research grants from the National Institute on Drug Abuse. Surveys have been carried out each year since 1975 by the University of Michigan's Institute for Social Research. The annual senior samples are comprised of roughly 17,000 seniors in 135 public and private high schools nationwide, selected to be representative of all seniors in the continental United States. They complete self-administered questionnaires given to them in their classrooms by University of Michigan personnel. Beginning in 1991, similar surveys of nationally representative samples of eighth- and 10th-graders have been conducted annually. The 10-grade samples involve about 15,000 students in 125 schools each year, while the eighth-grade samples have approximately 18,000 students in 160 schools.

The Monitoring [of] the Future Study has been conducted since 1975 at the University of Michigan's Institute for Social Research, under research grants from the National Institute on Drug Abuse. A nationally representative sample of about 17,000 high school seniors has been surveyed in school each year since 1975. A subsample of each senior class is followed each year thereafter for fourteen years by a mail survey, with retention rates generally averaging between 70%-80%. Among each year's respondents, who are from one to fourteen years

beyond high school, the "college student" sample is taken from those one to four years beyond high school. (Such samples have been available each year since 1980, and the sample size has ranged from 1,000 to 1,500 cases per year.) Only those actively enrolled full-time in a two-year or four-year college during March of that year are counted in the definition of college students used here.

The young adult sample discussed here is defined as all follow-up respondents one to ten years past high school (modal ages 19-28) in the survey year. There are about 6,600 to 6,900 such respondents per year, including the college students, who comprised about 15% of these young adults in 1980 and nearly 22% by 1992.

The Major Drugs of Use and Abuse

Perhaps the most important lesson we can learn in any realistic study of drug use is that different drugs have different effects. Smoking marijuana does not feel the same, or do the same things to the human mind and body, as injecting heroin; snorting cocaine is very different in most respects from swallowing a tab of LSD or drinking a gin and tonic. In order to know what drugs do—and are—it is absolutely essential to examine each drug or drug type individually.

Pharmacologists—scientists who study the effect that drugs have on humans and animals—classify drugs into categories. To begin with, some drugs are *psychoactive*, that is, they influence the workings of the mind; others are strictly medicinal, influencing the body but not the mind. Although some drugs that are not psychoactive, such as certain over-the-counter medications, are improperly used, psychoactive drugs are far more likely to be misused, abused, and overused; clearly, they are more interesting to us here.

Psychoactive drugs are generally classified into the following types:

General depressants depress, inhibit, or slow down a wide range of organs and functions of the body and retard signals passing through the central nervous system, that is, the brain and spinal cord—in most cases, they slow down, relax us, make us drowsier, less alert, less anxious. In most cases, they facilitate sleep. Examples include alcohol, tranquilizers, and sedatives. In sufficiently large doses, depressants can produce intoxication and, if taken over a long enough period of time, physical dependence. If too large a dose is taken at one time, it is possible to die of an overdose of a depressant drug—alcohol included.

Narcotics, or *narcotic analgesics*, dull the perception of pain, produce an intense "high" upon administration—and are highly addicting. They include heroin, morphine, opium, codeine, and the synthetic narcotics. As with general depressants, overdosing is a strong possibility with a large dose of a narcotic drug. Some other analgesics or painkillers that are not as effective as the narcotics do not produce an intoxication. These include aspirin and ibuprofen.

Stimulants speed up signals passing through the central nervous system; they inhibit fatigue and produce arousal, alertness, even excitation. Animals—and humans—find stimulants extremely reinforcing; that is, they will repeat self-administered doses, even when these interfere with other things they want, such as food, water, and sex. Cocaine and the cocaine derivative, crack, are the most well known of the stimulants; they also include the amphetamines, or "speed," and an amphetamine cousin, methamphetamine ("crank" or "ice"), as well as caffeine and nicotine.

Hallucinogens, or "psychedelics," produce extreme mood, sensory, and perceptual changes; examples include LSD, mescaline, and psilocybin. The term "hallucinogen" implies that users always or typically experience hallucinations when they take drugs of this type; in fact, that is rarely the case. Most of the time when users under the influence "see" things that do not concretely exist, they are aware that it is the drug and not the real world that is causing the vision. The term *psychedelic*, a word taken from the ancient Greek, implies that the mind is "made manifest"—that is, it works best—under the influence, another extremely misleading notion. In some classifications, PCP or "angel dust," originally an animal tranquilizer, is regarded as a hallucinogen. In addition, "ecstasy," or MDMA, chemically related to the amphetamines, is also thought of as a hallucinogen. Marijuana, once thought to be a hallucinogen, does not quite fit into this category, and must be regarded as a separate type of drug altogether.

Over-the-counter (OTC) medications are not psychoactive and do not produce a high or intoxication; in order to become dependent on an OTC remedy, or overdose on one, it is necessary to take extremely large doses. They are not entirely "safe"—no drug is—but relative to the psychoactive drugs, they are relatively so. Aspirin and other analgesics or painkillers cause hundreds of deaths by overdose (nearly all of them suicides) each year in the United States, an indication that there is some measure of danger in any substance that causes bodily changes.

As we saw in the introduction to the unit on use, dependence, and addiction, in addition to the impact of the specific drug used, there is the factor of *route of administration*—that is, *how* a drug is used. Some drugs, used via certain routes or methods of use, generate an immediate, powerful, sensuous sensation; other routes of administration produce a slower, less intense, less immediate, or "mellower" feeling. Smoking and intravenous (IV) administration produce the quickest and most intense high; oral (swallowing) and intranasal (sniffing or "snorting") ingestion produce a slower, less intense high. Of course, some drugs cannot be taken certain ways; marijuana is not water-soluable, and, therefore, cannot be injected, does not get absorbed by the nasal membranes, and cannot be snorted. Alcohol—obviously—cannot be smoked. Still, what many drugs can do to the human mind and body is partly dependent on the way they are taken.

Looking Ahead: Challenge Questions

Which of the major drugs is most dangerous?

What is it about each drug or drug type that some users find appealing? How can two drugs with very different effects become equally popular in a given society at a given time? Why are some drugs more popular during one decade and very different ones during another?

Since cocaine and its derivative, crack, are so pleasurable and reinforcing, how is it possible to stop their spread?

What do drug users and abusers seek when they take certain drugs? What is the appeal of each one? What is so bad about certain drugs—marijuana and "ecstasy," for instance—if used in moderation?

Why do users take a drug that is clearly dangerous to their health and their very lives?

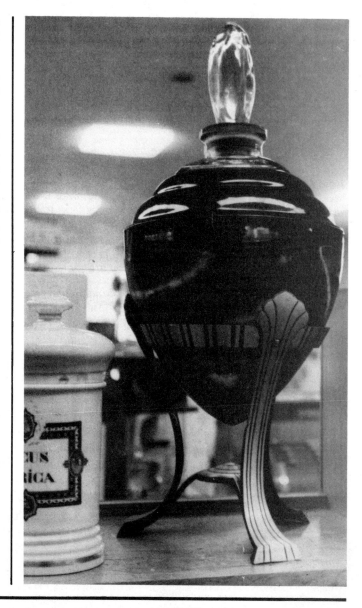

The How and Why of a Cocaine High

Advancing methods for treating addiction

William Booth
Washington Post Staff Writer

BALTIMORE—No one knows exactly what a squirrel monkey feels when it does cocaine. But government scientists at the Addiction Research Center here know this: A monkey will flip a switch for hours just to get another dose of cocaine. And just as some humans will go on a reckless binge of abuse, so too will a monkey hit the switch for more and more cocaine until researchers stop the experiment.

But scientists caution that just because they can get a monkey to feed its addiction so voraciously, it does not necessarily support the popular belief that cocaine is the most addictive of abused drugs.

Indeed, they say, the reason the animal keeps hitting the lever may just be because cocaine makes the monkey superalert and hyperactive.

A monkey might be just as addicted to alcohol, but after a few drinks, in contrast to cocaine's effect, the monkey might stop hitting the lever because it feels sleepy or dazed.

In the last few years, drug researchers have learned an enormous amount about cocaine. Not only do they know more about its true addictive properties, they now at last have a rough idea of how cocaine produces its high.

Addiction scientists have learned, for example, that the drug stimulates a still-mysterious pathway in the brain that is involved in feelings of pleasure and reward.

Indeed, some scientists think they now know at least one region of the brain where cocaine does its work, a structure called the nucleus accumbens, which is responsible for helping humans orient and move toward things they find pleasurable, whether the object of their desire is a member of the opposite sex, a fine wine or a rock of crack cocaine.

In addition, researchers know the exact molecular site in the nucleus accumbens where the cocaine molecule binds to its special receptor.

This in turn has led to a better understanding of how cocaine acts to overstimulate certain nerve cells in the brain, a phenomenon that makes users feel good.

Armed with this knowledge, new drugs are being developed to treat the worst symptoms of withdrawal, to suppress cocaine craving and to reduce cocaine-associated depression.

When a user smokes crack in a pipe, researchers believe, he is employing one of the most efficient drug delivery systems known.

In both animals and humans, scientists say, smoked cocaine reaches the brain so quickly that it is almost impossible to distinguish a dose delivered by intravenous injection from a dose delivered by a glass pipe.

"How fast does it get to the brain? We're not sure. It's too fast to measure in the lab," says Jonathan Katz, a behavioral pharmacologist at the Addiction Research Center, a branch of the National Institute on Drug Abuse.

Katz says he assumes crack cocaine reaches the brain in seconds.

Unlike snorting cocaine powder, a relatively slow and inefficient route, smoking crack delivers the drug directly to the lungs, where it is readily absorbed by the blood, pumped once through the heart and then up to the brain.

One researcher compared smoking crack to driving a nail of cocaine directly into one's forehead.

A "single significant dose" of cocaine—in other words, enough to get a person with a history of cocaine use high—increases breathing, boosts blood pressure and may double heart rate. Hunger, fatigue and depression fade. A subject feels vigorous, happy, hypersexual, friendly and alert. Some scientists describe this collection of sensations as euphoria.

Although a full explanation of how cocaine produces euphoria remains elusive, researchers do know that the drug appears to affect the limbic system, the part of the brain involved in the powerful emotional responses, of which the best-known are those important to human survival, such as the primal urges to feed, fight, flee and reproduce.

THE ANATOMY OF A HIGH

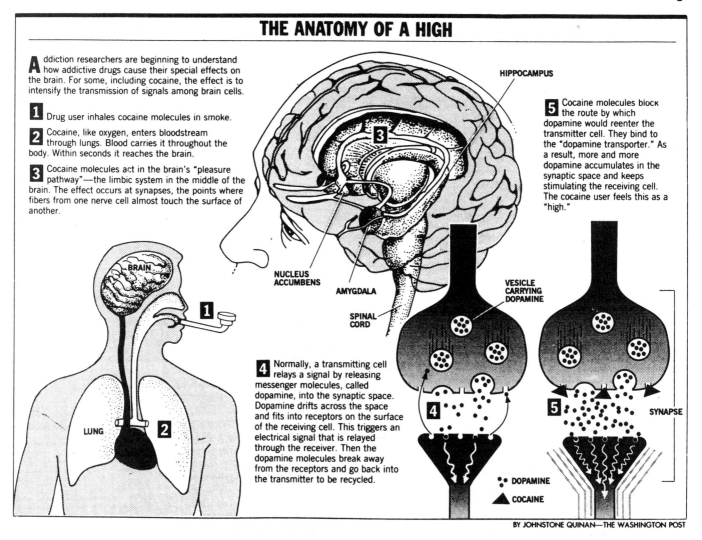

Addiction researchers are beginning to understand how addictive drugs cause their special effects on the brain. For some, including cocaine, the effect is to intensify the transmission of signals among brain cells.

1 Drug user inhales cocaine molecules in smoke.

2 Cocaine, like oxygen, enters bloodstream through lungs. Blood carries it throughout the body. Within seconds it reaches the brain.

3 Cocaine molecules act in the brain's "pleasure pathway"—the limbic system in the middle of the brain. The effect occurs at synapses, the points where fibers from one nerve cell almost touch the surface of another.

5 Cocaine molecules block the route by which dopamine would reenter the transmitter cell. They bind to the "dopamine transporter." As a result, more and more dopamine accumulates in the synaptic space and keeps stimulating the receiving cell. The cocaine user feels this as a "high."

4 Normally, a transmitting cell relays a signal by releasing messenger molecules, called dopamine, into the synaptic space. Dopamine drifts across the space and fits into receptors on the surface of the receiving cell. This triggers an electrical signal that is relayed through the receiver. Then the dopamine molecules break away from the receptors and go back into the transmitter to be recycled.

HIPPOCAMPUS

BRAIN

NUCLEUS ACCUMBENS

AMYGDALA

SPINAL CORD

VESICLE CARRYING DOPAMINE

SYNAPSE

LUNG

•• DOPAMINE

▲ COCAINE

BY JOHNSTONE QUINAN—THE WASHINGTON POST

Although several components of the limbic system are under study, the one area that appears to get the most action is the nucleus accumbens. The nucleus accumbens is uniquely situated to communicate between the limbic system and the part of the brain called the motor cortex, which directs movement.

"When you see a pretty girl and alert to her presence and orient toward her, or when you smell a good bordeaux wine sauce and move toward the smell, it is the nucleus accumbens that is helping you orient and move toward those things you perceive as pleasurable," says George Koob, a psychopharmacologist at the Research Institute of the Scripps Clinic in San Diego.

Scientists believe that cocaine stimulates the nucleus accumbens by meddling with a special chemical messenger called dopamine. In the nucleus accumbens, cocaine enters the tiny space where one nerve cell almost touches another, a sort of no man's

land called the synaptic space.

For one nerve cell to transmit a signal to another, it must make the signal cross the synaptic space. To do this a neuron releases a load of dopamine molecules. Each dopamine molecule travels across the space, briefly attaches itself to a receptor on the receiving cell and then heads back into the neuron from which it was released.

Cocaine, however, stops the dopamine from returning to the neuron that released it, according to Michael Kuhar of the Addiction Research Center. It forces the dopamine to remain in the synaptic space, where it keeps stimulating the receiving neuron over and over again.

In a sense, it is not the cocaine that makes a user high, it is the dopamine that lingers in the synaptic space, overstimulating the nucleus accumbens.

"It jazzes it up," says Koob.

In a normal person, Koob says, the nucleus accumbens may be activated from time to time. But under the influence of cocaine a person is feeling full-blown pleasure almost non-stop, wallowing in a kind of "brain hedonism."

In fact, a common complaint among former cocaine addicts is that they have difficulty getting enjoyment from life's simple, undrugged pleasures, such as sex and eating.

Indeed, Koob believes that one reason cocaine may be so addictive is that it not only makes users feel good, but it also makes them more active, enabling them and motivating them to take more and more of the drug—just like the laboratory animal in the experimental chamber that keeps hitting the lever for more cocaine—until overdose and death overtake them.

"That's what makes cocaine so powerful," says Koob.

The New View From On High

Trends: A wave of drugs floods the clubs

Most Americans reacted to the death of River Phoenix in October with at least a sigh of sympathy. Among a certain set, though, it sparked a grim curiosity. Early press reports of the actor's death by overdose mentioned GHB, an obscure and dangerous steroid substitute occasionally gulped down by West Coast thrill seekers. Never mind that according to a Los Angeles coroner's report GHB was not found in the actor's body. And never mind, too, that it's scarcely available outside a few Los Angeles night-spots. The hunt was on. "I'd never heard of GHB before. No one in New York had," said a Manhattan drug user last week. "This month it's the only drug."

Even drug abuse is subject to the whims of fashion. It's not that the old standards have quit the scene. Phoenix's death was apparently caused by a mixture of morphine, cocaine and other drugs. But members of his generation, mainly middle class and well educated, have turned to other, more exotic highs to fuel their nights. Whether it's Ecstasy at raves or DMT to launch the mind travel of self-styled "psychonauts," there's an alphabet soup of designer drugs to choose from. "It's a different culture of use," says Carlo McCormick, an editor of the New York trendsheet Paper and a student of drug culture. "These drugs are serving the same function that has existed for 20 years. They're just specific to a new generation."

And they're in plentiful supply. Alexander Shulgin, a pharmacologist at the University of California, Berkeley, has researched 179 potential intoxicants in one psychedelic chemical family alone, the phenethyl-amines. Forced to play a game of catch-up, last week the Drug Enforcement Administration hastily added one of them, 2C-B, to its schedule of controlled substances. But an informal survey last week by Miami club personality Julian Bain found that 2C-B, sold under the name Nexus, has already become the number-three drug of choice in South Beach.

Of all the drugs in the designer pharmacopeia, the most popular nationwide is MDMA, or Ecstasy. It's

Club Pharmacopeia

Special K (ketamine)
Cost $40-$50 per half gram
Effect Apparent weightlessness, disorientation
Who Uses Mainly New York gays

Ecstasy (MDMA)
Cost $20-$30 per pill
Effect Introspection, euphoria
Who Uses Ravers nationwide; British ravers and soccer fans

GHB
Cost $20 per ounce
Effect Alcohol-like drowsiness
Who Uses Body-builders, West Coast clubgoers

DMT
Cost $200 per gram
Effect Extreme perceptual alteration; "out-of-body" hallucination
Who Uses Serious "psychonauts"

Nexus (2C-B)
Cost $25-$35 per capsule
Effect Giddiness, visual effects
Who Uses Denizens of dance clubs in California and Florida

D Meth (methamphetamine)
Cost $60-$120 a gram
Effect Long-lasting manic energy
Who Uses Formerly bikers/blue collar, now West Coast ravers

been 10 years since "X" hit the bars, including some in Dallas where it could be bought with a credit card. Considered by many the ultimate "dance drug," X is often described as less disturbingly "trippy" than LSD and more serene than cocaine, which are considered cruder drugs. The white pills of MDMA give feelings of empathy and togetherness coupled with an up-all-night amphetamine rush. Despite nine MDMA laboratory busts in 1992, the Department of Health and Human Services reported 236 emergency-room visits involving the drug that year.

Designer-drug use tends to follow regional and demographic trends. With all the high-tech choices, getting high can now mean getting fairly specific. The New York City nightclub Bump! isn't named after the goofy disco dance, says staffer Marc Berkley. It's a tongue-in-cheek reference to a dose of ketamine (street name: Special K), a surgical anesthetic snorted by much of the club's mainly gay clientele in an attempt to magnify dance-floor sensations like lights, music and rhythm. The club has a 100-foot twisting slide lined with flashing lights. It's called the "K-Hole," the slang term for the episodes of numbed confusion that ketamine can induce.

Head rush: San Francisco's small but devoted DMT scene is a far more serious set. The orange powder causes a violent head rush that devotee Terence McKenna, author of "True Hallucinations," says can be used as an "epistemological tool" to understand the world. McKenna's trancelike public readings attract hundreds of fans. But if anyone's actually smoking the stuff, he's far from the crowd—anathema to the herd mentality bred by MDMA and ketamine. DMT has a nasty side effect: total physical collapse. "You're supposed to have someone there with you to take the pipe out of your hand," says Lon Clark, 27, a rave lighting designer who's seen it smoked.

In the clubs, advocates of the designer drugs claim psychological benefits including everything from enhanced self-image to emotional insight. Scientists, however, know little about the drugs' effects. Dr. George Ricaurte of Johns Hopkins recently found signs of damage to the nerves that release the neurotransmitter serotonin in former MDMA users. But Rick Doblin, president of the Multidisciplinary Association for Psychedelic Studies, a North Carolina group that promotes MDMA testing worldwide, disputes whether such effects are lasting or significant. Dr. Charles Grob of UC, Irvine, plans to test MDMA for possible medical applications like pain management for the terminally ill. Step one, set to begin at Harbor-UCLA Medical Center in Torrance, Calif., this month, will seek to determine the drug's toxic effects on the body. That's information from which young clubgoers could profit.

PATRICK ROGERS *with* PETER KATEL *in Miami*

CHOOSE YOUR POISON

While the government boasts that drug use has fallen, the range of intoxicants has increased, ensnaring a new generation

JILL SMOLOWE

IN NEW YORK CITY'S SPANISH HARLEM, the highs come cheap. To create a "blunt," teenagers slice open a cigar and mix the tobacco with marijuana. To enhance the hit, they fashion "B-40s" by dipping the cigar in malt liquor. In Atlanta, police observed 100 teenagers and young adults at a rave party in an abandoned house—the rage among middle-class youths everywhere with money to burn—and their rich assortment of hooch: pot, uppers, downers, heroin, cocaine and Ecstasy, a powerful amphetamine. In Los Angeles, Hispanic gangs chill out by dipping their cigarettes in PCP (phencyclidine, an animal tranquilizer), while black gangs still favor rock cocaine. Some of the city's Iranians go in for smoking heroin, known as "chasing the tiger," while Arabs settled in Detroit prefer khat, which gives an amphetamine-like high and is also the drug of choice in Somalia.

The high times may be a changin', but America's drug scene is as frightening as ever. Last week the University of Michigan released a survey showing a rise in illicit drug use by American college students, with the most significant increase involving hallucinogens like LSD. Meanwhile a canvas of narcotics experts across the country indicated that while drug fashions vary from region to region and class to class, crack use is generally holding steady and heroin and marijuana are on the rise. Junior high and high school students surveyed by the government report a greater availability of most serious drugs. Law officials and treatment specialists on the front lines of the drug war report that the problem transcends both income and racial differences. "When it comes to drugs, there is a complete democracy," says Clark Carr, executive di-

rector of Narconon Professional Center in North Hollywood, California.

The government paints a much brighter picture. According to the 1992 Household Survey on Drug Abuse, released last month by the Department of Health and Human Services, the nationwide pattern of drug abuse is in decline. The study shows an 11% dip in illicit drug use by Americans 12 years or older, from 12.8 million in 1991 to 11.4 million in 1992. The drop is pronounced in all age groups except those 35 and over, who use drugs at a rate comparable to 1979 levels. Yet the number of hard-core abusers remains unchanged. And a smorgasbord of nouvelle intoxicants is being served up to a new generation of users.

The frenetic '80s infatuation with stimulants has become the mellower '90s flirtation with depressants. Heroin, which has a calming effect, is gaining on crack, which produces high agitation. Some drug experts sense a sociological sea change. "It's really relevant that in the '80s the drug of choice was one that the second you did it, you wanted more," says Carlo McCormick, an editor at a culture and fashion monthly who was the host of LSD parties in New York City in the '80s. "At this point with the current crop of drugs, you're set for the night." Others have a wider perspective. "If you look historically at a large population that has been using a stimulant like cocaine," says James Nielsen, a 26-year veteran with the Drug Enforcement Administration, "they will then go on to a depressant like heroin."

Ironically, the heroin surge also reflects a new health consciousness on the part of drug abusers. Youthful offenders, scared off by the devastation of crack, are dabbling in heroin instead, while

chronic crack addicts are changing over to heroin because of its mellower high and cheaper cost. Among both groups, fear of HIV transmission has made snorting, rather than injection, the preferred method of ingestion. "The needle is out, man," says Stephan ("Boobie") Gaston, 40, of East Harlem, a 26-year abuser. "All they're doing is sniffing." Even so, the risks remain high. Heroin-related incidents jumped from 10,300 during a three-month period in 1991 to 13,400 during a comparable period in 1992, according to a Federal Drug Abuse Warning Network survey of hospital emergency rooms. Heroin-treatment admissions have also increased over the past year.

The turn toward heroin is coupled with a sharp recognition among youthful abusers of the dangers of crack. Anthony M., 13, who is detoxifying from a marijuana habit at the Daytop Village Bronx Outreach Center in New York City, estimates that 20 or so of his 200 classmates use heroin or other drugs, but among them, only one goes in for crack. "That kid wanted others to do it too," he says, "but the other kids were like, 'Nah,' because some of the kids, their parents had died because of crack."

Other hard-learned lessons seem not to affect young people today. LSD use among high school seniors reached its highest level last year since 1983, according to an annual study by the University of Michigan's Institute for Social Research. In the rave clubs of Los Angeles, $2 to $5 buys a teenager a 10-to-12-hour LSD high. "LSD may be a prime example of generational forgetting," says Lloyd Johnston, principal investigator for the study. "Today's youngsters don't hear what an earlier generation heard—that LSD may cause bad trips, flashbacks, schizophrenia, brain damage, chromosomal damage and so on."

Marijuana, usually the first illegal drug sampled by eventual hard-core abusers, is also back in vogue. Of the 11.4 million Americans who admitted to using drugs within a month of the 1992 Household Survey, 55% referred solely to pot; an additional 19% abused marijuana in combination with other drugs. "Cannabis is the drug that teaches our kids what other drugs are all about," says Charlie Stowell, the DEA's cannabis coordinator in California. He says today's marijuana is considerably more potent and expensive than the pot of the '60s because the amount of THC—the ingredient that provides the high—has risen from 2% or 3% to 12%.

The '90s has also ushered in some drug novelties. Since the turn of the decade, gamma hydroxy butyrate, known as GHB, has been used illegally in the body-building community to reduce fat. Recent-ly, however, youths have begun to abuse the drug to achieve a trancelike state. In New York City kids concoct a "Max" cocktail by dissolving GHB in water, then mixing in amphetamines. A different mix resulted in several overdoses in the Atlanta area in the past few months. Manhattan's hard-core sex community has also turned on to "Special K," or Cat Valium, an anesthetic that numbs the body.

The Administration appears to be pursuing several drug strategies simultaneously. The President has asked for a 7% rise in the budget for law enforcement as well as $13 billion for drug-control programs, an increase of $804 million over the current year. Last month Lee Brown, the Administration's drug czar, told a Senate subcommittee that the drug-control programs would now emphasize "demand-reduction programs" would now emphasize young people. Attorney General Janet Reno has also adopted a high profile on drugs, campaigning for a "national agenda for children" that would attack the root causes of drug abuse and violence.

Meanwhile the daily challenge of containing the drug epidemic falls largely to local cops and DEA field offices. Ingenuity is the name of the game. In California, where 19% of the state's marijuana is grown indoors to evade detection, the DEA tracks purchases of illicit equipment, such as high-pressure sodium lights, to pick up the trail of growers. Minneapolis police have grown more sophisticated in tracking crack dealers who no longer keep cars, residences or bank accounts in their own names. "We've begun using financial records and become more knowledgeable in accounting and the flow of money," says Lieut. Bernie Bottema, supervisor of the city's narcotics unit. "We've had to rise to the level of our competition." It appears that level is not going to drop off anytime soon. —*Reported by Ann Blackman/ Washington, Massimo Calabresi/New York and Jeanne McDowell/Los Angeles*

A Prozac Backlash

Does America's favorite antidepressant make sane people crazy?
Despite a string of dramatic accusations, the jury is still out.

Miracles are hard to come by, but to many Americans Prozac looked just like one. Introduced in 1987, the new antidepressant took the market, and the public imagination, by storm. Not only was it easier to prescribe than the other available treatments, but it seemed to alleviate a wider range of afflictions, from depression and anxiety to bulimia and obsessive-compulsive disorder. Best of all, it didn't cause the weight gain, low blood pressure or irregular heart rhythms common to many treatments. In just three years, Prozac became the nation's top-selling antidepressant (a title it still holds, with nearly a million prescriptions being filled every month). Instead of complaining about its price—20 times that of older drugs—happy customers lined up to bear their testimonials. "Prozac has made us a celebrity," says Eugene L. Step of the Indianapolis-based Eli Lilly & Co., which makes the drug. "I have become a far more avid viewer of talk shows." But the talk-show chatter has lately taken a radical new turn.

Self-described "Prozac survivors" now appear on "Donahue" to accuse the drug of turning sane people into murderers and self-mutilators. Scores of unhappy customers are filing lawsuits against Lilly, seeking huge awards for misfortunes they blame on Prozac (box). Some are using the drug as a criminal defense, saying they shouldn't be held accountable for crimes they committed while taking it. One activist group, an offshoot of the Church of Scientology, is even demanding that the Food and Drug Administration remove Prozac from the market. Lilly, meanwhile, is standing staunchly by its product, and psychiatrists have lost little of their initial enthusiasm. Many fear the current uproar will scare patients away from a potentially lifesaving treatment. "This drug is transporting a lot of people from misery to well-being," says Dr. Jerrold Rosenbaum of Harvard Medical School and Massachusetts General Hospital. "A flurry of sensational anecdotes shouldn't stop that."

The horror stories vary in texture, but they share a common theme. Joseph Charles Gardner Jr. started taking the drug in December 1988 to ease the depression that had settled over him after his father died of a heart attack. The 32-year-old resident of St. George, Utah, had always been quiet and conservative, serving as a Mormon missionary, attending Brigham Young University, holding jobs as a schoolteacher, a sheriff's deputy and a medical worker. Everything changed during 1989. Acquaintances say Gardner became restless and irritable after he started taking Prozac, and took to hanging out in bars. In April of that year, he married a Nevada casino worker named Nancy Snow, but she left him after three weeks. By the end of the year, he had twice tried to kill himself with overdoses of barbiturates. "People thought something was wrong," says his lawyer, Alan Boyack, "but nobody ever associated it with Prozac. He just kept taking this drug on the advice of his physician, and he starts going dingy."

Nancy Snow's divorce became final in September 1989, but Gardner didn't want to let go. The following July he approached her in a St. George bar and her best friend, a 32-year-old nurse named Janice Fondren, told him to leave her alone. Gardner was enraged. Later the same week, according to police, he showed up armed at Fondren's apartment. After a brief argument, he allegedly shot her through the heart, drove 22 miles to a remote section of the Shivwit Indian Reservation and left her naked body in the dirt. Gardner is now in a state hospital, where court-appointed psychiatrists have found him temporarily incompetent to stand trial. If he is finally arraigned, his lawyer says he will admit killing her, but will attribute his behavior to Prozac.

Rhonda Hala didn't kill anyone during the 18 months she took Prozac, but she blames the drug for nearly killing her. The 41-year-old Long Island secretary says she had never had any serious problems until late 1988, when a hospital psychiatrist prescribed Prozac (along with a muscle relaxant and later a tranquilizer) to alleviate the aftereffects of major back surgery. After 10 days on the drug, Hala says she became unbearably restless. "You sit down and every nerve in your body has to move," she recalls. "You feel like you're going to jump right out of your skin."

Then came an unaccountable longing for pain, which she satisfied by tearing at the flesh on her thighs, arms and torso. Over the next year she gouged herself with anything she could lay her hands on—screws, bottle caps, shower hooks, tacks, pens, razors. She had a dozen scenarios for suicide, but death was never the main objective. "I had to hurt," she says. "I never thought of taking an overdose of drugs. That would have been too painless." Last year, after her doctor took her off Prozac, Hala says she promptly stopped mutilating herself.

Kentucky massacre: Today she is one of roughly 60 clients from around the country for whom Leonard Finz, a New York personal-injury lawyer, is filing separate suits against Lilly. Finz's Prozac plaintiffs include everyone from the widow of rock star Del Shannon, who killed himself while taking Prozac in February 1990, to the families of several men killed by Joseph Wesbecker of Louisville, Ky. Wesbecker, a 47-year-old pressman with a history of psychiatric problems, was taking Prozac and several other medications in September 1989 when he stormed through the Standard Gravure printing plant with an AK-47. He shot 20 co-workers, eight of them fatally, before taking his own life. That Prozac caused the massacre is, to Finz, self-evident. "Lilly," he claims, "had its finger around the trigger of Joe Wesbecker's rifle."

Juries will have to decide whether Lilly is legally to blame for this carnival of misfortune. Scientists, meanwhile, are grappling with the more important question of whether Prozac can actually make people suicidal and violent. The evidence is still open to different interpretations. On at least two points, though, there is no debate.

The first is that depression itself can cause suicide and violence, even in people receiving treatment. Fully 15 percent of all clinically depressed patients end up taking their own lives. Since no antidepressant—neither Prozac nor any of the alternatives—has more than an 80 percent success rate, it stands to reason that some users will continue to think and act erratically. "Prozac tends to be used by people with psychiatric problems," says Dr. W. Leigh Thompson of Lilly Research Laboratories. "Some people with psychiatric problems happen to be violent."

Experts also agree that virtually any antidepressant could prompt a depressed person to act on impulses he already harbored, simply by making him restless. Roughly a quarter of all antidepressant users experience jitteriness and agitation as side effects. Various antidepressants can also cause an unbearable muscle restlessness called akathisia. Most people don't become violent or suicidal just because they feel restless. But the sensation can be too much for a mentally ill person to bear.

The question is whether Prozac, unlike other antidepressants, can directly induce violent or suicidal thoughts—thoughts that don't stem from an underlying illness. Dr. Martin Teicher, of Harvard Medical School and McClean Hospital, believes that it can. Teicher became something of a celebrity last year after he published a paper in the American Journal of Psychiatry, describing a strange thing that happened in his clinic. Six patients, depressed but not suicidal, had suddenly developed an "intense, violent suicidal preoccupation" after taking Prozac for two to seven weeks. Teicher couldn't rule out depression as the source of their self-destructive impulses—all six patients had considered killing themselves in the past. But their suicidal thoughts came on so suddenly during treatment that Teicher suspected Prozac had actually caused them.

Other researchers have since reported a handful of similar cases. In a recent letter to The New England Journal of Medicine, doctors in Syracuse, N.Y., described two previously non-suicidal patients—a depressed man and a depressed, bulimic woman—who became suicidal within weeks of starting Prozac. According to the letter, the obsessions receded after they stopped taking the drug. And last month psychiatrists at the Yale Medical School's Child Study Center reported the emergence of intense self-destructive thoughts

in several adolescents receiving Prozac for obsessive-compulsive disorder. The Yale researchers, led by Drs. Robert King and Mark Riddle, speculate that by disrupting production of the chemical messenger serotonin, Prozac may directly affect the brain's ability to regulate aggression. But they couldn't be sure that the patients' underlying conditions weren't the real culprit. Besides suffering from obsessions and compulsions, the report said four of the six children had been depressed or suicidal in the past.

Dark thoughts: Do these case reports reflect a unique, Prozac-related syndrome? Should violent thoughts be counted among the drug's direct side effects? The obvious way to find out is to study large groups of patients. But when researchers have gone looking for the "Teicher syndrome," they haven't found it. In one of Lilly's clinical trials, researchers randomly assigned 3,065 depressed patients to Prozac, a placebo or one of five other antidepressants. At the beginning of the six-week treatment period, all seven groups were equally prone to suicidal thoughts. By the end of the trial, the Prozac group was the least suicidal of the seven. More recently, in a one-year study, researchers at Rush-Presbyterian-St. Luke's Medical Center in Chicago monitored 100 Prozac users and found no increase in the risk of suicide or violence. And

'The Drug Did It': A Tough Sell in Court

Joseph Wesbecker gained a kind of immortality in death. After his 1989 rampage in Louisville, Ky., he became a symbol: the best-known violent Prozac user. Widows of three of Wesbecker's victims and his son are suing Eli Lilly & Co., Prozac's maker—just a few of about 60 pending civil suits. Prozac has made its way into criminal court, too. More than 20 defendants claim a "Prozac defense": the drug, they say, made them do it.

Most of the cases are a long shot, legal experts agree. Civil plaintiffs and criminal defendants alike have to prove that Prozac caused the violent behavior—a hard sell when the patients had histories of illness. In other cases against big pharmaceutical companies over such products as the Dalkon Shield and thalidomide, the damage was physical—more obvious than a psychological shift.

Civil plaintiffs have other hurdles to jump. Those suing doctors for malpractice must show the physicians didn't follow Lilly's prescription guidelines. Those suing Lilly must prove the company was reckless or negligent to let the drug out on the market, a difficult argument that will focus on the reliability of the drug's prerelease testing. Leonard Finz, the lead lawyer in many Prozac suits, says that Lilly's tests were inadequate and excluded patients with suicidal tendencies—the very users who appear most affected by the drug.

Deep pockets: Lilly says it is so confident of its testing that it will not settle any civil cases. Its tests of the drug go back to 1976, and Lilly can prove that it included suicidal patients. Says Eugene L. Step, executive vice president at Lilly: "The message is really simple: depressed people commit suicide." And Lilly spokesman Edward West says the "Prozac defense" hasn't produced a single "not guilty" verdict. Yet three criminal defendants received reduced penalties with the Prozac defense, claims the Citizens Commission on Human Rights, an interest group linked to the Church of Scientology. The group often speaks out against psychiatry, and collects horror stories about psychiatric drugs.

Though Lilly's position seems strong, juries have a way of evening the odds. In the battle of expert witnesses and technical testimony, issues can become clouded. And juries often show sympathy for the little guy—especially against a big corporation with deep pockets. "You take these cases before a jury and who the hell knows what might happen," says Robert Litan of the Brookings Institution, a legal liability expert. "It's a lottery." And while the Prozac defense is creative, it's not unique. Criminal conduct is being blamed on everything from drugs to junk food. Prozac parties are watching one case especially closely: in 1989 a Utah judge freed Ilo Grundberg, who killed her mother while under the influence of the insomnia drug Halcion. Now Grundberg is pursuing a $21 million civil suit against Halcion's maker, Upjohn. Upjohn denies that its drug is responsible—but if the company loses in court, the case could make the going tougher for Lilly.

JOHN SCHWARTZ and BOB COHN with bureau reports

two Boston psychiatrists have just published results from a survey intended to gauge suicidal thinking among 1,017 patients treated with various antidepressants during 1989. Drs. Maurizio Fava and Jerrold Rosenbaum, both of Harvard Medical School and Massachusetts General Hospital, found that no drug was associated with significantly more suicidal thinking than any other. A number of patients became suicidal while receiving treatment, but never in the sudden, inexplicable manner Teicher described.

Maybe Prozac does make some people crazy; the available evidence doesn't settle the question. But if the Teicher syndrome is real, it is exceedingly rare—too rare to show up in studies designed to detect it, and too rare in the view of most psychiatrists to warrant big changes in prescribing practices. Teicher hopes that future research will enable doctors to predict how individual patients will react to the drug. But even he has no plans to stop prescribing it in the meantime. Antidepressants are not cough drops. Dr. Joseph

Lipinski of Harvard Medical School and McLean Hospital likens them to loaded pistols. They all pose hazards. But until better treatments come along, Prozac remains a vital weapon against a formidable illness.

GEOFFREY COWLEY *with* KAREN SPRINGEN *in Indianapolis,* JEANNE GORDON *in St. George and* CARLA KOEHL *on Long Island*

SELLING POT

THE PITFALLS OF MARIJUANA REFORM

"Whatever the cultural conditions that have made it possible, there is no doubt that the discussion about marihuana has become much more sensible," Harvard psychiatrist Lester Grinspoon wrote in 1977. "If the trend continues, it is likely that within a decade marihuana will be sold in the United States as a legal intoxicant."

Jacob Sullum

Jacob Sullum is associate editor of REASON.

This was not a silly prediction. At the time, there was good reason to believe it would come true. Six years before, the National Commission on Marihuana and Drug Abuse, appointed by Congress and the Nixon administration, had recommended that the federal government and the states legalize both private possession of marijuana for personal use and casual, nonprofit transfers of the drug in small amounts.

In 1973 Oregon became the first state to "decriminalize" marijuana, making possession of less than an ounce a civil offense punishable by a maximum fine of $100. In 1975 Alaska removed all state penalties for private cultivation and possession of up to four ounces. By the end of the decade, 11 states had decriminalized marijuana possession, a policy endorsed by President Carter, the American Bar Association, the American Medical Association, and the National Council of Churches. Every other state had reduced the penalty for simple possession, nearly all of them changing the offense from a felony to a misdemeanor. Most allowed conditional discharge, without a criminal record.

So Grinspoon's optimism was justified. Yet the year after his prediction, things started to turn around: In 1978 the federal government's policy of spraying Mexican marijuana crops with the herbicide paraquat, which can cause lung fibrosis and death when swallowed in small doses, prompted a nationwide panic among pot smokers. That same year, Carter drug adviser Dr. Peter Bourne, who was sympathetic to reform, was forced to resign after press reports that he had used cocaine at a party sponsored by the National Organization for Reform of Marijuana Laws. His replacement, Lee Dogoloff, took a hard line on illegal drugs, including pot. And the percentage of Americans favoring marijuana legalization in the Gallup poll dropped from the first time in a decade, from 28 percent in 1977 to 25 percent in 1978. (By the late '80s, the figure was down to about 16 percent.)

OVERPLAYING THE BENEFITS OF CANNABIS MAY PROVE JUST AS RISKY AS UNDERPLAYING ITS POTENTIAL HARMS.

The '80s and early '90s saw a series of further setbacks:

❖ In 1983, the Drug Enforcement Administration began spraying paraquat on marijuana crops in the United States. Throughout the decade, the federal government pursued an aggressive domestic eradication policy, especially in California.

❖ The Reagan administration announced a "zero tolerance" program, imposing draconian seizure penalties for marijuana possession, even in tiny amounts.

❖ In 1987 Supreme Court nominee Douglas Ginsburg withdrew under pressure from his erstwhile supporters after admitting that he had smoked pot as a law professor.

❖ In 1989 the federal government launched Operation Green Merchant, raiding the homes of people suspected of growing marijuana because they had purchased gardening equipment.

❖ In 1990 Alaska voters passed a referendum, pushed vigorously by Bush administration drug czar William Bennett, that recriminalized marijuana possession.

❖ That same year, Congress approved a transportation appropriations bill that threatens to withhold funding from states that do not suspend the driver's licenses of drug offenders, including marijuana users, for at least six months.

❖ In 1992 the Department of Health and Human Services canceled a federal program that was supposed to supply patients with medical marijuana.

Under the Clinton administration, there's reason to hope that the pendulum may begin to swing in the other direction again. Both President Clinton and Vice President Gore have used marijuana, and both recall more with nostalgia than with hostility the counterculture of the '60s that many older Republicans still associate with the drug. Clinton has slashed the staff of the Office of National Drug Control Policy, and he has sought advice from scholarly critics of the Bush war on drugs, at least one of whom supports marijuana legalization. Perhaps most significantly, the woman Clinton plans to appoint as surgeon general, Dr. Joycelyn Elders, has said patients who can benefit from medical marijuana should be able to receive it.

But before reformers try to take advantage of what promises to be a more tolerant policy environment, they need to understand what went wrong the first time around. Since marijuana is both the most widely used and the least harmful of the major illegal drugs, the lessons of the anti-pot backlash have broad implications. If reformers cannot succeed in the case of marijuana, where the arguments for legalization seem to be strongest, it's not likely they will succeed elsewhere.

Several factors contributed to the reversals that began in the late '70s, but the most important was a persistent misperception: Both opponents of reform and the general public seemed to believe that the argument for legalization was based on the premise that "marijuana is harmless." So far as I can tell, no serious scholar or prominent activist who favored changing the marijuana laws ever made this claim. Rather, the reformers argued that pot was less harmful than other drugs and less harmful than the government had led people to believe. But by the time the policy debate filtered into local newspapers, college campuses, and suburban living rooms, these nuances were lost—partly because, in the experience of most users, marijuana *was* harmless.

This perception established a test that marijuana was bound to fail, since no drug is safe in every dose and circumstance. Consequently, the growing public and official tolerance of marijuana use was vulnerable from the start. Confronted by a powerful counter-reform movement in the late '70s and early '80s, it withered.

Current attempts to revive progress toward legalization run the risk of repeating this pattern. One major approach to reform emphasizes the medical uses of cannabis; another emphasizes the remarkable versatility of the hemp plant, from which mari-

juana is derived. There is good evidence for these claims. But like the notion that marijuana is completely safe, they tend to establish excessively ambitious criteria for legalization. Overplaying the benefits of cannabis may prove just as risky as underplaying its potential harms.

This is partly a matter of emphasis, but also a matter of style. If you're trying to convince the average American that legalization is a wise policy, it's deadly to come across as a marijuana enthusiast. The most successful reformers have been sober, cautious people far removed from pothead stereotypes—people like Harvard's Grinspoon, author of the 1971 book *Marihuana Reconsidered*.

Grinspoon set out to present credible evidence of marijuana's harms to pot-smoking kids who were ignoring the government's warnings. "I was concerned about all these young people who were using marijuana and destroying themselves," he says. But after examining the research on marijuana's effects, "I realized that I had been brainwashed, like everybody else in the country." In his book, he methodically debunked the many spurious claims about pot, including fears that it causes crime, sexual excess, psychosis, brain damage, physical dependence, and addiction to other drugs.

The following year, the National Commission on Marihuana and Drug Abuse reached broadly similar conclusions: that the dangers of pot had been greatly exaggerated and could not justify punitive treatment of its users. The commission introduced the concept of decriminalization, which the newly formed National Organization for the Reform of Marijuana Laws soon adopted as a goal. At a time when some 600,000 people were being arrested each year on marijuana charges, most for simple possession, the strategy had broad appeal. Liberals were concerned about the injustice of sending college students to jail for carrying a joint or two. Conservatives worried about the mass alienation and disrespect for the law that the policy was breeding.

"There was the beginning of a consensus," says NORML founder Keith Stroup. "It said, 'I don't like marijuana smoking, but I don't think it should be treated as a criminal matter.' " Stroup argues that decriminalization was a necessary first step toward legalization. "Otherwise," he says, "you'd never get beyond the fear that, without criminal penalties, everybody would be stoned all the time, and the whole state would go down the tube."

But, as Grinspoon noted in the 1977 edition of *Marihuana Reconsidered*, decriminalization is inherently unstable. "As long as marihuana use and especially marihuana traffic remain in this peculiar position neither within nor outside the law, demands for a consistent policy would remain strong," he wrote. "We would have to ask ourselves why, if using marihuana is relatively harmless, selling it is a felony; then we would have to decide whether to return to honest prohibition or move on to legalization."

Americans did indeed ask this question, and since the late '70s the trend has been back toward "honest prohibition." An important harbinger of this reaction came in 1974, when

Sen. James Eastland (D-Miss.) convened hearings on the "marijuana-hashish epidemic" with the avowed purpose of countering the "good press" that pot had been receiving. Dr. Gabriel Nahas, author of *Marijuana: Deceptive Weed* and *Keep off the Grass*, led a group of researchers who testified that marijuana may cause lung damage, birth defects, genetic abnormalities, shrinkage of the brain, impairment of the immune system, reduction in testosterone levels, and sterility.

Of these hazards, only lung damage has been well established by subsequent research. All the other claims have been discredited or remain controversial. Much of the research cited in the Eastland hearings was heavily criticized soon after it appeared. Some of it was laughably bad, with skewed samples and no control groups.

Despite the poor quality of these studies, anti-marijuana activists continue to cite them. "Those papers, and the ideas they brought forth, are at the heart of the anti-marijuana movement today," says Dr. John P. Morgan, professor of pharmacology at the City University of New York Medical School. "Nahas generated what was clearly a morally based counter-reform movement, but he did a very efficient job of saying that he was actually conducting a toxicological, scientific assessment."

The Eastland hearings left the impression that Americans had been duped by reformers about the nature of marijuana. The title of a piece in the June 10, 1974, issue of *U.S. News & World Report* is revealing: THE PERILS OF 'POT' START SHOWING UP. The writer was clearly confident that the speculation offered by Nahas and his colleagues was only the tip of the iceberg.

The testimony seemed to have a similar impact on Dr. Robert L. DuPont, then director of the National Institute on Drug Abuse. Although he initially supported reducing the penalties for marijuana possession, DuPont renounced decriminalization in 1979. "I have learned that it is impossible to be pro-decrim and anti-pot," he told an anti-marijuana group, "because no matter how you try to explain it to them, young people interpret decrim as meaning that pot must be okay because the government has legally sanctioned it."

DuPont's remarks reflect one of the main concerns that drove the anti-pot backlash: rising marijuana use among teenagers. According to NIDA's National Household Survey, the percentage of Americans between the ages of 12 and 17 who had ever used marijuana rose from about 14 percent in 1972 to about 31 percent in 1979, after which it declined steadily. NIDA's High School Senior Survey shows a similar trend: About 47 percent of seniors reported having used marijuana in 1975 (when the survey began); this figure rose steadily to a little over 60 percent in 1979, after which it declined. The most alarming and frequently cited NIDA pot statistic is for "daily" use by high-school seniors: It rose from 6 percent in 1975 to a peak of nearly 11 percent in 1978.

These numbers overstate the percentage of seniors who got stoned every day in the late '70s. First of all, they don't represent actual daily use throughout the year—only use on 20 or more of the previous 30 days. Granted, that's still pretty heavy. But the numbers include kids who had recently gone

through a brief period of heavy use. And as Mark Kleiman, associate professor of public policy at Harvard's John F. Kennedy School of Government, notes in *Marijuana: Costs of Abuse, Costs of Control*, the data are probably inflated by error or exaggeration: Experience with marketing surveys indicates that questions about habitual activities like "On how many of the last 30 days did you use marijuana?" tend to elicit systematic overreporting. Furthermore, the 11-percent "daily use" figure appears to be inconsistent with information from NIDA's household survey.

NO ONE HAS EVER DIED FROM A MARIJUANA OVERDOSE. MARIJUANA ITSELF (AS OPPOSED TO THE ACT OF SMOKING) DOESN'T CAUSE ORGAN DAMAGE.

In any event, it seems that teen-age marijuana use, like adult marijuana use, rose dramatically in the '70s, peaking around 1979. Many parents were alarmed at this trend, and there was reason to be concerned. Both supporters and opponents of legalization agree that it's not a good idea for unsupervised minors to use pot. Whatever the health hazards of the drug, they are likely to be more serious for children. Furthermore, frequent marijuana intoxication can interfere with emotional development, and there's no question that stoned kids have trouble absorbing and recalling information.

But the hysterical reaction of what came to be known as the Parent Movement for Drug-Free Youth, which attracted the active support of the federal government, cannot be understood merely as a response to these dangers. After all, the same concerns could be raised about alcohol use, which was also rising markedly among teenagers during this period. These parents focused their wrath on marijuana because it was an illegal, alien presence in their middle-class, suburban lives—a presence that was tolerated, if not condoned, by a large and growing number of Americans.

The police were looking the other way as tens of millions lit up. College professors, doctors, and lawyers were smoking pot. Movies and music glamorized drug use. There were water pipes in the local record store, for heaven's sake. Morgan, the CUNY pharmacologist, says the reform movement was caught off guard by the parental backlash: "We didn't know the revulsion and hatred that middle-class parents felt about marijuana and their kids getting high. We didn't have any idea how strongly they felt." The outraged parents who would eventually form the backbone of the anti-marijuana movement saw the drug as a lurking threat that would turn out to be far more hazardous than everyone seemed to believe.

Those fears were reinforced by a series of articles that appeared in mainstream magazines in the late '70s and early '80s—articles with titles like "All the Evidence on Pot Isn't In!" (*Seventeen*), "How I Got My Daughter to Stop Smoking

Pot" (*Good Housekeeping*), "Marijuana Alert: Enemy of Youth" (*Reader's Digest*), "Marijuana: Now the Fears Are Facts" (*Good Housekeeping*), "Marijuana: The Latest Dope on Its Dangers" (*Mademoiselle*), and "The Perils of Pot" (*Discover*). The articles delivered the same message as the Eastland hearings: You have been deceived. Marijuana is a lot more dangerous than you think.

The most influential anti-marijuana writer was probably the late Peggy Mann, a journalist who started writing about pot in 1978. After attending a conference in France on the dangers of marijuana, organized by Nahas and other anti-pot researchers, she wrote "The Case Against Marijuana Smoking," which appeared on the front page of *The Washington Post*'s Outlook section. During the next few years she wrote many magazine articles on pot, including a four-part series in *Reader's Digest* that prompted a record 6.5 million reprint requests. In 1985 Mann published *Marijuana Alert*, which Nancy Reagan describes in the foreword as "a true story about a drug that is taking America captive."

Marijuana Alert gathers together almost every scrap of research that reflects badly on marijuana, including thoroughly discredited studies, while virtually ignoring anything that would give a different impression, including major surveys of the literature. This is not simply the mirror image of the approach taken by reformers. Scholars such as Grinspoon, John Kaplan, Norman Zinberg, Edward Brecher, and Andrew Weil were forced to deal with speculation about marijuana's harms and the research supporting it. Indeed, their task was precisely to confront those claims.

Mann, on the other hand, deals with the opposition's arguments and evidence mainly by omitting them. While she describes Nahas's studies finding that marijuana impairs cellular immunity, she neglects to mention that other researchers have tried but failed to replicate them. She discusses Harold Kolansky and William T. Moore's 1971 study suggesting that marijuana use causes a host of psychological problems, but not the storm of criticism it prompted. She cites A. M. G. Campbell's 1971 study finding that marijuana causes cerebral atrophy but leaves out the methodological flaws that made it worthless: All 10 subjects were psychiatric patients, and there was no nonpsychiatric control group; the study also failed to control for epilepsy, head injuries, mental retardation, and the use of other drugs, including alcohol. When Mann does mention criticism, it's only to dismiss it.

This approach is quite effective. If you haven't already heard about the studies and surveys she ignores, Mann's book may well convince you that marijuana is a very dangerous drug. Largely because of Mann and other anti-pot propagandists, many Americans have a vague sense that recent scientific findings show marijuana to be considerably more hazardous than people thought it was in the '70s (a notion reinforced by a similar impression about cocaine). Yet the basic picture remains the same: No one has ever died from a marijuana overdose; based on extrapolations from animal studies, the ratio of the drug's lethal dose to its effective dose is something like 40,000 to 1 (compared to between 4 and 10 to 1 for alcohol and between 10 and 20 to 1 for aspirin). Unlike alcohol used to excess, marijuana itself (as opposed to the act of smoking) does not appear to cause organ damage. And virtually all of marijuana's negative effects are associated with heavy use (the equivalent of several joints a day).

In his 1992 book *Against Excess*, Kleiman writes: "Aside from the almost self-evident proposition that smoking anything is probably bad for the lungs, the quarter century since large numbers of Americans began to use marijuana has produced remarkably little laboratory or epidemiological evidence of serious health damage done by the drug."

Anti-marijuana activists commonly claim that today's pot is more dangerous because it is "much more potent" than the pot of the early '70s, with an average THC content 10 times greater. This claim, which was influential in the successful drive for recriminalization in Alaska, is doubly wrong. As Morgan has noted, the assertion that pot is 10 times more powerful than it used to be is based on a spurious comparison of low-grade Mexican marijuana from fewer than 20 seizures tested in the early '70s with high-grade domestic marijuana from more than 200 seizures tested in the early '80s. The average THC content of domestic seizures tested by the federal government has been pretty stable—around 2 percent to 3 percent—since 1979, the first year for which reliable data are available.

But even if average THC content were significantly higher now than in the '70s, this is more likely a health benefit than a hazard. Since marijuana users generally smoke until they achieve a desired effect, higher potency means less inhalation—a positive result, since lung damage is the only well-established physical risk associated with marijuana use by otherwise healthy adults.

Although they talk about the physical effects of smoking pot, anti-marijuana activists seem to worry more about its psychological impact. *Marijuana Alert*, for example, is full of horror stories about sweet, obedient, courteous, hard-working kids transformed by marijuana into rebellious, lazy, moody, insolent, bored, apathetic, sexually promiscuous monsters. The most striking thing about these accounts is the extent to which the symptoms of marijuana use overlap with the symptoms of adolescence. "It was very easy for parents to blame marijuana for all the problems that their children were having, rather than to accept any responsibility," Grinspoon observes. "It became a very convenient way of dealing with and understanding various kinds of problems."

In addition to confusing correlation with causation, anti-marijuana activists blur the distinction between short-term and long-term effects. Under the influence of marijuana, for example, users appear listless; their thinking may seem disordered, and their short-term memories are impaired. But to judge by the anecdotes that Mann offers, these are persistent traits of pot smokers, intoxicated or not. She says the problems may not disappear for months after the last joint, if at all.

For anyone who knew a pothead or two in high school or college, this depiction of marijuana's effects may have the ring of truth. One of my colleagues cites the impact that pot seemed to have on some of his fellow students: They sat around getting stoned all day, skipping classes, accomplishing nothing. But since the vast majority of people who use marijuana don't end up this way, it's clear that heavy pot use is more likely to be the expression of psychological problems or personality traits than the cause of them. Of course, being stoned all the time would exacerbate almost anyone's problems, but that doesn't mean pot can magically transform a straight-A student into a burned-out hippie.

Another frequently cited behavioral result of smoking pot is the so-called gateway effect. In 1985 I covered a pot bust in northeastern Pennsylvania, following a long line of state police cars up winding dirt roads through the woods until we arrived at a modest marijuana farm. Watching the troopers uproot the tall, bright-green plants, I asked the officer in charge what all the fuss was about. He gave the standard response: "Marijuana may not be so bad, but it leads to harder drugs. I've seen it a thousand times."

I've been mulling that over, on and off, for the last eight years. My initial reaction was, "That's not true." I have since arrived at a more sophisticated position: "*What's* not true?" The gateway theory is deliberately ambiguous and therefore impossible to disprove. It's not clear what it means to say that marijuana "leads to" other drugs.

For example, heroin use is usually preceded by marijuana use, but marijuana use is rarely followed by heroin use. Those who use marijuana are statistically more likely to use other drugs (as are users of alcohol and tobacco), but this tells us nothing about causation. In particular, it does not tell us whether eliminating marijuana from the planet would have any impact at all on cocaine or heroin use. And to the extent that a "gateway effect" works by introducing pot users to the black market, prohibition is the real problem. In short, the most useful thing that can be said about the gateway theory is that it's not very useful—as a scientific concept, that is; it's very useful as a rhetorical device.

Y ou could say the same for the entire case against marijuana. From a scientific perspective, it's not very impressive. But it has made a real difference in the hearts and minds of many Americans. The main reason the anti-pot campaign has been so successful is that many people believed they'd been told marijuana should be legalized because it was harmless. Therefore it did not take much evidence to discredit the reform movement. Just as the advocates of decriminalization drew strength from the actual lies the government had been telling about marijuana for decades, the anti-pot movement drew strength from the perceived lies of the reformers.

The "myth of harmlessness" shows up again and again in Mann's writings; it's her favorite foil. It also appears in essays by political commentators. In a 1983 *National Review* article, for example, Richard Vigilante refers to "much rhetoric about marijuana's being 'a harmless recreational drug' " and describes the task of reformers as "having to argue for the drug's legality by proving its harmlessness." News coverage confirms

that many people thought they were hearing the message that pot is harmless during the '70s. In its article on the 1974 Eastland hearings, for example, *U.S. News* reported: "The researchers…agreed that the claim that cannabis is an innocuous drug is ill-founded." In 1980 *Newsweek* could casually refer to "the widely accepted public view today that [pot] is probably harmless."

"This is just bizarre," says Richard Cowan, who became NORML's national director last year. "No one here ever claimed that marijuana is harmless. That's an easy straw man, since nothing is harmless." A charter member of Young Americans for Freedom, Cowan wrote an influential piece for *National Review* in 1972, "American Conservatives Should Revise their Position on Marijuana." In the two decades since then, he has repeatedly encountered the "marijuana is harmless" straw man.

No doubt anti-marijuana propagandists have sometimes deliberately mischaracterized the arguments of their opponents. But there is also an element of genuine misunderstanding here, rooted in the limitations of the English language. There is no convenient, shorthand way to express what the reformers have been trying to say: Marijuana is not so harmful, compared to other (legal and illegal) drugs, compared to a wide range of recreational activities, compared to its image as portrayed by the government, and compared to the laws aimed at suppressing its use. There is no word that means "acceptably risky" or "not all that dangerous," no word that expresses a low relative evaluation of harmfulness in the same way that *inexpensive* expresses a low relative evaluation of cost.

So reformers trying to be pithy have had to make do with

"NO ONE HERE EVER CLAIMED MARIJUANA IS HARMLESS," SAYS MORML'S NATIONAL DIRECTOR. "NOTHING IS HARMLESS."

modified versions of *safe*, *innocuous*, and *harmless*, as in "comparatively safe," "relatively innocuous," or "harmless for most people." When their arguments are summed up by others, the crucial modifiers are often lost.

For today's reformers, then, it's not enough to have the facts straight and to formulate solid arguments. They have to be aware of how their arguments will be perceived. In this connection, there are serious pitfalls for activists pursuing either of the two approaches to reform that are now prominent within the marijuana movement.

T he problems with the hemp-as-wonder-plant strategy are pretty obvious. Marijuana activists Jack Herer of California and Gatewood Galbraith of Kentucky are among the leading advocates of this approach, which has also attracted the support of *High Times* and country singer Willie Nelson. In his 1985 book *The Emperor Wears No Clothes*, which *High Times* editor Steve Hager calls "the bible of the hemp movement," Herer explores the history and the many uses of the hemp plant: In addition to medicine, it can be a source of food, oil, fuel, paper, building materials, and fiber for rope and fabric. He argues that hemp derivatives could successfully compete with current products, and he implies that the pharmaceutical, paper, and petroleum industries have conspired to suppress marijuana. He contends that substituting methane, methanol, and charcoal from hemp-based biomass for fossil fuels would halt global warming and thereby "save the world."

There are some good things to be said for Herer's approach. His book demonstrates how our view of hemp, which was once a very important legal crop in the United States and other countries, has been warped by the government's campaign against marijuana. And it is no doubt true that entrepreneurs would rediscover profitable, nonpsychoactive uses for the plant if legal barriers were removed.

Perhaps most important, the hemp movement has attracted interest from a lot of people—mostly young and leftish, but also libertarians, including *Orange County Register* columnist Alan Bock and some readers of this magazine. Herer's organization, HEMP (Help Eradicate Marijuana Prohibition), sets up a stand on weekends in Venice, California, touting the plant's uses and offering passers-by the opportunity to examine hemp rope and clothing. People stop and chat, and some of them sign a petition to get a marijuana legalization initiative on the ballot. Rallies and the sale of hemp products by mail also help to arouse curiosity.

Still, it would be fair to say that the hemp movement has limited appeal. What goes over in Venice does not necessarily go over in Provo—or in Washington, D.C. Kevin Zeese, vice president of the Drug Policy Foundation, praises the Hererites for getting young people involved in the fight against prohibition. But he observes: "That wing [of the movement] presents the marijuana user as a stereotype that frightens society—the long-haired hippie. It scares people."

In addition to the image problem, there's the substance of Herer's arguments. Even leaving aside the idea of a "marijuana conspiracy," Herer asks people to accept a host of claims about hemp—some clearly true, some dubious. And not only about hemp: To believe that this plant can "save the world," you have to buy (at least) the global-warming theory—as if marijuana legalization weren't controversial enough. Regardless of how truthful Herer's claims are, it's just *too much*. As Zeese puts it: "It comes across as, 'This is the wonder drug that can save the world, the environment, the trees, the fuel supply; it can heal the blind and crippled.' It really sounds like a snake-oil salesman, even though there's a lot of truth to it."

The Herer approach also seems like a ploy to distract people from the real issue. After all, hemp's main use in the United States today is not for paper or cloth or fuel. Any mildly skeptical person, upon hearing a guy with a long beard in a tie-dyed shirt talk about the wonderful versatility of the hemp plant, is going to have a pretty good idea what's *really* on his mind. The appearance of deceit only makes getting high seem all the more sinister: If there's nothing wrong with it, what are they trying to hide?

The issue of medical marijuana presents some of the same problems, but it's much harder for people to dismiss. For one thing, there is strong evidence that marijuana can relieve pain, help treat glaucoma, control nausea and vomiting, and stimulate appetite. There's also some indication that it's helpful for controlling seizures and muscle spasms. In 1988, after hearing 13 days of testimony and reviewing 18 volumes of evidence, the DEA's chief administrative law judge, Francis Young, concluded that marijuana has significant potential as a medicine and called it "one of the safest therapeutically active substances known to man." Furthermore, there is a real, potentially huge, and very sympathetic constituency for medical marijuana. Polls find that a large majority of Americans agree the drug should be available to these patients.

Most of the reformers I interviewed for this article predicted that medical marijuana would be legally available soon, perhaps within the first year of the Clinton administration. The change would not require legislation, or even direct presidential action. "I don't expect President Clinton to touch the marijuana issue, after his inhaling comments," Zeese says. But Clinton could instruct people at the DEA, HHS, and the Food and Drug Administration either to resume the federal government's medical marijuana program or to reclassify the drug so it could be available by prescription. Either way, if the new policy is for real, thousands of cancer, glaucoma, and AIDS patients could start receiving legal pot.

That prospect raises the complicated question of what connection, if any, medical marijuana has to broad legalization. Anti-pot activists such as Peggy Mann have long argued that medical marijuana is a red herring, a tactic to make the drug more acceptable and thereby promote legalization. Robert Randall, president of the Alliance for Cannabis Therapeutics, notes that, logically, marijuana could be legally available as a medicine but not as a recreational or social drug.

"We do that with almost every drug on the planet," he says. "It's illegal for you to have Valium if you don't have the scrip. So what's the big difference here?"

The big difference may be that marijuana is a lot more popular. Tens of millions of Americans smoke pot from time to time, and more might if it were easier to get or if it became more socially acceptable. Marijuana is also easier to manufacture than Valium. Still, it's wrong to argue, as Mann and the DEA do, that the drive for medical marijuana is merely a ruse. Many people want marijuana because it can help save their sight or relieve their suffering. There is a humanitarian argument for medical marijuana that is distinct from the argument for broad legalization. Nonetheless, it's clear that medical availability would affect the legalization debate.

The question is, how? Zeese, who ran NORML from 1983 to 1986, suggests medical access could hurt the drive for legalization in the same way decriminalization did: by eliminating sympathetic victims (in that case, the middle-class college kids who were going to jail for marijuana possession). "You'd be taking a lot of the steam out of the legalization movement, because you'd be putting a kinder and gentler face on the drug war," he says. "We wouldn't have those cancer patients and AIDS patients and glaucoma patients at our side as allies. We'd no longer have that compassionate argument."

Cowan offers a more optimistic scenario: Hundreds of thousands of people will be using legal pot, free to speak out about its effects without fear of repercussions. "The cat will be out of the bag," he says. "That is going to totally change the dynamics of the issue....If we get medical access, we're going to get legalization eventually. The narcocracy knows this; it's the reason they fight it so much."

Grinspoon, too, suggests that medical access would be difficult to contain. "The problems connected with that are so vast that it will not work," he says. He estimates that legal pot would retail for about $10 an ounce, much less than current black-market prices, typically $100 to $300 an ounce, depending on quality and availability. "Everybody will be going to the doctor and saying, 'Oh, I've got a backache, I've got this, I've got that.' The doctors are not going to want to be gatekeepers."

Moreover, any preparation of marijuana that was available by prescription would have to receive FDA approval. Grinspoon notes that pharmaceutical companies are not likely to pay for the expensive tests that would be necessary to meet the FDA's strict standards for efficacy, since marijuana could not be patented. In any case, he says, "why should people wait? They're suffering."

If the government didn't reclassify marijuana, Grinspoon says, it would need "an army of bureaucrats" to supervise any workable medical marijuana program. And what the bureaucracy gives, it can take away. A new administration could once again block medical access. Since availability would be based on claims about marijuana's therapeutic value, the government could always decide that new research or the development of "better" alternatives justified cutting off the legal supply. For all these reasons, Grinspoon argues that legalization is the best way to achieve medical availability, rather than the other way around.

If Grinspoon is right, it may be time to plow through the research again and dig up all those arguments from the '70s. In fact, this is what's happening in Alaska, where the challenge to recriminalization will involve rehashing the debate over marijuana's hazards. A Superior Court judge there has concluded that the 1990 anti-pot initiative can be upheld only if the drug's effects have changed significantly since 1975, when the Alaska Supreme Court ruled that the state constitution's privacy clause protects marijuana use in the home.

Putting marijuana on trial is an approach that's designed to favor the prohibitionists. It requires, if not proof of harmlessness, something very close to it. And even if the opponents of recriminalization can meet the burden of proof, the issue can always be raised again in 10 or 15 years. It is never finally settled.

Part of the problem is that most Americans do not view marijuana simply as a drug—a substance with certain bene-fits and certain hazards, one that can be used moderately or excessively, responsibly or irresponsibly. As a subject of public concern, marijuana has always been fraught with symbolism, and it has always represented something foreign to white, middle-class America: Mexicans, jazz musicians, ghetto blacks, hippies.

Decriminalization succeeded—and, despite the setbacks, it largely remains a success—because reformers were able to take the focus off the drug, with all its potent symbolism, and put the law on trial instead. But once the penalties for possession were reduced, the spotlight shifted back to marijuana's harmfulness. "A poor job was done, from the late '70s on, of framing the arguments," Cowan says. "We stayed on the defensive, allowing the debate to be focused on 'the latest research.' What we needed to do was to start telling people about the effects of the laws." If legalization is to succeed, reformers will have to

THE HEMP MOVEMENT HAS LIMITED APPEAL. IT PRESENTS THE MARIJUANA USER AS A STEREOTYPE THAT FRIGHTENS SOCIETY: THE LONG-HAIRED HIPPIE.

stress the injustice of prohibition—not just for the college kid caught with a few joints or the woman who gives pot brownies to AIDS patients, but for anyone who grows or sells marijuana. Not long ago REASON received a letter from a reader:

"I am a 42 year old male and married to a wonderful woman. We have three children who I love very much. My desperation is derived from the fact that I was taken away from my wife and children by the U.S. government and sent to prison in another state for a conviction of conspiracy to import and distribute marijuana. Although I have never been in trouble before with the law and always have been a productive, tax-paying citizen, the Government sentenced me to 25 years in prison without the possibility of parole. There was no violence or guns involved in this alleged conspiracy, and I can honestly proclaim that I have never broken any of God's Ten Commandments, but the Government has taken the rest of my life away from me. My children are ages 12, 2, and 1. I will never see or feel any of the cherished moments of their childhood, which breaks my heart. More importantly, they will grow up without a father, which hurts me more than anything."

I suspect that the average American would have little sympathy for this man. Unless that changes, marijuana will never be legal again.

HIGH ANXIETY

The most widely used tranquilizer in America is more addictive than Valium—and is often less effective than nondrug treatments for anxiety.

The woman we'll call Rachel G.—now age 31—had experienced attacks of anxiety since she was a child. But those occasional incidents did not prevent her from marrying and taking a responsible job at an East Coast biotechnology company. Then, in late 1990 and early 1991, her life took a stressful turn. There was turmoil at the lab where she worked, her mother fell seriously ill, her grandmother committed suicide, and her marriage deteriorated. In early April of 1991, after a confrontation with her boss, she had a full-blown panic attack.

"I broke into a cold sweat," she recalls. "My heart was palpitating. I swore I was having a heart attack. I was scared that I was dying . . . . I couldn't walk. I couldn't even move." The attacks went on for two days.

Rachel G. went to a psychologist for help, and simultaneously asked her regular internist for a pill to ease her suffering. Her physician prescribed *Xanax* (alprazolam). That was no surprise. In 1990, *Xanax* had become the only drug ever approved by the U.S. Food and Drug Administration for the treatment of panic disorder—repeated, intense bouts of anxiety that can make life almost unbearable.

The drug gave her some relief, but she felt it wasn't really solving her problem. After about three months on *Xanax*, she tried to cut her dose in half. Within 48 hours, she recalls, "I couldn't sleep. My heart was racing, and I was getting dizzy spells." Only going back up to an intermediate dose would suppress the withdrawal symptoms.

In February 1992, Rachel G. began having frightening thoughts of killing herself. She visited a psychiatrist, who prescribed *Tofranil* (imipramine), an antidepressant that also works against panic. Today, she is doing well, still taking imipramine—and also *Xanax*. Though she feels the *Xanax* is no longer helping her, she can't bring herself to try to quit. "I know I'm going to have to experience the withdrawal symptoms," she says, "and those are the exact symptoms that I went on it to escape from in the first place."

Rachel G.'s problem is far from unusual. *Xanax* is not only the most common treatment for panic attacks, but also the drug most often prescribed for run-of-the-mill anxiety—the kind that anyone might experience during a rough period in life. It is now the nation's largest-selling psychiatric drug; more than that, it is the fifth most frequently prescribed drug in the U. S.

Even if you've never taken *Xanax* yourself, you almost certainly know someone who has. Yet the risks are significant. Anyone who takes *Xanax* for an extended period—even as little as a few weeks—risks developing a stubborn dependency on the drug.

Xanax is just the latest in a long line of tranquilizers that have promised to deliver psychiatry's holy grail: relief from anxiety with no significant side effects. And like the pills that came before it, *Xanax* has fallen short. As psychiatrists and their patients are discovering, *Xanax* does have some serious drawbacks—even more than the drugs it was supposed to improve on.

Like the sleeping pill *Halcion* (triazolam), its closest chemical relative, *Xanax* demonstrates that no pill can deliver peace of mind without a price. It also raises a troubling question: How did such a flawed drug become a pharmacological superstar?

The selling of *Xanax* has been fueled by a vigorous promotional campaign. The drug's manufacturer, the Upjohn Co., has made *Xanax* highly visible in the medical community by promoting it as a uniquely effective drug for panic disorder. But *Xanax* does not represent a remarkable treatment advance so much as a marketing coup. In fact, it is little different from other, related tranquilizers—members of the drug fam-

For anxiety with associated depressive symptoms

Xanax

Anxious and blue? This ad suggests Xanax is especially useful for anxious people who are also depressed. While the FDA has approved this claim, many clinicians take issue with it.

ily known as benzodiazepines, which have held an uneasy place in American culture for three decades.

Beyond Valium

Though the word "benzodiazepine" is meaningless to most people, the trade names of the drugs in this family are almost as familiar as *Kleenex* or *NutraSweet*. The first drug in this category, *Librium* (chlordiazepoxide), came on the market in 1960; *Valium* (diazepam) came along three years later.

In 1979, a survey showed that 11 percent of Americans were taking antianxiety drugs, mostly benzodiazepines. The figure has dropped only slightly since then.

That was also the year the hazards of these drugs gained national attention through hearings held by Senator Edward Kennedy. As the hearings made clear, *Valium* and similar drugs caused two major problems: Physical dependency and sedation. People on benzodiazepines often found that they couldn't stop taking the drugs, and that they couldn't function well while they were on them. The drugs accumulated in the body; over time, they made the user more and more sluggish, drowsy, and forgetful.

Ironically, while the Kennedy hearings offered frightening testimony on *Valium*, they also set the stage for the arrival of its successor, *Xanax*. Introduced in 1981, *Xanax* was hailed as the first of a new chemical class

The more things change . . . A 1967 CU report on Xanax's predecessor, Valium, pointed out that it didn't work much better than an inactive placebo in soothing the symptoms of anxiety.

of benzodiazepines that were completely eliminated from the body in less than half a day. Since *Xanax* didn't accumulate, the hope was that it wouldn't make people increasingly drowsy or slow them down as they continued to take it.

In addition to this chemical advantage, *Xanax* gave Upjohn a marketing edge. The patent on *Valium* expired in 1984, just as sales of *Xanax* were beginning to build. As generic competitors undercut *Valium's* sales, the drug's manufacturer promoted it less actively, and sales of *Valium* dropped further. Upjohn took advantage of the opportunity. By 1986, *Xanax* had overtaken *Valium* as the most widely prescribed benzodiazepine. By 1987, it reached fourth place on the national sales list of all prescription drugs. And in 1991, *Xanax* accounted for almost one-fifth of Upjohn's worldwide sales.

The trouble is, *Xanax* has now turned out to be more addictive than *Valium* itself.

Stuck on Xanax

All benzodiazepines produce physical dependency if you take them long enough. Over time, it seems, the brain "learns" to expect a certain level of the drug. If the drug is removed, the brain reacts with agitation, sleeplessness, and anxiety—the symptoms that led people to take the drug in the first place. Frequently, these symptoms are worse than the original ones, a phenomenon known

as the "rebound" effect. In addition, abrupt withdrawal from the drugs can cause muscle cramps and twitches, impaired concentration, and occasionally even seizures.

Unlike people who are addicted to cocaine and heroin, users of benzodiazepines don't develop a psychological craving for the drugs, or escalate the doses they take over time. But they do have a true physical dependency, and their withdrawal symptoms make the benzodiazepines extremely difficult to kick.

A number of clinical studies have found that *Xanax* and other benzodiazepines that are eliminated rapidly from the body produce a quicker, more severe rebound effect than drugs like *Valium* that are eliminated more slowly. Some people who take *Xanax* three times a day, a standard schedule for panic disorder, find that they even have symptoms as the drug wears off between one dose and the next.

In one major study, Dr. Karl Rickels and his colleagues at the University of Pennsylvania took 47 anxious patients who had been on benzodiazepines for a year or more and tried to take them off their medication. Fully 57 percent of the patients on *Xanax* and similar drugs simply could not stop taking them—but only 27 percent of the people on drugs like *Valium* were that physically dependent.

Other studies have produced similar results. A Yale study of patients

ALL-PURPOSE PRESCRIPTIONS

WHO TAKES XANAX, AND WHY?

Xanax presents a paradox: It is a powerful psychiatric drug, but it is most often prescribed for people who have no psychiatric diagnosis at all. While many of those people may be suffering from a serious problem with anxiety that is never recorded on a diagnostic chart, others may simply be people who ask their doctors for some relief from stress.

We analyzed data from the 1990 National Ambulatory Medical Care Survey, a representative sample of doctor's visits conducted periodically by the U.S. Government. Our analysis shows that the drug is prescribed by a wide range of different kinds of doctors, for people with a wide range of conditions—a situation that increases the odds of misuse.

Xanax is usually prescribed by physicians in general practice. In the 1990 study, only 30 percent of *Xanax* prescriptions were written by psychiatrists, whereas nearly half were written by family, general, and internal-medicine practitioners. (Various other specialists wrote the rest.)

Of all *Xanax* prescriptions, only 28 percent were written for people who were diagnosed with clinical anxiety or panic attacks.

Another 21 percent were for people diagnosed with depression, a condition for which the use of *Xanax* is still controversial. The rest were generally written for people who had no diagnosed psychiatric problem at all, although they did have a variety of medical diagnoses, the most frequent being high blood pressure. The statistics are similar to those obtained in another large national survey: IMS America, a private organization that monitors drug sales, found that only about one-fourth of all benzodiazepines prescribed in 1989 were given for anxiety-related conditions.

Many of those *Xanax* prescriptions may have been written appropriately for people suffering from short-term anxiety triggered by a medical problem. But the data, combined with the huge sales volume of *Xanax*, suggest that the drug may often be prescribed as an all-purpose stress reliever. The FDA-approved package insert (which can be requested from the pharmacist) states specifically that *Xanax* should not be given simply to help people deal with the "stress of everyday life," and that the drug should be given only as a short-term treatment for clear symptoms of anxiety, or as a treatment for full-blown anxiety or panic disorders.

who had taken *Xanax* in a four-month treatment program for panic attacks found that most of those who were still using the drug two years later had shifted to a lower dose—but only 30 percent had been able to quit the drug entirely. Similarly, a study of long-term *Xanax* users done at Toronto's Addiction Research Foundation found that two-thirds had tried to stop using the drug and failed.

The experience of individual doctors underscores the problem. In 1988, researchers at the Johns Hopkins School of Medicine interviewed 31 American physicians who specialized in helping people withdraw from the benzodiazepines. Asked which drugs were especially hard for patients to give up, 84 percent of the doctors specifically mentioned *Xanax*, while only 29 percent cited *Valium*. Even under the best of circumstances, clinicians have found that, to get people off *Xanax*, they must reduce the dose in tiny steps—a process that often takes months.

An 'eraser' for the mind?

The fact that so many people try so hard to quit *Xanax*—as difficult as that is to do—shows that it is not an entirely pleasant drug to take. One woman we spoke with, a 41-year-old technical writer in San Francisco, started taking *Xanax* to deal with bouts of anxiety that made her feel "like I was going headlong toward some frightening and dangerous unknown." After taking *Xanax* for 14 months, she decided to stop because, as she puts it, "It made me too stupid. I just couldn't function professionally. People would say things to me, and I'd be in a sort of fog and not be able to respond appropriately." (She ultimately succeeded in quitting, but had to go through a very difficult withdrawal process—even though she was taking a low dose, one her psychiatrist told her would not cause dependency.)

A 1990 report by the American Psychiatric Association backs up this woman's experience. It found that the benzodiazepines tend to impair memory; a person on one of these drugs may have difficulty retaining new information.

Clinicians report the same problem. "One patient of mine, a physician who took *Xanax*, described it as 'a big eraser.' It sort of wipes out people's attention to things," says Dr. Robert J. Gladstone, a psychiatrist in Carlisle, Mass. "I think all benzodi-

azepines cause memory lapses, especially in the elderly," says Dr. Stuart Yudofsky, chairman of the Department of Psychiatry at Baylor College of Medicine in Houston.

Yudofsky also refers to evidence that the drugs impair coordination. And in his own experience, he says, patients who have used benzodiazepines for years have often suffered falls and head injuries.

Xanax can also have the paradoxical effect of causing rage and hostility rather than tranquility. While this is relatively rare, it's another reason for caution in using a drug that many people will be all but unable to quit.

Despite the risks, benzodiazepines have one clear use: They can be helpful for people in crisis who need short-term anxiety relief. "They're appropriate for what are called adjustment reactions," says Dr. Peter Tyrer, a professor of psychiatry at St. Mary's Hospital Medical School in London and a longtime benzodiazepine researcher. "For example, if someone has been in a car accident and is nervous afterward when he goes out into the street, he could take *Xanax* for a short time after that."

The problem, though, is that many people who start taking tranquilizers for the short term end up staying on them over the long haul. "For anxiety, in general, these medications tend to be used much too long and in too high doses," says Dr. Yudofsky. "People get put on a drug, the reason for taking it passes, but they're maintained on it week after week, year after year. That's misuse." Even Upjohn, in its own labeling for *Xanax*, cautions that the drug has never been established as effective for use over more than four months.

Pushing the panic button

The people most at risk for becoming dependent on *Xanax* are those with panic disorder, because they are prescribed high doses of the drug for an extended period of time to deal with their chronic panic attacks. Since they suffer from severe or disabling anxiety, they might find dependency an acceptable price to pay for effective relief. But even though Upjohn built *Xanax's* reputation on studies of people with panic attacks, it's not at all clear how much they were really helped.

A panic attack is intense anxiety in a concentrated dose. Victims with a severe case may suffer several full-scale attacks a day, during which

their hearts race and they hyperventilate, sweat, tremble, and feel a profound sense of terror. According to the largest, most thorough survey of psychiatric problems, conducted in the 1980s by the National Institute of Mental Health (NIMH), between 4 and 7 percent of Americans have panic attacks that are frequent enough to be considered a panic disorder. The majority of people with panic disorder also have a related condition, agoraphobia—a term now used to describe a fear of ordinary activities, such as driving a car or shopping at the supermarket, that can leave the sufferer housebound.

By the early 1980s, researchers had begun to recognize that at least some types of benzodiazepines, in addition to easing ordinary anxiety, could also stop panic attacks. Upjohn proceeded to spend lavishly on studies to see whether *Xanax* could be used to treat panic disorder, and enlisted highly respected consultants in the effort. "The most senior psychiatrists in the world were . . . flooded with offers of consultancies [from Upjohn]," recalls Dr. Isaac Marks, a professor of experimental psychopharmacology at the University of London's Institute of Psychiatry.

In fact, the research could just as well have been done with another benzodiazepine—one called lorazepam (*Ativan*)—that is also cleared from the body quickly, and has also been shown to stop panic attacks. But this drug has not been under patent protection for years—and since it has not had the profit potential that *Xanax* has, it has not been aggressively tested and promoted. Today, a bottle of 100 one-milligram *Xanax* tablets costs $72.55, according to the Red Book, a standard drug price guide. The same amount of generic lorazepam in a therapeutically equivalent dose costs as little as $3.75.

Upjohn's major study on panic was a two-phase project called the Cross-National Panic Study. Phase One, conducted in the U.S., Canada, and Australia, involved more than 500 subjects with severe panic attacks; half received *Xanax* and half, a look-alike placebo. Phase Two, conducted in North and South America and Europe, enrolled 1122 subjects to compare *Xanax* not only with a placebo, but also with imipramine, an antidepressant from a different chemical class that also blocks panic attacks (even though it has never received formal FDA approval for

Street abuse
Drug abusers traffic in Xanax because of an unusual property: When combined with methadone, Xanax produces a 'high' much like heroin, the drug methadone is meant to replace.

this use). At the time, the two studies were among the largest ever done on psychiatric drugs.

Well before the results were published, Upjohn used the research to promote its drug. The company sponsored conferences and symposiums on drug treatment for panic and anxiety, and then invited its consultants to speak at them—a strategy now used by many large pharmaceutical companies (see "Pushing Drugs to Doctors," CONSUMER REPORTS, February 1992). Many of those meetings were then written up in Upjohn-sponsored supplements to scientific journals, sent to thousands of psychiatrists in the U.S. and abroad.

When the Phase One results were finally published, they made a huge splash: Four articles on the study consumed the better part of the May 1988 issue of the *Archives of General Psychiatry*, the most prestigious psychiatric journal in the U.S. By that time, however, the international psychiatric community had already been hearing about *Xanax* as a treatment for panic for several years. Upjohn's publicity had made psychiatrists—and, later, general-practice physicians—more aware of *Xanax* than they were of other, similar drugs. It

HIGH NOTORIETY

HALCION AND PROZAC

Though *Xanax* is the best-selling psychiatric drug in the U.S., it's not the most notorious. Vying for that distinction are *Prozac*, a drug for depression, and *Halcion*, a benzodiazepine sold as a sleeping pill.

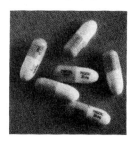

Both *Halcion* and *Prozac* have been reported to induce irrational behavior, including outbursts of murderous violence and suicide attempts. (*Halcion* was even blamed by some observers for President Bush's illness on his trip to Japan.) Lawsuits have been brought against their manufacturers, seeking damages for cases of suicide and assault committed by people taking the drugs. The accusations against both drugs prompted the U.S. Food and Drug Administration to ask expert committees to look at them more closely. Here's an update.

Prozac (fluoxetine)

Introduced in 1987 by the Eli Lilly Co., *Prozac* rocketed up the pharmaceutical bestseller list on the strength of Lilly's strenuous promotional efforts, its evident effectiveness against mild depression, and its relative absence of side effects. Overlooked in the initial enthusiasm for the drug, however, was the lack of evidence that *Prozac* worked well against *major* depression, a prolonged, serious psychiatric disorder that puts victims at high risk of suicide.

In any event, *Prozac*'s honeymoon ended three years ago, when a psychiatrist published a report on six chronically depressed patients who developed obsessive, violent suicidal thoughts after starting on the drug. The psychiatrist did emphasize that these six patients had unusually severe cases of depression; they had not responded to any other treatments, and five had had suicidal thoughts, though less severe ones, before they ever took *Prozac*. But those distinctions disappeared in the uproar that followed.

The FDA review panel, convened late in 1991, concluded that people taking *Prozac* did not seem to have any more suicidal or violent thoughts than patients on other antidepressants (though the panel recommended further monitoring of the drug, just in case). In the panel's view, the suicidal thinking some patients experienced was caused by the depression itself, not the drug.

Psychiatrists point out that patients can react "paradoxically" to almost any powerful drug, including *Prozac*, and therefore should be monitored closely—especially early in treatment, when they're getting used to the new drug. Meanwhile, *Prozac* remains the nation's best-selling antidepressant.

Halcion (triazolam)

Though marketed as a sleeping pill, not an antianxiety drug, *Halcion* is actually *Xanax*'s close chemical cousin. Like *Xanax*, *Halcion* is a benzodiazepine that's eliminated from the body very rapidly, meaning you can take it to get to sleep at night without being drowsy the next day. Upjohn started marketing *Halcion* in 1982; by 1987, the peak of its popularity, it was the 18th largest-selling prescription drug and the largest-selling sleeping pill in the U.S.

The disadvantages of *Halcion* eventually made themselves known. People who used it for any length of time found that, when they tried to stop, they experienced "rebound" insomnia worse than the original. There were also reports that *Halcion* seemed to make some people hostile or paranoid. The FDA was worried, and analyzed the thousands of voluntary reports of adverse reactions to *Halcion* the agency had received from doctors. *Halcion* indeed was linked to more hostility reactions than any other sleeping pill, relative to the numbers prescribed.

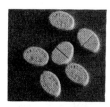

Another troublesome side effect also emerged: Some people who took even small doses experienced a bizarre reaction called anterograde amnesia. The day after they took *Halcion* to get to sleep they were up and about, apparently functioning normally. But later, they would have absolutely no memory of their actions. In 1991, *Halcion* was banned in the United Kingdom.

An FDA advisory committee decided, in May of 1992, to let *Halcion* stay on the U.S. market. But the panel agreed that the original recommended dose of 0.5 milligrams a day was too high, especially for elderly people; a lower dose of 0.25 milligrams was less likely to cause side effects (though it could also make the drug less effective). The committee also recommended strengthening the package insert's warnings on rebound insomnia and hostility reactions.

While the controversy over *Prozac* didn't seem to affect its upward sales trajectory, *Halcion*'s sales have suffered. By 1991 it had fallen to 38th place. And last November, in a widely publicized case, a Dallas jury decided *Halcion* had been partly responsible for driving a man to murder—a decision that may damage the drug's reputation even more.

almost certainly was responsible for the rapid growth of *Xanax* as a drug for all sorts of anxiety problems, not just panic disorder.

"The Cross-National Study was the best advertising ever done," says Dr. Rickels of the University of Pennsylvania. "Upjohn sold millions of doses of this drug before they even got it approved for panic."

No panacea for panic

Since receiving FDA approval to market *Xanax* for panic disorder, Upjohn has been using data from Phase One of the Cross-National Study in ads for the drug—including ads in journals for general-practice physicians. These doctors are likely to be unfamiliar with the actual results of the study, and to take Upjohn's word for what it showed. But despite the ads' claims, the study produced highly ambiguous results.

In the first four weeks of the eight-week study, *Xanax* looked much better than placebo treatment. By the fourth week, 50 percent of patients taking *Xanax* were completely free of panic attacks, versus 28 percent of those on an inactive placebo.

Many of Upjohn's ads for *Xanax* quote results from this midpoint of the study. But the drug's effectiveness was much less clear by the study's end. A look at the people who stayed in the study for the full eight weeks shows a remarkable picture: At the end of the study, there was no significant difference in the average number of panic attacks—or in functioning in work, home, and social life—between the people who had been taking *Xanax* and those who were taking placebos.

In addition, the Phase One study showed clearly how severe the "rebound" effect of *Xanax* withdrawal is. At the two study locations in Canada, 109 patients who had completed the eight weeks of treatment were observed as the dose of the drug (or placebo) was tapered down over a month's time. The *Xanax* group had averaged only 1.7 panic attacks a week—and the placebo group, 2.1 attacks a week—at the end of the eight-week treatment phase. But just two weeks after they stopped medication entirely, patients in the *Xanax* group were back up to 6.8 attacks a week—slightly worse off than they had been at the beginning of the study. By contrast, two weeks after the patients on placebo discontinued their "drug," they averaged only 1.8 panic attacks a week.

The findings are complicated by the Phase One study's greatest flaw:

About 10 percent of the people on *Xanax*, and half of those on placebo, dropped out between the fourth and the eighth week. At the time they left the study, the dropouts from the placebo group had more symptoms than people taking *Xanax*—a fact that would suggest the drug was doing some good. But many people on placebo may have been suffering from withdrawal symptoms, since many had been taking benzodiazepines just *before* they entered the study. There's also no way to tell whether they would have felt better by the end of the eight-week study if they had stuck it out, as other people in the group taking placebos did.

The findings of the Phase Two study were similar to Phase One's, except they also demonstrated that the antidepressant drug imipramine worked as well as *Xanax*. At the end of the eight weeks, 78 percent of people taking *Xanax* were panic-free, compared with 81 percent of those on imipramine and 75 percent of the people on placebo—virtually identical numbers.

Upjohn researchers and their supporters believe *Xanax* came out the clear winner in the studies. They point out that it acts much more quickly than imipramine and is easier to take. Imipramine is one of a class of antidepressants that can cause a range of unpleasant side effects, including sedation, dry mouth, severe constipation, blurred vision, weight gain, and impotence.

But other psychiatrists focus on the fact that people taking placebos did nearly as well as those on *Xanax* by the end of the study—and avoided the rebound effect that plagued people on the real drug. That suggests that for many people, the mere act of visiting a doctor might have been reassuring enough to produce a measurable decrease in symptoms. It also suggests that nondrug treatment could help many other panic sufferers learn how to control their symptoms.

The same may be true for people who have more generalized anxiety—a form of chronic, excessive worrying, combined with physical and emotional symptoms, that affects about 4 percent of Americans, according to NIMH estimates. *Xanax* itself, surprisingly, has never been tested as a long-term treatment for such chronic anxiety disorders. But Dr. David Barlow, a clinical psychologist who directs the Center for Stress and Anxiety Disorders of the State University of New York at Albany, points out that the benzodi-

azepines in general have not proved effective for treating these problems—except to offer temporary relief of symptoms.

Barlow reviewed two decades' worth of studies that used benzodiazepines to treat chronic anxiety. He observed that patients in the "control" groups for these studies—that is, patients who received inactive placebo pills—generally improved over time. In many cases, their anxiety decreased as much as that of the people who were on the real drugs. This suggests that chronic anxiety waxes and wanes over time, and that drugs may have little effect after their initial benefit.

Recommendations

If anxiety is an inevitable part of the human condition, then the wish for a magic potion to banish anxiety is probably a timeless human desire. In our own time, drug companies have marketed one tranquilizer after another, each one supposedly safer and more effective than the one before. But tranquilizers—in particular, the benzodiazepines—are still powerful, potentially dangerous drugs, subject to abuse and misuse.

Given the hazards and their widespread use, we still know surprisingly little about the risks and benefits of long-term benzodiazepine use—and too little in particular about *Xanax*, now the leader of the pack.

No one knows how many people are physically dependent on *Xanax* and how they may be affected by it. But there are some warning signs. A recent FDA analysis of reports of adverse reactions to drugs, which physicians send to the agency voluntarily, showed a number of cases in which the drug seemed to cause bouts of rage and hostility. Those side effects were rare, and were much less common with *Xanax* than with *Halcion*. But they were six times more common with *Xanax* than with *Ativan*, relative to each drug's sales. And *Ativan's* suspected side effects have been cited in a pending British class-action lawsuit against its manufacturer.

Consumers Union believes that more information is necessary to determine the frequency of side effects from *Xanax*—not only its effects on mood, but its potential for impairing memory and causing other cognitive problems. Careful surveillance of the drug's clinical use could do much to resolve these questions.

As time goes by A 1991 Upjohn ad ran the chart below showing that nearly half of Xanax patients were panic-free after four weeks of treatment, versus just one in four people on placebo. What the ad didn't show: By the eighth week, placebo patients who finished the study were panic-free almost as often as patients on Xanax were.

XANAX USUALLY BLOCKS PANIC ATTACKS WITHIN 1 WEEK
Percentage of patients free of panic attacks

WEEK 1

Placebo (n=259)	16.9%
XANAX (n=267)	33.2%

WEEK 4

Placebo (n=259)	27.1%
XANAX (n=267)	46.8%

In the meantime, if you or a loved one has a serious problem with anxiety, you need to understand your options clearly.

If you're not normally an anxious person, but are going through a particularly difficult time—a divorce or the death of a parent, for instance—you may be able to handle your anxiety with no professional help, or perhaps with a few visits to a psychotherapist to talk about the immediate stress. According to Dr. Yudofsky of Baylor, exercise, dietary changes (such as giving up caffeine), and other lifestyle changes can also help keep anxiety in check.

It can also be useful, and appropriate, to take *Xanax* or another benzodiazepine to cope with acute stress—as long as you take the drug carefully. If your doctor prescribes one of these drugs, take it at the lowest dose possible and for the shortest time possible. Remember that even a few weeks of daily *Xanax* use can lead to dependency.

If you're suffering from panic disorder, agoraphobia, or chronic anxiety, you have a serious problem that requires professional evaluation and treatment by a psychiatrist or psychologist. It's not clear, however, that drug treatment should be your first option. CU's medical consultants recommend seeing a mental-health professional who is familiar with cognitive-behavioral therapy (described below) before resorting to tranquilizers. Our consultants who have experience in both drug and nondrug therapy generally try the nondrug approaches first.

Whatever your problem is, you should avoid *Xanax* and its chemical cousins if you have any history of alcohol abuse or previous problems with other benzodiazepines. Those factors in your personal history make it more likely that you will become dependent on the drug. Alternative forms of drug therapy may be less risky. Antidepressants like imipramine can block panic attacks as effectively as *Xanax* can. For people with chronic anxiety who do not have panic attacks, a drug called *BuSpar* (buspirone) can frequently reduce anxiety and does not cause the sedation or physical dependency produced by the benzodiazepines.

Finally, if your physician does prescribe *Xanax* or another benzodiazepine, question him or her closely about how long you are expected to take the medication and exactly how you are to withdraw from it. While on the medication, use extreme caution when driving, since these drugs can impair coordination. Do not exceed the prescribed dose, and do not drink alcohol while on the drug. (The interaction can be disastrous; at the least, it can worsen the slurred speech, poor coordination, drowsiness, and mental slowness that often stem from use of benzodiazepines.) Inform your doctor immediately of any unexpected side effects, such as feelings of rage or agitation. And seriously consider trying some sort of psychotherapy to gain insight into your problem.

Long-term users Among people who use benzodiazepines for a year or more, about 70 percent are older than 50; about 60 percent are women.

SHORT-TERM PSYCHOTHERAPY

RELIEF WITHOUT DRUGS

People with serious anxiety—including those with panic attacks—don't need to choose between a life on tranquilizers and a life under severe stress. The past decade has seen the development of a new type of nondrug treatment called cognitive-behavioral therapy. While it doesn't give the immediate relief of a drug like *Xanax*, it does produce results quickly—and may be the most helpful approach over the long term.

Cognitive-behavioral therapists believe that many people, perhaps even most, have panic symptoms at one time or another—a stressful situation, for example, may trigger a racing heartbeat or rapid breathing. These symptoms usually pass quickly, and most people never give them a second thought. But a few people overreact intensely when they experience panic symptoms; they misinterpret them as symptoms of impending insanity or death.

"They tend to catastrophize their symptoms," explains Dr. Robert Liberman, who treats panic-attack patients at the UCLA Neuropsychiatric Institute. "Anyone might feel dizzy getting suddenly out of a chair. A person vulnerable to panic might exaggerate that feeling, leading to sustained feelings of panic."

Cognitive-behavioral therapy works by teaching panic victims a new way of thinking about their physical symptoms. "The therapies consciously induce panic sensations—spinning patients on a chair to get dizzy, or having them run up and down stairs to get out of breath," Liberman says. "Even when their heart is pounding, and they're short of breath and dizzy, they learn that nothing terrible happens and that these sensations naturally subside."

This technique and variations on it have been studied at a number of centers, with consistent results: After an average of a dozen weekly sessions, patients have few or no panic symptoms. More important, they maintain their improvement for a year or more.

Dr. David Barlow and his colleagues at the Center for Stress and Anxiety Disorders in Albany conducted one such study, comparing cognitive-behavioral therapy with *Xanax* and placebo over 15 weeks. The *Xanax* and behavior-therapy groups experienced roughly equivalent declines in general anxiety. But two weeks after the study ended, 87 percent of the behavior-therapy patients were completely free of panic attacks, while half of those in the *Xanax* group were still having attacks, even though almost all were still on the drug. Late in 1991, cognitive-behavioral therapy was endorsed by an expert panel convened by the National Institutes of Health to evaluate treatments for panic disorder.

Short-term therapy for depression had similarly positive results in a study conducted over the past decade by the National Institute of Mental Health. For people with mild to moderate depression, both cognitive therapy and a form of short-term treatment called interpersonal psychotherapy worked as well as drug treatment (in this case, imipramine). For patients with severe depression, drug treatment worked slightly better than either kind of therapy.

Despite the evident advantages of cognitive-behavioral therapy, it is still less accessible to most people than drug treatments. Relatively few psychologists and psychiatrists are trained in this form of therapy. Most health-insurance plans reimburse poorly for psychotherapy. And without the kind of expensive publicity that the drug companies can put behind their products, nondrug approaches have received less attention than they deserve.

Not everyone is a good candidate for cognitive-behavioral therapy. "You have to have someone who is highly motivated, and some people having prolonged and frequent panic attacks are just not able to endure the pain," says Dr. John Pecknold, a McGill University psychiatrist who participated in Upjohn's *Xanax* study.

Nevertheless, CU's medical consultants believe psychiatrists and their patients should more frequently consider this kind of short-term therapy as a treatment for anxiety and other psychological problems. These focused, effective methods entail less risk and offer better long-term results than drug therapy generally produces. They may also have the potential to be highly cost-effective. One recent study, for example, found even a single therapy session helped many people with panic attacks to overcome the problem.

Alcohol in perspective

True or false?

1. An ounce-and-a-half of 80-proof vodka or whiskey contains more alcohol than a 12-ounce can of beer.
2. A woman gets more intoxicated than a man from the same amount of alcohol.
3. Most Americans drink little or no alcohol.
4. Fatalities caused by alcohol-impaired driving are declining.
5. Measured in real dollars, the cost of alcoholic beverages has risen steadily during the last 40 years.

Answers

1. False. They contain the same amount. So does a five-ounce glass of wine.
2. True. The box on page 5 explains why.
3. True. Abstainers account for about 35% of the adult population, and light drinkers another 35%. Light drinkers, in the official definition, are those consuming two drinks a week or less. Moderate drinkers, who average one-half to two drinks a day, account for another 22%. Heavier drinkers—8% of us—consume more than two drinks a day.
4. True. The percentage of road crashes involving alcohol declined from 57% to 49% over the past decade. And the greatest decline was among teens and young adults. This is attributed to new laws setting the minimum drinking age at 21 in all states and to widespread educational efforts.
5. False. It cost less (in inflation-adjusted dollars) to drink in 1992 than it did in 1951. That's not a good thing—see below.

Double messages

Alcohol, a natural product of fermentation, is probably the most widely used of all drugs. It has been a part of human culture since history began and part of American life since Europeans settled on this continent. "The good creature of God," colonial Americans called it—as well as "demon rum." At one time, beer or whiskey may have been safer to drink than well water, but there have always been many other reasons for drinking: the sociability of drinking, the brief but vivid sense of relaxation alcohol can bring, and the wish to celebrate or participate in religious and family rituals where alcohol is served. In some cultures, abstention is the rule. In others, the occasional use of alcohol is regarded as pleasurable and necessary—but such use is carefully controlled and intoxication frowned upon. Tradition and attitude play a powerful role in the use of this drug.

Some people, unfortunately, drink because of depression and/or addiction to alcohol. Apart from such needs, powerful social and economic forces encourage people to drink. For starters, alcoholic beverages are everywhere—from planes and trains to restaurants and county fairs. Also, drink is cheap. The relative cost of alcohol has declined in the last decades. Since 1967 the cost of soft drinks and milk has quadrupled, and the cost of all consumer goods has tripled, but the cost of alcohol has not even doubled. This is because the excise tax on alcohol is not indexed to inflation. Congress has raised the federal tax on beer and wine only once in 40 years (in 1990). The tax on hard liquor has been increased only twice—small raises in 1985 and 1990. Opinion polls have shown that the public is in favor of raising federal excise taxes on alcohol, but the alcohol industry successfully fights increases. Furthermore, about 20% of all alcohol is sold for business entertainment and is thus tax deductible, making it that much less costly to whoever pays the bar bill.

Finally, the alcohol, advertising, and entertainment industries tirelessly promote the idea that it's normal, desirable, smart, sophisticated, and sexy to drink. In print, on television, and at the movies, we see beautiful, healthy people drinking. Beer ads associate the product with sports events, fast cars, camaraderie, and sex. Hollywood's stars have always imbibed plentifully, on and off camera: "Here's looking at you, kid," echoes down the ages. Among modern American male writers, alcoholism has been a badge of the trade: Hemingway, Fitzgerald, and Faulkner were all alcoholics. In *The Thirsty Muse*, literary historian Tom Dardis cites the deadly effect of alcohol on male American writers, many of whom made a credo of heavy drinking.

Considering all these pro-drinking forces, it is amazing that 35% of us over 18 never drink, and another 35% drink lightly and only occasionally. It's equally amazing that our drinking levels have been declining for the past 10 years. But it's estimated that only 8% of us consume more than half of all the alcohol. Still, out-and-out alcoholism is only one factor in the grief caused by drinking, and alcohol problems are not a simple matter of the drunk versus the rest of us.

Alcohol's toll

It's a rare person in our society whose life goes untouched by alcohol. Alcohol causes, or is associated with, over 100,000 deaths every year, often among the young. In 1990, alcohol-related traffic crashes killed more than 22,000 people—almost the same number as homicides. Half the pedestrians killed by cars have elevated blood alcohol levels. At some time in their lives, 40% of all Americans will be involved in an alcohol-related traffic crash. Alcoholism creates unhealthy family dynamics, contributing to domestic violence and child abuse. Fetal alcohol syndrome, caused by drinking during pregnancy, is the leading known cause of mental retardation. After tobacco, alcohol is the leading cause of premature death in America. The total cost of alcohol use in America has been estimated at $86 billion annually, a figure so huge as to lose its meaning. But money is a feeble method for measuring the human suffering.

In a free society, banning alcohol is neither desirable nor acceptable. But government, schools, and other institutions could do more than they do to protect the public health, teach the young about the dangers of alcohol, and treat alcoholics. As individuals and as citizens, we could all contribute to reducing the toll alcohol exacts on American life.

Alcohol and the body: short-term effects

Five ounces of wine, 12 ounces of beer, and 1.5 ounces of 80-proof spirits—all average servings—put the same amount of pure alcohol (about 1/2 to 2/3 ounce) into the bloodstream. But how fast it gets into the blood depends on many things. Some alcohol is absorbed through the stomach lining, enabling it to reach the bloodstream very quickly. If the stomach is empty, absorption is even faster: food slows it down. Aspirin in the stomach can hasten alcohol absorption. Since the alcohol in beer and wine is less concentrated, it tends to be absorbed more slowly than straight whiskey (and presumably you drink beer and wine more slowly than a shot of whiskey). But downing two beers in an hour raises blood alcohol concentration (BAC) more than one drink of whisky sipped for an hour. It's the alcohol that counts. A BAC of 0.10 is defined as legal intoxication in most states (0.08 in California, Maine, Oregon, Utah, and Vermont). It's hard to predict BAC accurately, since so many factors affect it. But a 150-pound man typically reaches a BAC of 0.10 if he has two or three beers in an hour. Any BAC impairs driving ability.

It takes the body about two hours to burn half an ounce of pure alcohol (the amount in about one drink) in the bloodstream. Once the alcohol is there, you can't hurry up the process of metabolizing it. You can't run it off, swim it off, or erase the effects with coffee. Leaner, larger people will be less affected by a given amount of alcohol than smaller ones with more fatty tissue—women, for instance. The effects of a given BAC are also greater in older people than in younger.

Every cell in the body can absorb alcohol from the blood. Of the short-term effects, none is more dramatic than those on the central nervous system. At first the drinker gets a feeling of ease and exhilaration, usually short-lived. But as BAC rises, judgment, memory, and sensory perception are all progressively impaired. Thoughts become jumbled; concentration and insight are dulled. Depression usually sets in. Some people get angry or violent. Alcohol induces drowsiness but at the same time disrupts normal patterns of sleeping and dreaming. It also adversely affects sexual performance.

The most unpleasant physical after-effect of too much alco-

Different for a woman

The alcohol industry has tried for some time to hitch a ride on women's quest for equality. Liquor ads promote the idea that if a woman can work like a man, she can, and indeed should, drink like a man. Nothing could be further from the truth.

Today 55% of women drink alcoholic beverages, and 3% of all women consume more than two drinks a day. But the ads don't tell a woman that she'll get more intoxicated than a man from the same amount of alcohol. Alcohol is distributed through body water, and is more soluble in water than in fat. Since women tend to be smaller than men and have proportionately more fatty tissue and less body water than men, the blood alcohol concentration resulting from a given intake will be higher for a woman than for a man of the same size. Recent research also shows that the stomach enzyme that breaks down alcohol before it reaches the bloodstream is less active in women than in men.

This may explain why excessive drinking seems to have more serious long-term consequences for women. They develop cirrhosis (liver disease) at lower levels of alcohol intake than men, for instance, and alcohol also puts them at increased risk for osteoporosis.

Finally, pregnant women who drink heavily risk having babies with fetal alcohol syndrome—characterized by mental retardation, structural defects of the face and limbs, hyperactivity, and heart defects. Because no level of alcohol consumption during pregnancy is known to be safe, pregnant women (as well as women planning pregnancy or having unprotected intercourse) are advised not to drink and to continue to abstain while breastfeeding. The amount of alcohol that passes into breast milk is smaller than the amount that crosses the placenta during pregnancy, but recent studies suggest that even a small amount can inhibit motor development in an infant. The idea that drinking beer promotes milk supply and benefits the baby is a myth.

hol is a hangover: dry mouth, sour stomach, headache, depression, and fatigue. Its cause is over-indulgence—not, as some believe, "mixing" drinks or drinking "cheap booze." No remedy has ever been found for hangovers.

The heart effect: worth drinking for?

Much recent research shows that moderate drinkers have a lower risk of developing heart disease. Supposedly, this beneficial effect comes from alcohol's ability to raise HDL cholesterol, the "good" type that protects against atherosclerosis. Some researchers have suggested that only one kind of beverage—for example, red wine—is protective. But it's more likely to be alcohol itself. Still, it's only moderate drinking that's helpful, and some people can't stick to moderation, while others (pregnant women) shouldn't drink at all. Few doctors suggest that nondrinkers begin drinking to protect their hearts.

Heavy drinking: long-term effects

Chronic, excessive use of alcohol can seriously damage nearly every organ and function of the body. When alcohol is burned in the body it produces another, even more toxic substance, acetaldehyde, which contributes to the damage. Alcohol is a stomach irritant. It adversely affects the way the small intestine transports and absorbs nutrients, especially vitamins and minerals. Added to the usually poor diet of heavy drinkers, this often results in severe malnutrition. Furthermore, alcohol can produce pancreatic disorders. It causes fatty deposits to accumulate in the liver. Cirrhosis of the liver, an often fatal illness, may be the ultimate result. Though alcohol is not a food, it does have calories and can contribute to obesity.

The effects of heavy drinking on the cardiovascular system are no less horrific. For many years doctors have observed that hypertension and excessive alcohol use go together, and according to a number of recent studies, heavy drinkers are more likely to have high blood pressure than teetotalers. Heavy alcohol consumption damages healthy heart muscle and puts extra strain on already damaged heart muscle. And it can damage other muscles besides the heart.

Some of the worst effects of alcohol are directly on the brain. The most life-threatening is an acute condition leading to psychosis, confusion, or unconsciousness. Heavy drinkers also tend to be heavy smokers and are also more likely to take and abuse other drugs, such as tranquilizers. Excessive drinking, particularly in combination with tobacco, increases the chance of cancers of the mouth, larynx, and throat. Alcohol appears to play a role in stomach, colorectal, and esophageal cancers, as well as possibly liver cancer.

What causes alcoholism?

Alcoholism is a complex disorder: the official definition, recently devised by a 23-member committee of experts, is "a primary, chronic disease with genetic, psychosocial, and environmental factors influencing its development and manifestations. The disease is often progressive and fatal. It is characterized by impaired control over drinking, preoccupation with the drug alcohol, use of alcohol despite adverse consequences, and distortions in thinking, most notably denial."

Alcohol use, by itself, is not sufficient to cause alcoholism. Medical science cannot yet explain why one person abstains or drinks rarely, while another drinks to excess—or why some heavy drinkers are able to stop drinking, while others continue until they die of cirrhosis. One area currently under intensive investigation is heredity. Are children of heavy drinkers more likely to fall victim to alcohol than others?

The answer is yes, but not just because these children were raised in an adverse environment. Studies have shown that, even when raised in nonalcoholic households, a significant number of children of alcoholic parents become alcoholics. This suggests that the ability to handle alcohol may be in part genetically determined. Not long ago, researchers claimed to have located an alcoholism gene, setting off a bitter controversy and raising the possibility of testing children, job applicants, and even fetuses for latent alcoholism. But if there are alcoholism genes, they remain to be identified, and a test for potential alcoholism is a long way off. Researchers point to differences in blood enzymes among alcoholics and non-users—but do not know whether the difference is responsible for the alcoholism or the result of it. Perhaps the chemistry of the body will prove to be the key to whether a person can drink moderately or not. Though most investigators believe that alcoholism has genetic, as well as environmental, causes, this does not mean that any individual is "doomed" to be an alcoholic. Alcoholic parents don't always produce alcoholic children. And many alcoholics come from families where no one ever drank.

Alcoholism is treatable

One problem in treating alcoholism is that it is hard to recognize. A person who is chronically drunk in public is obviously an alcoholic. But not all alcoholics display their problem by falling down in the street, losing their jobs, causing traffic crashes, or getting arrested. Many drink secretly or only on weekends, only in the evening, or even only once a month. Some may drink from depression, while others are sensation-seekers. They may successfully hold down a job or practice a profession. Yet at some point, whatever their drinking patterns, they have lost their ability to control their use of alcohol.

Many of the serious physical and personal consequences of alcoholism can be halted or reversed if drinking is discontinued soon enough. There are many different approaches to alcoholism: Alcoholics Anonymous and similar 12-step programs, individual or group psychotherapy, hospitalization and detoxification, and other methods. No single system will work for everyone. For some people, a combination of methods can help. Others may do as well with individual counseling. Family therapy may help others. The families of alcoholics also need therapy and other forms of social support. Scientific data about treatment are inconclusive. The crucial factor, most experts agree, is for the drinker to recognize that a problem exists and to seek the kind of treatment he or she needs.

The Drug Scene's New

"ICE" AGE

More potent than crack cocaine and easy to synthesize from commercially available chemicals, ice is becoming the latest scourge to hit America.

Dominick A. Labianca

Dr. Labianca is professor of chemistry, Brooklyn College of The City University of New York.

"ICE" is a purified form of crystalline methamphetamine hydrochloride, whose biologically active ingredient is the drug's methamphetamine component, the name reflecting the transparent, icelike crystals that characterize it. Methamphetamine, a central nervous system stimulant similar in its physiological actions to cocaine, is not new to the illicit drug scene; its current, potent form is, however. A "48 Hours" special telecast on May 4, 1989, that referred to ice as "crystal," confirmed these points. At the beginning of the program, titled "Crystal U.S.A.," host Dan Rather described the formidable character of this drug: "If you haven't run into crystal, chances are you will. . . . Back in the '60s, it was called speed, but today it's . . . a high octane version that brings with it a cruel addiction and a police blotter full of trouble."

In Hawaii—where, in 1987, ice smoking may have made its initial American appearance—Rather's chilling assessment of the devastating effects of methamphetamine intake essentially was common knowledge among police and medical personnel when "48 Hours" aired. In 1989, for example, Honolulu's police chief, Douglas Gibb, already had noted that instances of methamphetamine overdose were being observed with alarming frequency by the medical community. Furthermore, the problem has the potential to take on the epidemic proportions currently associated with crack usage because, unlike the cocaine precursor to crack that must be imported from Latin America, ice easily can be prepared in this country from readily available chemicals.

The menacing nature of methamphetamine is attributable to the fact that its hydrochloride salt easily can be vaporized. Therefore, ice—like crack cocaine—is smokable. This method of intake guarantees a considerably more rapid and efficient delivery to the user's brain than oral ingestion and is comparable to intravenous administration of the drug. Smoking eliminates the need for the hypodermic needles that constitute an obvious hazard in this age of AIDS.

The "high" that's induced by methamphetamine is similar to that of cocaine, but, in contrast to the latter, which lasts for minutes, it endures for hours. To the user, this is indeed a luxury and was emphasized rather nonchalantly and in typical salesman-like fashion by an illicit manufacturer of the drug, as quoted in *Time* (Apr. 24, 1989), who bragged that, "Dollar for dollar [ice] is better than coke; coke is just a little sexier, but [ice] goes eight times as far." No wonder, then, that ice was termed the "poor man's cocaine" by San Diego police officer Manny Hernandez, whose numerous arrests involving methamphetamine usage led to his interview on "48 Hours."

The inherent chemical makeup of methamphetamine allows it to exist in two forms that, on the molecular level, are mirror images of each other. One of these is substantially more potent. The difference in biological effectiveness between these forms best can be understood if they are thought of in terms of the obvious difference between a person's left and right hands. Since each hand is the non-superimposable mirror image of the other, it can not fit into a glove intended for the other. Moreover, the left hand of a right-handed individual is considerably less effective than the right hand, and vice versa. In a similar fashion, one of the two mirror-image forms of methamphetamine is considerably more potent than the other, and it is this more biologically active form that is known as ice. Its potency stems from its better fit—compared to its less active partner—into the appropriate components of the central nervous system that are structured to respond to such stimulants.

Ice's degree of purity depends on the synthetic route used to produce it. One approach results in the production of the 50/50 mixture of the two mirror-image forms of methamphetamine that constituted the speed of the 1960s. The physiological response elicited by such a mixture should not be underestimated, as can be gleaned from its detrimental effects on the "speed freaks" of that era. Nevertheless, speed can not induce the high produced by ice, even if taken intravenously, for a given weight of speed would contain only half the more potent form of methamphetamine found in the same weight of a pure sample of ice. Furthermore, if speed is taken orally, it becomes even less effective, compared to the inhalation of ice vapor. The oral route necessarily would expose the ingested drug to the liver before it could affect the brain and also would delay its absorption into the general circulation if food simultaneously was present in the stomach. These factors further would reduce the level of the more active form of methamphetamine that would reach the brain.

A far more effective synthetic approach to the production of methamphetamine, from the viewpoint of both the drug abuser and the illicit drug manufacturer, has superseded the method previously used to prepare speed. The more current route, as pointed out by UCLA pharmacologist Arthur Cho in *Science* magazine (Aug. 10, 1990), is a facile chemical transformation that utilizes a major participant called ephedrine and results in the formation of very pure samples of ice. The form of ephedrine critical to the success of this synthetic route is a commercially available chemical that has legitimate application as a bronchodilator and decongestant. Thus, ephedrine normally is used in the treatment of patients with asthma and nasal congestion. In fact, it is a key ingredient of the popular, over-the-counter Vicks' NyQuil Nighttime Colds Medicine. It is not too surprising, therefore, that ephedrine is one of the select chemicals currently regulated by the Chemical Diversion and Trafficking Act, which is part of the Antidrug Abuse Act of 1988. Accordingly, distributors of ephedrine must monitor sales of this chemical and are required to inform law enforcement authorities of any sales that are deemed suspicious.

One of the factors that determines the degree of effectiveness of a particular drug, whether used legally or illicitly, is the period of time that it persists in the blood. This factor necessarily governs prescribed dosage levels when a particular drug is used legitimately, for the longer it remains in the blood, the greater the extent of its physiological impact. The standard measure of this time factor is the drug's half-life, which reflects the time that must elapse before half of a given quantity that enters the bloodstream loses its activity via metabolic transformation. Compared to cocaine, whose half-life is approximately 12 minutes, methamphetamine's is about 60 times longer—or 12 hours. This substantial time difference stems from significant differences in the chemical makeup of these two drugs. Whereas cocaine is transformed rapidly in the bloodstream to biologically inactive metabolites, the molecular structure of methamphetamine is not conducive to this type of transformation. A large portion of any ingested dose of methamphetamine is excreted from the body unchanged, and those quantities of metabolites that eventually do form also are biologically active.

Repeated intake of ice, therefore, is accompanied by a substantial accumulation of methamphetamine in the body. While this ensures the prolonged high that has made ice such an attractive drug of abuse, it also poses a serious threat to the user's health.

The form of methamphetamine that comprises ice also is marketed as a legitimate therapeutic agent under the brand name Desoxyn. This drug is prescribed for oral intake to treat obesity and, in this capacity, is classified as an "anorectic" or "anorexigenic." Its usage as an appetite suppressant, however, must be regulated carefully by physicians, in accord with the following warning that appears in the *Physicians' Desk Reference* (PDR): "Methamphetamine has a high potential for abuse. It should thus be tried only in weight reduction programs for patients in whom alternative therapy has been ineffective. Administration of methamphetamine for prolonged periods of time in obesity may lead to drug dependence and must be avoided. Particular attention should be paid to the possibility of subjects obtaining methamphetamine for non-therapeutic use or distribution to others, and the drug should be prescribed or dispensed sparingly."

Desoxyn also is used to treat hyperactivity in children. The condition formally is designated "attention deficit disorder with hyperactivity," and the PDR specifies that oral treatment with this drug be restricted to children six years of age or older having "a behavioral syndrome characterized by moderate to severe distractibility, short attention span, hyperactivity, emotional lability and impulsivity." As with the treatment of obesity, careful monitoring of hyperactive children receiving Desoxyn therapy is warranted.

The PDR is quite explicit in its description of the symptoms of oral methamphetamine overdosage. These characterize ice smokers as well, although they undoubtedly are more pronounced among such individuals, given that the mode of intake associated with their use of the drug results in a more enhanced detrimental effect on the central nervous system. Typical among these symptoms are restlessness, tremor, rapid respiration, confusion, violent behavior, hallucinations, and panic. Since methamphetamine abuse is accompanied by an increase in tolerance to it, the regular user is likely to indulge in prolonged periods of drug intake. At the conclusion of these periods, the user is very tired and craves sleep, which can last for more than 24 hours. This does not reduce the craving for methamphetamine, however, as the fatigue and depression that follow sleep generally trigger the need for additional stimulation of the central nervous system. Thus, another bout of intake usually begins. This dangerous cycle can lead to fatal over-

dosage, or, at the very least, to a toxic psychosis that the PDR describes as "clinically indistinguishable from schizophrenia."

Parents, in particular, should be aware of the symptoms of methamphetamine abuse, as this drug is becoming increasingly popular among teenage drug users. Charles Carroll, whose firm, ASET Corporation, conducts undercover drug investigations, described for the New York *Daily News* (Dec. 19, 1989) the telltale symptoms that parents should recognize: "Look for dilated pupils, extreme talkativeness and short attention spans. Later, you'll see paranoia and wide mood swings." He stressed that *all* forms of methamphetamine—"not just the smokable version [ice] that the media have been publicizing"—are cause for concern. He added, "People are being real creative with the drug. They're putting it in coffee and food [which prolongs the effects, but also diminishes their impact, as noted previously], as well as snorting, smoking and shooting it." Carroll did not mention two additional points, although he probably was aware of them: Smoking ice, like cigarette smoking, damages the lungs and pulmonary arteries; and babies of women who smoke ice are likely to be born addicted and seriously ill. These additional damaging effects of ice are matters of concern among the parents of teenagers and also should serve to discourage adults who might consider flirting with ice smoking.

Impact on society

One of the more serious consequences of methamphetamine abuse is the violence it engenders. Tom Street, a homicide detective in the San Diego County Sheriff's Department who was interviewed by the "48 Hours" staff in 1989, concluded that 35% of the murders in San Diego County at the time could be attributed to methamphetamine and that no "other drug [could] make that claim." CBS News correspondent David Dow, in commenting on Street's disturbing assessment of the methamphetamine problem, emphasized the "violent trail of San Diego's methamphetamine epidemic." The spread of this epidemic and the contribution of the profit motive toward fueling it were summarized by another San Diego police officer in his description of an illicit, methamphetamine-producing laboratory that had been seized by undercover narcotic agents in "a sedate city neighborhood": "We have worries about houses blowing up, safety of the neighborhood, the contamination factor of undiscovered labs being in homes where people may later be exposed to hazardous chemicals. Plus, methamphetamine itself physiologically makes these violators very paranoid. They're normally very heavily armed. This lab could produce eight to 10 pounds of methamphetamine every three days. Retail, the street value of each pound of methamphetamine is $170,000, so 10 pounds is $1,700,000 every three days. It's a significant amount of money.. . . We're seeing labs in Oklahoma, in Texas, Nevada. It's spreading.''

In fact, the insidious allure of the ice high, the profits to be made from the manufacture and sale of the drug, and the accompanying violence are spreading rapidly beyond the West and Southwest and are becoming matters of nationwide concern. There also is the potential threat to innocent bystanders, stemming not only from the violence common to illicit drug transactions and the inherent dangers of clandestine neighborhood laboratories, but from methamphetamine users whose work-related activities affect significant segments of the general population. Specifically, truckers are known to use methamphetamine. Lori Woods, who patrols the highways of California's farm belt as a member of ''Snow Trucking,'' an undercover unit of the California Department of Narcotic Enforcement, was unable to provide ''48 Hours'' viewers with an estimate of the number of truckers who regularly use the drug, but stressed that ''The thought of driving down the highway next to [a trucker] who might be loaded is a terrifying thought.'' She added, ''I know that there were 560,000 traffic accidents in California [in 1988] and about 40,000 were truckers.''

Also terrifying is the thought that people in positions of responsibility, such as airline pilots and physicians, could take up smoking ice. This is not an unlikely scenario, as similar instances involving abuse of cocaine were documented in the 1980s. For example, Miami Beach physician Jules Trop detailed for *Time* (Apr. 11, 1983) the extent to which his addiction to cocaine-smoking, which ultimately reached a $2,000-a-day habit, nearly destroyed his professional and personal lives. *Time* (March 17, 1986) also reported on the case of a pilot for a major airline who called a New Jersey-based cocaine hotline in 1984, shortly before he was scheduled to fly a passenger jet to Europe. He had been on a three-day cocaine-snorting binge and admitted to feeling exhausted and paranoid. The pilot claimed, however, that he would be in sufficient control to meet his professional responsibilities and that ''he could stay awake and alert if he just kept taking drugs.'' The counselor to whom he spoke, and who emphasized that such calls were not unusual, frantically urged him to ''call in sick and get some sleep,'' but never was able to determine if the pilot had taken the advice.

Cases such as these are not likely to disappear, as cocaine usage is not expected to cease. The concern among drug experts and government officials, however, is that similar cases are bound to occur with methamphetamine as its abuse continues to expand. This obviously will compound an existing social problem, since methamphetamine and cocaine are essentially equivalent both in addictive character and ability to induce paranoid and psychotic behavior. Pharmacologists Avram Goldstein and Harold Kalant reported in *Science* (Sept. 28, 1990) that—compared to drugs such as alcohol, caffeine, marijuana, nicotine, various opiates, and hallucinogens such as LSD and PCP—cocaine and methamphetamine rate higher on a five-point scale assessing relative risk of addiction. These drugs possess a rating of one, which reflects the most severe risk. Should cocaine become scarce as the U.S. continues its efforts to stem the tide of incoming supplies, methamphetamine would be expected to become its likely successor as the stimulant of choice among users.

As with all types of substance abuse, there are no easy solutions to the methamphetamine problem. The consensus of opinion among various experts, however, is that, while law enforcement authorities must continue their war on drugs and research into the physiological nature of addiction must proceed, the only sure way to achieve any semblance of control over the situation is to increase, and to maintain, the emphasis on treating the underlying causes of usage. Elliot Currie, a sociologist at the University of California, Berkeley, made this point rather emphatically in 1989, when he testified at a hearing on the methamphetamine problem convened by Rep. Charles Rangel (D.-N.Y.), chairman of the House Select Committee on Narcotics Abuse and Control: ''As long as we continue to create, and to exacerbate, the social conditions that encourage serious drug abuse in whatever community in America —white, black, Hispanic—there will be little difficulty in producing attractive chemicals to fill the resulting demand.''

Ice currently is one of those attractive chemicals, and its complete elimination from the drug scene is as unlikely as getting rid of cocaine, heroin, or marijuana. In the final analysis, the only real hope for a society that aspires to remain substantially drug-free lies in continued emphasis on identifying and correcting the social ills that Currie alluded to and on expanding the role of drug-prevention education in our schools.

PUMPED UP

With the goal of being bigger, stronger and faster, many American teenagers are playing a risky game of chemical roulette. Their credo:
Die young die strong

It's a dangerous combination of culture and chemistry. Inspired by cinematic images of the Terminator and Rambo and the pumped-up paychecks of athletic heroes with stunning physiques and awesome strength, teenagers across America are pursuing dreams of brawn through a pharmacopeia of pills, powders, oils and serums that are readily available—but often damaging. Despite the warnings of such fallen stars as Lyle Alzado, the former football player who died two weeks ago of a rare brain cancer he attributed to steroid use, a *U.S. News* investigation has found a vast teenage subculture driven by an obsession with size and bodybuilding drugs. Consider:

■ An estimated 1 million Americans, half of them adolescents, use black-market steroids. Countless others are choosing from among more than 100 other substances, legal and illegal, touted as physique boosters and performance enhancers.

■ Over half the teens who use steroids start before age 16, sometimes with the encouragement of their parents. In one study, 7 percent said they first took "juice" by age 10.

■ Many of the 6 to 12 percent of boys who use steroids want to be sports champions, but over one third aren't even on a high-school team. The typical user is middle-class and white.

■ Fifty-seven percent of teen users say they were influenced by the dozen or so muscle magazines that today reach a readership of at least 7 million; 42 percent said they were swayed by famous athletes who they were convinced took steroids.

■ The black-market network for performance enhancers is enormous, topping $400 million in the sale of steroids alone, according to the U.S. Drug Enforcement Administration. Government officials estimate that there are some 10,000 outlets for the drugs—mostly contacts made at local gyms—and mail-order forms from Europe, Canada and Mexico can be found anywhere teenagers hang out.

■ The nation's steroid experts signaled the state of alarm when they convened in April in Kansas City to plan the first nationwide education effort.

■ Even Arnold Schwarzenegger, who has previously been reluctant to comment on his own early steroid use, has been prompted to speak out vigorously about the problem. The bodybuilder and movie star is the chairman of the President's Council on Physical Fitness and Sports (see 'Steroids don't pay off').

Performance drugs have an ancient history. Greek Olympians used strychnine and hallucinogenic mushrooms to psych up for an event. In 1886, a French cyclist was the first athlete know to die from performance drugs—a mixture of cocaine and heroin called "speedballs." In the 1920s, physicians inserted slices of monkey testicles into male athletes to boost vitality, and in the '30s, Hitler allegedly administered the hormone testosterone to himself and his troops to increase aggressiveness.

The use of anabolic steroids by weight lifters in the Eastern bloc dates back at least to the 1950s, and the practice has been spreading ever since among the world's elite athletes. But recent sensations in the sports world—Ben Johnson's record-shattering sprints at the Seoul Olympics and the signing of Brian Bosworth to the largest National Football League rookie contract ever *after* he tested positive for steroids—have attracted both young adults and kids to performance enhancers like never before, say leading steroid experts. These synthetic heroes are revered rather than disparaged in amateur gyms around the country, where wannabe Schwarzeneggers rationalize away health risks associated with performance-enhancing drugs.

Weighing in. The risks are considerable. Steroids are derivatives of the male hormone testosterone, and although they have legitimate medical uses—treatment of some cancers, for example—young bodybuilders who use them to promote tissue growth and endure arduous workouts routinely flood their bodies with 100 times the testosterone they produce naturally. The massive doses, medical experts say, affect not only the muscles but also the sex organs and nervous system, including the brain. "Even a brief period of abuse could have lasting effects on a child whose body and brain chemistry are still developing," warns Neil Carolan, who directs chemical dependency programs at BryLin Hospitals in Buffalo and has counseled over 200 steroid users.

Male users—by far the majority—can suffer severe acne, early balding, yellowing of the skin and eyes, development of female-type breasts and shrinking of the testicles. (In young boys, steroids can have the opposite effect of painfully enlarging the sex organs.) In females, the voice deepens permanently, breasts shrink, periods become irregular, the clitoris swells and hair is lost from the head but grows on the face and body. Teen users also risk stunting their growth, since steroids can cause bone growth plates to seal. One 13-year-old who had taken steroids for two years stopped growing at 5 feet. "I get side effects," says another teen who has used steroids for three years. "But I don't mind; it lets me know the stuff is working."

In addition to its physical dangers, steroid use can lead to a vicious cycle of dependency. Users commonly take the drugs in "cycles" that last from four to 18 weeks, followed by a lengthy break. But during "off" times, users typically shrink up, a phenomenon so abhorrent to those obsessed with size that many panic, turning back to the drugs in even larger doses. Most users "stack" the drugs, taking a combination of three to five pills and injectables at once; some report taking as many as 14 drugs simultaneously. Among the most commonly used are Dianabol ("D-Ball"), Anavar and Winstrol-V, the same type of steroid Ben Johnson tested positive for in 1988. "You wouldn't believe how much some guys go nuts on the stuff," says one teen bodybuilder from the Northeast. "They turn into walking, talking pharmacies."

Despite massive weight gains and sharply chiseled muscles, many steroid users are never quite happy with their physiques—a condition some researchers have labeled "reverse anorexia." "I've seen a kid gain 100 pounds in 14 months and not be satisfied with himself," reports Carolan. If users try to stop, they can fall into deep depressions, and they commonly turn to recreational drugs to lift their spirits. Even during a steroid cycle, many users report frequent use of alcohol and marijuana to mellow out. "I tend to get really depressed when I go off a cycle," says one Maryland teen, just out of high school. "On a bad day, I think 'Gee, if I were on the stuff this wouldn't be happening.' "

"Juicers" often enjoy a feeling of invincibility and euphoria. But along with the "pump" can come irritability and a sudden urge to fight. So common are these uncontrolled bursts of anger that they have a name in the steroid culture: "roid rages." The aggression can grow to pathological proportions; in a study by Harvard researchers, one eighth of steroid users suffered from "bodybuilder's psychosis," displaying such signs of mental illness as delusions and paranoia. So many steroid abusers are ending up behind bars for violent vandalism, assault and even murder that defense attorneys in several states now call on steroid experts to testify about the drugs' effects.

What steroids do in the long run is still unknown, largely because not one federal dollar has been spent on long-term studies. Although Lyle Alzado was convinced that steroids caused his brain cancer, for example, there is no medical evidence to prove or disprove the link. But physicians are concerned about occasional reports of users falling ill with liver and kidney problems or dropping dead at a young age from heart attacks or strokes. Douglas McKeag, a sports physician at Michigan State University, is compiling a registry of steroid-related illnesses and deaths to fill the gaping hole in medical

A roid dictionary

RIPPED: Refers to the sheer size of a bodybuilder's muscles.

CUT OR CHISELED: Clear muscular definition, another goal.

PINS, DARTS, POINTS: The hypodermic needles used to shoot steroids deep into the muscles.

SHOTGUNNING: Consuming any and every steroid available.

JOY RIDER: One who takes steroids not for athletic performance but just to achieve the ripped and cut look.

BLANKS: The 30 to 50 percent of black-market drugs that turn out to be ineffective fakes.

DESIGNER STEROIDS: Steroids manufactured in foreign or underground labs exclusively for the black market.

ROIDED OUT: Physically and mentally burned out from excessive steroid use.

knowledge. McKeag sees preliminary evidence that steroid use might cause problems with blood-cell function that could lead to embolisms in the heart or lungs. "If that turns out to be true," he says, "then bingo—we'll have something deadly to warn kids about."

Dianabol desperadoes. Unfortunately even that sort of documented health threat is unlikely to sway committed members of the steroid subculture. One widely shared value among users is a profound distrust of the medical community. Their suspicion is not totally unjustified. When steroid use was first becoming popular in the late 1950s, the medical community's response was to claim that they didn't enhance athletic ability—a claim that bulked-up users knew to be false. When that failed to deter users, physicians turned to scare tactics, branding steroids "killer drugs," again without hard evidence to back up the claim. As a result, self-styled "anabolic outlaws" and "Dianabol desperadoes" have sought guidance not from doctors but from the "Underground Steroid Handbook," a widely distributed paperback with detailed instructions for the use of more than 80 performance enhancers. "I know that proper steroid therapy can enhance your health; it has enhanced mine," writes author Daniel Duchaine. "Do you believe someone just because he has an M.D. or Ph.D. stuck onto the end of his name?" Or kids simply make up their own guidelines. "If you take more kinds at once, you get a bigger effect, and it's less dangerous because you're taking less of each kind," reasons one 18-year-old football player who has been taking steroids for two years.

"It's a whole different ballgame today, what some people are taking. When I hear about the dosages, I almost can't believe what I'm hearing. . . . It's like russian roulette."

Arnold Schwarzenegger

Although even the steroid handbook mentions health risks particular to children and adolescents, in the end most young users seem unfazed by the hazards. In one poll, 82 percent said they didn't believe that steroids were harming them much, and even more striking, 40 percent said they wouldn't stop in any case. Their motto: "Die young, die strong, Dianabol."

The main drawback to steroids, users complain, is that many brands must be administered with huge syringes. The deeper the needle penetrates the muscle, the less juice squandered just under the skin. Inserting the 1½-inch needles into their buttocks or thighs leaves many teens squeamish, and they often rely on trusted friends to do the job. "The first time I tried to inject myself, I almost fainted, and one of my friends did faint," remembers a 19-year-old from Arizona. "Sometimes one of the guys will inject in one side of his butt one day and the other the next. Then, we all laugh at him because he can barely sit down for the next three days."

Local "hard core" gyms, patronized by serious weight lifters, are the social centers of the steroid culture. Teenagers caught up in the body-building craze—typically white, middle-class suburbanites—commonly spend at least three hours a day almost every day of the week there, sometimes working out in the morning before school and again after school is out. Here they often meet 20-to-30-year-old men using steroids to bulk up for power lifting and bodybuilding shows or members of what steroid experts call the "fighting elite"—firefighters, bouncers, even policemen—synthetically boosting the physical strength they need to do their jobs. "Our role model is this older guy, the biggest guy at the gym," says one 17-year-old. "He's not a nice guy, but he weighs 290 pounds without an ounce of fat . . . that's our goal."

The older steroid veterans not only inspire kids to try the drugs but often act as the youngsters' main source for the chemicals. Sometimes, it's the gym owner who leads kids to a stash of steroids hidden in a back room; sometimes, it's a lifter who keeps the drugs in a dresser drawer at home and slips kids his phone number. Once in a while, it's a doctor or veterinarian who writes out endless prescriptions for the boys or for an unscrupulous coach. And too often, it's overzealous parents who push the drugs on their children. "My stepdad says he's going to start me up on steroids as soon as I'm done growing," says one freshman who wants to play pro football, "But I think he's just joking." Greg Gaa, director of a Peoria, Ill., sports-medicine clinic, says he has gotten calls from up to a dozen parents a year who want him to supply illegal performance enhancers to their children.

A vast black market across America guarantees kids ready access to steroids in big cities and small towns alike. Typically, the drugs are shipped via private couriers from sources in other countries. Two order forms obtained by *U.S. News* require a minimum order of $75, offer 14 different steroids (ranging from $15 to $120 per bottle) and promise 48-hour delivery for an extra $20. Though the order forms, sent out six months apart, are identical and obviously the work of the same operation, the company name and address have been changed, apparently to outsmart investigators. In the earlier mailing, it's Mass Machine, located in Toronto. In the later form, it's Gym Tek Training, located in New Brunswick, Canada. Jack Hook, with the U.S. Drug Enforcement Administration in San Diego, describes a sting operation in which undercover agents from the DEA and the California Bureau of Narcotics posing as bodybuilders met up with a European gym owner and ordered $312,000 worth of steroids; the seller was nabbed in February when the shipment arrived via Federal Express.

"The root of steroid use is society's addiction to bigger, faster, stronger. The win-at-all-costs mentality leads to cheating and unethical behavior. I regret few things, but I do regret selling myself out by using drugs to compete."

Steve Courson,
former Pittsburgh Steeler

Sometimes, kids themselves get into the act. Twenty-five percent say they sell the drugs to support their expensive habit. One Virginia 12th grader tells of fellow students who stole steroids from a drugstore when

SCHWARZENEGGER SPEAKS
'Steroids don't pay off'

Arnold Schwarzenegger, chairman of the President's Council on Physical Fitness and Sports, gave his first extensive interview about steroid use to Senior Writer Kenneth T. Walsh. Excerpts:

On competition. We are in a very fast world now, and we're always looking for a shortcut. We always want to get rich the fastest way, we want to get famous the fastest way, we want to get strong and be competitive the fastest way. But really there is no shortcut. It all comes down to one thing, and this is why sports and fitness activities are so important: The more hours we put in and the more we struggle, the more we fight against resistance and obstacles, the better we will get and the more it will pay off for other activities in life.

On the temptation of drugs. There is no one who has ever gone the long haul relying on drugs. So many kids have this misconception that all you need to do is take a few pills and work out a little bit, and that will take you over the top. But that's not the way it works. That extra 20 pounds that you may lift from using those steroids is not going to be worth it. No one will know about it. But you will know when you get sick and when the side effects come out. It doesn't pay off. I think it is very important that someone like myself who has been there—someone they

idolize—gets that message out.

On his steroid use. In those days you didn't have to deal with the black market. You could go to your physician and just say, "Listen, I want to gain some weight, and I want to take something." Then the physician would say, "Do it six weeks before the competition, then it will be safe." And that's what you would do. The dosage that was taken then versus what is taken now is not even 10 percent. It's probably 5 percent.

On his own performance. It was not the drug that made me the champion. It was the will and the drive and the five hours of working out, lifting 50, 60 tons of weights a day, being on a strict diet and training, my posing and doing all the different things that I had to do.

On the media and steroids. My concern is that the more steroids are played up and the more exposure that they have gotten, the more the kids have been using them. It's counterproductive to think that a 16-year-old kid will not use steroids because he reads that [Olympic track star] Ben Johnson has taken them. The press means well, but it doesn't have that effect. So many kids don't read the paper; all they read are the headlines, and they say, "Well, I should try that, too. It may be dan-

gerous, but let me give it a shot."

On ways to reduce steroid use. That doesn't mean we should stop education. The media should continue [exposing the dangers] because they're doing a great service. And we should continue educating our kids in school about all kinds of drugs, every substance that kids are using. We should let them know what the side effects are and show them footage of people who used to be big and famous how they die in a horrendous way and with cancer—show them things like they do in traffic school. And we should also get rid of the coaches who put pressure on the kids because there are all kinds of other complications that come with the pressure. The school is under pressure; the school raises money because of athletic activities and they have to be No. 1. Otherwise they don't get the funding and the donations. It's a very tricky thing.

On his philosophy for young people. Don't take drugs, get off the junk food, exercise every day, educate yourself every day, don't sit around in front of the TV set all night long. No one ever got smart or became champion by just watching TV. Don't sit there like a couch potato and just watch. That's my message. Get into discipline and accomplish things in your life.

they worked and made "a killing" selling them around school. "Everybody knows you just go to this one guy's locker, and he'll fix you up," says the teen. A typical 100-tablet bottle of steroids—a month's supply—usually runs from $80 to $100 on the black market, but naive high schoolers often pay three times that amount.

"The challenge of getting ahold of the stuff is half the fun," admits one

17-year-old from Iowa, who tells of meeting dealers in parking lots and taste-testing drugs that look like fakes. Drug-enforcement agents estimate that 30 to 50 percent of the illegal muscle builders teens buy are phony. One Chicago-area youth spent $3,000 on what turned out to be a saline solution. Investigators have seized pills that turned out to be penicillin—deadly to some—and phony oils that were poorly packaged and

rampant with bacteria. In April, two Los Angeles dealers were convicted of selling a counterfeit steroid that caused stomach pain, vomiting and a drop in blood pressure; the substance was a European veterinary drug used in show animals.

Subbing dangers. Since February 1991, when nonmedical steroid distribution became a federal offense punishable by five years in prison, several drugs touted as steroid alternatives have also flourished underground. The top seller this year is a compound called clenbuterol, which is used by veterinarians in other countries but is not approved for any use in the United States. The drug recently led to problems in Spain, where 135 people who ingested it fell ill with headaches, chills, muscle tremors and nausea.

"I'd like to play in the NFL. Most of my friends and I would never take steroids. I tried this liquid mix from the health store, but it was nasty stuff. Some things work, and some are rip-offs. You have to keep trying products until you find good ones."

Scott Bullock, 15,
Rock Island, Illinois

Human growth hormone, the steroid alternative Lyle Alzado used during his failed efforts at an NFL comeback, is medically used to treat dwarfism by stimulating growth. Its price, up to $1,500 for a two-week supply, is formidable, yet 5 percent of suburban Chicago 10th-grade boys surveyed in March by Vaughn Rickert of the University of Arkansas for Medical Sciences claim to have used the hormone. Although the body produces the substance naturally, too much can cause acromegaly or "Frankenstein's syndrome," which leads to distortion of the face, hands and feet and eventually kills its victim.

Gamma-hydroxybutyrate (GHB) is a dangerous substance now poplar among size seekers because it stimulates the release of human growth hormone. It also leads to comas. One Midwestern teen drank a GHB formula before going out to his high-school prom. He never made it. Within 20 minutes, he fell comatose

and was rushed to the hospital to be revived. The Centers for Disease Control reports 80 recent hospitalizations from GHB use.

Many of the steroid alternatives that kids turn to come from an unlikely source: the local health-food store. For years, well-meaning coaches have persuaded kids to stay off steroids by opting for legal (and presumably safe) performance aids advertised ad nauseam in muscle magazines and sold in every shopping mall. Kids, happy to find a legal boost, empty their pockets on colorful packages that can cost up to $200 for a month's supply. But chemicals marketed as dietary supplements—essentially as food—undergo far less scrutiny than those marketed as drugs. "We have virtually no idea what's inside some of these products," warns Food and Drug Administration supplement specialist Don Leggett. "Just the other day someone asked about three new chemical compounds, and we couldn't even identify them. The substances aren't even on the books yet." Not long ago, he points out, clenbuterol and GHB were available in some health stores. Leggett is part of a task force now trying to assess the safety of a dozen common ingredients found in the bulking-up formulas, including chromium, boron and plant sterols.

Cracking the culture. Meanwhile, the ambience of gyms and health-food stores serves to cloak the use of performance-enhancing drugs in the veneer of a healthy lifestyle. Since all of the trappings of their world have to do with hard work, fitness and vitality, kids who use the substances see them as just another training aid, not much different from Gatorade or a big steak dinner. "We're not freaks or addicts," asserts one teen. "We're using modern science to help us reach our goals."

Educators agree that users tend to be mainstream kids. "These kids aren't your typical drug abuser," says Dick Stickle, director of Target, the high-school sports association that hosted a meeting in April of 65 experts who worked to plot a strat-

egy for educating teens about the drugs' risks. "They have goals, they have pride; we've got to play on that pride." The group plans to send a book of guidelines for combatting the use of steroids and other performance enhancers to every secondary school, 37,000 in all, early this fall. But reaching secondary schools may not be enough: A Peoria, Ill., teacher was recently taken aback by a fourth grader who said he'd like to try the steroids his sixth-grade brother uses. Previous education efforts have at times backfired; in Oregon, students who learned about the dangers of steroids were more likely to use them than those who didn't. Testing all high-school football players alone would cost $100 million and be nearly useless, since most teens know how to beat the tests with the use of "masking" drugs available underground.

At the forefront of education efforts are Charles Yesalis, professor of health policy at Pennsylvania State University and the nation's premier steroid expert, and Steve Courson, a former NFL star who used steroids. Both say that curbing steroid use requires nothing less than a revamping of American values. "We don't allow our kids to play games for fun anymore," says Yesalis. "We preach that God really does care who wins on Friday night, when we should be teaching our children to be satisfied to finish 27th, if that's their personal best."

Courson, in his recent book, "False Glory," tells of being introduced to steroids at age 18 by a college trainer, using steroids throughout his college and pro career and developing an accelerated heartbeat during his heaviest cycle. He is currently awaiting a heart transplant. "In the NFL, I was nothing more than a highly paid, highly manipulated gladiator. I was spiritually bankrupt," says Courson, now a Pennsylvania high-school football coach. "I want kids to know they can be greater than gladiators, that they can use a sport to learn lessons about life and not let the sport use them."

Ultimately to reach children, educators will have to crack the secretive steroid subculture. So inviting is the underground world that, according to one study 1 in 10 users takes steroids primarily out of desire to belong to the tightknit group. Those who opt out are quickly ostracized. Bill, a 17-year-old junior from New England, says he was a wallflower with only a couple of friends before he got into steroids. Two and a half years and 16 cycles of steroid use made him part of the fellowship. But Bill vividly remembers one day last winter: It's the day his parents found a needle he forgot to discard. Since then, he hasn't seen much of his friends. "I had to switch gyms because they were all teasing me about shrinking up and pressuring me to use the stuff," he says. "I never see them now—we don't have anything to talk about anymore—but they're all betting I'll go back on it. Right now, the only way I know I'll stay off steroids is if I can find a guarantee that I'll reach 220 pounds without them. No, make that 230."

—*Joannie M. Schrof*

The Impact of Drug Use on Society

Drugs and drug use cause at least two different types of impact—objective and subjective. An objective impact is what a drug does, while a subjective impact is what a drug is thought to do—rightly or wrongly—that is, what kind of *concern* the members of a society have *about* the drug and its use.

First, what is a drug's *objective* impact? Illegal drug users often argue that society has no right to concern itself with their drug taking. "I'm only harming myself," they will insist. "Society has no right to interfere with my private life." Legal and moral arguments aside, the fact is, users do more than increase the likelihood of harming themselves when they take drugs. They can harm others as well, both directly and indirectly—directly, by upping the odds of accidents, crime, and violence, and indirectly, by increasing the cost of caring for them and their offspring, lowering productivity, and stimulating the underground economy, thereby undermining the viability of certain neighborhoods. In short, drugs can have a number of undesirable long-term consequences.

Of all drugs, experts agree, cigarettes cause the greatest loss of life over the long run. The surgeon general of the United States estimates that over 400,000 Americans die prematurely every year as a consequence of cigarette smoking. The increased cost of medical care for those who have contracted diseases as a consequence of smoking is incalculable, running at the very least into the tens of billions of dollars per year—considerably more than the government earns in taxes from tobacco products. Smokers have three times the chance of dying before the age of 65 as nonsmokers, and twice the chance of dying before the age of 75; a nonsmoker has about the same chance of living to the age of 75 as a smoker does of living to 65! Smokers of more than 2 packs a day have 23 times the chance of dying of lung cancer as nonsmokers. But since tobacco is legal, and the deaths it causes are slow and long-term and likely to strike only the middle-aged and the elderly, most of us do not become overly distressed about its use.

Alcohol causes some 150,000 premature deaths a year, perhaps half from the increased likelihood of accidents and violence and the other half from the various diseases. One estimate links 3 out of every 100 deaths directly to the consumption of alcohol—and admits that this is probably a gross underestimation. Estimates of the dollar cost of alcohol consumption to American society, including medical care and loss of productivity, range between $100 and $200 billion per year. Just the deaths from the increased likelihood of automobile crashes—over 20,000 per year—probably outweigh the number of premature deaths caused by all the illegal drugs combined. Of all the long-term impacts of heavy alcohol consumption, perhaps the most poignant and painful is that on the family of the heavy drinker. The children of alcoholics are victims who have to spend their entire adulthood struggling with the pain of the childhood they spent with an alcohol-dependent parent.

Illegal drug use has a serious impact on the user and on society generally, but it is likely to be very different from that of the legal drugs. Most users of heroin and cocaine die not from the chronic, long-term effects of their drugs of choice, but from overdoses. Through a program called DAWN (the Drug Awareness Warning Network), the federal government collects and complies drug overdose data, which are divided into *emergency room episodes* and *medical examiners reports* (or lethal overdoses). In 1990, DAWN estimated that there were roughly 370,000 drug episodes in the United States that required some hospital or clinic care. The drug mentioned the most in causing these nonlethal overdoses was *alcohol* (and alcohol was mentioned only if taken in conjunction or in combination with another drug), with 115,000 mentions. After that, cocaine, with 80,000 mentions, and the narcotics, with close to 60,000 mentions, most often caused acute hospital and clinic emergencies. The drugs that caused the greatest number of deaths by overdose were the same three that caused hospital emergencies—alcohol (in combination), in third place, cocaine, in second place, and narcotics, still the champion death-dealing drugs used in the United States today. All drugs do not necessarily kill in the same way. Cigarettes never appear in DAWN's data because they kill over the long run; their effects are *chronic* and not *acute*. Alcohol's effects are both chronic and acute—that is, one can die as a consequence of long-term use or as a result of a single episode of use. The lethal effects of illegal drugs such as heroin and cocaine are acute; they usually kill during a single episode of use, which means it is the young rather than the old who die from heroin and crack use.

Drugs often have an impact far beyond the society in which they are used. Illegal drugs usually transform the countries where they originate and from which they are exported. The use of cocaine in the United States, for example, has introduced "dirty money" into the economies of Colombia and Peru, corrupted local and even federal law enforcement officials, launched violent confrontations on a vast scale, and destroyed vast tracts of wilderness. We live in a global society—the societies of the world are all connected in important ways—and drug use and sale offer dramatic testimony to that fact.

In the late 1980s and early 1990s, it was feared that cocaine-dependent—especially crack-dependent—mothers would give birth to a whole generation of medically damaged children, babies who, because of their mother's addiction, would be born with a variety of ailments and pathologies, require special and costly medical and psychiatric care, become a multibillion-dollar burden to society, and never be normal, even when they entered the public school system at the age of five and six. This fear has proven to be unfounded, since the many other factors that are often associated with pregnant women who use cocaine and crack—alcoholism, cigarette smoking, poor nutrition, sexually transmitted diseases, and little or no medical attention during pregnancy—have a more harmful effect on the fetus and the baby than does the cocaine. Still, this fear demonstrates that public concern is far greater for illegal drugs than it is for legal drug use.

Looking Ahead: Challenge Questions

Is the overall impact on society of the legal drugs—tobacco, alcohol, prescription and over-the-counter drugs—more positive or negative? Are the troublesome effects of the legal drugs (including medical problems and violence) simply the price we have to pay for tolerating substances whose use is too firmly entrenched to eliminate? If the impact on society of tobacco and alcohol has been as disastrous as experts claim, why is their use tolerated?

Does drug abuse contribute to the "downfall of civilization," as some observers have argued?

If legal drugs contribute to far more premature deaths than illegal drugs do, why do the latter receive so much more media attention? Why are most people so much more interested in the use of cocaine, crack, and heroin than in cigarettes and alcohol?

If alcohol abuse causes such pain to those the alcoholic loves most, why can't he or she simply given up drinking?

Faced with overwhelming evidence that cigarettes kill, why do some people continue to smoke? How can cigarette companies continue to claim, as they do, that no conclusive proof exists that cigarettes cause disease or death?

If a pregnant woman becomes a crack addict and endangers the life of her child, should she be criminally liable for her behavior? Is she committing a crime?

Do the members of society overreact to the illegal use of drugs by a relatively small statistical minority? Why is this reaction more intense to the supposed impact of illegal drugs than to the already known impact of legal

Mothers Against Drunk Driving

Tie this red ribbon to a visible location on your vehicle as a symbol that you join Mothers Against Drunk Driving in its hope for a safe and sober holiday season.

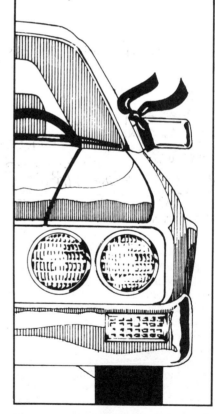

drugs? Is there a panic about drug abuse in the United States?

Does the United States owe a responsibili   the countries that have been drastically transfor   use and sale of illegal drugs here? Does the   cash into these countries offset the more s   such as corruption of officials and d   environment?

Dealing with Demons of a New Generation

Tom Dunkel

Summary: A decade ago society was awakened to what were seen as unique problems facing grown-up children of alcoholics. But now research shows that these problems plague offspring of all sorts of dysfunctional families. As the pool of subjects grows, answers are harder to find.

On the kind of sweltering summer afternoon that's guaranteed to fill empty stools in air-conditioned bars, 15 men and women gather inside the second-floor conference room of a nondescript office building in suburban Washington. They've come to talk about inner demons that, if they didn't know better, might very well drive them to drink.

Robert, a middle-aged recovering alcoholic, takes the floor and tells how he "was forced into the role of becoming an adult at 7 or 8 years old" because his father was a problem drinker. "As things are," he adds with a sad smile that covers the scar tissue of memory, "I survived and came out [the] other end of the sausage maker." [He's] a burly, 51-year-old ex-

Marine who describes himself as "an adult child of an alcoholic and a crazy person," is still sorting through the pieces of his fractured upbringing. "Thirty years ago I needed combat," he says. "It was a great therapeutic release to blow something up."

It is nothing new for members of a mutual support group to reveal intimate details about themselves to sympathetic listeners who have traveled the same emotional road. What is new is that Robert and John aren't unburdening themselves just to fellow children of alcoholics. Their group includes participants whose youths were misshapen by sexual abuse, physical abuse and a variety of other homegrown dysfunctions. In fact, three years ago the group stopped identifying itself as Adult Children of Alcoholics and adopted the more generic name Adult Children Anonymous. A few old hands initially resented widening the focus.

"I felt that way for about three meetings; you know, let them go start their own group," John recalls after the hour-long session. "But then the sharing was such a contribution. Anybody that's got a story to tell is a help."

John's less restrictive attitude reflects changes taking place on the professional level. Advocates for the estimated 29 million Americans who can be classified as "children of alcoholics" are backtracking from prior claims that these are people plagued by unique backgrounds and challenges.

A decade ago, when the abbreviation ACOA first came into use, ACOAs were granted almost de facto syndrome status. Telltale symptoms — ranging from low self-esteem and fear of intimacy to depression and poor job performance — were quickly identified. Umbrella organizations such as the National Association for Children of Alcoholics, or NACOA, came into being. A "co-dependency" movement evolved, championing the notion that innocent family members often are damaged by the psychological ripple effects that come from trying to cope with an alcoholic parent or spouse.

But now winds of revisionism are blowing as a body of contrary research — which includes recent studies done under the auspices of Duke University and the University of Missouri — piles high. Maybe being the child of an alcoholic isn't the psychological equivalent of having a new strain of virus, after all.

"Up until now there's been an assumption sometimes that all alcoholic families are similar," notes Deborah Wright, a psychologist at the University of Missouri who, along with colleague Paul Heppner, recently completed an analysis of 80 campus freshmen. "There's an assumption that kids raised in these types of environments will all have similar outcomes and be experiencing similar things. I didn't find that necessarily [true]."

A battery of personality and aptitude tests was given to the Missouri students. Wright and Heppner found just one distinction between those who came from alcoholic families and those who did not: The former were more likely to be abusers of alcohol or drugs. Any additional emotional or behavioral problems were ascribed to other factors, such as parental divorce or the family having had to relocate multiple times.

"I actually think that that writing was helpful at the time," says Wright, referring to the early, largely nonprofessional fieldwork done on COAs, "because we didn't know anything about alcoholic homes. But I think now we need to step back and say this is not necessarily true for everybody, and what is it in particular in those homes that will lead some [children] to struggle as adults, whereas others seem to get by."

A similar caution flag is raised by Shelly F. Greenfield, a psychologist at McLean Hospital in Belmont, Mass. She and a group of researchers at Duke recently went back and pored over statistics culled during an intensive mental health study of 3,000 North Carolina residents conducted in the early 1980s. After screening out potential influences such as divorce and poverty, they isolated some effects of familial alcoholism. Their conclusions were published in the *American Journal of Psychiatry* in April.

"There's so many contradictions in the literature and the field," says Greenfield. "What we were trying to get at in a broad, population-based way is: What are these people really at risk for? Because there is this sort of notion about these people as being an entity unto themselves. . . . What we found out is they're at risk for some things and not for other things."

Greenfield found that children of alcoholics show a strong predisposition toward having "psychiatric symptoms" as adults, as well as a "moderately significant" pattern of marital trouble. However, they are no more likely than the general population to have difficulties on the job or in their other personal relationships.

On the surface, those findings would seem to at least partially bolster the assertions of COA proponents. Not so. Greenfield is now involved in a second phase of number crunching on the North Carolina survey that will compare children of alcoholics with children of other dysfunctional parents. Preliminary results indicate that those who suffered sexual or physical abuse also have high rates of psychosis.

"My impression," explains Greenfield, "is that people who have had these very negative experiences early on, many of the things they wind up being at risk for — in terms of psychiatric symptoms and disorders — are similar. There's a lot of overlap."

But still there is conflicting clinical and anecdotal evidence fueling the debate, adds Greenfield. For example, a University of Cincinnati study compared 3-year-old sons of alcoholic and nonalcoholic fathers: The

> "When people begin getting clearer about this — that you can't grow up in an alcoholic home without it affecting you and creating some pain — then they'll look at alcoholism a little more seriously."

children of the alcoholics displayed more impulsive behavior and were not as advanced in language development, fine motor coordination and sociability. Similarly, Ralph Tarter, a professor of psychiatry and neurology at the University of Pittsburgh Medical School, remains a skeptic of COA theory even though he can cite several studies in which infants were removed from alcoholic families and placed in more stable, adopted homes — yet didn't emerge unscathed. "You still see a higher incidence of cognitive disorders," says Tarter, adding that such second-generation effects indicate how much still needs to be learned about the interplay of heredity and environment in alcoholism.

Nonetheless, the tide is running against COA purists who cling to unique-syndrome beliefs. Timmen Cermak is clinical director of Genesis Psychotherapy and Training Center in San Francisco and serves on the advisory board of NACOA. He has argued in the past that schoolteachers should be trained to identify COAs and that school health workers should be allowed to intercede without the consent of parents. But today Cermak, who himself was raised in an alcoholic family, downplays how different COAs are: "I've never felt it was an exclusive [syndrome]."

Cermak points out that peculiar, egg-before-the-chicken circumstances may have caused some pioneering therapists to be overzealous.

"What happened with adult children of alcoholics is that we've come about looking at people from a different direction than what normally happens," Cermak says. "Oftentimes we discover a disease and then go out to look for the population that has that disease. This is opposite. We've identified a population and then are looking at that population to see what special needs that population might have."

Claudia Black, a cofounder and former chairwoman of the NACOA, agrees with Cermak's assessment and even takes it a step further: There may be adult child syndromes more debilitating than COA. "I think that most professionals — and those of us specifically in the adult children of alcoholics movement — in all fairness recognize that what's true for people in alcoholic homes is very generalizable, particularly to other strongly dysfunctional family systems. . . . I believe there's probably more aspects of uniqueness when you're dealing with a home where there's physical and sexual abuse, where one's body is violated, versus when we're talking about . . . psychologically and emotionally greater dysfunctions."

Even those who think the COA syndrome has been overstated concede that the movement has made positive contributions. Most important, it brought secondary problems of addiction out of the closet and let the forgotten victims of alcoholism know they were not alone. That in itself was therapeutic for many people. Then, too, the attention paid to COAs brought to light the devastating toll exacted by addictions of every stripe.

Cermak hopes that the end result will be a sea change of opinion akin to the public outcry against secondhand smoke. "When people begin getting clearer about this — that you can't grow up in an alcoholic home without it affecting you and creating some pain — then they'll look at alcoholism a little more seriously," he predicts. "It's not something people do by themselves. I think that [m_____age] has not been received by _____ ulation at large."

The downside of the ____ ment, detractors say, ____ emergence of a rem____ dustry in which po____ querades as serious psychotherapy.

"There are economic benefits to treating people and giving labels," notes Pittsburgh's Tarter.

There's also a danger in creating a cult of victimhood in which COAs not only use the syndrome as a crutch to evade personal responsibility (the "it's-all-my-parents'-fault" rationalization), but also accuse fellow COAs of being in a stage of acute denial if they, too, don't feel weighed down by baggage from childhood. Thus, Atlanta psychiatrist Frank Pittman wrote last year in the *Family Therapy Networker* that "the adult child movement . . . has trivialized real suffering and made psychic invalids of those who once had a bad day."

Even if one assumes that the scientific underpinnings are specious, it's uncertain whether the COA movement has had a benign or deleterious effect. "That's the $64,000 question," says Tarter. "Nobody knows."

To date, most research studies have been short-term and have focused on a skewed subset of people who are being clinically treated for one alcohol-related problem or another. That leaves unanswered a host of questions besides the $64,000 variety. Among them: Are there distinctions between children of male alcoholics and children of female alcoholics? Do children of alcoholics experience different problems at different stages of their lives?

Finding answers will require a comprehensive, decades-long effort analogous to the Framingham, Mass., study of heart disease. No one yet has been willing to devote that amount of money and time to understanding alcoholism.

The University of Pittsburgh Medical School, however, is taking a step in that direction. In 1989, Tarter selected a group of 10-year-old children from 1,000 families. Data will be collected from them until they reach age 30. One statistical curiosity discovered so far indicates that a disproportionate number of children born to alcoholic or drug-addicted parents have abnormal brain wave patterns.

"Those brain wave differences correlate very strongly with certain types of behavioral characteristics, such as impulsivity and social deviance and lower IQ," explains Tarter.

Again, Tarter is not sure how those brain wave patterns might compare with those of children from other types of dysfunctional families. The phenomenon harks back to those hereditary and environmental factors waiting to be untangled. Nonetheless, Tarter thinks science-minded researchers and children of alcoholics are "coming to some common ground," though there is still a lot of distance between the two camps.

"My own position on this," he says, "is that being a COA in and of itself is not pathognomonic. That's where the scientific community departs from the movement. . . . Even if there's a genetic propensity, it's not necessarily going to be manifest unless a number of key environmental conditions are met. Unfortunately, we haven't studied that part of it very much."

The University of Missouri's Wright is less optimistic about the possibility of ever attaining that elusive common ground: "I don't think we'll ever come to a definitive answer because we can't say all COAs are COAs. It isn't that simplistic, unfortunately. I don't think we'll ever get to a place where we can make definitive statements about this large, large group. Because this large, large group is very heterogeneous. It's just a type of dysfunctional family."

Alcohol and Kids:
It's Time for Candor

A series of recent government studies shows that alcohol abuse is by far the biggest drug problem facing America's youth, and existing laws do little to address it

Antonia C. Novello

One pressure young people face makes my job, and our hopes for the future, inherently more difficult: the pressure to drink alcohol.

Alcohol is truly the mainstream drug-abuse issue plaguing most communities and families in America today.

We must realize how confusing the mixed messages are that we send to our children about alcohol. We've made progress in the war against illicit drugs because our youth have gotten consistent messages from their families, their schools, their churches, their communities, their nation—and their media.

We're losing the war against underage use of alcohol, however, because our youth receive some very mixed messages. Advertisements and other media images tell them, "Drink me and you will be cool, drink me and you will be glamorous, drink me and you will have fun!" Or even worse, "Drink me and there will be no consequences."

Our health message is clear—"use of alcohol by young people can lead to serious health consequences—not to mention absenteeism, vandalism, date rape, random violence, and even death." But how can that be expected to compete with the Swedish bikini team or the Bud Man?

In June 1991, I released "Youth and Alcohol: Drinking Habits, Access, Attitudes and Knowledge, and Do They Know What They Are Drinking?"

This collection of studies showed that:

■ At least 8 million American teenagers use alcohol every week, and almost half a million go on a weekly binge (or 5 drinks in a row)—confirming earlier surveys by the National Institute on Drug Abuse.

■ Junior and senior high school students drink 35 percent of all wine coolers sold in the United States (31 million gallons) and consume 1.1 billion cans of beer (102 million gallons) each year.

■ Many teenagers who drink are using alcohol to handle stress and boredom. And many of them drink alone, breaking the old stereotype of party drinking.

■ Labeling is a big problem. Two out of three teenagers cannot distinguish alcoholic from nonalcoholic beverages because they appear similar on store shelves.

■ Teenagers lack essential knowledge about alcohol. Very few are getting clear and reliable information about alcohol and its effects. Some million, to be exact, learn the facts from their peers; close to 2 million do not even know a law exists pertaining to illegal underage drinking.

In September 1991, we released a second set of reports, this one on enforcement of underage drinking laws. It was called, "Laws and Enforcement: Is the 21-year-old Drinking Age a Myth?"

These reports showed that:

■ The National Minimum Drinking Age Act of 1984 started out with five exemptions that in some states have become loopholes.

■ The federally mandated 21-year-old minimum drinking law is largely a myth; it is riddled with loopholes. Two-thirds of teens who drink, almost 7 million kids, simply walk into a store and buy booze.

Police point out that parents do not like their children arrested for "doing what everyone else does." One official described enforcement of alcohol laws as "a no-win" situation. And another commented, "Local police have another priority—[illicit] drugs. They ignore alcohol."

And by and large, there are only nominal penalties against vendors and minors when they violate th̶ ̶e laws. While vendors may have fines or their lic̶ ̶ ̶s-pended, license revocations are rare.

The penalties against the youth who v̶i are often not deterrents. Even when stri̶c courts are lenient and do not apply t̶h

6. THE IMPACT OF DRUG USE ON SOCIETY

We are seeing over and over again the potential for the kind of tragedy that occurred last year on Maryland's eastern shore where Brian Ball, 15 years old, drank 26 shots of vodka at an "all you can drink" party and died two days later—parties where underage drinking gets out of hand, and no adult is held liable. Only 10 states have adopted so-called "social host" laws that hold the host adult or parent liable for the consequences of underage drinking on their property.

Finally, last Nov. 4, we released a final report titled, "Youth and Alcohol: Controlling Alcohol Advertising That Appeals to Youth."

■ Much alcohol advertising goes beyond describing the specific qualities of the beverage. It creates a glamorous, pleasurable image that may mislead youth about alcohol and the possible consequences of its use.

■ A 1991 poll done by the Wirthlin Group said 73 percent of respondents agreed that alcohol advertising is a major contributor to underage drinking.

Additionally, the majority of Americans think that alcohol industry ads "target the young."

Most recently, as honorary chair of Alcohol Awareness Month, I released a fourth report which deals with usually unreported consequences of teen drinking.

Drinking and driving certainly puts many lives at risk, but an alcohol-impaired person doesn't need to get behind the wheel of a car to do harm to himself and to others. Depression, suicides, random violence, and criminal acts—such as date rape, battery, and homicide—all have strong links to alcohol use. So do the unintentional alcohol-related injuries that result from falls, drownings, shootings, residential fires, and the like.

Crime is a major consequence of alcohol consumption. Approximately one-third of our young people who commit serious crimes have consumed alcohol just prior to these illegal actions.

According to the Department of Justice, alcohol consumption is associated with almost 27 percent of all murders, almost 33 percent of all property offenses, and more than 37 percent of robberies committed by young people. In fact, nearly 40 percent of the young people in adult correctional facilities reported drinking before committing a crime.

Alcohol has also shown itself to be a factor in being a victim of crime. Intoxicated minors were found to provoke assailants, to act vulnerably, and to fail to take normal, common-sense precautions.

Among college student crime victims, for example, 50 percent admitted using drugs and/or alcohol.

Rape and sexual assault are also closely associated with alcohol misuse by our youth. Among college age students, 55 percent of perpetrators were under the influence of alcohol, and so were 53 percent of the victims. Administrators at one US university found that 100 percent of sexual assault cases during a specific year were alcohol-related.

Who can honestly tell me that alcohol is not adversely affecting the future of these young people?

I want to share with you another finding I find particularly shocking and revolting: Among high school females, 18 percent—nearly 1 in 5—said it was okay to force sex if the girl was drunk, and among high school males, almost 40 percent—2 out of every 5—said the same thing.

We found other startling links, such as:

■ 70 percent of attempted suicides involved the frequent use of drugs and/or alcohol.

■ Water activities—of special interest and concern in summer—often result in alcohol use and danger. Forty to 50 percent of young males who drown had used alcohol before drowning. Forty to 50 percent of all diving injury victims had consumed alcoholic beverages.

Clearly, something must be done about this pervasive problem confronting our youth. Two things are clear: First, we all have a role to play in solving this problem; second, by working together we can solve it.

I have urged the alcohol industry to come to the table, to work with us, to become part of the solution. I have also urged schools to make alcohol education a central part of the health curriculum from the earliest grades on. This curriculum must include teaching resistance and risk-avoidance techniques.

And, finally, I have urged families—parents and children—to talk to each other about alcohol, about distinguishing truth from fiction.

This article is adapted from a recent speech given by US Surgeon General Antonia C. Novello before the Town Hall of California in Los Angeles.

Alcohol and the Family

The children of problem drinkers are coming to grips with their feelings of fear, guilt and rage

Believe it or not, there are still people who think that the worst thing about drinking is a hangover.

Oh, yeah, on New Year's Day I had a hangover that . . .

No. Forget hangovers.

Huh? So what should we talk about? Cirrhosis?

If you wish, but the liver, with its amazing powers of regeneration, usually lasts longer than the spouse, who tends to fall apart relatively early in the drinker's decline.

You're making it hard for a man to drink in peace.

Sorry, but even if spouses do not abuse alcohol, they can come to resemble drunks, since their anger and fear are enormous: way beyond what you'd find in a truly sober person.

I know, I know, it's terrible what goes on behind closed doors.

You make it sound like there are no witnesses. You're forgetting the children. They grow up watching one out-of-control person trying to control another, and they don't know what "normal" is.

I suppose it's hard for the kids, until they move out.

They may move out, but they never leave their parents behind.

Hmm. Listen, can we talk?

We already are. A lot of people already are.

We are, just now, learning more about heavy drinking, and, simultaneously, putting behind us the notion that what alcoholism amounts to is just odd intervals of strange, and sometimes comic, behavior: W. C. Fields, Dean Martin, Foster Brooks. Since 1935 the members of Alcoholics Anonymous have been telling us, with awesome simplicity, that drinking made their lives unmanageable; Al-Anon brought us the news that relatives and friends of drinkers can suffer in harmony; and then came Alateen and even Alatot, where one picture of a stick person holding a beer can is worth a thousand slurred words. The Children of Alcoholics (COAs)—loosely organized but rapidly growing throughout the United States— reaffirm all of the previous grass-roots movements and bring us new insight into alcoholism's effects on the more than 28 million Americans who have seen at least one parent in the throes of the affliction. The bad news from COAs: alcohol is even more insidious than previously thought.

The good news: with the right kind of help, the terrible damage it does to nonalcoholics need not be permanent.

Imagine a child who lives in a chaotic house, rides around with a drunk driver and has no one to talk to about the terror. Don't think it doesn't happen: more than 10 million people in the United States are addicted to alcohol, and most of them have children. "I grew up in a little Vietnam," says one child of an alcoholic. "I didn't know why I was there; I didn't know who the enemy was." Decades after their parents die, children of alcoholics can find it difficult to have intimate relationships ("You learn to trust no one") or experience joy ("I hid in the closet"). They are haunted—sometimes despite worldwide acclaim, as in the case of

There's a Problem in the House

In "Adult Children of Alcoholics," Janet Geringer Woititz discusses 13 traits that most children from alcoholic households experience to some degree. These symptoms, she says, can pose lifelong problems.

Adult children of alcoholics . . .

- guess what normal behavior is.
- have difficulty following a project from beginning to end.
- lie when it would be just as easy to tell the truth.
- judge themselves without mercy.
- have difficulty having fun.
- take themselves very seriously.
- have difficulty with intimate relationships.
- overreact to changes over which they have no control.

- constantly seek approval and affirmation.
- feel that they are different from other people.
- are super-responsible or super-irresponsible.
- are extremely loyal, even in the face of evidence that the loyalty is undeserved.
- tend to lock themselves in course of action without g consideration to conseq

134

artist Eric Fischl—by a sense of failure for not having saved Mommy or Daddy from drink. And they are prone to marry alcoholics or other severely troubled people because, for one reason, they're willing to accept unacceptable behavior. Many, indeed, have become addicted to domestic turmoil.

'Hurting so bad': Children of alcoholics are people who've been robbed of their childhood—"I've seen five-year-olds running entire families," says Janet Geringer Woititz, one of the movement's founding mothers. Nevertheless, the children of alcoholics often display a kind of childish loyalty even when such loyalty is clearly undeserved. They have a nagging feeling that they are different from other people, Woititz points out, and that may be because, as some recent scientific studies show, they are. Brain scans done by Dr. Henri Begleiter of the State University of New York College of Medicine in Brooklyn reveal that COAs often have deficiencies in the areas of the brain associated with emotion and memory. In this sense and in several other ways—their often obsessive personalities, their tendency to have a poor self-image—the children of alcoholics closely resemble alcoholics. In fact, one in four becomes an alcoholic, as compared with one in 10 out of the general population.

The anger of a COA cannot be seen by brain scans. But at a therapy session at Caron Family Services in Wernersville, Pa., Ken Gill, a 49-year-old IBM salesman, recently took a padded bat and walloped a couch cushion hard enough to wake up sleeping demons. "I came because I was hurting so bad and I didn't know why," he says. "A lot of things were going wrong. I was a workaholic, and I neglected my family." It took Gill only a few hours of exposure to the idea that he might be an "adult child," he says, to realize that his failings as a parent may be if not excused, then at least explained. Like a lot of kids who grew up in an alcoholic household, Gill, who is also a recovering alcoholic, never got what even rats and monkeys get: exposure, at an impressionable age, to the sight and sound of functioning parents. Suzanne Somers, the actress and singer, spent years working out her anger in the form of a just published book called "Keeping Secrets." "I decided that this disease took the first half of my life, and goddam it," she says, "it wasn't going to take the second half of it."

'Control freak': Not every COA has all of the 13 traits (see chart) ascribed to them by Woititz in her landmark work, "Adult Children of Alcoholics" (1983. *Health Communications, Inc.*), and not all have been scarred. (President Reagan, who has written of sometimes finding his father passed out drunk on the front porch, does not appear, from his famous management style, to suffer ~~~from~~ any tendency to be a "control freak," a

COURTESY CLAUDIA BLACK

■ A nine-year-old's nightmare: Living in denial

most common COA complaint.) Some children of alcoholics are grossly overweight from compulsive eating while others are as dressed for success as, well, Somers. A few COAs are immobilized by depression. Another runs TV's "Old Time Gospel Hour." What these people *do* have in common is a basic agreement with George Vaillant, a Dartmouth Medical School professor who says that it is important to think of alcoholism not as an illness that affects bodily organs but as "an illness that affects families. Perhaps the worst single feature of alcoholism," Vaillant adds, "is that it causes people to be unreasonably angry at the people that they most love."

The movement is only about six years old, but expanding so rapidly that figures, could they be gathered for such a basically unstructured and anonymous group, would be outdated as soon as they appeared. We do know, though, that five years ago there were 21 people in an organization called the National Association for Children of Alcoholics; today there are more than 7,000. The 14 Al-Anon-affiliated children-of-alcoholics groups meeting in the early '80s have increased to 1,100. With only word-of-mouth advertising, Woititz's book has sold about a million copies; indeed, "Adult Children of Alcoholics" reached the number-three spot on The New York Times paperback best-seller list long before it was available in any bookstore—at a time, in other words, when getting a copy meant

collaring a clerk to put in an order and *saying the title out loud.*

"We turned on the phones in 1982," says Migs Woodside, founder and president of the Children of Alcoholics Foundation in New York, "and the calls are still coming in 24 hours a day." The COAs Foundation sponsors a traveling art show that features the work of young and adult COAs; often, says Woodside, an attendee will stand mesmerized before a crude depiction of domestic violence or parental apathy ("Mom at noon," it says beneath the picture of someone huddling beneath the bedcovers)—and will then go directly to a pay phone to find help. "The newcomers all tend to say the same thing," says Woodside. '"Wait a minute—that's my story, that's *me!*'"

"It's private pain transformed into a public statement," says James Garbarino, president of the Erikson Institute for Advanced Study in Child Development, in Chicago, "a fascinating movement." But when you consider that denial is the primary symptom of alcoholism and that COAs tend by nature to take on more than their share of blame for whatever mess they happen to find themselves in, the rapid growth of the COAs movement seems just short of miraculous—something akin to a drunken stockbroker named Bill Wilson cofounding AA, now *the* model for a vast majority of self-help programs throughout the United States. After all, who would want to spill the family's darkest secret after years of telling teachers, employers and friends that everything was fine? ("A child of an alcoholic will always say 'Fine'," says Rokelle Lerner, a counselor who specializes in young COAs. "They get punished if they say otherwise.") Who would voluntarily identify themselves with a group whose female members, according to some reports, have an above-average number of gynecological problems, possibly due to stress—and whose men are prone to frequent surgery for problems, doctors say, that may be basically psychosomatic?

The answer is, only someone who had, in some sense, bottomed out, just the way a drinker does before he turns to AA.

The concept of codependency is at the center of the COAs movement. Eleanor Williams, who works with COAs at the Charter Peachford Hospital in Atlanta, defines codependency as "unconscious addiction to another person's dysfunctional behavior." Woititz, in a recent Changes magazine interview, referred to it more simply as a tendency to "put other people's needs before my own." A codependent family member may suspect that he has driven the alcoholic to drink (though that is impossible, according to virtually all experts in the field); he almost certainly thinks that he can cure or at least control the drinker's troublesome behavior. "I actually thought that I could make a difference by cooking my husband better meals and by taking the kids out for drives on weekends [so he could rest]," says Ella S., a Westchester, N.Y., woman. "For all I know, it's a deeply ingrained psychological, and possibly genetic, disease, and here I am going at it with a lamb chop."

Mental movies: Obsessed with her husband's increasingly self-destructive behavior, Ella's next step, in typical codependent fashion, was to hide Bob's six-packs, which made him, to put it mildly, angry. Soon they were fighting almost daily and Ella was running mental movies of their scenes from a marriage all night long. "I was wasting a lot of time and energy trying to change the past, while he kept getting worse," she says. "There was a kind of awkward violence between him and me all the time; our hearts weren't really in it, but it wasn't until he had an affair with an alcoholism counselor *that I got him to* that I left." If you're wondering about children, Ella has a seven-year-old daughter, Ann. Her omission is significant. If life were a horse race, then Ann has been, as they say on the past performance charts, "shuffled back" among the also-rans.

What COAs—all people affected by alcohol—need to learn is that the race is fixed: when there is no program of recovery—either through the support of a group or the self-imposed abstinence of an individual—the abused substance will always win, handily, no matter what the competition. The first step of AA begins, "We admitted we were powerless . . ." But what will become of Ann, who is codependent on *two*

■ **The fighting never stops: Living with fear**

people? Perhaps, sensing that she is not exactly the center of attention, she will reach adulthood with a need for constant approval, a common COA symptom. Or maybe she will, even as a child, react to the chaos by trying to keep everything in her life under control, and thus give the impression that she is, despite everything, quite a trouper, a golden child.

"[Some] don't fall apart until they're in their 20s or 30s," says Woititz, and in some cases, especially those marked by violence or incest and sexual abuse (three times more common in alcoholic households than in the general population), that's the wonder of it all. One eight-year-old patient at Woititz's Verona, N.J., counseling center

woke up in the middle of the night to see her alcoholic mother shoot herself in the head. "The child called the 911 emergency number, got her mother to the hospital and basically saved her mother's life," says Woititz. "When I saw her she was having nightmares—that she wouldn't wake up and witness this suicide attempt. This is not a normal nightmare. The child had become mother to her own mother."

Each unhappy family, as Tolstoy said, is unhappy in its own way. Artist Eric Fischl, 39, in a short videotape he made for the COAs Foundation called "Trying to Find Normal," speaks of stepping over his passed-out mother, in their comfortable-looking (from the outside) Port Washing-

■ **Out of control: Remembering hurts**

Heredity and Drinking: How Strong Is the Link?

Research on the genetics of alcoholism took a curious turn a few weeks ago when Lawrence Lumeng analyzed his DNA to demonstrate why he can't tolerate liquor. Lumeng, a biochemist at the Indiana University School of Medicine, is among the 30 to 45 percent of Asians whose response to spirited beverages is a reddened face, headaches or nausea. This "Oriental flush," past studies have shown, arises in those who have an inefficient version of a liver enzyme that is crucial to the body's breakdown of alcohol; this "lazy" enzyme allows the buildup of an alcohol product, acetaldehyde, which is sickening and leads many Asians to shun alcohol. Working with biochemist Ting-Kai Li, Lumeng says that he pinpointed the gene that instructs cells to make the odd enzyme. The experiment offers dramatic evidence that a bodily response to alcohol is genetically dictated—and is thus inherited as surely as eye color.

There is no evidence for the opposite proposition: that a specific gene makes a person *crave* alcohol. Considering the wide variety of reasons why people consume the stuff, it seems unlikely that a "drinking gene" exists. But researchers have firmly established that, compared with other children, an alcoholic's offspring are around four times more likely to develop the problem, even if they were raised by other, nonalcoholic parents. In families with a history of alcoholism, explains C. Robert Cloninger, a psychiatrist and geneticist at Washington University in St. Louis, "what is inherited is not the fact that you are destined to become an alcoholic but varying degrees of susceptibility" to the disorder. So real is the predisposition that many researchers advise adult children of alcoholics (COAs) to drink no alcohol whatsoever.

Even the brains of COAs show faint signs of unusual activity, according to controversial studies by psychiatrist Henri Begleiter of the State University of New York in Brooklyn. Begleiter has found that young boys who have never consumed alcohol produce the slightly distorted brainwave patterns typical of their alcoholic fathers. Such signature brain waves, he says, may mark the son of an alcoholic as likely to develop a drinking problem and perhaps alert him to the risk. However, it remains to be seen whether such brain scans are sufficiently reliable and informative to distinguish potential social drinkers from future alcoholics. The technique, comments psychologist Robert Pandina, scientific director of the Center of Alcohol Studies at Rutgers University, is "at this time not any more valuable" as a predictor of future drinking behavior "than collecting a good family history on an individual."

Other studies show that many COAs respond uniquely to booze. Marc Schuckit, a psychiatrist at the Veterans Administration Hospital in San Diego, has found that college-age sons of alcoholics often react less to a few drinks than other college men; in his studies, the drinkers' sons were generally not as euphoric or tipsy after three to five cocktails. Schuckit believes that this lower sensitivity makes it harder for the alcoholics' sons to know when to stop drinking, starting them down the road to alcohol problems. Preliminary experiments by Barbara Lex of McLean Hospital in Belmont, Mass., confirm that daughters of alcoholics respond similarly. Women from families with a history of alcohol abuse tend to keep their balance better on a wobbly platform after having a drink. Apparently women, too, can inherit traits that might predispose them to addiction, although there are far fewer female than male alcoholics.

Half a beer: The key unresolved issue, of course, is why some individuals from alcohol-scarred families succumb to alcoholism while others don't. Genes play some role in the development, most notably in abstinence. "People say that whether you drink or not has to do only with willpower," explains Indiana's Lumeng, "but the reason I can drink only half a beer is biological."

Yet heredity alone obviously isn't to blame for alcoholism's appalling toll. In fact, about 60 percent of the nation's alcohol abusers are from families with *no* history of the disorder. How much people drink is influenced by factors as prosaic as cost; partly to curb consumption, the National Council on Alcoholism is lobbying to raise federal excise taxes on beer and wine, which haven't changed since 1951. Social influences like cost and peer pressure "are just as important as genes," says Dartmouth psychiatrist George Vaillant. "All the genes do is make it easier for you to become an alcoholic." For now, the value of genetic studies is to warn COAs that they may well have a real handicap in the struggle against the family trouble.

TERENCE MONMANEY *with* KAREN SPRINGEN *in New York* *and* MARY HAGER *in Washington*

---

ton, N.Y., home and seeing her "lying in her own piss." His work, which has been the subject of a one-man show at the Whitney Museum in New York, is not autobiographical, he says, and yet "the tone [of it] has everything to do with my childhood." His painting "Time for Bed" "relates to my memory of all hell breaking loose," he says. "I guess you could say the boy is me and his shame, embarrassment and sadness is mine as well. The little boy's Superman pajamas are on backwards, so it's like looking in a mirror. I painted the woman standing on a glass table with spiked heels on to give it a sense of fragility and danger. The man only has one arm because I wanted a sense of impotence."

Alcohol leaves every alcoholic and codependent who does not admit his powerlessness over the substance in a constant state of longing. Fischl didn't realize how sad he'd been until his mother died, in an alcohol-related car accident, in 1970. "The thing about having a sick parent is that you think it's your problem," he says. "You feel like a failure because you can't save her." Even when there is no incest, there is seduction. Fischl's mother kept "signaling," he says, "that if you could just come a little bit further with me in this, you can save me."

Some of the other things that alcohol ruins, before it gets to the liver: family meals ("Alcohol fills you up. My father was never interested in eating with us"); gloriously run-of-the-mill evenings around the hearth ("Alcohol makes you tired. My father was in bed most nights at 8"). When enough C_2H_5HO is added to a home, vases may start to fly across the room and crash into walls. All kinds of paper—court-issued Orders of Protection, divorce decrees, bounced checks—come fluttering down. The lights go on and off. Does that mean Daddy's forgotten to pay the bill again, or that the second act is starting?

Every alcoholic household is, in fact, a pathetic little play in which each of the members takes on a role. This is not an idea that arrived with the COAs movement; a 17-page booklet called "Alcoholism: A Merry-Go-Round Named Denial" has been distributed free of charge by Al-Anon for almost 20 years. Written by the Rev. Joseph L. Kellerman, the former director of the Charlotte, N.C., Council of Alcoholism, "Merry-Go-Round" takes note of the uncanny consistency with which certain characters appear in alcoholic situations. These include the Enabler ("a 'helpful' Mr. Clean . . .[who] conditions [the drinker] to believe there will always be a protector who will come to his rescue"); the Victim ("the person who is responsible for getting the work done if the alcoholic is absent") and the Provoker (usually the spouse or parent of the alcoholic, this is "the key person . . . who is hurt and upset by repeated drinking episodes, but she holds the family together . . . In turn, she feeds back into the marriage her bitterness, resentment, fear and hurt . . . She controls, she tries to force the changes she wants; she sacrifices, adjusts, never gives up, never gives in, but never forgets").

Some of the earliest books in the COAs movement explored the drama metaphor more deeply and defined the roles that children play. Sharon Wegscheider-Cruse, in her 1981 book, "Another Chance" *(Science and Behavior Books, Inc. Palo Alto, Calif.),* wrote about the Family Hero, who is usually the firstborn. A high achiever in school, the Hero always does what's right, often discounting himself by putting others first. The Lost Child, meanwhile, is withdrawn, a loner on his way to a joyless adulthood, and thus, in some ways, very different from the Scapegoat, who appears hostile and defiant but inside feels hurt and angry. (It is the Scapegoat, says Wegscheider-Cruse, who gets attention through "negative behavior" and is likely to be involved in alcohol or other drugs later.) Last and least—in his own mind— is the Mascot, fragile and immature yet charming: the family clown.

'Good-looking' kids: Virtually no one was publishing those kinds of thoughts when Claudia Black, a Laguna Beach, Calif., therapist, began searching for literature on the subject of the alcohol-affected family in the late '70s. "Half of my adult [alcoholic] patients had kids my age and older," she remembers, "but all I found was stuff on fetal alcohol syndrome and kids prone to juvenile delinquency." One thing that fascinated her about young COAs, she says, was that despite their developmental problems "they were all 'good-looking' kids"—presentable and responsible albeit not terribly verbal. "They had friends but weren't honest with them. Everything was 'fine and dandy'."

The title of Black's important 1981 book, "It Will Never Happen to Me" *(M.A.C.*

■ Trauma: Parental neglect

Denver, Colo.), reflects the typical codependent's mix of denial and false bravado. In it, she makes the point that the children in an alcoholic household never have an environment that is consistent and structured, two of the things they need most—and she, too, talks of such stock juvenile "roles" as the Responsible One and the Adjuster. Her unique

warning was that children who survive a parent's alcoholism by displaying unusual coping behavior often experience "emotional and psychological deficits" later on. They are also likely to become alcoholics, says Black, because "alcohol helps these persons become less rigid, loosen up and relax. When they drink they aren't quite so serious." Though those things happen to almost everyone who imbibes, Black says that "for those who are stuck in unhealthy patterns, alcohol may be the *only* thing that can provide relief."

Well, she guessed wrong there: a movement, manifested by often joyous meetings, has come along in the interim. At hundreds of COAs gatherings around the country tonight, people will talk and listen to each other's stories, to cry, to laugh and generally, as Ken Gill says, "recharge their batteries." "This program kept me from being an alcoholic myself," said a woman named Heather at a gathering in an affluent section of San Francisco last week. "Because I was the oldest, everything was always my fault. It's like when you make your parents breakfast and you bring them one scrambled egg and one fried egg—in my house I always scrambled the wrong egg." Heads bobbed in agreement. Who else but COAs could identify with a story about what happens when kids cook for their own mother and father?

Discovering self-esteem: Talking and listening: this is the way we've learned to

■ Physical abuse: An adult remembers

deal with problem drinking. And though it sounds wimpy, don't knock it; it's the surest way to alleviate not just the imbibing but the whole range of symptoms we call alcoholism. A woman named Nina stood up at a meeting in Boston last week, practically glossed over the fact that both her parents were alcoholics—and proceeded to speak about how well she was feeling and doing. COAs meetings and literature, she said, had allowed her to discover self-esteem. At another meeting, Carolyn told a story of complaining to her doctor about depression—and hearing the doctor shoot back a question about whether one of her parents was an alcoholic. "I was shocked," she said, and well she might be. Doctors, as a group, have yet to play a major role in helping mitigate the effects of alcohol, perhaps because the average medical-school student spends a grand total of between zero and 10 hours studying the affliction that kills 100,000 people annually.

An avalanche of information is coming, nevertheless, from another kind of M.D.—call them the Masters of Disaster, the people who've lived with alcoholism or worked with alcoholics so closely that they might as well be their kin. Robert Ackerman, a professor of sociology at Indiana University of Pennsylvania, has been studying the children of alcoholics for an exceedingly long time by the standards of the movement—since the early '70s. In his recent book "Let Go and Grow" *(Health Communications, Inc.)*, he reports on a survey he took to test the validity of Woititz's 13 generalizations about COAs, as well as seven more observations of his own. What he found was that "adult children of alcoholics identified about 20 percent more with these characteristics" than did the general population. Other professionals are reporting success with therapies involving hugging, acting out unresolved scenes from long ago and even playing one of several board games for children of alcoholics called Family Happenings and Sobriety. Cathleen Brooks, executive director of a program called Next Step in San Diego, reports that her clients often make life-changing strides after six to 18 months of primary treatment and make the decision never to drink or take drugs.

The 7 million COAs who are under the age of 18 are harder to help, if only because their parents' denial tends to keep them out of treatment. For these children who never know what to expect when they come home from school each day, life, says Woititz, "is a state of constant anxiety."

Some pediatricians think there is a link between such anxiety and childhood ulcers, chronic nausea, sleeping problems, eating disorders and dermatitis. Migs Woodside, from the COAs Foundation, says that the trained teacher can pick the child of an alcoholic out of a crowded classroom. "Sometimes you can tell by the way they are dressed or by the fact that they never have their lunch money," she says. "Sometimes you can tell by the way they suddenly pay attention when the teacher talks about drinking, and sometimes you can tell by their pictures."

Someday, 20 or 30 years from now, those children may feel a vague sense of failure or depression and be hard pressed to explain why. In the meantime, it's their Crayolas that are hard pressed. Beer cans—and not liquor or wine bottles—form a leitmotif in the work of young children of alcoholics. Occasionally, Woodside says, looking a little sad, the big stick figures can be seen tipping the cans into the mouths of the little stick figures.

CHARLES LEERHSEN *with* TESSA NAMUTH *and bureau reports*

Cocaine Effect on Babies Questioned

New study challenges the prevailing view

Neala S. Schwartzberg

Newsday Special Correspondent

During the early 1980s, researchers reported that babies born to mothers who used cocaine were in greater danger of mental and emotional problems than children born to mothers who were drug-free. Cocaine, especially in its smokable form, crack, was considered the most dangerous legal or illegal drug around, as far as babies were concerned.

But new evidence is challenging that view. Though everyone agrees that cocaine is far from benign, many researchers say its effects seem milder and vary more from child to child than once thought. And many say that the damage attributed to crack was often caused by a mix of substances, legal and illegal.

Nanci Stewart Woods and associates at the University of Florida examined 35 babies exposed to cocaine in the womb and a control group of 35 babies born to mothers who did not use the drug. Researchers found no evidence of cognitive or motor deficits either at birth, or at one month. Further, the babies exposed to cocaine performed at the same level as babies in the control group even when the investigators looked at the infants' ability to cope with their environment and to achieve and maintain an alert state.

"We expected to find them more easily overstimulated and overwhelmed given the statements that had been made about the behavior of cocaine-exposed babies," Woods said of the study, which followed the babies for one month. The group plans to publish its findings in an upcoming issue of the journal, Infant Behavior and Development.

The Florida results are not unique. Research at North Central Bronx Hospital, published in 1991, found no differences between a group of 51 cocaine- and crack-exposed infants and a group of 60 control babies when tested shortly after birth and approximately one month later on standard scales of development. Researchers at the University of Miami School of Medicine, reporting in 1991, found only minor effects due to cocaine exposure. Scientists looked at 26 cocaine-exposed babies and found they were more likely to respond to lights, sounds and sensations even after seeing them several times, compared to the same number of babies not exposed to cocaine prenatally. It seemed to take them longer to become familiar with these stimuli. But the tremors, irritability and restlessness thought to be cocaine-related were discovered to be the result of obstetrical complications and maternal alcohol use.

The idea that babies exposed to cocaine were in deep peril came mainly from anecdotal evidence. Researchers reported seeing that such children had sharply reduced development: A 3-year-old functioned on the level of a 4-month-old, a 5-year-old sat stone-faced one minute and ran riot the next for no apparent reason.

There were some studies that showed toddlers exposed to drugs prenatally showed more disorganized play, more scattering and batting of toys rather than fantasy play or exploration normally found in toddlers. Researchers also reported these babies had difficulty establishing a secure relationship with their mother. However, these studies ignored the effects on the child of living with a drug-abusing parent. These studies also mixed the impact of cocaine with the effects of other legal and illegal substances, ranging from heroin to marijuana to alcohol and even tobacco. In effect, some researchers now say, the studies really examined the misuse of multiple drugs, while attributing a disproportionate share of the blame on cocaine.

Even investigators who had decried the effects of cocaine have begun to soften their message. "These children cover a wide range. Some look perfectly fine, others do very poorly, the great majority are in the middle," notes Dr. Ira Chasnoff of the National Association for Perinatal Addiction Research and Education.

The closer researchers looked, the more difficult they say it has been to document the effects of cocaine. Cocaine is surely harmful. Babies exposed to cocaine prenatally are more likely to be premature, to be smaller for gestational age and experience more birth complications.

But women rarely use only cocaine. They also use tobacco and alcohol as well as illicit drugs ranging from marijuana to PCP. Alcohol has been linked to birth defects and mental retardation and smoking tobacco is one of the leading causes of growth retardation in the newborn. "There is no way to say which drug is worse," said Chasnoff.

Nor is there any way to predict whether cocaine will affect different babies in the same way or whether it will affect them at all. For example, Andy and Jenny both were exposed to cocaine through their mothers. But the similarity ends there.

A lively 4-year-old, Andy likes to run, ride his bike as fast as he can and in general be in charge. "He'll set his mind on something and he refuses to be distracted," says his adoptive mother Kathy, who asked that her son not be identified. "If he decides he wants a peanut butter sandwich with the peanut butter spread all the way to the edges and the ends cut off, that's what he wants and he won't be put off.

"He's a sweet and loving child, the protector of the little ones. If someone is hurt he runs over to comfort them and kiss them," said Kathy. Adopted by Kathy and her husband as an infant, Andy had to stay in the hospital for six weeks after birth because he tested positive for drugs and was considered "medically frail."

Andy still has problems, especially with his speech and language. "He talks constantly," his mother says, "but most people can't understand what he says and he's four years old. He's 100 percent better after a year in a preschool program, but he has a long way to go. And he gets so frustrated because people can't understand him."

One child who has experienced no lasting effects of prenatal cocaine exposure can only be identified as Jenny. It would be impossible to tell Jenny from any other child of above-average intelligence, yet her mother used crack while pregnant.

In effect, the studies really examined the misuse of multiple drugs, while attributing a disproportionate share of the blame on cocaine.

Jenny came to the attention of a special needs program only because she was born with a cleft palate which interfered with her speech. Checking into her history, the staff discovered that Jenny's mother had used both crack and alcohol. Although not premature, Jenny weighed less than three pounds at birth. Now, almost 3 years old, she is bright, always testing limits, trying to see how much she can get away with. Jenny's physical problem has long since been corrected, no one would ever suspect that she was the child of a crack user.

Focusing on the effects of cocaine not only obscures the pernicious effects of other legal and illegal drugs; it also sets up these babies to be stigmatized, say researchers.

"We are concerned that premature conclusions about the severity and universality of cocaine effects are in themselves potentially harmful to children," writes a team of doctors from Yale, Boston University and the National Institute of Child Health and Human Development near Wash-ington. They warned in a January commentary in the Journal of the American Medical Association, that society might be too harsh in its rush to judge the effects of cocaine on babies. The team included Drs. Linda Mayes and Richard Granger, of Yale, Dr. Marc Bornstein, of the national institute and Dr. Barry Zuckerman, of the Boston University School of Medicine.

The stigma attached to cocaine-exposed babies might also scare potential foster parents. "With current image of these babies as being brain-damaged," Woods said, "it is very scary for adoptive, natural or foster parents to consider raising the child. The anecdotal reports about attachments and emotional problems scare them."

Cocaine had been the catch-all, the simplest explanation for a child's difficulties. "When we get a target like crack," asserts Sandra Wolkoff, coordinator of the Early Childhood Training Institute, a professional and parent education unit at North Shore Child and Family Guidance Center, "It becomes all too easy to say 'if we take care of crack we'll have healthy babies.' But the truth is even if we got rid of crack tomorrow we'd still have high-risk babies."

The focus on cocaine as a major cause of difficulties obscured the importance of environmental factors, said Zuckerman, who is also chief of developmental and behavioral pediatrics at Boston City Hospital. Whether substance-exposed or not, children living in poverty are more likely than their more advantaged peers to suffer from low birthweight, prematurity, malnutrition, anemia, pre- and postnatal lead poisoning, and congenital infections. "By focusing on cocaine and not on lack of adequate nutrition, health care, and education," he said, "we conveniently can blame mothers and not the conditions of poverty."

Families vs. the lure of the streets

How a drug corner casts its long shadow of death

Scott Shane

Staff Writer

After Corey Baker was murdered last December, Angela Baker searched her only child's bedroom for clues to how she might have saved him from the devouring drug corner. She found a cassette, and played it on the stereo she'd bought him in a fruitless attempt to keep him off the streets.

In a wavering, adolescent attempt at a rap song, the 15-year-old chanted his own epitaph, an epitaph for dozens of boys and young men who have died around Park Heights and Woodland avenues in Northwest Baltimore:

So living on Park Heights there's only one thing you can do.

Go up and sell some blue tops. . . .

Running up to men and women saying, Do you want a dime?

Park Heights, Park Heights, the girls and the money and all the good stuff.

Not so long before he died, Corey Baker was a cheerful kid who liked to play Monopoly and Othello and was getting better at chess, who played guard on the Little League football team that won the championship in 1991, who spoke of becoming a pilot or a surgeon.

Then he started dabbling in the drug trade, and soon his name went onto the long roll of the dead in this nation's undeclared urban war, a war waged with the finest of modern firearms in the name of no cause greater than adolescent pride and a pocketful of $10 bills. Since 1988, within a half-mile of the intersection of Park Heights and Woodland, a territory pockmarked with drug dealing, 83 people have been murdered, 75 of them male and all of them black, with an average

age of 26. Approximately another 300 people have been shot and survived.

In a year in which the murder rate heads for a new record in the city as a whole, the Park Heights violence is growing worse. The number of gun assaults in the area has climbed from 52 in 1988 to 96 last year. At least five people have been killed in the neighborhood this summer.

It is a rate of violence not exceeded in many places in the world, apart from the shattered world, apart from the shattered cities of the former Yugoslavia, Mideast hot spots, South African townships and a few other places ripped by civil war. But it is mayhem quite typical of America's street drug markets, of which Park Heights and Woodland is not even Baltimore's worst.

Most of those murdered have been sons of the neighborhood. They have given their lives for the sparkle of a little gold, the right brand name on their tennis shoes, perhaps a sports car to draw a girl's gaze. Like Corey Baker, a striking number have left behind strict, working parents who had struggled to pull their children from the vortex of the corner.

Corey, his mother remembers with tears in her eyes, loved money. He loved to dream about the money he would have some day, loved to read books about making money. When he was 13, he took a grocery cart to the Preakness and hauled coolers between the parking lots and the racetrack all day for picnickers' change. "He came home that night with calluses on his feet and said, 'Mom, I made $40,' " his mother recalls.

The next summer, at 14, he got his first job through a Forest Park High School program. "When he got his first paycheck, $100 and something, he had such

a smile," says Ms. Baker, 33, an MTA bus driver. But he also complained about how slowly he had earned it: "He said, 'I have to work so long to get that little paycheck.' I said, 'Corey, that's life. Now you know what I go through.' "

That same summer, Corey discovered another way to make money, a shortcut around the tedious discipline of a real job for modest pay. He was recruited as a street salesman for the Woodland drug crew. His mother found out when police caught him sitting on some steps on Park Heights, holding two vials of cocaine.

Angela Baker, who prided herself on her close relationship with her son, pleaded with him to stay away from the drug corner. But the intoxication of the easy money overwhelmed her warnings. He began skipping his ninth-grade classes, drifting back to the corner.

One winter evening, as he and some buddies played with a dog in the drug zone, a young man walked up, pulled a gun, and ordered the boys to the ground.

"Give me the ring," the guy said.

Corey began to tug off the gold ring bearing his initial, "C." He'd bought it the year before for $49, saved from his $5-a-week allowance money. He'd wanted a bigger, thicker ring in a herringbone pattern, but his mother said no, afraid it would just make him a target for robbery.

"It's stuck, man," Corey told the gunman.

The man answered in the language of the drug corner. The single, .357-caliber Magnum bullet passed through Corey's heart and liver. The boy lay unconscious at Sinai Hospital for two days while his mother stood sleepless watch.

"The doctor said, 'Your son's a fighter.' But I saw the pain in his face," says Ms. Baker, 33. "He lasted about two days.

Then his body started blowing up, and I knew it wouldn't be long."

Public opinion is horrified by Baltimore's homicide rate, which corrodes the city's image, scares off business and fuels the exodus to the suburbs. But the drug-corner homicides that account for half of all murders have become dreary routine. "Drug-related" has come to carry more than a hint of "deserved," even though the category lumps neophyte ninth-graders like Corey Baker together with 30-year-old enforcers who have left a trail of bodies.

The media reflect this attitude and shape it: This newspaper gave Corey Baker's shooting a few lines in a police blotter and never reported his subsequent death. It is violence viewed through the wrong end of the telescope, a distant abstraction.

Turn the telescope around by talking with the grieving families and their neighbors, and the wrenching meaning of the statistics comes back into focus. In these green neighborhoods south of Pimlico Race Course, where patches of poverty alternate with solidly middle-class streets gunplay has long cast a pall over what might otherwise be quiet suburbia. Names like Woodland have lost the pastoral connotation that developers a few decades ago used as a selling point.

Today, this is a place where families can point out bullet holes in their cars and windows; where law-abiding homeowners adjust their lives and restrain their words for fear of offending teen-agers not half their age; where the contagion of the drug trade reaches into neat, well-furnished homes. It is a place where tragedy is played out, again and again, in private.

GUNFIRE AT NIGHT

No one knew what a "drug corner" was 25 years ago, when Charles and Deloris Langley came to Baltimore from North Carolina to visit relatives and stayed to build a better life. For a long time, it seemed they had found what they were looking for.

Mr. Langley, a cement finisher, worked steadily in the construction trade, traveling as far as Virginia, Pennsylvania and Delaware to find work in slow times. Mrs. Langley went to trade school and worked for 20 years as a data entry clerk.

In the cozy, tree-shaded house they bought on Woodland Avenue, they raised four sons, Cornelius, Charles Jr., Michael

and the baby of the family, Nicholas. The boys were "average, overactive, very athletic," says Mrs. Langley, 43, sitting on her living room sofa with family photos and plaques bearing inspirational poetry on the wall.

The Langley boys walked to neighborhood schools, haunted their local pool until they were made unofficial lifeguards, played with the family dog, Kramer, took overnight camping trips with their Boy Scout troop, accompanied by their father. There were weekend picnics on the Chesapeake at Sandy Point and family treks to Kings Dominion and Hershey Park. The boys spent part of most summers with Mrs. Langley's parents in Mount Olive, N.C.

Had the family lived, say, a few blocks farther east, that might have been the end of the story. But just two blocks west of their home on Woodland, a drug market was taking shape just as her sons reached their teen-age years. The parents worried about it and, from 1985 on, as occasional gunfire could be heard at night, spoke periodically of moving. Each time they decided they couldn't swing it financially.

One day in 1986, a neighbor called Mrs. Langley to tell her that Cornelius, who should have been in school, was at home with a large group of teen-agers. She sped home on her lunch hour and surprised her sheepish son, who mumbled "lame excuses."

Soon, Cornelius and Michael were coming home in expensive tennis shoes and sweat suits. "They would say somebody bought it for them," she recalls. She knew they were lying.

"I talked to them till I was blue in the face," she says. "We would have our conversations, and I'd say I knew what they were doing. When I came down real hard on them, they'd say, 'We're going to stop.' But they never did."

There are limits to a parent's control, she says. By the time Cornelius was 18 or 19, he would simply stay with friends when his parents pressured him to stop selling drugs.

"I've had people say it's the way they're brought up. But I'm a perfect example of how you can bring up your kids right, and it still can happen," she says.

What, she asks, should a loving parent do? "You don't want your kids selling drugs on the street," she says, "but you don't want them locked up, either. It involves kids you love, kids you brought into the world."

While she and her husband agonized, and went to their jobs, the inexorable logic of the drug world took its own course. One afternoon in August 1988, dealers from the area around North Avenue and Pulaski Street drove up to Park Heights and Woodland to put out "testers," drug samples. Cornelius and Michael confronted them, Michael using threatening words, and the interlopers left.

A few hours later two cars screeched up. Their occupants leapt out and gunned down Cornelius. Mrs. Langley, on her way home from work, drove up while her eldest son's body was still lying in the road.

The Langleys buried Cornelius, 21, in the family plot in North Carolina. When they returned, Michael was devastated by feelings of guilt, since he felt that his threats had prompted the attack.

"Michael didn't ever come back to himself," his mother says. "He didn't care. He said, 'My brother's dead, and I'd just as soon be dead.'"

One January midnight, five months after Cornelius was killed, Mrs. Langley lay awake in her bed and heard Michael and his cousin, Terrence, slam the door behind them. A few minutes later, she heard gunfire, by then a nightly routine. But when she heard Terrence burst through the door, she feared the worst.

"Michael's been shot," Terrence cried.

"My feet had already hit the floor," Mrs. Langley says. "I said to my husband, 'You'd better go out there, he's probably already dead.'"

She says she never learned the motive for the slaying. Michael, 19, was carrying two bags of heroin when he fell on nearby Palmer Avenue. Another veteran dealer says Michael's death was part of a feud between rival drug gangs; police believe it may have been a dispute over money.

Police arrested the man Michael had identified as Cornelius' killer. But Michael was the chief witness against him, and prosecutors were forced to drop the charges after Michael was killed. The case of Michael's murder languished for more than a year. Finally, a witness came forward, and Kevin Brooks, another young dealer, pleaded guilty to second-degree murder and was sentenced to 15 years.

Mrs. Langley was in North Carolina the day of the guilty plea: Tragedy had struck a third time, and she was burying her youngest son, 12-year-old Nicholas, killed when his bike was hit by a car 100 yards from his home.

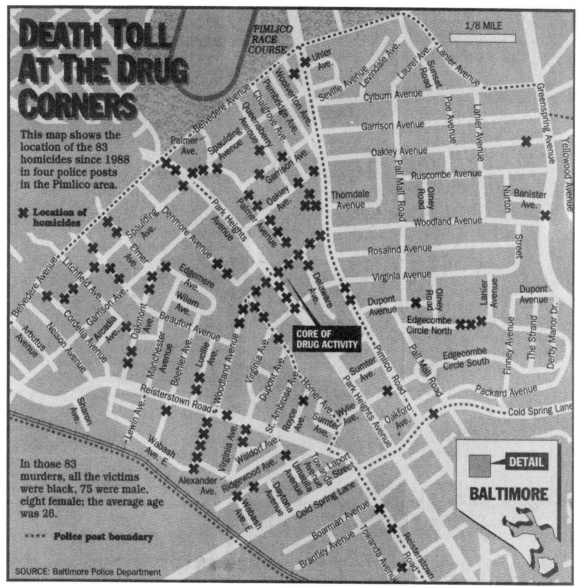

DEATH TOLL AT THE DRUG CORNERS

This map shows the location of the 83 homicides since 1988 in four police posts in the Pimlico area.

✖ **Location of homicides**

CORE OF DRUG ACTIVITY

In those 83 murders, all the victims were black, 75 were male, eight female; the average age was 26.

• • • • **Police post boundary**

SOURCE: Baltimore Police Department

DETAIL BALTIMORE

1/8 MILE

ROBERT CRONAN/STAFF GRAPHIC

For Michael's funeral program, composed on her sister's computer, Mrs. Langley had written: "As it has pleased the Almighty God to take from our midst our beloved son, though we cannot explain His reasons, yet we still trust in His almighty wisdom. He never makes a mistake."

After Nicholas' death, Mrs. Langley says, her faith was shaken. "I'd put a question mark after that," she says.

No matter what route she takes from her home, she says, "I see one of my sons lying in the street." In July, she returned to North Carolina to look for work, with the idea of leaving Baltimore and its memories behind for good. The Langleys' only living son, Charles, has settled in Mount Olive and is working as a moving man.

Asked for the names of contempor-aries of Cornelius and Michael who would remember them, Mrs. Langley thinks for a minute. Then she shakes her head.

"Just about everybody the kids associated with," she says quietly, "is dead."

'YOU WANT TO FIT IN'

The drug corner exacted from the Langley family such a price that you might expect to find nothing comparable in all of Baltimore. In fact, you only have to walk a few blocks, across the intersection of Park Heights and Woodland, to the Toles' house on Homer Avenue.

Dallas Toles Jr., 55, lost both of his sons. Then, in a decision that baffled a judge, he saved his second son's killer from prison.

For years, friends say, Mr. Toles has commuted to Virginia to a job as a tun-neler, tough, dirty work that paid a decent wage. He knew the neighborhood drug dealing might become a temptation to his sons, and he worked to make sure they would never have to turn to the streets for money.

But money is only part of the attraction. The drug corner entices because it conveys status. When some of the Woodland dealers and their musical friends taped a rap cassette last year, calling themselves "YBM," for "Young Black Mafia," they posed on the cover with their guns—and sold several thousand copies. The corner dealers are the big shots of a teen-agers' world.

"You want to fit in," says Jerome Bris-coe, an assistant state's attorney who

143

often prosecutes drug cases. "Fitting in on the drug corner means carrying a Tec-9 [assault pistol]. Fitting in there means at least hanging out with the guys who are twirling [dealing] drugs."

And so Mr. Toles' older son, also Dallas, 17, started hanging out. One evening in 1989, 11 months after Michael Langley's death, he was shot in the head at C&C Grocery, on the southwest corner of Park Heights and Woodland. Police found 14 bags of cocaine and $270 on his body.

As often is the case, the motive was never quite clear: Friends said it was a dispute over a girl; another says it was a botched robbery; police concluded it was a fight for drug territory. A young man named Michael Calloway was convicted of the murder and sentenced to 50 years in prison.

Then, one afternoon last January, Mr. Toles' second son, whom everyone called Scooter, was tussling in front of the house on Homer Avenue with another kid, named Tony. Mr. Toles came running out to see what the trouble was. Scooter's best friend, Clifton Mosley, aimed his revolver at Tony and fired once. The aim of a 15-year-old being what it is, the bullet hit Scooter, 16, in the upper left chest.

"Cliff, why'd you do that?" Scooter asked. Those were his last words. Clifton had killed his best friend.

The police caught Clifton a month later in an apartment a half-mile from the murder scene. They arrested him along with Bryant Warren, 22, a longtime dealer on the west side of Park Heights and Woodland, for whom both Scooter and Clifton had been selling, and confiscated a kilogram of cocaine and two handguns. From jail Clifton wrote to Scooter's parents to say he was sorry.

A man who has lost two sons in the drug wars might be expected to look to the courts for vengeance. But the drug corner consumes some young lives by means of bullets and others by means of long prison terms. For the people who live nearby, the two can come to seem like flip sides of the same fate.

Mr. Toles told prosecutors that he didn't want Clifton to go to prison, and he stuck to his position. Without his eyewitness testimony, they had no choice but to accept a guilty plea to manslaughter, a 10-year suspended sentence and five years on probation.

Judge Elsbeth L. Bothe accepted the plea but was frustrated by the result.

"Where'd this gun come from?" she demanded in court last June.

"From a junkie," said Clifton.

"Why'd you buy it, so you could kill your best friend?" the judge pressed.

Clifton didn't answer.

"Well, the problem is, that's what happens when people have guns. Guns don't know who they're killing," she said.

Then the judge turned to Scooter's father and stepmother, Jeanette Harcum. "How can you agree to this kind of thing?" she asked.

Mr. Toles remained silent. Ms. Harcum spoke up.

"This was an accident. They were best friends," she said. "It's hard to explain. He's 15. He's got a chance. It's not going to bring our son back."

'KILLING YOUR COMMUNITY'

At the funeral in December for Corey Baker, the big March Funeral Home chapel on Wabash Avenue was filled to capacity. Gregory Harris, Corey's best friend from school read a poem he'd written to comfort the family. An a cappella quartet, the Undercovers, sang.

The Rev. Frank M. Reid 3rd gave a spellbinding sermon on "the dark side of Christmas," urging the young African-Americans present to learn from Corey's death.

"God, we've got to admit we're tired of burying our children. No, God, it's not the Ku Klux Klan that's killing our children. It's us. . . . More and more of our young men and young women are having their lives stolen not by their oppressor, but by young people who look just like them."

Mr. Reid suggested that the ultimate responsibility for the guns and drugs rested with the larger society of whites, which manufactures the guns and imports the drugs. But he told his audience that if they take part in the drug trade, they are accomplices in the wars that are costing so many young, black lives.

"Every time you sell a little bit of crack, a little bit of rock, you're killing your community," he said. "If you don't change your life, we'll be back here next year, crying over you."

Several people had witnessed Corey's killing, and at least one witness eventually identified the alleged killer to police. Keith Minor, 22, a convicted cocaine dealer who lived about three blocks away, was arrested six weeks after the murder and jailed.

But, as frequently occurs after drug-corner shootings, no witnesses were willing to risk the gunslingers' retribution by

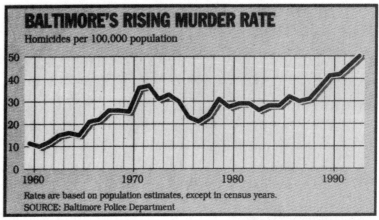

BALTIMORE'S RISING MURDER RATE
Homicides per 100,000 population

Rates are based on population estimates, except in census years.
SOURCE: Baltimore Police Department

ROBERT CRONAN/STAFF GRAPHIC

going to court to testify. The charges were dropped and Keith Minor was freed less than two months after his arrest.

He was released from jail March 22. Police say that on April 16 Keith Minor abducted and raped a 12-year-old girl who was walking home from school. He awaits trial on the rape charge, and police say he is still considered a suspect in Corey's murder.

There was little comfort for Angela Baker from the legal system. But, devastated by her son's death, searching for a useful way to express her grief, Ms. Baker turned to the community for help.

Mr. Reid's sermon had expressed the hope that Corey's death would mark a turning point, a sacrifice that would begin the slow process of "turning Baltimore City around." He called for "a spiritual army of young men and women" who would "take this community back."

When Angela Baker heard about Scooter Toles' death a few weeks after Corey's, she, her relatives and friends decided to try to rally the neighborhood against the killing. They began by distributing 300 flyers calling for a candlelight vigil one February evening at Park Heights and Woodland, in the heart of the drug market.

The night of the vigil, a score of Corey's family and friends from around the city arrived, holding handmade signs that said "Black on Black Crime Must Stop" and "Let's Save Our Children." Angela Baker held one bearing a photograph of her son: "I Miss You, Corey," it said.

However, from the immediate neighborhood, only three people joined the vigil. One boy, riding past on his bike, stopped to tell Ms. Baker he was the one who put a foam pillow under Corey's head as he lay on the pavement. A clutch of teen-agers marred the ceremony by walking past with cassette player defiantly turned up to a deafening pitch.

Angela Baker was deeply upset, puzzled that so few neighbors would come out to protest the continuing catastrophe of the drug corner. "The response I got, it just hurt me," she said, choking up at the memory months later. "It's like people lock themselves in their homes and just don't care.

"Part of it's fear, I guess, and part just don't care," Ms. Baker said. "Until we all get together, nothing's going to change."

The Economy of Drug Use

Drugs are not simply used; they are also bought and sold. They are the foundation for a number of major economic enterprises. The alcoholic beverage industry earns $50 billion at the retail level in the United States each year; some $30 billion is spent on tobacco products and $30 billion on pharmaceuticals; $10 billion is spent for over-the-counter medications. The size of the illegal drug industry is more difficult to determine because, as we saw, its sales are not taxed and, therefore, not officially recorded anywhere. Estimates range from $40 to $100 billion; if we average the estimates, this would make the illegal drug trade—if combined into a single industry—the most profitable business in the country, with a dollar volume larger than that of General Motors. Several journalists claim that more money is spent on illegal drugs than for any other existing product or service—more than on food, clothes, housing, education, or medical care. No one doubts that the drug trade is huge and extremely profitable.

Each drug is bought and sold in a somewhat different way, by a somewhat different cast of characters. Some drugs are legal, and their manufacturers are seen as respectable pillars of their communities. Other drugs are illegal, and their sellers are designated as villains, denounced in the media by politicians and other upstanding citizens. Some drugs are produced from plants that grow naturally in the wild or in an agricultural setting: Marijuana is made up of the leaves and flowering tops of the cannabis plant; opium is exuded when the mature pod of a type of poppy is lanced; peyote is the dried, sliced "buttons" of a desert cactus; psilocybin is the active ingredient in several species of mushroom, *Psilocybe mexicana* among them, that grow in the southwest. Other drugs, referred to as semisynthetics, were derived from natural substances that were chemically transformed— cocaine's origin was the coca plant, heroin's the opium poppy. Still others are completely synthetic chemicals, manufactured from other chemicals in a laboratory. A particular source necessitates a particular type of distribution, as well as a distinct economic activity.

One of the most painful ironies of the drug scene is the toleration and even encouragement that the legal drug trade receives, and the aggressiveness with which it pursues its business. True, some restraints have been placed on the tobacco and alcohol industries. In the United States, cigarettes cannot be advertised on televi-sion; warning labels must be placed on all packs of cigarettes sold; television commercials cannot depict alcoholic beverages being drunk; still-active athletes cannot advertise alcohol or cigarettes. But these are relatively moderate measures. (In some countries, alcohol and tobacco products cannot be advertised at all.) The legal drug industry lobbies forcefully against restrictions of any kind, and is often successful in blocking legislation that would cut into its profits or impede business in any way. For instance, the tobacco industry is waging a (in the long run, losing) campaign to convince the public and legislators that smoking in public is a basic right, comparable to the right of free speech, guaranteed by the Bill of Rights. And so far, the alcoholic beverage industry has been successful in blocking legislation to require that the contents of alcoholic beverages be listed on bottles sold to the public.

The economic activities of the illegal drug trade impact upon society in somewhat different ways. Dealers and smugglers are less likely to attempt to influence legislation or win the hearts and minds of the general public. In contrast, their methods tend to be cruder and more direct. Colombian cocaine kingpins offer the police and judges in their jurisdiction the choice of *plata o plomo* (silver or lead), that is, money or a bullet, a bribe in exchange for not arresting, prosecuting, or convicting them for their crimes, or death for doing so. In the United States, drug dealers have less unopposed powers, but they often dominate certain neighborhoods through intimidation and violence.

In short, those who sell drugs, whether legal or illegal, generally take steps to protect their profits. The economic character of the drug trade translates into power, or, at least, attempts to wield power. While this power is often struggled against and often overcome, it is a fixture of the drug scene and determines many crucial aspects of drug use and abuse specifically, and the structure and dynamics of the society generally. The economic dimension in the world of drug use is so important that it is ignored only at the risk of serious distortion.

Looking Ahead: Challenge Questions

Does the profit earned by the legal drug industry justify its acceptance? Can the same be said of the illegal drug trade? Should drug dealers and smugglers pay taxes?

Are the taxes paid by the cigarette and alcohol industries enough to cover the damage their use does to the society?

Should the alcohol and tobacco industries be more tightly regulated than they are? Should alcohol and cigarette ads be banned altogether? Must the contents of alcoholic beverages be listed on bottles sold to the public? Do we have the right to know what we are drinking? Should the tobacco industry be forced to pay for antismoking ads to counter their own commercials?

Is the right to smoke in public a basic right equivalent to free speech, guaranteed by the Bill of Rights? What about the right of the person near the smoker who finds cigarette smoke irritating?

Given the fact that drug dealers enforce their will through violence, how can their activities ever be eliminated?

Does the economic character of the drug trade influence drug use and abuse? How? If there were no profits in drugs, would anyone use them?

Worldwide Drug Scourge

The Expanding Trade in Illicit Drugs

This article is the first of a two-part series examining the global drug challenge in the post-Cold War era. The first part outlines how the revolutionary changes in the international system are altering patterns of drug production, trafficking, and consumption. The second part* will examine current U.S. drug control strategy and suggest how it might be revised to secure better results both at home and abroad.

Stephen Flynn

Lieutenant Stephen Flynn is a Coast Guard officer who is serving as a guest scholar in the Brookings Foreign Policy Studies program. This article presents the findings of a year-long project that he directed while serving as an adjunct fellow at the Center for Strategic and International Studies and as a Council on Foreign Relations International Affairs fellow. The author gratefully acknowledges the assistance of Rens Lee, Lamond Tullis, Richard Clayton, Bob Nieves, Felix Jimenez, David Long, Bill Taylor, Georges Fauriol, and Greg Grant.

Now that the Cold War is over, calls for a greater emphasis on the American domestic agenda have reached a crescendo. The problem of illicit drugs is invariably mentioned as one of the leading domestic ills deserving the full measure of the federal government's attention. But the drug issue is no more purely a domestic problem than are ozone depletion and disease control. As with greenhouse gas emissions and the AIDS epidemic, the drug scourge is a global phenomenon, and it is expanding at an alarming pace. Further, even the most aggressive domestic response cannot insulate the United States from the political, economic, and social fallout associated with the explosive growth in illicit drugs worldwide.

In the Central Asian republics, for instance, thousands of acres have been given over to the cultivation of opium poppies and cannabis. Over the past year, Hungary and Czechoslovakia have become major transit countries for Asian heroin destined for West Europe. Recently, Polish health officials warned that a dramatic rise in intravenous drug abuse in Warsaw has unleashed an AIDS epidemic. Especially ominous are reports of expanding organized criminal networks engaged in drug trafficking with the former Soviet Union, Central Europe, and Latin America.

The surge in the illicit narcotics trade in Eurasia and elsewhere has been first and foremost fueled by its tremendous profitability. Today drugs are a $100 billion a year transnational

[*See *Brookings Review,* Spring 1993. Ed.]

industry. The illicit stockholders and operatives come from every continent and include Colombians, Mexicans, Italians, Nigerians, Poles, Turks, Chinese, Lebanese, and Georgians.

Second, the recent unraveling of socialism and the move toward freer trade among industrialized countries has created a fertile environment for international businesses—even illicit ones—as deregulation and integration gather momentum. As commercial banks, investment firms, insurance companies, full-service brokers, and asset managers have all globalized their operations, the menu of financial institutions through which both clean and dirty money can be moved has never been so extensive. With the North American Free Trade Agreement, EC '92, the Asia-Pacific Economic Cooperation effort, and the collapse of the Iron Curtain, torrents of people, goods, and services are pouring across borders. In their midst, drug shipments can move with little risk of detection by customs authorities.

Third, the colossal social and economic dislocations connected with both the implosions of the communist world and the desperate standard of living in much of the third world are creating the ideal climate for widespread drug production and abuse. In the third world, the loss of superpower benefactors, declining rates of per capita GNP, unstable commodity prices, and rising domestic and foreign debt make the hard currency and profits connected with the drug trade almost irresistible. For many of the destitute and disaffected survivors of impoverished third world states and once rigidly controlled communist societies, drugs offer a seductive reprieve from an unpleasant world.

Finally, the recent resurgence of ethnic, religious, and nationalistic conflict slows or precludes altogether the development of new regional and international regulatory regimes to control illicit activities within the global community. It also hampers intelligence sharing and cooperation among neighboring law enforcement agencies, a development of which criminal drug organizations are a direct beneficiary.

The results: the production of heroin, cocaine, cannabis, and synthetic drugs is at a record high and will continue to

From *The Brookings Review,* Winter 1993, pp. 6-11. © 1993 by The Brookings Institute. Reprinted by permission.

rise; narcotics traffickers are moving drugs and money throughout the international economy with virtual impunity; and drug consumption is exploding in many countries that had hitherto escaped the drug scourge.

Global Drug Production

Because drug production is illicit, estimating its worldwide extent can be no more than an exercise in guesswork. But clearly the production of opium poppy, coca, and cannabis is on the rise. According to U.S. government estimates, in 1991 cocaine production in Latin America grew by 85 tons—a 7 percent increase over 1990. Opium production was estimated to be 4,200 tons in 1991, a 33 percent increase since 1988. Hashish production from the four major producing countries grew 65 percent between 1990 and 1991 to 1,244 tons.

More disturbing than the rise in global drug production is the sudden proliferation of producers. Within Peru, the world's leading producer of coca, illicit cultivation has spread out of the Upper Huallaga Valley into the Cuzco, Ayacucho, Pasco, and Puno Departments. New coca cultivation has been reported in remote regions in Brazil, Ecuador, and Venezuela. Cocaine refinement, once restricted to Colombia, now takes place in Peru, Bolivia, Venezuela, Argentina, Ecuador, and Brazil. Brazil's involvement is particularly ominous since it is the only South American country where acetone and ether, the chemicals used to turn coca base into cocaine, are manufactured in industrial quantities. Over the past year, European authorities have even discovered cocaine processing laboratories in Portugal, Spain, and Italy.

Opium cultivation has spilled over from the traditional production regions of Mexico, the Golden Triangle (Burma, Thailand, and Laos), and the Golden Crescent (Pakistan, Afghanistan, and Iran). Guatemala and Colombia are now major source countries in the Western hemisphere. U.S. officials estimate that Colombia may have produced about 4 tons of heroin in 1992—close to Mexico's 6.8 tons in 1990. The Colombians almost certainly have the means to become the chief world heroin suppliers of the 21st century.

In Eurasia, extensive opium poppy cultivation has been reported in Poland, Ukraine, Moldova, the Caucasus, and Central Asia. In January 1992 Sergey Tershchenko, the prime minister of Kazakhstan, legalized the cultivation of the opium poppy. The government of Kyrgzstan toyed with the idea, but backed away. In Central Asia, per capita income is approximately 40 percent below, and unemployment nearly 70 percent above, the average of the other former Soviet states. The economic incentives for poppy production will be even greater when Moscow ends its annual subsidy of billions of rubles to the region. Central Asia could very well become the "Andean region" of Eurasia.

Opium cultivation has also reemerged in China after being virtually eliminated by the communists when they seized power in 1949. Law enforcement authorities have spotted poppies in at least 13 of China's 23 provinces and 5 autonomous regions, with the largest plots in the remote southern province of Yunnan and in the northern province of Inner Mongolia.

Among traditional source countries for cannabis (the United States ranks second), production fell in 1991 because of bad weather and stepped-up eradication efforts. Still, the capacity for large-scale cultivation is spreading quickly. Brazil has become a major producer, with illegal cultivation taking place in at least 20 of its 26 states. In the former Soviet Union cannabis plants grow freely on more than 2.5 million acres, mostly in Kazakhstan, Kyrgzstan, Siberia, and the Far East. Cannabis is being grown throughout Africa. Hashish production soared in 1991, with Lebanon increasing its total production almost sixfold over 1990.

Production of synthetic narcotics also appears to be spreading. Laboratories in Taiwan and South Korea are the chief source of "ice," a high-purity methamphetamine developed during the mid-1980s. Poland has recently become one of the largest producers of amphetamines for the European market. According to police lab analyses, in 1991 some 20 percent of the amphetamines seized in West Europe and 25 percent of those seized in Germany originated in Poland. Underground laboratories for synthetic drugs have been discovered in Moscow, St. Petersburg, Sverdlovsk, and many other large cities in the former Soviet Union. Methaqualone ("mandrax") is produced throughout India, primarily for the large market in Southern Africa.

Spreading Like Weeds

Neither geography nor laboratory technology can constrain the cultivation of illicit drugs. Poppy, coca, and cannabis can be grown almost anywhere, and the ability to refine them or to produce synthetic drugs is widely available. All the coca and opium poppy plants being grown in the world would fill a space not much larger than the Eastern Shore of Maryland. The global capacity for cultivating these drugs is virtually untapped.

Illicit drug production is taking root most quickly in areas with few other meaningful economic options. Sub-Saharan Africa, Inner Mongolia, southern China, Central Asia, Afghanistan, and northeastern Brazil are among the most remote and impoverished places on the planet. Although peasants rarely get rich growing coca, poppies, or cannabis, they can earn up to 10 times what they can by growing traditional farm products. That can mean the difference between providing for the most basic needs of one's family or exposing it to life-threatening poverty.

Throughout much of the developing world, national currencies are nonexchangeable and worthless. Businessmen trying to finance capital improvements, insurgents and terrorists seeking the weapons and resources to fight their causes, and governments struggling to keep their economies afloat are in desperate need of hard currency at a time of global capital shortage. For them, too, the drug trade is almost the only answer.

The temptation to produce drugs may also prove almost irresistible in Eastern Europe and the former Soviet Union.

In Eurasia, extensive opium poppy cultivation has been reported in Poland, Ukraine, Moldova, the Caucasus, and Central Asia.

---

7. THE ECONOMY OF DRUG USE

One-third of the people in Hungary now live below the poverty level. By the end of 1991 unemployment in eastern Germany was 30 percent. In Russia as many as 10–11 million people, or 15 percent of the work force, may be unemployed by the year's end.

Drugs are usually produced where they are most difficult to stop—generally in remote areas safely outside a government's reach, often in territory under the sway of insurgency groups. The criminal organizations that support drug production have the resources to corrupt, intimidate, or bypass the authority of governments that, in addition, often face political problems that are more pressing than drugs or cannot take effective enforcement action because of a lack of political legitimacy.

The "Big Business" of Drug Trafficking

In essence, drug trafficking is a form of commodities trade conducted by transnational consortiums. Acquiring chemicals to produce drugs, transporting the drugs to wholesale distributors, and laundering the profits require interacting with and blending into legitimate markets. The size and complexity of these operations mandate that the drug industry pattern itself after the modern multinational corporation. Yet unlike traders in oil, automobiles, or microchips, traders in illicit drugs must outwit a dynamic enforcement environment designed to defeat them. Consequently, over the past two decades the drug trade has undergone something of a Darwinian evolution, the survivors of which have developed into sophisticated and highly flexible organizations. As one senior American drug enforcement official put it, "Lee Iacocca could learn a heck of a lot from these people!"

For those in the business of moving illicit drugs and money, the post–Cold War era has much to offer: a trend toward privatization and liberalization; an increase in the volume and diversity of world trade; the deregulation of national economies; the integration of global transportation, communications, and financial systems; and increasingly open and unmonitored borders between states. And since trafficking organizations are not bound by the legal constraints of domestic and international commerce regulation, they are particularly well placed to respond rapidly and with considerable ingenuity to these changes in the international economic system.

A prime example of the modern drug trafficking organization is the Cali "cartel." Like its better known counterpart from Medellin, the Cali cartel is a loose conglomeration of Colombian families based in a major Colombian city. But unlike the often violent Medellin cartel, which conjures up images of well-heeled thugs surrounded by private armies, the Cali cartel operates more like the senior management team at Exxon or Coca Cola. Its transportation, distribution, and money-laundering networks cover the globe. Outside the Western hemisphere, Cali operatives work in Japan, Hungary, Czechoslovakia, Poland, Germany, Italy, Spain, Portugal, the Netherlands, France, and Great Britain.

Because the huge U.S. and European markets are so far from coca production areas, transportation is critical to the cocaine business. Contrary to popular belief, most drugs do not cross American borders on low-flying Cessnas or aboard fast-moving "cigarette" boats. Most reach their markets by way of commercial conveyances. Containerized shipments, bulk cargo, false documentation, and front companies conceal the movement of cocaine by water. By land, most co-caine crosses the U.S.-Mexican border in hidden compartments of tractor trailers and other vehicles or in commercial cargo itself. For these border crossings, the Cali cartel relies on Mexican smugglers.

The Cali organization uses international shipping centers in Central and South America, particularly in Brazil, Venezuela, Surinam, and Panama, to ship cocaine by sea to Europe and to the eastern United States. It conceals the drugs in a variety of imaginative ways, one of the most creative of which was to hide 15.7 tons of cocaine in 2,000 concrete cement posts (U.S. authorities seized that shipment in September 1991). Occasionally drugs are shipped to the United States circuitously, passing through Europe or Canada before arriving.

When commercial airliners are used for shipping cocaine, the drug is hidden on the plane itself, or it is carried by human "mules," who swallow condoms containing pellets of cocaine. It is also concealed in luggage with false bottoms, in aerosol cans, and sneakers with hollowed-out soles. Sometimes it is converted to liquid and smuggled in bottles of shampoo, mouthwash, and liquor.

By blending shipments within the growing volume of international trade, the Cali cartel greatly reduces the chance of discovery. Interdicting drugs has always been a "needle-in-a-haystack" exercise for customs authorities, but when those drugs are hidden among general merchandise or on the person of international travelers, the task becomes overwhelming. In 1991, for example, 1.8 million containers arrived in the Port of Newark alone, but U.S. customs inspectors there were able to search thoroughly only 15–18 containers a day.

Getting the Goods to the Wholesalers

Once the drug arrives, it must be distributed. The Cali cartel has set up wholesale distribution networks throughout the country and exercises complete control over the New York and Washington, D.C., markets. If a load of cocaine arrives at Kennedy International Airport or at the Port of Newark, one of the 10 to 12 Cali distribution cells in New York receives it. Each cell, made up of 15–20 Colombian employees who earn monthly salaries ranging from $2,000 to $7,500, conducts an average of $25 million of business a month. Each cell is self-contained, with information tightly

---

The surge in the illicit narcotics trade in Eurasia and elsewhere has been first and foremost fueled by its tremendous profitability.

---

compartmentalized. Only a handful of managers know all the operatives. The cell has a head, bookkeeper, money handler, cocaine handler, motor pool, and 10 to 15 apartments serving as stash houses.

Communications are conducted in code over facsimile machines, cellular phones, and pay phones. To eliminate any risk of interception, cellular phones are purchased and discarded, often two or three times a week. When a wholesale customer wants to make a purchase, a cell member is notified by a pager system. That cell member proceeds to a public phone and arranges a rendezvous site. He then gets, from the motor pool, a rental car that is returned to the rental agency after the transaction. The transaction itself, including any travel receipts, is logged by the bookkeeper, and the money is turned over to the money handler to be shipped to the financial network set up by the cartel to hide and invest it. A favorite way to ship within the United States is the U.S. Postal Service's "Express Mail."

Such tactics stretch traditional law enforcement surveillance to the limit and beyond. Most national police authorities are finding themselves completely "outgunned" by technologies that are relatively cheap for organized crime but financially out of reach for the law enforcement community. The situation in Poland is suggestive. Between 1990 and 1991, Poland's police budget fell 13 percent. The use of patrol cars was limited to 60 kilometers a day, and police abandoned plans to modernize their vehicles or buy new car radios. Throughout the country only 30 police officials were assigned full-time to antidrug operations.

Once the cartel has received the money for its drug sales, it moves it into and through the legal financial system to conceal its origins. If the Cali cell broken up by federal authorities in December 1991 is typical, the Cali financial network must launder up to $300 million each year per cell. Money laundering typically involves three independent phases. First, drug proceeds are "placed," or used to make deposits or to purchase monetary instruments or securities that can be turned into cash elsewhere. Second, the money is "layered," or sent through multiple electronic funds transfers or other transactions to make it difficult to track and blur its illicit origin. Finally, the source of the money disappears as it is "integrated," or invested into seemingly legitimate accounts and enterprises.

The revolution under way in the global financial and banking markets has made all three of these jobs easier. Drug traffickers have a vast new array of possibilities for the placement of funds as national currencies become convertible and new and largely unregulated private banking institutions spring up throughout the former Soviet bloc and the third world. Many of the new banks have primitive accounting practices, no computers, and little or no experience with international banking practices. The integration and increased efficiency of the global banking system allows money launderers to layer money with virtual impunity. The sheer volume of electronic funds transfers makes them almost impossible to track. In 1991, for example, the Clearing House Interbank Payment System handled some 37 billion transactions worth $222 trillion. Finally, the sudden shift away from state to private ownership throughout the former communist world provides launderers with an array of "front" organizations to integrate their money into seemingly legitimate enterprises. The Cali cartel set up a number of such companies in Hungary, Czechoslovakia, and Poland in 1991.

Of course, the Cali cartel is not the only beneficiary of the changing international business environment. Italian, Polish, Turkish, Georgian, Chinese, Vietnamese, Lebanese, Pakistani, Nigerian, and many other transnational trafficking organizations are profiting as well.

Trends in Global Drug Consumption

Predicting with any precision the character and dimension of the global drug market is difficult. Most drug abuse research has been done on population groups within advanced societies, and epidemiologists are understandably hesitant to apply these findings to the developing world. Too, drug epidemics typically refuse to stay within tidy political, cultural, or geographical boundaries. Islamic fundamentalism seems to help explain why drug abuse is uncommon in Saudi Arabia, but not why more than a million Iranians and 1.7 million Pakistanis use drugs.

But although it may not be possible to anticipate precisely which specific locations are likely to suffer from widespread abuse and when, forecasting the overall trend in global drug consumption is less problematic. The prospect for growing drug abuse worldwide can be correlated with the prevalence of its three requisite ingredients: an awareness of drugs, access to them, and the motivation to use them.

The awareness of drugs has become almost universal. In the third world, demographic pressures are forcing millions of people out of their isolation in remote villages and into large cities, where it is impossible not to know about drugs. And the collapse of the communist regimes in the former Soviet bloc has ended the state's monopoly on information and has made it possible for people to travel freely both at home and abroad. Word of a drug that has acquired popularity somewhere can spread quickly almost everywhere.

Access to drugs is also increasing with the projected rise in production and trafficking. Further, if democratization and economic liberalization persist, individuals will have greater personal freedom, mobility, and control over their personal incomes, facilitating contacts with drug distributors and their purchases.

People in most third world societies are also increasingly motivated to use drugs. For one thing, the population of the developing world is growing younger. More than half the people in Nigeria and Kenya, and more than 40 percent in Latin America, are under the age of 20—an age group known for risk-taking behavior and the willingness to challenge social conventions. In addition, rapid population growth rates are causing people, particularly young men, to move to big cities. Separated from their families, often unemployed or underemployed, and with little opportunity for schooling, more and more of these disillusioned young people are at great risk of taking up drugs.

Peer pressure and the mass media can also push vulnerable young people to become drug users. Many European and American movies and television programs—even programs like "Miami Vice" and movies like "Scarface" that presumably show that "drug crimes don't pay"—portray drugs as luxury goods consumed by wealthy Americans. As such, drugs end up serving as status symbols, or as one Nigerian addict recently put it, as a way to "become like an American."

Finally, the dislocations associated with the end of the socialist experiment and the desperate economic plight of much of the third world are increasing the willingness of people, young and old, to violate the law.

Drug Use on the Rise

What evidence is there that global drug consumption is in fact on the rise? Although the data are soft, health officials around the globe are becoming increasingly alarmed. In Poland, 75 percent of all alcoholics are also addicted to either licit or illicit drugs. Most of these drug abusers in Poland are infected with the AIDS virus as a result of sharing intravenous needles. In Yugoslavia there are 300,000–400,000 addicts, with more than 15,000 in Belgrade alone. Estimates of drug abuse in the former Soviet Union range anywhere from 1.5 million to 7.5 million people. In all three areas, the spread of drug abuse is worst among the young. Almost two-thirds of Polish drug abusers are under 21 years of age.

In Eastern and Southern Asia nearly every country is reporting rising drug abuse. As the Burmese heroin trade has spilled increasingly into the subcontinent, Nepal, Bangladesh, and India all confront burgeoning user populations. In Pakistan, heroin users have grown from a few hundred to more than a million in little over a decade. Drug use in Thailand appeared to be stabilizing after an initial surge in large-scale opium poppy production in the 1970s, but new reports indicate that many villagers are shifting from traditional opium consumption to the more debilitating heroin addiction. As noted, opium and heroin are making a comeback in China, where police estimate that 300,000 use drugs, despite a relentless enforcement effort that featured the public execution of 250 drug traffickers in 1991.

In the barrios of Central and South America, cocaine addiction is becoming more prevalent, with the most worrisome trends in Colombia, Peru, Bolivia, Brazil, Ecuador, and Panama. One of every three secondary school students in Peru uses drugs. In Chile, Argentina, and Brazil, drug consumption is rising most dramatically among young people from upper-income families.

Africa represents the greatest unknown in the consumption picture, though it has virtually all the high-risk factors. Nigeria, Kenya, and South Africa, the wealthiest countries on the Sub-Saharan continent, are witnessing a rising incidence of drug abuse. In South Africa the drug of choice is "mandrax," a synthetic drug imported from India. In Nigeria and Kenya cannabis is the most widely abused drug, although there have been a growing number of reports of cocaine and heroin use.

The seductiveness of mood-altering substances is age-old and virtually universal. As the conditions that support widespread abuse become more prevalent within much of the global community, the prospect of expanding drug markets appears almost inevitable.

Needed: An International Response

The profound changes connected with the passing of the Cold War era have transformed the drug trade into a transnational challenge of the first order. As with other such challenges—weapons proliferation, disease control, migration, ozone depletion—states can do little on their own to stand up against the rising tide of drug production, trafficking, and consumption.

Acknowledging that the drug trade has become a transnational activity that is outstripping the traditional tools available to governments to combat it has important implications for current U.S. drug control strategy. In 1992, 93.6 percent of the $11.9 billion national drug control budget was spent on domestic enforcement, demand reduction, and border control. Of the rest, 6.3 percent went to bilateral programs to help governments in source and transit countries fight illicit narcotics. One-tenth of one percent ($15.5 million) of the total budget supported multilateral drug programs.

What these budget allocations tell us is that U.S. policymakers see drugs as essentially a domestic problem that can be resolved with a national response. At home, it is assumed that large doses of law enforcement, prevention, and treatment programs will erode the market for illicit narcotics. Likewise, along the borders, we seem to believe that a full-scale investment in interdiction will keep traffickers at bay. Overseas, selected governments are enlisted in an American effort to disrupt the production and transit of drugs destined for our shores.

Even if a national strategy to combat the scourge of drugs were to succeed at home, Americans would still face the effects of a flourishing drug trade overseas. As recent events in Peru illustrate, large-scale drug production can disrupt national economies and destroy democratic institutions. When drug trafficking can infiltrate with virtual impunity the commercial conveyances, migrant labor forces, banks, and securities markets that service a global economy, it provides fuel for protectionist forces who seek to slow or reverse the global trend toward greater economic liberalization. Finally, the reduced worker productivity and the public health consequences, including the spread of AIDS, associated with widespread drug abuse jeopardize further the limited development prospects of many third world countries, weakening their potential to become strong U.S. trading partners and stable allies.

The surging global drug epidemic requires an international drug control response and sooner rather than later. What this response should look like and what role the United States should play in it will be considered in the second part of this series. [See *The Brookings Review,* Spring 1993, for second part of series. Ed.]

The Tobacco Lobby:

Maintaining Profits, Distorting Issues, Costing Lives

William T. Godshall

WILLIAM T. GODSHALL, M.P.H. IS
EXECUTIVE DIRECTOR OF SMOKEFREE
PENNSYLVANIA, BASED IN PITTSBURGH, PA.

WARNING: Tobacco Industry Lobbying May Endanger Your Health

Nearly everyone agrees that government should protect people from the harm caused by toxic hazards. In urging tougher laws, many politicians go even further arguing that the public needs protection from unproven and speculative environmental risks. But what about tobacco?

Instead of protecting the public from cigarettes, most tobacco-related laws protect the nicotine industry from being held accountable for their outrageous actions and deadly products. These laws were enacted as a result of the massive political and legislative influence purchased by tobacco companies. The major purpose of their lobbying efforts is to increase or maintain huge profits for the tobacco companies, which means keeping as many people addicted to nicotine as possible.

The tobacco lobby has grown rapidly over the past few years especially at the state level. During 1991 in California alone, the tobacco industry spent $2.7 million on contributions to politicians. Last year in Pennsylvania more than 35 lobbyists worked for the tobacco industry. Such lobbying can effectively block legislation that would decrease smoking rates, reduce the sale of cigarettes to minors and protect nonsmokers from passive smoke in public places.

From *Priorities*, Summer 1992, pp. 44-46. Reprinted with permission from *Priorities*, a publication of The American Council on Science and Health, Inc., New York, NY 10023.

7. THE ECONOMY OF DRUG USE

Exempting Tobacco from Drug Programs

Causing nearly 500,000 deaths annually, nicotine addiction is without a doubt the deadliest drug abuse in America. But drug war proponents in our government have outrageously exempted this number one killer from almost every substance abuse policy and program. Massive public funding and attention on substance abuse have been diverted to drugs that harm and kill far fewer people. The nicotine exclusion effectively keeps millions of Americans smoking.

The major media, which receive billions of advertising dollars annually from tobacco companies and their subsidiaries, assist with this cover-up by almost never portraying nicotine as an addictive and deadly drug. Famous for their anti-drug fried egg commercial, the Partnership for a Drug Free America includes tobacco advertisers.

Targeted by advertising and promotions, more than two million American youth become addicted to nicotine each year. About one billion packs of cigarettes are sold annually to minors through retailers and vending machines. No other type of drug pushing to teenagers is more blatant, widespread or profitable. But most national and state government officials have chosen to ignore the outrageous activities of tobacco pushers, which will probably result in 100 times more deaths than those caused by cocaine and heroin combined.

Vending Machines

Many studies have documented how easily children can buy cigarettes through vending machines. One survey commissioned by National Automatic Merchandizing Association (NAMA) found that 13 year olds were 11 times more likely than were 17 year olds to buy cigarettes from the machines. Although less than one percent of adult smokers buy cigarettes primarily from vending machines, there are more than 600,000 of these mechanical drug dealers in America, accounting for more than half of all locations where cigarettes are sold.

Pro-health activists have lobbied to enact more than 140 local ordinances in the past three years that eliminate or restrict the placement of cigarette vending machines. Vending machine companies have joined with the tobacco lobby in opposing the the ordinances. Lawsuits have even been filed to strike down these local laws. None of these court challenges, however, has yet to succeed.

The tobacco lobby is also trying to get state statutes enacted that would pre-empt (outlaw) all local cigarette vending machine ordinances. In order to succeed, tobacco lobbyists have been drafting and promoting state legislation that deceptively appears to protect minors from illegal vending machine sales. But careful analysis of the wording in these bills reveals that few, if any, vending machines would be eliminated and that only those who profit from illegal cigarette sales would receive any type of protection.

Licensure

Although most states already have laws prohibiting tobacco sales to minors, these laws are almost never enforced. Even if they are enforced, they carry very small fines for retail clerks and do not hold accountable those who profit most from these illegal sales, the cigarette industry. To reduce over-the-counter sales to minors, pro-health groups are lobbying to license tobacco retailers in a similar way as liquor re-

Famous for their anti-drug fried egg commercial, the Partnership for a Drug Free America includes tobacco advertisers.

tailers are currently licensed. Businesses caught selling tobacco to minors would face stiff fines and temporary license suspension. In opposing licensure, the industry claims that the current laws are tough enough.

During 1991 in California alone, the tobacco industry spent $2.7 million on contributions to politicians.

In an effort to shift the legislative focus from the industry and retailers, the tobacco lobby is now trying to blame children by urging state legislatures to criminalize minors for buying or possessing cigarettes. This can effectively stop teens from exposing retailers that illegally sell tobacco and prevent addicted youth from seeking treatment to overcome nicotine addiction.

Taxation

The tobacco lobby spends a lot of money to oppose legislation that raises cigarette taxes because increasing prices have been shown dramatically to reduce nicotine addiction rates and corresponding cigarette sales. A ten percent price hike for cigarettes results in a four percent reduction in smoking. Younger smokers are affected disproportionately; half of those who quit are under age 26.

As a percentage of the retail price, cigarette taxes have dropped dramatically during the past twenty years, while state and federal expenditures for tobacco-related diseases have increased rapidly. In opposing cigarette tax hikes, the tobacco industry tries to fool the public into thinking that these taxes have sky-rocketed and that smokers are being dis-criminated against. The industry has also created front groups, appearing to represent concerned taxpayers, smokers and tobacco farmers to join them in their lobbying efforts to stop cigarette tax hikes.

Liability Reform

In an effort to immunize themselves from lawsuits by tobacco victims, tobacco companies have been spending much time and money lobbying for product liability reform. Any successful litigation would encourage an onslaught of similar suits and force manufacturers finally to be legally accountable for their deadly products and egregious actions. Manufacturers would then be forced to raise cigarette prices substantially to cover plaintiff awards and court costs. Like tax increases, these price hikes would further reduce the nicotine addiction rate.

In lobbying for product liability legislation, the tobacco companies have organized powerful coalitions with multinational manufacturers of other products. For public relations purposes, these coalitions claim that they want to reduce frivolous lawsuits against small local employers, who are given token status in the coalitions.

Passive Smoke and Clean Air Legislation

Meta-analysis of scientific studies has shown that environmental tobacco smoke kills about 50,000 Americans each year. If burned in an auditorium, just one cigarette creates greater concentrations of ammonia, benzene, arsenic, hydrogen

As a percentage of the retail price, cigarette taxes have dropped dramatically during the past twenty years, while state and federal expenditures for tobacco-related diseases have increased rapidly.

cyanide, methane, formaldehyde, carbon monoxide and particulates than would be permitted outdoors by the Clean Air Act

if their source were cars or a factory. Even though people spend 90 percent of the time indoors, indoor air has been

The number of deaths attributed to passive smoke is far higher than those attributed to all other types of environmental pollution combined.

shielded from clean air legislation by the efforts of the strong tobacco lobby.

The number of deaths attributed to passive smoke is far higher than those attributed to all other types of environmental pollution combined. But protecting humans from forced exposures to tobacco smoke has not been much of a concern for national and state legislatures or the major media. Neither has tobacco smoke pollution been on the agendas of most self proclaimed environmental activists, who create mass hysteria about levels of other pollutants that are virtually undetectable and have not been shown to harm humans.

The only smokefree legislation at the national level, where the tobacco lobby has maintained a strong power base, is the airline smoking ban passed in 1989. However, with little money, the non-smokers' rights movement has been able to make impressive progress at the local level in the past ten years. Smoking pollution control laws have been passed in hundreds of municipalities, with California leading the way. The original ordinances provided some protections, but many now require smokefree indoor environments at most work and public places, even in bars.

Unlike Congress, municipal councils are less easily influenced by tobacco PAC money and lobbyists who cut deals in back rooms. Realizing this vulnerability, the tobacco industry recruited local restaurant and tavern associations and

some labor union officials to provide visible opposition to clean indoor air laws. At the local level, tobacco lobbyists prefer to remain behind the scenes.

Preemption Strategy

Another tobacco industry reaction to local smokefree laws is to greatly expand its lobbying presence at the state level. In 1988 and 1989 the industry successfully lobbied half a dozen state legislatures, including Florida, Pennsylvania and Illinois, to enact statutes that specifically preempt local laws, but provide little or no protection from tobacco smoke. Although the tobacco lobby publicly claimed to oppose these so-called state indoor air laws, the tobacco industry was their only beneficiary.

Recognizing that state indoor air laws which preempt local laws rarely promote health, pro-health activists have successfully prevented their enactment in other

A ten percent price hike for cigarettes results in a four percent reduction in smoking.

states. Non-preemptive clean indoor air laws have also been enacted at the state level, but most of these provide very little protection from tobacco smoke. In fact, at the state level, most of the laws that affect tobacco protect the industry.

Conclusion

Clearly, the tobacco lobby has purchased extensive influence from our federal and state governments and is now expanding at the local level. This is one of the most tragic examples of corruption in our public policy process.

Special privileges continue to be bought by tobacco companies, whose products kill more people than AIDS, alcohol, crack, cocaine, heroin, suicide, fires and automobile accidents combined. At the same time, thousands of pages of laws and regulations exist to protect the public from insignificant or nonexistent health risks.

High in the Hollows

Fenton Johnson

Fenton Johnson, author of the novel "Crossing the River," was born and raised in New Haven, Ky.; he now lives in San Francisco.

Driving the side winding roads of the Kentucky knobs, even the casual observer notices islands of prosperity among the jagged limestone cliffs and river valleys. Many of the peeling clapboard farmhouses of my childhood have been torn down and replaced with brick ranch-style homes. A new truck or car sits in the driveway—at times of day you'd expect the owner to be away at work. A few of the old farmhouses have been lavishly restored, their orgy of Victoriana (beveled glass, wicker porch furniture, gingerbread trim in contrasting colors) standing in jarring contrast to the stark, frugal lines of the houses themselves. Accompanying me along these roads, an elderly friend points. "Pot houses," she sniffs.

For most of the last five years, the rural counties of Kentucky, Tennessee and Missouri have been among the national leaders in marijuana production. This usually surprises outsiders, but surprises no one who grew up or lives among these hills. "Used to be a hell of a thing to find out your next door neighbor grew," a local farmer said to me. "Now nothing surprises you."

Once most of these farmers relied on tobacco, a high-yield, low-acreage crop that has been the ideal moneymaker in a coun-

tryside where flat land and salaried jobs are about equally scarce. In recent years, given the instability of the tobacco market, they were faced with some hard choices: sell the farm (or lose it to the bank) and move to the city; commute two hours and more to an assembly-line job in a small-town factory; or grow pot.

Some of these people would never grow marijuana; others would grow it if it were legal. And there are others, with a long tradition of making their own laws, who have turned to it readily. This is whisky-making country, after all, where people survived Prohibition and the Depression by making moonshine for Midwestern cities.

There's a complex struggle going on here, between the

intricate interweavings of small-town Southern life.

I know those interweavings well, for I grew up in this country—where 60 years ago nearly every family (including mine) was involved with moonshining; where today marijuana production and distribution are a part of the local scene; where a way of life is changing. Or, as many argue, staying the same.

Marijuana has not always been illegal. Throughout the 19th century, marijuana, then known as hemp, provided an important cash crop in those same South Central states that currently lead in its illicit production. The fiber of the hemp plant was (and is) considered at least the equal of

KENTUCKY, ITS MOONSHINE DAYS OVER, IS INTO MARIJUANA AS A MAJOR CASH CROP. AND THE LAW IS ONCE AGAIN COMBING THE HILLS.

farmers' strict ethics and what they need to do to make a living; between those who grow and those who don't; between the farmers who grow to survive, and those who grow to get rich; between the law and people who have never had much use for it; between and among all these groups, whose members are usually related to one another by blood and by the

other fibers, natural or synthetic, for rope and cord. Kentucky built its first public roads to convey the hemp crop to market.

In 1937, the Marijuana Tax Act outlawed marijuana. Since then, the cultivation of hemp has been illegal, except during World War II, when the shortage of petroleum-based synthetic fibers led the

Government to issue permits to grow hemp.

After the war, the permits were revoked, and hemp retired to the fence rows of middle America — where, as ditch weed, it grew in abundance. Then, in the 1960's, hemp — a k a marijuana, pot, dope, grass — came into widespread use for another of its properties, this one known for years among jazz singers and old country folks suffering from rheumatism: smoking it got you high.

The 1960's generation of college-age pot smokers looked abroad for their stash — first to Mexico. Then, after the Ford Administration began to destroy Mexican fields with chemical sprays, attention turned to Colombia as a source.

During the 1980's, the Reagan Administration undertook a high-profile law-enforcement program to embargo the importation of marijuana. Mark A. R. Kleiman, lecturer at Harvard's John F. Kennedy School of Government and author of "Marijuana: Costs of Abuse, Costs of Control," calls this "the only successful piece of agricultural policy of the Reagan years."

In fact, the policy's success had at least one unintended side-effect. Facing intensified Federal enforcement, Colombian drug lords turned from exporting bulky, difficult-to-conceal marijuana to vastly more portable — and more lucrative — cocaine.

The Reagan Administration's efforts had indeed closed off the importation of marijuana; domestic producers moved in.

At the time, many farmers needed a lucrative new crop. During the 1970's, the Government had promoted expansion on the farm, financing purchases of expensive equipment, construction of outbuildings, and acquisition of land. During the 1980's, the Reagan Administration abruptly tightened farm credit and reduced commodity supports, leaving farmers saddled with debt and facing a bleak market.

As one Kentucky farm housewife told me: "In the early 1970's, banks were eager to loan money. Then, in the 1980's, Government policy changed, the banks called in the loans, the bottom fell out of the tobacco market — all at once. Lots of people were close to foreclosure and felt the Government had betrayed them. So why not grow a little pot?"

Country boys returning from Vietnam and an influx of counterculture, back-to-the-land hippies, had already popularized marijuana smoking among the area's young people. All that remained was for times to get hard enough for their folks to consider growing it.

"The typical guy we see growing marijuana is a 55-year-old farmer with a 20-year-old son," says a chaw-chewing lawman, a ham of a man with a huge paw of a handshake. "He's got maybe 150 acres, he's trying to farm, he started 30 years ago when he could make a living at it. Now he's got kids in college or about to go there and is hard up. Some are about to lose their farms, some have already gone on their son's notes for their farm.

"Then the 20-year-old son comes home and talks about planting 20 marijuana plants here, five plants there. He tells the father, 'Let's grow $20,000 worth,' and they do it and it works. The son provides the connection. If the old guy grew it, he wouldn't know how to get rid of it."

These are tobacco farmers, experienced in working with a plant that requires intensive labor and individual attention. They grew, made money, put that money into the local economy. "We'd hit September, early October, the slowest time of year in a tobacco-based economy," says a local bank official. "And you'd walk down Main Street and see all these people buying clothes and extra food and supplies — the pot crop was in."

How much money we're talking about depends on who's talking, though nobody doubts that directly or indirectly pot has financed many of the new homes and businesses in the area. This is a farm economy, after all; people are accustomed to dealing in cash and asking no questions. A local bank official says assets in his bank dropped $5 million — a sizable sum for a rural bank — when he began asking depositors to complete the forms required by the Internal Revenue Service for cash transactions of over $10,000. A bank teller talks of counting a pile of bills that was still frozen in the middle — "deep freeze money, we call it around here." A local lawyer tells of being called to a farm auction to help count the down payment — $24,000 in small bills.

"It don't hurt to spread that money around in the community," one grower said. When asked whether an indictment on marijuana charges was impossible in the local courts, a judge studied the ceiling. "I think you could say that's a fair statement," he said. Several other judges I spoke to, as well as a number of lawyers, agreed.

During the 1970's, that policy was consistent with the national trend toward reducing penalties for marijuana possession. Federal efforts to eradicate marijuana were spotty and half-hearted; state and local police usually looked the other way. If a property owner and longtime communi- ty citizen was arrested, juries and judges were lenient. In Kentucky, first-time growers routinely received a fine of $500 and a suspended sentence.

Under the Reagan Administration, the Federal Government did an about-face. It began to underwrite state police search-and-destroy efforts. Federal district attorneys began to pursue marijuana convictions, and Federal sentencing guidelines became so strict that judges have virtually no discretion in sentencing. The grower who only a few years ago faced a fine and a year in prison may now be looking at 20 to 25 years without parole. Last August, the state Agricultural Stabilization and Conservation Service sent Kentucky farmers a letter notifying them that "if marijuana is grown on your land the law provides that the U.S. government may TAKE YOUR FARM unless you can affirmatively show that such unlawful conduct was carried on without your knowledge."

It is difficult to prove one *doesn't* know something, so this in effect empowers Federal agents to seize property on which marijuana is grown, even if the property owner is unaware of its existence — even if, according to the United States District Attorney for the Western District of Kentucky, Joseph M. Whittle, the property owner is acquitted of marijuana-growing charges.

In other words, this is hardball. One local law-enforcement official reflects a widespread view when he insists there's a hidden agenda here, with Federal agencies searching for heads to prove that they're making progress in the war on drugs. What better place to crack down, he argues, than in the rural countryside, free from the entanglements of international law and the violence of city streets?

IN OCTOBER 1987, FEDeral, state and local officials converged on a farm outside New York Mills, Minn., and seized 62 dump- truck loads of marijuana. The raid was the first of a series attacking what the Justice Department calls "the largest domestic marijuana-producing organization in the history of the United States." The final tally came to 182 tons of marijuana seized from 29 sites, including farms in Illinois, Indiana, Michigan, Missouri, Kansas, Wisconsin, Minnesota, Nebraska and Kentucky. The farms were managed by a loosely connected group called the "Cornbread Mafia," a name coined by the police, the press or the growers themselves, depending on who's talking. Of the 78 persons arrested and charged so far in the Cornbread Mafia case, 59 are from Marion County, an enclave of 17,000 people tucked in the knobs of south-central Kentucky.

According to Assistant United States Attorney David P. Grise, who helped publicize and prosecute the case, the Cornbread Mafia growers rented, or purchased, farmland across the Midwest. They planted the land in alternating rows of corn and marijuana (corn grows faster, helping conceal the pot but letting sunlight through). To minimize contact with local communities, imported laborers, most of them from Kentucky, tended the plants. Once the harvest was in, the growers disappeared, leaving only a caretaker to look after the farm.

Grise insists that the name "Cornbread Mafia" originated with the growers themselves. Local journalists scoff at that assertion, pointing out that such headline-hype terminology hardly comes naturally to rural Kentucky farmers. These local observers describe the "Mafia" as a group of guys who had known one another since childhood and operated largely independently, sharing (and concealing) information like any cagey farmer. If they constituted a mafia, it was in their absolute loyalty to one another and their roots. As Grise says: "Elsewhere in Kentucky, people will reveal information as part of the plea-bargaining process. Not in Marion County."

NOT EVERY RURAL area that engages in marijuana production has a history of encounters with the law as troubled and thorny as that of Marion County. In most of the Midwest and much of Kentucky, the pattern falls closer to that described by a farmer in a neighboring county: a farm economy gets sidetracked when farmers and their children, with only a high school diploma from poor, rural school systems, begin searching for some way to make money that will allow them to stay near their families and to work with their hands. But Marion County, though not the most isolated, or the poorest, or the least developed of marijuana-producing counties, epitomizes the phenomenon. Here some locals have developed lawlessness into an art, while family, friends, and the local business community have acquiesced in looking the other way.

"Well, Marion has always been a wide-open county," says Dee Davis, executive director of Appalshop Films, a division of Appalshop, eastern Kentucky's widely acclaimed cultural center. He hails from Hazard, a town 200 miles from Marion not exactly known for its law-abiding ways, but still he has heard of Marion County. "What about that stolen-car fence? Is that still going?"

"That stolen-car fence" — actually, a stolen-goods fence — was a notorious ring of thieves that operated during the 1950's and 60's out of Raywick, a Marion County town of maybe 300. People point to one man as the brain behind that operation — the "Robin Hood of Raywick," Charley Stiles.

Charley terrorized the state and the region. A judge told me how he had bought a new car for his son, then realized he had no room for it in his garage. Though he lived miles from Raywick, he was afraid to park it on the street, a fear he confided to a friend. A few days later, a stranger showed up at the judge's door. "Charley said to tell you to park that car wherever you want," the man said. "You got no need to worry about *that* car."

The police arrested Charley again and again; just as often, juries let him go. Days after the jury let Charley off, a brand new refrigerator would appear on some poor widow's porch, or a struggling farmer would get a hefty, interest-free loan. "He would do anything for you, Charley would" — this was the refrain of Charley Stiles stories.

On Sept. 10, 1971, Charley was gunned down in a cornfield several counties removed from Raywick, shot once, or a dozen, or more than a dozen times, in his chest or in his back — depending on whether you believe the state troopers who shot him, or the people who tell the story now. The troopers contended they fired in self-defense, a story that hardly anyone believed, then or now.

"I hate to see it get to the point," a local judge said, choosing his words carefully, "where the police feel they have no recourse in the courts." Another chronicler, after an hour of telling Charley stories (how Charley helped this person out, or pulled the wool over that cop's eyes), shook his head. "He was one hell of a guy," he said, and paused. "But it was a good thing they took him down."

As I grew up I heard multiple versions of Charley Stiles stories. When I visited last month, I heard them retold in spades — this time by the marijuana growers, for whom Charley is a folk hero. His story is a crucial piece of this jigsaw puzzle, not because he inspired the Marion County growers to go interstate (though there may be some truth to this), but because he is the latest in a series of outlaw heroes — the best role model going in this neck of the woods.

One grower's 6-year-old son, asked by his teacher what he wanted to be when he grew up, piped up, "I want to be a doper, like my father." I heard that story more than once, but from the grower's friends, not from the grower himself; he's in jail, denied bond, facing 20-plus years for his role in the Cornbread Mafia case. "These guys are the robber outlaws — you'll hear all the moonshiner stories from them," said one ex-grower, formerly of the Cornbread crowd. "Years from now you'll hear the same stories, except they'll be about the pot growers."

Or so they hope. These are people who will do just about anything for the sake of a good story; for the sake of fame, however local. "If they don't talk about you," an 80-year-old moonshiner told me, "hell, you ain't no count." As for the risk of going to prison, one ex-grower said, "When your father has been in the pen, and most of the people you know, their fathers have been in the pen, well, there's not anything wrong with it."

LAWLESSNESS IS THE common thread between the years of moonshining and the years of marijuana growing. And not the least important question this raises is how, as an outsider who now lives in Marion County put it, "people can go through such rigid moral training and not know right from wrong."

Some part of the answer to that question lies in that remarkable Southern talent for sustaining a double standard. "Now, I don't know anybody that grows," one farmer told me. He dug at the dirt with the toe of his boot. "Well — in my *heart* I know they grow. But I don't *know* they're growing. Understand?"

I understand. Around here no one grows pot — just as no one's daughter gets pregnant before she gets married, no one's son is gay. The facts of the matter may contradict this (25,000 plants eradicated last summer in a single raid, to cite only one such fact). The demographics may stand in contradiction (among a stable, intimately connected population of 17,000, how can there be secrets?). The geography may stand in contradiction (in a county where there are no secrets, how can you hide 25,000 marijuana plants?). But only by accepting the contradiction between what is said and what is done can the outsider begin to understand how it is possible to sustain such a large illicit economy in such a very small place.

But the answer to the question "How is it possible?" goes deeper than that. It finds its roots in a deep-seated instinct to preserve family and self in the face of hindrance from the law. For people raised as farmers, for whom welfare is a disgrace not very much better than prison, there is pride in growing pot.

The marijuana raids, with their low-flying helicopters and camouflage-clad state policemen, represent the most visible federally supported effort this area has seen since the Civil War — or, perhaps, since the invasion of revenue officers during Prohibition. And local people view these raids together with more broadly harmful Federal policies: local farmers hear the politicians extolling family virtues, but they also can see in their grocery stores — stocked with products from American and foreign agribusinesses — evidence that Government farm policy is not working to benefit them and their families.

"From their previous experience with moonshining, there's a historical attitude that those who control the legal system do not represent them," says Ronald D. Eller, director of the University of Kentucky's Appalachian Center. "The legal system became something to get around. ... This translates into an attitude of 'us versus them,' 'them' being the rest of America, or the America they see on TV. 'We' live here and have to survive. There's a certain pride in the ability to survive and beat a system that's not equitable."

Of course, not all growers are upstanding farmers driven to pot by desperation. A lot of them, as one ex-grower put it, "just can't stand prosperity" — they made their first bundle just to get over a rough spot, then can't stand to leave that relatively easy money behind. Others get caught up in the mystique of rural machismo, in a long-running game of cops and robbers. Speaking of the Marion County growers, Grise said: "They don't see this as a crime. They see themselves as doing their job, which is to grow pot; they see us as doing our job, which is to bust them for growing pot." As one grower said, "Where else can you have the chance of making this much money with this much excitement?"

Though the growers are a minority of the Marion County community, the county has profited from several years' vigorous cash flow, and the last people to welsh on that are those who have benefited: the bankers who look the other way when large cash deposits come through the window, the lawyers who joke with the sheriff about allowing defendants to harvest enough of their crops to pay their legal fees.

Then there are those just entering the job market, who face the choice of earning a minimum wage cooking hamburgers at a fast-food joint or earning $100 a day for working outside, working with their hands — working marijuana.

"Young people are very bitter about not being able to live on the farm, not being able to have the kind of life

their parents had," said one local lawyer. That bitterness translates into a loss of respect for institutions, into a sense that it's every one for himself, and don't get caught. A young law officer I spoke with — whom a lawyer identified as "very actively looking the other way" in his dealings with local growers — put it this way: "I don't give a damn. I just don't give a goddamn."

TODAY, THE LARGest open fields of pot are gone from Marion County; all parties on both sides of the law agreed on this (though the 25,000-plant bust occurred only a few months ago). But nobody thinks pot cultivation has disappeared. "We'll just go underground," said one grower, speaking literally — caves and basements are being turned into greenhouses. Outside, plants are now scattered in bunches of two and three, making detection difficult and lowering the chances of losing an entire crop to thieves or the police. "This is America," one grower said. "If there's a demand for a product, there'll be somebody to produce it."

That same ethic drove moonshining in Prohibition times, and the view seems prevalent in Marion County that history is repeating itself. Once again the Government has outlawed a previously legal substance. Once again the courts are allowing the police greater leeway to seize property, search individuals and breach privacy, in an effort to eliminate consumption of a widely used drug.

So far, at least in Kentucky,

the Federal crackdown has not led to open violence. Local law-enforcement officers and growers alike agree that growers are far more likely to run than shoot.

This is not to say the growers never use violence. Stories of extortion are common — a grower might offer $5,000 to a farmer, say, if he doesn't venture onto the back few acres for four months. The farmer who refuses can expect retaliation: barns burned, equipment vandalized. And the county has seen an increase in unsolved murders that everyone attributes to quarrels among growers.

But during the last few years the Government has raised the stakes dramatically. Now that growers face 25 years in jail and the loss of the family farm, many people believe they will decide, as one lawyer put it, to hold on to the guns they've been dropping.

"I sense a strong analogy between the marijuana phenomenon of central Kentucky — and the crime that comes with it — and the crack epidemic in New York," said the Rev. Thomas P. O'Dell, a Kentucky clergyman who has worked in Manhattan's Bellevue Hospital. "Hopelessness, bred by changing local economies and neglect, is a common thread ... the decline of tobacco as a meaningful cash crop hereabouts has left behind folks who likely find themselves in circumstances similar to New York City youths now that the industrial jobs are gone."

NOT LONG AFTER THE Federal Government started seriously prosecuting marijuana growers, Kentucky

game wardens began pulling from the murky rivers scuba divers who were illegally scooping up thousands of washboard mussels. The shell of these mussels, ground into bits and introduced into Japanese pearl oysters, provides the perfect catalyst for the formation of cultured pearls. The divers truck the shells out of state, where they're sold to Japanese buyers.

Moonshining, marijuana, mussels. In those parts of the world that the 20th century has more or less left behind, people find ways to get by.

How can this be changed? Some people around here think that the answer lies in education. "You're not going to break the grandfather — he's too strong, and it's in his blood," says one law-enforcement official. "But you can get to the kids, or the kids of the kids." Others say that changing the way these people work will require, more or less, the end of the family farm. "The only way you change the animal is to change the environment," a local teacher said. "Bring in industry, new jobs, new blood — that'll change the countryside. The way they live will follow."

And there are others, the older people from the moonshining families, who have seen it all before; they have a different view, more cynical or realistic, depending on your perspective. Sixty years from now, they say, different Federal agents will be here, cracking down on a different product or substance, trotting out a different story for different reporters. And the same people, or their children, or their children's children, will find themselves on the other side of the law.

PUSHING DRUGS TO DOCTORS

A young doctor listened intently to a panel of distinguished physicians discuss advances in hypertension treatment at the annual meeting of the American Academy of Family Physicians. By the end of the three-hour presentation, he was thinking seriously about switching some of his hypertensive patients to a drug called a calcium channel blocker, which was much discussed at the presentation. The seminar was sponsored by the pharmaceutical company G.D. Searle and Co., as the young physician knew. But he didn't realize that Searle—which was then running a promotional campaign for *Calan,* one of several calcium channel blockers—had carefully picked speakers who were well-known advocates for this class of drugs.

◻ On one recent Sunday, physicians who tuned in to the Lifetime Cable Network, which runs special medical programming for doctors, saw a 30-minute presentation called "Physician's Guide to Gallstone Disease." The program urged doctors to use medication instead of surgery to treat gallstones. It omitted the fact that gallbladder surgery remains the preferred treatment for almost all patients. The video was produced and paid for by CIBA-Geigy, maker of *Actigall,* the medication being recommended. After the U.S. Food and Drug Administration declared the program false and misleading, the company agreed to clear future *Actigall* promotions with the FDA in advance.

◻ At the American Psychiatric Association's annual meeting in 1991

psychiatrists attended a symposium on new research in the treatment of manic-depression. Despite the broad topic, the session mainly focused on the use of anticonvulsant drugs, even though the FDA has never approved them for this use. The symposium was sponsored by Abbott Laboratories, maker of *Depakote* — an anticonvulsant that speakers at the session discussed as a manic-depression treatment.

◻ Two years ago, cancer specialists around the country were sent several issues of a serious-looking publication called "Oncology Commentary '90," which summarized symposia that dealt with unapproved uses of several anticancer drugs. The publication was produced by the maker of those drugs, Bristol-Myers Squibb, which did not disclose its

The way that drug companies sell their wares is a prescription for inefficient medicine— and a major contributor to soaring health-care costs.

involvement anywhere on the publication. After months of regulatory wrangling, the FDA forced the company to send a letter to every doctor who received the mailing, confessing its behind-the-scenes influence.

Over the past 15 years or so, the $63-billion-a-year pharmaceutical industry has made physicians the targets—sometimes willing, sometimes unwitting—of sophisticated, subtle, and highly effective marketing techniques that permeate nearly every aspect of medical practice. Drug companies organize "educational symposia" that are actually disguised promotional efforts for their products. They pay for sober-looking "supplements" to respected medical journals and fill those supplements with articles selected and edited to make their products look good. They pay doctors to use drugs in "clinical trials" organized not by drug researchers but by drug marketers. And they offer doctors all sorts of gifts and perks, from ballpoint pens to lavish banquets and concerts.

Sometimes the drugs being marketed really are more effective, less costly, or safer than their competitors. But others are unoriginal products seeking to take market share away from established, and frequently less expensive, formulations. Of the 20 or so new drugs the FDA approves in a typical year, the agency usually rates no more than four as truly meaningful therapeutic advances. That leaves the rest to slug it out in the arena of image, promotion, and marketing.

The industry carefully avoids adding up its annual promotional tab, but independent sources place it conservatively at around $5-billion. It must be money well spent; the pharmaceutical industry has long been the nation's most profitable. The top 10 U.S. drug companies averaged 16 percent profit on sales in 1990, more than triple that of the average Fortune 500 company.

But what's good for Searle and CIBA-Geigy may not be good for the rest of us. Between 1980 and 1990, while general inflation was 58 percent, overall health-care costs rose 117 percent—and the cost of drugs rose 152 percent. Every unnecessary prescription, and every unnecessary choice of an expensive, brand-name drug over a cheaper alternative, contributes to these excessive costs.

Besides the money spent directly on drug-company promotion, current marketing practices have a high indirect cost as well. Companies have

the greatest incentive to promote costly drugs, even if they're no more effective than cheaper ones.

High drug prices are a special burden for elderly people, who make up 12 percent of the population but consume 34 percent of prescription drugs. Surveys by the American Association of Retired Persons have found that prescription drugs are the single largest out-of-pocket medical expense for three out of four Americans over 5, and that four out of ten have no prescription drug insurance coverage whatever. One in

seven say they have failed to take prescribed medicine because it was too expensive.

The new age of marketing

For many years, pharmaceutical companies sold their wares the way any business-to-business company does. They sent representatives out to call on doctors with samples and sales patter and placed ads in medical journals—methods that are still the core of their marketing efforts. But then, in 1977, came *Tagamet.* In addition to being a genuine break-

---

SELF-PROTECTION FOR PATIENTS

ARE YOU GETTING THE RIGHT DRUG?

If you visit the doctor for a lingering cough and cold and come away with a $90 prescription for a brand-name antibiotic, are you getting state-of-the-art treatment or an inappropriate, overpromoted drug? Unfortunately, it's hard to tell. As a patient, you hold very few of the cards in the prescribing game; in the end, only a doctor can write a prescription. That said, however, patients can still improve their chances of getting an effective prescription at a reasonable price. Here are some strategies to keep in mind.

Look for red flags. Brand-name drugs for arthritis, high blood pressure, ulcers, high cholesterol, and respiratory infections are among the most heavily promoted and thus the most likely to be prescribed. If your doctor prescribes one of these drugs, question him or her closely: Why choose this particular drug? Are there other, possibly cheaper, choices? If so, why not prescribe one of them? You may also want to look the drug up in one of the consumer drug guides now available.

Ask about nondrug therapies. You don't have to take a pill for everything that ails you. For example, using a vaporizer, salt-water gargles, plenty of fluids, and acetaminophen may work about as well as a prescription combination product in treating a viral respiratory infection, without causing such side effects as drowsiness. Exercise, salt restriction, and weight loss can successfully treat some people who have cases of mild hypertension.

Don't demand the latest drug. The latest, most expensive drug isn't necessarily the best, despite what you may have read or heard. The oldest antibiotic of all, penicillin,

remains the drug of choice for treating strep throat. Diuretics have a long record of safety, if you can tolerate their mild side effects, and can successfully treat many cases of high blood pressure at a much lower cost than newer agents. Old drugs that are still widely used have generally stayed around for a reason—they're effective and their side effects are well known. Newer drugs are more likely to have unpleasant surprises in store.

Ask about generic or over-the-counter alternatives. Prescription-strength *Motrin,* a brand-name version of the antiarthritis drug ibuprofen, costs $31 for a 30-day supply. The same amount of generic prescription-strength ibuprofen costs about $17. Although specific procedures vary from state to state, pharmacists are now allowed to substitute generics for brand-name drugs. If you don't mind taking three or four tablets at a time, you can also buy ibuprofen over the counter in pills of lower dosage, and simply take more pills to raise the dosage level. That would cost you even less—about $13 a month for a therapeutically equivalent dose.

If you've taken a drug for a long time, remind your doctor occasionally. It may be time to stop. For example, many patients continue to take *Tagamet* or *Zantac,* two ulcer medications, long after their ulcers have healed. They may no longer need the drug at all: Their doctors may simply have neglected to review the need for renewing the prescription.

through in the treatment of ulcers, it was a breakthrough in marketing.

"This was the first prescription drug to open the nightly news," David Jones, a former industry marketing and public relations executive, recalled in a recent speech. "People were asking for it before it was available. . . . The industry quickly realized that . . . if this kind of publicity, generating this kind of demand, could happen naturally with one drug, it could be made to happen with others."

Nowadays, company marketing departments, frequently with the help of outside consultants, draw up elaborate plans to launch and position new products, defend proven sellers against new competition, or increase the market share of existing products. More and more, pharmaceutical companies are promoting their drugs directly to consumers—an ominous trend we'll cover in an upcoming issue. But their major efforts have been directed at doctors. Drug companies use advanced market-research techniques to probe the psyches of unsuspecting physicians, and use the results to fine-tune their pitches. "Basically, industry has been almost in a feeding frenzy, competing to win the attention of physicians by various promotional efforts," says Dr. Stephen Goldfinger, faculty dean for medical education at Harvard Medical School.

Though doctors insist their scientific training, high intelligence, and sophistication enable them to resist manipulation, the truth is that skillful marketers can influence M.D.s just as easily as they can sway the rest of us. A landmark 1982 study by Dr. Jerry Avorn of Harvard showed that doctors' opinions of two popular, heavily advertised drugs came straight from the ads and sales pitches. The doctors believed they'd gotten their information from objective scientific sources, but those sources, in fact, had said all along that the drugs were not effective for their advertised uses.

Even a thorough medical-education campaign may be no match for a drug company's marketing efforts, as Avorn and his colleague Stephen B. Soumerai have shown in analyzing the case of *Darvon*. Between 1978 and 1980, the FDA organized a nationwide effort to reduce the prescribing of this heavily marketed painkiller: The drug had proven to be addictive and was very easy to use as a means of suicide. *Darvon's* manufacturer, Eli Lilly, was supposed to support the FDA's effort, but an FDA

audit found that the company had in fact continued to promote the drug to doctors. During this period, sales of the drug hardly budged. What finally knocked *Darvon* off the sales charts was the expiration of its patent, which made further marketing efforts uneconomical. Lilly then turned to marketing *Darvocet-N,* a combination of *Darvon* and acetaminophen then still under patent; it swiftly rose to become the 10th-most prescribed drug in the U.S.

Ethics and evasions

During the Reagan era, the FDA, which regulates the advertising and promotion of prescription drugs, suffered from both budget cuts and the Administration's anti-regulatory philosophy. The agency took a hands-off attitude toward the new promotional techniques. Its understaffed Division of Drug Marketing, Advertising, and Communications tried valiantly to police the more flagrant abuses, but was no match for the industry in size or resources. "We wrote letters, we wrote letters, and we wrote more letters," the agency's new commissioner, Dr. David Kessler, said in a press conference shortly after taking office last year.

Things began to change somewhat in late 1990. Senator Edward M. Kennedy's Committee on Labor and Human Resources held hearings that spotlighted the most extravagant promotional practices, such as CIBA-

Geigy's sending doctors and their spouses to all-expenses-paid "symposia" at Caribbean resorts to hear about *Estraderm,* an estrogen-dispensing skin patch, or Wyeth-Ayerst's offering physicians frequent-flyer mileage for prescribing *Inderal LA,* a hypertension drug. Not coincidentally, in the weeks before the hearing, the American Medical Association and the drug industry's trade group, the Pharmaceutical Manufacturers Association, hastily adopted new codes of ethics that prohibited such lavish incentives. "The promotional practices of some companies had plainly crossed the line of ethical behavior and had to be stopped," says Kirk B. Johnson, the AMA's general counsel.

The FDA also began to awaken from its decade-long slumber. Last year, Dr. Kessler, the new, activist commissioner, gave the marketing office new staff and authority. Kessler also personally put the profession on notice with a stern, much-quoted article in the New England Journal of Medicine.

The new, more ethical climate is having some effect. "Drug companies are no longer flying physicians around the country or exchanging cash," says the AMA's Johnson. Doctors we interviewed agreed that invitations to resort junkets and offers of cash "honoraria" for merely attending meetings have dried up.

But if consumers can now feel somewhat more confident that a drug prescribed for them did not gain its pride of place through a thinly disguised bribe, they still cannot be sure that a medication's efficacy and price are the only considerations driving the doctor's prescribing habits. The pharmaceutical trade press is now filled with articles about techniques that can keep companies in technical compliance with the new guidelines even if they seem to go against their spirit.

Consider, for instance, the rapid evolution of the dinner meeting. A widely used innovation of the late 1980s, dinner meetings worked like this: A company would invite selected physicians to dinner at an expensive local restaurant. Before eating, they would listen to a product presentation and afterwards would be handed a $100 "honorarium" for their time and attention. According to industry market studies, 80 percent of dinner meetings produce increased sales of the target drug among doctors who attend.

Under the new guidelines, the

dinner meetings are continuing. Except now, instead of a $100 cash "honorarium," attendees get to pick a $100 gift, such as a medical textbook or office equipment, out of a catalog. Consulting firms who design and run campaigns for drug companies are even placing ads in trade publications bragging of their ability to put on sales-boosting dinner meetings that comply with the AMA rules.

The gift obligation

The gifts handed out at dinners are hardly the only ones doctors receive. A staple of the pharmaceutical salesperson's trade is something called "reminder items."

Allen F. Shaughnessy, a pharmacist at the Medical University of South Carolina, actually counted the promotional items in his school's family medicine center. Its 24 examination rooms, waiting room and nursing stations contained 5 pens, 36 notepads, 55 pamphlets and posters, and 43 trinkets such as pushpins, key rings, cups, and tote bags bearing company names or product logos. And this was a clinic at an academic institution; private doctors' offices have many more such items.

Another category of gift is the "hospitality" that drug companies dispense—everything from pizza for hospital residents and interns to banquets and performances by famous entertainers at medical conventions. The money spent is substantial. For its 1991 convention, the American College of Rheumatology responded to the new ethical climate by turning down pharmaceutical money for evening dinners and receptions and paying for those events itself. The College's meeting planner estimates the decision cost $200,000.

Many doctors believe that trivial gifts and entertainments can't possibly influence them. But others contend that the very act of receiving a gift, no matter how small, sets up a culturally conditioned obligation to reciprocate. It's worth noting that the Pharmaceutical Manufacturers Association of Canada, in its ethics code, has banned "reminder items." And in the U.S., the Veterans Administration prohibits its physicians from accepting gifts from companies.

"I learned a lot about gift-giving from my father, who was a very ethical businessman," says Dr. David Schiedermayer, an internist and associate director of the Center for the Study of Bioethics at the Medical College of Wisconsin. "He would never accept a gift without returning it in kind. A gift has strings attached; we all know that. That's why gift-giving is important in our culture."

Evidence that this is so comes from the industry itself. One trade publication, Medical Marketing & Media, recently ran an admiring account of a campaign on behalf of *Anaprox,* one of a number of anti-arthritic drugs jostling for position in a lucrative market. Physicians received direct-mail invitations to send away for a series of exercise-related gifts bearing the drug's logo: a Walkman-type stereo; a jumprope; hand and ankle weights; a fanny pack; an exercise log. Presumably, most physicians could easily afford these items. Yet the promotion appeared to work; after one year, *Anaprox*'s share of prescriptions for exercise-related injuries increased from 33 to 43 percent. The trade journal didn't seem troubled by the fact that *Anaprox* offers no demonstrable benefits over generic ibuprofen, a similar drug which costs much less.

"The costs of gifts to physicians are ultimately passed on to the public," says a report from the AMA's Council on Ethical and Judicial Affairs. "In effect, then, patients may be paying for a benefit that in some cases is captured primarily by their physicians."

Undercover messages

Ambiguous as the gift obligation may be, another pharmaceutical practice concerns industry critics even more: the use of money and marketing expertise to subvert the medical profession's elaborate system of scientific exchange. Since it's an insidious, subtle means of influence, it's also difficult to police.

From medical school on, physicians are taught to regard medical school faculty, medical journals, and professional meetings as sources of unbiased information. Pharmaceutical companies have found ingenious ways to influence all three. In the process, the distinction between promotion and true scientific exchange has been blurred and, in some cases, totally erased.

The confusion is no accident; it serves drug companies well. "From a propagandist's perspective, the less the audience knows it's being manipulated, the greater the opportunity, because its defenses are down," says David Jones, who worked as a public relations executive for several major drug companies before resigning in 1986. He resigned, he says, because he decided that marketing manipulation had gotten out of control.

Promotion disguised as scientific exchange has another very important advantage for drug companies. "Regular" promotions, such as advertisements, direct mail, and sales presentations, must comply with strict FDA rules. Among other things, the regulations prohibit discussion of non-approved uses—uses of a drug that have not been officially sanctioned by the FDA—and require disclosure of a drug's drawbacks and side effects. Truly independent scientific exchange is under no such restrictions. Researchers speaking at scientific meetings can, for example, talk at length about unapproved uses that are still experimental. By appropriating these means of exchange,

Medical Convention Notes

SYMPOSIA, SUPPERS, AND STUFF

Family doctors treat chronic conditions that may require drug therapy for months or years: asthma, high blood pressure, heart disease, depression, menopause. They also prescribe lots of antibiotics for sore throats, ear infections, and respiratory ailments. So the annual meeting of their specialty society, the American Academy of Family Physicians, represents a not-to-be-missed marketing opportunity for drug companies.

One of our reporters spent three days at the AAFP's most recent annual meeting, held last September in Washington, D.C., and found the drug companies' presence there ubiquitous. Most visible were the commercial exhibits that covered two immense floors of the Washington convention Center.

Critics often write of the "carnival" atmosphere of these exhibits, and the comparison is apt: Companies, especially larger ones, had put up bright, fanciful pavilions and staffed them with barkers and magicians. At one point, 14 people were clustered in Wyeth's booth watching a pitchman demonstrate a wooden puzzle as he interwove a sales message for *Premarin,* a drug commonly prescribed for menopausal women. Ortho showed sales messages on a Sony high-definition television. Well-groomed salespeople handed out prizes—stuffed animals, T-shirts, umbrellas, sports bags, and the like—to M.D.s who filled out cards agreeing to see a sales rep when they got back home.

As a non-M.D., our reporter wasn't offered these more valuable gifts. Still, she wound up carrying four tote bags sagging with items laid out for the taking: pens, rulers, notepads, posters, luggage tags, clipboards, over-the-counter product samples, refrigerator magnets, and more, all with company names and logos. In the lobby, a vendor called "Sack Sitters" was doing a huge business packing cartons of freebies for shipment home.

During companies picked up the tab for many of the convention's social programs, including two private performances by Mstislav Rostropovich and the National Symphony Orchestra (Ortho Pharmaceutical, McNeil Pharmaceutical, Janssen Pharmaceutica) and a reception and dance (Eli Lilly). Meeting-goers also received invitations to other social events that weren't part of the official program: a cooking demonstration and four-course meal with a noted cardiologist (Pfizer); an "All Things Chocolate" late-night reception featuring chocolate goodies (Syntex); a concert by Frankie Valli and the Four Seasons (McNeil). Until the new AMA guidelines were released last year, the AAFP also allowed companies to hand out "family travel grants" to member physicians.

Of 35 continuing-education courses given for credit at the convention, 22 had industry sponsors. In most cases, the commercial tie-ins were easy to discern: Ortho, a major manufacturer of birth-control pills, sponsored a session on oral contraceptives; Bristol-Myers Squibb, which

makes a cholesterol-lowering drug, funded a course on treating high cholesterol; Marion Merrell Dow, maker of drugs for asthma and allergies, paid for a course on asthma and allergy treatment. Upjohn sponsored a "Doctor's Lounge," featuring case histories of patients with various conditions. The opening vignette concerned a patient with panic disorder, a condition for which *Xanax,* an Upjohn product, had just received approval from the FDA. Videotapes and viewing stations were also commercially sponsored.

For this convention, as for previous conventions, pharmaceutical companies and their hired consultants were allowed to submit entire courses for inclusion on the educational program. The AAFP's staff and program committee would accept or veto the programs. But the content and faculty were otherwise left up to the sponsors, who paid the faculty directly and frequently supplied slick portfolios and syllabuses for course attendees.

The pharmaceutical industry's presence is likely to diminish noticeably at the next convention: Delegates to the Washington meeting adopted a new, much stricter code of ethics. The new code prohibits commercial sponsors from picking faculty and subjects for educational seminars. From now on, the AAFP will accept industry money for educational programs only if it comes in the form of unrestricted grants—though by following this policy, the AAFP believes it "may risk some reduction in funding in the short-term."

---

then, drug companies have managed to free themselves from the FDA's restraints.

"We haven't regulated it, even though we have the authority, because it's been hidden from us and, I think it's fair to say, hidden from some of the audiences," says Ann Witt, the newly appointed acting director of the FDA's Division of Marketing, Advertising and Communications. Now, however, the FDA is preparing to draw a clear boundary between scientific and promotional activities—starting with continuing medical education.

Education or promotion?

For most physicians, medical education doesn't stop with the completion of their formal training. If they want to retain hospital privileges, keep their specialty certifications, and, in some states, even keep their medical licenses, they must obtain a certain number of hours a year of continuing medical education credits. Approval of CME programs is granted by institutions—mainly hospitals, medical schools, and medical societies—that meet the standards set by the independent Accreditation

Council for Continuing Medical Education.

Despite its professed reverence for continuing education, the medical establishment hasn't fully supported it with hard cash. One typical medical school, Albert Einstein College of Medicine in New York, provides less than 5 percent of the annual budget for its busy CME department; the rest comes through tuition charges and grants, in roughly equal amounts. The drug industry has been only too happy to help out. Dr. Martin Schickman, a cardiologist and assistant dean for CME at the

University of California at Los Angeles, estimates that 50 percent of CME courses get some sort of commercial support.

The drug industry's public position is that it supports medical education out of concern for the safe and appropriate use of its products and for the professional advancement of its customers, physicians. Indeed, even the industry's most vocal critics concede that some industry-supported education is genuinely impartial and useful. But all too often, it has been turned into a deliberate vehicle for product promotion.

Industry support for CME can take many forms, ranging from subsidies for travel money and speakers' fees to the creation of entire courses, complete with faculty, syllabus, slides, and handouts. The sponsoring drug company may exercise considerable control over the choice of speakers for a CME session—often recruiting nationally recognized experts, who are paid well for their demonstrated ability to attract large audiences.

"It can be a major supplemental source of income for a physician to make 10 to 15 presentations a year to conventions, grand rounds, and so on," says David Jones. "The fee can be $1000 to $5000 per presentation for an important physician, plus the perks of first-class travel."

Drug companies insist they have little if any control over the content of such experts' presentations, and physicians who participate say the same thing. But critics point out that the drug companies needn't influence physician speakers outright in order to meet their marketing objectives. Doctors who frequent the lecture circuit generally have well-known opinions on medical issues; a drug company need only select the speaker whose opinion matches its marketing needs. Dr. Marvin Moser, a hypertension specialist and clinical professor of medicine at Yale University, was able to identify the type of drug being promoted through the hypertension panel described above merely by hearing the speakers' names.

In a revealing article on public relations that appeared in Pharmaceutical Executive, a trade magazine, medical publicist Julie C. Wang advised that "third-party endorsement by opinion leaders" is better than ordinary advertising because "experts . . . without a direct material interest in a product make apparently spontaneous and objective observa-

tions about products." And, of course, some doctors seem to be all too willing to follow the company line. "We had a speaker for grand rounds last month, talking about patients who come into the emergency room with severe headache," recalls John Mitchell, the director of pharmacy at Garden City Hospital, a small community teaching hospital near Detroit. "Roche sponsored his presentation. The speaker mentioned only three drugs by trade name during his lecture, all of which were made by Roche. I was absolutely in awe that he was able to work all of them in."

Drug companies, understandably, don't publicize whatever evidence they have that CME sponsorship increases sales. But, in a provocative series of studies, Dr. Marjorie Bowman of the Bowman Gray School of Medicine in South Carolina found clear evidence of that.

Bowman and her colleagues analyzed the content of two industry-supported, university-accredited CME courses. Both were on calcium channel-blocker drugs for high blood pressure, but one was sponsored by Pfizer, which makes *Procardia,* and the other by Marion Merrell Dow, maker of *Cardizem.* In each case, speakers mentioned positive effects more often in connection with the sponsoring company's drug, and negative effects more often with competitors' drugs. Bowman followed up by monitoring the prescribing practices of doctors who attended the courses. In each case, the doctors began prescribing more of the drugs made by the company that sponsored the course they took.

CME sponsorship has proven so cost-effective that an entire category of consulting firms has come into being to organize educational programs on behalf of pharmaceutical companies. A big part of the consultants' job is to shop around for accredited CME providers who will put on such a canned presentation. According to Dr. Goldfinger of Harvard and others, several medical schools and professional societies are well known as willing to accept such programs.

Conversely, CME providers also shop around for drug companies to help pay for their educational programs. The chairman of Wyeth-Ayerst Laboratories said that in a single year, 1989, his company received more than 6000 requests for CME funding.

The CME system has become so

intertwined with pharmaceutical companies that some form of regulation now seems all but inevitable. As things now stand, "the whole academic-scientific process runs a significant risk of taint," says Dr. Kessler of the FDA. "We've got to make sure true scientific exchange doesn't lose its value."

Unfortunately, the same can now also be said of drug research itself.

Research: Science for sale?

Research is, of course, vital to the development of new drugs. The law requires that drugs be tested before approval to make sure they have the desired therapeutic result, are safe, and don't produce unacceptable side effects. Much of this research is conducted by doctors at academic medical centers and paid for by pharmaceutical companies.

For many, industry support is a major source of research funds. In a 1990 survey, the American Federation for Clinical Research found that 34 percent of its members received corporate research grants; the average grant was for $31,000 a year. While such grants may play a legitimate role in research funding, a University of Arizona study found that industry research projects at the University were actually a profit center for the scientists who conducted them. They took in far more money—$2000 to $5000 per enrolled patient—than they actually spent on the research.

Traditionally, premarket testing has been overseen by drug companies' research-and-development divisions, which are staffed by scientists trained in the rigors of the scientific

method. But the new pharmaceutical marketing experts have inexorably invaded this area. Writing in the New England Journal of Medicine, Dr. Alan Hillman and colleagues from the University of Pennsylvania, who perform cost-benefit analyses for pharmaceutical firms, outlined some of the ways that companies influence research:

"They fund projects with a high likelihood of producing favorable results. . . . They exclude products that may compare favorably with the sponsor's own. Sometimes, only favorable clinical data are released to investigators. . . . Negative studies may be terminated before they are ready for publication. . . . Corporate personnel may seek to control the content and use of the final report, including the decision to publish."

These manipulations do have a measurable effect. In a review of 107 published studies comparing a new drug against traditional therapy, Dr. Richard Davidson of the University of Florida found that drug company-supported studies of new drugs were far more likely to favor those drugs than were studies supported by non-commercial entities.

Other types of clinical research are even more easily used for commercial purposes. So-called "Phase IV" studies, conducted *after* a drug reaches the market to detect any unexpected side effects, involve large numbers of doctors, and have proven useful for drug-company promotion.

In 1989, Pharmaceutical Executive ran a detailed description of how to design Phase IV studies to "support promotional efforts" while "defusing the critics." As the article in the trade journal stated, "Some companies have implemented very simple studies . . . to directly increase product sales by involving large numbers of investigators who increase their own prescribing as a result of participating in the study. . . . Such studies usually are not intended to yield publishable information."

The physicians shouldn't be given easy-to-criticize incentives like travel junkets, the writer helpfully noted. Instead, the company can make a donation to the physicians' favorite school or research organization, or list them as "authors in papers prepared by company writers and placed in single-sponsor journals."

The publication ploy

Doctors consistently name medical journals as one of their main sources of unbiased information. Especially valued are peer-reviewed journals, journals whose articles are reviewed by experts in the field before being accepted for publication.

Drug companies have found an effective way to use these journals' credibility for their own purposes by subsidizing the publication of "supplements." Piggybacked onto regular issues of the journal, supplements use the same sober-looking design and typography as the regular articles. Frequently, the supplements are based on symposia sponsored by the same companies that pay for the publication.

"Repeatedly, we have found these publications not to be balanced, objective sources of information regarding current drug research or drug treatment," David Banks, an FDA enforcement officer, said in a speech last year.

Select supplements virtually at random from the shelves of a medical library, and it's clear that objectivity is not their goal.

A March 1990 supplement to the American Journal of Medicine carried a write-up of a Squibb symposium focusing on the "continuing efficacy and safety" of *Azactam*, an injectable antibiotic made by Squibb, for a wide variety of patients and conditions. Squibb's marketing department apparently found this supplement so helpful it handed out reprints as a promotion, with prescribing information bound in. By contrast, the Medical Letter, an independent, noncommercial publication that reviews drugs and medical devices, does not cite *Azactam* as the drug of first choice for a single category of infection. (The drug that is the preferred alternative to *Azactam*, Hoechst-Roussel's *Claforan*, costs slightly less.)

A September 1991 supplement to the Journal of Clinical Psychiatry, sponsored by Wallace Laboratories, dealt with "selecting appropriate benzodiazepine hypnotic therapy." The benzodiazepines are a widely prescribed class of tranquilizer that includes a number of drugs, such as *Valium* and *Xanax*. But virtually every article in the supplement focuses on favorable information about *Doral*, Wallace's entry into the furiously competitive sleeping-pill market.

A supplement to the journal Hospital Formulary, entitled "Issues in Reperfusion for the '90s," was sponsored by Genentech. Based on a symposium and "coordinated for publication" by a CME consulting firm, the supplement repeatedly attacked a widely publicized European study showing that Genentech's $2000-a-dose drug *Activase* is no more effective in breaking up heart attack-causing blood clots than its $200-a-dose generic competitor streptokinase. Nowhere in the supplement was the European study defended, even though many experts have done so in professional meetings and the national media.

Many journals actively market their willingness to publish supplements. The American Society of Hospital Pharmacists bought an advertisement in the trade journal Medical Marketing & Media, offering "sole sponsor opportunities." Those opportunities included supplements to its two professional magazines as well as educational symposia and other publications.

Even the American Medical Association, putative guardian of medical ethics and publisher of the Journal of the AMA, found it difficult to resist the lure of such easy money. It planned to charge $25,000 to $150,000 per issue to publish single-topic, industry-sponsored collections of articles. An outcry from consumer advocates and a warning from the FDA eventually persuaded the AMA to drop the plan.

The FDA cracks down

Under Commissioner Kessler, the FDA is now looking for ways to restore balance to a system of research, publication, and education that has clearly been compromised.

Last fall, the agency circulated a "draft concept paper" that, for the first time, proposed general rules and principles governing drug company-supported continuing education. The paper proposed that a company-supported CME program would be considered promotional, and regulated as such, unless it was truly independent—meaning that the sponsoring company had virtually no role in the selection of speakers and that the content was unbiased and scientifically rigorous. Speakers would have to disclose any potential conflicts of interest, such as being on a company's speakers' bureau or accepting company research grants.

The paper specifically stated that the FDA had no intention of meddling in true scientific exchange, which was, in any event, far outside the agency's jurisdiction. But Kessler and his staff also pointed out that the FDA has the clear legal responsibility to regulate drug advertising and promotion, whether those marketing efforts take place in a traditional or a nontraditional guise.

Predictably, the Pharmaceutical Manufacturers Association, the industry's influential trade group, denounced the proposal on sight. If such guidelines were adopted, the PMA said, then drug companies would simply stop funding continuing education programs.

Organized opposition also came from something called the "Coalition of Healthcare Communicators." Operating out of a post-office box in Connecticut, the coalition was made up of nine trade groups that represented medical advertising, public-relations, and marketing interests. In a "Dear Doctor" letter that was circulated widely, the coalition painted the FDA proposals as a threat to free speech and academic freedom. "We must work together to protect scientific independence and integrity from bureaucratic interference," the five-page letter concluded. Whether coincidentally or not, protests from academic physicians soon began descending on the FDA regulators as well.

We support the FDA's efforts to disentangle marketing from scientific exchange, and hope Kessler and his colleagues will be able to resist the pressure to back off. The very source and intensity of the opposition—the mightily profitable drug companies and the well-paid consultants and academicians they employ—itself suggests the degree to which science and commerce have become interdependent.

A careful inspection of the FDA proposal reveals that, far from threatening scientific independence and integrity, it aims to rescue them from commercial influences. The rules wouldn't affect drug companies who practice what they preach and subsidize CME programs that are truly balanced and scientifically rigorous. But the rules would seriously limit the behind-the-scenes manipulation of superficially "independent" scientific presentations.

The FDA, however, does not bear sole responsibility for policing the drug industry's activities. The medical-academic establishment also

needs to continue its efforts to create a more ethical environment for the profession:

▣ The medical profession should adequately fund its own continuing education instead of depending on pharmaceutical companies for the bulk of funding.

▣ Physicians who accept honoraria, research grants, or placement on industry speakers' bureaus should be required to disclose all such connections whenever they speak at symposia or scientific meetings on subjects related to the companies' products. Those disclosures should also be printed on any brochures announcing their speaking engagements or CME courses, so that doctors could weigh the speakers' objectivity before they decide to attend.

▣ Medical-journal editors should design their single-sponsor supplements to distinguish them clearly from regular editorial matter—by means of prominently displayed notices, different typography, different page layout, or, preferably, all

three—just the way newsmagazines already do.

▣ Medical schools and residency programs should train students to recognize and evaluate drug-marketing messages, since those messages will surround them for the rest of their working lives.

▣ Professional medical associations should consider setting specific limits for the amounts their members can accept as honoraria for speaking engagements. In addition, all physicians should continually ask themselves whether accepting industrial largesse—whether a takeout lunch for the office staff, an expensive textbook, a speaker's fee, or a research grant—has compromised their intellectual and their clinical judgment.

The relationship between physicians and drug companies needs to change dramatically. We believe that can be done quickly. And we believe that effective changes will make the medical marketplace a safer, more honorable one for doctors and patients alike.

[Ed. Note: This is Part 1 of a 2-part series. See Part 2, *Consumer Reports*, March 1992.]

The Cocaine
Money Market

Colombia's sophisticated laundering system
has stymied the authorities

Douglas Farah and Steve Coll

Washington Post Foreign Service

Farah reported from Colombia and Panama, Coll from Panama and Washington.

T

CALI, Colombia
he international dollar trade here has no exchange floor or electronic tickers or pontificating analysts. Yet the market's huge size, sophisticated structure and competitive daily bidding operations would be familiar to any Chicago futures broker. There's just one twist: In Cali, cocaine trafficking capital of the Western Hemisphere, most dollar traders operate in the illegal black market, and they are well-advised never to lose money for their clients. "If you lose drugs, people get upset," one narcotics specialist says. "You lose money and people die."

During the 1980s, Colombia's drug cartels brought home only an estimated 10 percent to 20 percent of the billions of dollars in cash proceeds from their sales of cocaine in the United States. But over the past two years, because of tougher U.S. banking law enforcement and other factors, they have been sending about half of their cash back to Colombia—an estimated $5 billion to $7 billion annually, according to investigators.

This change in the movement of cocaine money has presented U.S. and regional law enforcement agents with a formidable—some say unmanageable—challenge as they seek to disrupt the financial empires of Colombia's largest cocaine traffickers.

Over the past year, Colombian cocaine traffickers have refined and expanded a unique illicit money trading market. Independent Colombian money brokers allied with the cocaine cartels—at least several dozen brokers, and perhaps more, investigators say—have been allowed to bid competitively for the right to transport large blocks of illicit cash to Colombia. The blocks of cash are typically $1 million or more, and come from cocaine sales in U.S. cities.

Cali operatives call the system *bajando el dolar,* or "bringing down the dollar." For the money brokers at its center, the profit potential is huge: the payoff for buying piles of cash in the United States and getting them to Colombia can be as high as 25 percent of the amount transported, or $250,000 for every $1 million. But the risks of trading can be formidable.

For example, a Colombian broker wishing to purchase a cash block in the United States must first show to his cocaine exporting client that he is "bonded"—that is, that he can reimburse the trafficker even if the cash he purchases is lost, stolen or seized by police. This bonding is done either through cash, land or urban properties, according to law enforcement and Cali cartel sources.

Lacking market police equivalent to the Securities and Exchange Commission, which oversees Wall Street, the cocaine cartel often enforces fair trading by sending a few people to stay with the family of a money broker during the period of a trading contract, a cartel source says. When the money broker or his employees call home, these "friends" remind him that completion of the deal is anxiously awaited, the source says.

■

FOR U.S. AND COLOMBIAN LAW ENFORCEMENT officials, disrupting this burgeoning money market has become a major, if daunting, priority. Because of weak Colombian financial laws and the complex expansion of the Cali-based money brokerage system, law enforcement officers have yet to make a major case against the key Colombian brokers, officials say. Some vow this will change very soon; others are skeptical that a major success can ever be achieved.

The trouble in breaking up the money market comes as many law enforcement officials are acknowledging the failure of a long U.S. campaign to choke off production of cocaine in South America and to eradicate the coca leaf, the

MONEY TRAIL TO COLOMBIA

IN THE U.S.

■ Cocaine users buy drug on streets

■ Cash held at safe house

■ Broker buys cash held in United States at discount from cartel family, uses various means to get it into Colombia

ON THE TRAIL

■ "Smurfs" — small-time contractors — smuggle cash in modest amounts for the Colombia brokers, or deposit in banks

■ Cash moves in bulk in shipping containers and cocaine-smuggling planes returning empty

BACK TO THE SOURCE

■ "Tourists" change bulk money into pesos

■ Banks change drug money to stocks or bonds

■ Broker receives cash, sells to legitimate Colombian businessman for pesos at discount. Broker pays off contract with cartel in pesos, keeps profit.

THE WASHINGTON POST

raw product from which cocaine is derived. This setback has prompted the development of the "kingpin strategy," which focuses more time and resources on disrupting the astonishingly sophisticated, multi-billion-dollar financial networks of Colombia's biggest cocaine traffickers.

Since the decline of the cocaine cartel based in Medellin, the Colombian organizations based in Cali now manage about 80 percent of the world's cocaine trade, according to the U.S. Drug Enforcement Administration and other sources. Cali's main kingpins include brothers Miguel and Gilberto Rodriguez Orejuela, and their close friend and longtime associate Jose Santacruz Londono. Sources say the Rodriguez Orejuelas have a remarkably sophisticated operation, relying on a system of computerized bookkeeping, wire transfers and cellular phones to monitor business and keep the money flowing.

The trouble, as with past tactics in the U.S.-led drug war, is that it is one thing to talk about disrupting the financial operations of the Colombian cocaine cartels, and another to succeed.

"We celebrate our hollow little victories that don't mean anything because of the magnitude of the problem," says one weary anti-narcotics agent. "The truth is that every day the traffickers are stronger economically and politically."

Statistics make the point. The DEA estimates annual cash seizures from Colombia-based cocaine trafficking organiza-

tions at about $200 million. That's in a cocaine money industry generating an overall estimated $20 billion in illegal cash profits each year, a senior DEA official says.

"If we get 1 in 4 shipments, it's okay with [the traffickers], and we are getting 1 in 100," says one official. "It is going to take more manpower, resources and intestinal fortitude to get serious about this, and I have not seen that yet by any country."

In financial terms, Colombia's cocaine barons can be seen as ordinary commodity exporters faced with two unique business challenges. One problem is that all their customers pay in cash. The other is that this cash must be converted into forms of wealth that the cocaine exporters can use in Colombia.

During the 1980s, investigators say, the cartels generally solved these problems by depositing directly into U.S. banks the cash they received from retailing large loads of cocaine to smaller organizations that handle U.S. street sales. Then the cartels shifted their wholesale profits through front companies and international accounts until they could be safely invested or held for the benefit of cartel leaders.

■

TO A DEGREE, THAT SYSTEM IS STILL AVAILABLE, according to investigators. But tougher U.S. and European banking regulations, increased law enforcement efforts, economic liberalization in Colombia and high interest rates in Colombian banks have made direct deposits into U.S. banks less attractive and riskier than before, investigators and cartel sources say. Among other measures, U.S. authorities now require banks to keep a record of any deposit over $10,000, preventing traffickers from making large deposits without detection. So increasingly, Colombian cocaine exporters—of whom the largest and most powerful are based in Cali—are attempting to smuggle cash dollars out of the United States and to slip them into the legitimate international financial system elsewhere. The doorways for such cash deposits or other "money laundering" transactions are many, but the preferred points of entry into the banking system these days include Panama, Mexico, Brazil, Venezuela and Colombia itself, investigative and cartel sources say.

Specialists, investigators and cartel sources say that increasingly, the Colombian cartels have large amounts of cash backed up in the United States, waiting to be transferred outside U.S. borders.

In response to this problem, the Colombia-based illicit dollar trading market has expanded and evolved. An account of the way the market works was provided by Greg Passic, who directs money laundering investigations for the DEA; Fernando Brito, director of the Department of Administrative Security, Colombia's equivalent of the FBI; Colombian Attorney General Gustavo de Greiff; other law enforcement sources, and a source who has worked with the Cali cartel in its laundering operations.

■

WHEREAS THE COCAINE CARTELS FORMERLY INSISTED on receiving every dollar earned in the United States, they have lately decided to pay a share of their dollars to middlemen to make it easier to bring their profits back to Colombia, investigators say. The middlemen, who are Colombian money brokers, are now able, for example, to pay just $4 million to the cocaine traffickers in Cali for the right to take possession of $5 million in cash sitting in a safe house in Houston, according to investigators. The broker pockets the difference, in exchange for transporting the money to Colombia.

The size of the payoff to the middleman or broker varies, partly depending on location. Cash that is stashed in some cities is priced more attractively than in others, investigators say. After agreeing to buy a block of cash stored somewhere in the United States, a money broker guarantees to deliver the total amount—minus his commission—to the cocaine cartel family within 15 days of making the deal. He also pledges to deliver the money in Colombian pesos, rather than in dollars.

The broker's profit rests on his ability to smuggle or otherwise transfer the block of cash he has bought in the United States into a bank. He then sells the dollars to a legitimate Colombian businessman, who pays pesos for them and gets the dollars at a better exchange rate than normal. The broker's "spread," or profit, is the portion of the original dollar stash he gets to keep, minus his expenses and the money he loses by allowing a businessman to buy the rest of the dollars from him at a discount. The broker typically tries to reduce his risk in the market by subcontracting the cross-border smuggling aspect of his work to Mexican, Colombian or other gangs adept at finding low-level runners willing to take physical risks with cash, investigators say.

"What you have with the Colombians—it's not organized crime, it's modular crime," says the DEA's Passic. "They have fragmented each function and assigned that responsibility to an individual."

Typically, law enforcement officers in the United States can catch only the small-time subcontracted smugglers as they attempt to move relatively small blocks of cash out of the United States or deposit the money into banks in small amounts to evade the $10,000 bank reporting requirement.

These smugglers are referred to as "smurfs," a nickname based on television cartoon characters that reflects the runners' relative unimportance in the Colombian-based cocaine industry. For example, when police in Cali were sent in May to round up illegal aliens, they found long lines of tourists outside money exchange houses at the downtown Plaza de Caicedo, all with documents in order and all seeking to change $25,000, the legal limit for tourists under Colombian law, according to Brito.

Further investigation determined that the tourists were receiving their dollars from the Cali cocaine cartel and exchanging them in a vast operation involving more than $400,000 a day, Brito says.

Money is "smurfed" by operatives who buy thousands of small postal money orders in the United States and transfer them to virtually unregulated money exchange houses around Colombia. Brito says an investigation into 15 exchange houses in Colombia and 12 in the United States showed the orders were made out in the names of real people, with correct Colombian national identification numbers, obtained from newspaper announcements of deaths or lottery winners. False identifications are produced for smurfs allied with the cartels.

Cartel families stamp symbols on the backs of money orders—a shield, a swan in a circle, an eagle, a smiling moon face—to make clear which money orders are which, according to U.S. Postal Inspection Service investigators.

On the U.S. end, the preponderance of such cash smuggling has led to a relatively large number of cash seizures this summer at airports, other export terminals and safe houses, according to the DEA. In one case this summer, a man was arrested at New York's Kennedy airport after loading about $120,000 in cash into a number of condoms and swallowing them before boarding a flight to Bogota, a DEA official says. The official called this swallowing feat "a record."

Law enforcement officials in Colombia says bulk shipments of dollars, either by airplane or in shipping containers out of Miami to Panama or a Colombian port, are growing.

■

WITH THE ONCE HIGHLY PROTECTED ECONOMY OF Colombia opening rapidly to foreign imports and with dollar exchange restrictions easing, Colombian and law enforcement officials fear the problem will only grow.

"This whole process of [economic] liberalization has had a dark side," says University of Miami money laundering specialist Bruce Bagley. Adds Colombian Attorney General de Greiff, "What this means is that we have a $5 billion problem. . . . The criminals have an immense power to buy the things they want."

They are also hurting legitimate Colombian business. One popular dollar repatriation technique of late is use of "San Andresitos," sprawling retail markets in most Colombian cities that thrive on contraband consumer goods, says Salomon Kalmanovitz, an academic and banking director who has studied the practice. Cocaine traffickers launder an estimated minimum of $700 million annually through these markets, according to Kalmanovitz and others, by buying television sets, video recorders, liquor, cameras, cosmetics and other luxury goods for cash in Panama and the United States, then smuggling them into Colombia and selling them to consumers at a discount. The huge influx of drug-financed consumer goods is at least partly responsible for Colombia's wildly warped trade statistics, with the government recently reporting a 78 percent increase over 1992 in imports in the first half of this year. Meanwhile, the constant influx of dollars has revalued the Colombian peso internally, making the dollar worth less on the black market than in official exchanges. That hurts legitimate Colombian exporters, who can buy ever less with their dollars earned abroad.

With so much money washing back to the region, and with such a sophisticated cash flow market to be managed, another rising concern is that the Colombian cocaine cartels are moving aggressively into Latin American banking.

"They buy into stock instruments, government debt redemption certificates. There are increasingly sophisticated schemes that we're seeing in most parts of the world," says Rayburn Hesse, senior policy adviser in the U.S. State Department's Bureau of Narcotics, Terrorism and Crime. "There is literally no horizon."

Panama's proximity to Colombia and its booming Colon Free Trade Zone help explain its role in laundering cocaine money.

LARRY FOGEL—THE WASHINGTON POST

Cocaine Central: How the Invasion Didn't Stop Panama

Steve Coll and Douglas Farah
Washington Post Foreign Service

Coll reported from Panama and Washington, Farah from Panama and Colombia. Washington Post special correspondent Berta Thayer contributed to this report.

COLON, Panama
"Pure Coffee" reads the freshly painted sign on a tin warehouse in this tropical free trade port. But on Sept. 1, federal agents in Miami opened 318 coffee boxes routed from the warehouse and discovered an unusual blend: Panamanian-labeled coffee mixed with 5.2 metric tons of Colombian cocaine.

That large seizure, achieved after Drug Enforcement Administration and U.S. Customs agents penetrated a tangle of front companies and financial records in the United States, Panama, Colombia and elsewhere, is the latest of many signs that Panama remains a major center for cocaine trafficking and the handling of huge cocaine cash profits nearly four years after U.S. forces invaded the country.

The Dec. 20, 1989, invasion was aimed partly at clamping down on Panama's role in the Colombia-based cocaine trade. U.S. troops overthrew Panama's military leader, Gen. Manuel Antonio Noriega, who has been convicted and imprisoned in the United States on cocaine trafficking charges. Yet the State Department acknowledges today that aside from the United States itself, newly democratic Panama is the most active center for cocaine "money laundering" in the Western Hemisphere. Money laundering is the process by which Colombian-based cocaine producers and distributors transfer their illegal cash profits into legitimate bank accounts or other financial assets.

The major cocaine traffickers have begun transferring more and more of their cash profits back to Colombia, creating a vast new illegal market in the transport and exchange of cash dollars. Destabilizing the increasingly sophisticated financial networks of cocaine kingpins has become a priority for U.S. law enforcement and anti-narcotics foreign policy programs. As a result, officials and other experts see freewheeling, post-invasion Panama as one of the major obstacles in the multibillion-dollar U.S. effort to stem the flow of drugs from South America to the United States. Given Panama's proximity to Colombia, its longtime liberal banking rules and its use of the U.S. dollar as its national currency, enforcement officials say some cocaine trafficking and money laundering through the isthmus is inevitable.

But the more pressing issue is whether in democratic Panama the Colombia-based cocaine export industry and its illicit financial services system are just as embedded in major banking, business and government structures as they were under Noriega, when the United States routinely criticized the government.

"What the United States did, you see, was chop off the head but leave the whole rest of the structure intact," a U.S. investigator who concentrates on money laundering says. "The bottom line is that nothing has really changed."

The evidence accumulated so far suggests that Colombian cocaine traffickers today see Panama as a door through which they can move illegal cash profits back to Colombia or into legitimate assets such as bank deposits, real estate and luxury consumer goods.

In part, Panama is a popular gateway because there are no restrictions on the amount of cash that can be imported. There are requirements that large cash deposits to banks be recorded, but records are not analyzed or monitored effectively by the government, U.S. officials say.

7. THE ECONOMY OF DRUG USE

■

PANAMA'S PERVASIVE BUSINESS SECRECY LAWS, which apply to banks and corporations, also make it relatively easy for drug traffickers to build networks of front companies—or businesses that exist only on paper—to disguise, store and siphon cocaine profits into legitimate enterprises, investigators say.

Moreover, a trade in cash is booming in the Panamanian port city of Colon, where the government has set up a "free trade zone" in which items may be imported and sold duty-free. Some traffickers have set up businesses in the zone that are used to smuggle cocaine dollars into the country and deposit them in the Panamanian banking system; others buy luxury consumer goods such as televisions and cosmetics there with cocaine cash, then ship them to Colombia, where they can be sold for Colombian pesos that are "clean" of any taint of trafficking. The State Department recently called Colon a "money-laundering mecca for drug traffickers."

Investigators suspicious of how the Colon zone was being used by Colombian cocaine exporters recently received an education while poring over documents seized in July 1992 from a company called Celeste International. U.S. officials identify Celeste as a major front company that laundered cash for Cali, Colombia, cocaine kingpins Miguel and Gilberto Rodriguez Orejuela. Five tons of cocaine were seized on Celeste's Colon premises.

Situated on the Caribbean mouth of the Panama Canal, the Colon free zone is a teeming trade center for luxury and consumer goods flowing from Western and Asian manufacturers to Central and South American countries. About $9 billion changes hands here every year, roughly 20 percent of it in cash, according to zone officials. Showrooms along its narrow streets display $30,000 watches and glistening Chinese vases as well as duty-free blue jeans, electronics, perfumes and liquor.

Celeste exploited this milieu for the Rodriguez Orejuela trafficking organization by issuing false invoices showing that it received cash for consumer items it never delivered, U.S. officials say. Using these invoices as cover, millions of dollars in cocaine profits allegedly were moved to Celeste's Panamanian bank accounts. From there, they could be routed to wherever the Rodriguez Orejuela group wished—without raising the suspicions of law enforcement officials looking for drug money.

■

NO ONE KNOWS HOW MUCH OF NEARLY $2 BILLION in annual cash turnover in the Colon free zone is cocaine money washing into the international banking system. But some law enforcement officials are frustrated by what they see as Panama's lack of political will to attack the problem.

The zone's deputy administrator, Gerardo E. Harris, asked about Celeste and other cases of false invoice-based money laundering, replies: "It's not our responsibility. We have no ways or means to determine whether it's occurring or not."

With about 13,000 jobs in the zone at stake, Panamanian officials are reluctant to impose rules that would make Colon less attractive to regional traders. Some Panamanian officials argue that any illicit cash flowing through Colon's free zone most often reflects efforts by traders in a liberalized regional economy to evade tariffs and taxes rather than to launder cocaine profits.

Yet inside and outside the Colon zone, evidence and allegations of cocaine-related money-laundering schemes in post-invasion Panama—or questionable activities by senior officials in the Panamanian government—are plentiful and varied:

■ Panama's suspended attorney general, Rogelio Cruz Rios, has been charged with exceeding his authority when he released in August 1992 about $25 million in alleged Colombian cocaine profits that had been frozen in Panamanian bank accounts at U.S. urging at the time of the 1989 invasion.

Earlier charges that Cruz Rios personally profited by releasing the money have been dropped for lack of evidence. But Panamanian officials say others profited when Cruz Rios unfroze the accounts last year. After the move, a "substantial amount"—millions of dollars—was paid to Panamanian lawyers, according to Carlos Lucas Lopez, president of Panama's Supreme Court. Millions more were transferred out of Panama, he says.

The Panamanian lawyers who benefited say the money they received was for legal fees. "That's the excuse they have given," Lopez says. "But they are very big fees." Investigations are continuing, Lopez says.

■ Panama's Supreme Court recently authorized a more aggressive investigation into accusations that the former head of Panama's customs service, Rodrigo Arosemena, removed and placed in his car trunk $1.8 million in cash from a seized shipment of $7.2 million of suspected cocaine profits smuggled by boat into Panama. The cash was stuffed in cardboard boxes inside a shipping container. Arosemena, who resigned his post to run for the National Assembly, denied taking the cash and called the allegations politically motivated.

■ Last year, after seizing 1.5 metric tons of cocaine, Mexican officials alerted Panama's government that a company in the Colon free trade zone was involved in the shipment, according to sources familiar with the case. A Panamanian businessman was arrested, confessed and was imprisoned. But the U.S. government has learned the businessman has been inexplicably released from jail and has disappeared.

■ An investigation of Panama's booming construction industry has found evidence that many of the luxury towers going up on Panama City's Pacific shoreline have few of the proper permits, raising concerns that the buildings are being constructed to launder large-scale cocaine profits, as is common in Colombia, sources say. By paying cash to buy a piece of property and construct an office tower, investigators say, cocaine traffickers convert illegal cash profits from cocaine into a legal asset—real estate. Panamanian officials counter that such allegations are irresponsible without specific evidence of wrongdoing.

■ A New York judge this year froze millions of dollars held in New York bank accounts by the Hong Kong Bank of Panama on grounds the money represented cocaine profits smuggled into the banking system, consolidated in Panama, then shipped back to the United States, according to an affidavit filed by a U.S. postal inspector.

■ In Miami, two accused cocaine traffickers, Augusto Falcon and Salvador Magluta, are to stand trial on charges that, until 1991, they earned more than $2 billion importing illegal drugs. To disguise their alleged trafficking, the pair employed at least two dozen Panamanian front companies, according to U.S. investigators.

Some of those companies were established more than a decade ago by the law firm of Panamanian President Guillermo Endara. University of Miami money-laundering specialist Bruce Bagley has accused Endara of "willful ignorance" in this and other cases, a view echoed by other critics.

Endara vigorously denies the charge, saying he never

knew that Falcon and Magluta were clients of his large firm. Moreover, Endara's firm withdrew from the matter in 1987 following private warnings that the two clients were unsavory, the president has said.

Whether Endara's involvement will become an issue at the Miami trial is uncertain.

■ The 5.2 tons of cocaine seized in Miami on Sept. 1, routed through a Colon coffee warehouse, has exposed an international network of Panama-based companies and business deals reaching to Europe, the Middle East, the former Soviet Union, South America and the United States, according to sources familiar with that case. Whether investigators will be able to untangle the network fully is another matter.

Indeed, some law enforcement authorities and other critics argue that the cocaine economy has fundamentally poisoned Panama's embryonic democracy. These critics argue that the U.S. government is playing down the extent of cocaine-related organized crime burgeoning in Panama because Washington wants to promote the longevity of Panama's democratic leaders.

"The guys who are supposed to defend the system aren't doing it," says one investigator. "How serious are we? How much can we expect from the local Panamanian officials? . . . The problem is that DEA has nobody to trust here."

■

SENIOR U.S. AND PANAMANIAN OFFICIALS ARGUE that such criticism exaggerates Panama's problem and fails

to give its fledglling government credit for what it has accomplished since Noriega's ouster. They say the problem is not as great as it was in Noriega's time, that enforcement efforts are improving and that some difficulties are inevitable in a transition from authoritarian to democratic rule.

"Panamanian authorities are making a good faith and increasingly effective effort to stem the flow of narcotics into and out of Panama," U.S. drug policy director Lee P. Brown declared in an Aug. 11 speech. "But there is more to the problem than trafficking . . . . Panama's financial and business sectors should be at the forefront of [an] effort to help deprive the narco-traffickers of their profits. At stake is not only the reputation of banks and businesses, but the image of Panama."

Yet Panama continues to resist unlocking its bank and corporate secrecy laws or to improve oversight of illicit transactions. Moreover, some Panamanian officials argue that U.S. efforts in this area are hypocritical. From the 1930s, when Washington secretly used Panamanian companies to ship weapons to Britain, to the Iran-contra affair, when the Reagan administration secretly funded the Nicaraguan anti-Communist rebels, Western governments have long exploited Panama's rules for their own ends, Panamanians say.

"It happens now that they're all excited about drugs," Panama's controller general, Ruben D. Carles, says. "But for years, the [U.S.] government used it [the financial system]. Why should we change?"

Fighting the Drug War

Everyone agrees that the United States has a drug problem; in fact, until the crisis in the Middle East that began in May 1990 with Iraq's invasion of Kuwait, and the economic recession that gripped the country with the dawn of the 1990s, more Americans named drugs as the nation's number one problem than any other. But what should be done about drugs? How should we fight the drug war? Is there an answer to these questions—or is it a hopeless, unwinnable battle? Of all drug-related issues, perhaps this one is the most controversial.

There are at least three currently argued perspectives or models on the drug war. The first can be called the *punitive* model. The reason we are losing the war against drugs, the punitive model argues, is that we are not tough enough on users and dealers. The solution to the drug problem is tougher laws, more arrests, longer jail and prison terms for drug offenders, more police, more lethal police weapons, more interception of drugs smuggled into the country from abroad, more surveillance, fewer constitutional rights for dealers, users, and suspects, more planes, faster boats, more and bigger seizures of drug dealers' assets, more pressure on the governments of countries where drugs originate, and perhaps even the assistance of the armed forces.

The second model might be called the *maintenance* or the *medical* model. Addicts and drug abusers are not criminals, this model argues. Just as alcoholics are not committing any crime when they get drunk in the privacy of their own homes, abusers of the currently illegal drugs should not be arrested or imprisoned for their compulsive, self-destructive behavior. They are sick and in need of medical and psychiatric care, including, as a last resort, maintenance on an addictive drug such as methadone. Maintenance is typically proposed only for the narcotics; for the other illegal drugs, some alternative form of therapy, which includes, eventually, abstinence, is called for by this model.

The third perspective is the *decriminalization* or *legalization* model. This model proposes that the problem with the use of the currently illegal drugs is the profit motive. Eliminate the laws against the possession, sale, and use of drugs, and they will no longer be profitable to sell, and most of the problems associated with their use—the violence, corruption, and medical problems that sellers and users cause or experience—will disappear. Some proponents of legalization even argue that the use of drugs will actually decline when criminal penalties are removed.

Some people advocate one model only for certain drugs and another model for different drugs, while others argue that their model applies to all currently illegal drugs. Hardly anyone argues that currently legal drugs, such as tobacco and alcohol, should be criminalized. However, some observers do argue that legal penalties should be removed from marijuana, but should stay in place for drugs such as heroin and cocaine. In fact, in 11 states, making up a third of the United States population, small-quantity marijuana possession has been decriminalized; the possessor cannot be arrested, prosecuted, or jailed, and may receive only a citation equivalent to a traffic ticket. Nonetheless, most supporters of a strong version of the punitive model favor strictly enforced laws against all currently illegal drugs, and many supporters of legalization favor removing criminal penalties against all currently illegal drugs.

Much of the debate over the question of legalization hinges on whether national alcohol prohibition actually worked. In 1920, a constitutional amendment banning the sale of all alcoholic beverages in the United States took effect; it was repealed in 1933, and Prohibition was regarded as a failure. After all, the legalization model argues, if it is not possible to legislate against the sale of alcohol, how can the criminalization of the other drugs work any better? In fact, as historical research shows, Prohibition actually did reduce the consumption of alcohol. Rates of cirrhosis of the liver, traffic accidents, and arrests for drunken driving and public drunkenness all declined sharply. In addition, when alcohol was relegalized, sales in 1933, the first "wet" year after Prohibition, were far lower than in years just before Prohibition, indicating that many drinkers had given up the alcohol habit during that period. Of course, many other problems accompanied Prohibition, including the rise of organized crime and a number of medical maladies associated with drinking alcohol substitutes—but use did decline.

The argument over drug legalization may be little more than cocktail party chatter. Very, very few politicians can publicly support legalization and hope to get reelected.

Public opinion polls show that 9 out of 10 Americans oppose the legalization of currently illegal drugs, over half believe that legalization would lead to increased use, and two-thirds believe that legalization would lead to an increase in the crime rate. Only a quarter support the legalization of marijuana, considered the least dangerous of the illegal drugs; only slightly more than 1 in 20 support the legalization of heroin and cocaine. Given this sort of opposition, legalization is not a viable political option at this time.

Looking Ahead: Challenge Questions

What is the best way to fight the drug war? Should it be fought at all?

Would legalization take the profit motive out of drug selling? Would it result in diminished use? Or would use increase, as others have argued? Given the fact that the rate of marijuana use has not increased in the states that have decriminalized small-quantity possession, why shouldn't this also be the case for heroin and cocaine?

If Prohibition actually did decrease the use of alcohol, why was it discontinued? Is Prohibition an acceptable and workable model for the currently illegal drugs? Does arresting the drug user work?

Experts generally agree that interdiction—stopping drugs at the supply side—is not possible, and that demand should be reduced. How can we reduce the demand for drugs?

U.S. Drug Laws:

Two Views

U.S. Drug Laws — An Introduction

The two Sounding Board articles that follow address substance abuse. The first, by Lester Grinspoon and James Bakalar, argues for relaxing the laws against drug use; the second, by Herbert Kleber, favors retaining them. Because these laws are confusing and may not be widely understood by our readers, Rachel Hart, research assistant at the Journal, *prepared the following summary.*

Drug-control laws, which are established by both federal and state statutes, generally regulate three activities: the manufacture, distribution, and possession of drugs. Other illegal drug-related activities, such as possessing drug-related paraphernalia, laundering money, and driving while intoxicated, are regulated by a variety of other state and federal statutes. Narcotics offenders may be prosecuted under state or federal laws.

The federal government divides controlled substances into five categories, or schedules, with schedule I drugs — those with the highest potential for abuse and no accepted medical use — being the most strictly controlled. Examples of schedule I drugs include heroin, lysergic acid diethylamide (LSD), and "designer drugs" (unnamed chemical substances designed to mimic the pharmacologic effects of scheduled drugs). Schedule II drugs, which include morphine, cocaine, and codeine, have a high potential for abuse but also have limited accepted medical uses. Schedule III, IV, and V drugs all have accept-

ed medical uses and are considered by federal authorities to have a progressively lower potential for abuse — the higher the schedule number, the lower the potential.

State schedules are usually similar but not identical to the federal schedules. Marijuana, for instance, is classified by the federal government's Controlled Substances Act as a schedule I drug, whereas many states either create a separate category for it or leave it on the schedule of the most strictly controlled drugs but specify less severe penalties for its possession. The severity of penalties also varies from state to state. Possession of 2 oz of marijuana, for example, may be a misdemeanor in one state and a felony in another.

Drug violators apprehended by federal law-enforcement agents (usually the Drug Enforcement Administration or the Bureau of Alcohol, Tobacco, and Firearms) may, at the discretion of federal officials, be prosecuted under federal laws controlling substance abuse; violators apprehended by state or local law-enforcement officials are usually prosecuted under state laws. The federal government may also prosecute cases that fall under its constitutionally mandated jurisdiction. For instance, drug trafficking across state lines is a federal offense, since the federal government has the ultimate authority over matters involving interstate commerce.

Sanctions for violating drug laws depend on the type, category, and amount of the drug in question; the type of activity; and the law under which it is prosecuted. Specific provisions, such as the amount of a drug that differentiates simple possession from possession with the intent to sell, vary among the states and between the states and the federal government.

The War on Drugs —
A Peace Proposal

AFTER nearly 10 years of escalation, the government assault on illicit drugs has proved to be a costly failure. We have all been paying the price in misdirected resources, social tension, violent crime, ill health, compromised civil liberties, and international conflict.

The war on drugs is, in effect if not in intention, a war on drug users. The federal budget for the control of illicit drugs has increased more than eightfold since 1981, and more than two thirds of the total is devoted to the enforcement of increasingly harsh criminal laws.[1] These laws needlessly make criminals of at least 20 million Americans a year. Of the 1 million drug arrests each year, about 225,000 are for simple possession of marijuana, the fourth most common cause of arrest in the United States.[2] In the 1980s, while the number of arrests for all crimes was rising 28 percent, the number of arrests for drug offenses rose 126 percent.[3] Largely because we imprison so many drug users and petty drug dealers, the United States has a higher proportion of its population incarcerated than any other country in the world for which reliable statistics are available.

Mandatory-sentencing laws force judges to impose excessive penalties. Under federal law the sentence for possession (not sale) of a teaspoonful of "crack" cocaine is a mandatory five years with no chance of parole. Since drug offenders now have far less incentive to accept guilty pleas, the number of trials in federal district courts is rapidly increasing. Judges feel both the burden of conscience and the burden of labor; in every federal judicial circuit they have urged Congress to reconsider mandatory sentencing.

As everyone knows, prohibition of drugs also enriches gangsters, while promoting burglary, theft, and violence in the streets. Furthermore, relentless enforcement of the criminal law encourages the use of the most dangerous and addictive drugs in the most concentrated forms. Bulky marijuana is less profitable and more risky for smugglers and dealers than cocaine and heroin. These drugs are easier to conceal and adulterate, easier to discard during a raid, and since their traces do not last as long in the body, less likely to be exposed by drug testing.

The international campaign is a particularly futile and destructive feature of the war against drugs. Drug crops are repeatedly eradicated in one place, only to be cultivated in another; the total acreage needed to supply the U.S. market is relatively small. Vast resources devoted to a hopeless attempt to seal our southern borders have had little effect on the price of cocaine. By urging South American countries to militarize the enforcement of anti-drug laws, the U.S. government promotes large-scale corruption and violation of human rights. The threat to the livelihoods of peasants heightens endemic social conflict and civil violence.[4]

Enforcement of anti-drug laws is also restricting the liberties of U.S. citizens. The Bill of Rights is in danger of becoming meaningless in cases involving drugs. Tenants charged with no crime are evicted from homes where police believe drugs are being sold. Public housing projects are sealed for house-to-house inspections. The Supreme Court has permitted warrantless searches of automobiles, the use of anonymous tips and drug-courier profiles as the basis for police searches, and the seizure of lawyers' fees in drug cases. Property on which marijuana plants are found can be forfeited even if the owner is charged with no crime. Prosecutors have been allowed to try the same person at the state and federal levels for the same drug-related crime.[5]

Random drug testing is a spreading blight on civil liberties. In a 1989 case in which the Supreme Court allowed random urinalysis of Customs Service employees, Justice Antonin Scalia, who is not known as a liberal, correctly stated in his dissent that no evidence had been presented to show that this violation of privacy and human dignity served to improve job performance, the purpose for which it was ostensibly intended.[5] Drug testing is, in any case, dangerously unreliable. Since the proportion of workers using illicit drugs is low, any test with less than 100 percent specificity is likely to produce a high percentage of false positives.

Present drug policies also have disastrous effects on health and health care. The American College of Physicians and two organizations concerned with prisoners' health have objected to mandatory sentencing in a recent joint position paper; they point out that a new epidemic of tuberculosis is incubating in jails and prisons crowded with drug-law offenders.[6] Infection with the human immunodeficiency virus is spreading rapidly among intravenous drug users who cannot legally exchange contaminated for sterile needles. Federal laws and policies have strangled the medical potential of marijuana, a remarkably safe substance that is useful to patients with cancer, AIDS, glaucoma, multiple sclerosis, and other disorders. It remains officially a forbidden medicine in the United States for all but nine persons who are still receiving it under a Compassionate Investigational New Drug program that was discontinued in 1991.[7]

The benefits of a truce in the war against drugs are obvious. Police could spend more of their time and effort on the kinds of crime that most immediately threaten public order and safety. Resources now devoted to law enforcement could be devoted to combatting the chief causes of drug abuse and related social problems — poverty, unemployment, poor housing, illiteracy, and family disintegration. Gang warfare and drive-by shootings would no longer spread everyday terror in our cities. The profits of organized crime would decline precipitously. A threat to the Bill of Rights would be removed, and the prisons would be half empty. The many people for whom marijuana is medically useful could obtain it without fear of arrest or the need to bargain with illicit drug dealers. Funds would be available for more and better treatment of drug abuse. Drug education would be more plausible and convincing when freed of the false assumption that all currently illegal drugs have only destructive uses.

The most thoughtful and candid defenders of the war on drugs acknowledge its deleterious effects, while insisting that it is a burden society must bear. They admit that harsh enforcement policies promote corruption, endanger civil liberties, and increase violence among drug dealers. They admit that no more than a small fraction of the international traffic can be interdicted. They acknowledge that the campaign against illicit drugs does not necessarily reduce crime and in some ways endangers the public health.[8,9] But they contend that any retreat from the struggle would lead to an enormous increase in the use of illicit drugs, with disastrous consequences for the moral and social order. They say that any control system short of prohibition could not be enforced; if drugs were taxed at a rate high enough to cover their social cost, abusers would still have to commit crimes and turn to a black market.

But defenders of the war on drugs have not been able to prove that substantial changes in the laws or their enforcement would greatly increase the use of drugs that are now illegal. The percentage of the population using opiates in 1914, when they were first banned under federal law, may not have been very different from today's percentage,[10] and the social consequences of addiction were less serious. During the 1970s 10 states effectively decriminalized the possession of small amounts of marijuana by reducing the penalty to a fine (in Oregon, to a civil violation). The most careful study of these legal changes concluded that they led to a substantial reduction in the costs of law enforcement and criminal justice but did not affect the rate of marijuana use or public health and safety.[11] In 1983, 5.5 percent of American high-school seniors smoked marijuana daily, as compared with 0.5 percent of students at a roughly equivalent educational level in the Netherlands, where marijuana laws were rarely enforced and marijuana was sold openly in coffee shops.[12]

Public-opinion surveys also suggest that few people who do not now use illicit drugs would use them if the laws changed. The 1985 Household Survey of the National Institute on Drug Abuse found that only 3 percent of 18-to-25-year-olds who had ever used cocaine and only 10 percent of those who had used it in the past month had ever habitually used it even once a week.[13] Only 2 percent of people who do not use cocaine say they might try it if it were legalized, and 93 percent state vehemently that they would not.[14] Even if the use of some drugs increased, any resulting dangers might be offset by a decline in the use of drugs that are now legal. At least one study suggests that high-school students use less alcohol when they smoke

marijuana[15]; there are some good reasons to regard this as a desirable trade.

Cocaine is far more dangerous than marijuana, but even its addictive potential and health hazards are often overstated, especially when it is blamed for ills caused by poverty, unemployment, shattered families, and disintegrating neighborhoods. In one survey 4 percent of high-school students who had used cocaine, as compared with 18 percent of cigarette smokers, said they had tried to stop but could not.[16] Most cocaine users do not become dependent, and most who do eventually free themselves.[17] Although it is undesirable for pregnant women to use this or any other drug, recent research suggests that the dangers of exposure to cocaine in the womb have been exaggerated in both scientific reports and the popular press.[18] It appears that the effects of the drug are hard to distinguish from those of poor prenatal care, low birth weight, alcohol abuse, venereal disease, and the adverse family and social circumstances of the mother. There is little evidence that the vast majority of infants exposed to cocaine during pregnancy have permanent brain damage or suffer other irreparable harm. Certainly no effect of cocaine on the fetus has been shown to be as severe and as common as fetal alcohol syndrome.

There is evidence that the use of illegal drugs alone does not necessarily hurt job performance or reduce earnings.[19] Studies purporting to prove that it does often confuse association with cause.[20] Some research suggests that adolescents who occasionally use illicit drugs, especially marijuana, are actually healthier psychologically than those who have never used illicit drugs (as well as those who use them habitually).[21] Other research shows that college students who use illicit drugs and those who do not have similar grades and participate to the same extent in college activities.[22]

All sides of the debate on drugs can cite the precedent of national alcohol prohibition, because the historical evidence is scanty and unreliable. Everyone acknowledges that Prohibition, like our present drug policies, increased corruption and crime. Although Americans probably drank less in the 1920s than before, it is doubtful that Prohibition was the reason. As measured by deaths from cirrhosis of the liver, hospital admissions for alcohol-related psychosis, and arrests for drunkenness, consumption seems to have declined mainly in the early years of Prohibition. It began to rise again in the late 1920s and continued to rise more slowly, if at all, after repeal and the establishment of the present state regulatory systems for alcohol. In 1937 through 1940, years after repeal, consumption was at about the level it reached in the last years of Prohibition. It did not reach 1915 levels again until the late 1960s.[23]

In 1920, when the 18th Amendment went into effect, alcohol use had already been declining steadily in the United States for years. Alcohol-related admissions to Bellevue Hospital in New York City fell from 5.0 per 1000 population in 1910 to 0.73 per 1000 in 1920 and then rose to 2.4 per 1000 in 1933.[24] The few countries that instituted national prohibition were not the only ones in which alcohol consumption fell during the first quarter of the century. In the United States the death rate from cirrhosis of the liver fell from 14 per 100,000 in 1910 through 1914 to 7 per 100,000 during the Prohibition years. But in Great Britain, where alcohol remained legal, the rate fell from 10 per 100,000 in 1914 to 5 per 100,000 in 1920 and 2 per 100,000 in the 1940s, before it began to rise again.[25] Historical changes in alcohol consumption show that other influences are more important than availability and price. Although the rate of taxation on alcohol has fallen in real dollar terms during the past 40 years, and although the availability of this drug has certainly not decreased, its use has begun to decline along with use of illicit drugs.[26]

The educational campaign against tobacco conducted since the 1960s shows how to reduce drug consumption without the use of force. The campaign has been waged half-heartedly: the government still subsidizes tobacco growers and distributors, tobacco advertising is pervasive, and tobacco products are lightly taxed. Nevertheless, a strategy relying on common sense rather than coercion has substantially reduced our consumption of the most addictive drug of all. Unfortunately, it has been largely ignored as a model for the control of other drugs.

The peace process that ends the drug war can begin with some small changes. After the beneficial effects have been assimilated and recognized, we might consider further steps. This approach is modeled on the "harm reduction" policy that has been influential in the Netherlands and other European countries.[27]

Above all, the federal role in drug enforcement should be greatly reduced. Federal involvement emphasizes the unfortunate imagery of a patriotic war in which drugs and drug users are the enemy. Furthermore, the federal government has encouraged some of the most wasteful and self-defeating practices in enforcing the laws against drugs. Its withdrawal would give state and local governments an opportunity to adjust their policies to local conditions.

We suggest that the following steps be taken now:

1. The federal government should abandon or at least drastically reduce its effort to seal the borders against drugs and devote at least 90 percent of its drug-control funding (rather than the present 30 percent) to prevention and treatment.

2. Marijuana should be made medically available immediately by reclassifying it as a schedule II drug.

3. Cultivation of small amounts of marijuana for personal use should be legalized.

4. Possession of drugs without the intent to sell should not be a cause for imprisonment under federal law.

5. Local governments should be allowed and encouraged to establish needle-exchange programs.

6. Mandatory sentences for crimes involving drugs and forfeiture rules inapplicable in other types of crime should be eliminated.

7. Mandatory random drug testing in the workplace should not be permitted for most jobs.

At a later stage, several other steps should be considered. Federal and state laws that prohibit the sale and use of marijuana by adults could be eliminated.

The production and sale of less harmful forms of abused drugs, such as coca tea or coca chewing gum,[28] could be legalized. And health professionals could be allowed to provide opiates other than methadone, as well as stimulants (including cocaine), to addicts as part of a treatment program.

As Mayor Kurt Schmoke of Baltimore has suggested, a national commission might be established on the model of the Wickersham Commission appointed by President Herbert Hoover in 1929 to study the prohibition of alcohol. This commission could consider a comprehensive policy for all recreational drugs, which might include such features as a "harmfulness tax" — a consumption tax adjusted for each drug according to its social cost.[29]

Despite its superficial support of the war against drugs, the public is thoroughly confused about this issue. In a poll of 1401 people taken for the Drug Policy Foundation in 1990, a large proportion said they were willing to restrict civil liberties, and even accept warrantless searches of homes and cars, in order to reduce the use of illicit drugs. Yet more than two thirds preferred treatment and counseling to punishment for drug abusers, and fewer than half favored tougher penalties such as those imposed by recent federal laws. Forty-nine percent agreed that legal alcohol was more harmful than illicit marijuana, and only 33 percent disagreed. Half approved of needle-exchange programs for addicts, and two thirds favored the medical use of marijuana.[14]

In the face of this public confusion, as well as the massive evidence that their policies are failing, government officials have continued to raise a war cry. The National Drug Control Strategy of the Bush administration, as presented in 1989 by William Bennett, director of the Office of National Drug Policy, called for an emphasis on discouraging casual users, who were considered "contagious" because their existence conveys the message that it is possible to maintain a career and family while using an illicit drug.[30] The problem, apparently, is that this message is correct. James Q. Wilson, another supporter of the drug laws, has pointed out that the costs of changing the laws are difficult to measure because they are "to a large degree moral"; the illegality of drugs reflects society's obligation to sustain the character of its citizens.[9]

Taking refuge in this kind of vague and inclusive language sometimes betrays insecurity about one's arguments. It would be hard to justify in any other way a declaration of war on more than 20 million occasional users of illicit drugs (mainly marijuana), the vast majority of whom are harming neither themselves nor anyone else. Such language may also reflect a lack of historical and cultural perspective. Drugs have been used to alter consciousness in most societies throughout history, and different drugs have been considered acceptable at different times and places. In 1930 marijuana was legal in most states and alcohol was illegal; obviously, moral standards and the character of the citizenry did not change radically when the status of the two drugs was reversed a few years later.

8. FIGHTING THE DRUG WAR

Of all the Prohibition era mistakes we are now repeating, the most serious is trying to free society of drugs by the use of force. There is no reason to believe that the inclination to ingest substances that alter consciousness can be eradicated. A drug-free society is an impossible and probably an undesirable dream. It has been said that the worst and most corrupting lies are problems badly stated. As our contrasting policies on marijuana and alcohol suggest, what we call the drug problem has been very badly stated indeed. The philosopher John Dewey taught that moral ends are not fixed and absolute, but serve as guides that must be judged by the means needed to attain them. Our present drug policies are immoral because they require a war of annihilation against a wrongly chosen enemy. We will never be able to regulate the use of consciousness-altering drugs effectively until our ends are changed along with the means that serve them.

Harvard Medical School
Boston, MA 02115

LESTER GRINSPOON, M.D.
JAMES B. BAKALAR, J.D.

REFERENCES

1. Executive Office of the President. National drug control strategy: a nation responds to drug use. Washington, D.C.: Government Printing Office, 1992.
2. Federal Bureau of Investigation. Crime in the United States. Washington, D.C.: Government Printing Office, 1991.
3. Austin J, McVey AD. The 1989 NCCD prison population forecast: the impact of the war on drugs. San Francisco: National Council on Crime and Delinquency, 1989.
4. Nadelmann E. US drug policy: a bad export. Foreign Policy 1988;70:83-107.
5. Wisotsky S. A society of suspects: the war on drugs and civil liberties. Policy analysis 180. Washington, D.C.: Cato Institute, 1992.
6. Skolnick AA. Some experts suggest that the nation's "war on drugs" is helping tuberculosis stage a deadly comeback. JAMA 1992;268:3177-8.
7. Grinspoon L, Bakalar JB. Marihuana, the forbidden medicine. New Haven, Conn.: Yale University Press, 1993.
8. Moore MH. Buy and bust: the effective regulation of an illicit market in heroin. Lexington, Mass.: D.C. Heath, 1977.
9. Wilson JQ. Drugs and crime. In: Tonry M, Wilson JQ, eds. Drugs and crime. Chicago: University of Chicago Press, 1990.
10. Kolb L, Du Mez AG. The prevalence and trend of drug addiction in the United States and factors influencing it. Public Health Rep 1924;39:1179-204.
11. Single EW. The impact of marijuana decriminalization: an update. J Public Health Policy 1989;10:456-66.
12. Trebach A. The great drug war. New York: Macmillan, 1987.
13. National household survey on drug abuse, 1985. Rockville, Md.: National Institute on Drug Abuse, 1987.
14. Dennis RJ. The American people are starting to question the drug war. In: Trebach A, Zeese K, eds. Drug prohibition and the conscience of nations. Washington, D.C.: Drug Policy Foundation, 1990.
15. DiNardo J. Are marihuana and alcohol substitutes? The effect of state drinking age laws on the marihuana consumption of high school seniors. Santa Monica, Calif.: Rand Corporation, 1991.
16. O'Malley PM, Johnston LD, Bachman JG. Cocaine use among American adolescents and young adults. In: Kozel NJ, Adams EH, eds. Cocaine use in America: epidemiologic and clinical perspectives. NIDA research monograph 61. Washington, D.C.: Government Printing Office, 1985.
17. Erickson PG, Alexander BK. Cocaine and addictive liability. Social Pharmacol 1989;3:249-70.
18. Mayes LC, Granger RH, Bornstein MH, Zuckerman B. The problem of prenatal cocaine exposure: a rush to judgment. JAMA 1992;267:406-8.
19. Gill AM, Michaels RJ. Does drug use lower wages? Ind Labor Relat Rev 1992;45:419-34.
20. Horgan J. Your analysis is faulty: how to lie with drug statistics. New Republic. April 2, 1990:22-4.
21. Shedler J, Block J. Adolescent drug use and psychological health: a longitudinal inquiry. Am Psychol 1990;45:612-30.
22. Pope HG Jr, Ionescu-Pioggia M, Aizley HG, Varma DK. Drug use and life style among college undergraduates in 1989: a comparison with 1969 and 1978. Am J Psychiatry 1990;147:998-1001.
23. Levine HG, Reinarman C. From prohibition to regulation: lessons from alcohol policy for drug policy. Milbank Q 1991;69:461-94.
24. Jolliffe N. The alcoholic admissions to Bellevue Hospital. Science 1936;83:306-9.
25. Terris M. Epidemiology of cirrhosis of the liver: national mortality data. Am J Public Health 1967;57:2076-88.
26. Moore MH, Gerstein DR, eds. Alcohol and public policy: beyond the shadow of prohibition. Washington, D.C.: National Academy Press, 1981.
27. Nadelmann EA. Thinking seriously about alternatives to drug prohibition. Daedalus 1992;121(3):85-132.
28. Weil A. The marriage of the sun and moon: a quest for unity in consciousness. Boston: Houghton Mifflin, 1980.
29. Grinspoon L. The harmfulness tax: a proposal for regulation and taxation of drugs. N C J Int Law Commer Regul 1990;15:505-10.
30. The White House. National drug control strategy. Washington, D.C.: Government Printing Office, 1989.

Our Current Approach to Drug Abuse —
Progress, Problems, Proposals

MOST drug-abuse experts and historians agree that we are in the declining phase of a drug epidemic that began about 30 years ago. Still, drug abuse remains one of the nation's critical domestic problems, linked to crime, neglect of children, family violence, incomplete education, homelessness, AIDS, high health care costs, urban decay, and diminished economic competitiveness. Until we reduce the current level of addiction and the experimentation that leads many people to that end, individual tragedies and profound social problems will continue to undermine the quality of our lives.

Most people are poor judges of their own susceptibility to addiction. In 30 years of treating thousands of heroin and cocaine addicts, I have met few who anticipated addiction when they started using drugs. Most believed initially that they would have the willpower to use drugs casually. Some do, but as more people use drugs, the problems related to their use increase. Laws and regulations arise from the need to diminish the numbers of drug users and their impact on society.

I will argue here that our current approach to drug abuse is far preferable to proposals either to legalize drugs or to refrain from enforcing the laws prohibiting their use. I will briefly summarize the current situation in regard to illicit drug use, the dangers of the alternative proposals, and recommendations for change that could improve our drug problem.

CURRENT POLICIES — PROGRESS AND PROBLEMS

With the recognition that drug abuse cannot be entirely eliminated, the goal of current drug-abuse policy is to reduce the use of drugs through a combination of activities to reduce supply and demand. There has been substantial progress toward that goal. Marijuana use peaked in 1979 and is now at its lowest level since 1973. Cocaine use peaked around 1985, and since then, the number of current users (defined as those who have used drugs in the previous 30 days) has dropped by more than 75 percent, from 5.8 million in 1985 to 1.3 million in 1992.[1]

The sharp decrease in illegal drug use over the past decade — from 24 million users in 1979 to 11.4 million in 1992 — reflects a dramatic cultural shift that has yet to be widely appreciated. Progress in reducing drug use has resulted from a variety of forces: parent groups, community efforts, improved education and prevention programs, the activities of the Media Partnership for a Drug-Free America, the establishment of drug-free workplaces, and strong national leadership. The decline has had beneficial effects in our schools, neighborhoods, and places of work. Many people who would otherwise have gone on to become addicts have not started to use drugs.

Prevention is not perfect. The effect of legal availability on the use of drugs, even if such use remains

---

Proposed schemes for legalizing drugs vary from complete legalization to allowing medical dispensation of heroin or cocaine to those already addicted.

---

illegal for youngsters, can be examined by comparing tobacco use with marijuana and cocaine use by adolescents over the past decade. Despite greatly increased publicity about the dangers of smoking, stepped-up prevention programs, and the prohibition of television advertisements for cigarettes, tobacco use among adolescents barely declined from 1980 to 1990,[2] yet marijuana use declined dramatically during the same period (Table 1). In 1980, users of the two substances were almost equal in number; 10 years later, half as many students were using marijuana. The decrease in the use of marijuana did not lead to an increased use of alcohol. Both occasional and heavy use of alcohol declined — more than tobacco use but much less than marijuana use. The legal availability of tobacco and alcohol for use by adults and the corresponding social attitudes about the use of these substances make it

much more difficult to prevent their use by adolescents.

Problems certainly remain. The inadequate availability of treatment programs has kept casualties associated with heavy "crack" cocaine use on the rise,[3] although the number of new crack cocaine users appears to have been substantially reduced, which bodes well for the future.[4] The supply of high-quality heroin and the shift to heroin use by some burned-out cocaine addicts have led to some increase in heroin addiction. Crime, overcrowding of prisons and courts, and disease, especially AIDS and tuberculosis, remain major problems associated with addiction in many of our cities.

Large numbers of minority men are in prison, primarily for selling drugs or committing crimes to get money for drugs. As drug use drops, these numbers should drop sharply as well, if effective treatment is available for drug users in prison, with appropriate training and job opportunities after their release. Legalization of drugs would hit this group hardest, as it has in the case of alcohol.

Our current drug situation follows the pattern of earlier drug epidemics.[5,6] As the use of drugs

Table 1. Use of Various Drugs by High-School Seniors.*

DRUG	1980	1985	1990	1980–1990
		% of students		% change
Alcohol				
30-day prevalence	72	65.9	57.1	−20.7
Daily for past 30 days	6	5	3.7	−38.3
≥5 drinks in a row, previous 30 days	41.2	36.7	32.2	−21.8
Cigarettes				
30-day prevalence	30.5	30.1	29.4	−3.6
Daily for previous 30 days	21.3	19.5	19.1	−10.3
Half a pack or more per day	14.3	12.5	11.3	−21.0
Marijuana				
30-day prevalence	33.7	14.9	14	−58.4
Daily for previous 30 days	9.1	4.9	2.2	−75.8
Cocaine (excluding crack)				
30-day prevalence	5.2	6.7	1.9	−63.5
Daily for previous 30 days	0.2	0.4	0.1	−50.0
Crack cocaine				
30-day prevalence			0.7	
Daily for previous 30 days			0.1	

*Data adapted from Johnston et al.[2]

drops from epidemic to endemic levels, disadvantaged groups are more likely than others to continue using drugs because of their greater availability and fewer alternative opportunities. That is why minority communities want not only treatment facilities but also fair laws, justly applied, to reduce the horrendous toll of drug-related crime in their neighborhoods. The illegal open-air drug bazaars that flourish in southeastern Washington, D.C., and the South Bronx would not be tolerated in Georgetown or Scarsdale.

THE PROBLEMS WITH LEGALIZATION

Since current approaches have improved but not solved our drug problem, some people call for regulatory changes. Some do so from a misguided feeling of frustration: nothing is working, and the problem is getting worse. Others espouse the libertarian position:

in a free society, people should be free to experiment with substances and suffer any consequences.[7] Still others acknowledge that laws against the possession and sale of drugs may reduce their use but argue that such laws create more problems than they solve by leading to crime, violent drug wars, and wholesale imprisonment.[8] The general thrust of all these arguments is that legalization would lead to decreased crime without a substantial rise in addiction and would therefore result in an overall benefit to society.[9] Proposed schemes vary: legalize drugs completely and allow marketing similar to that of tobacco and alcohol, decriminalize personal use and possession of drugs, or allow a medical dispensation of heroin or cocaine to those already addicted. Detailed and persuasive rebuttals of all these positions have been made,[10-15] and space does not permit their repetition here. Instead, some common problems of legalization will be noted.

The Effect on Use

The crime, community disruption, and individual destruction that result from illicit drug use are caused mostly by the use of cocaine, especially the crack form, and heroin. Most proponents of regulatory change argue that we should proceed gradually, starting with marijuana, a drug considered to be less dangerous, before going on to those that are considered more dangerous. The reality, however, is that those who favor legalization lack a comprehensive plan to deal with cocaine. Cocaine is the *bête noire* of the legalization movement. Unlike sedatives, which depress their own use for hours, the use of cocaine stimulates further use. Binges are common, often ending only when no more cocaine or money is available or when the body, overwhelmed by the effects of the drug and sleep deprivation, collapses. Since crack cocaine is nothing but cocaine hydrochloride, heated with baking soda and water, regulatory changes that made cocaine hydrochloride more available would do the same for crack. Given the pharmacologic properties of these stimulants, the argument that legalization would lead to only a minimal rise in use seems disingenuous.

There are over 50 million nicotine addicts, 18 mil-

If cocaine were legalized, some researchers believe there would be no decrease in alcohol abuse.

---

lion alcoholics or problem drinkers, and fewer than 2 million cocaine addicts in the United States. Cocaine is a much more addictive drug than alcohol. If cocaine were legally available, as alcohol and nicotine are now, the number of cocaine abusers would probably rise to a point somewhere between the numbers of users of the other two agents, perhaps 20 to 25 million. A detailed systems analysis of the effect of different regulatory schemes on cocaine prevalence suggests that the number of compulsive users might be 9 times higher (range, 4.7 to 15.8) than the current number.[16] Anyone can use cocaine and become addicted. Although a psychiatric disorder increases the vulnerability to addiction, it is not a prerequisite. When drugs have been widely available — as heroin was to U.S. soldiers in Vietnam or cocaine was at the turn of the century — both use and addiction have risen.[17,18] This critical factor of availability speaks to the need for continued law-enforcement activities even while treatment and prevention efforts are increased.

The Effect on Crime and Other Social Costs

Crime would not decrease if drugs were legalized. If the cost of drugs were low, addicts would tend to spend more time using them and less time working, so they would continue to need to commit crimes in order to acquire money. If the total number of addicts rose sharply as availability increased, crime would also increase. Fewer crimes would be committed by each addict, but there would be substantially more crime overall. Drug-related social problems would also increase: disorders in infants of addicted mothers, psychiatric disorders, AIDS and tuberculosis, homelessness, auto accidents, and family violence. The only problems likely to decrease would be violence and crimes among drug dealers.

Prohibition of alcohol, it was argued in the 1920s, would almost eliminate crime and other social ills. The famous preacher Billy Sunday proclaimed, "We will turn our prisons into factories."[19] Those who favor legalizing drugs appear to be just as unrealistic in arguing the opposite point of view, that making heroin and cocaine legally available will decrease crime and violence. If it were legally available, cheap crack cocaine, with its tendency to lead to paranoia and aggression, would result in more crime and violence, just as alcohol does.

Preventing Increased Drug Use by Children and Adolescents

Legalization, of course, would not be complete; few propose legalizing drug use by minors. Would we be any more successful in keeping cocaine or heroin away from youngsters than we have been with alcohol or tobacco? The lower cost of legalized drugs would increase their availability for use by youngsters. A gram of cocaine costs $80 on the illegal market but less than $10 to import legally. At $10 a gram, a dose of cocaine would cost less than 50 cents — well within the reach of 10-year-olds with lunch money. If the price of legalized drugs were kept high, illegal cartels would continue to undercut it substantially. Addicts would still need to commit crimes to support their habit, unless drug use was subsidized at clinics. If the price of drugs were substantially lowered to drive out the cartels, the drugs would become more widely available. The people most likely to use drugs would be the young, the poor, and those with psychiatric problems.

The introduction of crack cocaine in the mid-1980s illustrates these issues. Cocaine, until then primarily available only by the gram, making it expensive to purchase, suddenly became available in small doses at $3 to $5 a "rock." The use of crack cocaine exploded, especially among the poor and the young.

The fact that alcohol causes problems in greater numbers reinforces the point. If cocaine were legalized, the likely result would be no decrease in the problems related to alcohol abuse and a sharp increase in those related to cocaine abuse. As McAuliffe notes, those who use the higher number of alcohol-related deaths to argue for the legalization of cocaine ignore this point.[14]

Marijuana and Other Drugs

Although marijuana is not as toxic or addictive as cocaine, like the latter drug, it can lead to a variety of physical, psychological, and social problems. Will we legalize 1 percent or 10 percent marijuana or very potent hashish? Marijuana is most hazardous to the well-being of those who are most interested in using it — the young. Its effects on short-term memory, motivation, and energy level can interfere with the cognitive and social development of adolescents. Legalizing marijuana would reverse the decline in its use by adolescents, who would obtain it from those over 21 or purchase it illegally themselves. This is especially likely since the cost (currently as high as $400 per ounce) would sharply decline under legalization. What about lysergic acid diethylamide (LSD), phencyclidine (PCP), and similar drugs? Which of the many mind-altering drugs are we willing to legalize to change our psychic reality?

As Kleiman recently noted, "Until success is achieved in imposing reasonable controls on the currently licit killers, alcohol and nicotine, the case for adding a third or fourth recreational drug . . . will remain hopelessly speculative."[20]

BETTER POSSIBILITIES FOR CHANGE

Substantial progress has been made in reducing some aspects of drug abuse but not others. I believe that the following changes would help.

Expanded and Improved Treatment

The most cost-effective way to decrease the number of hard-core addicts is to expand treatment. Crop eradication or interdiction activities cannot stem the flow of illegal drugs into this country.[21] Although it is important to maintain some pressure against offshore production and distribution, as well as against drug traffic in this country, the current federal ratio of expenditures to control supply and demand — 65 percent to reduce supply and 35 percent to reduce demand — is misguided. A 50:50 ratio is more likely to be effective.

Currently, we can treat only 1.7 million people a year, but 2.5 to 3 million need treatment. To rectify this shortfall, which is a function of both inadequate federal funding and declining state funding, would require approximately $2 billion per year above current expenditures. Although the problem may be solved by health care reform if adequate substance-abuse treatment is available to all, a reform will take years to implement, and expansion of treatment for drug abuse is needed now.

Most forms of drug treatment are effective for some people. The question is which treatment works for which person and under what circumstances. A well-run treatment system requires an extensive initial evaluation, a variety of approaches and settings, and careful case management to move patients among treatment settings as appropriate. The intensity of a treatment is often independent of its setting.[22] In addition, systematic research on outcomes is essential to improve the cost effectiveness of treatment and determine what works for whom and why. Such a system would be affordable, could be integrated into the mainstream of health care, and would save billions of dollars by offsetting costs. A recent study by the Center on Addiction and Substance Abuse suggested that treatment for drug and alcohol abuse, integrated into a managed system of overall health care, could be provided at a cost of $60 per American per year.[23] This figure would need to be increased to allow for the vocational, educational, and psychosocial services required by a substantial minority of addicts.

New programs need to be developed for the two groups of drug users with the largest gap between need for and availability of treatment: hard-core addicts in the criminal-justice system and pregnant addicts. Only about 10 percent of the latter are receiving treatment. Initiatives for the former group include more rapid but less severe sanctions; alternatives to incarceration, including expansion of therapeutic communities and methadone maintenance; the provision of effective treatment programs in prison; and new programs for released inmates, especially during the first 6 to 12 months after their release, when recidivism is most likely.

Improved Prevention

Since the drug problem will ultimately be solved at the local level, adequate local resources and knowledge are essential. The 1989 National Drug Control Strategy (a report issued by the White House) was

---

There is exciting research in progress that is investigating the mechanisms of drug actions in the brain, new behavioral interventions, and a search for new medications.

---

deliberately called national rather than federal to emphasize that federal efforts alone are insufficient.[24] A concerted effort is required, not just by government but by organized community partnership programs, especially those modeled after the Robert Wood Johnson Foundation's Fighting Back initiative (a 1988 program that funded drug-control efforts by broad-based community groups, including parent and service groups, schools, health care providers, and law-enforcement officials).

The federal government should disseminate information on models that have worked, help with appropriate funding, and ensure accountability. Education about the dangers of drug use is a necessary but not sufficient component of prevention. A recent review[25] concluded that the social-influence model and its variants showed the most promise in drug education. This model attempts to familiarize adolescents with the external and internal pressures to use drugs, provides answers to pro-drug arguments, and teaches techniques for resisting peer pressure to use drugs. This approach combined with parent programs, community-leader training, and media campaigns has been shown to be successful.[26]

Since many factors (for example, poverty and familial dysfunction) decrease the motivation to resist drug use and are difficult to ameliorate in the short term, increased emphasis should be placed on programs that provide protective measures, such as adult mentors.[27]

The importance of developing forms of prevention that are effective in the declining phase of an epidemic is underscored by reports of increased drug use and decreased perception of risk by eighth-graders.[2] As drug use declines, firsthand knowledge of associated problems declines, and the younger would-be users tend to have a more cynical attitude toward the messages of drug education.

Modification of Existing Laws

A judicial commission should examine possible changes in the mandatory minimal-sentencing laws. These laws, which were enacted out of frustration with increased drug-related crime, should be revised to deter or control the true "drug kingpins"[28] and to make better use of limited prison facilities. Over 40 percent of drug offenders serving five-year sentences in federal prisons are relatively minor participants in the drug trade, such as drivers and couriers in large transactions.[29] Likewise, state laws need to be modified to make drug-related penalties more consistent and fair.

Use of currently illicit drugs for medical purposes should be a scientific, not political, question. Proponents of "medical marijuana" argue that oral synthetic tetrahydrocannabinol, available under schedule II, is not sufficient to treat the side effects of chemotherapy for cancer or the AIDS-related wasting syndrome, that the whole marijuana plant needs to be given through smoking. This issue has become politicized: opponents fear that marijuana made available for medical use would become more available for illicit use, especially by adolescents, and that its image as a dangerous drug would be changed; proponents see the change as a first step in having marijuana use decriminalized.

The National Academy of Science or the National Institutes of Health should evaluate the evidence for the proposed medical uses of marijuana. If the evidence is persuasive, the drug can be moved to schedule II; if it is inconclusive, appropriate research can be conducted to resolve the question. Cocaine is a schedule II drug used in anesthesiology and otolaryngology, but it is still viewed as a very dangerous drug when used in a nonmedical fashion. Since marijuana is a complex mixture containing over 300 compounds, many not adequately characterized, and since it has been associated with harmful effects, the decision requires a careful risk–benefit analysis. It may be better, for example, to consider alternative routes for the administration of synthetic tetrahydrocannabinol. Whether a drug is moved to schedule II is a decision that should be made by the Department of Health and Human Services rather than by the Drug Enforcement Agency, as the current law provides, to reduce the suspicion that such decisions are not being made on scientific grounds.

More Research

Improvement of treatment and prevention requires a much larger investment in research. It is a disgrace that so little money is currently being spent for research and that recent increases have been lower than annual increases in the cost of living. There is exciting research in progress, including investigations of mechanisms of drug actions in the brain,[30] new behavioral interventions, and a search for new medications, such as a proposed anticocaine vaccine.[31] At a minimum, research on drug abuse should equal 5 percent of the budget for drug control, or approximately $650 million per year instead of the current $425 million.

Center on Addiction and Substance Abuse
Columbia University
New York, NY 10019   HERBERT D. KLEBER, M.D.

REFERENCES

1. National household survey on drug abuse, 1992. Rockville, Md.: National Institute on Drug Abuse, 1993.
2. Johnston LD, O'Malley PM, Bachman Jr. Monitoring the future: annual survey of American high school seniors. Ann Arbor, Mich.: Institute for Social Research, 1992.
3. Drug Abuse Warning Network (DAWN). Bethesda, Md.: Department of Health and Human Services, 1992.
4. Gladwell M. New York crack epidemic appears to wane. Washington Post. May 31, 1993:A-1.
5. Musto DF. Cocaine's history, especially the American experience. In: Bock GR, Whalen J, eds. Cocaine: scientific and social dimensions. West Sussex, England: John Wiley, 1992:7-14.
6. Musto D. America's first cocaine epidemic. Wilson Quarterly 1989;13:59-64.
7. Szasz T. Our right to drugs: the case for a free market. Westport, Conn.: Greenwood Press, 1992.
8. Nadelmann EA. Drug prohibition in the United States: costs, consequences, and alternatives. Science 1989;245:939-47.
9. Idem. Thinking seriously about alternatives to drug prohibition. Daedalus 1992;121(3):85-132.
10. Inciardi JA, McBride DC. Legalization: a high-risk alternative in the war on drugs. Am Behav Sci 1989;32:259-289.
11. Kaplan J. Taking drugs seriously. Public Interest. Summer 1988;92:32-50.
12. Kleiman MAR, Saiger AJ. Drug legalization: the importance of asking the right question. Hofstra Law Rev 1990;18:527-65.

13. Wilson JQ. The legalization of drugs. Commentary February 1990:21-8.
14. McAuliffe WE. Health care policy issues in the drug abuser treatment field. J Health Polit Policy Law 1990;15:357-85.
15. Inciardi A. The great drug war and the great drug debate: wrangling over control versus legalization. In: The war on drugs II: the continuing epic of heroin, cocaine, crack, crime, AIDS and public policy. Mountainview, Calif.: Mayfield Publishing, 1992:233-87.
16. Homer JB. Projecting the impact of law enforcement on cocaine prevalence: a system dynamics approach. J Drug Issues 1993;23:281-95.
17. Kaplan J. The hardest drug: heroin and public policy. Chicago: University of Chicago Press, 1983.
18. Musto DF. The American disease, origins of narcotic control. New York: Oxford University Press, 1987.
19. Farrell M, Strang J. The lure of masterstrokes: drug legalization. Br J Addict 1990;85:5-7.
20. Kleiman MAR. Legalizing drugs. Economist. June 12-18, 1993:8.
21. Reuter P. The limits and consequences of U.S. foreign drug control efforts. Ann Am Acad Polit Social Sci 1992;521:151-62.
22. McLellan AT, Grissom GR, Brill P, Durell J, Metzger DS, O'Brien CP. Private substance abuse treatments: are some programs more effective than others? J Subst Abuse Treat 1993;10:243-54.
23. Kleber HD. Center On Addiction and Substance Abuse's recommendations on substance abuse coverage and health care reform, March, 1993. Presented at Senate Committee on Labor and Human Resources Hearing, Washington, D.C., May 13, 1993.
24. The White House. National drug control strategy. Washington, D.C.: Government Printing Office, 1989.
25. Ellickson PL. School-based drug prevention: what should it do? What has it done? In: Coombs R, Ziedonis D, eds. Handbook on drug abuse prevention. Englewood Cliffs, N.J.: Prentice-Hall (in press).
26. Pentz MA. Dwyer JH, MacKinnon DP, et al. A multicommunity trial for primary prevention of adolescent drug abuse: effects on drug use prevalence. JAMA 1989;261:3259-66.
27. Sternberg L. Adolescent transitions and alcohol and other drug use prevention. In: Gopelrud EN, ed. Preventing adolescent drug use: from theory to practice. OSAP prevention monograph 8. Bethesda, Md.: Department of Health and Human Services, 1991:13-51. (Department of Health and Human Services publication no. (ADM) 91-1725.)
28. Kleiman MAR. Against excess: drug policy for results. New York: Basic Books, 1992.
29. Sentencing Commission. Special report to Congress: mandatory minimum sentences in the federal criminal justice system. Washington, D.C.: Government Printing Office 1991.
30. Shimada S, Kitayama S, Lin C-L, et al. Cloning an expression of a cocaine-sensitive dopamine transporter complementary DNA. Science 1991;254:576-8.
31. Landry DW, Zhao K, Yang GX-Q, Glickman M, Georgiadis TM. Antibody-catalyzed degradation of cocaine. Science 1993;259:1899-901.

PREGNANT, ADDICTED – AND GUILTY?

Should mothers be tried as criminals when their babies test positive for drugs? To the dismay of civil libertarians, more and more prosecutors around the country are saying yes.

Jan Hoffman

Jan Hoffman, a staff writer for The Village Voice, *was a journalism fellow at Yale Law School.*

Traveling west from Detroit about 200 miles along I-96, crack arrived in Muskegon County, Mich., late in September 1988. Or at least that's when the prosecutor Tony Tague first started noticing that a crime rampage was rocking this hard-scrabble, blue-collar county – the kind of siege that supposedly strikes only the nation's largest cities. With only 161,000 people scattered across 7 cities and 16 townships, Muskegon County, a scenic but tired factory area with an unemployment rate nearly double the national average, would appear to be scarcely worth the picking. "The Detroit drug dealers told us that Muskegon is such a welfare town that it's guaranteed income for them when the checks come it," recalls Detective Sgt. Al Van Hemert, a ruddy veteran narcotics cop.

Muskegon's murders, break-ins and muggings began to rise dramatically. District judges were spending three days a week instead of one on drug cases, and the county jail became dangerously overcrowded. A special 72-CRACK phone line rang constantly. Tague, the 32-year-old son of a retired local police chief, conducted a high-profile antidrug crusade, but his office simply became overwhelmed.

A year after crack hit the area, county social workers removed 27 children in just one month from crack-afflicted homes. Three of the children belonged to a 23-year-old black single mother named Kimberly Ann Hardy. Hardy came to the attention of the county's Department of Social Services because she was the first woman reported by Muskegon General Hospital to bear a child who tested positive for crack cocaine.

It was time, concluded Tony Tague, to send a message. Choosing a controversial new tactic already employed by prosecutors in Florida, Georgia, South Carolina and Massachusetts, Tague ordered Kimberly Hardy arrested on the same charge prosecutors routinely use against drug dealers: delivering drugs in the amount of less than 50 grams, a felony in Michigan carrying a mandatory minimum jail term of one year and a maximum of 20 years.

To avoid becoming embroiled in debates over when the fetus becomes a person, the prosecutor contended that hardy delivered crack to her son through her umbilical cord during the 90 seconds or so after the child had left the birth canal but before the cord was cut.

Almost from the outset, Tague maintained that his objective was not to send women to prison, but to protect children. As Sergeant Van Hemert says: "We want to avoid becoming a Detroit or a New York. Our attitude is, 'Hey, let's stop it now!' It's a form of caring."

Crack babies seem to be everywhere, and they will not go away. Cautionary images of shrieking infants, bug-eyed as if they are watching tape loops from hell, even march across public-service announcements during televised sports events. A frequently cited nationwide study claimed that last year, 375,000 children may have been affected by their mother's drug use during pregnancy. Strokes in utero and respiratory and neurological disorders are only a few of the most common problems plaguing these drastically underweight children.

Their suffering, to say nothing of the long-term social costs, is so staggering that people understandably want to turn on their perceived torturers: their mothers. "If the mother wants to smoke crack and kill herself, I don't care," Sergeant Van Hemert says flatly. "Let her die, but don't take that poor baby with her." In a 15-state survey by The Atlanta Constitution, 71 percent of the 1,500 people polled favored criminal penalties for pregnant women whose drug use injured their babies.

At their recent conventions, the National District Attorneys Association and the American Bar Association took up the national debate about law enforcement's increasingly aggressive role in penalizing these women: should the threat of criminal prosecution be used to drive them toward treatment?

Michael Barber, the Sacramento attorney who was chairman of the A.B.A.'s family-law section this year, favors discretionary criminal sanctions, such as supervised probation, as well as "threatened incarceration if, when she's pregnant, she's still taking drugs." Although many legal experts prefer that these cases remain in family courts, which can order treatment and removal of children but not jail sentences, Barber is dubious. "Family courts don't provide the control factor in the mother that we need to prevent the repetition of this activity," he says.

In the last few years, more and more judges and lawmakers have come to view these mothers as criminals who victimize children, rather than as victims themselves. Since 1987, 19 states and the District of Columbia have instigated more than 50 criminal proceedings against mothers for drug abuse during their pregnancies, according to the American Civil Liberties Union, which has vigorously opposed these measures. (With the exception of a few cases, prosecutors have not gone after pregnant alcoholics. In many states, giving alcohol to a minor is only a misdemeanor.)

Last summer, Jennifer Johnson of Florida became the first woman in the country to be convicted of making a drug delivery to her baby; she was sentenced to 14 years on probation. Most prosecutors concede that widespread prison terms for pregnant mothers are not feasible. But in May, a Kentucky woman who gave birth to three children during her 17-year addiction to pills and intravenous drugs was sentenced to five years in prison for criminal child abuse. In North Carolina a few months ago, a prosecutor charged an addicted mother whose newborn had a positive toxicology test with a more pernicious crime—assault with a deadly weapon.

"The war on drugs has degenerated into a war on women," says Alan S. Rapoport, Kim Hardy's attorney. "And why is it that all these straight white men are telling pregnant women how they should act and feel?"

Feminists and civil libertarians argue that prosecuting women for what is in essence their conduct during pregnancy abrogates constitutional rights to privacy and turns pregnant users into second-class citizens, deprived of equal protection. They also involve the "slippery slope" argument—if the line isn't drawn at drug abuse, will prosecutors go after pregnant women for drinking, smoking or even taking aspirin?

Prosecutors maintain that they are simply protecting children. But defense attorneys retort that law-enforcement officials are forcing a wedge between mother and child, making the relationship adversarial—"fetal rights" versus "maternal rights." Their interests should instead be seen as joined, argued a recent Harvard Law Review article on state intervention during pregnancy. "The harm to the fetus does not make the woman's addiction more criminal. Rather, it highlights the severity of her disease."

But at least eight states now include drug exposure in utero in their definition of child abuse and neglect—and many more have legislation pending. Some states and many local jurisdictions require nothing but a positive drug test to remove an infant from a mother.

Dr. Ira J. Chasnoff, who supplied an affidavit supporting Hardy, says that penalties against addicted mothers tend to fall much more heavily on poor minority women. As an example, Dr. Chasnoff, the founder and president of the National Association of Perinatal Addiction Research and Education, points to Florida's Pinellas County, where pregnant black users are nearly 10 times more likely to be reported for substance abuse than pregnant white users. Treatment programs for pregnant addicts are scarce enough, he warns; prosecutions only scare addicts away from seeking even basic prenatal care, for fear they'll be turned in.

Dr. Chasnoff doesn't have much regard for the legal theory that cocaine is passed through the umbilical cord just before it's clamped. "Good ethics and good law have to be based on good science," he says, "and we just don't have that kind of data."

State courts have been divided over whether indicting pregnant addicts is within the scope of existing drug-delivery statutes. Michigan is now considering the question. On June 2, a few days before Hardy was to go on trial, the Michigan Court of Appeals, in a highly unusual move, elected to hear arguments about whether her case should be tried in the lower circuit court or be thrown out altogether. A decision will probably not be reached until early this fall. The outcome of the Hardy case, which is being eagerly awaited across the country by law-enforcement officials, civil libertarians and feminists, as well as health-care officials, may help determine whether the door to future prosecutions will be open or closed.

But with the exception of Hardy herself, perhaps no one is awaiting the decision more eagerly than a 36-year-old attorney and single mother named Lynn Ellen

Bremer. On July 18, Bremer, who is white, became the second woman in Muskegon County to be bound over for trial on charges of drug delivery to her infant.

Kim Hardy smoked crack the night before she gave birth to her son, Aréanis, on Aug. 20, 1989, as she freely admitted to Sergeant Van Hemert. Lynn Bremer told him that 40 hours before her daughter, Brittany, was born on April 10 of this year, she snorted a gram of cocaine with some friends to celebrate her birthday.

The prosecution developed its case against each woman in similar fashion. It began with drug tests, performed during labor. Hardy's urine had been screened for drugs shortly after she showed up at Muskegon General. According to a policy adopted by many public hospitals, Hardy qualified as a "high-risk pregnancy"—she'd had no prenatal care and was six to eight weeks early. At Hackley Hospital, Bremer's own obstetrician ordered her tested because he had known about her cocaine addiction for nearly five months. Despite his threats to drop her as a patient if she didn't stop using, she had refused both residential and outpatient treatment.

But neither woman was asked to sign an informed consent for the screens on herself or her child—which defense attorneys across the country have turned into a key issue in many of these cases. Hardy's lawyers argued that the tests violated her rights to privacy and against self-incrimination. Meanwhile, the prosecution maintained that drug-testing constitutes sound medical practice and that permission could be considered to have been granted under the patient's general consent form.

Bremer's daughter weighed 6 pounds and was apparently healthy. But Hardy's 5-pound son was jaundiced, constipated and could not keep down his formula; he had a small head and developed a mysterious infection. After the women were discharged, the hospitals kept the infants for observation, tested them for drugs and reported the positive results to the Department of Social Services. Both Hardy and Bremer were given 24 hours' notice to appear at emergency hearings to determine the temporary removal of their newborns. Although social workers later remarked that neither of Hardy's older children, then 4 years old and 11 months old, respectively, appeared neglected, because of the positive tests on the newborn and her admitted use, they too were immediately sent to foster care.

In despair over losing their children, Hardy and Bremer used drugs one more time. Then they entered 30-day residential treatment programs. While Tague took credit for this, both women asserted that their motive was to clean themselves up and get their children back. Tague announced to the news media that they would be arrested once their treatment had been completed.

Drug use, which both women admitted, is a rarely applied misdemeanor in Michigan that's punishable by probation—especially in a first-offense case. But because they were pregnant when they used drugs, they were charged instead with the felony of drug delivery. "Arrest pregnant women for possession or use, the same thing you'd arrest a man for," says Lynn Paltrow of the A.C.L.U. "But these women are being prosecuted for the crime of becoming pregnant while having an addiction problem."

Tague has little patience for this line of thinking: "It's easy for the defense attorneys to throw out academic arguments about why we should not be proceeding. Why aren't they concerned about the constitutional rights of the child to be born drug free?"

Judge Frederic Grimm Jr. of District Court, who had ordered Hardy to stand trial after preliminary hearings, took a narrow focus in his ruling. "I feel sympathetic toward the defendant," he said recently, "but her behavior is proscribed criminal behavior. And you don't excuse it by saying she's disadvantaged or a mother."

Shortly after the birth of her second child, Nyéassa, in the fall of 1988, Kim Hardy had started smoking crack. A friend from New York had introduced her to the new drug. In Muskegon, crack comes in miniature Ziploc plastic bags and sells for an inflated $20 a rock. "It was the 'in' thing to do in Muskegon Heights," says Hardy. "I had no sense of the danger." Soon, she was snitching her boyfriend's household money and showing up at the low-rise projects in the Heights where young dealers clustered in the parking lots.

As she recounts her story, Hardy seems older than 23. She is blunt, with a no-nonsense gravity that occasionally makes way for a tart sense of humor. "I am not a welfare mother," she says evenly. "I am on assistance."

She grew up in Newton, Miss., where her three children have been living in the foster care of her parents. Her father, an auto mechanic, and mother, an industrial seamstress, used to drive the family around the country during summer vacations, which only whetted Hardy's appetite to leave town as soon as possible.

In her senior year of high school, she became pregnant, the last of her circle to do so. Abortion was not an option. Her parents were Jehovah's Witnesses, and a child, she felt, "was the one thing in the world that was mine. He was a part of me, my body." She managed to get her high-school diploma and four years ago moved with her son, Darius, to Muskegon, where she had relatives.

Muskegon is a rough place to make a fresh start, with thousands of Dutch, Polish and black workers laid off from auto-parts factories gone belly-up in recent years. She finally got a job on an assembly line at Stanco Metal Products. When she became pregnant with Nyéassa, the smell of burning oil exacerbated her nausea. She quit and went on assistance, intending to go back to work a few months after the baby was born.

Ronald Brown, her 35-year-old boyfriend, already had four children by a former wife when he met Kim. Those children, who had been exposed to drugs, alcohol and violence throughout their lives, were now scattered throughout foster-care homes and prison. One, according to the Department of Social Services, which has worked with Ronald and his family for 14 years, was born severely disabled because of the mother's drug abuse and alcoholism. Ronald himself has been in alcohol-treatment programs for years.

After the birth of Nyéassa, her daughter with Ronald, Hardy's menstrual cycle was irregular and, she recalls, it wasn't until March of last year that she realized she had probably become pregnant again—within months of delivering Nyéassa. But by then, Hardy was having a lot of domestic turmoil with Ronald. She also had a serious crack problem.

"I was in a lot of denial," she says now. "I thought I could cure myself."

Even if Hardy had been willing to consider it, residential treatment would have been almost impossible to obtain. Very few programs nationwide accept pregnant addicts, largely because of liability problems posed by high-risk pregnancies. Medicaid covers only 17 days of a typical 28-day treatment, which, given the high recidivism rate of crack users in recovery, is like "spitting in the ocean," says Barbara A. Klingenmaier, the Muskegon County foster-care supervisor.

Soon after she learned she was pregnant, Hardy, convinced she had to get away from her crowd of crack users as well as her crumbling relationship with Ronald, took the kids home to Mississippi for the duration of her pregnancy. But by moving, she lost all her welfare benefits, including Medicaid. Unable to pay for clinic visits, she had to go without prenatal care. In August, hoping to patch up things with Ronald, she returned to Muskegon to give birth. They were going to call the baby Aréanis, a name they had heard on a Star Trek episode.

Even though Muskegon County is cooled by shore breezes from Lake Michigan, it can smell pretty bad in the summer, when sour fumes from the paper mill or the waste-treatment plant blow in the wrong direction. Kim Hardy had been feeling heavy and uncomfortable all that steamy day, Aug. 19. A couple of Ronald's friends showed up in the evening and woke her up, offering her crack. Maybe, she thought groggily, it would help her relax and go into labor. The baby was so far along that a couple of hits couldn't possibly hurt.

Two months ago, Tague's office sent a letter to the Department of Social Services. The letter was a strongly worded request that the agency comply with a Michigan law requiring it to notify the prosecutor whenever it found instances of child abuse. By Tague's definition, child abuse included "substantial evidence of cocaine or alcohol abuse by a woman during pregnancy." Social-service workers would now be additionally compelled to report details of the woman's addiction, as well as whether her umbilical-cord fluid had been tested. (An issue in both the Hardy and Bremer cases has been the preservation of evidence: neither umbilical cord was tested, much less saved.)

The letter underscores the difficult and compromising position of the social workers, who are expected to both aid and inform on their clients. In Muskegon County, an unusual amount of interdepartmental quid pro quo is essential, because the prosecutor handles not only criminal matters but all Department of Social Services juvenile court cases as well. Social workers have to feed the prosecutor; otherwise, the cases may fall to the back of his calendar.

Vicki Birdsall, a social worker who investigated both Hardy and Bremer and alerted Sergeant Van Hemert, doesn't have misgivings about her role. She even believes that prosecution can be "therapeutic." But she thinks that drug delivery is too narrow a charge, and instead favors a statutory broadening of criminal child abuse to include fetuses. "One of my coke babies had retinal damage and seizures and to me that is just as severe as somebody waling on a kid," she says.

But Barbara Klingenmaier, the foster-care supervisor who helped place the Bremer and Hardy children, maintains that criminal prosecution of drug-addicted mothers undercuts their fragile self-esteem and can impede recovery. She says these cases should remain under the jurisdiction of juvenile court, which has the authority to punish the mother by ordering children removed. "That is the impetus to change their behavior in most of our cases," she says.

Tony Tague seems impervious to criticism that he's crossed over the line. "We have taken progressive steps in prosecution," he says, "and as a result have been engaged in a lot of controversy. Traditional means are no longer able to address the kind of problems we're confronting. There's a real need for innovative methods."

Tague, who trained in the Manhattan District Attorney's office, is emblematic of the "Thirtysomething" generation of prosecutors—tough, of course, but also politically astute and ambitious. In putting his own imprimatur on the war on drugs, Tague has become a bona fide Muskegon celebrity whose office passes out stickers and pins that say: "Help Tony Tague Fight Drugs!"

Tague maintains that a major goal of the Bremer and Hardy prosecutions has been accomplished: the women entered treatment. Because of his campaign, he says, more and more women have become aware of the dangerous connection between drugs and pregnancy: "When physicians make suggestions, it doesn't appear that's enough for them to seek treatment. The possibility of prosecution is a strong incentive."

Sitting in her attorney's office, which, in the way of small communities, happens to be in the same building at the Muskegon mall where she and Kim Hardy's attorney practice, Lynn Bremer vehemently shakes her head. "Tony Tague is telling women to get treatment and they won't be prosecuted. I'm a perfect example of someone who tried to reach out, and it's all coming back in my face."

Adds her attorney, Norman Halbower: "You're guilty of not getting a cure soon enough."

Bremer, who is from a well-to-do local family and clerked for several Muskegon County circuit judges, finally confessed her two-year cocaine addiction to her obstetrician about four months into her pregnancy. She was estranged from her family and, despite the admonitions of her boyfriend, also a cocaine user, she felt that the doctor was the only person she could turn to. "I knew I couldn't quit," she says, "and I wanted somebody to keep a check on me."

The doctor urged her to go into a residential treatment program, but Bremer, having recently joined a law firm, did not want to jeopardize her job. Then, too, Bremer's long work days pretty much ruled out the possibility of even a four-hour-a-week outpatient program. So, instead, she saw a drug counselor for a half-dozen sessions. She did manage to cut down her use, she says, but still flunked a number of urine tests administered by her obstetrician. One time, knowing she would not pass, she even brought someone else's specimen to his office.

"I tried, I really tried, but I couldn't do it," she says, in a whispery, halting voice. "I moved out of my boyfriend's house to get away from it, and I'd go along for a while, and then some people would come over and . . . it just looked good."

In addition to her criminal case, Bremer, like Hardy, still faces a juvenile court case for neglecting her infant daughter, Brittany, who has been placed temporarily in foster care. Meanwhile, she has volunteered for random drug tests and warily goes for counseling. "I feel betrayed," Bremer says. "Everyone I talked to about my drug problem has been subpoenaed."

Bremer, while awaiting trial, is back at work now, but it's particularly difficult to appear as an attorney when everyone in the courtroom knows she's also a defendant. She questions whether she can get an unbiased trial in a county where she's argued cases before all the judges.

These days Bremer is living apart from her boyfriend, Jeffrey Coon, a 32-year-old assembly-line worker, who is also in recovery. "Although we're on good

terms," she says, "sometimes it burns me up because he's not charged with anything, and he was right there doing it all with me. I wish he would have to do some squirming, too."

Bremer's spirits are low. "I'm embarrassed and sad," she says. "My reputation is gone, and I still don't have my daughter with me. This whole thing has turned making a baby into a tragic event."

On the last Saturday in June, hours before Muskegon's gala annual parade, Hardy is talking cheerfully about how things are finally looking up. "Life is a lot simpler now," she says with a laugh. "It's a lot cheaper without drugs."

Hardy's been clean since mid-October. Social workers describe her turnaround as "extraordinary." In a few short weeks, her kids, who are reportedly in fine shape, will be returned to her after a 10-month absence. She sees a drug counselor, has made a new circle of friends and has just rented a modest three-bedroom house in a predominantly white neighborhood of Muskegon. That gives her pause, but at least it's far away from her old haunts. Besides, she is thankful that someone was willing to rent to her.

Since her case broke in the papers, she's become a public figure. She can't find a job, she says, because she is recognized as *that drug mother*. "Some people look at me like I'm an infection," she says.

But this fall, she starts classes in Muskegon Community College's new chemical dependency program. Noting the lack of black female counselors, Hardy says she intends to get a master's degree and become a drug therapist.

In retrospect, although she doesn't believe that she should be facing the prospect of going to jail—to say nothing of being prosecuted in the first place—Hardy is actually grateful for what's happened to her: she's stopped smoking crack. "Why is it that we have to make women criminals before we can get them drug treatment?" asks Kary Moss of the A.C.L.U.

One of Hardy's attorneys, Alan Rapoport, has an answer to Moss's question. "This crusade is not about getting women into treatment or protecting babies," he says acidly. "It's about winning the war on drugs."

Moss points out that in spite of Tony Tague's insistence that he is inspiring addicted mothers to get help, the real choice is not between prosecution and treatment, but between prosecution and virtually nothing. Most drug programs were set up to treat male heroin addicts and have no obstetrician on staff. A recent study by Dr. Wendy Chavkin of the Columbia University School of Public Health and Beth Israel Medical Center found that 87 percent of New York City's drug-abuse programs turned away pregnant crack addicts, even though the women were eligible for Medicaid. And the rare clinics that do admit them almost never have child-care facilities—a critical shortcoming for most mothers.

The effects of Tague's prosecutions are certainly being felt at the recovery-care unit at Muskegon General Hospital, which now has 11 beds for residential treatment and four for detoxification. Cheryl Gawkowski, a staff psychologist, reports that some pregnant addicts have sought help specifically because of their fear of going to jail, while others have avoided prenatal care altogether for exactly the same reason. "I go back and forth on the issue," she admits.

Hardy's opinion doesn't waver at all. A pregnant addict should be encouraged as strongly as possible to enter treatment, she says, but not forced to go. "she has to do it for herself," Hardy says. "It's a disease—just like alcoholism—and women are not going to stop until they're ready."

Only if the child is born testing positive for drugs, Hardy believes, should social services use their authority to intervene, removing the baby until the mother gets treatment. "Prosecutors don't protect babies, child protective services workers do," she says.

She doesn't know how long her own case will be hanging over her head. "It could take years. But for today, things are O.K., and I'm just looking forward to my kids coming home."

Should We Legalize Drugs? History Answers

H ow are we to win our national struggle with cocaine, heroin, marijuana, and other illegal drugs? Everyone agrees that drug-related problems are a plague on our society, destroying lives, helping wreck neighborhoods, poisoning schools, feeding crime, bleeding the economy. Lately strong voices are saying that the war against them as we are now fighting it cannot be won, that the best solution is legalization, or at least decriminalization. What does history—with its case studies of past substance bans and attempts at regulation and decontrol—tell us might happen if drugs were no longer outlawed? Could we close the criminal marketplace? Make drugs safer for those who use them? Reduce demand? Cut enforcement costs and raise tax revenues? Or would things get worse? Two scholars, Ethan A. Nadelmann of Princeton University and David T. Courtwright of the University of North Florida, have studied the historical record closely. Their answers could hardly be more different.

Yes

Ethan A. Nadelmann

The better title for this article, let me suggest at the outset, would be "Drug Prohibition: Con." Most opponents of "drug legalization" assume that it would involve making cocaine and heroin available the way alcohol and tobacco are today. But most legalization supporters favor nothing of the kind; in fact, we disagree widely as to which drugs should be legalized, how they should be controlled, and what the consequences are likely to be. Where drug-policy reformers do agree is in our critique of the drug-prohibition system that has evolved in the United States—a system, we contend, that has proved ineffective, costly, counterproductive, and immoral.

Efforts to reverse drug prohibition face formidable obstacles. Americans have grown accustomed to the status quo. Alcohol prohibition was overturned before most citizens had forgotten what a legal alcohol policy was like, but who today can recall a time before drug prohibition? Moreover, the United States has succeeded in promoting its drug-prohibition system throughout the world. Opponents of alcohol prohibition could look to successful foreign alcohol-control systems, in Canada and much of Europe, but contemporary drug anti-prohibitionists must look further—to history.

The principal evidence, not surprisingly, is Prohibition. The dry years offer many useful analogies, but their most important lesson is the need to distinguish between the harms that stem from drugs and the harms that arise from outlawing them. The Americans who voted in 1933 to repeal Prohibition differed greatly in their reasons for overturning the system. They almost all agreed, however, that the evils of alcohol consumption had been surpassed by those of trying to surpress it.

Some pointed to Al Capone and rising crime, violence, and corruption; others to the overflowing courts, jails, and prisons, the labeling of tens of millions of Americans as criminals and the consequent broadening disrespect for the law, the dangerous expansions of federal police powers and encroachments on individual liberties, the hundreds of thousands of Americans blinded, paralyzed, and killed by poisonous moonshine and industrial alcohol, and the increasing government expenditure devoted to enforcing the Prohibition laws and the billions in forgone tax revenues. Supporters of Prohibition blamed the consumers, and some went so far as to argue that those who violated the laws deserved whatever ills befell them. But by 1933 most Americans blamed Prohibition.

If there is a single message that contemporary anti-prohibitionists seek to drive home, it is that drug prohibition is responsible for much of what Americans identify today as the "drug problem." It is not merely a matter of the direct costs—twenty billion dollars spent this year on arresting, prosecuting, and incarcerating drug-law violators. Choked courts and prisons, an incarceration rate higher than that of any other nation in the world, tax dollars diverted from education and health care, law-enforcement resources diverted from investigating everything from auto theft to savings-and-loan scams—all these are just a few of the costs our current prohibition imposes.

Consider also Capone's successors—the drug kingpins of Asia, Latin America, and the United States. Consider as well all the murders and assaults perpetrated by young drug dealers not just against one another but against police, witnesses, and bystanders. Consider the tremendous economic and social incentives generated by the illegality of the drug market—temptations so overwhelming that even "good kids" cannot resist them. Consider the violent drug dealers becoming the heroes of boys and young men, from Harlem to Medellín. And consider tens of millions of Americans being labeled criminals for doing nothing more than smoking a marijuana cigarette. In all these respects the consequences of drug prohibition imitate—and often exceed—those of alcohol prohibition.

Prohibition reminds us, too, of the health costs of drug prohibition. Sixty years ago some fifty thousand Americans were paralyzed after consuming an adulterated Jamaica ginger extract known as "jake." Today we have marijuana made more dangerous by government-sprayed paraquat and the chemicals added by drug dealers, heroin adulterated with poisonous powders, and assorted pills and capsules containing everything from antihistamines to strychnine. Indeed, virtually every illicit drug purchased at the retail level contains adulterants, at least some of which are far more dangerous than the drug itself. And restrictions on the sale of drug paraphernalia has, by encouraging intravenous drug addicts to share their equipment, severely handicapped efforts to stem the transmission of AIDS. As during Prohibition, many Americans view these ills as necessary and even desirable, but others, like their forebears sixty years ago, reject as perverse a system that degrades and destroys the very people it was designed to protect.

Prohibition's lessons extend in other directions as well. The current revisionist twist on that "Great Experiment" now claims that "Prohibition worked," by reducing alcohol

The late-nineteenth-century experience shows that in a legal market consumers prefer less potent drugs.

consumption and alcohol-related ills ranging from cirrhosis to public drunkenness and employee absenteeism. There is some truth to this claim. But in fact, the most dramatic decline in American alcohol consumption occurred not between 1920 and 1933, while the Eighteenth Amendment was in effect, but rather between 1916 and 1922. During those years the temperance movement was highly active and successful in publicizing the dangers of alcohol. The First World War's spirit of self-sacrifice extended to temperance as a means of grain conservation, and there arose, as the historian David Kyvig puts it, "an atmosphere of hostility toward all things German, not the least of which was beer." In short, a great variety of factors coalesced in this brief time to substantially reduce alcohol consumption and its ills.

The very evidence on which pro-prohibition historians rely provides further proof of the importance of factors other than prohibition laws. One of these historians, John Burnham, has noted that the admission rate for alcohol psychoses to New York hospitals shrank from 10 percent between 1909 and 1912 to 1.9 percent in 1920—a decline that occurred largely before national prohibition and in a state that had not enacted its own prohibition law.

At best one can argue that Prohibition was most effective in its first years, when temperance norms remained strong and illicit sources of production had yet to be firmly established. By all accounts, alcohol consumption rose after those first years—despite increased resources devoted to enforcement. The pre-Prohibition decline in consumption, like the recent decline in cigarette consumption, had less to do with laws than with changing norms and the imposition of non-criminal-justice measures.

Perhaps the most telling indictment of Prohibition is provided by the British experience with alcohol control during a similar period. In the United States the death rate from cirrhosis of the liver dropped from as high as 15 per 100,000 population between 1910 and 1914 to 7 during the twenties only to climb back to pre-1910 levels by the 1960s, while in Britain the death rate from cirrhosis dropped from 10 in 1914 to 5 in 1920 and then gradually declined to a low of 2 in the 1940s before rising by a mere point by 1963. Other indicators of alcohol consumption and misuse dropped by similar magnitudes, even though the United Kingdom never enacted prohibition. Instead wartime Britain restricted the amount of alcohol available, taxed it, and drastically reduced the hours of sale. At war's end the government dropped restrictions on quantity but made taxes even higher and set hours of sale at only half the pre-war norm.

Britain thus not only reduced the negative consequences of alcohol consumption more effectively than did the United States, but did so in a manner that raised substantial government revenues. The British experience—as well as Australia's and most of continental Europe's—strongly suggests not only that our Prohibition was unsuccessful but that more effective post-Repeal controls might have prevented the return to high consumption levels.

But no matter how powerful the analogies between alcohol prohibition and contemporary drug prohibition, most Americans still balk at drawing the parallels. Alcohol, they insist, is fundamentally different from everything else. They are right, of course, insofar as their claims rest not on health or scientific grounds but are limited to political and cultural arguments. By most measures, alcohol is more

dangerous to human health than any of the drugs now prohibited by law. No drug is as associated with violence in American culture—and even in illicit-drug-using subcultures—as is alcohol. One would be hard pressed to argue that its role in many Native American and other aboriginal communities has been any less destructive than that of illicit drugs in America's ghettos.

The dangers of all drugs vary greatly, of course, depending not just on their pharmacological properties and how they are consumed but also on the attitudes and beliefs of their users and the settings in which they use them. Alcohol by and large plays a benign role in Jewish and Asian-American cultures but a devastating one in some Native American societies, and by the same token the impact of cocaine among Yuppies during the early 1980s was relatively benign compared with its impact a few years later in impoverished ghettos.

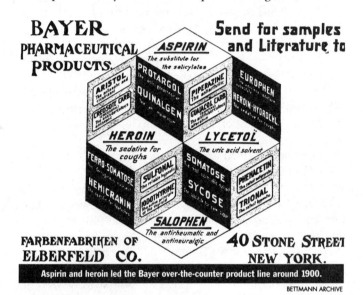

Aspirin and heroin led the Bayer over-the-counter product line around 1900.

BETTMANN ARCHIVE

The culture helps determine the setting of drug use, but so do the laws. Prohibitions enhance the dangers not just of drugs but of the settings in which they are used. The relationship between prohibition and dangerous adulterations is clear. So too is its impact on the potency and forms of drugs. For instance, Prohibition caused a striking drop in the production and sale of beer, while that of hard liquor increased as bootleggers from Al Capone on down sought to maximize their profits and minimize the risks of detection. Similarly, following the Second World War, the enactment of anti-opium laws in many parts of Asia in which opium use was traditional—India, Hong Kong, Thailand, Laos, Iran—effectively suppressed the availability of opium at the cost of stimulating the creation of domestic heroin industries and substantial increases in heroin use. The same transition had occurred in the United States following Congress's ban on opium imports in 1909. And when during the 1980s the U.S. government's domestic drug-enforcement efforts significantly reduced the availability and raised the price of marijuana, they provided decisive incentives to producers, distributors, and consumers to switch to cocaine. In each case, prohibition forced switches from drugs that were bulky and relatively benign to drugs that were more compact, more lucrative, more potent, and more dangerous.

In the 1980s the retail purity of heroin and cocaine increased, and highly potent crack became cheaply available in American cities. At the same time, the average potency of most legal psychoactive substances declined: Americans began switching from hard liquor to beer and wine, from high-tar-and-nicotine to lower-tar-and-nicotine cigarettes, and even from caffeinated to decaffeinated coffee and soda. The relationship between prohibition and drug potency was, if not indisputable, still readily apparent.

In turn-of-the-century America, opium, morphine, heroin, cocaine, and marijuana were subject to few restrictions. Popular tonics such as Vin Mariani and Coca-Cola and its competitors were laced with cocaine, and hundreds of medicines—Mrs. Winslow's Soothing Syrup may have been the most famous—contained psychoactive drugs. Millions, perhaps tens of millions of Americans, took opiates and cocaine. David Courtwright estimates that during the 1890s as many as one-third of a million Americans were opiate addicts, but most of them were ordinary people who would today be described as occasional users.

Careful analysis of that era—when the very drugs that we most fear were widely and cheaply available throughout the country—provides a telling antidote to our nightmare legalization scenarios. For one thing, despite the virtual absence of any controls on availability, the proportion of Americans addicted to opiates was only two or three times greater than today. For another, the typical addict was not a young black ghetto resident but a middle-aged white Southern woman or a West Coast Chinese immigrant. The violence, death, disease, and crime that we today associate with drug use barely existed, and many medical authorities regarded opiate addiction as far less destructive than alcoholism (some doctors even prescribed the former as treatment for the latter). Many opiate addicts, perhaps most, managed to lead relatively normal lives and kept their addictions secret even from close friends and relatives. That they were able to do so was largely a function of the legal status of their drug use.

But even more reassuring is the fact that the major causes of opiate addiction then simply do not exist now. Late-nineteenth-century Americans became addicts principally at the hands of physicians who lacked modern medicines and were unaware of the addictive potential of the drugs they prescribed. Doctors in the 1860s and 1870s saw morphine injections as a virtual panacea, and many Americans turned to opiates to alleviate their aches and pains without going through doctors at all. But as medicine advanced, the levels of both doctor- and self-induced addiction declined markedly.

In 1906 the first Federal Pure Food and Drug Act required over-the-counter drug producers to disclose whether their products contained any opiates, cocaine, cannabis, alcohol, or other psychoactive ingredients. Sales of patent medicines containing opiates and cocaine decreased significantly thereafter—in good part because fewer Americans were interested in purchasing products that they now knew to contain those drugs.

Consider the lesson here. Ethical debates aside, the principal objection to all drug legalization proposals is that they invite higher levels of drug use and misuse by making

Our drug prohibition can't be understood without recalling that it began along with alcohol prohibition.

drugs not just legal but more available and less expensive. Yet the late-nineteenth-century experience suggests the opposite: that in a legal market most consumers will prefer lower-potency coca and opiate products to the far more powerful concoctions that have virtually monopolized the market under prohibition. This reminds us that opiate addiction per se was not necessarily a serious problem so long as addicts had ready access to modestly priced opiates of reliable quality—indeed, that the opiate addicts of late-nineteenth-century America differed in no significant respects from the cigarette-addicted consumers of today. And it reassures us that the principal cause of addiction to opiates was not the desire to get high but rather ignorance—ignorance of their addictive qualities, ignorance of the alternative analgesics, and ignorance of what exactly patent medicines contained. The antidote to addiction in late-nineteenth-century America, the historical record shows, consisted primarily of education and regulation—not prohibition, drug wars, and jail.

Why, then, was drug prohibition instituted? And why did it quickly evolve into a fierce and highly punitive set of policies rather than follow the more modest and humane path pursued by the British? In part, the passage of the federal Harrison Narcotic Act, in 1914, and of state and local bans before and after that, reflected a belated response to the recognition that people could easily become addicted to opiates and cocaine. But it also was closely intertwined with the increasingly vigorous efforts of doctors and pharmacists to professionalize their disciplines and to monopolize the public's access to medicinal drugs. Most of all, though, the institution of drug prohibition reflected the changing nature of the opiate- and cocaine-using population. By 1914 the number of middle-class Americans blithely consuming narcotics had fallen sharply. At the same time, however, opiate and cocaine use had become increasingly popular among the lower classes and racial minorities. The total number of consumers did not approach that of earlier decades, but where popular opinion had once shied from the notion of criminalizing the habits of elderly white women, few such inhibitions impeded it where urban gamblers, prostitutes, and delinquents were concerned.

The first anti-opium laws were passed in California in the 1870s and directed at the Chinese immigrants and their opium dens, in which, it was feared, young white women were being seduced. A generation later reports of rising cocaine use among young black men in the South—who were said to rape white women while under the influence—prompted similar legislation. During the 1930s marijuana prohibitions were directed in good part at Mexican and Chicano workers who had lost their jobs in the Depression. And fifty years later draconian penalties were imposed for the possession of tiny amounts of crack cocaine—a drug associated principally with young Latino and African-Americans.

But more than racist fears was at work during the early years of drug prohibition. In the aftermath of World War I, many Americans, stunned by the triumph of Bolshevism in Russia and fearful of domestic subversion, turned their backs on the liberalizing reforms of the preceding era. In such an atmosphere the very notion of tolerating drug use or maintaining addicts in the clinics that had arisen after 1914 struck most citizens as both immoral and unpatriotic. In 1919 the mayor of New York created the Committee on Public Safety to investigate two ostensibly related problems: revolutionary bombings and heroin use among youth. And in Washington that same year, the Supreme Court effectively foreclosed any possibility of a more humane policy toward drug addicts when it held, in *Webb et al.* v. *U.S.*, that doctors could not legally prescribe maintenance supplies of narcotics to addicts.

But perhaps most important, the imposition of drug prohibition cannot be understood without recalling that it occurred almost simultaneously with the advent of alcohol prohibition. Contemporary Americans tend to regard Prohibition as a strange quirk in American history—and drug prohibition as entirely natural and beneficial. Yet the prohibition against alcohol, like that against other drugs, was motivated in no small part by its association with feared and despised ethnic minorities, especially the masses of Eastern and Southern European immigrants.

Why was Prohibition repealed after just thirteen years while drug prohibition has lasted for more than seventy-five? Look at whom each disadvantaged. Alcohol prohibition struck directly at tens of millions of Americans of all ages, including many of society's most powerful members. Drug prohibition threatened far fewer Americans, and they had

An addict gives himself a fix early in the century.

relatively little influence in the halls of power. Only the prohibition of marijuana, which some sixty million Americans have violated since 1965, has come close to approximating the Prohibition experience, but marijuana smokers consist mostly of young and relatively powerless Americans. In the final analysis alcohol prohibition was repealed, and opiate, cocaine, and marijuana prohibition retained, not because scientists had concluded that alcohol was the least dangerous of the various psychoactive drugs but because of the prejudices and preferences of most Americans.

There was, of course, one other important reason why Prohibition was repealed when it was. With the country four years into the Depression, Prohibition increasingly appeared not just foolish but costly. Fewer and fewer Americans were keen on paying the rising costs of enforcing its laws, and more and more recalled the substantial tax revenues that the legal alcohol business had generated. The potential analogy to the current recession is unfortunate but apt. During the late 1980s the cost of building and maintaining prisons emerged as the fastest-growing item in many state budgets, while other costs of the war on drugs also rose dramatically. One cannot help wondering how much longer Americans will be eager to foot the bills for all this.

Throughout history the legal and moral status of psychoactive drugs has kept changing. During the seventeenth century the sale and consumption of tobacco were punished by as much as death in much of Europe, Russia, China, and Japan. For centuries many of the same Muslim domains that forbade the sale and consumption of alcohol simultaneously tolerated and even regulated the sale of opium and cannabis.

Drug-related moralities have always been malleable, and their evolution can in no way be described as moral progress. Just as our moral perceptions of particular drugs have changed in the past, so will they in the future, and people will continue to circumvent the legal and moral barriers that remain. My confidence in this prediction stems from one other lesson of civilized human history. From the dawn of time humans have nearly universally shown a desire to alter their states of consciousness with psychoactive substances, and it is this fact that gives the lie to the declared objective of creating a "drug-free society" in the United States.

Another thing common to all societies, as the social theorist Thomas Szasz argued some years ago, is that they require scapegoats to embody their fears and take blame for whatever ails them. Today the role of bogeyman is applied to drug producers, dealers, and users. Just as anti-Communist propagandists once feared Moscow far beyond its actual influence and appeal, so today anti-drug proselytizers indict marijuana, cocaine, heroin, and assorted hallucinogens far beyond their actual psychoactive effects and psychological appeal. Never mind that the vast majority of Americans have expressed—in one public-opinion poll after another—little interest in trying these substances, even if they were legal, and never mind that most of those who have tried them have suffered few, if any, ill effects. The evidence of history and of science is drowned out by today's bogeymen. No rhetoric is too harsh, no penalty too severe.

Lest I be accused of exaggerating, consider the following. On June 27, 1991, the Supreme Court upheld, by a vote of five to four, a Michigan statute that imposed a mandatory sentence of life without possibility of parole for anyone convicted of possession of more than 650 grams (about 1.5 pounds) of cocaine. In other words, an activity that was entirely legal at the turn of the century, and that poses a danger to society roughly comparable to that posed by the sale of alcohol and tobacco, is today treated the same as first-degree murder.

The cumulative result of our prohibitionist war is that roughly 20 to 25 percent of the more than one million Americans now incarcerated in federal and state prisons and local jails, and almost half of those in federal penitentiaries, are serving time for having engaged in an activity that their great-grandparents could have pursued entirely legally.

Examples of less striking, but sometimes more deadly, penalties also abound. In many states anyone convicted of possession of a single marijuana joint can have his or her driver's license revoked for six months and be required to participate in a drug-treatment program. In many states

anyone caught cultivating a marijuana plant may find all his or her property forfeited to the local police department. And in all but a few cities needle-exchange programs to reduce the transmission of AIDS among drug addicts have been rejected because they would "send the wrong message"—as if the more moral message is that such addicts are better off contracting the deadly virus and spreading it.

Precedents for each of these penalties scarcely exist in American history. The restoration of criminal forfeiture of property—rejected by the Founding Fathers because of its association with the evils of English rule—could not have found its way back into American law but for the popular desire to give substance to the rhetorical war on drugs.

Of course, changes in current policy that make legally available to adult Americans many of the now prohibited psychoactive substances are bound to entail a litany of administrative problems and certain other risks.

During the last years of the Volstead Act, the Rockefeller Foundation commissioned a study by the leading police scholar in the United States, Raymond Fosdick, to evaluate the various alternatives to Prohibition. Its analyses and recommendations ultimately played an important role in constructing post-Prohibition regulatory policies. A comparable study is currently under way at Princeton University, where the Smart Family Foundation has funded a working group of scholars from diverse disciplines to evaluate and recommend alternative drug-control policies. Its report will be completed late in 1993.

History holds one final lesson for those who cannot imagine any future beyond drug prohibition. Until well into the 1920s most Americans regarded Prohibition as a permanent fact of life. As late as 1930 Sen. Morris Shepard of Texas, who had coauthored the Prohibition Amendment, confidently asserted: "There is as much chance of repealing the Eighteenth Amendment as there is for a humming-bird to fly to the planet Mars with the Washington Monument tied to its tail."

History reminds us that things can and do change, that what seems inconceivable today can seem entirely normal, and even inevitable, a few years hence. So it was with Prohibition, and so it is—and will be—both with drug prohibition and the ever-changing nature of drug use in America.

Ethan A. Nadelmann is assistant professor of politics and public affairs in the Woodrow Wilson School and the Department of Politics at Princeton University. He chairs the Princeton Working Group on the Future of Drug Use and Alternatives to Drug Prohibition.

8. FIGHTING THE DRUG WAR

No

David T. Courtwright

One thing that all parties in the American drug-policy debate agree on is that they want to eliminate the traffic in illicit drugs and the criminal syndicates that control it. There are two divergent strategies for achieving this end: the drug war and drug legalization, or, more precisely, controlled legalization, since few people want the government to simply abandon drug control

and proclaim laissez faire.

The drug war was launched during the Reagan administration. It is actually the fourth such campaign, there having been sustained legislative and governmental efforts against drug abuse between 1909 and 1923, 1951 and 1956, and 1971 and 1973. What distinguishes the current war is that it is more concerned with stimulants like cocaine than with opiates, it is larger, and—no surprise in our age of many zeros—it is much more expensive.

The war against drugs has included the treatment of addicts and educational programs designed to discourage new users, but the emphasis has been on law enforcement, with interdiction, prosecution, imprisonment, and the seizure of assets at the heart of the campaign. The news from the front has been mixed. Price and purity levels, treatment and emergency-room admissions, urinalyses, and most other indices of drug availability showed a worsening of the problem during the 1980s, with some improvement in 1989 and 1990. The number of casual cocaine users has recently declined, but cocaine addiction remains widespread, affecting anywhere from about 650,000 to 2.4 million compulsive users, depending on whose definitions and estimates one chooses to accept. There has been some success in stopping marijuana imports—shipments of the drug are relatively bulky and thus easier to detect—but this has been offset by the increased domestic cultivation of high-quality marijuana, which has more than doubled since 1985. Heroin likewise has become both more available and more potent than it was in the late 1970s.

But cocaine has been the drug of greatest concern. Just how severe the crisis has become may be gauged by federal cocaine seizures. Fifty years ago the annual haul for the entire nation was 1 or 2 pounds, an amount that could easily be contained in the glove compartment of a car. As late as 1970 the total was under 500 pounds, which would fit in the car's trunk. In fiscal year 1990 it was 235,000 pounds—about the weight of 60 mid-size cars. And this represented

a fraction, no more than 10 percent, of what went into the nostrils and lungs and veins of the approximately seven million Americans who used cocaine during 1990. Worse may be in store. Worldwide production of coca surged during 1989 to a level of 225,000 metric tons, despite U.S. efforts to eradicate cultivation. Global production of opium, marijuana, and hashish has likewise increased since President Reagan formally declared war on drugs in 1986.

The greatest obstacle to the supply-reduction strategy is the enormous amount of money generated by the illicit traffic. Drug profits have been used to buy off foreign and domestic officials and to secure protection for the most vulnerable stages of the drug-cultivation, -manufacturing, and -distribution process. These profits also hire various specialists, from assassins to money launderers to lawyers, needed to cope with interlopers; they pay for technological devices ranging from cellular phones to jet planes; and they ensure that should a trafficker die or land in jail, there will be no shortage of replacements.

It is hardly surprising that these stubborn economic realities, together with the drug war's uneven and often disappointing results, have led several commentators to question the wisdom of what they call the prohibition policy. What is unprecedented is that these disenchanted critics include mayors, prominent lawyers, federal judges, nationally syndicated columnists, a congressman, a Princeton professor, and a Nobel laureate in economics. They espouse variations of a position that is often called controlled legalization, meaning that the sale of narcotics should be permitted under conditions that restrict and limit consumption, such as no sales to minors, no advertising, and substantial taxation. They cite the numerous advantages of this approach: several billion dollars per year would be realized from tax revenues and savings on law enforcement; crime would diminish because addicts would not have to hustle to keep themselves supplied with drugs; the murders associated with big-city drug trafficking would abate as lower-cost, legal drugs drive the traffickers out of business. Because these drugs would be of known quality and potency, and because they would not have to be injected with shared needles, the risk of overdose and infection would drop. The issue of foreign complicity in the drug traffic, which has complicated American diplomatic relations with many countries, would disappear. Under a policy of controlled legalization, it would be no more criminal or controversial to import coca from Colombia than to import coffee.

The more candid of the legalization proponents concede that these advantages would be purchased at the cost of increased drug abuse. Widespread availability, lower prices, and the elimination of the criminal sanction would result in more users, some of whom would inevitably become addicts. But how many more? Herbert Kleber, a treatment specialist and former deputy director of the Office of National Drug Control Policy, has argued that there would be between twelve and fifty-five million addicted users if cocaine and heroin were legally available. While it is impossible to anticipate the exact magnitude of the increase, history does support Kleber's argument. In countries like Iran or Thailand, where narcotics have long been cheap, potent, and readily available, the prevalence of addiction has been and continues to be quite high. Large quantities of opium sold by British and American merchants created a social disaster in nineteenth-century China; that Chinese sailors and immigrants subsequently introduced opium smoking to Britain and America is a kind of ironic justice. Doctors, who constantly work with and around narcotics, have historically had a very serious addiction problem: estimates of the extent of morphine addiction among American physicians at the turn of the century ran from 6 percent to an astonishing 23 percent. In a word, exposure matters.

By 1980 half of all drug arrests were of minors. That black market would persist with legalization.

Kleber has also attacked the crime-reduction rationale by pointing out that addicts will generally use much more of an illicit substance if the cost is low. They would spend most of their time using drugs and little of it working, thus continuing to resort to crime to acquire money. If the total number of addicts rose sharply as availability increased, total crime would also increase. There would be less crime committed by any single addict but more crime in the aggregate.

The debate over decriminalization is, in essence, an argument about a high-stakes gamble, and so far the opponents represent the majority view. At the close of the 1980s, four out of every five Americans were against the legalization of marijuana, let alone cocaine. But if the drug war produces another decade of indifferent results, growing disillusionment could conceivably prompt experiments in controlled legalization.

The controlled-legalization argument rests on the assumption that legal sales would largely eliminate the illicit traffic and its attendant evils. The history of drug use, regulation, and taxation in the United States suggests otherwise. The very phrase *controlled legalization* implies denying certain groups access to drugs. Minors are the most obvious example. No one advocates supplying narcotics to children, so presumably selling drugs to anyone under twenty-one would remain a criminal offense, since that is the cutoff point for sales of beverage alcohol. Unfortunately, illicit drug abuse in this century has become concentrated among the young—that is, among the very ones most likely to be made exceptions to the rule of legal sales.

Until about 1900 the most common pattern of drug dependence in the United States was opium or morphine addiction, brought about by the treatment of chronic diseases and painful symptoms. Addicts were mainly female, middle-class, and middle-aged or older; Eugene O'Neill's mother, fictionalized as Mary Tyrone in *Long Day's Journey into Night*, was one. Habitual users of morphine, laudanum, and other medicinal opiates in their adolescence were extremely rare, even in big cities like Chicago.

Another pattern of drug use was nonmedical and had its roots in marginal, deviant, and criminal subcultures. The "pleasure users," as they were sometimes called, smoked opium, sniffed cocaine, injected morphine and cocaine in combination, or, after 1910, sniffed or injected heroin. Nonmedical addicts began much younger than their medical counterparts. The average age of addiction (not first use, which would have been lower still) for urban heroin addicts studied in the 1910s was only nineteen or twenty years. They were also more likely to be male than those whose addiction was of medical origin, and more likely to have been involved in crime.

Initially the pleasure users were the smaller group, but during the first two decades of this century—the same period when the police approach to national drug control was formulated—the number of older, docile medical addicts steadily diminished. There were several reasons: doctors became better educated and more conservative in their use of narcotics; the population grew healthier; patent-medicine manufacturers were forced to reveal the contents of their products; and the numerous morphine addicts who had been created in the nineteenth century began to age and die off. Drug use and addiction became increasingly concentrated among young men in their teens and twenties, a pattern that continues to this day.

In 1980, 44 percent of drug arrests nationwide were of persons under the age of twenty-one. There were more arrests among teen-agers than among the entire population over the age of twenty-five; eighteen-year-olds had the highest arrest rate of any age group. By 1987 the proportion of those arrested under twenty-one had declined to 25 percent. This was partly due to the aging of the population and to the effects of drug education on students. But when large numbers of "echo boomers"—the children of the baby boomers—become adolescents during the 1990s, the percentage of under-twenty-one drug arrests will likely increase.

THEIR SECURITY DEMANDS YOU VOTE **REPEAL**

BALLOT BOX

WOMEN'S ORGANIZATION
FOR
NATIONAL PROHIBITION REFORM

STRONG MUSEUM, ROCHESTER, N.Y.

A 1932 poster links repeal and family values.

So, depending on timing and demographic circumstances, at least a quarter and perhaps more than a third of all drug buyers would be underage, and there would be a great deal of money to be made by selling to them. The primary source of supply would likely be diversion—adults legally purchasing drugs and selling them to customers below the legal age. The sellers (or middlemen who collected and then resold the legal purchases) would make a profit through marking up or adulterating the drugs, and there might well be turf disputes and hence violence. Some of the dealers and their underage purchasers would be caught, prosecuted, and jailed, and the criminal-justice system would still be burdened with drug arrests. The black market would be altered and diminished, but it would scarcely disappear.

Potential for illegal sales and use extends far beyond minors. Pilots, police officers, fire fighters, drivers of buses, trains, taxis, and ambulances, surgeons, active-duty military personnel, and others whose drug use would jeopardize public safety would be denied access to at least some drugs, and those of them who did take narcotics would be liable to criminal prosecution, as would their suppliers. Pregnant women would also pose a problem. Drugs transmitted to fetuses can cause irreversible and enormously costly harm. Federal and local governments may soon be spending billions of dollars a year just to prepare the impaired children of addicts for kindergarten. Society has the right and the obligation to stop this neurological carnage, both because it cruelly handicaps innocents and because it harms everyone else through higher taxes and health-insurance premiums. Paradoxically, the arguments for controlled legalization might lead to denying alcohol and tobacco to pregnant women along with narcotics. Alcohol and tobacco can also harm fetal development, and several legalization proponents have observed that it is both inconsistent and unwise to treat them as if they were not dangerous because they are legal. If cocaine is denied to pregnant women, why not alcohol too? The point here is simply that every time one makes an exception for good and compelling reasons—every time one accents the "controlled" as opposed to the "legalization"—one creates the likelihood of continued illicit sales and use.

The supposition that this illegal market would be fueled by diversion is well founded historically. There has always been an undercurrent of diversion, especially in the late 1910s and 1920s, when black-market operators like Legs Diamond got their supplies not so much by smuggling as by purchases from legitimate drug companies. One possible solution is to require of all legal purchasers that which is required of newly enrolled methadone patients: consumption of the drug on the premises. Unfortunately, unlike methadone, heroin and cocaine are short-acting, and compulsive users must administer them every few hours or less. The dayrooms of drug-treatment clinics set up in Britain after 1968 to provide heroin maintenance were often clogged with whining addicts. Frustrated and angry, the clinic staffs largely abandoned heroin during the 1970s, switching instead to methadone, which, having the advantages of oral administration and twenty-four-hour duration, is far more suitable for clinic-based distribution. Confining the use of heroin or cocaine or other street drugs to clinics would be a logistical nightmare. But the alternative, take-home supplies, invites illegal sales to excluded groups.

Another historical pattern of black-market activity has been the smuggling of drugs to prisoners. Contraband was one of the reasons the government built specialized narcotic hospitals in Lexington, Kentucky, and Fort Worth, Texas, in the 1930s. Federal wardens wanted to get addicts out of their prisons because they were constantly conniving to obtain smuggled drugs. But when drug-related arrests multiplied after 1965 and the Lexington and Fort

Worth facilities were closed, the prisons again filled with inmates eager to obtain drugs. Birch Bayh, chairing a Senate investigation of the matter in 1975, observed that in some institutions young offenders had a more plentiful supply of drugs than they did on the outside.

Since then more jails have been crammed with more prisoners, and these prisoners are more likely than ever to have had a history of drug use. In 1989, 60 to 80 percent of male arrestees in twelve large American cities tested positive for drugs. It is hard to imagine a controlled-legalization system that would permit sales to prisoners. Alcohol, although a legal drug, is not sold licitly in prisons, and for good reason, as more than 40 percent of prisoners were under its influence when they committed their crimes. If drugs are similarly denied to inmates, then the contra-

Customs duties on opium produced not only revenues but smuggling. The same thing would surely happen today.

band problem will persist. If, moreover, we insist that our nearly three million parolees and probationers remain clean on the theory that drug use aggravates recidivism, the market for illegal sales would be so much the larger.

By now the problem should be clear. If drugs are legalized, but not for those under twenty-one, or for public-safety officers, or transport workers, or military personnel, or pregnant women, or prisoners, or probationers, or parolees, or psychotics, or any of several other special groups one could plausibly name, then just exactly who is going to buy them? Noncriminal adults, whose drug use is comparatively low to begin with? Controlled legalization entails a dilemma. To the extent that its controls are enforced, some form of black-market activity will persist. If, on the other hand, its controls are not enforced and drugs are easily diverted to those who are underage or otherwise ineligible, then it is a disguised form of wholesale legalization and as such morally, politically, and economically unacceptable.

One of the selling points of controlled legalization was also one of the decisive arguments for the repeal of Prohibition: taxation. Instead of spending billions to suppress the illicit traffic, the government would reap billions by imposing duties on legitimate imports and taxes on domestically manufactured drugs. Not only could these revenues be earmarked for drug treatment and education programs,

but they would also increase the prices paid by the consumer, thus discouraging consumption, especially among adolescents.

The United States government has had extensive historical experience with the taxation of legal narcotics. In the nineteenth and early twentieth centuries, opium was imported and subject to customs duties. The imports were assigned to one of three categories. The first was crude opium, used mainly for medicinal purposes and for the domestic manufacture of morphine. Foreign-manufactured morphine, codeine, and heroin made up the second class of imports, while the third was smoking opium, most of it prepared in Hong Kong and shipped to San Francisco.

The imposts on these imported drugs fluctuated over the years, but they were generally quite stiff. From 1866 to 1914 the average ad valorem duty on crude opium was 33 percent; for morphine or its salts, 48 percent. From 1866 to 1908 the average duty on smoking opium was an extraordinarily high 97 percent. This last was in the nature of a sin tax; congressmen identified opium smoking with Chinese coolies, gamblers, pimps, and prostitutes and wished to discourage its importation and use.

These customs duties produced revenue; they also produced widespread smuggling, much of it organized by violent criminal societies like the Chinese tongs. The smugglers were as ingenious as their latter-day Mafia counterparts. They hid their shipments in everything from hollowed-out lumber to snake cages. Avoiding the customs collectors, they saved as much as three dollars a pound on crude opium, three dollars an ounce on morphine, and twelve dollars a pound on smoking opium. Twelve dollars seems a trifling sum by modern standards, hardly worth the risk of arrest, but in the nineteenth century it was more than most workers earned in a week. Someone who smuggled in fifty pounds of smoking opium in 1895 had gained the equivalent of a year's wages. One knowledgeable authority estimated that when the duty on smoking opium was near its peak, the amount smuggled into the United States was nearly twice that legally imported and taxed. Something similar happened with eighteenth-century tobacco imports to the British Isles. More than a third of the tobacco consumed in England and Scotland circa 1750 had been clandestinely imported in order to avoid a duty of more than five pence per pound. The principle is the same for domestically produced drugs: If taxes are sufficiently onerous, an illegal supply system will spring up. Moonshining existed before and after, as well as during, Prohibition.

The obvious solution is to set taxes at a sufficiently low level to discourage smuggling and illegal manufacturing. But again there is a dilemma. The most important illicit drugs are processed agricultural products that can be grown in several parts of the world by peasant labor. They are not, in other words, intrinsically expensive. Unless they are heavily taxed, legal consumers will be able to acquire them at little cost, less than ten dollars for a gram of cocaine. If drugs are that cheap, to say nothing of being 100 percent pure, the likelihood of a postlegalization epidemic of addiction will be substantially increased. But if taxes are given a stiff boost to enhance revenues and limit consumption, black marketeers will re-enter the picture in numbers proportionate to the severity of the tax.

Tax revenues, like drugs themselves, can be addictive. In the twelve years after the repeal of Prohibition, federal liquor tax revenues ballooned from 259 million to 2.3 billion dollars. The government's dependence on this money was one important reason anti-liquor forces made so little progress in their attempts to restrict alcohol consumption during World War II. Controlled drug legalization would also bring about a windfall in tax dollars, which in an era of chronic deficits would surely be welcomed and quickly spent. Should addiction rates become too high, a conflict between public health and revenue concerns would inevitably ensue.

When both proponents and opponents of controlled legalization talk about drug taxes, they generally assume a single level of taxation. The assumption is wrong. The nature of the federal system permits state and local governments to levy their own taxes on drugs in addition to the uniform federal customs and excise taxes. This means that total drug taxes, and hence the prices paid by consumers, will vary from place to place. Variation invites interstate smuggling, and if the variation is large enough, the smuggling can be extensive and involve organized crime.

The history of cigarette taxation serves to illustrate this principle. In 1960 state taxes on cigarettes were low, between zero and eight cents per pack, but after 1965 a growing number of states sharply increased cigarette taxes in response to health concerns and as a politically painless way of increasing revenue. Some states, mainly in the Northeast, were considerably more aggressive than others in raising taxes. By 1975 North Carolina purchasers were paying thirty-six cents per pack while New Yorkers paid fifty-four cents. The price was higher still in New York City because of a local levy that reached eight cents per pack (as much as the entire federal tax) at the beginning of 1976.

Thus was born an opportunity to buy cheap and sell dear. Those who bought in volume at North Carolina prices and sold at New York (or Connecticut, or Massachusetts) prices realized a substantial profit, and by the mid-1970s net revenue losses stood at well over three hundred million dollars a year. Much of this went to organized crime, which at one point was bootlegging 25 percent of the cigarettes sold in New York State and *half* of those sold in New York City. The pioneer of the illegal traffic, Anthony Granata, established a trucking company with thirty employees operating vehicles on a six-days-a-week basis. Granata's methods—concealed cargoes, dummy corporations, forged documents, fortress-like warehouses, bribery, hijacking, assault, and homicide—were strikingly similar to those used by illicit drug traffickers and Prohibition bootleggers.

Although high-tax states like Florida or Illinois still lose millions annually to cigarette bootleggers, the 1978 federal Contraband Cigarette Act and stricter law enforcement and accounting procedures have had some success in reducing over-the-road smuggling. But it is relatively easy to detect illegal shipments of cigarettes, which must be smuggled by the truckload to make a substantial amount of money. Cocaine and heroin are more compact, more profitable, and very easy to conceal. Smuggling these drugs to take advantage of state tax differentials would consequently be much more difficult to detect and deter. If, for example, taxed cocaine retailed in Vermont for ten dollars a gram and in New York for twelve dollars a gram, anyone who bought just five kilograms at Vermont prices, transported them, and sold them at New York prices would realize a profit of ten thousand dollars. Five kilograms of cocaine can be concealed in an attaché case.

Of course, if all states legalized drugs and taxed them at the same rate, this sort of illegal activity would not exist, but it is constitutionally and politically unfeasible to ensure uniform rates of state taxation. And federalism poses other challenges. Laws against drug use and trafficking have been enacted at the local, state, and federal levels. It is

DARING DRUG EXPOSE

SHAME HORROR DESPAIR

MARIHUANA

WEED with ROOTS In HELL

NOT RECOMMENDED FOR CHILDREN

MISERY

Smoke That Gets In Youth's Eyes

LUST CRIME SORROW

HATE SHAME DESPAIR

What Happens at Marihuana Parties

WEIRD ORGIES WILD PARTIES UNLEASHED **PASSIONS**

The original poster for a movie revived in the 1960s as *Reefer Madness*.

probable that if Congress repeals or modifies the national drug laws, some states will go along with controlled legalization while others will not. Nevada, long in the legalizing habit, might jettison its drug laws, but conservative Mormon-populated Utah might not. Alternately, governments could experiment with varying degrees of legalization. Congress might decide that anything was better than the current mayhem in the capital and legislate a broad legalization program for the District of Columbia. At the same time, Virginia and Maryland might experiment with the decriminalization of marijuana, the least risky legalization option, but retain prohibition of the non-medical use of other drugs. The result would again be smuggling, whether from Nevada to Utah or, save for marijuana, from the District of Columbia to the surrounding states. It is hard to see how any state that chose to retain laws against drugs could possibly stanch the influx of prohibited drugs from adjacent states that did not. New York City's futile attempts to enforce its strict gun-control laws show how difficult it is to restrict locally that which is elsewhere freely available.

I referred earlier to the legalization debate as an argument about a colossal gamble, whether society should risk an unknown increase in drug abuse and addiction to eliminate the harms of drug prohibition, most of which stem from illicit trafficking. "Take the crime out of it" is the rallying cry of the legalization advocates. After reviewing the larger history of narcotic, alcohol, and tobacco use and regulation, it appears that this debate should be recast. It would be more accurate to ask whether society should risk an unknown but possibly substantial increase in drug abuse and addiction in order to bring about an unknown *reduction* in illicit trafficking and other costs of drug prohibition. Controlled legalization would take some, but by no means all, of the crime out of it. Just how much and what sort of crime would be eliminated would depend upon which groups were to be denied which drugs, the overall level of taxation, and differences in state tax and legalization policies. If the excluded groups were few *and* all states legalized all drugs *and* all governments taxed at uniformly low levels, then the black market would be largely eliminated. But these are precisely the conditions that would be most likely to bring about an unacceptably high level of drug abuse. The same variables that would determine how successful the controlled-legalization policy would be in eliminating the black market would also largely determine how unsuccessful it was in containing drug addiction.

David T. Courtwright is a professor of history at the University of North Florida and the author of *Dark Paradise: Opiate Addiction in America Before 1940* (Harvard University Press, 1982) and *Addicts Who Survived: An Oral History of Narcotic Use in America, 1923–1965* (University of Tennessee Press, 1989).

"Altered States: and Other Drugs in America," a lively and wide-ranging exhibit on substance use and abuse, will be on display at the Strong Museum in Rochester, New York, through mid-1994. It will then travel to other cities under the auspices of the Smithsonian Institution.

Testing Workers for Drugs Reduces Company Problems

Joseph B. Treaster

Back in the mid-1980's, Daniel Burke worried about the growing national drug problem and whether his children might be tempted to experiment. But he never thought of drugs as a problem for his company until an employee in New York City died of a cocaine overdose in an office stairwell.

"It turned out this guy had been dealing, too," said Mr. Burke, the president of Capital Cities/ABC Inc. "And a great number of our employees knew it."

That incident became the catalyst for a program of drug testing, anti-drug education and counseling at Capital Cities/ABC, and similar programs have quietly become fixtures in nearly every major American company. These efforts, costing hundreds of millions of dollars, have sharply reduced drug use in factories and offices, executives and industrial drug experts say, and resulted in fewer accidents, lower absenteeism and less employee turnover. Moreover, the experts say, corporate anti-drug campaigns have contributed to an overall decline in casual drug use around the country.

"Corporate programs make drug use more of a hassle and make it seem less socially acceptable," said Dr. Robert B. Millman, the director of alcohol and drug abuse programs at the New York Hospital–Payne Whitney Psychiatric Clinic. "There's no question they have driven down drug use."

Dr. Kent W. Peterson, a vice president of the American College of Occupational and Environmental Medicine and a consultant to companies on drug problems, said there is clearly a "spin-off effect" on the rest of society.

"Company drug policies are often discussed with spouses," Dr. Peterson said. "They get communicated to children and they affect one's social and recreational life. They have also sensitized community leaders to the fact that something can be done and that this is not something they have to passively accept."

Two of the largest drug-testing companies, Roche Biomedical Labs, and SmithKline Beecham Clinical Laboratories estimate that 15 million Americans or 13 percent of the work force are being required to give urine samples for testing annually, up from half that five years ago and costing $600 million.

Between 5 and 8 percent of those tested by the two big labs are found to have drugs in their system, com-pany officials said. Of those, 40 to 50 percent have been using marijuana, 20 to 25 percent cocaine, and about 10 percent opiates, mainly codeine, but occasionally heroin. The rest test positive for either amphetamines; an animal tranquilizer known as PCP, or angel dust, or a variety of mainly prescription drugs that are sometimes abused. Medical doctors review the results and verify legitimate prescription drug use.

Drug experts say that people can beat drug tests by presenting a clean sample of someone else's urine, adulterating their own sample or by taking certain substances that diminish the percentage of drugs in the system. But they say research suggests that only the most committed drug users are persistently willing to put their jobs—or their chance of getting a job—in jeopardy.

Tests Brought Civil Suits

While some surveys show employees strongly support drug testing because it promises greater safety and harmony at work, scores of civil suits in the early and mid-1980's challenged the procedure as an invasion of privacy. The courts, however, have upheld most testing programs, and many fewer suits are being filed these days.

Even the American Civil Liberties Union, which filed many of the suits, acknowledges that drug testing has reduced drug use. But Lewis Maltby, an A.C.L.U. specialist on the issue, said that instead of taking urine samples companies should be testing reflexes and general performance with electronic devices similar to computer games that are now becoming available.

Many employers say their new approach has reduced accidents.

"These tests are non-invasive," Mr. Maltby said. "They're a lot like playing Pac Man. There's a TV screen in front of you and you move a dot with a joy stick. No one has got to drop their pants to take these tests."

David G. Evans, a lawyer who has written books on drug testing and employee rehabilitation programs, says that performance tests measure hand-eye coordination, but not judgment and memory.

People have objected most to random drug testing, which is mainly limited to Government and private jobs that affect public safety, like those at nuclear power plants, airlines, railroads and trucking companies. More than 90 percent of the testing, experts say, is of job applicants. But most of these same companies also test after accidents and when suspicions are aroused through erratic behavior. Fewer than 10 percent of the companies test randomly or at the time of annual physicals.

Regardless of the type of testing, the experts say, the bedrock of every corporate drug program is a simple policy statement banning drugs which, in itself, serves as a powerful deterrent. Research has found that testing, combined with education

and rehabilitation, is most effective in reducing drug use.

Small and medium-size companies have trailed large corporations on drug programs, but many are now banding together to get lower rates on drug testing and rehabilitation services. Last Wednesday, for example, the New Jersey State Chamber of Commerce announced that it would begin helping small businesses make group purchases of these services.

At the impetus of former President Ronald Reagan, who campaigned for a "drug-free workplace," the military and many Federal agencies pioneered institutional anti-drug programs that became models for industry. Now anti-drug programs are being recognized as so effective in cutting health costs that some states and private insurance companies are offering incentives for setting them up. Florida, for example, provides a 5 percent reduction in workers' compensation payments to companies with anti-drug programs, and Blue Cross and Blue Shield of Virginia is paying for drug testing for small businesses in a pilot program.

For all their success, corporate drug programs have received little attention beyond the legal challenges, in part because of a reluctance of executives to associate their companies with drugs in any way. "Even if they've been successful, companies are afraid of tarnishing their image by talking about drug problems," said J. Michael Walsh, the former executive director of the President's Drug Advisory Council under George Bush.

Every company that has instituted drug programs has recorded steep drops in drug incidents. When Pfizer Inc., the New York-based pharmaceutical company, started testing job applicants in 1987, 9.9 percent turned up with evidence of having recently used drugs. But by last year, the percentage had fallen to 3.2 Hoffmann-LaRoche, the big pharmaceutical company with its United States headquarters in New Jersey, found about 7 percent of its job applicants were using drugs when the

company began testing a decade ago. Now it is fewer than 1 percent.

Many companies offer counseling and treatment to employees found using drugs and give them a second chance, sometimes even a third. But applicants get no help. They are simply not hired and many never learn why. At the least, Dr. Millman, of New York Hospital, said, job applicants should be confronted with their drug use and referred to rehabilitation services.

Assessing the Need for Tests

Some companies say they started drug programs without knowing whether they had a problem. But at many others, like Texas Instruments, in Dallas, there was no doubt.

"It was not unusual for us to get reports of drugs being used or sold in one of our plants," said Chuck Nielson, the vice president for human resources. "I'm sure we would have at least 10 to 15 incidents a year."

But now, nearly four years after the company began its program, Mr. Nielson says drug incidents have become "almost nonexistent."

"I can't remember when we had the last one," he said.

Harold C. Green, the owner of a paving and painting company with 50 employees in Laurel, Md., knew he had a problem, too. One of his dump truck drivers drove off a bridge. Two others crashed into each other, and a heavy equipment operator ran down a foreman and broke his leg. His annual workers compensation costs soared to nearly $100,000.

Mr. Green put a drug program with random testing, rehabilitation and seminars on drug and alcohol abuse, stress and safety procedures that is costing $6,000 to $8,000 a year and his spending on workers compensation plunged to $30,000.

"Also," he said, "it's going to cost you a lot less to treat an individual than to go out and put an advertisement in the newspaper, hire, train and bring someone up to speed on how the company operates."

Everything seemed to be going smoothly at the fruit-juice processing plants and warehouses of Tropicana Products Inc. in Florida, New Jersey and New York, but Robert L. Soran, the president, and Martin J. Gutfreund, the vice president for human resources, noticed employees' names popping up in newspaper reports of drug arrests.

They started testing and found 25 percent of their job applicants were using drugs. Soon, 75 percent of the company's 3,800 employees, mainly those who operated machinery, were being tested randomly.

A Blunt Statement

Before testing started, everyone was notified of the new anti-drug policy and drug rehabilitation was made available. Tropicana did not spend money on anti-drug education, but issued a blunt statement: Illicit drug use would not be tolerated; anyone who asked for help could get it without penalty, but anyone caught using drugs would be dismissed.

Accidents dropped by 50 percent, he said, and employee turnover fell by 20 percent. After six years of testing, he said, 5 to 6 percent of the job applicants were testing positive.

Last year, Mr. Soran and Mr. Gutfreund moved to Uniroyal Technology Corporation, which also is based in Florida and does business in New Jersey, Connecticut and elsewhere in the country. Early this year, they introduced the kind of drug program they had developed at Tropicana.

Though casual drug use has fallen sharply in the country in recent years, the two executives know how hard it is to eliminate it. Only last month, Mr. Gutfreund said, Uniroyal in Sterling, N.J., offered a mechanic's job to four people before it found one who had not been using drugs.

TOWARD A POLICY ON DRUGS

Decriminalization? Legalization?

Elliott Currie

Elliott Currie is the author of the award-winning Confronting Crime: An American Challenge.

One of the strongest implications of what we now know about the causes of endemic drug abuse is that the criminal-justice system's effect on the drug crisis will inevitably be limited. That shouldn't surprise us in the 1990s; it has, after all, been a central argument of drug research since the 1950s. Today, as the drug problem has worsened, the limits of the law are if anything even clearer. But that does not mean that the justice system has no role to play in a more effective strategy against drugs. Drugs will always be a "law-enforcement problem" in part, and the real job is to define what we want the police and the courts to accomplish.

We will never, for reasons that will shortly become clear, punish our way out of the drug crisis. We can, however, use the criminal-justice system, in small but significant ways, to improve the prospects of drug users who are now caught in an endless loop of court, jail, and street. And we can use law enforcement, in small but significant ways, to help strengthen the ability of drug-ridden communities to defend themselves against violence, fear, and demoralization. Today the criminal-justice system does very little of the first and not enough of the second. But doing these things well will require far-reaching changes in our priorities.

Above all, we will have to shift from an approach in which discouraging drug use through punishment and fear takes central place to one that emphasizes three very different principles: the reintegration of drug abusers into productive life, the reduction of harm, and the promotion of community safety.

This is a tall order, but, as we shall see, something similar is being practiced in many countries that suffer far less convulsing drug problems than we do. Their experience suggests that a different and more humane criminal-justice response to drugs is both possible and practical. Today, there is much debate about the role of the justice system in a rational drug policy—but for the most part, the debate is between those who would intensify the effort to control drugs through the courts and prisons and those who want to take drugs out of the orbit of the justice system altogether. I do not think that either approach takes sufficient account of the social realities of drug abuse; and both, consequently, exaggerate the role of regulatory policies in determining the shape and seriousness of the problem. But those are not the only alternatives. In between, there is a range of more promising strategies— what some Europeans call a "third way"—that is more attuned to those realities and more compatible with our democratic values.

One response to the failure of the drug war has been to call for more of what we've already done—even harsher sentences, still more money for jails and prisons—on the grounds that we have simply not provided enough resources to fight the war effectively. That position is shared by the Bush administration and many Democrats in Congress as well. But the strategy of upping the ante cannot work;

From *Dissent*, Winter 1993, pp. 65-71. Excerpted from "Rethinking Criminal Justice" from *Reckoning: Drugs, the Cities, and the American Future* by Elliott Currie. © 1993 by Elliott Currie. Reprinted by permission of Hill and Wang, a division of Farrar, Straus & Giroux, Inc.

and even to attempt it on a large scale would dramatically increase the social costs that an overreliance on punishment has already brought. We've seen that the effort to contain the drug problem through force and fear has already distorted our justice system in fundamental ways and caused a rippling of secondary costs throughout the society as a whole. Much more of this would alter the character of American society beyond recognition. And it would not solve the drug problem.

Why wouldn't more of the same do the job?

To understand why escalating the war on drugs would be unlikely to make much difference—short of efforts on a scale that would cause unprecedented social damage—we need to consider how the criminal-justice system is, in theory, *supposed* to work to reduce drug abuse and drug-related crime. Criminologists distinguish between two mechanisms by which punishment may decrease illegal behavior. One is "incapacitation," an unlovely term that simply means that locking people up will keep them—as long as they are behind bars—from engaging in the behavior we wish to suppress. The other is "deterrence," by which we mean either that people tempted to engage in the behavior will be persuaded otherwise by the threat of punishment ("general deterrence"), or that individuals, once punished, will be less likely to engage in the behavior again ("specific deterrence"). What makes the drug problem so resistant to even very heavy doses of criminalization is that neither mechanism works effectively for most drug offenders—particularly those most heavily involved in the drug subcultures of the street.

The main reason why incapacitation is unworkable as a strategy against drug offenders is that there are so many of them that a serious attempt to put them all—or even just the "hard core"—behind bars is unrealistic, even in the barest fiscal terms. This is obvious if we pause to recall the sheer number of people who use hard drugs in the United States. Consider the estimates of the number of people who have used drugs during the previous year provided annually by the NIDA (National Institute on Drug Abuse) Household Survey—which substantially *understates* the extent of hard-drug use. Even if we exclude the more than 20 million people who used marijuana in the past year, the number of hard-drug users is enormous: the survey estimates over six million cocaine users in 1991 (including over a million who used crack), about 700,000 heroin users,

and 5.7 million users of hallucinogens and inhalants. Even if we abandon the aim of imprisoning less serious hard-drug users, thus allowing the most conservative accounting of the costs of incapacitation, the problem remains staggering: by the lowest estimates, there are no fewer than two million hard-core abusers of cocaine and heroin alone.

If we take as a rough approximation that about 25 percent of America's prisoners are behind bars for drug offenses, that gives us roughly 300,000 drug offenders in prison at any given point—and this after several years of a hugely implemented war mainly directed at lower-level dealers and street drug users. We have seen what this flood of offenders has done to the nation's courts and prisons, but what is utterly sobering is that even this massive effort at repression has barely scratched the surface: according to the most optimistic estimate, we may at any point be incarcerating on drug-related charges about one-eighth of the country's hard-core cocaine and heroin abusers. And where drug addiction is truly endemic, the disparity is greater. By 1989 there were roughly 20,000 drug offenders on any given day in New York State's prisons, but there were an estimated 200,000 to 250,000 *heroin* addicts in New York City alone. To be sure, these figures obscure the fact that many prisoners behind bars for *non*drug offenses are also hard-core drug users; but the figures are skewed in the other direction by the large (if unknown) number of active drug dealers who are not themselves addicted.

Thus, though we cannot quantify these proportions with any precision, the basic point should be clear: the pool of *serious* addicts and active dealers is far, far larger than the numbers we now hold in prison—even in the midst of an unprecedented incarceration binge that has made us far and away the world's leader in imprisonment rates.

What would it mean to expand our prison capacity enough to put the *majority* of hard-core users and dealers behind bars for long terms? To triple the number of users and low-level dealers behind bars, even putting two drug offenders to a cell, would require about 300,000 new cells. At a conservative estimate of about $100,000 per cell, that means a $30 billion investment in construction alone. If we then assume an equally conservative estimate of about $25,000 in yearly operating costs per inmate, we add roughly $15 billion a year to our current costs. Yet this would leave the majority of drug dealers and hard-core addicts still on the streets and, of course, would do nothing to prevent new ones from emerging in otherwise unchanged communities to take the place of those behind bars.

It is not entirely clear, moreover, what that huge expenditure would, in fact, accomplish. For if the goal is to prevent the drug dealing and other crimes that addicts commit, the remedy may literally cost more than the disease. Although drug addicts do commit a great deal of crime, most of them are very minor ones, mainly petty theft and small-time drug dealing. This pattern has been best illuminated in the study of Harlem heroin addicts by Bruce Johnson and his co-workers. Most of the street addicts in this study were "primarily thieves and small-scale drug distributors who avoided serious crimes, like robbery, burglary, assault." The average income per nondrug crime among these addicts was $35. Even among the most criminally active group—what these researchers called "robber-dealers"—the annual income from crime amounted on average to only about $21,000, and for the great majority—about 70 percent—of less active addict-criminals, it ranged from $5,000 to $13,000. At the same time, the researchers estimated that the average cost per day of confining one addict in a New York City jail cell was roughly $100, or $37,000 a year. Putting these numbers together, Johnson and his co-workers came to the startling conclusion that it would cost considerably more to lock up all of Harlem's street addicts than to simply let them continue to "take care of business" on the street.

If we cannot expect much from intensified criminalization, would the legalization of hard drugs solve the drug crisis?

No: it would not. To understand why, we need to consider the claims for legalization's effects in the light of what we know about the roots and meanings of endemic drug abuse. First, however, we need to step back in order to sort out exactly what we *mean* by "legalization"—a frustratingly vague and often confused term that means very different things to different interpreters. Many, indeed, who argue most vehemently one way or the other about the merits of legalization are not really clear just what it is they are arguing *about*.

At one end of the spectrum are those who mean by legalization the total deregulation of the production, sale, and use of all drugs—hard and soft. Advocates of this position run the gamut from right-wing economists to some staunch liberals, united behind the principle that government has no business interfering in individuals' choice to ingest whatever substances they desire. Most who subscribe to that general view would add several qualifiers: for example, that drugs (like alcohol) should not be sold to minors, or that drug advertising should be regulated or prohibited, or (less often) that drugs should be sold only in government-run stores, as alcohol is in some states. But these are seen as necessary, if sometimes grudging, exceptions to the general rule that private drug transactions should not be the province of government intervention. For present purposes, I will call this the "free-market" approach to drug control, and describe its central aim as the "deregulation" of the drug market.

Another approach would not go so far as to deregulate the drug trade, but would opt for the controlled dispensation of drugs to addicts who have been certified by a physician, under strict guidelines as to amounts and conditions of use. Something like this "medical model," in varying forms, guided British policy toward heroin after the 1920s. Under the so-called British system, addicts could receive heroin from physicians or clinics—but the private production and distribution of heroin was always subject to strong penalties, as was the use of the drug except in its medical or "pharmaceutical" form. (A small-scale experiment in cocaine prescription is presently being tried in the city of Liverpool.) Since the seventies, the British have largely abandoned prescribing heroin in favor of methadone—a synthetic opiate that blocks the body's craving for heroin but, among other things, produces less of a pleasurable "high" and lasts considerably longer. The practice of dispensing methadone to heroin addicts came into wide use in the United States in the 1960s and remains a major form of treatment. Methadone prescription, of course, does not "legalize" heroin, and the possession or sale of methadone itself is highly illegal outside of the strictly controlled medical relationship.

Still another meaning sometimes given to legalization is what is more accurately called the "decriminalization" of drug *use*. We may continue to define the production and sale of certain drugs as crimes and subject them to heavy penalties, but not punish those who only *use* the drugs (or have small amounts in their possession), or punish them very lightly—with small fines, for example, rather than jail. Something close to this is the practice in Holland, which is often wrongly perceived as a country that has legalized drugs. Though drug use remains technically illegal, Dutch policy is to focus most law-enforcement resources on sales, especially on larger traffickers, while dealing with users mainly through treatment programs and other social services, rather than the police and courts.

Another aspect of Dutch policy illustrates a further possible meaning of legalization: we may selectively decriminalize *some* drugs, in some amounts, and not others. The Dutch, in practice—though not in law—have tolerated both sale and use of small amounts of marijuana and hashish, but not heroin or cocaine. A German court has recently ruled that possession of small amounts of hashish and marijuana is not a crime, and, indeed, marijuana possession has largely been decriminalized in some American states, though usually as a matter of practical policy rather than legislation.

Let me make my own view clear. I think much would be gained if we followed the example of some European countries and moved toward decriminalization of the drug user. I also think there is a strong argument for treating marijuana differently from the harder drugs, and that there is room for careful experiment with strictly controlled medical prescription for some addicts. For reasons that will become clear, decriminalization is not a panacea; it will not end the drug crisis, but it could substantially decrease the irrationality and inhumanity of our present punitive war on drugs.

The free-market approach, on the other hand, is another matter entirely. Some variant of that approach is more prominent in drug-policy debates in the United States than in other developed societies, probably because it meshes with a strongly individualistic and antigovernment political culture. Indeed, the degree to which the debate over drug policy has been dominated by the clash between fervent drug "warriors" and equally ardent free-market advocates is a peculiarly American phenomenon. Much of that clash is about philosophical principles, and addressing those issues in detail would take more space than we have. My aim here is simply to examine the empirical claims of the free-market perspective

in the light of what we know about the social context of drug abuse. Here the free-market view fails to convince. It greatly exaggerates the benefits of deregulation while simultaneously underestimating the potential costs.

There is no question that the criminalization of drugs produces negative secondary consequences—especially in the unusually punitive form that criminalization has taken in the United States. Nor is there much question that this argues for a root-and-branch rethinking of our current punitive strategy—to which we'll return later in this essay—especially our approach to drug *users*.

But proponents of full-scale deregulation of hard drugs also tend to gloss over the very real primary costs of drug abuse—particularly on the American level—and to exaggerate the degree to which the multiple pathologies surrounding drug use in America are simply an unintended result of a "prohibitionist" regulatory policy. No country now legalizes the sale of hard drugs. Yet no other country has anything resembling the American drug problem. That alone should tell us that more than prohibition is involved in shaping the magnitude and severity of our drug crisis. But there is more technical evidence as well. It confirms that much (though, of course, not all) of the harm caused by endemic drug abuse is intrinsic to the impact of hard drugs themselves (and the street cultures in which drug abuse is embedded) within the context of a glaringly unequal, depriving, and deteriorating society. And it affirms that we will not substantially reduce that harm without attacking the social roots of the extraordinary demand for hard drugs in the United States. Just as we cannot punish our way out of the drug crisis, neither will we escape its grim toll by deregulating the drug market.

The most important argument for a free-market approach has traditionally been that it would reduce or eliminate the crime and violence now inextricably entwined with addiction to drugs and with the drug trade. In this view it is precisely the illegality of drug use that is responsible for drug-related crime—which, in turn, is seen as by far the largest part of the overall problem of urban violence. Criminal sanctions against drugs, as one observer insists, "cause the bulk of murders and property crime in major urban areas." Because criminalization makes drugs far more costly than they would otherwise be, addicts are forced to commit crimes in order to gain enough income to afford their habits. Moreover, they are forced to seek out actively criminal people in order to obtain their drugs, which exposes them to even more destructive criminal influences. At the same time, the fact that the drug trade is illegal means both that it is hugely profitable and that the inevitable conflicts and disputes over "turf" or between dealers and users cannot be resolved or moderated by legal mechanisms, and hence are usually resolved by violence.

For all of these reasons, it is argued, outlawing drugs has the unintended, but inevitable, effect of causing a flood of crime and urban violence that would not exist otherwise and sucking young people, especially, into a bloody drug trade. If we legalize the sale and use of hard drugs, the roots of drug-related violence would be severed, and much of the larger crisis of criminal violence in the cities would disappear.

But the evidence suggests that although this view contains an element of truth, it is far too simplistic—and that it relies on stereotypical assumptions about the relationship between drugs and crime that have been called into serious question since the classic drug research of the 1950s. In particular, the widely held notion that most of the crime committed by addicts can be explained by their need for money to buy illegal drugs does not fit well with the evidence.

In its popular form, the drugs-cause-crime argument is implicitly based on the assumption that addict crime is caused by pharmacological compulsion—as a recent British study puts it, on a kind of "enslavement" model in which the uncontrollable craving for drugs forces an otherwise law-abiding citizen to engage in crime for gain. As we've seen, however, a key finding of most of the research into the meaning of drug use and the growth of drug subcultures since the 1950s has been that the purely pharmacological craving for drugs is by no means the most important motive for drug use. Nor is it clear that those cravings are typically so uncontrollable that addicts are in any meaningful sense "driven" to crime to satisfy them.

On the surface, there is much to suggest a strong link between crime and the imperatives of addiction. The studies of addict crime by John Ball and Douglas Anglin and their colleagues show not only that the most heavily addicted commit huge numbers of crimes, but also that their crime rates seem to increase when their heroin use increases and to fall when it declines. Thus, for example, heroin addicts in Ball's study in Baltimore had an average of 255 "crime days" per year when they were actively addicted, versus about 65 when they were not. In general, the level of property crime appears in these studies to go up simultaneously with increasing intensity of drug use. One explanation, and perhaps the most common one, is that the increased need for money to buy drugs drives addicts into more crime.

But a closer look shows that things are considerably more complicated. To begin with, it is a recurrent finding that most people who both abuse drugs and commit crimes began committing the crimes *before* they began using drugs—meaning that their need for drugs cannot have caused their initial criminal involvement (though it may have accelerated it later). George Vaillant's follow-up study of addicts and alcoholics found, for example, that, unlike alcoholics, heroin addicts had typically been involved in delinquency and crime well before they began their career of substance abuse. While alcoholics seemed to become involved in crime as a *result* of their abuse of alcohol, more than half of the heroin addicts (versus just 5 percent of the alcoholics) "were known to have been delinquent *before* drug abuse." A federal survey of drug use among prison inmates in 1986, similarly, found that three-fifths of those who had ever used a "major drug" regularly—that is, heroin, cocaine, methadone, PCP, or LSD—had not done so until after their first arrest.

Other studies have found that for many addicts, drug use and crime seem to have begun more or less *independently* without one clearly causing the other. This was the finding, for example, in Charles Faupel and Carl Klockars's study of hard-core heroin addicts in Wilmington, Delaware. "All of our respondents," they note, "reported some criminal activity prior to their first use of heroin." Moreover, "perhaps most importantly, virtually all of our respondents reported that they believed that their criminal and drug careers began independently of one another, although both careers became intimately interconnected as each evolved."

More recent research shows that the drugs-crime relationship may be even more complex than this suggests. It is not only that crime may precede drug use, especially heavy or addictive use, or that both may emerge more or less independently; it is also likely that there are several *different* kinds of drugs-crime connections among different types of drug users. David Nurco of the University of Maryland and his colleagues, for example, studying heroin addicts in Baltimore and New York City, found that nine different kinds of addicts could be distinguished by the type and severity of their crimes. Like earlier researchers, they found that most addicts committed large numbers of crimes—mainly drug dealing and small-scale property crime, notably shoplifting, burglary, and fencing. Others were involved in illegal gambling and what the researchers called "deception crimes"—including forgery and con games—and a relatively small percentage had engaged in violent crime. On the whole, addicts heavily involved in one type of crime were not likely to be involved in others; as the researchers put it, they tended to be either "dealers or stealers," but rarely both. About 6 percent of the addicts, moreover, were "uninvolved"—they did not commit crimes either while addicted or before, or during periods of nonaddiction interspersed in the course of their longer addiction careers.

The most troubling group of addicts—what the researchers called "violent generalists"— were only about 7 percent of the total sample, but they were extremely active—and very dangerous; they accounted for over half of all the violent crimes committed by the entire sample. Moreover, revealingly, the violent generalists were very active in serious crime *before* they became addicted to narcotics as well as during periods of nonaddiction thereafter—again demonstrating that the violence was not dependent on their addiction itself. Nurco and his colleagues measured the addicts' criminal activity by what they called "crime days" per year. Addicts were asked how many days they had committed each of several types of crime; since on any given day they might have committed more than one type of crime, the resulting figure could add up to more than the number of days in the year. The violent generalists averaged an astonishing 900 crime days a year over the course of their careers. The rates were highest during periods when they were heavily addicted to drugs. But even *before* they were addicted, they averaged 573 crime days, and 491 after their addiction had ended. Indeed, the most active group of violent generalists engaged in more crime *prior* to addiction than any other group did *while* addicted. And they continued to commit

crimes—often violent ones—long after they had ceased to be addicted to narcotics.

None of this is to deny that serious addiction to heroin or other illegal drugs can accelerate the level of crime among participants in the drug culture, or stimulate crime even in some users who are otherwise not criminal. Higher levels of drug use *do* go hand in hand with increased crime, especially property crime. Certainly, many addicts mug, steal, or sell their bodies for drugs. The point is that—as the early drug researchers discovered in the 1950s—both crime and drug abuse tend to be spawned by the same set of unfavorable social circumstances, and they interact with one another in much more complex ways than the simple addiction-leads-to-crime view proposes. Simply providing drugs more easily to people enmeshed in the drug cultures of the cities is not likely to cut the deep social roots of addict crime.

If we take the harms of drug abuse seriously, and I think we must, we cannot avoid being deeply concerned about anything that would significantly increase the availability of hard drugs within the American social context; and no one seriously doubts that legalization would indeed increase availability, and probably lower prices for many drugs. In turn, increased availability—as we know from the experience with alcohol—typically leads to increased consumption, and with it increased social and public-health costs. A growing body of research, for example, shows that most alcohol-related health problems, including deaths from cirrhosis and other diseases, were far lower during Prohibition than afterward, when per capita alcohol consumption rose dramatically (by about 75 percent, for example, between 1950 and 1980). It is difficult to imagine why a similar rise in consumption—and in the associated public-health problems—would not follow the full-scale legalization of cocaine, heroin, methamphetamine, and PCP (not to mention the array of as yet undiscovered "designer" drugs that a legalized corporate drug industry would be certain to develop).

If consumption increased, it would almost certainly increase most among the strata already most vulnerable to hard-drug use—thus exacerbating the social stratification of the drug crisis. It is among the poor and near-poor that offsetting measures like education and drug treatment are least effective and where the countervailing social supports and opportunities are least strong. We would expect, therefore, that a free-market policy applied to hard drugs would produce the same results it has created with the *legal* killer drugs, tobacco and alcohol—namely, a widening disparity in use between the better-off and the disadvantaged. And that disparity is already stunning. According to a recent study by Colin McCord and Howard Freeman of Harlem Hospital, between 1979 and 1981—that is, *before* the crack epidemic of the eighties—Harlem blacks were 283 times as likely to die of drug dependency as whites in the general population. Drug deaths, combined with deaths from cirrhosis, alcoholism, cardiovascular disease, and homicide, helped to give black men in Harlem a shorter life expectancy than men in Bangladesh. That is the social reality that the rather abstract calls for the legalization of hard-drug sales tend to ignore.

U.S. Aid Hasn't Stopped Drug Flow From South America, Experts Say

James Brooke

Special to The New York Times

LIMA, Peru, Nov. 20—It was the summer of 1989, and drug lords were gunning down presidential candidates in Colombia and flooding American cities with cocaine. Declaring that there was "no match for an angry America," President Bush announced that he was expanding the war on drugs.

Though his main pledge was to crack down on street sales, Mr. Bush also asked Congress to increase spending to help cut off the drug supply at its source in Peru, Colombia and Bolivia.

Four years and roughly $2 billion later, drug policy experts interviewed throughout the Andes share a conclusion: The flow of drugs from South America to North America has not slowed.

"We haven't had any real impact on the drug flow," one official at the United States Embassy here said. He noted that Peru seized 7 tons of cocaine and cocaine base last year out of an estimated 650 tons produced there. "That's peanuts," he said.

Failed Campaigns

American drug enforcement agents have tried forcible eradication of crops of coca leaf, the essential ingredient of cocaine; substituting other crops for coca; destroying cocaine

The New York Times

At Santa Lucia, the United States has spent about $100 million for a base in fighting coca leaf cultivation in the Huallaga Valley.

laboratories, and tightening customs controls on refining chemicals. They have patrolled the skies to interdict flights by drug planes and widened investigations of money laundering by traffickers.

Aid to Peru, Bolivia, Colombia and Ecuador is being cut.

But in a market dictated by supply and demand, the American-financed efforts have at best raised operating costs in a highly profitable business. In one indication that there is no shortage on the streets, the prices and purity levels of illegal drugs sold

in the United States have remained relatively stable over the last four years.

Today Washington is sending crossed signals to South America on the future of the drug war. Clinton Administration officials are talking about "tracking down the bees in the hive" and devoting more money to catching cocaine traffickers in the source countries.

"We can't stop our efforts—that would be to doom a number of these countries to even greater attack by narco-traffickers," said Timothy E. Wirth, a State Department counselor who advises the White House on drug policy.

Congress Cuts Funds

But Congress is cutting aid to Peru, Bolivia, Colombia and Ecuador for military and police action to block drug shipments by about one third this year, to roughly $90 million. Overall American aid for anti-drug efforts in Peru, Colombia and Bolivia is also declining.

"The Clinton Administration is afraid to say that an international drug war can't work," said Kevin B. Zeese, vice president of the Drugs Policy Foundation, a Washington-based group.

The reaction in the Andean countries has been muted. Many South Americans say their governments joined the so-called drug war only to soothe the United States and were always skeptical that its enforcement strategies would work.

"Drugs are only on the agenda in Peru when Fujimori goes to the U.S. or when Lee Brown comes through Lima," said Roberto Lerner Stein, a local drug expert, referring to Alberto K. Fujimori, the Peruvian President. On the day that Mr. Brown, President Clinton's top drug policy official, visited Lima last August, Peru's Congress approved a bill requiring that convicted traffickers get life sentences.

A case study of the obstacles to enforcement is offered at Santa Lucia, a mountain base in Peru's Huallega Valley that has cost American taxpayers about $100 million over the last five years. Four years ago, American Embassy officials talked enthusiastically of using Santa Lucia as a base for eradicating coca leaf cultivation in the valley, Peru's prime growing area.

Air and Land Attack

Initially joint teams of Peruvians and Americans descended by helicopter to mountain slopes and attacked fields of coca bushes with weed cutters. But Shining Path guerrillas fired on the helicopters, forcing police officers to abandon the manual eradication exercise.

Then the United States experimented with aerial spraying of herbicides in an attempt to kill the crops. Peru's Government then blocked that move out of fear of driving unemployed and desperate peasants into the ranks of the Shining Path.

Cocaine laboratories and drug planes were the next targets. Guided by American-supplied radar, Peruvian Air Force pilots have shot down or forced down eight small planes used for trafficking this year—a tiny fraction of the hundreds that are estimated to carry drugs from Peru annually.

And when cocaine trafficking is pressured in one area, it shifts to another. Colombian planes now often fly over Brazil before darting into Peru for pickups.

On the ground, traffickers have shifted refining operations in Peru from enormous factory-size laboratories to mobile, easily concealed jungle labs. To reduce transportation costs, leaders of Colombia's powerful cocaine cartels also increasingly refine cocaine in Bolivia. Cocaine now accounts for two-thirds of Bolivia's drug exports, up from one-third at the start of the drug war.

Change of Route

Police efforts have also prompted traffickers to diversify their export routes. Today the lion's share of South America's cocaine exports slips through countries that are not significant producers, including Argentina, Brazil, Ecuador, Mexico and Venezuela.

On Nov. 6, the Venezuelan police broke up a trafficking ring that was reported to be shipping one ton of Colombian cocaine a month to the United States. Underscoring Venezuela's role as a transit country, United States officials acknowledged on Friday that a C.I.A. anti-drug program there accidentally allowed a ton of nearly pure cocaine to be shipped to the United States in 1990.

Similarly, coca leaf cultivation in Peru has shifted out of helicopter range of Santa Lucia, which is in the Upper Huallaga River Valley. Moving into the central and lower valley, about 200,000 farmers now grow

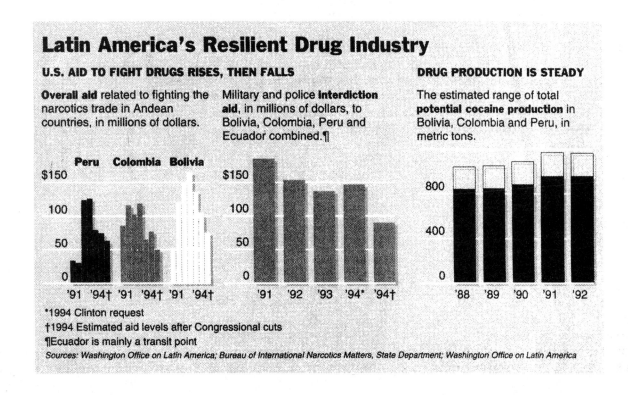

Latin America's Resilient Drug Industry

U.S. AID TO FIGHT DRUGS RISES, THEN FALLS

Overall aid related to fighting the narcotics trade in Andean countries, in millions of dollars.

Peru Colombia Bolivia

$150
100
50
0

'91 '94† '91 '94† '91 '94†

Military and police **interdiction aid**, in millions of dollars, to Bolivia, Colombia, Peru and Ecuador combined.¶

$150
100
50
0

'91 '92 '93 '94* '94†

DRUG PRODUCTION IS STEADY

The estimated range of total **potential cocaine production** in Bolivia, Colombia and Peru, in metric tons.

800
400
0

'88 '89 '90 '91 '92

*1994 Clinton request
†1994 Estimated aid levels after Congressional cuts
¶Ecuador is mainly a transit point

Sources: Washington Office on Latin America; Bureau of International Narcotics Matters, State Department; Washington Office on Latin America

coca in an area that was largely rain forest only four years ago. New coca cultivation destroys 500,000 acres of Peru's Amazon rain forest every year, according to Peru's National Institute of Natural Resources, a Government agency.

"You can win in some areas, but then they are replaced by other areas," said Dr. Lerner, a Peruvian psychologist who studies drug issues here. "Supply depends on the consumer market."

Next month American drug advisers are to leave the Santa Lucia base as part of a 50 percent cut in total anti-drug aid to Peru. "By the end of the year we have to wrap it up," said one American official here. "We are already moving out equipment."

Mr. Fujimori, the Peruvian President, has bluntly criticized the Americans' anti-drug strategies. An agronomist by training, Mr. Fujimori has long argued that the best aid would be economic incentives to persuade coca leaf growers move to alternative crops.

"Many people would accept alternative crops, but there are no loans," Mr. Fujimori said in a recent news conference here. "For weapons, there's money. But to develop agriculture, there's no money."

In Colombia, which has the strongest economy of the Andean countries, President César Gaviria recently told President Clinton that Colombia would make up any cuts in American aid from its own budget. One of the American-financed programs, an effort to reform and protect Colombia's judiciary, is highly popular with the public.

But, in Bolivia, the poorest nation of the region, officials warn that American aid is essential for maintaining anti-drug efforts.

Because Bolivian cocaine is also exported to Europe, Bolivia's new Minister of Government, Germán Quiroga, said in a recent interview that his country would have to turn to countries like France and Germany for help.

American drug enforcement officials interviewed early this month in Bolivia, Colombia, Peru and Venezuela preferred to emphasize individual successes in the anti-drug fight.

They note that Peruvian Air Force planes regularly fire on trafficking planes, sending them crashing into the Amazon jungle. In Colombia, the police have killed or jailed most of the top leaders of the Medellín cocaine cartel. In Bolivia, crop substitution programs have encouraged peasants to eradicate about 20 percent of the nation's coca plants since 1989.

Cocaine Still No. 1 Export

But cocaine powder and semi-refined cocaine remain the largest single export items for Bolivia, Colombia and Peru. In Bolivia and Peru, about 5 percent of the population depend on coca crops as a livelihood. Peruvians grow about two-thirds of the world's coca leaf, a market share that has changed little during four years of the drug war.

"You can't declare war on three million peasants," said Hernando de Soto, who coordinated Peru's anti-drug strategy two years ago. "When I was Peru's drug czar, the only people I could talk to in Washington were cops or people who wanted peasants to raise silkworms."

After years of research, American and Peruvian Governments have failed to come up with a product that competes with coca leaf or with incentives that rival those of the Colombian cocaine cartels.

The cartels often provide agricultural credit. They pick up products at the farm gate. They pay cash. And they circumvent the red tape surrounding legal exports.

Little Farm Credit

In contrast, Peru's cash-strapped Government provides virtually no farm credit. Guerrilla violence has damaged the nation's road and bridge networks to such an extent that Amazon farmers cannot afford to send products to cities like Lima on the Pacific Coast. Bureaucratic demands involving licensing and paperwork close export markets to all but the most sophisticated farmers.

Experts say that hundreds of millions of dollars in aid—far more than Western nations are willing to provide—would be needed to develop alternative agricultural programs and transportation systems to get the crops to market.

Seizures of drug shipments declined in the Andes last year.

"In Lima, it is cheaper to import a redwood tree from California than to bring a log from the Amazon," Mr. de Soto said. "The peasants say they want to substitute coca. But to do that you have to create a market environment."

Widespread Corruption

Not only has the coca leaf harvest defied Washington's wishes, but poppy fields are appearing in Colombia and Peru. Virtually unknown to the country five years ago, poppies are now grown on an estimated 75,000 acres in Colombia. Today, Colombia is second only to Burma in production of poppies for heroin.

Official corruption is also a challenge in countries where policemen make $90 a month and judges earn $200 a month. In Peru, 15 policemen were recently jailed on charges of accepting a $100,000 bribe in return for freeing one of the Huallaga Valley's biggest drug traffickers, a Colombian named Waldo Vargas, a day after he was detained in May.

In Colombia, a Deputy Attorney General, Guillermo Villa, was dismissed last month after it was discovered that he was a friend of Gilberto Rodríguez Orejuela, who with his brother, Miguel, controls the country's powerful Cali cocaine cartel.

In Venezuela, President Ramón J. Velásquez nearly resigned this month after he discovered that he had pardoned a major cocaine trafficker. The 78-year-old President maintains that one of his secretaries was to blame for slipping the pardon into a pile of documents awaiting signature. But the police are investigating reports that the family of the trafficker, Larry Tovar Acuña, paid $800,000 to win his release.

Although seizures of drug shipments actually declined throughout the Andes last year, United States officials argue that American aid has strengthened police forces and court systems in South America by fostering an attitude that drug-related payoffs are still scandalous.

"We have prevented the country from falling into the hands of the 'narcos,' " a United States Embassy official said in Bolivia. "If we leave Bolivia, corruption will go to all levels."

Drug Prevention and Treatment

How do we convince nonusers not to become involved with drugs in the first place? How do we get abusers who are involved off drugs—and convince them to stay off? Regardless of the legal question, we are still faced with the twin problems of prevention and treatment.

What is the best way of making sure that young people do not experiment with and become seriously involved with illegal drugs? In the 1980s, then-first lady Nancy Reagan's "Just Say No" slogan became the best-known statement on the drug scene. But did it work? Did it deter many, or any, young people from the path of drug abuse? This issue is still being debated. Ads appear on television and in magazines and local newspapers claiming that one's brain on drugs is roughly the same as an egg frying in a hot skillet. Does this campaign—its truth value aside—actually dissuade youngsters from using drugs? Again, the evidence is not conclusive. Celebrities appear regularly in the media denouncing drug use and urging that young people not try any drug. Again, is this effort effective? Once again, the answer is not clear. Nonetheless, the issue of prevention is a much-discussed, hotly debated question.

Once someone does become ensnared in a compulsive, destructive pattern of drug abuse, what is to be done? What works? What treatment is most successful—or successful at all—in getting abusers off drugs—permanently?

Some treatment programs entail the addict living in a *therapeutic community* (or TC) for a period of time, usually with strict supervision by ex-addict supervisors, eventually emerging back into society a changed person, purged of the impulses that caused him or her to abuse drugs in the first place. Therapeutic communities are a controversial mode of treatment, since they require a sizable investment of resources; the "split" rate—addicts leaving the program prematurely, against the advice of the staff, to return to the streets—tends to be very high; and proponents often develop a dogmatic, sectarian attitude toward other treatment modalities. Still, for a minority of drug abusers, the therapeutic community clearly works.

Some experts believe that programs based on the Alcoholics Anonymous (AA) model will work for most, or some, drug abusers. Here, addicts living in the community meet on a regular basis, sharing testimony about their lives with one another. Still other observers believe that drug abusers need to be threatened with a jail or prison term in order to force them into a mandatory treatment program. Others argue that, at least for the long-term, hard-core heroin addict, methadone maintenance is the only viable program. Some insist that the environment in which abusers live—including friends, family, and employment—has to be changed before their drug use can be addressed. Others opt for a multimodality approach; they feel that abusers of each drug or drug type, as well as different kinds of drug abusers, are sufficiently distinct as to require a variety of programs, each tailored to the drug and its abuser.

Regardless of which approach to drug abuse treatment is correct, three facts remain widely agreed-upon. First, there are not enough spaces in treatment programs to handle all the drug abusers who wish treatment. Second, there are not enough financial resources currently allocated to drug treatment to make a serious dent in the problem of abuse and addiction. And third, not enough is known about the outcome of the various treatment programs that are used to say definitively which one works best, or even which one works best for which type of drug abuser.

Looking Ahead: Challenge Questions

What is the best drug treatment? Is there any such thing as a single "best" treatment program?

Will an AA-type program work for drug addicts?

Does the threat of incarceration work as a way of motivating addicts to enter—and profit from—treatment?

Why hasn't the government allocated sufficient resources to drug treatment programs?

Why are so many addicts on the street reluctant or unwilling to enter treatment? What can we do to get them to get help?

UNITED NATIONS
POSTAL ADMINISTRATION

CONTROL NARCOTICS

GETTING JUNKIES TO CLEAN UP

And inducing teenage mothers, high school dropouts, and drunken drivers to change their behavior. It isn't easy, but some new approaches are beginning to make progress.

Lee Smith

CHANGING human behavior is like reshaping concrete. The material is stubborn. Over the past couple of decades government agencies as well as corporations and private foundations have spent billions trying to blunt destructive habits that create grim casualty lists: four million cocaine and heroin addicts, one million pregnant teenagers a year, and 700,000 high school dropouts.

Can anything hold down the mounting toll? The answers come at a maddeningly slow pace. A hard-pressed drug clinic would rather spend money to keep a program rolling than to study whether its graduates remain clean. Promising ideas don't circulate fast enough, and failed ones persist, partly because theorists are inclined to stick with treatments that ought to work—but often don't.

Though evidence from the field is incomplete, enough exists to sketch some general conclusions. There are four basic approaches to changing behavior: education, punishment, financial incentives, and—often the last resort—treatment. Under the right circumstances, all work some of the time and none work all of the time, despite the attempts of advocates to portray one or another as a panacea.

In all four cases programs for the very young will likely produce the best results. New York City stumbled when it spent $120 million in the late 1980s to persuade 150,000 wavering students to stay in high school. The city hired extra guidance counselors, offered wilderness training to

REPORTER ASSOCIATE *Suneel Ratan*

some youngsters to build their confidence, and rigged up an automatic telephone dialing system that rang the truants' homes and reminded them to come to class. The effort failed; the dropout rate remained at 28%.

The program almost certainly came too late. The 16-year-old who drops out in New York probably started to make that decision, unconsciously, a decade before. Dr. Sheppard G. Kellam, chairman of the mental hygiene department at Johns Hopkins School of Public Health, has tracked hundreds of youngsters from 6 to 16. His statistics show that those likely to drop out—and become heavy drinkers and drug users as well—can be spotted early. Most are what he calls the shy-aggressive type, belligerent loners who emerge from their solitude mostly to strike a schoolmate or defy a teacher.

Working with the Baltimore public school system, Kellam is trying to figure out how to reform these tiny classroom bullies before they cause grown-up trouble. Some are put in classes where teachers divide students into teams. Privileges are awarded on the basis of how well the team, rather than any individual in it, behaves. The idea is to reform delinquents through peer pressure. Preliminary results are mildly encouraging. Some 20% of the children described by teammates as "mean" at the beginning of the year were rated "nice" at the end.

But no classroom remedy is likely to work unless the parents or grandmother or big sister backs it up at home. As Harvard psychologist Jerome Kagan puts it, "It's hard to treat a child for diarrhea if you send him back to a swamp every night." So Kellam's next daunt-

ing step will be to get the guardians to cooperate. They will likely have to alter their own behavior, even more deeply embedded than that of the children.

EDUCATION is a potent force, though proponents are inclined to exaggerate its power. Senator Edward Kennedy (D-Massachusetts), for one, insists that instruction can inoculate children against the drug epidemic. Not likely. Many schools don't even understand what it is they are supposed to teach. Simply laying out the physiology of drugs or alcohol or sex doesn't help much; it is familiar to youngsters anyhow.

It is better, say experts, to focus on what you might call the social aspects surrounding such activity. What the 15-year-old girl doesn't know is how to bring up the subject of contraception with her new boyfriend. "For many kids it's easier to jump into bed than discuss sex," says Joan Lipsitz, a director at the Lilly Endowment, a private foundation in Indianapolis. "Sex isn't a difficult act for them; talking is." The boy of 13 doesn't know how to turn down marijuana when it's offered by the most popular 16-year-old in school.

One drug program, Project Star in Kansas City, has produced measurable results in helping youngsters cope with such situations. Begun in 1984 with the support of Ewing Kauffman, founder of Marion Laboratories and owner of the Kansas City Royals, it relies on role playing and other training techniques familiar to business.

Kauffman insisted on market research of sorts. Says he: "I'm a penny pincher, so I wanted to test this program just as I would a new pharmaceutical." Some 15,000 sixth-

and seventh-graders were divided into two groups: The experimental group got an hour a week on substance abuse. Rather than giving lectures, teachers encouraged students to discuss their curiosity and fears and develop their own standards, which sometimes turn out to be remarkably conservative. Thus, no matter what the pressures outside the classroom, the students would know that at least one community shared their values.

The other group of students, intended as a control, had no special instruction on the subject. University of Southern California researchers periodically surveyed and tested both groups. The experimental group used all substances less frequently. Half of the control group drank alcohol, compared with 35% of the experimental; 32% smoked cigarettes, vs. 24%; 20% used marijuana, vs. 14%.

Getting accurate information about what their peers were doing proved especially important. At the start the youngsters in the experimental group assumed that two-thirds of their classmates had tried forbidden fruit. Fewer than a third actually had, which greatly reduced social pressure on the abstemious.

Each student was encouraged to develop a particular strategy to resist peer pressure, then practice it repeatedly in minidramas with classmates, much the way a business executive might rehearse an upcoming confrontation with a difficult client. How to resist the big man on campus when he offers marijuana? Maybe the BMOC has no clear idea of whether he is testing his junior or simply making a perfunctory gesture, so the 13-year-old might demur gracefully with a terse "No, thanks." (Take a small bow, Nancy Reagan, but the "Just" in the "Just say no" campaign makes it sound too easy.)

Indianapolis has copied the plan, and Washington, D.C., is testing it in a few schools. Some of the elements that helped it work in Kansas City, however, cannot be easily duplicated. Kauffman's prominence as owner of a major league baseball team helps too, by attracting media attention. The Midwestern city has its social and economic troubles (9% of the population lives below the poverty level) but not on the scale of Chicago or Los Angeles. What happens to peer pressure, for example, when the 13-year-old discovers that a critical mass of his classmates are indeed substance users? One possible solution: Start the program at a lower grade.

PUNISHMENT can be a powerful deterrent, psychologists say, but only when the wayward perceive it as swift and sure. That greatly limits its effectiveness in a society that cherishes due process. An impressive exception is the campaign against drunken driving, where punishment has been far more effective than either treatment or education.

Attacking the problem as a treatable disease misses the mark. It is not the archetypal alcoholic who poses the greatest danger on the road. Says James L. Nichols, an authority on drunken driving at the Department of Transportation: "A 20-year-old male who has had eight beers is more likely to drive recklessly than a 40-year-old with a severe alcohol problem." Mandatory safe-driving classes don't help much either.

What does work are well-publicized campaigns in Florida, California, and 18 other states to thwart drunken drivers by suspending their licenses for 30 days or more. At random police checkpoints, drivers have to pass Breathalyzer exams or perhaps simple arithmetic quizzes. Those who flunk must hand over their licenses, although police give temporary permits to allow a chance for appeal.

That's about as sure and swift a punishment as the Constitution allows, but its effectiveness is not as straightforward as lawmen would like to think. Says Nichols: "Most of those who lose their licenses continue to drive. But because they're worried about getting caught, they drive carefully." Compared with drunken drivers who are merely warned or put through education programs, drivers whose licenses are suspended have 40% to 50% fewer crashes for as long as five years after their arrests.

Some clinics report they can help smokers quit with shock therapy. In a typical setup the smoker, who sits in a room with a wire attached to one wrist, gets a small jolt after reaching for a cigarette. Away from the clinic the person snaps a rubber band on the wrist after lighting up to recall the punishing shock.

When the consequences don't have to be faced immediately, punishment is far less fearsome. Teenagers are careless about using condoms, despite the risk of AIDS. Ruth Wooden, president of the Advertising Council, says interviews with teenagers show that what worries them about tobacco is not so much emphysema at 60 as bad breath on Saturday night.

FINANCIAL INCENTIVES, even small ones, are surprisingly effective. But, as with punishment, the payoff must be quick. In 1984, Planned Parenthood of the Rocky Mountains in Denver offered girls under 16 who had previously had babies, abortions, or miscarriages $1 a day not to get pregnant again.

Once a week they come in to pick up the wages of virtue. Though they don't have to, many hang around to talk about baby care or their own health or to gossip. Says Dr. Margaret LaTourrette, a Planned Parenthood board member: "They wouldn't come without the money. Some buy diapers, some buy hair spray."

On average half of teenage girls who get pregnant once do so again as adolescents. Over the past year only two of the 57 girls in the Rocky Mountain program have become pregnant. That is a very small sample on which to base big conclusions, but the program is so inexpensive that it seems worth trying elsewhere.

Dr. Larry Culpepper, who runs the Blackstone Valley Perinatal Network in Rhode Island, attracts poor pregnant women to his program by offering them a chance to win a lottery of from $25 to $500. Traffic is up 30% since the payoffs began more than a year ago. "These women want healthy babies just like other mothers," says Culpepper. "They don't know help is available, and they don't read pamphlets. But if someone wins $100, the word gets around the housing project fast."

Even if only one woman carries her baby to full term as a result, the lottery will justify its grants, $15,000 from the March of Dimes and $5,000 from the federal government. A premature baby costs an average of $22,000 more to care for than one carried to full term. And taxpayers usually pay the bill.

Financial penalties work in at least one case better than many economists have assumed. The conventional wisdom about smoking is that the habit is not sensitive to changes in prices. But according to a study by the National Bureau of Economic Research, smoking decreased between 1955 and 1985 in states where excise taxes rose.

While New York City attempted to coax kids to stay in school, Wisconsin threatened their mothers. With Learnfare, a program developed under Republican Governor Tommy G. Thompson, recipients of aid to families with dependent children (AFDC) forfeit a share of their benefits if their teenage children skip school. The program appears to be bringing children back to the classroom, but it isn't clear whether the returnees are studying or just filling seats.

Economics by itself doesn't seem to hold a drug addict's attention for long. Dr. Roger Meyer, head of the department of psychiatry at the University of Connecticut, recalls a treatment program for heroin addicts he helped direct in the mid-1970s. As long as the patients were in the hospital and under supervision, they performed well for rewards, such as $4 for writing a job résumé.

After they were released they were supposed to show up daily at a local pharmacy, swallow a potion that blocks heroin, and collect $1. Many fell away. Those who stuck with the program tended to be the ones with strong family ties.

TREATMENT follows when all else fails, but how effective is it? Most drug clinics don't keep track of their discharged patients closely enough to answer the question statistically. The anecdotal evidence suggests that the failure rate is high. Addicts generally relapse at least once or twice, says Dr. Herbert D. Kleber, deputy director of demand reduction for the Office of National Drug Control Policy. The trouble is, an addict doesn't enter treatment the first time to get rid of his habit. Rather, says Kleber, "he wants to get back to that honeymoon when the drug felt great and he could control it."

Nonetheless, like smokers, a lot of drug addicts and alcoholics keep trying to reform. Dr. Roger Weiss, who runs the alcohol and drug treatment program at McLean Hospital near Boston, says that, contrary to the cliché, the most promising candidate is not one who has hit bottom but one who is just an arm's length away. Says Weiss: "He is the guy who thinks about selling his mother's wedding ring but hasn't done it yet." The combination of a downside risk in continuing and an upside opportunity in stopping seems to provide the best incentive.

Government and private agencies could do a much better job of directing drug abusers to the appropriate place. Says Kleber: "Where an addict gets treatment depends very much on which door he happens to knock on. It is senseless to put someone with no skills into a 28-day rehabilitation program. He has to be habilitated." Learning a trade, as well as the discipline to show up for work and take orders, could require as much as 18 months.

Also, says Kleber, states should require hospitals and other treatment centers to achieve a minimum success rate in order to get government funding; perhaps one-half to two-thirds of their patients should be drug free a couple of years after release. Programs that take the toughest cases could have more lenient standards.

Partisans of all strategies would do well to acknowledge that none are more than moderately effective. Programs that don't meet standards should be junked, no matter how compelling the educational or punitive theory behind them. And programs that do work should be analyzed more critically to find out what it is that makes them effective. Even a modest improvement in suicidal human behavior would be reason for the rest of society to cheer.

Alonzo's Battle

For a former crack hustler, leaving the streets and living right is 'hard, man'

Katherine Boo

Washington Post Staff Writer

Alonzo Washington has lost more than most to the D.C. streets. First his father, gunned down in a robbery when Alonzo was 7. Then his mom, lost in a more complicated, private way. Then a brother, who now resides at Lorton, the District of Columbia's prison in Virginia. Yet something in the streets still called seductively to Alonzo. It registered on his hip, where a small black pager hung.

At sweet 16, Alonzo wasn't just a veteran salesman in the District's bustling crack trade. This Hugo Boss-sporting teenage father—with his eighth-grade education, nagging family troubles and canny disregard for the law—was the embodiment of one of America's most intractable urban conundrums. And today, a few months out of juvenile detention, just days into official adulthood, Alonzo is already, by the odds, a marked man.

Now he lives on the fault line of the District's juvenile justice system: a system that invests tens of millions a year to lock kids up for a while and then abandons them, at 15, 16, 17, in the center of their temptations. Of the thousands of teenagers shuttled through the system every year, a remarkable three-quarters will tangle again with the law, adding their bodies to that stubborn statistic: more young black men in jail than in college. There are many stories such numbers do not tell. One is about how tough it is to beat the odds when the world you know doesn't give you much to fight with.

This fall, Alonzo Washington is holding down his first legit job, as a barber's apprentice. He's trying to be a father to his 22-month-old son, he's studying for his GED. He's getting, embarrassingly enough at 18, his learner's permit. Yet even this "businessman on a mission," as he calls himself—this shrewd, candid kid with the conquering smile and a slew of self-help mantras: Even he struggles to turn his back on the way of life he knows best. And that battle reflects something more than personal character, or lack thereof. It reflects a city's character too.

Alonzo would like his story to be one about the power and exhilaration you feel when you cash in the bad life for the good.

But he knows there's a truer story: about the soul-crushing struggle to keep believing, despite the evidence, that the straight life is better than the street life you've left behind.

It's 2 o'clock, Monday, at Alonzo's apartment, so this must be "As the World Turns." And here on the screen is the lovely Emily, once a fugitive-harboring vixen, now Mother Teresa in a cat suit. Character transformations are apparently easier in the leafy soap opera village of Oakdale. "In D.C. life," says Alonzo, his son busily prodding his cheekbone, "it's complicated being good."

"I see it kind of like this," he explains at the commercial. "When you're bad, everyone knows you're bad and that's that. But I think temptation is even more after you when you're trying to be straight. Satan works harder on you. You're more of a challenge."

This afternoon, Alonzo's one day off from the barbershop, you can sort of see what he means. It takes a lot to wipe the grin off Alonzo's face, but now baby Alonzo lets loose a howl that would test Saint Emily herself. "Dadd-eee! Dadd-eeeeee!" Oh jeez.

Like everyone else in this tiny Silver Spring, Md., apartment, the baby's hot, sweating; it's 100 degrees outside, and in. Alonzo leaps to pour his son a drink of water. Nope. The Barney song. Forget it. He's eaten, right? Napped?

"The diaper?" volunteers a friend who has stopped in for a visit. "It's all crooked. Look how it's sticking out at the back."

Alonzo grows doleful. "We don't have any more Pampers. . . ."

Pampers, he has recently discovered, are expensive.

Alonzo thinks a lot about money these days—what he'd do if he had more. He'd get a Honda Accord so he could drive to his GED classes and ditch those unreliable buses. He'd get, for sure, a phone and a VCR for the apartment where he's lived on and off for the past few years. And maybe more Ralph Lauren outfits for the baby, born while he was in detention and now his charge once a week or so, when the mother, an old girlfriend, Letitia Kirkland, needs a break.

Not that he's complaining. No, it's not so bad now, really—sitting here watching TV, as he does most days off, in the two-bedroom space he shares with his unemployed mother, her

From *The Washington Post National Weekly Edition,* October 18-24, 1993, pp. 6-7. © 1993 by The Washington Post. Reprinted by permission.

boyfriend and Alonzo's lifelong roommate, his mentally disabled twin brother, Antonio. "I'd go out, but I don't really have any friends anymore," Alonzo says, "just associates. But I don't mind. I'm holding my head high."

Money, friends, adventures more real than a TV movie: Those were the accouterments of the old life, in the working-class neighborhood in Northwest Washington, where he and his brothers grew up and where his now-invalid grandmother still lives. Mom, struggling after the murder of her husband, was off "getting her stuff together." That was the life Alonzo lived before realizing "the future is now," "the past is irrelevant" and "success comes when you keep it strictly business." As for what exactly this new, righteous life should consist of, well, that requires a pretty enormous act of imagination.

"You know those steps in 'The Exorcist'?" he asks one day. "Someone told me they were in Georgetown. Is that right?" He'd kind of like to see them. But that's light-years from the world he knows best: a rambunctious slice of Kennedy Street, where he first learned how to hustle, how to live.

"Now, in 1993, this is no time to be getting into hustling, with the sentences they're handing out," Alonzo advises, balancing the baby on a Gore-Texed knee. "But '86, '87, that was the hustling time, man." Just thinking about it revives the grin. "Suddenly people I knew started getting fast cars and houses— well, okay, at least the older guys had houses, and someone I knew had an 850 BMW, a gold one. It had always been going on, I guess, but about 12 or 13 I got to thinking about how they got that." He got to realizing that he could get that too.

Like most kids in the drug trade, of course, he never got that, even after three years busting tail. Just a Honda scooter (promptly stolen), a lot of Polo stuff and an undeniably fine array of shoes. He did, though, get something else.

Every morning at 6 or 7, on a shopping strip flanked by a nude-dancing lounge and a social services agency called the Righteous Men's Commission, Alonzo would settle in to sell. And he'd stay there until late at night, and sometimes all night, if business was good. He had already learned how to count change, work the crowds, make a sale; like many inner-city boys, he hawked chocolate on the streets for a candy company called Teen Advancement. But this new job offered more than income. At its best, dealing gave him a heady, thoroughly unfamiliar jolt of confidence.

"You're not thinking, just reacting, and it's exciting that way. And after a while I felt good at it. I wasn't as good as I thought I was—I had a lot more learning to do to get really good. Still, people liked to be around me. No one was ever saying 'Eh, I don't know about that Alonzo. . . .' I had a responsibility, and they could trust me."

"They" were, of course, his crew, his friends, a few of whom could always be unearthed, whatever the hour, to trade jokes or provide running commentary on passersby. He hates to think of it today, now that things are so different. But back then those friends mattered. A lot. It wasn't like he hadn't had friends before, but strange hours, shared danger—stuff like that draws people tight. And among these "friends to the end," Alonzo for

once felt—how can he put this?—"right. Just right about everything."

His eyes track Alonzo Jr. through the stifling little room. "No, I guess it was never just about the money. That, you make it and it leaves just like that—bye! And it never seems like enough, because even if you're making a couple grand a day your friends might be making twice that, and what you have seems like nothing. No, I guess I thought hustling was, for the first time, really living. Really being yourself. The money, the clothes, the herb, the people—that was being you. And to tell you the truth, it was fun."

Fun. Like nagging girlfriends, like muggy bus rides, like empty bank accounts are not. "You know what I think?" he says one afternoon, taking a breather from his sweeping duties at the barbershop. "Society has taken the play out of life. Everything has to be so serious, so strict. And I don't think that's right." Despite his grandmother's love and attention ("That woman did everything but bore me," he says), Alonzo's has been a pretty serious life, beginning with the murder of his father near the old Children's Hospital in Shaw. "I got over it," is all he'll say about it now.

Far harder were the prolonged absences of his mother. "Her, I missed just about every day." Still, there was little time for self-indulgence. Even as a child, he had business to attend to: the business of his twin, Alonzo's image except for the sloping shoulders, the clotted voice. "Antonio, he's my home-piece, my man," says Alonzo. "Always was."

"I was always mature for my age, I think," he says. "I'd ride bikes and play ball, but I was always a step ahead. I guess in part because I was always watching out for my brother. It wasn't that people made fun of Antonio or anything," he hastens to add. "He was just—when he was younger, you know, he was real sensitive about people crying. When he saw someone cry, he'd bust out crying too. I was like that too, I guess. I grew out of it."

By 14 or so, as Alonzo became increasingly caught up in the street life, many such childish things whirled out of his field of vision. "Dropping out—at the time I didn't even think about it," he says. "School had never really took. There was one teacher in sixth grade—Dr. Jacqueline Bates. She told me I was smart and wanted to get at my lack of willpower. But I could never really pep up. I wasn't enthused about it. No youth I know is enthused about it."

Of course, the alternative, hustling, wasn't always a blast either. All around him, for instance, other dealers were getting arrested and sentenced to 10, 20 years' hard time. And a few, inevitably, were getting killed. Drive-bys. Executions. Sporadic, generalized gunspray that caught more than one luckless pizza delivery guy in the cross-fire. But at 14 or 15, Alonzo simply wasn't worrying about such things. He was "highly, highly focused" on the hustling, until his own number came up.

At 15, four blocks from his grandmother's house, he served up zip-lock bags of crack to three undercover cops. He was sentenced to home detention. "It was nothing," says Alonzo. He high-tailed it back to his friends. Six months later, when the cops pulled over a Chevrolet in which he was riding, he would demonstrate just how important those friends were.

It was 4 in the morning, and Alonzo's pockets were clean. One of his buddies, though—he was carrying half a dozen bags of rock. As Alonzo watched the police handcuff the other young man, he found he couldn't just stroll back to his corner. "Don't lock him up," Alonzo told the officers. "The crack is mine. Take me."

They did. And when the gavel came down a few weeks later, he had a sentence at one of the city's most troubled junior jails.

Don't let its leftish tendencies on other social policy issues mislead you: D.C.'s juvenile justice system—anchored by costly prisonlike facilities known for turning boys into expert thugs—makes those of Utah and Georgia seem positively Scandinavian. Until shuttered by a federal court order this spring, D.C.'s Cedar Knoll was nationally renowned for overcrowding and undernurturing, and the frequent escapes of its guests.

When Alonzo arrived at Cedar Knoll in 1991, he was well aware of its reputation. But hell is a relative concept, and Alonzo found the place not so much a disruption of his old life as an intensification. Yes, the food was terrible, the fighting constant and bedtime aggravatingly early. And, sure, "there were some knuckleheads in there, and some guys who tried to eat light bulbs to kill themselves—there's stuff like that goes on." But most of the time, he says, "it was like a playground—a kids' world, just kind of wild."

"When I first got there," he says, "I still had the idea that I would just hold on, come out and go back to the streets. I just thought I was a little smarter than all this." But then something changed.

In his first weeks at Cedar Knoll, an image sometimes swam comfortingly in his head: a slice of Kennedy Street sidewalk held open in his honor. *Wonder how Alonzo's doing,* the crew would say. Man, when Alonzo gets back. . . . He wrote to his friends about detention, about their lives, about the fun he was missing. And at the end of those letters he asked each of them a favor—to send him change to buy snacks from the vending machines at Cedar Knoll.

"These were people," says Alonzo slowly, "with hundreds of dollars in their pockets. But they never wrote back. None of them."

This simple betrayal penetrated as pleas by lawyers, judges, counselors, his grandmother did not. Loneliness and depression overwhelmed him. Until God and a baby came to set him straight.

Shortly after Alonzo's arrival at Cedar Knoll, Letitia, a soft-spoken girl he'd fallen for at 14, gave him a baby son, a son who bears his name. A photo of the newborn now challenged him as nothing had done before. *Do it,* said this baby, *for me.*

But how? There was only one way Alonzo could think of. He'd been hauled to church by relatives all his life; he now dredged up some of the words. "Alone in my room, I had this feeling that God was a real thing, that He was there. So I said, please, God, let me leave this place. I'll walk a new life. I'll give my son a real provider."

Before long, with the help of his court-appointed lawyer, he was transferred to Act Two, a smaller, more structured institution in Northeast, where his new attitude—the smile, the willingness to work, the courtly manners his grandma had given him—was noticed by a counselor, Samuel Brice. Unlike some other kids, Brice recalls, "Alonzo wanted to be helped." Alonzo also wanted to keep busy; in his free time he'd cut other residents' hair. Watching, an idea took shape in Brice's mind. One day, getting a trim from his barber of 20 years, he asked Ronald Mitchell to give one of his more promising kids a part-time job. This impromptu exchange is now rich with meaning for Alonzo: His Creator had answered his prayers.

To a red vinyl chair in a fern-filled barbershop—this is where Alonzo has been delivered, to sweep, to clean, to cut hair. As WPGC blares in his ear one Saturday afternoon, as scissors click and customers chat around him, Alonzo is a study in furrowed concentration. Clippers in hand, he adjusts the head of a man in polo shirt and moccasins and stares fiercely into the mirror. Then the clippers, held delicately in extended fingers, begin to fly across the plane of hair. Stroke. Stroke. There. A perfect high-top fade.

So he may have nicked the man a little. The man didn't seem to notice. Instead he asked for Alonzo's—*Alonzo's*—card.

To Alonzo, this is not just a workday at the Park-Ritchie Barber Shop in a Takoma Park, Md., condo complex. This is "cookies and ice cream." Working between GED classes, he earns a couple hundred dollars in a good week and learns something almost as important to him as how to cut fades.

"This isn't a storefront shop, you know," he says pointedly during a break. "I'm getting a chance to find out how the middle-class people live. Doctors, lawyers, everything—black people. And, man, they're conservative. About everything. . . ."

Lost for a moment in thoughts of personal gentrification, he fingers the gold charm on his neck chain. A scissors and comb in the shape of an X.

There's no room for Hugo Boss attitude at the Park-Ritchie. A white zip-up smock goes better with a razor and a broom. Still, under Ronald Mitchell's astringent and affectionate tutelage, Alonzo has missed only one day of work in a year. That may be because, in spite of the intermittent grunge jobs, Alonzo is occasionally swept up by the surge of self-confidence that Kennedy Street used to offer.

There are quite a few parallels between hustling and cutting heads, he's discovered. It won't do, for instance, to gossip about your customers. You can never let your personal troubles fuzz you out. And then there's the matter of making accurate change. This Alonzo excels at.

Ronald Mitchell doesn't like to make predictions. In 20 years as co-owner and master barber of the shop, he's had more than one promising kid let him down, lured away by faster cash and fresher vocations. But Alonzo tempts him out onto a limb. "I knew when Alonzo first got here that he has the motivation—he always walks in here with a smile across his face. He minds his manners, keeps his station clean, and sometimes he really surprises me with what he can do with a razor. He's picking it all up; the customers love him. Now all he's got to do is stay the course."

The course: buttressed by barbershop banter and Mitchell's endless assignments, Alonzo sees it clearly when he's working. He speaks surely of going to barber school and becoming a master barber like Mitchell, who with his own business, devoted customers and sleek black Acura Legend has become Alonzo's "personal hero—the only man I've known to stick around." At work with Mitchell, Alonzo feels most like that "businessman on a mission." At work, only one problem dogs him. At the end of the day he'll have to leave.

After the bottles of talc and Black Magic Sheen are arranged neatly on his shelf, after the smocks are folded into squares, Alonzo sheds his uniform for a Ralph Lauren T-shirt with an American flag on the chest. "Back to the streets," he says wryly as he waits at the bus stop, wolfing his dinner, a Quarter Pounder with cheese. "Notice there are *no* middle-class people on the streets." Five minutes later, he's off the bus and on Blair Road, where he promptly runs into a friend—make that an associate—out on a weekend pass from juvenile detention. With few words, they arrange to hook up later.

Just a month ago, Alonzo's contact with his associates was mostly a "hi-bye thing." They'd disrespect his barbershop ambitions; he'd think of his son and keep walking. He felt right. He felt righteous. Today, things aren't as clear.

"The streets, it's about making money and surviving," he's saying now, hiking up Blair, flashing a peace sign at yet another associate hanging on the curb. "Until society changes, until the Creator changes society, people are going to be on the streets and a lot of us are going to fall by the wayside. . . ."

Then up the stairs to the steamy apartment, where Mom's annoyed because he hasn't bought the groceries and Antonio is quietly watching music videos. Alonzo retreats to the room he and Antonio share—the one with the big stuffed bears and the poster of Michael Jordan. Collapsing into a chair, he fingers a cigar and yawns. Saturday night. Perhaps, like last weekend, he'll burrow in, turn on the TV and try not to wonder if, back on Kennedy Street, something livelier is going on. Or perhaps, like yesterday, he'll actually pop by for a visit. Just a curbside beer, old times' sake. See some friends. You know.

"There are lines I won't cross, though. I stay away from the danger. I watch my p's and q's. And when push comes to shove, I'm out of there. I'm home by 12 o'clock. . . ."

He knows, he knows. Stupid. After so much work, so many plans. Just stupid. But that's how it is sometimes, especially lately. Somehow, his moves are a step behind his mantras. "How do you change your skin, your soul?" he asks one day, his voice hard-edged with impatience. "I mean, people are always saying to me, 'Hey, Alonzo, are you behaving yourself?' I'm not behaving myself. I'm just trying to be more careful. But I'm always going to be doing something stupid."

And what exactly does his city have to offer him, to stop him from being stupid, to cool him down in this season of temptation? In the struggle to make his tentative transformation a real one, a barbershop and a baby may not be enough. He'll make it, says Samuel Brice. He'll make it, says Ronald Mitchell. Only Alonzo seems unsure. "I'm scared, I'm always scared. I don't ever, ever want to be there again. The Lord has welded that into my head. But every day I'm scared to death."

Watching, listening, it's hard not to share his fear.

Late one afternoon, after reeling off his resolutions to keep positive, stay the course and keep it strictly business, he picks up his toddler and bounds down the stairs—Grandma's manners—to escort his guest out. As he stands at the metal door, baby spittle shiny on his good black T-shirt, his son begins to cry. And cry.

"It's hard, man," Alonzo says almost inaudibly before retreating, child in arms, into the shadowy hallway. "That's what you should make the headline. It's really, really hard."

Prisoners, and Prisons, Gain From Drug Therapy

Joseph B. Treaster

Until Alex Maldonado was arrested a few weeks ago, his life was dominated by crack. It was on his mind when he awoke around noon, and it was behind one of his first decisions of the day: Should he go shoplifting or break into a car to get money for the drug? Either way, after smoking for a couple of hours he would need more crack and "go out and steal something else."

The first time he tried a bigger target, a Park Avenue apartment, he was caught and sent to Rikers Island, New York City's sprawling prison colony in the East River. But instead of idling away the time while his case meandered through the courts, the 25-year-old Mr. Maldonado joined 1,200 other prisoners in a schedule of 13-hour days of group therapy and classes intended to end drug addiction.

Across the nation, more and more jails and prisons are offering rehabilitation to prisoners like Mr. Maldonado. Nationally, researchers say, perhaps 15 to 20 percent of the more than one million prisoners are now receiving drug treatment, up from hardly anything in the mid-1980's.

Behind this trend is the notion that prisons and jails are ideal places to interrupt the pattern of drug use. More than 70 percent of the inmates have abused drugs, experts say, and they have been responsible for a huge number of robberies, burglaries and assaults.

The hope is that time spent fighting addiction helps fight future crime.

Once behind bars and coils of razor wire, some heavy drug users, who seem to thrive on the excitement and euphoria of their illicit lives and rarely seek rehabilitation, become a pliable audience for therapists.

Mr. Maldonado, for instance, had tried drug programs before, unsuccessfully, but has become an enthusiastic about the program at Rikers Island. He says he hopes to continue treatment when he's released.

'You're Being Soft'

In addition, prison officials get a bonus: they are discovering that inmates in programs like those at Rikers Island follow rules better and fight less, making it easier and cheaper to manage institutions.

"Some people say that with drug treatment you're being soft on criminals," said Catherine M. Abate, the Commissioner of the New York City Department of Correction. "But it's not that. It just makes good, common sense. In the long term, this is the only way to reduce crime."

Researchers have data demonstrating that drug rehabilitation reduces both drug abuse and crime. But they note that drug treatment is usually a cumulative process, with people dropping in and out of programs over several years.

As time goes on, drug users stay in treatment longer and have longer periods of sobriety on their own. Their drug use and crime stops, or at least declines, while they are in treatment and remains in abeyance or diminished for some time afterward.

Cost Effectiveness Argued

Many experts argue that drug rehabilitation is much less expensive than prison construction. The cost of building a single prison cell, for example, is $100,000, and New York City spends $58,000 a year to house a prisoner at Rikers Island.

A year in the most intense drug rehabilitation programs in prison costs about $4,000 more than merely housing a prisoner. The most expensive treatment that might be prescribed as a follow-up outside prison for the toughest cases runs about

$18,000 annually. Perhaps most importantly, proponents say, drug treatment strives to change patterns of behavior so that the need for new prisons might be curtailed.

Under President Bush, spending for drug rehabilitation and education nearly doubled, to $3.2 billion. About 70 percent of that money went to law enforcement, and only a small fraction to prison treatment. Less than a third of the nation's heavy drug users have been able to receive treatment.

Even though the treatment program at Rikers Island has mushroomed since its beginning three years ago with 50 inmates, it now serves only about 10 percent of the city's prisoners.

Islands of Quiet

President-elect Bill Clinton is expected to commit more money to the health side of the anti-drug ledger.

"He thinks drug treatment is important and ought to be available to everyone who wants it," said Bob Boorstin, who served as deputy communications director during the Clinton campaign and who has studied drug policy. "It's ultimately going to repair a lot of lives and save a hell of a lot of money."

At Rikers Island, the dormitories or barracks that have been set aside for drug treatment are islands of quiet in a gray, seething world of tension and violence. On most of Rikers, prisoners steal one another's sneakers. They settle scores with homemade knives and razor blades and, some say, drugs are easily available.

"In the other sections you could look at a guy wrong and he could break your jaw," said Jose Torres, who is 46 years old and was arrested for selling crack. "Here, it's different. They say, 'Hold your belly,' meaning keep yourself intact, don't overreact. There's a feeling of unity. You're able to communicate."

On most of Rikers Island, inmates hang around killing time. They sprawl on their bunks, play cards or watch television, go to meals or not. Discarded newspapers and magazines lie like throw rugs on the linoleum tiles, and laundry dangles between lockers.

90 Percent First-Timers

But the drug-treatment units are boot-camp tidy. Everyone's feet must be on the floor by 7:45 A.M. Wool blankets are drawn tightly over cots and trimmed with a narrowly folded white towel, tucked diagonally across one corner. Everyone has cleaning chores; everyone is expected to dress neatly.

Each barracks of 50 inmates gathers in a circle of plastic armchairs with a pair of counselors for group therapy four or five times a day. The inmates, all volunteers, also meet with counselors privately. Some participants are studying for high school diplomas. Others are learning how to become professional bakers or to work with computers.

"It's very much an effort to socialize or resocialize people," said Robert Gangi, the executive director of the Correctional Association of New York, which monitors prison systems. "It tries to enhance their self-esteem and develop discipline, so as to better control their impulses, and better equip them to hold jobs and relate to their families."

For 90 percent of the prisoners, this is the first taste of drug rehabilitation.

"Our goal is to help them recognize they have a problem and see how that drug problem has been affecting their lives," said Mark Van Denburgh, a supervising counselor. "That's the first step."

Treatment Averts Crime

For years many researchers believed that rehabilitation had little effect on prisoners. But the tide began to turn in the late 1980's. Then Dr. Harry K. Wexler, a senior researcher at the National Development and Research Institutes in New York, which specializes in drug issues, started publishing the results of a study of the Stay'n Out program at the Arthur Kill state prison on Staten Island.

Three years after intensive therapy in that program, Dr. Wexler found, three out of every four prisoners had stuck to their pledge to give up drugs and had not been in trouble with the police.

Conversely, said Dr. Douglas S. Lipton, a colleague of Dr. Wexler at the research center: "If you don't treat these people, most of them are going to return to drugs and active, predatory crime, and they'll be back in custody within three years."

In a study of nearly 500 heroin addicts, Dr. Marcia R. Chaiken, who heads a private research center near Boston, found that the addicts committed 15 times as many robberies and 20 times as many burglaries as non-drug using criminals. Dr. Lipton said several other studies suggested that the crime rates for people using crack are as high or higher. Yet another study, by Dr. Bruce D. Johnson, found that using drugs did not turn people into robbers and burglars, but that it more than quadrupled the rate of offenses by people already involved in crime.

'Stress Level Is Lower'

No one has quantified, in dollars and cents, the absence of violence in the drug units at Rikers Island. But Ms. Abate said the savings is indisputable. "You're not having to deal with injuries," she said, "not having to deal with overtime costs and hospital runs. The stress level is lower. We're even seeing lower absenteeism among the officers on those units."

The most effective drug treatment in prisons, Dr. Lipton and other researchers say, runs 9 to 12 months in self-contained units called therapeutic communities and needs to be followed up with at least outpatient treatment and regular attendance at meetings of support groups like Alcoholics Anonymous and Narcotics Anonymous.

By its nature, as a kind of penal way station where most prisoners are either awaiting sentencing or transfer to state prisons, Rikers Island usually holds people for only a few weeks to a few months: not long enough to imprint a new life style.

Counselors at Rikers try to find places in therapeutic communities outside the jail for those being released. But most often there is nowhere to turn. In New York City, state officials estimate, there are about 600,000 heavy drug users and

room in treatment centers for about 39,000. Last year, 10,679 prisoners received drug treatment at Rikers Island, but only 214 went on to rehabilitation programs outside the jail.

Still, Dr. Lipton said he thought the effort at Rikers was worthwhile. "It's an opportunity to expose inmates to treatment and to initiate a process," he said. "They begin to see what it's like, overcome some of the fears and the folk lore. So it's a valuable experience."

Mr. Maldonado, who said he first tried cocaine when he was 17 years old, after discovering a packet of it as he went through his father's coat

looking for change, jumped at the chance to be in the Rikers Island program.

Now, as he tries to negotiate an assignment to a drug-treatment program for 18 to 24 months in lieu of prison for the Park Avenue burglary, his lawyer has told him that the prison sentence, with allowances for good behavior, would probably mean less time away from his family. But that did not dissuade him.

"I told him I don't care," Mr. Maldonado said. "I want a drug program because I really know I need it."

Maintenance isn't cure, but it's limiting HIV, crime in Britain's drug picture

Richard O'Mara

Staff Writer

WIDNES, England—Siobhan Monaghan smokes 15 heroin reefers a day. She gets them free, here at the Widnes Drug Dependency Clinic.

The clinic takes up a few rooms above an insurance office in an old house on Victoria Road. Lives are being reclaimed there. It is the largest of about a dozen similar establishments throughout Britain that prescribe heroin, cocaine and amphetamines to addicts.

Ms. Monaghan is 36 and a functioning heroin addict; she gets paid for her work as an outreach worker at the clinic. An addict for 21 years, she's not certain she will ever stop using the stuff: "It's quite pleasant and enjoyable you know, if you use it in the right way."

The idea of maintaining an addict on heroin or cocaine, rather than trying to break the addiction, is controversial and is not widely practiced, not in Britain, not anywhere.

A task force on drug reform appointed by Baltimore Mayor Kurt L. Schmoke looked at a variety of maintenance programs in Britain and other European countries, though none was seriously considered for Baltimore. Instead, two weeks ago, the panel recommended starting a needle exchange program, focusing on arrests of drug traffickers over users, and retraining doctors to offer more treatment to addicts.

At the Widnes clinic, 61 addicts are under treatment. Of them, 18 are injecting maintenance doses of heroin, and two are injecting cocaine. Nine are smoking heroin reefers. Others are taking methadone—a more benign alternative to heroin—or amphetamines orally, while one is taking cocaine through a nasal spray.

Dr. John Angus Marks, the resident psychiatrist, said each year about 5 percent of the clinic's 150 addicts go off drugs entirely. A study of the lives of 89 of them between 1982, when the clinic opened, and 1989 revealed 20 had given up drugs completely.

> *"They all live more or less normal lives, aren't always in trouble with police. And they don't die."*
>
> **DR. JOHN ANGUS MARKS**
> **Widnes** *Drug Dependency Clinic*

"This is not a great cure rate," he said. "But they all live more or less normal lives, aren't always in trouble with the police. And they don't die."

The nine staff people inside these stark white rooms who do the work of counseling, assessing addicts' needs, or prescribed drugs believe they have ameliorated the scourge of drug abuse within their part of the economically blighted Merseyside region.

They have saved lives, not only those of addicts but of people with no connection to the addicts' world: the citizens who would be victimized by the crime that accompanies drug addiction.

The experiences of Britain and the United States in the matter of drug abuse and how to deal with it couldn't be more different, their policies more divergent. Both were set after World War I.

The United States opted for total prohibition of opiates (and alcohol), and Britain chose to ration them. Neither country has abandoned its original policy, though Britain has modified its practices.

Originally, some 20,000 British general practitioners were authorized to prescribe opiates, cocaine and other drugs to addicts, as patients. That was many more physicians than needed. According to Dr. Marks, the number of addicts was always low in Britain and reached only "about 540 in 1960."

Late in that decade, as the incidence of drug abuse grew dramatically in the United States, dealers made their way to England, found physicians to prescribe narcotics for large profits, then returned and marketed them at home. More dealers came; more British drugs found their way to the United States.

"The Americans hated this," said Dr. Marks, "so the British government, deciding its relationship with America was more important than a few addicts, passed the Misuse of Drugs Act of 1971."

This reduced to about a thousand the number of physicians who could legally prescribe opiates. It wasn't a total abandonment of the rationing policy, but many of the authorized physicians—psychiatrists for the most part—weren't interested in treating addicts.

Thus, the old maintenance system was diminished, and, as a consequence, the number of addicts grew, though at nothing similar to the rate in the United States. Today, according to Dr. Marks, there are about 50,000 addicts among

Britain's 55 million people. Baltimore alone may have as many addicts as that.

Dr. Marks and those who favor giving hard drugs to addicts believe it reduces their number within the population, and also lowers the mortality rate among them. How? Free, legally obtained drugs remove the addict's need to deal to support the habit, so there is less pressure to seduce others into that life.

Also, legal clinics prescribe drugs free of dry milk or some of the more lethal substances that are mixed with street drugs.

Supporters of maintenance see another benign effect: The antiseptic practices used in clinics reduce the incidence of AIDS in the population. Sharing of dirty needles by addicts is a major factor in the spread of HIV (human immunodeficiency virus), which causes AIDS.

Statistics independently gathered by Russell Newcombe, a professor at the University of Manchester, compare Widnes with another Merseyside community, Bootle, which has no maintenance programs.

They show that the incidence of crime, deaths from narcotics and the numbers of new addicts registered greatly favor Widnes.

There is disagreement, though, over the effect on the crime rate. Widnes Police Inspector Terry White said drug-related crime has not diminished in Widnes, though he said it is not growing.

Hugh Dufficy, of the Standing Conference on Drug Abuse, a national umbrella group that speaks for all the clinics, says of Widnes: "There certainly appears there is a decrease in drug-related crime. It is hard to prove, but it would be logical there would be."

But Dr. Sue Rubin, who runs a drug dependency clinic in Liverpool, is disinclined to prescribe hard drugs such as heroin, as are most clinics authorized to do so throughout the country. She thinks it is too difficult for an addict to stabilize on heroin.

She has more than 800 addicts on methadone, but only one on heroin. "My position is that I am not a legal drug dealer," she said. She regards her job as stabilizing addicts the best way she can, to wean them away from narcotics, and do her best to prevent the spread of HIV.

She ascribes Liverpool's very low HIV rate (.02 percent) among injecting addicts to the maintenance and needle exchange programs.

It was the growing incidence of AIDS in Baltimore (38 percent of the AIDS cases in Baltimore are needle-using addicts) that moved Mayor Schmoke to seek reform of drug policies. "AIDS is what led me to advocate a public health strategy for drug abuse," he told the General Assembly last October.

Said Dr. Marks: "We were really saved from HIV in the 1970s by this program. This was the time when HIV was seeded and spread, but, as a consequence of the [maintenance] system, Liverpool has no HIV problem."

Trying to Break Addictions, But in Less Time

Joseph B. Treaster

They were young men and women with eyes showing lots of hard mileage, and they were dumping their most shameful secrets. One woman told of stealing her mother's rent money. Another had slammed a cranky child into a wall. A man in a light windbreaker and expensive sneakers told of trading his girl friend to another man for a few vials of crack.

The confessions, drawn out during a weekend seminar at Odyssey House in Manhattan, were part of an effort to break down the streetwise addict's resistance to treatment.

Packing psychological exercises into hours usually reserved for leisure, the seminar is among a range of new approaches that experts are trying in the hope of making drug treatment cheaper and more effective.

There is a lot at stake. Many drug experts believe the ranks of the estimated six million heavy drug users in the country could be thinned considerably, sharply reducing drug markets and violent crime, if treatment was available for all. But many Washington officials are skeptical of the benefits of drug treatment and have been unwilling to allocate money to augment programs that now treat fewer than a third of the addicts.

The skepticism is understandable. Dropout rates have been high, relapse is common and treatment specialists concede that no one really knows how to cure drug addiction. For elected officials the least controversial route has been to designate most anti-drug money for law enforcement.

Yet drug specialists argue that treatment, which consists mainly of individual and group therapy, has a significant impact on crime. It provides varying periods of sobriety during which the need to rob and steal to support drug habits is diminished. Some addicts find jobs or return to school after treatment and, living healthier lives, become less of a burden on hospitals and clinics.

In an effort to reduce costs and speed treatment, Odyssey House, like many other treatment organizations, has cut the duration of its programs to about a year, down from 18 to 24 months. Others are trying to break drug habits in as little as three months. "This is a way to get more people into treatment," said John Caban, the executive vice president in charge of treatment at Odyssey House. "Also, if you tell some people they're going to be staying 18 or 24 months, they think it's an eternity. They don't even bother to think about it. One year is much easier to digest."

Not everyone favors the new approach. "This is being budget-driven rather than research-driven," said Dr. Mitchell S. Rosenthal, who founded Phoenix House in New York and serves as its president. "The population being treated today may be more disabled than ever, with greater psychological, educational and social deficits. One probably ought to think, in some cases, about lengthening treatment."

Reducing Free Time

Treatment specialists who have chosen shorter programs argue that they are providing more engaging treatment. They have reduced free time, which can breed boredom, and increased daily therapy sessions. They have also shifted the most experienced counselors to the earliest parts of the treatment, when dropouts have been highest. And they have started giving therapy to relatives of addicts.

To make treatment more appealing to women with young children, some organizations, like Amity in Tucson and Operation Par in St. Petersburg, Fla., are operating centers in which women and their children live together. Not long ago, Amity began emphasizing women's issues in a program for both men and women. Rod Mullen, the executive director, said both sexes have been staying in treatment longer.

Mr. Caban said he considers the seminars, which he developed, to be crucial to making Odyssey House's shortened program effective. The confessions and other jarring exercises get the addicts' attention, he said, and provoke discussions that might not previously have occurred until after six or seven months of treatment, a point many never reached.

In telling their stories, the addicts discover that nothing the others can throw at them is as terrible as they had imagined.

Getting Rid of Shame

"They see they're surviving, and controlling it," Mr. Caban said. "They get rid of the shame and the guilt. They lower their defenses and they make room for treatment."

Mr. Caban, a former addict with a doctorate in education from Columbia

University, says the seminars, given within the first 90 days of treatment, have sharply reduced the number of dropouts and may soon be presented at affiliates around the country. Of 212 addicts treated at Odyssey House immediately before the seminars began, 161 left within six months. But the next group, the first to participate in the seminar, started with 160 addicts and, in the same period, lost 57 members, more than reversing the rate of retention.

Current therapies reach only a third of drug addicts.

Some treatment centers, like Gaudenzia in Philadelphia, are offering programs covering a range of durations, from 3 to 18 months, based on assessments of addicts' needs when they enroll.

Michael Harle, Gaudenzia's executive director, said: "It used to be, 'Here's the program. It's 18 months. You do it or you don't.' But different people had different needs. About 30 percent of the people in the 18-month program used to graduate. Now about 60 percent are completing the various programs."

Mainly because of cost, most drug treatment is done on an outpatient basis. Some clinics dispense methadone, a synthetic narcotic that blocks the craving for heroin. But the most intense treatment is provided in residential centers that style themselves as therapeutic communities, seeking to create a new world, a new ethos and a new circle of friends for people who have spun out of control on drugs.

Not Boot Camps, but Close

Therapeutic communities are not quite boot camps and not quite prisons. But they are strict places at which freedom to come and go is limited, visitors and letter-writing are considered privileges and every minute is accounted for. As in the Army, duties include menial chores: answering telephones, waiting on tables and cleaning the kitchen.

"The tradition used to be almost of hazing, of seeing if people could survive the therapeutic communities," said Dr. Robert B. Millman, the director of drug and alcohol abuse programs at the New York Hospital-Payne Whitney Psychiatric Clinic. "Now they're becoming much more user-friendly."

Once, clients used to leave therapeutic communities with a smile and a handshake. But now, as a way of reinforcing treatment, especially shortened treatment, many programs provide up to a year of outpatient treatment and almost all encourage attendance at such self-help programs as Alcoholics Anonymous, Narcotics Anonymous and Cocaine Anonymous.

On a recent weekend, the Odyssey House seminar began with 52 addicts sitting stiff and apprehensive in a circle of steel folding chairs. Mr. Caban strode before the addicts with a microphone on a long cord. One moment he was a television evangelist; then he was tugging at his hooded sweatshirt, adjusting his dark glasses and sounding like an old friend, someone who had been to the bottom and knew the way back. Verbally rubbing their shoulders, he began persuading the addicts that they were part of a family. Stony faces began to soften and pretty soon they were looking into themselves and reporting back to the group.

Drug addicts often don't think highly of themselves. They construct elaborate facades to cover up weaknesses and, Mr. Caban has found, they rarely look people directly in the eyes. So he has them stand up and lock eyes with a neighbor. Some give their coldest killer stares. Others giggle. A man in an orange sweatshirt said he saw a lot of pain in the others "and I wondered if it was in my eyes, too."

Then the subject of trust came up. The addicts blindfolded their partners and led them around the lawn outside the auditorium, zigging and zagging, brushing close to walls and fences and pulling back at the last minute. Nobody crashed into anything and they were supposed to conclude that they could actually trust someone. But not everyone did.

A man named Leonard said he had put himself totally in the hands of his partner. But, he complained, the other man had not reciprocated. He shouldn't take it personally, his partner told the group. "I've been hurt a lot," he said. "I've been led by a lot of bad people. If I can't see where I'm going, I'm not going."

■ CONDONING THE LEGAL STUFF?

Hard Sell in The Drug War

CYNTHIA COTTS

Cynthia Cotts writes about drug policy.

"This is your brain on drugs," goes the fried-egg ad. "Any questions?" After seeing the ad, some teenagers have stopped taking drugs—and some 4-year-olds have stopped eating eggs. "Fried Egg" is one of hundreds of ads released under the imprimatur of the Partnership for a Drug-Free America. Launched in 1986 in New York City, this nonprofit group uses advertising to reduce the demand for illegal drugs. It's a flashy concept, but, as "Fried Egg" demonstrates, propaganda can breed misconceptions.

The Partnership means well, but it sends a self-serving message. The ads themselves exaggerate and distort, relying on scare tactics to get people's attention. Ad strategies are based on market research rather than public health policy. Even worse, the Partnership has accepted $5.4 million in contributions from legal drug manufacturers, while producing ads that overlook the dangers of tobacco, alcohol and pills. This "drug-free" crusade is actually a silent partner to the drug industry, condoning the use of "good" drugs by targeting only the "bad" ones.

Of course, the pharmaceutical and advertising industries have long been intertwined. James Burke, who resigned as chairman and C.E.O. of Johnson & Johnson in 1989 to become chairman of the Partnership, is no stranger to marketing. In the mid-1980s, he engineered a classic campaign to restore public confidence in Tylenol after the cyanide scare. A few years later, Johnson & Johnson sued Bristol-Myers Squibb for claiming in its advertising that Aspirin-Free Excedrin is a better pain reliever than Extra-Strength Tylenol. At the Partnership, Burke has implemented a concept borrowed from the pharmaceutical industry: If ads can sell drugs, they can unsell them, too.

More than 100 agencies have made Partnership ads pro bono, and the media kick in ad space and airtime for free. The incentive? Creative directors get to show off, giving their ads titles like "Candy Store" and "Tricks of the Trade" and submitting them for industry awards. The actors involved get exposure, and the media outlets can pat themselves on the back for contributing to a good cause.

Typically, Partnership ads are melodramatic. They trade on scare tactics (the school-bus driver snorts coke) and stereotypes (black boys sell crack in the schoolyard). With their hard line on marijuana, Partnership ads revive an old message: One puff, and you're hooked. Dr. Gil Botven, who studies drug abuse prevention programs at Cornell Medical College, thinks "what the Partnership is doing is great." But, he adds, "scare tactics have never been demonstrated to be effective."

Partnership spokeswoman Theresa Grant doesn't like the term "scare tactics." "We feel it's appropriate to arouse people's attention," she says. A recent print ad shows a preteen in a denim jacket under the headline, "What she's going through isn't a phase. It's an ounce a week." The ad copy alerts parents to the dangers of pot smoking, and in doing so, it exaggerates slightly—not many 10-year-olds could afford an ounce of marijuana a week, let alone smoke it and stay on their feet. When questioned about the exaggeration, Grant said the ad had just come under review. A few weeks later, the "Not Just a Phase" girl was back, taking up a full page in *The New York Times*.

Fact checking is a sensitive issue for the Partnership. They've caught so much flak over the years for inaccuracies that the review process has been overhauled; now, the factual content of all ads is scrutinized before they're produced. The first screamer was a 1987 TV ad depicting the brain wave of a 14-year-old smoking pot. It was actually the brain wave of a coma patient. In 1990 *Scientific American* uncovered some cooked figures in a cocaine ad. Those early mistakes were really "born of naïveté," says Grant. "Nobody intentionally distorted facts. In those days, they really thought they had the kind of substantiation they needed."

A 1990 print ad reels off marijuana slang terms and concludes, "No matter what you call it, don't call it harmless." The ad cites potential damage to the lungs and reproductive system. But calls to the National Cancer Institute and the National Institute on Drug Abuse (N.I.D.A.) didn't turn up any casualties, just a lot of inconclusive studies. One study did find "reduced gas exchange capacity" in the lungs of fifteen women who were chronic pot smokers. As for reproductive risks, scientists have injected a lot of pregnant monkeys with THC, the key psychoactive chemical in marijuana, but they've yet to come up with hard evidence. In fact, the health issue is "nebulous," Grant concedes, so the Partnership is switching its tack on marijuana. Future ads won't tell you it's dangerous, just that it's uncool.

Like its mentors in the pharmaceutical industry, the Partnership has learned to backpedal. In the fall of 1990 the campaign sent ads to Alaskans for a Drug-Free Youth, a parent group that was campaigning to put recriminalization of marijuana on the ballot. Recriminalization was passed that November, and the Partnership crowed about the victory in its Winter 1991 newsletter.

When asked about the Partnership's effort, Grant denies a political motive. "It wasn't any different than if we provided messages to a community group in Iowa," she says. "I must be remiss, because I never looked at it from the perspective of assisting in a political campaign."

To maintain its good reputation, the Partnership has to offer hard proof of advertising's impact on drug abuse. So, even though experts have concluded that media campaigns do not in themselves change behavior, Burke goes around trumpeting the power of the media to save children from drugs. Burke is echoed by Mathea Falco, a former Assistant Secretary of State for International Narcotics Matters, who is now writing a book on drug prevention programs. The Partner··· greatest achievement, says Falco, is to convey the me "that using drugs is silly. They're making it socially unac able, and that's the best way to bring about social cha

No one can prove that the ads are responsible for decl drug use, or indeed that all drug use is down. The latest government surveys show a rise in the use of cocaine and heroin by urban youth, and in the use of LSD by college students nationwide.

When he needs proof Burke can quote the Partnership Attitude Tracking Survey (PATS), conducted annually at the Partnership's behest by the Gordon S. Black Corporation. The PATS research suggests a correlation between teens who have seen the antidrug ads, teens who disapprove of drug use and teens who say no to drugs. But when Burke cites PATS, he doesn't mention that Gordon Black is a market research firm, or that PATS is based on "mall intercepts." That is, participants fill out questionnaires anonymously at shopping malls in sample locations. Confidentiality is thus guaranteed, but accuracy is not.

At the University of Michigan, Dr. Lloyd Johnston, a research scientist, conducts an annual survey of high school students for N.I.D.A. According to Johnston, the mall intercepts are an inexpensive method of measuring trends, but they lack the sampling precision of a household survey. Nonetheless, Johnston's surveys do bolster the PATS conclusions. Most teens remember the antidrug ads and report being in-

fluenced by them. "There's no guarantee advertising did it per se," says Johnston, "but it's clear things have moved in the right direction."

The PATS five-year summary reports that illegal drug use by students is dropping, but fails to mention that tobacco and alcohol are still teenagers' drugs of choice. Johnston's latest statistics show that 40 percent of tenth graders report drinking within the past month and getting very drunk within the past year. "The other thing that comes out of our surveys," says Johnston, "is that smoking has not dropped among young people for almost a decade." Nineteen percent of high school seniors are daily tobacco smokers, and hundreds of thousands of them, Johnston sadly predicts, will die of lung cancer one day.

The Partnership has traditionally attacked marijuana, cocaine and crack, drugs deemed widely available to schoolchildren. But if the Partnership's mission is to stop kids from experimenting in the first place, why not go after cigarettes and beer? The answer is obvious. According to Falco, "It would be *suicidal* if the Partnership took on the alcohol and tobacco industries. The Partnership is living off free advertising product and space, and the media and ad agencies live off alcohol and tobacco advertising." Theresa Grant acknowledges that the decision to focus on illegal drugs was "pragmatic," based on the desire to "get the airtime and space and not alienate the people who are making this possible."

The Partnership ignores cigarettes,

The Partnership's condoning of legal drugs doesn't bother Falco. "The message may not be complete," she chirps, "but it's better than nothing!" Many public health researchers, however, are concerned about a new generation of teens who smoke, drink and pop pills.

Experts believe that children begin using drugs in the order of availability, and they're more likely to try marijuana if they've already tried alcohol and cigarettes. "The natural thing in a prevention campaign," says Dr. Botven, "would be to focus on the three gateway substances: alcohol, tobacco and marijuana. The Partnership starts with marijuana, and my concern is they're skipping the most important ones in terms of fatality." Johnston believes the Partnership has the ability to target legal drug abuse, and says he "would be delighted if they would." When asked if he thinks that could happen, he pauses. "A betting man would say no."

In the Partnership's early days, its primary supporter was the American Association of Advertising Agencies. That group knew better than to alienate the legal drug industry. But the mandate must have been reinforced in 1989, the year Burke came from Johnson & Johnson, bringing with him a $3 million grant from the Robert Wood Johnson Foundation, a prominent health care philanthropy. The foundation described its unusually handsome grant to the Partnership as "pivotal in leveraging . . . support from other private foundations."

On cue, the other foundations rolled over. In 1989 and 1990, the ten largest foundation grants for alcohol and drug abuse totaled $12.4 million. The Partnership took $4.7 million from that pool, or 38 percent. Many an individual donor gave its largest antidrug grant to the Partnership. In other words, the Robert Wood Johnson Foundation accelerated a trend: the channeling of foundation money into public awareness, which is considered a less effective form of drug-abuse prevention than school- and community-based programs.

The Partnership's funders are usually kept secret, says Grant, to protect them from other grant seekers and from the legalization lobby. But the Partnership's 1991 tax return reveals another motive for secrecy: conspicuous support from the legal drug industry. From 1988 to 1991, pharmaceutical companies and their beneficiaries contributed as follows: the J. Seward Johnson, Sr., Charitable Trusts ($1,100,000); Du Pont ($150,000); the Procter & Gamble Fund ($120,000); the Bristol-Myers Squibb Foundation ($110,000); Johnson & Johnson ($110,000); SmithKline Beecham ($100,000); the Merck Foundation ($75,000); and Hoffman-La Roche ($50,000).

Pharmaceuticals and their beneficiaries alone donated 54 percent of the $5.8 million the Partnership took from its top twenty-five contributors from 1988 to 1991. That 54 percent is conservative. It doesn't include donations under $90,000, and it doesn't include donations from the tobacco and alcohol kings: The Partnership has taken $150,000 each from Philip Morris, Anheuser-Busch and RJR Reynolds, plus $100,000 from American Brands (Jim Beam, Lucky Strike).

Coincidence? Hardly. The war on drugs is a war on illegal drugs, and the Partnership's benefactors have a huge stake in keeping it that way. They know that when schoolchildren learn that marijuana and crack are evil, they're also learning that alcohol, tobacco and pills are as American as apple pie.

This glossary of 185 drug terms is included to provide you with a convenient and ready reference as you encounter general terms in your study of drugs and drug and alcohol abuse that are unfamiliar, technical, or require a review. It is not intended to be comprehensive, but, taken together with the many definitions included in the articles themselves, it should prove to be useful.

Absorption The passage of chemical compounds, such as drugs or nutrients, into the bloodstream through the skin, intestinal lining, or other bodily membranes.

Acetylcholine A cholinergic transmitter that forms salts used to lower blood pressure and increases peristalsis, and thought to be involved in the inhibition of behavior.

Addiction Chronic, compulsive, or uncontrollable behavior.

Adrenergic System The group of transmitters, including epinephrine, norepinephrine, and dopamine, that activates the sympathetic nervous system.

Alcohol Abuse *See* Alcoholism.

Alcoholics Anonymous (AA) A voluntary fellowship founded in 1935 and concerned with the recovery and continued sobriety of the alcoholic members who turn to the organization for help. The AA program consists basically of "Twelve Suggested Steps" designed for the personal recovery from alcoholism, and AA is the major proponent of the disease model of alcoholism.

Alcoholism Any use of alcoholic beverages that causes damage to the individual or to society. *See also* Disease Model.

Amphetamines A class of drugs, similar in some ways to the body's own adrenaline (epinephrine), that act as stimulants to the central nervous system.

Analgesics Drugs that relieve pain.

Anesthetics Drugs that abolish the sensation of pain, often used during surgery.

Angel Dust Slang term for phencyclidine.

Anorectic A drug that decreases appetite.

Antagonist Programs Drug treatment programs that use antagonist agents, like naltrexone (antagonist of heroin) or antabuse (used in treating alcoholism), to block the effect of drugs on the body.

Antianxiety Tranquilizers Tranquilizers, like Valium and Librium, used to relieve anxiety and tension, sometimes called minor tranquilizers.

Anticholinergics Drugs that block the transmission of impulses in the parasympathetic nerves.

Antidepressants Drugs that relieve mental depression. *See also* Depression, Mental.

Antihistamines Drugs that relieve allergy or cold symptoms by blocking the effects of histamine production.

Antipsychotic Tranquilizers Drugs used to treat psychosis; include Thorazine (chlorpromazine). Also called major tranquilizers or neuroleptics. *See also* Tranquilizers.

Atropine An alkaloid derivative of the belladonna and related plants that blocks responses to parasympathetic stimulation.

Autonomic Nervous System (ANS) That part of the nervous system that regulates involuntary action, such as heartbeat; consists of the sympathetic and parasympathetic nervous systems.

Axon The core of the nerve fiber that conducts impulses away from the nerve cell to the neurons and other tissue.

Barbiturates Drugs used for sedation and to relieve tension and anxiety.

Binding The attachment of a transmitter to its appropriate receptor site.

Blood Level The concentration of alcohol in the blood, usually expressed in percent by weight.

Caffeine An alkaloid found in coffee, tea, and kola nuts, that acts as a stimulant.

Caffeinism Dependence on caffeine.

Cannabis *See* Marijuana.

Capsule A container, usually of gelatin, that encloses a dose of an oral medicine.

Central Nervous System (CNS) The brain and spinal cord.

Chewing Tobacco A form of tobacco leaves, sometimes mixed with molasses, that is chewed.

Chlorpromazine An antianxiety tranquilizer, manufactured under the name of Thorazine, used for treating severe psychoses. Also used as an antagonist to LSD panic reactions.

Choline A transmitter, part of the cholinergic system.

Cholinergic System Group of transmitters that activate the parasympathetic nervous system.

Cocaine A white crystaline narcotic alkaloid derived from the coca plant and used as a surface anesthetic and a stimulant.

Codeine A narcotic alkaloid found in opium, most often used as an analgesic or cough suppressant.

Coke Slang term for cocaine.

Cold Turkey Slang expression for abrupt and complete withdrawal from drugs or alcohol without medication.

Compulsive Drug Use Drug use that is frequent, with intensive levels of long duration, producing physiological or psychological dependence.

Constriction Narrowing or shrinking.

Contraindication A condition that makes it inadvisable or hazardous to use a particular drug or medicine.

Controlled Drinking Moderate drinking by recovered alcoholics, discouraged by AA.

Controlled Drug Use Use of drugs over a period of time without abusing them.

Controlled Substances All psychoactive substances covered by laws regulating their sale and possession.

Controlled Substances Act of 1970 Federal act that classifies controlled substances into five categories and regulates their use. Schedule I drugs are those most strictly controlled, and include heroin, marijuana, LSD, and other drugs believed to have high abuse potential. Schedule II drugs are also strictly controlled but have some medicinal uses. These drugs include morphine, methadone, and amphetamines. Schedule III, IV, and V substances include drugs that have increasingly less abuse potential. Over-the-counter medicines not subject to any refill regulations fall into Schedule V.

Craving Refers to both physical and psychological dependence; a strong desire or need for a substance.

Crisis Intervention The process of diagnosing a drug crisis situation and acting immediately to arrest the condition.

Decriminalization The legal process by which the possession of a certain drug would become a civil penalty instead of a criminal penalty. *See also* Legalization.

Deliriants Substances, like some inhalants, that produce delirium.

Delirium State of temporary mental confusion and diminished consciousness, characterized by anxiety, hallucinations, and delusions.

Dendrite The part of the nerve cell that transmits impulses to the cell body.

Dependence, Drug A physical or psychological dependence on a particular drug resulting from continued use of that drug.

Dependence, Physical The physical need of the body for a particular substance such that abstinence from the substance leads to physical withdrawal symptoms. *See also* Addiction; Withdrawal Syndrome.

Dependence, Psychological A psychological or emotional reliance on a particular substance; a strong and continued craving.

Depression, Mental The state of mind that ranges from mild sadness to deep despair, often accompanied by a general feeling of hopelessness.

Detoxification Removal of a poisonous substance, such as a drug or alcohol, from the body.

Dilation Widening or enlargement.

Disease Model A theory of alcoholism, endorsed by AA, in which the alcoholism is seen as a disease rather than a psychological or social problem.

DMT Dimethyltryptamine, a psychedelic drug.

DNA Deoxyribonucleic acid, the carrier of chromosomes in the cell.

Dopamine An indoleaminergic transmitter necessary for normal nerve activity.

Downers Slang term for drugs that act to depress the central nervous system.

Drug Any substance that alters the structure or function of a living organism.

Drug Abuse Use of a drug to the extent that it is excessive, hazardous, or undesirable to the individual or the community.

Drug Misuse Use of a drug for any purpose other than that for which it is medically prescribed.

Drug Paraphernalia Materials, like hypodermic syringes, that are used for the preparation or administration of illicit drugs.

Drunkenness The state of being under the influence of alcohol such that mental and physical faculties are impaired; severe intoxication.

DWI Driving while intoxicated.

Dysphoria Emotional state characterized by anxiety, depression, and restlessness, as opposed to euphoria.

Ecstasy A derivative of nutmeg or sassafras, causing euphoria and sometimes hallucinations; also known as XTC, Adam, or MDMA.

Endorphins Any group of hormones released by the brain that have painkilling and tranquilizing abilities.

Epinephrine An adrenal hormone that acts as a transmitter and stimulates autonomic nerve action.

Ethical Drugs Drugs dispensed by prescription only.

Euphoria Exaggerated sense of happiness or well-being.

Experimental Drug Use According to the U.S. National Commission on Marijuana and Drug Abuse, the short-term non-patterned trial of one or more drugs, either concurrently or consecutively, with variable intensity but maximum frequency of ten times per drug.

Fetal Alcohol Syndrome (FAS) A pattern of birth defects, cardiac abnormalities, and developmental retardation seen in babies of alcoholic mothers.

Flashback A spontaneous and involuntary recurrence of psychedelic drug effects after the initial drug experience.

Food and Drug Administration (FDA) Agency of the U.S. Department of Health and Human Services that administers federal laws regarding the purity of food, the safety and effectiveness of drugs, and the safety of cosmetics.

Habituation Chronic or continuous use of a drug, with an attachment less severe than addiction.

Hallucination A sensory perception without external stimuli.

Hallucinogen Or, hallucinogenic drugs. Drugs that cause hallucinations. Also known as psychedelic drugs.

Harrison Narcotics Act Federal act passed in 1914 that controlled the sale and possession of prescription drugs, heroin, opium, and cocaine.

Hash Oil An oily extract of the marijuana plant, containing high levels of THC.

Hashish The dried resin of the marijuana plant, often smoked in water pipes.

Herb Commonly, any one of various aromatic plants used for medical or other purposes.

Heroin Diacetylmorphine hydrochloride, an opiate derivative of morphine.

High Intoxicated by a drug or alcohol; the state of being high.

Illicit Drugs Drugs whose use, possession, or sale is illegal.

Illusion A distorted or mistaken perception.

Indole An indoleaminergic transmitter.

Indoleaminergic System A system of neurotransmitters, including indole and serotonin.

Inebriation The state of being drunk or habitually drunk.

Intoxication Medically, the state of being poisoned. Usually refers to the state of being drunk, falling between drunkenness and a mild high.

Involuntary Smoking Involuntary inhalation of the cigarette smoke of others.

Ketamin A general anesthetic, also used as a deliriant.

Legalization The movement to have the sale or possession of certain illicit drugs made legal.

LSD Lysergic acid diethylamide-25, a hallucinogen.

Maintenance Treatment Treatment of drug dependence by a small dosage of the drug or another drug, such as methadone, that will prevent withdrawal symptoms.

Marijuana The dried leaves of the cannabis plant, usually smoked and resulting in feelings of well-being, relaxation, or euphoria. Also spelled: Marihuana.

MDMA *See* Ecstasy.

Medical Model A theory of drug abuse or addiction in which the addiction is seen as a medical, rather than a social, problem.

Medicine A drug used to treat disease or injury; medication.

Mescaline A hallucinogenic alkaloid drug, either derived from the peyote plant or made synthetically.

Metabolism The set of physical and chemical processes involved in the maintenance of life; or, the functioning of a particular substance in the body.

Methadone A synthetic opiate sometimes used to treat heroin or morphine addiction. *See also* Maintenance Treatment.

Methaqualone A non-barbiturate sedative/hypnotic drug, used to bring on feelings of muscular relaxation, contentment, and passivity. Also known as Quaaludes.

Morphine An organic compound extracted from opium, a light anesthetic or sedative.

Multimodality Programs Programs for the treatment of drug abuse or alcoholism involving several simultaneous treatment methods.

Multiprescribing   The situation in which a person is taking more than one prescription or over-the-counter drug simultaneously.

Narcotic   Any drug that dulls a person's senses and produces a sense of well-being in smaller doses, and insensibility, sometimes even death, in larger doses.

Nervous System   In human beings, the brain, spinal cord, and nerves. *See also* Somatic Nervous System; Autonomic Nervous System.

Neuroleptic   Any major, or antipsychotic, tranquilizer.

Neuron   The basic element responsible for the reception, transmission, and processing of sensory, motor, and other information of physiological or psychological importance to the individual.

Neurotransmitter   *See* Transmitter.

Nicotine   The main active ingredient of tobacco, extremely toxic and causing irritation of lung tissues, constriction of blood vessels, increased blood pressure and heart rate, and, in general, central nervous system stimulation.

Norepinephrine   Hormone found in the sympathetic nerve endings that acts as an adrenergic transmitter and is a vasoconstrictor.

Opiate Narcotics   A major subclass of drugs that act as pain relievers as well as central nervous system depressants; includes opium, morphine, codeine, and methadone.

Opiates   The drugs derived from opium—morphine and codeine—as well as those derived from them, such as heroin.

Opium   Narcotic derivative of the poppy plant that acts as an analgesic.

Opoids   The group of synthetic drugs, including Demerol and Darvon, that resemble the opiates in action and effect.

Overmedication   The prescription and use of more medication than necessary to treat a specific illness or condition.

Over-the-Counter Drugs   Drugs legally sold without a prescription.

Parasympathetic Nervous System   The part of the autonomic nervous system that inhibits or opposes the actions of the sympathetic nerves.

Parasympathomimetics   Drugs that produce effects similar to those of the parasympathetic nervous system.

Parkinson's Disease   A progressive disease of the nervous system characterized by muscular tremor, slowing of movement, partial facial paralysis, and general weakness.

Patent Medicines   Drugs or other medications protected by a patent and sold over the counter.

Peristalsis   Wave-like muscular contractions that help move matter through the tubular organs (e.g., intestines).

Phencyclidine (PCP)   A synthetic depressant drug used as a veterinary anesthetic and illegally as a hallucinogen. Also known as angel dust.

Placebo   An inactive substance used as a control in an experiment.

Placenta   The membranous organ that develops in the uterus of a pregnant female mammal to nourish the fetus. Though the fetus and mother are thus separated, drugs and alcohol are often still able to reach the developing fetus.

Polyabuse   Abuse of various drugs simultaneously.

Pot   Slang term for marijuana.

Potency   Term used to compare the relative strength of two or more drugs used to produce a given effect.

Prescription Drugs   Drugs dispensed only by a physician's prescription.

Primary Prevention   Efforts designed to prevent a person from starting to use drugs.

Proprietary Drugs   Patent medicines.

Psilocybin   A hallucinogenic alkaloid, found in various types of mushrooms, chemically related to LSD.

Psychedelic Drugs   Hallucinogens.

Psychoactive   Any drug that can cause alterations in the user's mood or behavior.

Psychopharmacology   The study of the effects of drugs on mood, sensation, or consciousness, or other psychological or behavioral functions.

Psychosis   Severe mental disorder, characterized by withdrawal from reality and deterioration of normal intellectual and social functioning.

Psychotherapeutic Drugs   Drugs that are used as medicines to alleviate psychological disorders.

Psychotomimetics   Drugs that produce psychosis-like effects.

Receptors   The input organs for the nervous system.

Recidivism   Return to former behavior.

Recombinant DNA   DNA prepared in the laboratory by the transfer or exchange of individual genes from one organism to another.

Recreational Drug Use   Drug use that takes place in social settings among friends who want to share a pleasant experience; characterized by less frequency and intensity than addictive drug use. Also called social-recreational drug use.

Rehabilitation   Restoration of a person's ability to function normally.

Reinforcement   A stimulus that increases the probability that a desired response will occur.

Rush   Slang term for an immediate feeling of physical well-being and euphoria after the administration of a drug.

Schedules   Categories of drugs as defined in the Controlled Substances Act of 1970.

Schizophrenia   A psychosis characterized by withdrawal from reality accompanied by affective, behavioral, and intellectual disturbances.

Scopolamine   Poisonous alkaloid found in the roots of various plants, used as a truth serum or with morphine as a sedative.

Secondary Prevention   Early treatment of drug abuse to prevent it from becoming more severe.

Sedative/Hypnotics   Class of non-narcotic depressant drugs that calm, sedate, or induce hypnosis or sleep. Sedative/hypnotics are divided into four categories: barbiturates, alcohol, antianxiety tranquilizers (minor tranquilizers), and nonbarbiturate proprietary drugs.

Serotonin   An indoleaminergic transmitter found in the blood serum, cells, and central nervous system, that acts as a vasoconstrictor.

Set   The combination of physical, mental, and emotional characteristics of an individual at the time a drug is administered.

Setting   The external environment of an individual at the time a drug is administered.

Side Effects   Secondary effects, usually undesirable, of a drug or therapy.

Snuff   A preparation of pulverized tobacco that is inhaled into the nostrils.

Sobriety   The quality of being free from alcohol intoxication.

Social-Recreational Drug Use   *See* Recreational Drug Use.

Socioeconomic   Both social and economic.

Somatic Nervous System   That part of the nervous system that deals with the senses and voluntary muscles.

Somatic Nervous System That part of the nervous system that deals with the senses and voluntary muscles.

Speed Slang term for methamphetamine, a central nervous system stimulant.

Stereospecificity The matching of both electrical and chemical characteristics of the transmitter and receptor site so that binding can take place.

Stimulants A major class of drugs that stimulate the central nervous system, causing mood elevation, increased mental and physical activity, alertness, and appetite suppression. Primary stimulants include the amphetamines and cocaine. Secondary stimulants include nicotine and caffeine.

STP Early slang term for phencyclidine.

Subcutaneous Beneath the skin.

Substance Abuse Refers to overeating, cigarette smoking, alcohol abuse, or drug abuse.

Sympathetic Nervous System That part of the autonomic nervous system that acts to release sugars from the liver, slow digestion, and increase heart and breathing rates.

Sympathomimetic Any drug that produces effects like those resulting from stimulation of the sympathetic nervous system.

Synapse The space, or gap, between two neurons.

Tars The dark, oily, viscid substances created by burning tobacco, known to contain carcinogenic agents.

Temperance The practice of moderation, especially with regard to alcohol consumption. The Temperance Movement was a popular movement in the nineteenth and twentieth centuries to restrict or prohibit the use of alcoholic beverages.

Tertiary Prevention Treatment to prevent the permanent disability or death of a drug abuser.

THC Tetrahydrocannabinol, a psychoactive derivative of the cannabis plant.

Therapeutic Community Setting in which persons with similar problems meet and provide mutual support to help overcome those problems.

Titration The ability to determine desired drug dosage.

Tolerance The capacity to absorb a drug continuously or in large doses with no adverse effect.

Trance Dazed or hypnotic state.

Tranquilizers Drugs that depress the central nervous system, thus relieving anxiety and tension and sometimes relaxing the muscles, divided into the major tranquilizers, or antipsychotics, and minor tranquilizers, or antianxiety tranquilizers. *See also* Antianxiety Tranquilizers; Antipsychotic Tranquilizers.

Transmitters Also known as neurotransmitters. Any substance that aids in transmitting impulses between a nerve and a muscle. Three known categories of transmitters are the cholinergic system, adrenergic system, and indoleaminergic system.

Treatment Drug treatment programs can be drug-free or maintenance, residential or ambulatory, medical or nonmedical, voluntary or involuntary, or some combination of these.

Uppers Slang term for amphetamines, and, sometimes, cocaine.

Withdrawal Syndrome The group of reactions or behavior that follows abrupt cessation of the use of a drug upon which the body has become dependent. May include anxiety, insomnia, perspiration, hot flashes, nausea, dehydration, tremor, weakness, dizziness, convulsions, and psychotic behavior.

Index

Credits/ Acknowledgments

Cover design by Charles Vitelli

1. Thinking About Drugs

Facing overview—Dushkin Publishing Group, Inc., photo by Pamela Carley. 10—Yale Medical School Library. 12—American Institute of Pharmacy, University of Wisconsin-Madison. 14—Rancy Santos, Randolph Photographer. 15—Time Warner, Inc. © 1981, 1986.

2. Use, Addiction, and Dependence

Facing overview—United Nations photo by John Isaac.

3. Why Drugs?

Facing overview—United Nations photo by Gaston Guarda.

4. Patterns and Trends in Drug Use

Facing overview—American Cancer Society photo. 77—The Dushkin Publishing Group, Inc., photo by Pamela Carley.

5. The Major Drugs of Use and Abuse

Facing overview—Photo courtesy of Jean Bailey.

6. The Impact of Drug Use on Society

Facing overview—MADD photo.

7. The Economy of Drug Use

Facing overview—Dushkin Publishing Group, Inc., photo by Pamela Carley. 153—Photo by Leslie Sawin.

8. Fighting the Drug War

Facing overview—United States Customs photo. 196—Photo by UPI/Bettman.

9. Drug Prevention and Treatment

Facing overview—United Nations photo.

ANNUAL EDITIONS ARTICLE REVIEW FORM

■ NAME: _____ DATE: _____

■ TITLE AND NUMBER OF ARTICLE: _____

■ BRIEFLY STATE THE MAIN IDEA OF THIS ARTICLE: _____

_____

_____

_____

_____

■ LIST THREE IMPORTANT FACTS THAT THE AUTHOR USES TO SUPPORT THE MAIN IDEA:

_____

_____

_____

_____

_____

_____

■ WHAT INFORMATION OR IDEAS DISCUSSED IN THIS ARTICLE ARE ALSO DISCUSSED IN YOUR TEXTBOOK OR OTHER READING YOU HAVE DONE? LIST THE TEXTBOOK CHAPTERS AND PAGE NUMBERS:

_____

_____

_____

_____

_____

_____

■ LIST ANY EXAMPLES OF BIAS OR FAULTY REASONING THAT YOU FOUND IN THE ARTICLE:

_____

_____

_____

_____

■ LIST ANY NEW TERMS/CONCEPTS THAT WERE DISCUSSED IN THE ARTICLE AND WRITE A SHORT DEFINITION:

_____

_____

_____

_____

_____

*Your instructor may require you to use this Annual Editions Article Review Form in any number of ways:
for articles that are assigned, for extra credit, as a tool to assist in developing assigned papers, or simply
for your own reference. Even if it is not required, we encourage you to photocopy and use this page;
you'll find that reflecting on the articles will greatly enhance the information from your text.

ANNUAL EDITIONS:
DRUGS, SOCIETY, AND BEHAVIOR 94/95
Article Rating Form

We Want Your Advice

Here is an opportunity for you to have direct input into the next revision of this volume. We would like you to rate each of the 52 articles listed below, using the following scale:

1. Excellent: should definitely be retained
2. Above average: should probably be retained
3. Below average: should probably be deleted
4. Poor: should definitely be deleted

Your ratings will play a vital part in the next revision. So please mail this prepaid form to us just as soon as you complete it.
Thanks for your help!

Annual Editions revisions depend on two major opinion sources: one is our Advisory Board, listed in the front of this volume, which works with us in scanning the thousands of articles published in the public press each year; the other is you—the person actually using the book. Please help us and the users of the next edition by · completing the prepaid article rating form on this page and returning it to us. Thank you.

Rating	Article	Rating	Article
	1. Drugs 'R' Us		27. High Anxiety
	2. Opium, Cocaine, and Marijuana in American History		28. Alcohol in Perspective
	3. Alcohol in America		29. The Drug Scene's New "Ice" Age
	4. Coke Inc.: Inside the Big Business of Drugs		30. Pumped Up
	5. Addiction and Dependence		31. Dealing with Demons of a New Generation
	6. The Battlefield of Addiction		32. Alcohol and Kids: It's Time for Candor
	7. High and Hooked		33. Alcohol and the Family
	8. Smoking—Why Is It So Hard to Quit?		34. Cocaine Effect on Babies Questioned
	9. Drugs and Free Will		35. Families vs. the Lure of the Streets
	10. Intoxicating Habits		36. Worldwide Drug Scourge: The Expanding Trade in Illicit Drugs
	11. High Times in the Wild Kingdom		37. The Tobacco Lobby: Maintaining Profits, Distorting Issues, Costing Lives
	12. The Lure of Drugs: They 'Organize' an Addict's Life		38. High in the Hollows
	13. Probing the Complex Genetics of Alcoholism		39. Pushing Drugs to Doctors
	14. A Pleasurable Chemistry		40. The Cocaine Money Market
	15. Executive's Secret Struggle with Heroin's Powerful Grip		41. U.S. Drug Laws: Two Views
	16. Just Say Maybe		42. Pregnant, Addicted—and Guilty?
	17. With Teens and Alcohol, It's Just Say When		43. Should We Legalize Drugs? History Answers Yes—No
	18. U.S. Reports Sharp Increase in Drug-Caused Emergencies		44. Testing Workers for Drugs Reduces Company Problems
	19. Up in Smoke		45. Toward a Policy on Drugs
	20. With Supply and Purity Up, Heroin Use Expands		46. U.S. Aid Hasn't Stopped Drug Flow from South America, Experts Say
	21. Smoking, Drinking, and Illicit Drug Use among American Secondary Students, College Students, and Young Adults, 1975		47. Getting Junkies to Clean Up
			48. Alonzo's Battle
	22. The How and Why of a Cocaine High		49. Prisoners, and Prisons, Gain from Drug Therapy
	23. The New View from on High		50. Maintenance Isn't Cure, But It's Limiting HIV, Crime in Britain's Drug Picture
	24. Choose Your Poison		51. Trying to Break Addictions, But in Less Time
	25. A Prozac Backlash		52. Hard Sell in the Drug War
	26. Selling Pot: The Pitfalls of Marijuana Reform		

(Continued on next

ABOUT YOU

Name_____ Date_____

Are you a teacher? ☐   Or student? ☐

Your School Name _____

Department _____

Address _____

City _____ State _____ Zip _____

School Telephone # _____

▬▬▬▬▬▬▬▬▬▬▬▬▬▬▬▬▬▬▬▬

YOUR COMMENTS ARE IMPORTANT TO US!

Please fill in the following information:

For which course did you use this book? _____

Did you use a text with this Annual Edition? ☐ yes ☐ no

The title of the text? _____

What are your general reactions to the Annual Editions concept?

Have you read any particular articles recently that you think should be included in the next edition?

Are there any articles you feel should be replaced in the next edition? Why?

Are there other areas that you feel would utilize an Annual Edition?

May we contact you for editorial input?

May we quote you from above?

▬▬▬▬▬▬▬▬▬▬▬▬▬▬▬▬▬▬▬▬

ANNUAL EDITIONS: DRUGS, SOCIETY, AND BEHAVIOR 94/95

BUSINESS REPLY MAIL

First Class   Permit No. 84   Guilford, CT

Postage will be paid by addressee

The Dushkin Publishing Group, Inc.
Sluice Dock
DPG **Guilford, Connecticut 06437**